Pat...
Kevi...
Mar...

New Discovery

Leaving Certificate Poetry Anthology
for Higher and Ordinary Level 2014

Edco
The Educational Company of Ireland

First published 2012

The Educational Company of Ireland
Ballymount Road
Walkinstown
Dublin 12

www.edco.ie

A member of the Smurfit Kappa Group plc

© Patrick Murray, Kevin McDermott,
Mary Slattery, 2012

ISBN 978-1-84536-518-9

Editor: Jennifer Armstrong
Design : Design Image
Layout: DTP Workshop
Cover Design: Graham Thew
Cover photographs: Topfoto, Corbis

All rights reserved. No part of this publication may be reproduced, stored in a retrieval system, or transmitted in any form or by any means, electronic, mechanical, photocopying, recording or otherwise, without either the prior permission of the publisher or a licence permitting restricted copying in Ireland issued by the Irish Copyright Licensing Agency,
25 Denzille Lane, Dublin 2

Any links to external websites should not be construed as an endorsement by EDCO of the content or view of the linked material.

Foreword

This anthology, which includes all the poems prescribed for the Higher and Ordinary Level English Leaving Certificate Examinations of 2014, has been prepared by three experienced teachers of English. Each of the contributors has been able to concentrate on a limited number of the prescribed poets and their work, thus facilitating a high standard of research and presentation.

Guidelines are given which set each poem in context. In addition, each poem is accompanied by a glossary and appropriate explorations, designed to allow the student to find his/her authentic response to the material. Relevant biographical details are provided for each poet. A list of examination-style questions is provided for each prescribed poet at Higher Level along with a snapshot of the poet's work and a sample examination-style essay to aid revision.

Guidelines are included for students on approaching the Unseen Poetry section of the course. There is also advice on approaching the prescribed question in the examination. Students will also find the glossary of poetic terms a valuable resource in reading and responding to poetry.

The poetry course for Leaving Certificate English demands a personal and active engagement from the student reader. We hope that this anthology makes that engagement possible and encourages students to explore the wider world of poetry for themselves.

Teachers can access the New Discovery for Leaving Certificate Higher and Ordinary Level e-book by registering on www.edcodigital.ie

Contents

* denotes poem included for Ordinary Level English Leaving Certificate

Acknowledgements	x
Elizabeth Bishop	1
Biography	2
Social and Cultural Context	3
Timeline	6
The Fish*	7
The Bight	14
At the Fishhouses	19
The Prodigal*	26
Questions of Travel	31
The Armadillo	37
Sestina	41
First Death in Nova Scotia	47
Filling Station*	51
In the Waiting Room	58
Exam-Style Questions	65
Sample Essay	66
Snapshot	70
Emily Dickinson	71
Biography	72
Social and Cultural Context	76
Punctuation and Capital Letters	77
Timeline	78
"Hope" is the thing with feathers	79
There's a certain Slant of light	81
I felt a Funeral, in my Brain*	84
A Bird came down the Walk	89
I Heard a fly buzz – when I died*	92
The Soul has Bandaged moments	96
I could bring You Jewels – had I a mind to	100
A narrow Fellow in the Grass	103
I taste a liquor never brewed	106

After great pain, a formal feeling comes	108
Exam-Style Questions	111
Sample Essay	113
Snapshot	116

Seamus Heaney — 117

Biography	118
Social and Cultural Context	121
Timeline	124
The Forge	125
Bogland	128
The Tollund Man	132
Mossbawn: Two Poems in Dedication: (1) Sunlight	137
A Constable Calls*	141
The Skunk	146
The Harvest Bow	151
The Underground*	155
The Pitchfork	162
Lightenings, viii: 'The Annals Say'	166
A Call*	170
Postscript	175
Tate's Avenue	179
Exam-Style Questions	182
Sample Essay	184
Snapshot	188

Thomas Kinsella — 189

Biography	190
Social and Cultural Context	191
Timeline	194
Thinking of Mr D.*	195
Dick King	199
Chrysalides	203
Mirror in February*	207
Hen Woman	211
Tear	218
His Father's Hands	224
from Settings: Model School, Inchicore	231
from The Familiar: VII	236
from Glenmacnass: VI Littlebody	239
from Belief and Unbelief: Echo	244

Exam-Style Questions	246
Sample Essay	247
Snapshot	251
Philip Larkin	**252**
Biography	253
Social and Cultural Context	257
Timeline	259
Wedding-Wind	260
At Grass	263
Church Going	267
An Arundel Tomb	273
The Whitsun Weddings	278
MCMXIV	284
Ambulances*	288
The Trees	292
The Explosion*	294
Cut Grass	299
Exam-Style Questions	301
Sample Essay	303
Snapshot	306
Derek Mahon	**307**
Biography	308
Social and Cultural Context	309
Timeline	311
Grandfather*	312
Day Trip to Donegal	316
Ecclesiastes	320
After the Titanic*	324
As It Should Be	328
A Disused Shed in Co. Wexford	331
The Chinese Restaurant in Portrush	339
Rathlin	342
Antarctica*	346
Kinsale	351
Exam-Style Questions	353
Sample Essay	354
Snapshot	358

Sylvia Plath	359
Biography	360
Social and Cultural Context	363
Timeline	365
Black Rook in Rainy Weather	366
The Times Are Tidy	371
Morning Song	374
Finisterre	377
Mirror	382
Pheasant	385
Elm	389
Poppies in July*	397
The Arrival of the Bee Box*	402
Child*	409
Exam-Style Questions	413
Sample Essay	415
Snapshot	419
William Butler Yeats	420
Biography	421
Social and Cultural Context	422
Timeline	424
The Lake Isle of Innisfree	425
The Wild Swans at Coole*	427
An Irish Airman Foresees His Death*	432
September 1913	437
Easter 1916	441
The Second Coming	448
Sailing to Byzantium	452
from Meditations in Time of Civil War: VI: The Stare's Nest by My Window	456
In Memory of Eva Gore-Booth and Con Markiewicz	459
Swift's Epitaph	463
An Acre of Grass	466
Politics	469
from Under Ben Bulben: V and VI	470
Exam-Style Questions	473
Sample Essay	475
Snapshot	478

Patricia Beer	479
Biography	479
The Voice*	480
Carol Ann Duffy	485
Biography	485
Valentine*	486
Tess Gallagher	491
Biography	491
The Hug*	492
Kerry Hardie	499
Biography	499
Daniel's Duck*	500
George Herbert	505
Biography	505
The Collar*	506
Brendan Kennelly	513
Biography	513
Night Drive*	514
Liz Lochhead	519
Biography	519
Kidspoem/Bairnsang*	520
Howard Nemerov	524
Biography	524
Wolves in the Zoo*	525
Julie O'Callaghan	530
Biography	530
The Net*	531
Marge Piercy	535
Biography	535
Will we work together?*	536

Penelope Shuttle	540
Biography	540
Zoo Morning*	541
Peter Sirr	546
Biography	546
Madly Singing in the City*	547
Dylan Thomas	553
Biography	553
Do Not Go Gentle into that Good Night*	554
David Wheatley	559
Biography	559
Chronicle*	560
William Carlos Williams	566
Biography	566
This is just to say*	567
Enda Wyley	572
Biography	572
Poems for Breakfast*	573
Reading Unseen Poetry	578
Guidelines for Answering Questions on Poetry	590
Glossary of Terms	596
Poets Examined at Higher Level in Previous Years	600

Acknowledgements

The poems in this book have been reproduced with the kind permission of their publishers, agents, authors or their estates as follows:

'The Armadillo', 'At The Fishhouses', 'The Bight', 'Filling Station', 'First Death in Nova Scotia', 'The Fish', 'In the Waiting Room', 'The Prodigal', 'Questions of Travel', 'Sestina' by Elizabeth Bishop from *The Complete Poems 1927-1979*. © 1979, 1983 by Alice Helen Methfessel. Reprinted by permission of Farrar, Straus and Giroux LLC.

'The Forge' and 'Bogland' from *Door into the Dark* (1969); 'The Tollund Man' from *Wintering Out* (1972); 'Mossbawn: Two Poems in Dedication (1) Sunlight' and 'A Constable Calls' from *North* (1975); 'The Skunk' and 'The Harvest Bow' from *Fieldwork* (1979); 'The Underground' and 'Lightenings viii (The annals say...)' from *Station Island* (1984); 'The Pitchfork' from *Seeing Things* (1991); 'Postscript' and 'A Call' from *The Spirit Level* (1996); 'Tate's Avenue' from *District and Circle* (2006) by Seamus Heaney, published by Faber and Faber Ltd.

'Thinking of Mr D.', 'Dick King', 'Mirror in February', 'Chrysalides', from 'Glenmacnass VI Littlebody', 'Tear', 'Hen Woman', 'His Father's Hands', from 'Settings: Model School, Inchicore', from 'The Familiar VII' and 'Belief and Unbelief: Echo' by Thomas Kinsella from *Collected Poems* (2001) by Carcanet Press Limited, reproduced by kind permission of the poet and Carcanet Press, Manchester.

'An Arundel Tomb', 'The Whitsun Weddings', 'MCMXIV', 'Ambulances' from *The Whitsun Weddings* (1964); 'The Trees', 'The Explosion', 'Cut Grass' from *High Windows* (1974) by Philip Larkin published by Faber and Faber Ltd. 'At Grass', 'Church Going' and 'Wedding Wind' from *The Less Deceived* (1955) by Philip Larkin by The Marvell Press.

'Grandfather', 'Day Trip to Donegal', 'Ecclesiastes', 'After the Titanic', 'At it Should Be', 'A Disused Shed in Co Wexford', 'Rathlin', 'The Chinese Restaurant in Portrush', 'Kinsale', 'Antarctica' by Derek Mahon from *New Collected Poems* (2011) by kind permission of the author and The Gallery Press, Loughcrew, Oldcastle, Co Meath.

'Pheasant', 'Finisterre', 'Mirror', 'Child', 'Morning Song', 'Elm', 'The Arrival of the Bee Box', 'Poppies in July', 'Black Rook in Rainy Weather', 'The Times are Tidy' by Sylvia Plath from *Collected Poems* (1981) published by Faber and Faber Ltd.

'The Voice' by Patricia Beer from *Friends of Heraclitus* (1993), Carcanet Press, Manchester.

'Valentine' by Carol Ann Duffy from *Mean Time* (1993) published by Anvil Press Poetry.

'The Hug' by Tess Gallagher from *Midnight Lantern: New and Selected Poems* © 1984, 1987. Reprinted with the permission of The Permissions Company, Inc, Graywolf Press, Minneapolis, Minnesota. www.graywolfpress.org.

'Daniel's Duck' by Kerry Hardie from *The Sky Didn't Fall* © 2003. By kind permission of the author and The Gallery Press, Loughcrew, Oldcastle, Co Meath.

'Night Drive' by Brendan Kennelly from *The Essential Brendan Kennelly, with CD readings*, Bloodaxe Books 2011, reprinted by permission of the publisher.

'Kidspoem/Bairnsong' from *Colour of Black and White* by Liz Lochhead published by Polygon Press. An imprint of Birlinn Ltd. www.birlinn.co.uk

'Wolves in the Zoo' from *The Western Approaches* (1975) by Howard Nemerov, published by University of Chicago Press.

'The Net' by Julie O'Callaghan from *Tell Me This is Normal: New and Selected Poems* (2008) reproduced by kind permission of the publishers Bloodaxe Books.

'Will we work together?' by Marge Piercy, © 1977, 1980 by Marge Piercy and Middlemarsh, Inc. Used with permission of the Wallace Literary Agency, Inc.

'Zoo Morning' by Penelope Shuttle, from *Selected Poems 1980-1996*, published by OUP. Reproduced by kind permission of the poet and David Higham Associates.

'Madly Singing in the City' by Peter Sirr from *Bring Everything* © 2000. By kind permission of the author and The Gallery Press, Loughcrew, Oldcastle, Co Meath.

'Do Not Go Gentle into That Good Night' by Dylan Thomas from *Collected Poems* published by Orion. Used by permission of the author.

'Chronicle' by David Wheatley from *Misery Hill* © 2000. By kind permission of the author and The Gallery Press, Loughcrew, Oldcastle, Co Meath.

'This is Just to Say' by William Carlos Williams from *Collected Poems Volume I* (2000) Carcanet Press, Manchester.

'Poems for Breakfast' by Enda Wyley from *Poems for Breakfast* (2004), Dedalus Press Dublin.

'Thistles' by Ted Hughes from *Collected Poems* (2005) published by Faber and Faber.

'Eating Poetry' by Mark Strand from *Reasons for Moving: Darker; The Sargentbille Notebook* © 1971 by Mark Strand. Used by permission of Alfred A.Knopf, a division of Random House, Inc.

'Lay Back the Darkness' by Edward Hirsch from *Lay Back The Darkness: Poems* © 2003. Used by permission of Alfred A. Knopf, a division of Random House, Inc.

'Dreams' by Langston Hughes, from *Collected Poems of Langston Hughes* published by Alfred A. Knopf Inc/Vintage. Reproduced by kind permission of the poet and David Higham Associates.

'A Blessing' by James Wright from *Collected Poems* © 1971. Reprinted by permission of Wesleyan University Press.

While every care has been taken to trace and acknowledge copyright, the publishers tender their apologies for any accidental infringement where copyright has proved untraceable. They would be pleased to come to a suitable arrangement with the rightful owner in each case.

Topfoto p. 1, 117, 189, 252, 307, 420, 458, 479, 485, 505, 519, 540, 553, 566. Corbis p. 71, 359, 524. Dorothy Alexander p. 491. Paddy Jolley/The Gallery Press p. 499. Photocall Ireland p. 513. Kim Haughton p. 530. Richard Rosenthal p. 535. Peter Sirr by The Gallery Press p. 546. John Wheatley/The Gallery Press p. 559. The Dedalus Press p. 572. Other photos, Shutterstock.

Elizabeth Bishop

1911–79

THE FISH*
THE BIGHT
AT THE FISHHOUSES
THE PRODIGAL*
QUESTIONS OF TRAVEL
THE ARMADILLO
SESTINA
FIRST DEATH IN NOVA SCOTIA
FILLING STATION*
IN THE WAITING ROOM

Biography

Elizabeth Bishop was born on 8 February 1911 in Worcester, Massachusetts. She was the only child of William T. Bishop and Gertrude May Bulmer Bishop. William, who was vice-president of his father's successful building firm, died of Bright's disease when Elizabeth was eight months old. Gertrude was so traumatised by her husband's death that it led to a mental breakdown that resulted in her being hospitalised five years later. Elizabeth never saw her mother again, although she lived until 1934.

Although Elizabeth left published accounts of only two memories of her life with her mother – one of them a short reference in her poem 'First Death in Nova Scotia' – it is clear that the experience left an indelible impression on her, influencing her emotional life and possibly accounting for her later struggles with depression and alcoholism.

Elizabeth was cared for initially by her maternal grandparents at Great Village, a tiny town in Nova Scotia, a time she recollected later with affection. Her grandparents were simple and loving people, and there was a family of aunts and uncles who were caring and kind to her. In 1917, however, her paternal grandparents, the wealthy Bishops, arrived in Great Village by train to take the six-year-old Elizabeth back to live with them in Worcester. Her departure was so sudden that she recalled it as a 'kidnapping' from the happy home she knew to a much more austere environment, a violent change that seems to have created a sense of loss in the child, a sense which remained with her as an adult.

Bishop's unhappiness showed itself in the many illnesses she suffered from – asthma, bronchitis, eczema. The Bishops felt unable to cope with her after only nine months, and her mother's older sister, Aunt Maude, took the ill and nervous child to live with her and her husband in the upstairs apartment of a run-down tenement in an impoverished neighbourhood in Revere, Massachusetts. Bishop later said that Aunt Maude had saved her life.

Education

Ill-health meant that Bishop had very little formal schooling before the age of fourteen. Her formal education began at Walnut Hill School for Girls. Academically she made great progress. Her literary gifts were apparent and she wrote fiction and poetry for the school magazine. By the time she attended the exclusive all-girls' college at Vassar in New York, where she majored in English literature, she was already considered to have great talent. She was also an accomplished musician and painter.

Following graduation Bishop remained in New York, writing poems for small magazines and using money from her inheritance to travel to France, England, North Africa, Spain and Italy. In 1938 she moved to Key West, Florida. In 1946 her first collection of poems, *North & South*, the fruit of ten years' work, received the Houghton Mifflin Poetry Award. Awarded a Guggenheim Fellowship in 1947, she became consultant in poetry at the Library of Congress.

Brazil

Bishop's life changed again in 1951 when, on a visit to Brazil, she met Lota de Macedo Soares. The two women settled together near Rio de Janeiro in a lesbian relationship that was to last until Lota's death in 1967. Bishop described this period as the happiest time of her life: for the first time she had a home and a sense of family with Lota's adopted children. She also continued her travels, visiting Mexico and Europe, and in 1961 she took a trip up the Amazon River to see Indian tribes.

Her second collection, *A Cold Spring*, was published in 1955. Combined with *North & South*, it won the Pulitzer Prize for Poetry. Her literary reputation was recognised by the Fellowship of the Academy of American Poets awarded in 1964. In 1965 her third collection, *Questions of Travel*, appeared.

After Lota's death in 1967 Bishop lived for a year in San Francisco, then taught for a number of years at Harvard University, Cambridge, Massachusetts. In 1976, maintaining her pattern of producing a book of poems roughly every ten years, she published *Geography III*. Numerous prizes and awards followed until her death in Boston in 1979. Bishop's *Complete Poems* was published in 1991.

Social and Cultural Context

Bishop is now recognised as one of the best American poets of the twentieth century, although she published only four small volumes of poems over a span of forty years. During her lifetime she was by no means a well-known writer, even though her work was praised by many critics as it appeared. One of the possible reasons for this may be that she was not identified with any particular school or movement in poetry.

Although Bishop's copious letters to her friends and acquaintances reveal her awareness of most of the important cultural movements of her day, she retained to the end a sense of her own independence and integrity. In her work with students at New York and Harvard, she stressed the importance of poetry and observed that it must be worked at if it is to be rewarding – a philosophy that could be said to underlie her considerable poetic achievement.

Literary and artistic influences

Bishop was, however, influenced by many major literary movements. Her earliest published work, which explores imaginary worlds, shows her interest in the ideas of the Symbolist poets of the late nineteenth and early twentieth centuries. She was also influenced by the theories of the early twentieth-century poetic movement Imagism, in which the image is central to a poem's meaning. Her mastery of these techniques is clear in her mature work, but she moved above and beyond them in forging her own distinctive style.

She assimilated other important literary and artistic ideas of the twentieth century. Critics have remarked on the extent to which her poems share the Surrealists' fascination with perspective and vision, for instance, which is not surprising for a poet who was also a gifted amateur painter. (Surrealism, popular in the 1920s and 1930s, seeks to break down the boundaries between rationality and irrationality, to liberate the imagination from reality.) Bishop is on record as saying that, for her, the best poetry conveys 'the most fantastic thoughts in the most correct and natural language'. In 'The Fish', for instance, we can see how her unusual description of the fish is conveyed in a direct, conversational style.

Child psychology

In her poems about childhood, Bishop is seen to have absorbed the teachings of famous child psychologists of her time such as Melanie Klein and Benjamin Spock. Both of these psychologists emphasised the importance of recognising the child as an individual with his or her own perspective and understanding. Klein in particular wrote about the idea of 'knowing and not knowing' in childhood, when the depth of understanding exceeds the ability to articulate thoughts and emotions. She also recognised the importance of play and fantasy as a means of emotional communication in a child's life. These ideas are particularly relevant in poems such as 'First Death in Nova Scotia', 'Sestina' and 'In the Waiting Room'.

In turn, Bishop is acknowledged to have influenced many contemporary and younger poets, in particular John Ashbery and her great friend Robert Lowell. Indeed Ashbery recognised her influence by calling her 'the writer's writer's writer'.

Travel

Bishop's lifelong interest in travel was an important source of her creative inspiration. She lived for some years in Key West, Florida (the setting for her poems 'The Fish' and 'The Bight'). Having moved back to New York, and feeling unhappy there, she decided to travel. In 1951 she came to Brazil. In her poems about that country (including 'Questions of Travel') we can see her desire to see things afresh and her sense of curiosity about other cultures and ways of life. But she often linked the concept of home with the concept of travel, questioning not only the idea of going but also of remaining in one place.

Many critics have remarked that she is a poet who is more concerned with geography than with history, so that although she lived through World War II in the United States and through turbulent times in Brazil, these are not subjects that engage her poetic attention. Rather, she is more concerned to describe the changing landscape and weather of Brazil or the different cultural customs she finds there. In 'In the Waiting Room' we can see how this interest in other lands and peoples fascinated her from an early age.

Feminism

Nor was Bishop interested, as a poet, in being part of the feminist movement of the 1960s and 1970s. Although she described herself as having been a feminist from about the age of six – her poem 'In the Waiting Room' would suggest this – she rarely engaged with the issue directly in her work. **She preferred to think of art as being outside gender.**

Bishop was reluctant to be pigeon-holed as a woman poet, believing it would limit her power to reach a wider audience. Throughout her life she refused to allow her poems to be included in all-women anthologies. She was the sort of feminist who believed that a talented woman could compete successfully in any area of life. She regarded overtly feminist poetry as propaganda and disapproved of the new 'confessional' type of poetry in which personal relationships were laid bare. Her relationship with Lota de Macedo Soares never featured directly in her work.

Timeline

1911	Born on 8 February in Massachusetts; father dies
1916	Mother hospitalised; lives with grandparents in Nova Scotia
1917	Lives with grandparents and later Aunt Maude in Massachusetts
1930–34	Attends Vassar College, New York
1938	Moves to Key West, Florida
1946	Publishes her first collection of poems, *North & South*; wins Houghton Mifflin Poetry Award
1951	Meets partner, Lota de Macedo Soares; settles in Brazil
1955	Publishes her second collection, *A Cold Spring*; wins Pulitzer Prize for Poetry
1964	Awarded Fellowship of the Academy of American Poets
1965	Publishes her third collection, *Questions of Travel*
1967	Lota dies; Elizabeth lives in San Francisco for a year
1970	Poet-in-residence at Harvard University, Massachusetts
1976	Publishes her fourth collection, *Geography III*
1979	Dies in Boston
1991	*Complete Poems* published

The Fish

I caught a tremendous fish
and held him beside the boat
half out of water, with my hook
fast in a corner of his mouth.
He didn't fight. 5
He hadn't fought at all.
He hung a grunting weight,
battered and venerable
and homely. Here and there
his brown skin hung in strips 10
like ancient wallpaper,
and its pattern of darker brown
was like wallpaper:
shapes like full-blown roses
stained and lost through age. 15
He was speckled with barnacles,
fine rosettes of lime,
and infested
with tiny white sea-lice,
and underneath two or three 20
rags of green weed hung down.
While his gills were breathing in
the terrible oxygen
– the frightening gills,
fresh and crisp with blood, 25
that can cut so badly –
I thought of the coarse white flesh
packed in like feathers,
the big bones and the little bones,
the dramatic reds and blacks 30
of his shiny entrails,
and the pink swim-bladder
like a big peony.
I looked into his eyes
which were far larger than mine 35
but shallower, and yellowed,

the irises backed and packed
with tarnished tinfoil
seen through the lenses
of old scratched isinglass.
They shifted a little, but not
to return my stare.
– It was more like the tipping
of an object toward the light.
I admired his sullen face,
the mechanism of his jaw,
and then I saw
that from his lower lip
– if you could call it a lip –
grim, wet, and weaponlike,
hung five old pieces of fish-line,
or four and a wire leader
with the swivel still attached,
with all their five big hooks
grown firmly in his mouth.
A green line, frayed at the end
where he broke it, two heavier lines,
and a fine black thread
still crimped from the strain and snap
when it broke and he got away.
Like medals with their ribbons
frayed and wavering,
a five-haired beard of wisdom
trailing from his aching jaw.
I stared and stared
and victory filled up
the little rented boat,
from the pool of bilge
where oil had spread a rainbow
around the rusted engine
to the bailer rusted orange,
the sun-cracked thwarts,
the oarlocks on their strings,
the gunnels – until everything
was rainbow, rainbow, rainbow!
And I let the fish go.

Glossary

8	*venerable*:	worthy of respect on account of age, character, position, etc.
16	*barnacles*:	crustaceans or shellfish that cling to rocks, large fish, etc.
31	*entrails*:	inner parts of the fish
33	*peony*:	a large, showy flower
40	*isinglass*:	a whitish, semi-transparent gelatinous substance
52	*wire leader*:	a short piece of wire connecting fish-hook and fish-line
53	*swivel*:	a ring or link that turns round on a pin or neck
59	*crimp*ed:	curled, wavy
68	*bilge*:	filth that collects in the bottom of a boat
71	*bailer*:	a bucket for ladling water out of a boat
72	*thwarts*:	seats or benches that the rowers sit on
73	*oarlocks*:	devices for holding and balancing the oars on the side of a boat
74	*gunnels*:	gunwale, the upper edge of a boat's side

Guidelines

'The Fish' was written when Bishop lived in Florida in the 1930s. It is included in her first collection, *North & South*. **As with so many of her poems, it is based on a real experience that she had of catching a large Caribbean jewfish at Key West.**

Commentary

Lines 1–20

In the first few lines of the poem the speaker tells us that she caught a 'tremendous fish' (line 1) that did not resist capture at all, probably because, as she says, he was 'battered and venerable' (line 8). 'Battered' suggests that he has suffered. 'Venerable' is a word often applied to elderly people and hints at the respect Bishop feels for him from the beginning. **It also suggests that she is giving the fish some of the attributes of a human being**.

She then describes in detail what the fish looked like, using some unusual and original images that appeal to our senses of sight and touch. His skin is compared to 'ancient wallpaper' (line 11), complete with patterns and stains. Vivid colours enable us to visualise the fish: 'brown' and 'darker brown' skin (lines 10 and 12) speckled with lime green and white (lines 16 to 19), as well as suggestions of pink in 'roses' (line 14). **She** gives us a realistic picture of the fish, seeing him not only in imaginative terms but also taking care to present him as he really is, his fishy texture and physical characteristics. He is covered in barnacles and infested with sea-lice. From underneath him hang 'rags of green weed' (line 21), seaweed of course, but somehow suggesting the beard of a 'venerable' old man.

Lines 22–33

In these lines Bishop focuses on the fish as an alien creature, leaving aside for a time any human characteristics he might have. The 'frightening gills / fresh and crisp with blood' (lines 24–25) and the 'coarse white flesh' (line 27) appeal to our sense of touch, while we can see the 'dramatic reds and blacks / of his shiny entrails' (lines 30–31). The pattern of flower imagery is continued as his pink swim-bladder is compared to a 'big peony' (line 33).

Lines 34–65

Despite the barrier between animal and human, **Bishop begins to empathise with the fish**: 'I looked into his eyes' (line 34). She describes the eyes with great care. **Details are important to her**, such as whether the fish's eyes are larger or shallower than those of humans, and how the irises seem 'backed and packed / with tarnished tinfoil' (lines 37–38). As is part of her characteristic method of description, she clarifies the last image: not just any tinfoil but tinfoil 'seen through the lenses / of old scratched isinglass' (lines 39–40). (Isinglass is a gelatinous substance that causes an object viewed through it to seem somewhat hazy.) The adjectives 'tarnished' and 'old' continue the notion of age that has been introduced from the beginning.

The narrator is under no illusion that the creature responds to her, but she certainly responds to him. She admires 'his sullen face / the mechanism of his jaw' – the features belong to humans, as does the 'lip' and 'mouth' she mentions with the pieces of fish-line hanging from it (lines 45 to 55). She describes the hooks and fish-lines as 'weaponlike' (line 50), and sees that the fish has struggled many times to escape capture. Words such as 'strain and snap' (line 59) emphasise how difficult it must have been for him.

The achievement of the fish in escaping capture becomes like that of a war hero who has endured conflict and is now honoured for it. We visualise a battle-scarred general, decorated for bravery: the fish-lines are 'like medals with their ribbons / frayed and wavering' (lines 61–62). Now the fish seems really to have earned the adjective 'venerable' used earlier in the poem.

The images, metaphors and similes Bishop uses here display her ability to go beyond surface description to display the metaphorical significance of the fish for her. Her unusual, almost fantastic description of the fish (half creature, half human) displays the extent to which she was influenced by Surrealism (the artistic movement of the early twentieth century that sought to liberate the imagination from the real and actual).

Lines 65–76
For the remainder of the poem Bishop is concerned with her own response to capturing the fish. When she says that she 'stared and stared' (line 65), it suggests that she has an important moment of recognition that influences what she now does. She is recording her admiration for the uniqueness of the fish. She also sees the fish as a creature with rights within his own environment, the sea. He has a right to an existence that is independent of humans.

There are a number of aspects to her sense of 'victory' (line 66). It was a great achievement to have caught such a 'tremendous fish'. There is also her victory in achieving an insight into the experience of the fish, how he has struggled and overcome difficulties. Given the circumstances of Bishop's life, it is possible that she sees in the fish a fellow creature, suffering and struggling like herself.

For all these reasons, **Bishop is overjoyed at this moment of recognition. She expresses her joy in a lovely metaphor of beauty and hope, a rainbow**. The metaphor has its origin in the oil that had spread around a 'pool of bilge' (line 68) that lay at the bottom of the boat. With her usual eye for details she describes parts of the boat as 'rusted' (line 70) and 'sun-cracked' (line 72), creating a link between the well-used boat and the 'venerable' fish. It seems appropriate that even the boat shares in the 'victory' that finally belongs to the fish: 'And I let the fish go' (line 76).

Tone of the poem

The tone of the poem goes beyond any conventional delight a person might feel at having 'caught a tremendous fish' (line 1). **Bishop reveals her growing interest and emotional involvement in the fish and his struggle, past and present.** The admiring tone of the language used to describe him suggests that she recognises the difficulties he has had, and his achievements in overcoming them.

She also recognises that he is a creature from another element far removed from that of humans. She is full of wonder at the difference between them. Finally, she is humble in her recognition that the fish has a right to his own freedom. There is no regret in the last line: 'And I let the fish go.'

Fable

The poem can be read as a fable (a poem with a message or a moral). In many traditional fables there is an encounter between a human and an animal in which the human learns an important lesson. From the beginning of the poem the fish seems more than just a creature of nature. Bishop gives him some human characteristics, as in a traditional fable. He is a 'venerable' (well-respected) and aged general, who has received awards for his bravery in battle. He has struggled and has gained 'wisdom' from those struggles. It may be that the lesson of the poem (the reason why she finally let the fish go) is connected with her awareness that the fish has a moral right to his own survival. Such an interpretation would indicate that Bishop recognised the complex relationship human beings have with the natural world. Writing in the 1930s, she would have been ahead of her time in having such a modern, ecologically aware attitude to nature.

Form of the poem

The poem is written as one long narrative with a clear beginning, progression and ending. It is unrhymed, which helps to give the impression of the speaking voice, with the exception of the last two lines, where a rhyming couplet gives a sense of closure.

The metre Bishop chooses is dimeter, with two stresses per line (as in 'He didn't fight') or trimeter with three stresses ('He hadn't fought at all'). This form of metre echoes speech rhythms and is particularly suitable for telling a story.

Sound patterns in the poem

Although the poem does not rhyme, Bishop makes use of sound patterns such as assonance, consonance and alliteration. For example, you may notice the repeated 'u' sound in 'hung a grunting', 'i' sound in 'skin . . . strips' (assonance); alliteration in 'big bones' and 'tarnished tinfoil'; and consonance in the phrase 'speckled with barnacles'. Such sound patterns are to be found throughout the poem and contribute to its harmonious effect.

Thinking about the poem

1. 'I caught a tremendous fish'. In lines 1 to 9 of the poem, how does Bishop show that the fish was 'tremendous'?
2. How does Bishop describe the fish in lines 16 to 21?
3. Choose the word that in your view best defines Bishop's description of the fish: attractive, imaginative or realistic. Explain your choice.
4. Where in the poem does Bishop present the fish as having human characteristics?
5. Where in the poem, however, are we made aware that this is an illusion?
6. 'I stared and stared' (line 65). Why is this a significant moment in the poem?
7. How do Bishop's feelings about the fish change as the poem progresses?
8. Why, in your opinion, does she release the fish? Who has had the 'victory' here, in your opinion?

9   What sort of person do you imagine Bishop to be, from your reading of this poem?
10 Bishop once said, 'I simply try to see things afresh.' Does she achieve this in 'The Fish'? Support your answer by reference to the poem.

Taking a closer look

1   The fish is compared to wallpaper (lines 10 to 15) and to an old army general (lines 61 to 64). Which of the comparisons do you find more convincing? Give a reason for your view.
2   Choose **two** more examples of similes (comparisons) used in the poem and say whether you liked them or not. Give reasons.
3   Comment on Bishop's use of colour in describing the fish.

Imagining

1   You wish to include 'The Fish' in an anthology entitled *Nature*. Give reasons why this poem would be suitable for the anthology.
2   You wish to make a short film or video of this poem. Describe how you would use lighting and music to create atmosphere.

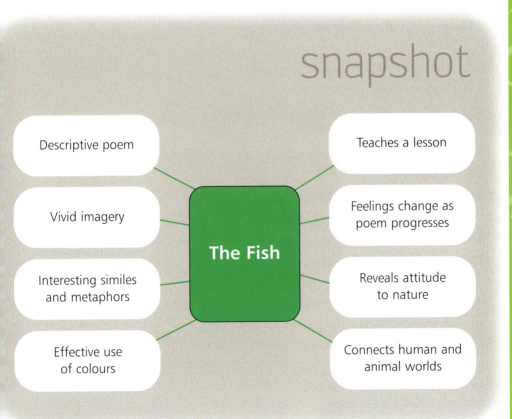

snapshot

- Descriptive poem
- Vivid imagery
- Interesting similes and metaphors
- Effective use of colours

The Fish

- Teaches a lesson
- Feelings change as poem progresses
- Reveals attitude to nature
- Connects human and animal worlds

The Bight
(On my birthday)

At low tide like this how sheer the water is.
White, crumbling ribs of marl protrude and glare
and the boats are dry, the pilings dry as matches.
Absorbing, rather than being absorbed,
the water in the bight doesn't wet anything, 5
the color of the gas flame turned as low as possible.
One can smell it turning to gas; if one were Baudelaire
one could probably hear it turning to marimba music.
The little ocher dredge at work off the end of the dock
already plays the dry perfectly off-beat claves. 10
The birds are outsize. Pelicans crash
into this peculiar gas unnecessarily hard,
it seems to me, like pickaxes,
rarely coming up with anything to show for it,
and going off with humorous elbowings. 15

Black-and-white man-of-war birds soar
on impalpable drafts
and open their tails like scissors on the curves
or tense them like wishbones, till they tremble.
The frowsy sponge boats keep coming in 20
with the obliging air of retrievers,
bristling with jackstraw gaffs and hooks
and decorated with bobbles of sponges.
There is a fence of chicken wire along the dock
where, glinting like little plowshares, 25
the blue-gray shark tails are hung up to dry
for the Chinese-restaurant trade.
Some of the little white boats are still piled up
against each other, or lie on their sides, stove in,
and not yet salvaged, if they ever will be, from the last bad storm, 30
like torn-open, unanswered letters.

The bight is littered with old correspondences.
Click. Click. Goes the dredge,
and brings up a dripping jawful of marl.
All the untidy activity continues, 35
awful but cheerful.

Glossary

title	*Bight*: a wide bay	
2	*marl*: a thick, clay-like soil	
3	*pilings*: timber posts driven into the ground to make a foundation	
7	*Baudelaire*: Charles Baudelaire (1821–67), a French Symbolist poet	
8	*marimba music*: African xylophone music played by jazz musicians	
9	*ocher dredge*: orange-brown-coloured ochre machine for clearing mud	
10	*claves*: musical keys	
16	*man-of-war birds*: large tropical seabirds	
20	*frowsy*: ill-smelling, untidy	
21	*retrievers*: dogs trained to find and fetch things	
22	*jackstraw gaffs*: splinters of wood used as hooks to land large fish	
24	*chicken wire*: wire netting	
25	*plowshares*: the detachable part of a plough that cuts and turns the soil	
29	*stove in*: broken	

Guidelines

'The Bight' was probably written in 1948 and is found in the collection *A Cold Spring* (1955).

Some of the details in this poem appeared first in a letter Bishop wrote when she lived in Key West, Florida, to her friend and fellow poet Robert Lowell. Excavations being carried out at Garrison Bight, Key West, left the harbour, as she describes it, 'always in a mess . . . it reminds me a little of my desk'. This remark might help us to appreciate her reference to Baudelaire, and indirectly to his 'theory of correspondences'. This Symbolist poet believed that there was a connection between the spiritual and physical worlds, so that one could express one's thoughts and feelings by describing objects and scenes.

It could be said that this is what the poem does. **It moves from description of ordinary activity (the dredging of the harbour) – what it looks and sounds like – to discovery of a more private world.** What Bishop sees and hears as the bight is excavated seems to lead her to contemplate the connections ('correspondences', line 32) between what is going on there and her work as a creative artist searching for material and trying to put shape on it.

Commentary

Stanza 1

The poem begins by describing the scene at low tide in the bight (or bay). Although the objects she sees are ordinary – the clay deposits (marl), the boats and the wooden posts (pilings) – she describes them using unusual metaphors and similes. The marl is shaped like 'ribs' that stick out from a body; with the adjectives 'white' and 'crumbling' the image she creates is surreal and a little menacing (line 2). The boats are dry, as are the wooden posts.

The water that 'doesn't wet anything' is 'the color of the gas flame turned as low as possible' (lines 5 and 6). She develops this image further when she says, 'One can smell it turning to gas' (line 7). Taken together with the phrase 'dry as matches' (line 3) there may be an underlying sense of anxiety about the scene, a fear of fire or a gas explosion.

At this stage Bishop introduces the name of Baudelaire, the French Symbolist poet mentioned in the overview above. If she were he, she says, perhaps she could make even more connections – not only see and smell the gas but also hear it turning to something completely different, like music. (In his poetry Baudelaire frequently used synaesthesia, or a combination of senses in one image.) Despite sounding slightly dismissive here, we should be aware that Bishop is in fact making such connections right though the poem.

Lines 9 to 15 show Bishop's remarkable ability to observe ordinary reality and present it in a new way through unusual metaphors and similes. The dredge that is carrying out the excavation sounds as if it is playing music (ironically recalling the reference to Baudelaire). She describes the pelicans as if they are machines rather than creatures. They are 'like pickaxes' in the way they 'crash' into the gas-like water, coming up with nothing to show for it.

Stanza 2

In lines 16 to 19 she describes large 'man-of-war birds' in similarly mechanised terms, with their tails open 'like scissors' but ending in a 'tremble'. Like the pelicans, they cannot find any food in the shallow water. Other objects, too, are seen as ineffective:

the ill-smelling boats, compared to 'retrievers', that keep coming in with useless things such as bits of fishing line (lines 20 to 24).

The whole impression is one of pointlessness and is continued when she describes other random objects that catch her attention. **Once again the comparisons she makes are unusual.** The 'blue-gray shark tails' (line 26) bound for Chinese restaurants that are drying on the chicken-wire fence along the dock are 'like plowshares' (line 25) – another word depicting a machine. The little boats that were damaged during the last storm still have their sides broken and may never now be salvaged; she compares them to 'torn-open, unanswered letters' (line 31).

Significantly, she comments, 'The bight is littered with old correspondences' (line 32). This line has interesting connotations. It echoes the French word used by Baudelaire (*correspondances*, meaning connections), but it is also of course a play on the idea of letter writing. Perhaps this is why she told Lowell that the bight reminded her of her desk.

The last four lines bring us back to the sound of the dredge as it digs up more and more mud. The activity goes on, not beautiful, not uplifting, but nevertheless 'cheerful' (line 36).

Interpreting the poem

As in many poems, the last lines offer a clue to the central idea of the poem. Might Bishop be saying that life itself, like the activity in the bight, is not always beautiful, and sometimes seems fruitless, but still has its own energy and purpose?

The subtitle '*(On my birthday)*' is revealing. (As it was not actually Bishop's birthday, it is perhaps even more significant in drawing attention to itself.) A birthday is a time of celebration, but also a time to take stock, to look at the past as well as the future and to think about one's life and work. Although she hardly appears in the poem directly, it is possible that the poet is reviewing her life and achievements by exploring the activity in the bight. From this point of view, the last line would suggest a hopeful if realistic attitude that reveals a great deal about Bishop as a person.

A poet's imagination

Bishop's unusual choice of images and similes, the seemingly random objects she mentions, may also reflect the untidiness of the subconscious that is the basis of a poet's imagination. Sometimes the work of the imagination yields nothing that is useful or beautiful, as the images of ineffectiveness and waste that are found in the poem suggest. There is no attempt to make the bight picturesque. In fact the opposite is true. The emphasis seems to be on the untidiness or even ugliness of the scene.

Yet, we should be aware of the irony, for this poet at least, that despite the struggle of artistic creation, a poem has been written. She has produced a clear and precise description of the activity going on in the bight, including the many details and technical terms that make the scene realistic. Almost all of the senses have been used to describe the sounds, textures and visual impact of what she sees before her.

Sound patterns in the poem

Appropriately for a poem that describes the dredging of a bay, the language the poet uses emphasises the untidiness and even ugliness of the scene. This lack of harmony is reflected in the sounds of the words, which are anything but harmonious. You will notice this if you try saying the lines aloud. Polysyllabic words and harsh consonants add to the effect. For example, the hard 'c' and 'k' sounds used in lines 9 to 13, echoing the harsh sounds of hard work.

Thinking about the poem

1. Look at the methods Bishop uses to describe the bight – sensuous images, similes and metaphors – and discuss her ability to really 'see' her surroundings.
2. Would you agree that her description is extremely individual, even unusual? Which images strike you as being particularly so?
3. Most poets love to use the sounds of words to create atmosphere. Point out where Bishop does this most effectively.
4. Bishop was an accomplished painter. How is this indicated, if at all, in this poem?
5. How would you describe the poet's mood in the poem: depressed, optimistic, humorous or celebratory? Perhaps you would suggest another word?
6. Do you like the way the poet has used language in this poem? Explain your answer.
7. Can 'The Bight' give us an insight into Bishop's personality and her attitude to her work? Explain your answer.
8. You wish to include 'The Bight' in a talk entitled 'Introducing Elizabeth Bishop'. Write out what you would say in your talk. You might consider such aspects as her powerful descriptions, her unusual use of language, and how you responded to the poem.

At the Fishhouses

Although it is a cold evening,
down by one of the fishhouses
an old man sits netting,
his net, in the gloaming almost invisible,
a dark purple-brown, 5
and his shuttle worn and polished.
The air smells so strong of codfish
it makes one's nose run and one's eyes water.
The five fishhouses have steeply peaked roofs
and narrow, cleated gangplanks slant up 10
to storerooms in the gables
for the wheelbarrows to be pushed up and down on.
All is silver: the heavy surface of the sea,
swelling slowly as if considering spilling over,
is opaque, but the silver of the benches, 15
the lobster pots, and masts, scattered
among the wild jagged rocks,
is of an apparent translucence
like the small old buildings with an emerald moss
growing on their shoreward walls. 20
The big fish tubs are completely lined
with layers of beautiful herring scales
and the wheelbarrows are similarly plastered
with creamy iridescent coats of mail,
with small iridescent flies crawling on them. 25
Up on the little slope behind the houses,
set in the sparse bright sprinkle of grass,
is an ancient wooden capstan,
cracked, with two long bleached handles
and some melancholy stains, like dried blood, 30
where the ironwork has rusted.
The old man accepts a Lucky Strike.
He was a friend of my grandfather.
We talk of the decline in the population
and of codfish and herring 35

while he waits for a herring boat to come in.
There are sequins on his vest and on his thumb.
He has scraped the scales, the principal beauty,
from unnumbered fish with that black old knife,
the blade of which is almost worn away.   40

Down at the water's edge, at the place
where they haul up the boats, up the long ramp
descending into the water, thin silver
tree trunks are laid horizontally
across the gray stones, down and down   45
at intervals of four or five feet.

Cold dark deep and absolutely clear,
element bearable to no mortal,
to fish and to seals . . . One seal particularly
I have seen here evening after evening.   50
He was curious about me. He was interested in music;
like me a believer in total immersion,
so I used to sing to him Baptist hymns.
I also sang 'A Mighty Fortress Is Our God.'
He stood up in the water and regarded me   55
steadily, moving his head a little.
Then he would disappear, then suddenly emerge
almost in the same spot, with a sort of shrug
as if it were against his better judgment.
Cold dark deep and absolutely clear,   60
the clear gray icy water . . . Back, behind us,
the dignified tall firs begin.
Bluish, associating with their shadows,
a million Christmas trees stand
waiting for Christmas. The water seems suspended   65
above the rounded gray and blue-gray stones.
I have seen it over and over, the same sea, the same,
slightly, indifferently swinging above the stones,
icily free above the stones,
above the stones and then the world.   70

If you should dip your hand in,
your wrist would ache immediately,
your bones would begin to ache and your hand would burn
as if the water were a transmutation of fire
that feeds on stones and burns with a dark gray flame. 75
If you tasted it, it would first taste bitter,
then briny, then surely burn your tongue.
It is like what we imagine knowledge to be:
dark, salt, clear, moving, utterly free,
drawn from the cold hard mouth 80
of the world, derived from the rocky breasts
forever, flowing and drawn, and since
our knowledge is historical, flowing, and flown.

Glossary		
4	*gloaming*:	twilight
6	*shuttle*:	tool used to repair fishing nets
10	*cleated*:	strips of wood that have been nailed on to prevent slipping
10	*gangplanks*:	narrow movable walkways
15	*opaque*:	not transparent
18	*translucence*:	light shining through
24	*iridescent*:	coloured like the rainbow
24	*coats of mail*:	pieces of armour
28	*capstan*:	revolving cylinder used for winding cable
32	*Lucky Strike*:	a brand of cigarette
52	*total immersion*:	form of baptism practised by some Christians
74	*transmutation*:	change from one form into another
77	*briny*:	very salty

Guidelines

'At the Fishhouses' comes from *A Cold Spring* (1955).

In 1946 Bishop paid a visit to the place of her childhood, Nova Scotia. It was her first time to go there since her mother's death in 1934. For a time she stayed in Halifax, across the bay from Dartmouth where her mother had lived and eventually died. Bishop's letters suggest that she was depressed during this visit, possibly due to the resurfacing of painful memories. 'At the Fishhouses' contains some echoes of notes she made while there. She wrote that other parts of the poem came to her in a dream.

Commentary

Lines 1–12

Like many of Bishop's poems, 'At the Fishhouses' opens with an objective description, in this case of the fishhouses and the old man who sits there, mending his nets. **The atmosphere of the place is conveyed vividly in images that engage almost all our senses.** Images of light and colour appeal to our visual sense. 'The air smells so strong of codfish / it makes one's nose run and one's eyes water' (lines 7–8) combines the sense of smell and touch, making us feel as if we are there in person. The fishhouses are carefully described in everyday, conversational language as places where ordinary business is conducted.

Lines 13–25

The phrase 'All is silver' in line 13 introduces a change in atmosphere and language. **The poem moves from the concrete world of the senses – the place itself, what can be seen and heard – to the world of the imagination.**

The sea symbolises the depth of this world: it is opaque and mysterious, an idea that is followed through as the poem progresses. In contrast, the silver light that shines on 'the benches / the lobster pots, and masts' is clear (lines 15–16). It is caused by a covering of fish scales and moss, signs of age and mortality. The detailed description in lines 21 to 25 shows the effects of light on the wheelbarrows and the fish scales. The language transforms them from ordinary objects into romanticised images. In this light even the flies are 'iridescent' or rainbow-coloured (line 24).

Lines 26–40

Now the poet directs her attention to what is behind the fishhouses, where there is a capstan (a machine used for winding cable) that has fallen into disuse. This 'ancient' device has 'some melancholy stains' on it, 'like dried blood', which reminds us that this is a place of death, if only for the fish (lines 28 to 30).

She encounters the old fisherman, 'a friend of my grandfather' (line 33); the personal reference suggests the importance of this place for Bishop as memories of her childhood resurface. The old man's way of life is fast disappearing, but, like the rest of the scene, he is given a strange sort of glamour, transformed by the poet's imagination.

Lines 41–46

This short section seems to form a bridge between the two longer parts of the poem. The ramp where boats are hauled down into the sea is made of 'thin silver / tree trunks' (lines 43–44) that descend further and further into the water, just as Bishop is also leading the reader into an imaginative experience with the sea and the seal she sees there. Images of light and colour, and the sense of depth created by the repetition of the word 'down', add to the atmosphere of romance and mystery.

Lines 47–66

From these lines on Bishop enters imaginatively into the sea as part of elemental nature, 'Cold dark deep and absolutely clear' (line 47). This image of icy beauty emphasises the otherness of the sea. It implies an utter contrast with the decaying human world as represented by the fisherman and the fishhouses.

Bishop's encounter with the seal and her interpretation of it give us another insight into how we can perceive the world in an imaginative way. As in 'The Fish', the seal seems to communicate with her at some, almost religious, level, so that she (humorously) sings Baptist hymns to him. But he does not leave his natural element of water for a moment, and the poet cannot enter it ('total immersion' is impossible), and so any communication she establishes with him is ultimately an illusion. She had, however, experienced a sort of communication with him, in contrast with the sea, which is absolutely separate from the human world.

As she does throughout the poem, Bishop now switches her attention from the sea back to the land behind her, focusing on the fir trees that stand waiting to be cut down for Christmas, before returning to contemplate the mystery of the sea.

Lines 67–77

'I have seen it over and over' – these words introduce a richly evocative description of the sea. Repetition, alliteration of 's' sounds and assonance combine to create an almost hypnotic effect. Sensuous images evoke the power and mystery of the sea. There are images of touch ('If you should dip your hand in', line 71) and taste ('it would first taste bitter', line 76), visual images and similes ('as if the water were a transmutation of fire', line 74). The overall impression is that Bishop is trying to understand the sea through the senses, which is the way we experience the world, but the images are all qualified with the word 'if'. Might this suggest that it is impossible to have a perfect understanding of the sea?

Lines 78–83

The poem ends in a beautiful lyrical passage, when Bishop compares the sea to human knowledge and contemplates the complex nature of that knowledge. The language she uses suggests that she has had a moment of vision. The sea is not the source of all knowledge, but it is like what 'we imagine knowledge to be' (line 78). It is both sensory and abstract. We can know the world through our senses. It is 'dark, salt, clear, moving' (line 79). These sensuous words are placed alongside abstract ideas of time, such as 'forever' and 'historical' (lines 82 and 83). Thus knowledge is both sensory and abstract.

The poet earlier described the sensations we would experience if we were to dip our hands into the sea. In the same way, knowledge may be painful. It may even be unbearable. Bishop's insight in these final lines is that knowledge may even be disillusioning, as the images of 'cold hard mouth' and 'rocky breasts' imply (lines 80 and 81). Knowledge, like the sea, is 'utterly free' (line 79); it can never be static but must instead constantly change and move. And like the sea, knowledge may be utterly indifferent to human beings with their preoccupations with death and loss.

Interpreting the poem

It could be said that the poem has as its underlying theme questions not only of what we know about the world, but also of how we know the world. Does our perspective shift constantly, as the sea does? Is knowledge (by which Bishop seems to mean understanding rather than reason or external facts) dependent upon a particular time and place (historical)? Is it merely temporary, ongoing (flowing), soon to become flown, or past, since we will take our understanding with us when we die? These are complex questions that have occupied philosophers for centuries.

How the poem is organised

To an extent Bishop has answered the question of how we know the world through how she has organised her poem. For instance, her perspective is constantly shifting, from the concrete world of the senses (what she sees and hears around her), to the transforming power of the imagination (the light and beauty of the scene) to the world of contemplation of the sea. She seems to suggest that we 'know' the world in many ways.

We should also take into account that Bishop does not actually equate the sea with knowledge. Rather, the sea 'is like what we imagine knowledge to be' (line 78). Here it is the poet herself who is making the comparison rather than discovering an absolute meaning that was already there. The distinction is significant because, as the critic Robert Dale Parker points out, 'First she sees . . . then wonders if she is wrong'.

Personal experience

Brett Millier comments on the possible personal basis of the poem. He suggests that the 'chill maternal image' at the end of the poem – 'the cold hard mouth' and 'the rocky breasts' (lines 80 and 81) – remind us that Bishop is returning to her motherland, the place of her disturbed and disturbing childhood. He goes on to say:

> Having spent a good part of the previous two years working with Dr. Ruth Foster on the origins of her depression and alcoholism, Elizabeth must have felt that her inheritance from her mother, what she 'derived' from that troubled relationship – her 'knowledge' of herself and her Nova Scotia past – was indeed 'flowing and drawn' and hopelessly temporal and irremediable, 'historical, flowing and flown'.

Perhaps, from this point of view, 'knowledge' of her mother and of her own past was indeed unbearable.

Bishop and nature

Bishop's early reputation as a poet was as a meticulous observer of the world around her. The critic Randall Jarrell claims that each of her poems should have written about it: 'I have seen it.' Others have recognised that what interests her is more complex. It is what her biographer, David Kalstone, describes as the mysterious relation between what she observes in nature and what it 'spiritually' signifies. So her encounter with the fish in 'The Fish' and her description of the activity in 'The Bight', as well as her descriptions in 'At the Fishhouses', have their spiritual side as metaphors of a deeper meaning to be found in nature than appreciation of it for its own sake.

Thinking about the poem

1. Discuss the descriptions of the five fishhouses and the old fisherman mending his nets. Would you agree that Bishop makes us feel as if we are actually there?
2. From the beginning we are made aware of the sea. How is it presented at first? What characteristics is it given?
3. Why, in your opinion, does the poet introduce the character of the old fisherman, whom she describes as 'a friend of my grandfather' (line 33), into the poem? What atmosphere does she create by the language she uses to describe him and his work?
4. Explore the second section of the poem (lines 40 to 46). Do you detect a change of tone in these lines? Why is the word 'down' repeated? Might it be interpreted metaphorically as a comment on the poet's changing perspective?

5   How do you respond to the poet's encounter with the seal? What kind of relationship does she have with him?
6   There are a number of religious references in the poem. Give possible reasons for this.
7   How does the poet's sense of being able to communicate with the seal differ from her attitude to the sea?
8   What does the poet learn from the sea? Comment on the language she uses to describe it.
9   Would you agree with the view that the sea becomes a metaphor for human knowledge? If so, what might her description suggest about Bishop's understanding of what human knowledge may be?
10 Do you like this poem? Would you include it in an anthology of Bishop's best poems?

The Prodigal

The brown enormous odor he lived by
was too close, with its breathing and thick hair,
for him to judge. The floor was rotten; the sty
was plastered halfway up with glass-smooth dung.
Light-lashed, self-righteous, above moving snouts,   5
the pigs' eyes followed him, a cheerful stare –
even to the sow that always ate her young –
till, sickening, he leaned to scratch her head.
But sometimes mornings after drinking bouts
(he hid the pints behind a two-by-four),   10
the sunrise glazed the barnyard mud with red;
the burning puddles seemed to reassure.
And then he thought he almost might endure
his exile yet another year or more.

But evenings the first star came to warn.   15
The farmer whom he worked for came at dark
to shut the cows and horses in the barn
beneath their overhanging clouds of hay,
with pitchforks, faint forked lightnings, catching light,

safe and companionable as in the Ark. 20
The pigs stuck out their little feet and snored.
The lantern – like the sun, going away –
laid on the mud a pacing aureole.
Carrying a bucket along a slimy board,
he felt the bats' uncertain staggering flight, 25
his shuddering insights, beyond his control,
touching him. But it took him a long time
finally to make his mind up to go home.

Glossary		
title	*Prodigal*: wasteful, spendthrift	
10	*two-by-four*: a length of timber with a cross-section measuring two inches by four inches	
20	*companionable*: sociable, suitable as a companion	
23	*aureole*: a halo of light around a blessed figure or saint	

Guidelines

The poem was written in 1951 and is included in the collection *A Cold Spring* (1955).

Bishop began to drink destructively during her college days and by 1939 she was an alcoholic. As she had no real family and no permanent home, her drinking often led to her leaving embarrassing situations and making herself effectively homeless. Her drinking may have had a genetic basis as her father, grandfather and three uncles all drank heavily. Furthermore, the circumstances of her life led to depression, which in turn she tried to alleviate by drinking. She tells us that 'The Prodigal' sprang from an experience in Nova Scotia in 1946 when 'one of my aunt's stepsons offered me a drink of rum, in the pig sties at about nine in the morning'. In the same letter, she speaks of the poem as having resulted from her experience of undergoing psychoanalysis.

The poem, a double sonnet, is based on the story of the prodigal son told in the Gospel of Luke, chapter 15, verse 15. The parable describes how the younger son of a rich man claims his inheritance early and leaves home. He squanders all his money and is forced to work as a swineherd, living with the pigs he tends. Eventually he returns home, where he is welcomed and forgiven by his father, who is so delighted to see him that he prepares a feast of a fatted calf. This leads to resentment on the part of the elder son, who had remained at home and helped his father.

Commentary

Stanza 1

Bishop dramatises the time before the prodigal returns home rather than the homecoming itself. She does not flinch from describing the squalor in which the prodigal lives among the pigs in the pigsty, with their 'brown enormous odor', 'breathing' and 'thick hair' (lines 1 and 2). We can almost smell and hear the animals among which the prodigal lives. We can see the rotten floor and 'glass-smooth dung' (line 4) that plasters the walls. His life has been degraded, so much so that he does not even know how far he has fallen: he lives too close to the animals 'for him to judge' (line 3).

Bishop describes the pigs in a non-judgemental, almost approving, way. They offer the prodigal some comfort and companionship. Their eyes follow him with 'a cheerful stare –/ even the sow that always ate her young' (lines 6–7). Such a realistic detail makes us realise how low the prodigal has sunk, especially since he scratches the sow's head in spite of being sickened at what he sees. It is a measure of his self-deception that he has come almost to accept his living conditions.

He also deceives himself (and perhaps others too) about his drinking: 'he hid the pints behind a two-by-four' (timber plank; line 10). But the poem also suggests that he is still capable of seeing beauty and hope in his surroundings. He appreciates the sunrise that 'glazed the barnyard mud with red' and the 'burning puddles' (lines 11 and 12). However, his self-deception also allows him to think that 'he almost might endure / his exile' (lines 13–14) for some time longer. Clearly he is not yet ready to face his problems and change his life.

Lines 15–23

The second stanza, in effect a second sonnet, opens with the word 'but', which signals another perspective on the situation. There may be a possibility of hope, as the imagery of light used throughout the stanza suggests: the 'star' (line 15), the 'faint forked lightnings' (line 19), the 'lantern' and the 'sun' (line 22) and a 'pacing aureole' (halo of light; line 23) on the mud. The image of the star is particularly appropriate in a poem that carries biblical echoes. But there is also a sense of isolation in the image of the farmer going about his business, shutting up the cows and horses in the barn. They may have been 'safe and companionable as in the Ark' (line 20), but there is no indication of any human contact between the farmer and the prodigal.

Lines 24–28

The prodigal's **moment of truth** occurs when he becomes aware of 'the bats' uncertain staggering flight', which gives him 'shuddering insights' (lines 25 and 26). He does not want to recognise the truth, but at last he realises his terrible isolation. The bats terrify him because their blind flight resembles his stumbling through life and his uncertain future.

But the decision 'to go home' is not an easy or inevitable one: it takes him 'a long time' to make it (lines 27 and 28). The implication is that the idea of 'home' is not without problems for the prodigal. **Home may be seen as the last resort rather than the first place of refuge.**

Personal experience

The last line recalls Bishop's circumstances as someone for whom 'home' did not truly exist. Home often signifies the notion of parental love and support, which Bishop lacked throughout her childhood due to her father's early death and her mother's mental illness. Home may be a difficult place if you do not feel loved there. On the other hand, in accepting love at home you make yourself vulnerable. These underlying concerns, and our awareness of Bishop's struggles with alcoholism, make 'The Prodigal' one of her most revealing poems.

Form of the poem

'The Prodigal' is a double sonnet, twenty-eight lines in length. It does not conform to a regular rhyme scheme. (Its rhyme scheme is *abacdbcedfeggf* in the first sonnet and *abacdbecfedfgh* in the second.) It has been pointed out that the last word, 'home', does not have a true rhyme and this has the effect of isolating that word (and the idea) within the poem.

Thinking about the poem

1. Which words and phrases best convey the squalor and degradation of the prodigal's living conditions, in your view?
2. Do you like Bishop's description of the pigs? Give a reason for your view.
3. Does the poem show an understanding of the prodigal's behaviour and state of mind? Give a reason for your opinion.
4. Which one of the following words best describes Bishop's attitude to the prodigal: sympathetic, compassionate or judgemental? Explain your choice.
5. 'The second sonnet gives the reader a different perspective from the first.' Would you agree with this statement? Give a reason for your opinion.
6. What role does the farmer play in the story told in the poem?
7. Why, in your opinion, does the prodigal make the decision he does at the end of the poem?
8. The poem has been said to be full of 'pain, alienation and bitterness'. Would you agree with this view? Give a reason for your opinion.
9. On the other hand, others have found the poem to be 'optimistic'. Would you agree with this finding? Give a reason for your opinion.
10. Would you agree that this poem reveals a great deal about Bishop, although it is not written in the first person? Refer to the poem in your answer.

Taking a closer look

1. 'The floor was rotten; the sty / was plastered halfway up with glass-smooth dung' (lines 3–4). What do you find interesting about the sounds in this line?
2. 'And then he thought he almost might endure / his exile yet another year or more' (lines 13–14). Explain why the prodigal thought he could go on living as he did.
3. 'But it took him a long time / finally to make his mind up to go home' (lines 27–28). What might Bishop means to convey by this final line of the poem?

Imagining

1. Imagine that you are the prodigal. In a series of **three** diary entries, describe the life you lead and how you feel about it.
2. You have been asked to make a short film to accompany a reading of the poem. Explain how you would use music, sound effects, images, colour, etc. to capture the atmosphere.

snapshot

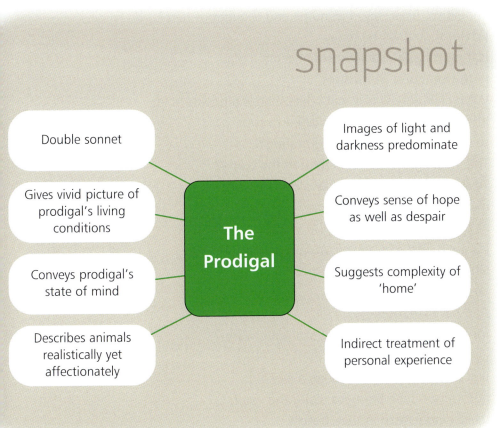

The Prodigal
- Double sonnet
- Gives vivid picture of prodigal's living conditions
- Conveys prodigal's state of mind
- Describes animals realistically yet affectionately
- Images of light and darkness predominate
- Conveys sense of hope as well as despair
- Suggests complexity of 'home'
- Indirect treatment of personal experience

Elizabeth Bishop

Questions of Travel

There are too many waterfalls here; the crowded streams
hurry too rapidly down to the sea,
and the pressure of so many clouds on the mountaintops
makes them spill over the sides in soft slow-motion,
turning to waterfalls under our very eyes.   5
– For if those streaks, those mile-long, shiny, tearstains,
aren't waterfalls yet,
in a quick age or so, as ages go here,
they probably will be.
But if the streams and clouds keep travelling, travelling,   10
the mountains look like the hulls of capsized ships,
slime-hung and barnacled.

Think of the long trip home.
Should we have stayed at home and thought of here?
Where should we be today?
Is it right to be watching strangers in a play
in this strangest of theatres?
What childishness is it that while there's a breath of life
in our bodies, we are determined to rush
to see the sun the other way around?
The tiniest green hummingbird in the world?
To stare at some inexplicable old stonework,
inexplicable and impenetrable,
at any view,
instantly seen and always, always delightful?
Oh, must we dream our dreams
and have them, too?
And have we room
for one more folded sunset, still quite warm?

But surely it would have been a pity
not to have seen the trees along this road,
really exaggerated in their beauty,
not to have seen them gesturing
like noble pantomimists, robed in pink.
– Not to have had to stop for gas and heard
the sad, two-noted, wooden tune
of disparate wooden clogs
carelessly clacking over
a grease-stained filling-station floor.
(In another country the clogs would all be tested.
Each pair there would have identical pitch.)
– A pity not to have heard
the other, less primitive music of the fat brown bird
who sings above the broken gasoline pump
in a bamboo church of Jesuit baroque:
three towers, five silver crosses.
– Yes, a pity not to have pondered,
blurr'dly and inconclusively,

on what connection can exist for centuries
between the crudest wooden footwear   50
and, careful and finicky,
the whittled fantasies of wooden cages.
– Never to have studied history in
the weak calligraphy of songbirds' cages.
– And never to have had to listen to rain   55
so much like politicians' speeches:
two hours of unrelenting oratory
and then a sudden golden silence
in which the traveller takes a notebook, writes:

'Is it lack of imagination that makes us come   60
to imagined places, not just stay at home?
Or could Pascal have been not entirely right
about just sitting quietly in one's room?

Continent, city, country, society:
the choice is never wide and never free.   65
And here, or there . . . No. Should we have stayed at home,
wherever that may be?'

Glossary		
1	*here*: Brazil
11	*hull*: outer body or frame
12	*barnacled*: covered with crustaceans
20	*the other way around*: seen from the southern hemisphere
34	*pantomimists*: people taking part in a pantomime
37	*disparate*: dissimilar, completely different
45	*Jesuit baroque*: ornate seventeenth-century architectural style often found in churches in Brazil
51	*finicky*: overdone, fussy
52	*fantasies*: fanciful designs
54	*calligraphy*: the art of handwriting; refers here to the design of the cages
57	*oratory*: public speaking
62	*Pascal*: Blaise Pascal (1623–62), French mathematician and philosopher

Guidelines

This poem is the title poem of the collection *Questions of Travel* (1965).

Bishop travelled a great deal throughout her life, visiting, among other places, Europe, various parts of the United States and Mexico before her trip to Brazil in 1952. Although she remained in Brazil for many years with her partner, Lota de Macedo Soares, she continued to be interested in travel.

The poem takes a quizzical look at the notion of travel and why we feel the need to do it. It also questions our ability to understand other people's cultures.

Commentary

Stanza 1

The poem is set in Brazil. At the beginning there is a slight touch of travel-weariness, as if the speaker has seen and done too much. Everything seems excessive and crowded, but beautiful too, as the language she uses suggests. Similes and metaphors help the reader to visualise the landscape, while sound effects such as sibilance ('soft slow-motion', line 4) and alliteration ('travelling, travelling', line 10) help create a harmonious aural effect.

Stanza 2

In the second stanza Bishop raises some of the 'questions of travel' that she would like to ask. In line 14 she wonders whether it would have been better to have stayed at 'home' (in her case, the United States) and 'thought of here' (Brazil). In other words, would imagining some place be as good as travelling to it?

Other questions occur to her. What ethical right do tourists have to watch the people of other cultures, as if they are watching a play? The metaphor of theatre emphasises the unreality of travel as opposed to living in a place. The question also touches on what has become a modern concern, the notion of 'ethical tourism'.

Possibly addressing the poem to herself as an enthusiastic traveller, Bishop wonders why people feel compelled to seek out different and strange sights. Is it childishness? Her tone is wryly humorous as she describes the usual tourist experience of staring 'at some inexplicable old stonework, / inexplicable and impenetrable' (lines 22–23). Here she implies the limitations we all have in understanding the culture of others. She also comments on the clichéd response most tourists make to the sights that are 'instantly seen and always, always delightful' (line 25).

Stanza 3
Bishop said that she was always interested in her poems showing the mind in action instead of in repose. Characteristically, then, the third stanza shows her working out some of the answers to the questions she has asked. But she continues to recognise uncertainty in her own mind, while at the same time delighting herself and the reader with her quirky observations of Brazilian life and culture. The details she chooses bring this world alive to us by appealing to our senses and focusing on the aspects of culture that make Brazil unique. She suggests that the claims of reality are more pressing than those of the imagination. It would surely 'have been a pity / not to have seen the trees along this road' (lines 30–31). These are particular trees, 'gesturing / like noble pantomimists' (lines 33–34) and not just any generalised view.

In lines 35 to 39 she recalls hearing 'the sad, two-noted, wooden tune' of clogs 'carelessly clacking' over the floor of a petrol station. This, too, is a specific sound, peculiar to the footwear of Brazil and therefore part of its unique culture. Another example she chooses is the 'fat brown bird' (line 43) that sings in its elaborately designed birdcage, a kind seen throughout South America. Her conclusion is that by studying such artefacts as the wooden clogs and the birdcage, one can understand the culture of a people.

Her final observation about the rain in Brazil has a slightly humorous tone: it is 'unrelenting' as she says, 'like politicians' speeches' (lines 55 to 57). When it stops, the traveller may ask some final questions in a typical traveller's log or diary.

Stanzas 4 and 5
The last two stanzas are presented in italics, signifying the handwritten notes of a traveller's diary. Once again Bishop returns to the idea of the competing claims of the imagination versus reality. Does the act of travelling imply a lack of imagination, since one can imagine places even if one has not visited them? On the other hand, she questions the belief of the great French philosopher Blaise Pascal, who stated, 'I have discovered that all the unhappiness of men arises from one single fact, that they cannot stay quietly in their own chamber.'

Bishop suggests that the 'question of travel' is more complex. We may not be as free as we think to choose our destinations or to decide not to travel: for some people, staying at home may be impossible. Similarly, the notion of 'home' that we leave behind may not be as simple as it seems. We could take into account here the ambivalent attitude to 'home' expressed in 'The Prodigal'.

Personal experience

As in so many of her poems Bishop reveals a great deal about herself in this poem. As always, she shows her ability to describe the world around her, in this case some of the Brazilian landscape and culture. Underlying the 'questions of travel' that she raises are also questions relating to the opposite, to staying at home. Due to her disrupted childhood, Bishop had no experience of what a stable and happy home life might be like. So her last question about home, 'wherever that may be' (line 67) is a poignant reminder of the deep loneliness at the heart of so many of her poems.

Language of the poem

The language Bishop uses here is a blend of the poetic and the conversational, which seems appropriate to convey the notion of someone thinking aloud. She handles many variations of tone, including being speculative, tentative, humorous and lyrical.

Thinking about the poem

1. Describe the poet's attitude to the landscape suggested in the first stanza. How does she communicate her feelings?
2. Which of the questions about travel raised by Bishop in the second stanza do you find the most interesting? Write a short note in response to the question.
3. Explore the details of her travel experiences that Bishop focuses on in the third stanza. Do you find them revealing, unusual, eccentric? Perhaps you can suggest another term?
4. Comment on the variations of tone in the poem. What effect is created?
5. Examine the sound effects Bishop uses in the poem and say how they contribute to its meaning.
6. Would you agree that Bishop gives the impression in this poem of someone thinking aloud? Comment further on this view.
7. From your reading of the poem, did Bishop approve of travel and travellers?
8. Why, in your opinion, did Bishop write 'Questions of Travel'?
9. Compare the poem with any **two** of Bishop's other poems under the following headings:
   - The poet's attitude to nature.
   - The poet's use of striking images.
   - The poet's interest in cultures other than her own
   - What the poem reveals about the poet as a person.
10. Although it was written half a century ago, would readers nowadays still respond to the issues raised in the poem?

The Armadillo
for Robert Lowell

This is the time of year
when almost every night
the frail, illegal fire balloons appear.
Climbing the mountain height,

rising toward a saint								5
still honored in these parts,
the paper chambers flush and fill with light
that comes and goes, like hearts.

Once up against the sky it's hard
to tell them from the stars –							10
planets, that is – the tinted ones:
Venus going down, or Mars,

or the pale green one. With a wind,
they flare and falter, wobble and toss;
but if it's still they steer between						15
the kite sticks of the Southern Cross,

receding, dwindling, solemnly
and steadily forsaking us,
or, in the downdraft from a peak,
suddenly turning dangerous.							20

Last night another big one fell.
It splattered like an egg of fire
against the cliff behind the house.
The flame ran down. We saw the pair

of owls who nest there flying up						25
and up, their whirling black-and-white
stained bright pink underneath, until
they shrieked up out of sight.

The ancient owls' nest must have burned.
Hastily, all alone,
a glistening armadillo left the scene,
rose-flecked, head down, tail down,

and then a baby rabbit jumped out,
short-eared, to our surprise.
So soft! – a handful of intangible ash
with fixed, ignited eyes.

Too pretty, dreamlike mimicry!
O falling fire and piercing cry
and panic, and a weak mailed fist
clenched ignorant against the sky!

Glossary

title	*Armadillo*: a burrowing mammal found mainly in South America; it rolls up into a ball inside its bony armour if it is in danger
dedication	*Robert Lowell*: American poet and friend of Bishop; in response he dedicated 'Skunk Hour' to Bishop
1	*time of year*: 24 June
5	*saint*: San Juan (St John); his feast day, 24 June, is celebrated in Brazil
16	*Southern Cross*: constellation in the southern hemisphere; its four major stars form the shape of a cross
35	*intangible*: cannot be touched
36	*ignited*: on fire
37	*mimicry*: imitation
39	*weak mailed fist*: the armadillo rolled up into a ball looks like a fist made of armour (coat of mail), however, it is weak

Guidelines

First published in *The New Yorker* magazine in 1957, 'The Armadillo' is found in the collection *Questions of Travel* (1965). It is dedicated to the poet Robert Lowell, Bishop's friend, who considered the poem to be among her best work.

St John's Day, 24 June, is the winter solstice (the shortest day of the year) in Brazil, which is in the southern hemisphere. In order to honour the saint, it was the custom of the local people to send up fire balloons into the sky. These helium-filled balloons carried paper boxes, which then self-ignited. The idea was to let them drift towards the shrine of St John in the mountains. If the balloons fell into the forest before the fire was extinguished, they caused a forest fire. For this reason, and because of the damage done to the ecosystem and the animals, the practice was declared illegal, although it still occurred widely.

Bishop wrote to a friend in 1955 that she was in two minds about the fire balloons. She admired them as they lit up the sky, but she was horrified at the damage they caused. The poem expresses her feelings about the custom.

Commentary

Stanzas 1 to 4

As in many of Bishop's poems, she begins with a short narrative (starting: 'This is the time of year') that sets the poem in context. She writes as an observer rather than a participant in the custom. When you read the poem you can trace the differing attitudes she has to the balloons.

You can almost hear her thinking aloud as she describes the balloons as precisely as possible: what they look like, how they move through the sky. The tone at this stage is admiring. She sees the balloons as 'hearts' (line 8), as 'stars' (line 10), responding to their charm and recognising the loving reason for their existence.

In the fourth stanza the tone is still admiring as she describes how the balloons float upwards towards the major constellation in the southern hemisphere, the Southern Cross.

Change of tone

The balloons are described as 'steadily forsaking us' mere mortals looking up (line 18). There is a suggestion that they have a higher-bound purpose as they make their way towards the heavens. But quite soon we are made aware of the dreadful consequences when the balloons drop into the forest. The word 'dangerous' (line 20) takes the reader aback somewhat.

Images of suffering birds and animals, presented without comment, have an emotive effect on the reader. The owls, burnt out of their nest, 'shrieked up out of sight' (line 28) in pain and terror. The armadillo, having no defences against fire, is forced out into the open.

In the ninth stanza a 'baby rabbit' ('soft' and '*short*-eared') is seen in a horrifying image as 'a handful of intangible ash', its eyes 'ignited', destroyed by fire.

Final stanza

In the final stanza, placed in italics for emphasis, Bishop's indignation finally breaks through. It is not entirely clear to whom she is addressing the accusation '*Too pretty, dreamlike mimicry!*', but there are a number of possibilities.

Is she accusing the balloons of being deceptively pretty, as she had described them earlier? Unlike the stars that they resemble, they are dangerous to the animals on earth.

Or, as has been suggested, might she be addressing herself as a poet, criticising her depiction of the whole scene as too beautiful, too obviously poetic, when what is really happening is horrific? If we reread the poem in the light of the final stanza, we become aware of the poetic devices she has used – simile, metaphor, sound effects such as alliteration and rhyme and above all powerful imagery. The poet's art has been exposed for what it is – an act of pretty mimicry.

There is no mistaking the angry tone, however. The speaker is in complete sympathy with the natural world here. The armadillo, as depicted in the last two lines, is ignorant of evil and powerless to protect itself in the face of human cruelty.

Allegory

A possible allegorical reading of the last image of the armadillo may show Bishop's awareness of the links between all the elements of nature, including human beings, as they suffer from oppression and wrong. The mailed fist recalls human responses to oppression, past and present. This might lead us to reinterpret the fire balloons as instruments of war and destruction, set in motion by the forces of superstition. This is a pessimistic reading of the poem.

Thinking about the poem

1. Would you agree that this poem shows Bishop's remarkable gift for precise description? Comment on the techniques she uses in order to make us share in her experience of the event.
2. Is there a sudden change of tone as the poem progresses? Where precisely would you locate the change?
3. What consequences do the balloons have for the natural world? How does the poet convey these consequences?
4. How would you interpret the line '*Too pretty, dreamlike mimicry!*' in the last stanza? Justify your answer.
5. Comment on Bishop's use of language in the last stanza.
6. Why did Bishop choose the title 'The Armadillo' for her poem, in your view?
7. Compare Bishop's attitude to nature in 'The Fish' with the attitude she expresses here.
8. From your reading of this poem, what does it reveal about Bishop as a person?
9. Would you agree with Robert Lowell's opinion that 'The Armadillo' is one of Bishop's best poems?

Sestina

September rain falls on the house.
In the failing light, the old grandmother
sits in the kitchen with the child
beside the Little Marvel Stove,
reading the jokes from the almanac,
laughing and talking to hide her tears.

She thinks that her equinoctial tears
and the rain that beats on the roof of the house
were both foretold by the almanac,
but only known to a grandmother.
The iron kettle sings on the stove.
She cuts some bread and says to the child,

It's time for tea now; but the child
is watching the teakettle's small hard tears
dance like mad on the hot black stove,
the way the rain must dance on the house.
Tidying up, the old grandmother
hangs up the clever almanac

on its string. Birdlike, the almanac
hovers half open above the child,
hovers above the old grandmother
and her teacup full of dark brown tears.
She shivers and says she thinks the house
feels chilly, and puts more wood in the stove.

It was to be, says the Marvel Stove.
I know what I know, says the almanac.
With crayons the child draws a rigid house
and a winding pathway. Then the child
puts in a man with buttons like tears
and shows it proudly to the grandmother.

But secretly, while the grandmother
busies herself about the stove,
the little moons fall down like tears
from between the pages of the almanac
into the flower bed the child
has carefully placed in the front of the house.

Time to plant tears, says the almanac.
The grandmother sings to the marvellous stove
and the child draws another inscrutable house.

Glossary

title	*Sestina*: a poetic form (see guidelines)
4	*Little Marvel Stove*: a brand of solid-fuel stove
5	*almanac*: a calendar that gives details of weather predictions, tides, phases of the moon and other events on the basis of astrological calculations; for this reason, it was sometimes thought to have magic powers. Many of these annual publications feature other material such as jokes
7	*equinoctial*: at the time of the autumn equinox (i.e. September)
39	*inscrutable*: cannot be understood, mysterious

Guidelines

'Sestina' is included in the collection *Questions of Travel* (1965). It was originally given the title 'Early Sorrow', which offers us an insight into the origin of the poem and the nature of the experience depicted in it. It was among the first poems that Bishop wrote about her childhood. She was in her fifties, living in Brazil, before she was able to write about her traumatic experiences as a child in Nova Scotia, just before her mother's final departure to the psychiatric institution in which she was to spend her life.

It is thought that psychoanalysis helped Bishop to retrieve buried memories of that time. The poem shows her awareness of the crucial role of a fantasy world in communicating a child's emotions, as well as the significance, for children, of objects that can be named. These ideas were propounded by the child psychologist Melanie Klein and others. The repetitive form of the poem, a sestina, is particularly appropriate for its theme. (See Form of the poem, below.)

Commentary

Stanza 1
The domestic scene painted at the beginning of the poem seems cosy at first, in contrast to the wet and darkening conditions outside the house. We can picture the child and the grandmother reading from the almanac, surrounded by familiar and comforting objects. But as the poem progresses we become aware that all is not well. The grandmother is 'laughing and talking to hide her tears' (line 6).

Stanza 2

In the second stanza Bishop enters into the child's mind as she tries to make sense of what is taking place. She has no idea why her grandmother is crying, but thinks in her childish way that the almanac had foretold her tears, as it had the weather. As children do, she focuses on the familiar objects around her: the kettle, the stove. The rain is beating on the roof. This image is bleak and rather threatening. Again, it contradicts the apparent cosiness of the scene.

Stanza 3

From a child's perspective, objects often have a personality and a life. To the young Elizabeth, 'the teakettle's small hard tears' (overflow of water) seem to 'dance like mad on the hot black stove' (lines 14 and 15). This is a revealing image. The stove that seemed so cheerful, almost toy-like in the first stanza now appears threatening. The drops of water that dance 'like mad' jolts us into remembering that her mother was institutionalised for mental illness when Bishop was a young child. The phrase suggests something out of control that contrasts with the grandmother's actions in tidying the place and hanging up the almanac.

Stanza 4

The grandmother is clearly suffering grief at what has happened to her daughter and to her granddaughter, but hides her sorrow by drinking tea and pretending she feels chilly.

To the child, the almanac that hovers over them on the wall is like a bird – another rather menacing image. The cup in line 22 is described as being full of not tea, but 'dark brown tears'. The impression we get is that their grief would overwhelm them if it was expressed.

As in the previous stanzas, the language here is simple and childlike, focusing throughout on objects (linguistically on nouns). **Bishop's experience of psychoanalysis and her readings of child psychology taught her that young children tend first of all to name the world, without realising the significance of what it is these names represent.** In the poem these objects come to bear the weight of the child's emotions, without her being consciously aware that this is so.

Stanza 5

In the fifth stanza the child makes the stove and the almanac speak. Neither of them says directly what has happened or is happening in the family, since the child was unlikely to have been told exactly what that was. But psychoanalysis made Bishop familiar with the concept of a child's knowing and not knowing at the same time.

The pictures that a child who has been traumatised will draw are often quite revealing. So, for instance, the house, with the figure of a man in it, might be understood by a psychologist to represent the child's awareness of the father she had lost (Bishop's father died when she was a baby). The 'rigid' house with its 'winding pathway' may represent tension and difficulties that the family experienced.

Stanza 6
Although still poignant, the mood seems to lift somewhat in the sixth stanza. In her imagination the child sees the 'little moons' of the almanac (that denote the phases of the moon over the course of each month) falling 'down like tears' onto the flower bed that she has drawn in her picture. Might the flower bed suggest a sense of hope for the future? At the very least it points to a possibility of beauty and happiness in the future.

Envoy
In the envoy (shorter final stanza) Bishop makes the almanac speak again. It gives a rather cryptic message to the child: '*Time to plant tears*'. We can interpret this message in a number of ways. For some commentators, it suggests that for the adult Bishop it is time to bury tears, to put away the 'early sorrow' that was the first title of the poem. On the other hand, the line may look towards the child-poet's future rather than the adult-poet's past. It may suggest that the child will use her grief creatively, to express it through the medium of poetry and the imagination, as Bishop does here.

The final two lines appear to strengthen the second interpretation. The grandmother seems to have overcome the worst of her grief, and the child continues to draw her picture of an ideal house.

Tone of the poem

What Bishop leaves unsaid in this poem is almost as significant as what she says. No grief or sorrow is directly expressed, but there is an underlying atmosphere that is painfully emotional. While her relationship with her grandmother, who acts as a mother figure, is seen as positive, the poem begs the question as to where her mother and father are. It is another reminder that Bishop's concept of 'home' may not have been entirely happy.

Form of the poem

Bishop chose to deal with these painful memories in the form of a sestina. This is an archaic and difficult form of poetry, highly stylised and formal. In a sestina there are six unrhymed stanzas of six lines and a seventh stanza of three lines, known as an envoy.

Only six words are used at the end of the lines; in Bishop's poem the words are house, grandmother, child, stove, almanac, tears. Each stanza is linked by this intricate pattern of line-endings: the six words are repeated in a different order in each stanza so that the last word in each stanza recurs as the ending of the first line in the next. The word order is as follows: *abcdef, faebdc, cfdabe, ecbfad, deacfb, bdfeca*. The envoy uses all of the six end words, three of them (*ace*) at the ends of the lines and the other three (*bdf*) within the lines.

It can be seen that a sestina is a form that involves great discipline and control of one's material. It allows for ritual repetition, almost as a child's game does. Some critics have seen the form as particularly suited to the theme of the poem, childhood sorrow. Writing a sestina offers a formula within which grief may be repeated and yet contained.

When Bishop changed the title of the poem, she drew attention to the form of the poem, so that effectively it becomes a subject in the poem.

Thinking about the poem

1. Explore the changes of mood and atmosphere throughout the poem. How are they created, in your opinion?
2. What evidence is there to suggest that we are viewing the things in the kitchen – the stove, the kettle, the almanac – as well as the figure of the grandmother, from a child's perspective? In answering, try to imagine yourself as a child again and how you saw the world around you.
3. Describe the relationship between the child and the grandmother.
4. Explore the idea of time and the idea of family as they recur throughout the poem. How are they connected with the poem's theme, do you think?
5. What is the significance of the child's drawing in stanza 5?
6. Which of the six key words used in the poem is the most significant in your opinion? Explain your choice.
7. Write your response to this poem?
8. Compare 'Sestina' and 'First Death in Nova Scotia' as poems about childhood memories. Which poem do you find the more affecting?
9. 'Bishop's poems reveal a great deal about her life'. Discuss this statement, referring (among other poems) to 'Sestina'.

First Death in Nova Scotia

In the cold, cold parlor
my mother laid out Arthur
beneath the chromographs:
Edward, Prince of Wales,
with Princess Alexandra,
and King George with Queen Mary.
Below them on the table
stood a stuffed loon
shot and stuffed by Uncle
Arthur, Arthur's father.

Since Uncle Arthur fired
a bullet into him,
he hadn't said a word.
He kept his own counsel
on his white, frozen lake,
the marble-topped table.
His breast was deep and white,
cold and caressable;
his eyes were red glass,
much to be desired.

"Come," said my mother,
"Come and say good-bye
to your little cousin Arthur."
I was lifted up and given
one lily of the valley
to put in Arthur's hand.
Arthur's coffin was
a little frosted cake,
and the red-eyed loon eyed it
from his white, frozen lake.

Arthur was very small.
He was all white, like a doll

that hadn't been painted yet.
Jack Frost had started to paint him
the way he always painted 35
the Maple Leaf (Forever).
He had just begun on his hair,
a few red strokes, and then
Jack Frost had dropped the brush
and left him white, forever. 40

The gracious royal couples
were warm in red and ermine;
their feet were well wrapped up
in the ladies' ermine trains.
They invited Arthur to be 45
the smallest page at court.
But how could Arthur go,
clutching his tiny lily,
with his eyes shut up so tight
and the roads deep in snow? 50

Glossary

3	*chromographs*:	coloured copies of pictures
4	*Edward, Prince of Wales*:	(1841–1910), member of the British royal family, eldest son of Queen Victoria and Prince Albert, later became King Edward VII
5	*Princess Alexandra*:	married Edward in 1863
6	*King George*:	(1865–1936), British monarch, King George V
6	*Queen Mary*:	(1867–1953), wife of King George V
8	*loon*:	an aquatic bird, the great crested grebe
14	*kept his own counsel*:	kept his thoughts to himself
25	*lily of the valley*:	a white flower
34	*Jack Frost*:	a childish name given to frost
35	*Maple Leaf*:	emblem of Canada; 'Maple Leaf Forever' is a phrase from the Canadian national anthem at the time the poem was written
42	*ermine*:	white fur
46	*page*:	a boy attendant

Guidelines

This poem follows 'Sestina' in the collection *Questions of Travel* (1965). Like 'Sestina', it is one of the poems Bishop wrote in her fifties in which she recaptures childhood memories. She had recently undergone psychoanalysis to help her recognise the causes of her struggles with depression and alcoholism. As in 'Sestina', the perspective is that of a child.

The poem tells of Bishop's first disturbing encounter with death. It is interesting to note that it contains one of the few direct references to her mother found in Bishop's work, although her presence is implicit in many of Bishop's poems of loss. Set in her childhood home in Nova Scotia, the poem records the death of her cousin, whom she calls Arthur. Bishop was not quite four when he died.

Commentary

Stanza 1

The child-narrator describes the scene in the parlour where Arthur has been laid out, significantly enough by her mother. From the beginning, repetition plays a part in creating atmosphere. The parlour is 'cold, cold' (line 1).

As a child does, Bishop names the objects that she sees in the room where Arthur lies: the coloured pictures of the royal family on the walls, the stuffed bird that had been shot by Arthur's father.

Stanza 2

At first the child's interest appears to lie completely in the stuffed bird. She personifies the bird, saying that 'he hadn't said a word' (line 13) since he was shot. She focuses on the primary colours of the bird and his 'red' glass eyes. **She seems unable to distinguish between what is real and what is imaginary.** But her awareness of his silence and his motionlessness is perhaps a way of skirting around the subject of death rather than articulating it fully.

Stanza 3

Bishop remembers being lifted up by her mother to 'say good-bye' (line 22) to her little cousin. This is a poignant scene, all the more so when we consider that once again Bishop's memory of her mother is bound up with moments of loss. She uses a childlike image to describe Arthur's coffin: 'a little frosted cake' (line 28). In her childish way she imagines the 'red-eyed loon' (is he weeping too?) wanting it for himself (line 29).

Stanza 4

Again, Bishop describes Arthur in his coffin in terms a child might use. The language is simple. The images are appropriate for a little girl. Arthur is 'like a doll' (line 32).

'Jack Frost' is a name children often give to frost; here it allows Bishop to show how aware the child is of the coldness of death. At this point she associates the winter frost of Arthur's pallor with the Canadian flag and by extension the Canadian national anthem (at the time of writing). In her confusion she thinks that Jack Frost had begun to paint the child only to leave him unfinished, but by repeating the word 'forever' she reveals that somehow she knows that Arthur himself is gone forever.

Stanza 5

In this final stanza the child invents a sort of fairy-tale ending for Arthur. He is going to be a 'page at court' (line 46) for the royal family whose pictures are on the walls. They, like the loon, are seen to be in the colours of death: red and ermine (white fur).

But as she asks, how could Arthur go out in the snow all alone? **This is a terrifying image for a child, and suggests that deep down she knows that it is impossible.**

Child's experience of death

As the title suggests, 'First Death in Nova Scotia' describes Bishop's first encounter with death as a child and her confusion about what it really means. As in 'Sestina', the concept of the child's knowing and not knowing is crucial. It is clear that the child has a subconscious awareness of what it is to be dead. Repetition of key words and phrases – 'cold', 'white', 'frozen', 'painted', 'forever' – underline the fact that the child's understanding of death, though naïve and not analysed, is instinctive. Yet it is an imperfect understanding; the poem is psychologically credible when she invents the fairy-tale ending for the little boy, at the same time wondering how this could happen.

The atmosphere of the poem is strange and uncanny. Images of the sightless eyes of the loon, the pallor of the dead child, the speaker's confusion about her little cousin's whereabouts, all combine to create a surreal world where there is no distinction between reality and imagination. All objects seem to have the same importance to the child. Without expressing any emotion, Bishop dramatises a traumatic event in her childhood.

Form of the poem

The poem is divided into five ten-line, mostly unrhymed, stanzas. Longer stanzas allow Bishop to give the impression of someone looking about and thinking aloud. The metre chosen by Bishop in this poem, mainly three-stress lines (trimeter), has been regarded as the most speechlike of metres and therefore appropriate to telling a story (see also 'The Fish').

Thinking about the poem

1. The first stanza describes what the child saw in the 'cold, cold parlor'. What significance does each object have for her as the poem progresses?
2. How does she feel about the stuffed loon? What atmosphere is created by her description of the bird?
3. Would you agree that the poet's choice of language is remarkably childlike throughout? Explain your view.
4. How does the poem convey the child's natural confusion and naivety about death? Does she have any idea of what death means?
5. Do you find this poem disturbing, unusual, moving . . . ? Perhaps you would suggest another term?
6. Which of the two poems 'Sestina' or 'First Death in Nova Scotia' best conveys a childhood experience, in your view?
7. If you were to compile your choice of Bishop's poems for an anthology, would you choose this one? Make a case for or against its inclusion.

Filling Station

Oh, but it is dirty!
– this little filling station,
oil-soaked, oil-permeated
to a disturbing, over-all
black translucency.   5
Be careful with that match!

Father wears a dirty,
oil-soaked monkey suit
that cuts him under the arms,
and several quick and saucy   10
and greasy sons assist him
(it's a family filling station),
all quite thoroughly dirty.

Do they live in the station?
It has a cement porch
behind the pumps, and on it
a set of crushed and grease-
impregnated wickerwork;
on the wicker sofa
a dirty dog, quite comfy.

Some comic books provide
the only note of color –
of certain color. They lie
upon a big dim doily
draping a taboret
(part of the set), beside
a big hirsute begonia.

Why the extraneous plant?
Why the taboret?
Why, oh why, the doily?
(Embroidered in daisy stitch
with marguerites, I think,
and heavy with gray crochet.)

Somebody embroidered the doily.
Somebody waters the plant,
or oils it, maybe. Somebody
arranges the rows of cans
so that they softly say:
ESSO–so–so–so
to high-strung automobiles.
Somebody loves us all.

Glossary

3	*oil-permeated*:	saturated with oil
5	*translucency*:	shine
8	*monkey suit*:	dungarees, overalls
10	*saucy*:	cheeky
18	*impregnated*:	penetrated
24	*doily*:	an ornamental cloth
25	*taboret*:	a low seat or stool without a back or arms
27	*hirsute*:	hairy
27	*begonia*:	a flowering plant
28	*extraneous*:	not essential
31	*daisy stitch*:	a design
32	*marguerites*:	daisies
33	*crochet*:	a type of knitting done with a small hook
39	*ESSO*:	a brand of oil and petrol products
39	*so-so-so*:	as explained by Bishop: 'a phrase people used to calm and soothe horses'; here it also refers to the way in which the cans are arranged

Guidelines

'Filling Station' is from the collection *Questions of Travel* (1965). The poem describes a particular petrol station.

Commentary

Stanzas 1 and 2
The poet almost seems to enjoy describing the grease and grime she sees in the petrol station, where presumably she has stopped to fill up her car. Everything she sees appears oily and dirty: 'oil-soaked, oil-permeated' to the extent that it has an 'over-all / black translucency' or shine (lines 3 to 5). Humorously, she warns (herself or someone else) to be careful of a lighted match, as the place could quickly go up in flames.

Stanza 2 describes members of the family who own and work in the station: a father and 'several' (line 10) sons. Like their surroundings, they are 'greasy' (line 11) and 'quite thoroughly dirty' (line 13). The tone of voice here is light-hearted.

Stanza 3

With characteristic Bishop curiosity about the world around her, she begins to ask questions about what she sees here. She finds some evidence to answer her question as to whether the family live in the filling station, unlikely as it might seem at first. On the porch she can see a set of wicker chairs, 'crushed and grease- / impregnated' (lines 17–18) like everything else, and there is an equally 'dirty dog, quite comfy' (line 20), lying on the sofa. The colloquial word 'comfy' suggests she finds the scene pleasant despite the dirt. This is certainly not a soulless, alien place. It is a family environment, complete with a dog, though even at this stage we cannot fail to notice that there is no mention of a woman in this all-masculine setting.

Stanzas 4 and 5

In the fourth stanza other objects attract Bishop's attention: 'comic books provide / the only note of color – / of certain color' (lines 21–23). This detail highlights how impossible it is to know what colour anything here really is. She goes on to pick out a 'big dim doily' (decorative cloth) placed over a taboret (a type of seat) as well as a large hairy plant (lines 24–27). Then in stanza 5 she wonders aloud about these objects: 'Why the extraneous plant? / Why the taboret? / Why, oh why, the doily?' (lines 28–30). Although everything is dirty ('doily' even rhymes with 'oily'), these are objects that suggest a desire for a more ordered life. Someone has gone to the trouble of embroidering the doily; it may be 'gray' now but it has been carefully decorated by hand.

Stanza 6

Bishop answers her own questions in the final stanza. **Somebody cares about this place and has tried to improve it, even if their efforts are futile**: the begonia gets more oil than water, she humorously suggests. That same 'somebody' has taken the trouble to arrange the petrol cans in some kind of order, so that they 'softly say: / ESSO–so–so–so' (lines 38–39). Bishop has explained these sounds as those used to soothe restless horses, which accounts for the next witty line: 'to high-strung automobiles' (line 40). The words suggest a soothing, calming presence among the working atmosphere of the filling station.

The final line, 'Somebody loves us all', sums up her conclusion that there is an affectionate presence in the filling station, possibly a maternal figure that completes the family, although she is not visibly present.

Interpreting the poem

Although 'Filling Station' is quite simply written, it can be read on a number of levels. It can be interpreted as an expression of Bishop's optimistic view of life, despite her personal difficulties, especially the lack of a mother in her childhood.

She seems to suggest that a mother's presence may be always felt, even if she is not actually there. So the father, in his ill-fitting overalls, and the 'greasy' sons have had at least some experience of feminine care and affection. It does not matter that they are dirty and unattractive as somebody has loved them. By extension, might Bishop herself have benefited from her mother's love in her very earliest years, before illness caused her mother to disappear from her life? And despite her later problems, might 'somebody' have loved her too?

Regret

Some readers feel that the light-hearted tone of the poem is tinged with regret. After all, the filling station has been allowed to become so dirty. The mother is nowhere to be seen. Has she gone away or simply given up the battle against the oil and grease? Might this be an indirect expression of grief for Bishop's deprived childhood? From this point of view, the final line is somewhat ironic as not everyone has 'somebody' to love them.

Allegory

An allegory is a story with a symbolic meaning. Some people have interpreted 'Filling Station' as an allegory of human life. The filling station can be seen as a little world in itself, symbolic of the real world that is full of disorder and sordidness. Efforts to improve it with some kind of decoration (the doily, the begonia, the petrol cans) can be interpreted as a metaphor for our earthly efforts to create beauty out of ugliness and order out of randomness. 'Somebody loves us all' may then imply a divine perspective that oversees our efforts. The poet has placed the word 'Somebody' within the last stanza so that it takes a capital letter, a respect normally given to the word 'God'. The line recalls the phrase often embroidered on samplers (in this case a doily): God loves us all.

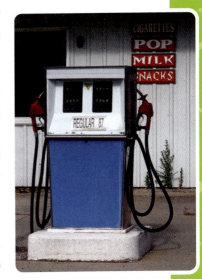

Satire

The critic Guy Rotella offers another view of the poem. He sees it as a satire (a poem that mocks or ridicules something) of a certain kind of nature poem in which nature is seen as containing a lesson or moral that the poet can discover. In such poems, details of the natural scene are revealed as part of God's eternal plan, and the poem leaves the reader with a message, as in the last line of this poem. Rotella argues that Bishop's description of the petrol station corresponds to the descriptive aspects of such nature poems. He suggests that the poem indicates her cynical attitude to such moral lessons or 'truths'. This is a rather bleak reading of the poem, since it implies that the statement in the last line is not at all valid.

Sound patterns in the poem

Bishop makes frequent use of sibilance (repetition of 's' sounds) in the poem – for instance in words such as 'soaked', 'translucency', 'saucy', 'greasy' and so on. This has an almost onomatopoeic effect as it suits the impression of oiliness and grease that she wants to give. The poem does not rhyme, as is appropriate when the impression is that of a speaking voice, but assonance (repetition of vowel sounds) in 'that match' for instance and alliteration in 'family filling' and 'dim doily' contribute to the harmony of the poem.

Thinking about the poem

1. How does the poet elaborate on her opening exclamation: 'Oh, but it is dirty!'?
2. How would you describe Bishop's attitude to the filling station? Does it change at any point?
3. What puzzles her about the filling station?
4. What conclusion does she come to when she sees the doily and the plant?
5. How does the poem give the impression of someone thinking aloud?
6. What picture of Bishop does the poem reveal to the reader? Do you find the personality revealed attractive?
7. Which one of the following statements is closest to your own view of the theme of the poem?

    Everybody is loved by somebody.
    We shouldn't judge by appearances.
    Life is full of surprises.

    Explain your view.
8. Is 'Filling Station' a serious or a light-hearted poem? Support your answer by reference to the poem.
9. A critic once remarked on the 'deceptive casualness' of Bishop's poems. Would you agree that this view could be applied to 'Filling Station'? Give reasons for your answer.
10. 'Good poetry creates vivid pictures in our minds.' In your view, is this true of 'Filling Station'?

Taking a closer look

1. Give **three** examples of Bishop's descriptive skill and say why you chose them.
2. Comment on the phrase 'high-strung automobiles' in line 40.
3. 'Somebody loves us all.' Is this a good ending to the poem? Explain your opinion.

Imagining

1. Imagine that you are the 'somebody' who has tried to look after this filling station. Write an entry from your diary explaining how you attempt to keep the place tidy and how you feel about it.
2. You have been asked to speak to your class about this poem. Write out the talk you would give, describing what the poem is about and giving your personal response to it.

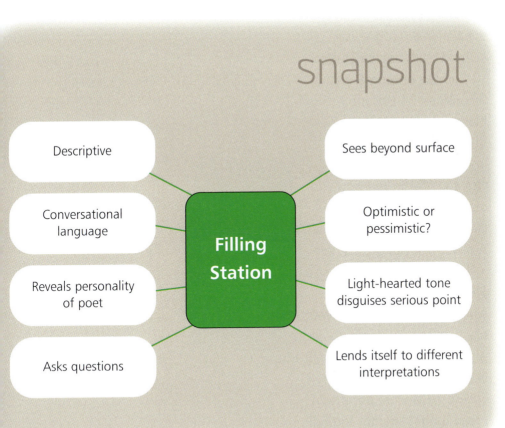

In the Waiting Room

In Worcester, Massachusetts,
I went with Aunt Consuelo
to keep her dentist's appointment
and sat and waited for her
in the dentist's waiting room.   5
It was winter. It got dark
early. The waiting room
was full of grown-up people,
arctics and overcoats,
lamps and magazines.   10
My aunt was inside
what seemed like a long time
and while I waited I read
the *National Geographic*
(I could read) and carefully   15
studied the photographs:
the inside of a volcano,
black, and full of ashes;
then it was spilling over
in rivulets of fire.   20
Osa and Martin Johnson
dressed in riding breeches,
laced boots, and pith helmets.
A dead man slung on a pole
– "Long Pig," the caption said.   25
Babies with pointed heads
wound round and round with string;
black, naked women with necks
wound round and round with wire
like the necks of light bulbs.   30
Their breasts were horrifying.
I read it right straight through.
I was too shy to stop.
And then I looked at the cover:
the yellow margins, the date.   35

Suddenly, from inside,
came an *oh!* of pain
– Aunt Consuelo's voice –
not very loud or long.
I wasn't at all surprised;
even then I knew she was
a foolish, timid woman.
I might have been embarrassed,
but wasn't. What took me
completely by surprise
was that it was me:
my voice, in my mouth.
Without thinking at all
I was my foolish aunt,
I – we – were falling, falling,
our eyes glued to the cover
of the National Geographic,
February, 1918.

I said to myself: three days
and you'll be seven years old.
I was saying it to stop
the sensation of falling off
the round, turning world
into cold, blue-black space.
But I felt: you are an *I*,
you are an *Elizabeth*,
you are one of *them*.
Why should you be one, too?
I scarcely dared to look
to see what it was I was.
I gave a sidelong glance
– I couldn't look any higher –
at shadowy gray knees,
trousers and skirts and boots
and different pairs of hands
lying under the lamps.

I knew that nothing stranger
had ever happened, that nothing
stranger could ever happen.

Why should I be my aunt,
or me, or anyone?
What similarities –
boots, hands, the family voice
I felt in my throat, or even
the *National Geographic*
and those awful hanging breasts –
held us all together
or made us all just one?
How – I didn't know any
word for it – how "unlikely" . . .
How had I come to be here,
like them, and overhear
a cry of pain that could have
got loud and worse but hadn't?

The waiting room was bright
and too hot. It was sliding
beneath a big black wave,
another, and another.

Then I was back in it.
The War was on. Outside,
in Worcester, Massachusetts,
were night and slush and cold,
and it was still the fifth
of February, 1918.

Glossary		
	1	*Worcester, Massachusetts*: Bishop lived there with her paternal grandparents; she was very unhappy
	2	*Aunt Consuelo*: this was in fact Bishop's Aunt Florence
	9	*arctics*: overshoes or galoshes
	14	*National Geographic*: magazine of the National Geographic Society, famous for its articles on geography and anthropology and its wonderful photographs
	20	*rivulets*: small streams
	21	*Osa and Martin Johnson*: famous husband and wife team of explorers
	23	*pith helmets*: sun helmets made from pithy swamp plant
	25	*Long Pig*: the dead man is to be roasted by the cannibals like a pig on a spit
	26	*pointed heads*: the babies' heads are bound with string to force them into a point
28–29		*necks . . . wire*: in certain cultures long necks are considered to be sexually attractive; the women's necks are extended by having metal rings wound around them

Guidelines

'In the Waiting Room' opens the collection *Geography III* (1976). She wrote the poem, like 'Sestina' and 'First Death in Nova Scotia', when she was in her fifties – almost half a century after the experience it recalls.

Bishop dated many of her adult attitudes back to the age of six, which was the age at which her paternal grandparents 'kidnapped' her and brought her to live with them in Worcester, Massachusetts, where the poem is set. She revealed in a letter to a friend that her memory of the experience she describes in the poem was detailed and vivid. At the age of six she became aware of herself, for the first time, as a member of the human race and specifically as a female member. In the letter she reveals that other men and women had told her that they had similar moments of realisation in their childhoods.

Commentary

Lines 1–17

As is typical of a poem by Bishop, 'In the Waiting Room' begins with a narrative account in a factual tone. In this poem it concerns a visit Bishop made as a child with her Aunt Consuelo (Aunt Florence in real life) to a dentist. The location and the time are described very precisely and with Bishop's usual eye for detail. We can visualise the people waiting, dressed appropriately for that time and place in 'arctics' (overshoes) and 'overcoats' (line 9), later elaborated upon as 'trousers and skirts and boots' (line 69). While she waits for her aunt, the child reads the *National Geographic* magazine and looks at the photographs.

Lines 18–35

The narrator records what she sees in the photographs: pictures of a volcano as it erupts and famous explorers dressed for their expeditions. **But other pictures surprise and disturb her, as visions of a world she hardly knew existed.** There are images of cannibalism (the 'Long Pig', line 25; 'slung on a pole', line 24) as well as babies with seemingly deformed heads and naked women with their necks 'wound round and round with wire / like the necks of light bulbs' (lines 29–30).

The reader may be aware that what she sees are the beautifying rituals and customs of other cultures. But the child has no such frame of reference. She can only stare in alarm at the 'horrifying' breasts of the women (line 31). She is so embarrassed that she is 'too shy to stop' (line 33).

But we can also see how the seemingly random choice of objects she describes may suggest the diversity of the world, as she is about to realise it, in the contrast between the heavily clothed people around her and the people of other cultures who have quite different values and attitudes. The shock of this contrast makes her reassure herself by looking at the cover of the magazine, and the date, wishing perhaps to locate herself once again within the world she knows.

Lines 36–53

Aunt Consuelo's cry of pain from the dentist's room becomes somehow blended with her own involuntary cry of surprise at what she has seen in the magazine, to the extent that she becomes rather disoriented for a short time.

For the first time she has become aware of herself as a human being with her own identity and place in the world. She realises that she and her aunt share the same identity as family, and as women and human beings with the people in the photographs. Her disorientation at this discovery is expressed in images of 'falling, falling' (line 50), almost fainting, trying to hold on to the present: February 1918.

Lines 54-74

The narrator clings to ordinary facts – that her seventh birthday is just three days away – to counteract the bewildering discovery she has made, which she continues to describe as having the 'sensation of falling off / the round, turning world / into cold, blue-black space' (lines 57-59). The image of the globe is revealing. It suggests that she is losing the sense of perspective that allows one to view the world from one's particular vantage point of location and culture.

As a child, of course, she could not have analysed her experiences in this way, and the narrator does not suggest that she does. Instead, she shows us the child coming to realise that she is an individual, and that she is also 'one of *them*' (line 62) – a member of the human race, but specifically, too, a female member. She asks the unanswerable question: '*Why* should you be one, too?' (line 63). She expresses her realisation that she is not unique in the world. Even as a child she senses how important this discovery is.

Lines 75-89

The child's questions continue. She wonders about the similarities between herself and her aunt and between them and the women in the photographs. **How could human beings all be individuals and yet so similar?** And how and why was she here in that particular place, at that particular moment, listening to the patient cry out in the dentist's room, when meanwhile others were elsewhere being mutilated (as she saw it)? These are fundamental, unanswerable questions, and Bishop does not attempt to answer them.

Lines 90-99

In the final two stanzas we see Bishop's characteristic ability to accept uncertainty. After the feelings of shock – she is still 'sliding / beneath a big black wave' (lines 91–92) – she is 'back in it' (line 94), that is, the world she knows: Worcester, Massachusetts, in February 1918, with seasonal weather outside and ordinary men and women in the dentist's waiting room.

Interpreting the poem

You will notice how many questions Bishop asks in the poem. They are simply phrased, but they are nonetheless profoundly philosophical. Bishop speculates about the nature of existence and how extraordinary it is to be one's self as well as part of the human race. She becomes aware of how arbitrary location is, and how it may determine culture and custom.

Aunt Consuelo allows an 'oh! of pain' to escape (line 37), and in the culture of Worcester, Massachusetts, 'it could have / got loud and worse but hadn't' (lines 88–89). This may be an implicit recognition of how repressed and inhibiting this society is. Yet in other parts of the world women allow themselves to be mutilated in order to be sexually attractive. In other parts of the world people expose their bodies; here, they are muffled up in 'trousers and skirts and boots' (line 69). These questions of the relative nature of human culture were of great interest to Bishop. We saw her touch on them in 'Questions of Travel' and 'The Armadillo'.

The title of the poem suggests further possible interpretations. The child is literally 'in the waiting room', but metaphorically she is also waiting to take her place as an adult, a conscious member of the human race with all its complexity. Such a reading is optimistic, especially if we emphasise her recognition that the human race has 'similarities' (line 77) that 'made us all just one' (line 83). But we cannot ignore the images of violence and death that pervade the poem, the volcano 'black, and full of ashes' (line 18), the 'dead man slung on a pole' (line 24), the cries of pain the child overhears, as well as the image of the 'big black wave' (line 92) that seems to engulf her. The reference in the final stanza to 'The War' that still raged in 'February, 1918' completes the sense of chaos that underlies all human society. From this point of view, to be 'in the waiting room' suggests something rather more sinister: waiting for the human fate of death that we all must eventually experience.

Thinking about the poem

1. Examine how the poet conveys the atmosphere in the waiting room.
2. What contrast is suggested between the people in the waiting room and the people in the magazine?
3. What is the child's response to the articles she read and the photographs she saw?
4. Where would you locate the central moment of realisation or discovery in the poem?
5. What questions does her discovery cause her to ask? How did you respond to these questions?
6. Why does she call her aunt 'a foolish, timid woman' (line 42)? Support your answer by reference to the poem.
7. Does she get across her feelings well in lines 55 to 74? Explain your answer.
8. The final lines of the poem bring us back to the waiting room. But does the child see the world as she saw it previously?
9. Was the 'moment of truth' strange or incredible for the child? Have you ever shared in such a realisation, or wondered about similar issues?
10. Compare the poem, as a memory poem, with 'Sestina' and 'First Death in Nova Scotia'. Which poem do you prefer?
11. Can you see, from this description of her childhood experience, any connection between the young Bishop and the poet she will later become?
12. Write out the talk you would give on the poems of Elizabeth Bishop, using this poem as an example of her style and concerns.

Exam-Style Questions

1. You have been asked to give a short presentation entitled 'Introducing Elizabeth Bishop'. Write out the text of the talk you would give.
   Here are some possible areas that you might focus on in your presentation:
   - Bishop's poems reveal a great deal about her life, especially her childhood, and her personality.
   - Her descriptions are always vivid and fresh, in line with her desire to see things in a new way.
   - You can see how, as a painter as well as a poet, she was interested in the shape, colour and texture of things around her, and this is reflected in her use of language.
   - Her poems are hardly ever purely descriptive, there is almost always a deeper theme.

2. Bishop once said, 'I simply try to see things afresh.' To what extent, do you think, does she achieve this in her poems?

3. 'Bishop's poems are rarely simply descriptive. They always have a deeper theme.' Would you agree with this view of Bishop's work? Explain your answer.

4. A critic once remarked on the 'deceptive casualness' of Bishop's poems. Would you agree with this assessment of her tone and poetic methods? Explain your answer.

5. 'Bishop has a remarkable ability to understand how a child's mind works.' Would you agree with this view of Bishop's work? Explain your answer.

6. 'Elizabeth Bishop: a personal response.' Write your response, which could include discussion of how you respond to the following aspects:
   - Her choice of themes – childhood experience, travel, the natural world, the creative imagination – do they appeal to you?
   - The speculative nature of her poems, the questions they raise and sometimes answer.
   - Her use of language, her striking imagery, the sounds of her poems, etc.
   - Her personality and outlook as revealed in her work.
   - The emotions her poems evoke.

   Remember to support your points with reference to or quotation from the poems on the course.

7. 'The poetry of Elizabeth Bishop appeals to the modern reader for many reasons.' Discuss. (Leaving Certificate exam, 2002.)
   Possible reasons include:
   - Her themes are varied – childhood memories, relationship with the natural world, family situations, travel, etc. The modern reader can identify with these themes and the issues she raises.

- Her powers of description (the sensuous imagery and painterly qualities in her poems) allow the reader to enter into her experiences.
- Her use of language – how she conveys both thought and emotion – is striking.
- The sounds and shapes of her poems (the varied forms in which she writes: sestina, sonnet, longer narrative poems) are interesting.

You must always support your points by reference to or quotation from the poems on the course.

8   'A sense of homelessness and not belonging is a central theme in the poetry of Elizabeth Bishop.' Discuss this statement.

9   'Bishop's narrative style and her use of conversational language make her poems accessible to the reader.' Would you agree with this view? Explain your answer.

10 'Bishop has written some deeply moving poems.' Write an essay in which you agree or disagree with this view.

Sample Essay

Elizabeth Bishop poses interesting questions delivered by means of a unique style.

Do you agree with this assessment of her poetry? Your answer should focus on both themes and stylistic features. Support your points with the aid of suitable reference to the poems you have studied.

I would agree that the questions Elizabeth Bishop poses in her poems are wide-ranging and interesting. She often creates the impression of someone thinking aloud, reflecting on the world about her, on her own experience and the issues it raises. She is preoccupied with what it means to be human in a world that she sees as uncertain and constantly changing. These questions – about identity, about death, about travel, about human beings' relationship with nature, about the experience of love and loss – are expressed in a unique and attractive style.

[Introductory paragraph refers to question asked and indicates areas that will be developed]

Bishop has frequently been praised for her ability to describe situations and objects clearly and precisely. This descriptive power extends also to emotions and abstract ideas. We can see her gift at work in 'In the Waiting Room'. The setting is described with her usual vivid detail. We are told the date (February 1918), the place (Worcester,

Massachusetts) and the name of her companion (Aunt Consuelo). The patients in the dentist's waiting room are described in terms of their clothes, 'arctics and overcoats', and later 'gray knees / trousers and skirts and boots'. She remembers her childish horror at seeing photographs in the *National Geographic* of 'Babies with pointed heads / wound round and round with string', 'naked women' with their necks 'wound round and round with wire / like the necks of light bulbs'. They had 'horrifying' breasts. Repetition of 'round and round' and the light bulb simile contribute to the impact of the descriptions.

As we read on further, we continue to identify with the young Elizabeth's growing disturbance at what she has seen. It causes her to consider fundamental human questions: Who am I? Why am I here rather than anywhere else? Although only seven years old, she experiences a moment of truth: 'But I felt: you are an *I*, / you are an *Elizabeth*, / you are one of *them*'. Her awareness of who she is – not only a particular person but also a woman, like the women in the magazine – leads her to a further question: 'Why should I be my aunt, / or me, or anyone?' That these deep philosophical questions are expressed in simple childlike language adds to the impact they have on the reader.

[Discussion of poem refers to themes (questions posed) and features of style]

In 'Questions of Travel' Bishop poses a series of questions about the human desire to leave home and seek out new experiences. The tone of this poem is more detached than that of 'In the Waiting Room'. She is clearly amused at the tendency of travellers to be impressed at 'any view, / instantly seen and always, always delightful?' and the clichéd description of 'one more folded sunset'. She wonders why people feel the need to see the 'tiniest green hummingbird in the world' or travel to 'stare at some inexplicable old stonework'. Unlike 'In the Waiting Room', she suggests answers to these questions.

We see her great love of Brazil, where she lived for many years, in the painterly way she evokes its trees 'like noble pantomimists, robed in pink'. She describes in precise detail some of the unique cultural artefacts of that country: the wooden clogs worn by the people and the ornate birdcages they make. The images she creates include sound effects: the clogs 'carelessly clacking' is onomatopoeic; as well as vivid visual metaphors: the birdcage is a 'bamboo church of Jesuit baroque'. When she compares the heavy rain of Brazil to 'politicians' speeches' we respond to her sense of humour as well as to the freshness of the description. Her conclusion is that it would have been 'a pity' not to have had such experiences.

In characteristic Bishop manner, however, she leaves her readers not with a definite conclusion but with an invitation to think for themselves. The eminent philosopher Blaise Pascal came to the conclusion a long time ago that travel was the source of much unhappiness. But Bishop appears to dispute this idea when she raises the question, in the last line, of where exactly 'home' may be, and why we should have stayed there. In so doing she touches once again on one of her most enduring themes: the nature of home. It may seem to be a simple idea for many people, but for a poet whose childhood was so unstable it is a legitimate question to consider. By ending her poem with a question mark Bishop leaves the question open.

[Discussion of second poem also includes references to themes and stylistic features; note how quotations and references are incorporated into sentences]

Another poem in which we see Bishop thinking aloud about a human problem is 'First Death in Nova Scotia'. In this poem, as in 'In the Waiting Room', the speaker is the child Elizabeth coming to terms with her first experience of death, of her 'little cousin Arthur'. Her surroundings, her interpretation of her cousin's death, her inability to distinguish between what is real and what is imaginary are all characteristic of a child's view of the world. The language she uses is simple, with lots of primary colours such as red and white, and the images are also childish: Arthur's coffin is a 'little frosted cake'.

As a child Bishop would have had endless questions about death, as we are aware as we read through the poem, but she invents a sort of fairy-tale ending for Arthur that is psychologically credible for a child. He is going to be a page in a royal court, like the picture she sees on the wall. But by her final question: 'But how could Arthur go . . . ?' the speaker shows that she knows that this cannot really happen. Although this is a child's confusion about the permanence of death, it has a moving effect on the reader.

[Personal response given to issues raised in the poem]

In a number of her poems Bishop is preoccupied with the relationship of human beings to nature. In poems such as 'The Fish' and 'The Armadillo' she shows that she understood how human beings and nature are inextricably linked in a moral chain. As usual, her style is not to lecture or to find fault but to allow her descriptions of the natural world to speak for themselves. By doing this she leaves the reader with questions relating to human responsibility towards other creatures.

In 'The Armadillo', for instance, she describes the custom in Brazil of sending fire balloons up into the sky to celebrate St John's Day in June. Her tone of admiration is clear in the beautiful images she creates: 'the paper chambers flush and fill with light / that comes and goes, like hearts'. She compares them to the stars and to planets like Venus and Mars. But she also sees the damage the fire balloons do to the birds and animals when they fall into the forest. Images of suffering are presented to the reader without comment. Visual details such as 'stained bright pink' and the onomatopoeic word 'shrieked' leave us in no doubt as to the destruction that is caused by the custom. The armadillo, forced out into the open and rolled up into a ball, looks like a fist made of armour ('mailed') but is merely a weak, defenceless creature. No one could fail to be moved by her picture of the 'baby rabbit' that becomes a 'handful of intangible ash'.

Once again Bishop is dealing with an important question. Why should human activities and culture bring about suffering in the natural world? This is the underlying theme of the poem. In her poem 'The Fish', she also implicitly questions the right of a human being to conquer such a majestic creature, 'battered and venerable' as he was. Her sense of respect, as well as sympathy, for the fish's struggles leads her to release the fish: 'And I let the fish go.'

[Theme of nature discussed; based mainly on one poem but reference to another to support the argument]

In conclusion it must be said that these questions of existence and death, of how we should live and be responsible in life, are only a few of the selection of interesting questions that Bishop raises in her poems. In posing them and in attempting to answer some of them we see her capacity for close observation, her ability to create vivid images and her emotional involvement. Her style is always appropriate to her theme, whether she is speaking in the voice of a child or as a well-travelled adult. Above all we respond to the humanity of the questions she poses.

[Conclusion refers to both themes and style, as terms of question required]

New Discovery Poetry Anthology

snapshot

- Great ability to describe situations, objects, emotions and ideas clearly and precisely
- Had a difficult childhood that influenced her writing
- Writes about travel, childhood experiences, the art of writing
- Close observer of the natural world
- Reveals personality and outlook in poems
- Well respected by fellow poets
- Regarded art as being genderless
- Interested in the shape and texture of the world
- Striking use of language: metaphors, similes, etc.
- Writes in variety of forms: lyric, narrative, sestina, sonnet
- Deeper themes underlie surface description

Emily Dickinson

1830–86

'HOPE' IS THE THING WITH FEATHERS
THERE'S A CERTAIN SLANT OF LIGHT
I FELT A FUNERAL, IN MY BRAIN*
A BIRD CAME DOWN THE WALK
I HEARD A FLY BUZZ – WHEN I DIED*
THE SOUL HAS BANDAGED MOMENTS
I COULD BRING YOU JEWELS – HAD I A MIND TO
A NARROW FELLOW IN THE GRASS
I TASTE A LIQUOR NEVER BREWED
AFTER GREAT PAIN, A FORMAL FEELING COMES

Biography

Emily Dickinson's life reads like a detective mystery. As a young woman she lived a social life, meeting up with friends, attending parties in her home town of Amherst and attracting the attention of several young men. By all accounts she was high-spirited and witty. From about the age of thirty she increasingly withdrew from society, choosing to live almost the entirety of her time as a recluse in her father's house, communicating with the outside world through a voluminous correspondence. In accordance with her wishes, after her death, her sister and sister-in-law destroyed all her correspondence. Fortunately, the thousand or so poems her sister found hidden in Emily's writing desk were saved.

Amherst

Emily Elizabeth Dickinson was born on 10 December 1830 in Amherst, a Calvinist town in Massachusetts. Apart from a brief period at Mount Holyoke Female Seminary, a trip to Washington and Philadelphia and a stay in Boston to receive treatment for an eye problem, all her life was spent there. She was the second child of Emily Norcross and Edward Dickinson. Her mother came from a prosperous family and her father was a lawyer, a politician and, later, the treasurer of Amherst College. In a letter to Thomas Wentworth Higginson, Dickinson was less than flattering of her parents: 'My Mother does not care for thought – and, Father, too busy with his Briefs – to notice what we do – He buys me many Books – but begs me not to read them – because he fears they joggle the Mind.' She had an older brother, Austin, and a younger sister, Lavinia. All three children were very close throughout their lives and all started school in the one-room local primary school.

Education

Dickinson received a sound education at Amherst Academy and Mount Holyoke Female Seminary. When they were young, Edward Dickinson encouraged his children in their education. In a letter, written when Emily was seven, he exhorted them to 'Keep school, and learn, so as to tell me when I come home, how many new things you have learned, since I came away.' Amherst Academy was a progressive school. It had a broad curriculum, from the classics to science, and the teachers were well qualified and motivated. The school was connected to Amherst College and students could attend college lectures in astronomy, botany, chemistry, geology, natural history and zoology. **This scientific emphasis is reflected in Dickinson's poetry: in her fascination with naming, her detailed descriptions, her choice of words and the range of her imagery.**

At the age of seventeen Dickinson entered Mount Holyoke Seminary, a boarding school run by a devout Christian headmistress, Mary Lyon. Many of the graduates of the seminary became evangelical missionaries. Her stay there was not happy. Evangelical fervour swept through the college and the students were invited to declare their faith in God openly and publicly. Dickinson refused to do so and was put into a category of students who were 'without hope'. Unhappy and homesick, she returned to Amherst. Thereafter her attitude to Christian belief was one of positive doubt. In 1850, when Amherst was infected with a bout of revivalist fervour, the nineteen-year-old Emily wrote: 'I am standing alone in rebellion'. Her rebellion, such as it was, was more private and interior than public in nature and found expression in her poetry. **Although Dickinson never declared herself a Christian, she spent a lifetime exploring the nature of the soul and the spiritual life. Her poems are influenced by the rhythms of Protestant hymns and the Bible is a major source of her diction and imagery.**

Young adulthood

As was the case with many unmarried daughters after the completion of their formal education, the future for Dickinson was one of domestic work. Because her family was a prominent one in Amherst, there were many visitors to the house. Not only were visitors to be received and entertained, but there was also an obligation to return social visits. In a letter written in 1850 Dickinson exclaimed: 'God keep me from what they call households.' Although she baked bread and worked in the garden, Dickinson refused to clean and dust the house. She also declined to make social calls, although she did maintain an active social life with her siblings and friends and read widely. Among the novels that had an electric effect upon her was *Jane Eyre* and she may well have identified with the novel's heroine.

In 1855 Dickinson travelled to Washington to visit her father who, by this time, had been elected to the US House of Representatives. She went on to Philadelphia to visit a friend from school. There, it seems, she met Charles Wadsworth, a Presbyterian preacher. There is much speculation that Wadsworth was the great secret love of her life.

In the following year Austin, her brother, married Susan Gilbert and set up home in an adjoining house. Dickinson spent many evenings in their company and the company of their friends. One of these friends was Samuel Bowles, editor of the *Springfield Republican*, an influential newspaper in Massachusetts, who published some of her poems. Dickinson maintained a correspondence with Bowles and his wife over the course of twenty-five years. Some critics suggest it was Bowles, and not Wadsworth, who was the love of her life.

Withdraws from society

When their mother's health began to decline in 1855, Emily and Lavinia took over the running of the house. Although she was still in her twenties, Dickinson began to withdraw from society. Gradually she became a recluse, rarely if ever leaving her home. The myth of the mysterious woman dressed in white, glimpsed in her garden, was formed during her lifetime. Mabel Loomis Todd, a writer who came to live in Amherst in 1881 and who became the lover of Dickinson's brother, Austin, wrote to her parents about the 'lady whom the people call the Myth: She has not been outside of her own house in fifteen years . . . she dresses wholly in white, and her mind is said to be perfectly wonderful. She writes finely, but no one ever sees her.'

There has been much speculation on the cause of her seclusion. Many early biographers favoured the explanation of disappointment in love. Charles Wadsworth visited her in 1860 and some biographers see a connection between this visit and her decision to withdraw from the world. The truth may have been more prosaic. Her brother, for example, suggested that her seclusion was simply a pose. Certainly, her family did not regard her behaviour as odd. Relieved of the necessity of visiting and entertaining, Dickinson pursued her interest in writing. She wrote poems and she wrote letters to friends. Indeed, she regarded letter writing as a form of visiting, although more focused and intense than the polite form of social visits that were common in Amherst at that time.

It is evident from the number of poems that she wrote in 1862 that Dickinson underwent some kind of personal crisis. Speculation suggests that this crisis was related to the failure of a love affair. Many of the poems written in this period explore despair and depressed states of mind.

Although Dickinson withdrew from society, she did have friends. Apart from her sister and brother, she was very close to her brother's wife, Susan Gilbert, whose family also came from Amherst. Susan was a trusted friend and one of Dickinson's most important readers. Indeed, she may well have read all of Dickinson's poetry and many poems were written for her. (Although they lived in neighbouring houses, Dickinson often preferred to write to Susan rather than meet face to face.) Helen Hunt Jackson was another literary friend who encouraged Dickinson to publish her work. And Dickinson was certainly romantically involved with Otis Lord, a family friend, to whom she wrote ardent letters, but whose proposal of marriage she declined in 1880.

An audience for her poetry

In 1862, when she was aged thirty-two, Dickinson wrote to Thomas Wentworth Higginson enclosing some of her poems. She wanted to know if her verse was alive and did it breathe. Higginson was widely known as a man of letters and a prolific essayist. An essay that Dickinson read in the *Atlantic Monthly* prompted her to write to him. He was also a radical theologian, an outspoken supporter of women's rights and an advocate for the abolition of slavery. Although he had a reputation for encouraging young writers, Higginson neither fully understood the nature of Dickinson's talent, nor recognised the scope of her achievement. Faced with her epigrammatic style, Higginson tried to regularise and smooth her poems. Determined and certain, Dickinson refused to compromise.

Despite not fully appreciating her peculiar genius, Higginson mentored and encouraged Dickinson for many decades and her correspondence with him was immensely important to her. Interestingly, fewer than twenty of her poems were published during her lifetime. However, Dickinson sent poems to nearly all her correspondents and, in this way, her poems were circulated among her friends. So, although little of her work was published, she did have an audience for her poetry.

After her death, Emily's sister, Lavinia, found a box containing 900 poems 'tied together with twine' in 'sixty volumes' or fascicles (bundles). A hundred poems were published in 1890, edited by Mabel Loomis Todd and Thomas Wentworth Higginson, with 'corrections' made by Higginson to rhymes, punctuation, rhythms and, in some cases, imagery. Because of problems with copyright and family feuds over the ownership of the poems, it was not until 1955 that her collected poems were published in the way that she had written them.

Final years

The three years between 1882 and 1885 were difficult for Dickinson. She lost her mother; her friends Otis Lord and Helen Hunt Jackson; and her young nephew, Gilbert. Austin began an affair with Mabel Loomis Todd, a family friend, and Emily was torn between her brother and her sister-in-law, Susan.

In 1884 Dickinson suffered the first attack of the kidney disease that eventually caused her death in 1886, at the age of fifty-five. She left precise instructions for her funeral, specifying the white dress she was to be buried in and the route to be taken from her house to the churchyard. At her funeral service, Thomas Wentworth Higginson read a line from her favourite Emily Brontë poem as her epitaph: 'No coward soul is mine.'

Social and Cultural Context

Although her father was a politician and she lived during the period of the American Civil War (1861–5), there is little indication that the war had any significant influence on the poetry of Emily Dickinson. Nor do the poems give much indication that the era in which she lived was one in which the campaign for the rights of women began or that the campaign for the abolition of slavery, which led to the Civil War, dominated national politics. Dickinson's poetry does, of course, speak to the cultural and literary context of her day. The Calvinist tradition of her family and the writings of Henry David Thoreau and Ralph Waldo Emerson are important influences. Equally important to an understanding of her poetry was the position of women in society in nineteenth-century New England.

The Calvinist tradition

The Calvinist tradition was brought to New England by the Pilgrim fathers who settled there in the seventeenth century. The Calvinist emphasis on sin and damnation led to a strict moral code and a focus on sinfulness. All life, it seemed, was directed at preparing for the Day of Judgement. For this reason, individuals were encouraged constantly to examine their conscience. Calvinism created an atmosphere in which individualism was curtailed and artistic expression was viewed as potentially proud and sinful. Although Calvinism was on the wane in the nineteenth century, its influence remained strong in Amherst. Indeed, when Dickinson was a student at Mount Holyoke Female Seminary, the headmistress instigated a series of Calvinist revivals, during which students were encouraged to declare their faith as Christians. Beset by doubts, Dickinson refused to do so and remained unconverted. Despite this, **the language of Calvinism and of the Bible is evident in her poetry and provides a rich source of imagery. The question of everlasting life was one to which she returned often in her poetry.**

Ralph Waldo Emerson

Dickinson was certainly influenced by the group of writers known as Transcendentalists, the most famous of whom was Ralph Waldo Emerson. The Transcendentalists believed that God dwelt or was immanent in nature and in humanity. This led to a celebration of the natural world as a sign of God's creative energy. If Dickinson did not convert to Calvinism, neither did she convert to Transcendentalism. She did, however, admire Emerson's emphasis on self-reliance, the primacy of individual experience over tradition and the importance of the interior life. Indeed, **Dickinson's reclusive lifestyle and her exploration of what she referred to as 'the undiscovered continent' echo some of the themes she found in Emerson's writing.**

Alone in rebellion

The position of women in New England society was one of subservience to men. Women were not expected to be full-time writers or intellectuals, or to be involved in public affairs. Their place was at home, living pious, domestic lives. At one level, the external facts of Dickinson's life suggest that she was content with a domestic role. However, her poetry speaks of extreme states of mind, hints at suppressed emotions and feelings, challenges religious orthodoxy and reveals an individual deeply at odds with the social and religious values of her day: one who stood alone in rebellion.

Punctuation and Capital Letters

Dickinson was very eccentric in her usage of punctuation and capital letters. Generally, her odd use has the purpose of emphasis. Her use of the dash is a device to indicate her own peculiar sense of rhythm, which she felt was not adequately served by regular punctuation such as the semi-colon and colon. The dash also works to create moments of suspense or dramatic pauses in the poems.

Timeline

1830	Born 10 December in Amherst, Massachusetts
1835	Attends local primary school
1840	Attends school in Amherst Academy
1847	Boarder at Mount Holyoke Female Seminary; declines to profess herself a Christian
1848	Withdraws from Mount Holyoke due to ill health and home sickness
1850	Back in Amherst: 'I am standing alone in rebellion'
1855	Travels to Washington to visit her father and then to Philadelphia; probable meeting with Charles Wadsworth; her mother's health begins to decline
1856	Her brother, Austin, marries her friend, Susan Gilbert; the couple live in an adjoining house
1858	Begins writing in earnest; assembles her poems into bound packets or fascicles
1861	Suggestion of a personal 'major crisis'; more and more withdrawn from the world
1862	Writes to Thomas Wentworth Higginson and encloses some poems; writes 366 poems
1863	Writes 141 poems
1864	Writes 174 poems; visits Boston for treatment for her eyes; may have met Judge Otis Lord, who later proposes to her
1874	Father dies
1882	Friendship with Susan strained by Austin's love affair with Mabel; mother dies; Charles Wadsworth dies
1883	Eight-year-old nephew, Gilbert, dies; Emily is heart-broken
1885	Bedridden with Bright's disease
1886	Writes to cousins 'Called Back' on 14 May; dies on 15 May
1890	First selection of her poems published
1955	First edition of her poems published as she wrote them

'Hope' is the thing with feathers

'Hope' is the thing with feathers –
That perches in the soul –
And sings the tune without the words –
And never stops – at all –

And sweetest – in the Gale – is heard –   5
And sore must be the storm –
That could abash the little Bird
That kept so many warm –

I've heard it in the chillest land –
And on the strangest Sea –   10
Yet, never, in Extremity,
It asked a crumb – of Me.

Glossary

1 | *the thing*: although she gives 'Hope' some of the characteristics of a bird, Dickinson also wishes to be true to its abstract nature of 'hope' as a quality or disposition

Guidelines

Dickinson wrote a number of 'definition poems' in which she uses physical details to define what an abstract experience is or is not. Often her definitions consist of a series of comparisons. However, she does not use the word 'like'. 'Hope' is not like a thing with feathers, it 'is the thing with feathers' (line 1). The directness and confidence of the statement makes her definition vivid and immediate. As in religious symbolism, Hope is imagined as having some of the characteristics of a bird. **Although Hope may seem something slight (it is only a 'little Bird', line 7), it is in fact something immensely powerful and comforting.** The poem, written in 1861, during what was a difficult period for Dickinson, has an optimistic, buoyant mood.

Commentary

Stanza 1

In the first stanza Dickinson **introduces the metaphor** (Hope is a feathered thing that resides in the soul) and develops it through the poem by telling us that Hope sings; that it is resilient in times of storm and distress; that it is found in all places; and that it seeks nothing for itself.

According to the first line, Hope is a thing with feathers, that is, something that can fly, and that can lift the spirit. The use of the word 'feathers' suggests the warm, comforting nature of Hope. Hope, the poem asserts, resides in the soul. By describing the song of Hope as 'the tune without words' (line 3), Dickinson suggests that Hope goes beyond logic and reason and their limitations. **Hope is resilient and unceasing. It never stops 'at all'.**

Stanza 2

The comfort that Hope gives in times of distress and uncertainty – emotional, spiritual, psychological – is recorded in stanza 2. The comfort of Hope is known to many. **The phrase 'the little bird' (line 7) suggests the poet's affection and admiration for Hope.**

Stanza 3

Stanza 3 records the poet's personal experience of Hope, in times of personal anguish. Hope has come to her in the 'chillest land' (line 9) and on 'the strangest Sea' (line 10). **In these periods of personal crisis, Hope offered comfort, without seeking anything in return.** Hope, in other words, is generous and other-seeking, asking nothing for itself. This final stanza of the poem strikes a solemn note, as if the poet wants to give hope the dignified celebration she believes it deserves.

Form of the poem

The poem is written in four-line stanzas. The second and fourth lines rhyme. The metre is based upon the common metre of hymns and ballads. Dickinson's punctuation, her use of slant rhymes and enjambment, and her skilled use of repetition and alliteration work to eliminate the sing-song effect of this metre.

Thinking about the poem

1. What is the most important quality of Hope, as suggested by the first stanza? What words or phrases capture this?
2. Think about the description 'the tune without the words' (line 3). Why might a tune without words be appropriate to Hope? Explain your answer.
3. How is the strength of Hope suggested in the second stanza?
4. The poem becomes more personal in the final stanza.
    a) What has been the poet's experience of Hope?
    b) What is the effect of the words 'chillest' (line 9) and 'strangest' (line 10)? Explain your answer.
5. What, do you think, does the poet have in mind in her reference to 'Extremity' in line 11?
6. Do you think that this poem would offer consolation to a reader in some kind of distress? How do you think it might do this? Give reasons for your answer.

There's a certain Slant of light

There's a certain Slant of light,
Winter Afternoons –
That oppresses, like the Heft
Of Cathedral Tunes –

Heavenly Hurt, it gives us –   5
We can find no scar,
But internal difference,
Where the Meanings, are –

None may teach it – Any –
'Tis the Seal Despair –   10
An imperial affliction
Sent us of the Air –

When it comes, the Landscape listens –
Shadows – hold their breath –
When it goes, 'tis like the Distance   15
On the look of Death –

Glossary	
3	*Heft*: weight
10	the *Seal Despair*: 'Seal' has the meaning of mark or sign, as in the wax seal placed on a letter. In the Calvinist tradition, the sacraments are seals of God's promise of salvation. In this poem, the hope of salvation is noticeably absent

Guidelines

'There's a certain Slant of light' explores a state of mind in which the comfort of hope is absent. In its place there is the despair associated with a certain kind of winter light falling on the landscape. The speaker in the poem sees the light, coming from heaven, as an affliction, affecting the inner landscape of the soul. The poem was probably written in 1861, during the period when it is believed Dickinson suffered a major personal crisis.

Commentary

Stanza 1

The fall of a certain kind of winter light is oppressive, according to the first stanza of the poem, as oppressive as the 'Heft / Of Cathedral Tunes' (lines 3–4). This is a striking simile. It links winter light and church music with a heaviness of the soul (the word 'heft' suggests weight). What starts off as a visual image is now described in terms of music, and the music is, in turn, described in terms of weight. **This blurring of the distinction between the senses (synaesthesia) creates a feeling of disturbance.**

Stanza 2

Dickinson states that this slant of winter light gives 'Heavenly Hurt' (line 5). **This is a hurt that leaves no physical wounds or scars but which affects the inner life or soul of the person and brings despair.** One can interpret this stanza as suggesting that the relationship between humanity and heaven is marked by a certain cruelty on the part of heaven.

Stanza 3

It is suggested that the hurt referred to in the second stanza cannot be understood, taught or explained away. It is without remedy. The slant of light is the mark or sign of despair ('Seal Despair', line 10), which is both a psychological and a spiritual condition. The word 'Seal' also suggests the message of a royal personage, a closed communication, something beyond contradiction. This meaning is reinforced by the phrase 'imperial affliction', which implies that the affliction associated with the winter light is sent by a higher or sovereign authority. Is the message of the winter light the message of human mortality that is beyond contradiction?

Stanza 4

The light causes the world to be still and hushed, as if nature itself is in awe of heaven's light, and passive in the face of it. In other words, the light impresses as much as it oppresses. Note how, in this stanza, the poem moves from the inner landscape back to the external one. The passing of the light does not lift the feeling of despair. On the contrary, the passing of the light leaves a chill, as if one had looked on the distance between the present and our death. It is only when the light disappears that its full meaning becomes clear. **The final dash in the poem suggests the unknown into which we all face.**

Form of the poem

The poem is written in four-line stanzas with a regular rhyming scheme. The sounds and rhyme of the poem add considerably to the feeling of seriousness and weighty matters. Note the use of final 't' sounds, which slow the rhythm and give a sense of definition and precision to the poem. **The poem itself works as a seal – it is written in an authoritative style that brooks no contradiction.**

Thinking about the poem

1. What is the effect of a certain kind of winter light, according to the first stanza of the poem?
2. What state of mind might regard 'Cathedral Tunes' (line 4) as heavy or oppressive? Explain your answer.
3. What, according to the second stanza, is the effect of the light? Where is the difference made by the light noticed or felt?
4. In the second stanza the words 'we' and 'us' are used by the poet. Do you think that 'I' and 'me' might have been more appropriate? Explain your answer.

5   a) What words or phrases in the third stanza suggest the powerlessness of those afflicted by despair?
    b) What, in particular, is the effect of the word 'Seal' (line 10) in relation to despair?
    c) Does the phrase 'imperial affliction' (line 11) suggest that the affliction is sent by a higher authority (God) or is the idea that affliction is itself majestic? Give reasons for your answer.
6   What, according to the speaker, is the feeling or situation when the light goes?
7   Examine the rhymes and the rhythm of the poem. In your view, how important are they in expressing the poet's concerns?
8   Consider the three phrases 'Heavenly Hurt' (line 5), 'An imperial affliction' (line 11) and 'the Seal Despair' (line 10). What view of providence or God emerges from them?
9   Discuss the poem as an expression of a religious crisis, in which the speaker feels betrayed by God.
10 What does this poem have in common with "Hope' is the thing with feathers'?
11 'internal difference, / Where the Meanings, are' (lines 7–8). What, do you think, does this statement suggest about Dickinson?

I Felt a Funeral, in my Brain

I Felt a Funeral, in my Brain,
And Mourners to and fro
Kept treading – treading – till it seemed
That Sense was breaking through –

And when they all were seated,   5
A Service, like a Drum –
Kept beating – beating – till I thought
My Mind was going numb –

And then I heard them lift a Box
And creak across my Soul   10
With those same Boots of Lead, again,
Then Space – began to toll,

As all the Heavens were a Bell,
And Being, but an Ear,
And I, and Silence, some strange Race 15
Wrecked, solitary, here –

And then a Plank in Reason, broke,
And I dropped down, and down –
And hit a World, at every plunge,
And Finished knowing – then – 20

Glossary

4	*Sense:*	waking consciousness or common sense
6	*Service:*	a church funeral service or ceremony
9	*Box:*	coffin
11	*Boots of Lead:*	the heavy tread of the mourners
12	*Space:*	the outside world into which the imagined funeral cortege moves
13	*Heavens:*	the sky or firmament
19	*World:*	the worlds which the poet imagines her soul passing through on its way to its final destination

Guidelines

In this celebrated poem we are given an account of the progress of a funeral from the startling perspective of the person lying in the coffin. The poem was probably written in 1861, during a difficult period in Dickinson's personal life, when she was beset by both religious and artistic doubts. In addition, there were also her complicated and disappointed feelings for Samuel Bowles, editor of the *Springfield Republican* newspaper.

Commentary

Stanzas 1 and 2

In the first line the speaker declares 'I Felt a Funeral in my Brain'. **The verb 'Felt' and the noun 'Brain' suggest an experience that is intense and physical.** By using these words, Dickinson abolishes the traditional boundary between experiences of the mind and those of the body. What the poet imagines is so vivid that it feels like a physical experience. The repetition of the word 'treading' in line 3, describing the impact of the activities of the mourners, emphasises this physicality.

The second stanza continues the first-person narrative account of the progress of the funeral. When the mourners were seated, the service began. **The stanza emphasises how hearing became the sense through which the 'I' received the world. The transition from 'Brain' in line 1 to 'Mind' in line 8 suggests, perhaps, that the physical intensity of the experience lessened, and it became more psychological in character.** However, Dickinson understood that there can be no absolute distinction between mind and body.

Stanzas 3 and 4

In stanza 3 the word 'Soul' is introduced (line 10). This suggests that the experience, which began as a physical one and became more psychological in character, developed a spiritual quality as it proceeded. This development did not make the experience any clearer. In fact the descriptions in stanzas 3 and 4 suggest that the 'I' became increasingly disoriented and the boundary between external and internal collapsed.

Furthermore, as it progressed, the experience was increasingly defined by a sense of contraction. Space was filled with the tolling of a bell and 'Being' (line 14) was reduced to just hearing. Just as bells mark time and differentiate one moment from another, so the tolling in the poem marks a decisive moment. **The sense of contraction experienced by the 'I' was accompanied by an overwhelming sense of isolation. The 'I' is described as shipwrecked from life, cut-off, along with silence, and left 'here'. The effect of 'here', placed as the last word in stanza 4, is to give a startling immediacy to the experience.**

Stanza 5

Before the 'I' and the reader can take stock of the situation and grasp the nature of stanza 4's 'here', the poem is on the move again. **'Reason', the faculty that could help to make sense of the experience, did not hold up** ('And then a Plank in Reason, broke', line 17) and the 'I' underwent a new sensation, that of falling, plunging deeper into the experience, down to new levels or worlds. And at the end of this plunging, we are told that the 'I' 'Finished knowing – then' (line 20). This may mean that the poet's knowledge of the beyond is finished at this point; or that the poet has finished her imagined funeral with the knowledge of something that she cannot express; or that knowledge itself finishes.

Different interpretations

Some critics read the plunge as the coffin's descent into the grave and the 'here' of stanza 4 as death. (The word 'Plank' in line 17 may suggest the planks placed across the open grave, before the final interment.) Such readers see stanzas 4 and 5 as describing the experience of entering into death. Others interpret the final stanza as describing the descent into madness or despair, while yet more read the plunge as a description of the loss of consciousness.

The final line is highly regarded by critics even as they disagree on its meaning. Some interpret it as a declaration that the plunge beyond reason yielded a new, deeper knowledge, although this knowledge is not expressed. At the end or finish of the fall, the 'I' had learned something, but this something is not revealed. Others read the final line as suggesting that thought and knowledge are lost in the fall. Another reading suggests that the poet, on the verge of gaining an imaginative insight into the nature of death, fails. However much she might desire to experience death, imaginatively, it is beyond the imagination's capacity to do so.

Looking at the poem as a whole, some critics see the funeral described in the poem as a metaphor for the breakdown of consciousness, and relate the poem to Dickinson's personal crisis. They read the poem as one of Dickinson's definition poems, where the progress of a funeral is a comparison (the vehicle) for despair or a mental breakdown (the tenor). Others take the poem at face value, regarding it as an unusual exploration of one of Dickinson's favourite themes – the transition between life and death, which she also explores in 'I heard a Fly buzz'. Some readers regard the poem as charting the failure of her poetic imagination, during a period when she was unable to write. **Whichever interpretation is given, the poem sees Dickinson straining her imagination to the limits of its power.**

Reading aloud

Just as there are several ways of interpreting the poem, so too there are several possibilities for reading it aloud. **On the one hand, it can be read as a narrative of a nightmarish, terrifying experience. In this reading, the dashes and punctuation may suggest the fragmented comprehension of the 'I'. On the other, the fact that the poem is narrated in the past tense may suggest that a tone of calm, puzzled wonder might be appropriate.**

Style and form of the poem

Dickinson uses the four-line stanza of the ballad or the hymn. An interesting stylistic feature is the repeated use of 'And' in the poem, especially in stanzas 4 and 5. This creates a sense of forward motion, as if the 'I' was powerless before the experience. Another notable effect is the repetition of the words 'treading' (line 3) and 'beating' (line 7) and the use of the dash after each use of these words, which emphasises the insistent nature of the noise.

Thinking about the poem

1. The poem tells a story. What, according to the speaker, happens in the opening two stanzas of the poem?
2. What is the effect of the repetition of 'treading' in line 3 and 'beating' in line 7?
3. In the third stanza the speaker says that the Mourners creaked across her Soul with 'Boots of Lead' (lines 10–11). What feeling is created by this description?
4. In terms of a person in a coffin, does it make sense to suggest that the whole of one's being might be reduced to the sensation of hearing, as one moves from life into death (lines 13–14)? Explain your answer.
5. The most dramatic moment of the poem occurs in stanza 5. Explain in your own words what happens.
6. In line 1 the poet uses the word 'Brain'; in line 8 it is 'Mind'; and 'Soul' is used in line 10. In your opinion, how do these changes contribute to the meaning of the poem? Explain your answer.
7. What, in your view, is the effect of the repeated use of the word 'and' in the poem?
8. Which of the following statements is closest to your interpretation of the poem?
   It is a poem about a funeral.
   It is a poem about a nervous breakdown.
   It is a poem about the limits of the imagination.
   You may choose more than one but you must explain your choice.
9. Prepare a reading of the poem that is calm and reflective. Prepare another that is panic-struck. Which reading, in your view, best captures the spirit of the poem?

Taking a closer look

1. Consider the use of the words 'Felt' and 'Brain' in the first line of the poem. What other words might Dickinson have used? What is the effect of using these words? Explain your answer.
2. Consider **two** examples of the use of the dash in the poem and comment on their effectiveness.
3. 'And Finished, knowing – then –' (line 20). What is your understanding of the final line of the poem?

Imagining

1. You have been asked to make a short film to accompany a reading of the poem. What music, sound effects, colour, images, etc. would you use to create the atmosphere of the poem? Explain your choices.
2. Suggest an alternative title for the poem. Explain your suggestion.

snapshot

I Felt a Funeral, in my Brain

- Startling perspective
- Description of funeral
- Imagery of heaviness and contraction
- Imagery of falling
- Terrifying, isolating experience
- Experience is physical, psychological and spiritual
- Use of 'and' and repetition creates sense of being overwhelmed
- Theme of death and dying
- Theme of breakdown
- Ends on a note of uncertainty

Emily Dickinson

A Bird came down the Walk

A Bird came down the Walk –
He did not know I saw –
He bit an Angleworm in halves
And ate the fellow, raw.

And then he drank a Dew   5
From a convenient Grass –
And then hopped sidewise to the Wall
To let a Beetle pass –

He glanced with rapid eyes
That hurried all around –   10
They looked like frightened beads, I thought –
He stirred his Velvet Head

Like one in danger, Cautious,
I offered him a Crumb
And he unrolled his feathers   15
And rowed him softer home –

Than Oars divide the Ocean,
Too silver for a seam –
Or Butterflies, off Banks of Noon
Leap, plashless as they swim.   20

Glossary

1	*Walk*: sidewalk, footpath	
3	*Angleworm*: a worm used as fish bait in angling	
7	*sidewise*: sideways, towards one side	
18	*Too silver for a seam*: the ocean's surface is so silvery that no division (such as made by oars) can be seen	
20	*plashless*: making no disturbance	

Guidelines

The poet observes a bird. She offers him a crumb. The bird flies away. **In her poetry, Dickinson describes many small moments in life, especially in meetings of the human and the animal world, which have a feeling of accident, surprise and favour about them.**

Stanzas 1 and 2

In the first stanza the narrator tells us of the bird straying into the human realm by coming down 'the Walk' (line 1). The narrator is unobserved by the bird and registers an amused surprise at the bird eating a 'raw' worm (line 4).

The narrator continues to observe the bird in stanza 2. Having dined, the bird quenches his thirst by drinking from the dewy grass. By referring to 'a Dew', **Dickinson particularises the image, and creates the impression of observing the event through a microscope, as a scientist might do.**

Having eaten and drank his fill, the bird courteously steps aside to 'let a Beetle pass' (line 8). This image captures the essence of Dickinson's technique in the poem. **On one hand, she observes the bird with a scientist's eye. On the other, she treats the events in a whimsical manner, by attributing human qualities and motives to the actions of the bird.**

Stanza 3

In the third stanza, there is a change in perspective. The bird is no longer the gentleman diner. Now his movements suggest the nervousness of one who might himself fall prey to a predator. The phrase 'Velvet Head' (line 12), accurately capturing the texture and appearance of the head feathers, also suggests the beauty of the bird.

Stanzas 4 and 5

Sympathetic to the bird's fears, the observer moves to allay them by offering him a crumb. In using the word 'Cautious' (line 13) to refer to both the bird and the observer, Dickinson creates a sense of identification between them. Despite this, the proffered gift is not taken and the bird flies away.

The flight is not undertaken in panic. **The sense of grace and ease in the flight of the bird is mirrored in the language of these lines (15–20), creating an impression of gentle motion.** Although the bird flies away, there is little sense of disappointment in the poem's conclusion. The observer takes pleasure in their accidental encounter. The vocabulary of the final stanza (Ocean, silver, Butterflies, Noon, Leap, swim) suggests a life of innocent, carefree pleasure. Like an Impressionist painting, there is harmony of air, water and light.

Form of the poem

The poem is written in four-line, rhyming stanzas. The long vowel sounds create a sense of quiet and hush. In this poem the dash is used to create pauses but it does not have the jarring effect that is evident in other poems. The overall effect of the poem is one of dreamy gentleness.

Thinking about the poem

1. What words and phrases in the poem convey the bird as (a) a predator; (b) a gentleman; and (c) prey? What is the poet's attitude to the bird in each of these guises?

2. The use and placing of the word 'Cautious' in line 13 is often admired by critics. Why, do you think, is this so?

3. The poem concludes with images of rowing and swimming. What do they suggest about the flight of the bird? What do they tell us about Dickinson? Explain your answer.

4. a) Where, in your view, is the humour and amusement of the poet most evident? Explain your answer.

    b) Does rhyme and punctuation contribute to the humour of the poem? Explain your answer.

5. 'In the poem, we see how Dickinson views the world with the eye of a scientist and the eye of an artist.' Give your response to this assessment of the poem.

6. What impression of Dickinson do you form from reading the poem? Explain your answer.

I heard a Fly buzz – when I died

I heard a Fly buzz – when I died –
The stillness in the Room
Was like the Stillness in the Air –
Between the Heaves of Storm –

The Eyes around – had wrung them dry –   5
And Breaths were gathering firm
For that last Onset – when the King
Be witnessed – in the Room –

I willed my Keepsakes – Signed away
What portion of me be   10
Assignable – and then it was
There interposed a Fly –

With Blue – uncertain stumbling Buzz –
Between the light – and me –
And then the Windows failed – and then 15
I could not see to see –

Glossary

4	*Heaves:*	wind surges of a storm
5	*Eyes around:*	the mourners around the bed keeping watch
7	*last Onset:*	final assault of death
7	*the King:*	God
8	*Be witnessed:*	inspired by their religious faith, all waited for the moment of death when, they believed, God would be present in the room (in the Calvinist tradition the moment of death is the moment the soul faces the judgement of God)
9	*Keepsakes:*	mementoes or souvenirs
11	*Assignable:*	could be left or bequeathed
12	*interposed:*	came between things; here, the fly got between the dying person and the solemn moment of death
13	*Blue:*	there is no noun to follow the adjective 'Blue' so it carries over to 'Buzz' at the end of the line and suggests a confused or disturbed apprehension of the world

Guidelines

Dickinson's fascination with death again provides the subject matter of this poem. It is written in the past tense, in the voice of the dying person, and describes the moment of death.

Commentary

Stanza 1
The startling perspective in the poem is announced in the first line: 'I heard a Fly buzz – when I died – '. The poem explores the moment of death. This moment is dominated, from the dying person's perspective, by the buzzing of a fly in the death-room. The fly interrupted the temporary silence in the room.

Stanza 2
In the second stanza we are told that, as death approached, the mourners gathered themselves and, inspired by their religious faith, waited for the moment when their God ('the King', line 7) would 'Be witnessed – in the Room' (line 8). In the Calvinist

tradition, the moment of death is the moment when the soul faces God's judgement. The mourners around the deathbed are filled with expectancy; the phrase 'Be witnessed' suggests the solemnity of a court.

Stanza 3

The dying person had tidied up her legal affairs and, thus prepared, waited for the moment of death. However, it was not the presence of God coming to claim her soul that filled her consciousness, but a Fly who 'interposed' (line 12). **The arrival of the fly, a symbol of human decay and corruption, suggests that death cannot be managed, arranged or ordered.** The word 'interposed' implies that the fly got between the dying person and the solemn moment of death.

Stanza 4

In the final stanza, as the moment of death is described, the syntax is fractured, suggesting the failure of consciousness as sight and sound blur and become one. As the last act in the drama of life, the buzzing fly suggests life as comedy rather than tragedy. The buzzing of the fly is unexpected, it is like a drunkard disturbing the solemnity of an important occasion. **The stumbling, buzzing fly comes between the dying person's sight and the source of light.** And then, as suggested by the imagery of light and darkness, the dying person was plunged into the darkness of death, and the moment had passed.

The poem is deliberately ambiguous on the nature of the light that the fly obscured. Was it natural or divine light? Were 'the Windows' of line 15 the eyes, the windows of the soul, or the windows of the room? **The ending of the poem, and the anti-climax it describes, suggests that humans have no way of knowing if the immortal life with God that their faith professes actually exists.** The final line implies that the dying person is robbed of both sight and understanding, a finality emphasised by the rhyme of 'me' and 'see' in this stanza. Is this the message of the voice from the dead – after dying all is darkness and emptiness? Is that the significance of the dash that ends the poem? For those who identify the narrator of the poem with Dickinson, the poem appears to offer evidence of her lack of faith in an afterlife with God.

Form of the poem

As befits a poem on a religious theme, 'I heard a Fly buzz' is written in the metre of a hymn, with a four-line stanza and a regular rhyming scheme. However, the use of the dash, with its jarring effect, and run-on lines takes away the sing-song effect of the form.

Thinking about the poem

1. What is the story that the poem tells?
2. In the second stanza what is the attitude of the mourners as they wait for the death of the narrator? Explain your answer.
3. What words and phrases in stanza 3 suggest that the speaker prepared carefully for her death?
4. What is the effect of the appearance of the fly in the room at the moment when 'the King' (line 7) is expected?
5. What happens at the end of the poem?
6. Given the ending, how would you describe the tone of the poem: amused, irritated, fearful, puzzled or disappointed? Explain your choice.
7. Consider each of these readings of the poem. Which of them, if any, corresponds to your own?

    The fly cheats the dying person of a glimpse of God before the moment of death.

    The appearance of the fly is a reminder that death cannot be controlled and managed.

    The poem calls into question faith in God and an eternal life.

    Explain your answer.
8. On the evidence of this poem, what kind of person do you imagine Dickinson to have been? Explain your answer.
9. Which of Dickinson's other poems bears the closest resemblance to this one? Explain your answer.

Taking a closer look

1. 'I heard a Fly buzz – when I died –' (line 1). In your view, is this an effective opening to the poem? Explain your answer.
2. 'when the King / Be witnessed' (lines 7–8). What view of death is suggested by these lines?
3. Comment on the use of the word 'stumbling' in line 13: 'With Blue – uncertain stumbling Buzz –'.

Imagining

1. Imagine that you are one of the mourners in the room. Write a letter to a friend in which you describe the moment of death and the feeling in the room afterwards.
2. You are asked to make a video version of the poem for YouTube. Describe as clearly as you can what your finished video will look and sound like.

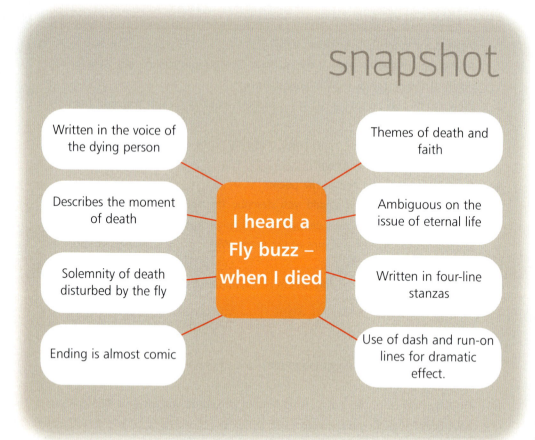

The Soul has Bandaged moments

The Soul has Bandaged moments –
When too appalled to stir –
She feels some ghastly Fright come up
And stop to look at her –

Salute her – with long fingers –   5
Caress her freezing hair –
Sip, Goblin, from the very lips
The Lover – hovered – o'er –
Unworthy, that a thought so mean
Accost a Theme – so – fair –   10

The soul has moments of Escape –
When bursting all the doors –
She dances like a Bomb, abroad,
And swings upon the Hours,

As do the Bee – delirious borne – 15
Long Dungeoned from his Rose –
Touch Liberty – then know no more,
But Noon, and Paradise –

The Soul's retaken moments –
When, Felon led along, 20
With shackles on the plumed feet,
And staples, in the Song,

The Horror welcomes her, again,
These, are not brayed of Tongue –

Glossary	
7	*Goblin*: an ugly demon
10	*Accost*: to approach and speak to someone; and also to solicit sexually
13	*abroad*: in different directions; out of doors
16	*Dungeoned*: imprisoned
20	*Felon*: convict or prisoner
21	*shackles*: rings fixed around a prisoner's ankles and joined by a chain
21	*plumed feet*: feathered feet; the image calls to mind the figure of Mercury, the messenger of the Gods, who had winged sandals
24	*These*: refers back to the 'retaken moments' of line 19
24	*not brayed of Tongue*: not spoken about or publicised

Guidelines

'The Soul has Bandaged moments' explores the contrasting highs and lows of the inner life. Images of horror and fright are contrasted with images of fulfilled happiness. Images of imprisonment are contrasted with images of freedom. The poem begins with the figure of Fright and ends with the figure of Horror, suggesting that the soul experiences more anguish than joy.

The poem may be read in a number of different, if related, ways: in psychological terms as an exploration of depression and elation; in spiritual terms as an exploration of hope and despair; in sexual terms as an exploration of the conflict between freedom and restraint; or in artistic terms as an exploration of the absence and presence of inspiration.

Commentary

Stanzas 1 and 2

'The Soul' is portrayed in the poem as a terrified woman, helpless before the attention of an unwelcome other: many critics interpret the 'Fright' of stanza 1 as death or death's servant. In stanza 2 the Fright is described as saluting and caressing the Soul's 'freezing hair' (line 6). The 'freezing hair' indicates the chill of fear and the coldness of death that the Soul experiences as the Fright pays her unwanted attention. **The dashes of the opening lines of stanza 2 capture the increasing fear of the soul.** The placing of the word 'unworthy' in line 9 makes the subject uncertain. Does it refer to the Lover, the Fright or the Soul herself? Does the word refer to the erotic turn the poem takes at this point?

Stanzas 3 and 4

Stanzas three and four break free of the atmosphere of threat, dread, claustrophobia and death that dominates the first two stanzas. Now the images suggest sensuous pleasure, freedom, warmth and fulfilment. The simile 'like a Bomb' (line 13), however, strikes a note of caution. The Soul's escape is too exuberant, too ecstatic. Like a bomb, it will explode and leave a sense of desolation. **These two stanzas suggest an intense period of psychological elation and, perhaps, artistic energy.**

Stanzas 5 and 6

The moments of escape come to an end and, like a prisoner, the Soul is welcomed again by 'The Horror' (line 23). **The imagery of shackles and staples is striking** and contrasts with the imagery of flight often used by Dickinson to denote joy and happiness. **The final two stanzas express the poem's despairing point of view: the interior life – psychological, spiritual, artistic, erotic – is characterised by feelings of oppression and despair, punctuated by periods of respite.**

The final line states that these moments when the Soul's is a prisoner 'are not brayed of Tongue'. In other words, they are not talked about. This may suggest that the subject of depression and despair is not one which is spoken of in public, and to do so would be to 'bray' or to speak in a way that might be considered rough and uncouth. **Thus, the experience of depression is, essentially, a lonely and isolating one. However, the tone of the final line can be read as a proud declaration of strength and pride.**

Form of the poem

The poem is divided into three sections, each containing two stanzas. Each section describes a condition of the soul. The first section (stanzas 1 and 2) suggests constraint and violation; the second (stanzas 3 and 4) celebrates the delirium of freedom; the third (stanzas 5 and 6) describes the soul's recapture.

The poem departs from Dickinson's usual four-line stanzas with one verse of six lines and a final concluding couplet. In the second stanza, the repetition of 'her', the alliteration and the hissing 's' sound combine to create a feeling of dread.

Thinking about the poem

1. 'The Soul has Bandaged moments' (line 1). Consider the possible meanings of 'Bandaged'. What does the word suggest about the condition of the Soul?
2. How is the figure of Fright portrayed (lines 3–6)? What words capture the Soul's terror before this Fright?
3. The image of Fright, the cold stranger menacing the Soul (portrayed as a vulnerable young girl), is taken from the tradition of Gothic Romance. Do you think that the word 'Goblin' (line 7) adds or takes away from the atmosphere of horror?
4. a) Who, do you think, is the 'Lover' referred to in line 8?
   b) Who or what is 'Unworthy' (line 9)? Explain your answers.
5. In your view, what does the word 'Bomb' (line 13) suggest about the nature of the Soul's escape described in stanza 3?
6. In stanza 4 the words 'Noon' and 'Paradise' are used as shorthand for happiness and fulfilment. Do you think that they are effective? Explain your answer.
7. Explain, as clearly as you can, what Dickinson means by the 'retaken moments' (line 19) of the Soul?

8   a) What, in your view, does Dickinson have in mind in her reference to 'The Horror' in line 23 of the poem?

   b) Does the verb 'welcomes' work in this line? Explain your answer.

9   In your view, what does the final line suggest about the sufferer's experience of depression? Give reasons for your answer.

10 Some critics read the poem as expressing the poet's depression at the loss of her creativity. What parts of the poem most support this reading?

11 Read the poem aloud. Do you think that the rhythm suits the mood of the poem? Explain your answer.

12 There is no first-person pronoun in the poem and, in the eyes of some critics, this lessens the impact of the poem. Do you agree with their point of view? Give reasons for your answer.

I could bring You Jewels – had I a mind to

I could bring You Jewels – had I a mind to –
But You have enough – of those –
I could bring You Odors from St. Domingo –
Colors – from Vera Cruz –

Berries of the Bahamas – have I –   5
But this little Blaze
Flickering to itself – in the Meadow –
Suits me – more than those –

Never a Fellow matched this Topaz –
And his Emerald Swing –   10
Dower itself – for Bobadilo –
Better – Could I bring?

Glossary

3	*St. Domingo*: San (or Santo) Domingo, capital of the Dominican Republic. The name is intended to suggest somewhere exotic. Like all the places mentioned in the poem, it is associated with the Spanish conquest of South America: the city was given its name by Christopher Columbus (1451–1506)
4	*Vera Cruz*: port in Mexico, founded by Hernán Cortés (1485–1547); an exotic place known for its colourful houses and tropical plants and flowers
5	*Bahamas*: a group of islands in the West Indies, where Columbus first made landfall in the New World in 1492; another exotic location
9	*Topaz*: a gem famous for its lustre and beautiful colours
10	*Emerald*: a precious stone, green in colour
11	*Dower*: gift, often used to describe the wealth brought to a man by a woman on their marriage
11	*Bobadilo*: Francisco de Bobadilla (d.1502), the Spaniard sent by Isabella and Ferdinand of Spain in 1499 to San Domingo to take over from Columbus as governor of the Indies. Bobadilla ordered Columbus to be returned to Spain in shackles and seized his gold and treasures

Guidelines

Although Dickinson is often described as a recluse, she had a wide circle of friends and corresponded with many of them throughout her life. **Many of her letters took the form of poems, or were written to accompany small gifts that she enclosed. These poems, many of them written as riddles, show the playful and humorous sides of Dickinson's personality.** Some of the letters/poems were clearly intended as tokens of her love, though she took considerable pains to disguise the identity of her beloved. 'I could bring You Jewels' is a good example of her letter-poems.

Commentary

Stanzas 1 and 2

The opening line of the poem strikes a note of confidence and playfulness, which is sustained to the end of the poem, making this the most joyful of Dickinson's poems on the Leaving Certificate course. The poem is also different in that it focuses on a relationship, rather than on the individual consciousness of the speaker.

In the first two stanzas the speaker considers the gift she will offer her beloved, the 'You' of the poem. She settles on a small meadow flower. **The chosen gift is a mark of the speaker's freedom and uniqueness, and a reflection, perhaps, of her unshowy personality.** The note of confidence and self-ease is striking in this choice. In the first stanza, the luxury of considering exotic gifts is reflected in the long lines that Dickinson employs. As she settles on her gift, the lines get shorter and the tone more decisive.

Stanza 3

A jaunty, confident tone is evident in the use of the word 'Fellow' in line 9. The concluding rhetorical question suggests that the flower is the best gift she could offer. Notice how, in this final stanza, the assured, confident tone is emphasised in the use of the word 'Never' (line 7) and in the rhyming of 'Swing' and 'bring', which closes her argument with a ring of authority. **In its playful, assured way, the poem establishes that the true value of gifts and the true nature of riches cannot be measured in material terms.**

Form of the poem

Dickinson employs the four-line stanza with the rhyme occurring between lines 2 and 4. Unlike other of her poems, there is a conversational feel to the opening lines, achieved by the length of the line and the phrase 'had I a mind to'. This is Dickinson at her most relaxed. As the poem proceeds, the tone becomes less conversational and concludes with the magisterial four-word last line.

Thinking about the poem

1. What do you learn about the 'You' of the poem, the person to whom the poem is addressed, from the first two lines? Explain your answer.
2. What, in your view, is the effect of the place names – St Domingo, Vera Cruz, Bahamas – used in lines 3 to 5?
3. In the first five lines a number of potential gifts are rejected. How does the gift that is eventually selected differ from them?
4. a) In your view, what does the choice of gift tell you about the speaker?
   b) What does it suggest about the nature of the relationship between the lovers?
5. What view of riches is suggested by the poem? Explain your answer.
6. 'The voice of the poem shows an absolute certainty and confidence in herself, in her choice of gift and in her beloved.' Give your response to this assessment of the poem.
7. What, in your view, is the mood of the poem?
8. Using 'I could bring You Jewels' as a model, write your own love poem.

A narrow Fellow in the Grass

A narrow Fellow in the Grass
Occasionally rides –
You may have met Him – did you not
His notice sudden is –

The Grass divides as with a Comb –   5
A spotted shaft is seen –
And then it closes at your feet
And opens further on –

He likes a Boggy Acre
A Floor too cool for Corn –   10
Yet when a Boy, and Barefoot –
I more than once at Noon
Have passed, I thought, a Whip lash
Unbraiding in the Sun
When stooping to secure it   15
It wrinkled, and was gone –

Several of Nature's People
I know, and they know me –
I feel for them a transport
Of cordiality –   20

But never met this Fellow
Attended, or alone
Without a tighter breathing
And Zero at the Bone –

Glossary

6	*spotted shaft*: the long thin mottled body of the snake
13	*Whip lash*: the part of the whip used for striking or lashing
14	*Unbraiding*: untwining like the leather thongs of a lash
19	*transport*: a strong emotion

Guidelines

This was one of the few poems published during Dickinson's life. It was published under the title 'Snake', though the word is never used in the poem. (In a letter discussing the poem, written in 1866, Dickinson did, however, refer to 'my Snake'.) Dickinson wrote many poems on the birds and small creatures that she observed in her garden. **Her attitude to animals is often one of amused absorption. However, the snake arouses a terrified fascination.** Interestingly, the poem is written in the persona of a male.

Commentary

Stanza 1
The opening two lines of the poem strike an off-hand note, as if the reader has joined a casual conversation. The word 'Fellow', for example, creates a sense of easy familiarity. By the fourth line, the tone has altered. The abruptness of line 4: 'His notice sudden is', and the menacing 's' sounds it contains, indicate an absence of fellow-feeling in the speaker for the snake. On second reading, it may well be the figure of the Devil on horseback that is brought to mind by the stanza's imagery.

Stanzas 2 and 3
The imagery in stanza 2 hints at the secrecy, danger and unpredictability of the snake. The word 'shaft' (line 6) suggests the danger and speed of an arrow-shaft.

The third, eight-line, central stanza returns to the casual-seeming air of the opening line and describes the favoured habitat of the snake. The poem changes direction in this stanza. There is a switch to the past tense as the speaker recalls a boyhood memory. **The word 'Barefoot' (line 11) suggests the vulnerability and simplicity of the boy, who is no match for the crafty snake.**

Stanzas 4 and 5
In the fourth stanza the speaker states that he knows 'Several of Nature's People' (line 17) and they know him, and he professes for them 'a transport / Of cordiality' (lines 19–20). There is a whimsical, even comic, air to this stanza. However, the snake stands apart from the 'Several of Nature's People' and the speaker's attitude to the snake is caught in the celebrated final stanza.

The last line of the poem, 'And Zero at the Bone – ', catches the inner terror caused in the speaker by this animal. The combination of the abstract 'Zero', with its association of void and emptiness, and the concrete 'bone' captures the physical sensation of a terror that is almost beyond words. The use of the word 'Fellow' in the final stanza reads as a measured irony.

Adam and Eve
In responding to a poem about a snake, it is almost impossible to ignore the figure of the snake in the story of Adam and Eve. There, the serpent, the Devil in disguise, deceived Adam and Eve into acting against God's command. This story predisposes us to view the snake as an evil deceiver.

Form of the poem

Dickinson rarely strays from the four-line stanza of the ballad or the hymn. When she does, as in the third stanza of this poem, there is very little innovation in the stanza form. Her success as a poet comes in the dramatic use of the dash, and the change in tone she achieves through the sound of words and her startling imagery, as evident in the final line of the poem.

Thinking about the poem

1. The word 'Fellow' (lines 1 and 21) has a feeling of familiarity about it. Does it capture the speaker's attitude to the snake? Explain your answer.
2. In six lines (lines 3–8), Dickinson succeeds in suggesting the danger, unpredictability and secrecy of the snake. How, in your opinion, does she do this?
3. What, in your view, does the snake's habitat (lines 9–10) tell us about him?
4. In your view, which of the following ideas are associated with the adjective 'Barefoot' in line 11: hardiness, innocence, vulnerability and/or foolishness? Explain your choice.
5. What do the words 'Whip lash' (line 13) suggest about the snake? Explain your answer.
6. a) What is the speaker's relationship with 'Nature's People', as described in stanza 4?
   b) In your view, is there anything contradictory in the idea of 'a transport of cordiality'?
7. What, do you think, is the effect of the 'But' placed at the opening of the fifth stanza?
8. Dickinson substitutes her phrase 'Zero at the Bone' (line 24) for the more usual 'chilled to the bone'. In your view, what does she gain by doing so?
9. Show how Dickinson uses rhythm and sound to capture the movements of the snake.
10. What, if anything, does the snake symbolise in the poem? Explain your answer.

I taste a liquor never brewed

I taste a liquor never brewed –
From Tankards scooped in Pearl –
Not all the Vats upon the Rhine
Yield such an Alcohol!

Inebriate of Air – am I –   5
And Debauchee of Dew –
Reeling – thro endless summer days –
From inns of Molten Blue –

When 'Landlords' turn the drunken Bee
Out of the Foxglove's door –   10
When Butterflies – renounce their 'drams' –
I shall but drink the more!

Till Seraphs swing their snowy Hats –
And Saints – to windows run –
To see the little Tippler   15
Leaning against the – Sun –

Glossary	
3	*Vats:* vessels for storing liquid, for example, wine
3	*Rhine*: a wine region of Germany on the banks of the River Rhine; there is another draft of this poem in which line 3 reads: 'Not all the Frankfort berries'
5	*Inebriate*: intoxicated
6	*Debauchee*: a person who pursues pleasure in a reckless way
8	*Molten*: melted; presumably, the shimmering effect on the blue sky caused by the heat of the sun
10	*Foxglove*: a tall purple or white flowered plant
11	*'drams'*: a small measure of alcohol
13	*Seraphs*: angels
15	*Tippler*: a frequent drinker (of alcohol)
16	*Leaning . . . Sun*: in the other draft of the poem, the final line reads 'From Manzanilla come.'

Guidelines

The poem was first published anonymously on 4 May 1861 in the *Springfield Republican* under the title 'The May Wine'. Two lines were altered by the editor to achieve an exact rhyme, and another line was changed to make the meaning clearer. **Richard Sewell, Dickinson's biographer, describes it as 'a rapturous poem about summer'.** The central metaphor of intoxication is ironic, given that Dickinson grew up in a Puritan household, and her father was a supporter of the Temperance League. A further irony is that the poem was written in the common rhythm of hymns.

Commentary

The central metaphor of the poem is one of intoxication brought on by a joyous appreciation of life. The poem describes the speaker's sense of delight in the beauty of the world around her. Dickinson strikes an exaggerated, playful tone, established from the first line, 'I taste a liquor never brewed'. The riddling quality of this line and the extravagance of the imagery capture the **mood of dizzy happiness** that infuses the poem. In the third stanza, the imagery of flowers as inns or taverns and bees as drunkards continues the vein of cartoon humour evident throughout the poem.

In the final stanza Dickinson does not present the world's beauty as a sign of God's creativity. The inhabitants of heaven are presented as faintly ridiculous, enclosed and, perhaps, envious of the freedom and of 'the little Tippler' (line 15), whose pose, leaning against the sun, strikes a note of **comic rebelliousness**, applauded by the angels as they swing their hats to honour her.

In many of her poems, the 'I' persona is shown as starving or thirsting. **This poem is a rarity in Dickinson's work in that it celebrates the joy of excess, a reckless, indulgent joy captured in the word 'Debauchee' (line 6).**

Christian interpretation

For some critics, the poem is not a celebration of excess and rebelliousness. They read the 'Sun' of the final stanza as a symbol of Christ. In this reading, the speaker announces an intention to enjoy the beauty of the world until she comes into the company of Christ, where her arrival will be greeted by the watching angels and saints.

Form of the poem

The poem is written in the common metre of hymns and flows along without any of the dramatic pauses or changes of tone evident in many of Dickinson's other poems.

Thinking about the poem

1. a) What kind of tankards are, in your view, 'scooped in Pearl' (line 2)?
   b) What does this suggest about the liquor to be drunk from them? Explain your answer.
2. Identify the words and phrases in the poem that are associated with intoxication. What, according to the second stanza, is the cause of the speaker's intoxication?
3. In your opinion, is the association of drunkenness with bees (lines 9–10) apt? Explain your answer.
4. 'I shall but drink the more!' (line 12). What, in your view, is the tone of this declaration?
5. What image of heaven is presented in stanza 4? In your view, is it an effective image?
6. One critic remarked that the Sun in stanza 4 is treated as a celestial lamppost. Would you agree that the entire poem is marked by a similar spirit of whimsy and joy? Explain your answer.
7. Comment on the use of comic exaggeration in the poem. What phrases strike you as being particularly humorous?
8. Compare the celebration of the summer sun, in this poem, with the meditation on winter light in 'There's a certain Slant of light'.

After great pain, a formal feeling comes

After great pain, a formal feeling comes –
The Nerves sit ceremonious, like Tombs –
The stiff Heart questions was it He, that bore,
And Yesterday, or Centuries before?

The Feet, mechanical, go round –　　　　　　　　　　　　5
Of Ground, or Air, or Ought –
A Wooden way
Regardless grown,
A Quartz contentment, like a stone –

This is the Hour of Lead – 10
Remembered, if outlived,
As Freezing persons, recollect the Snow –
First – Chill – then Stupor – then the letting go –

Glossary

3	*He*:	the reference is ambiguous, it could refer to the 'stiff Heart' or to Christ, whose suffering is brought to mind by the experience of great pain
3	*bore*:	has two possible meanings: to bear suffering or to accept blame
4	*And … before*:	the 'stiff Heart' feels disoriented, not able to distinguish between recent time ('Yesterday') and past time ('Centuries before')
6	*or Ought*:	or anything
7	*a Wooden way*:	the phrase suggests the unnatural movements of a puppet; it also suggests Christ's stumbling on the Way of the Cross
9	*Quartz*:	a very hard mineral
13	*Stupor*:	a dazed condition

Guidelines

'After great pain' was written in 1862, a year in which Dickinson wrote 366 poems. Many commentators believe that she was on the edge of madness during this time. **This is another poem that explores the effects of anguish upon the individual.** The source of the pain referred to in line 1 is not disclosed. It may be the result of loneliness, separation or bereavement, all of which Dickinson experienced. **The absence of personal statement gives the poem a universal quality, as if the poet is speaking for all who have suffered great pain.**

Commentary

Stanzas 1 and 2

The opening line strikes a note of dignified solemnity. The nature of the 'great pain' is not described. Interestingly, the opening line suggests that such pain leads not to a loss of control but to the constraint of formality. However, the sense of control is lost in the second stanza with its fragmented phrases and incomplete meanings. **The phrasing and punctuation of the second stanza suggest a series of unconnected sensations and thoughts, and reflect the way in which pain interrupts the mind's ability to make sense of experience and derive meaning from it.** The final line of the stanza suggests that great pain results in a hard, stone-like insensitivity, which brings its own kind of contentment, 'A Quartz contentment, like a stone'. The word 'contentment' is almost ironic.

Stanza 3

The opening line of the third stanza defines the nature of this 'contentment': it is the 'Hour of Lead'. It is the period of heavy and deadening oppression when all human sensations become frozen. This period is not forgotten, even if the sufferer survives it. The memory of this oppression is likened to 'Freezing persons' recollecting 'the Snow' (line 12). **The continuous present of the final line means that the reader cannot determine if the freezing person has survived the ordeal, or if it continues. Here, as in the rest of the poem, the thought is incomplete.**

Form of the poem

In keeping with its theme, 'After great pain' moves away from the regularity of the ballad and hymn form. The long lines of the opening stanza, with their steady stoicism and harmonious sounds, are in contrast to the staccato movement of stanza 2. Although the thought of the poem may be incomplete, each stanza concludes with a full rhyme that mirrors the formality mentioned in the first line of the poem.

Thinking about the poem

1. 'After great pain, a formal feeling comes –' (line 1). Explain, as clearly as you can, what is meant by 'formal' in this context?
2. What, in your view, is the effect of comparing the nerves, which convey feelings and sensations from the body to the brain, to tombs (line 2)?
3. The meaning of lines 3 and 4 is hard to unravel, due to the conciseness of the language. Give careful consideration to each of the following questions.
    a) What does the adjective 'stiff' suggest about the Heart?
    b) Does the Heart feel in some way guilty?
    c) If 'He' does not refer to the Heart, does it refer to Christ? Could it refer to both?
    d) Does 'bore' suggest suffering or blame? Might it suggest both?
    e) Does the line 'And Yesterday, or Centuries before?' suggest the Heart's confusion, or the fact that Christ's suffering is both past and present?
    In each case, explain your answer.
4. How, in stanza 2, is the dazed condition of the victim of great pain suggested? What words are particularly effective?
5. In your view, what kind of contentment is a 'Quartz contentment' (line 9)?
6. How well, do you think, does the phrase 'Hour of Lead' (line 10) sum up the mental and physical condition of the sufferer?

7 The final image of the poem 'Chill – then Stupor – then the letting go –' (line 13) is much admired. Do you read it as a pessimistic or an optimistic ending? Explain your answer.
8 Read the poem aloud. What sounds contribute to the mood of the poem?
9 'What Dickinson describes in "After great pain" is the numbed feeling that is caused by emotional or spiritual pain.' Give your response to this statement.

Exam-Style Questions

1 'Emily Dickinson's poetry explores extreme states of mind and emotion in an unusual way.' Discuss this statement.
2 Discuss the view that Dickinson's fascination with death leads to her best writing.
3 'It is less what Emily Dickinson has to say than her manner of saying it that is interesting.' Give your view of this statement.
4 From your reading of her poetry, do you agree that Dickinson's poetry offers us a glimpse into a fascinating mind and a fascinating writer?
5 'The loss of love and the loss of faith are dominant themes in Dickinson's poetry.' Discuss this view.
6 'Even when she is dealing with serious themes, Dickinson's poetry is marked by a sense of wit and a sense of humour.' Discuss this view of Dickinson's poetry.
7 'In Dickinson's poetry we see the world through the eye of an artist and the eye of a scientist.' Discuss this view of Dickinson's poetry.
8 'Dickinson's poetry is not hard to understand. It is, however, complex.' Give your response to this statement.
9 What, in your experience, is the effect of reading Dickinson's poetry?
10 'Dickinson's poetry is the poetry of small details and large ideas.' Discuss.
11 Write an introduction to Dickinson's poetry for readers new to her poetry. You should cover the themes and preoccupations of her poetry and how you responded to her use of language and imagery in the poems you studied.
Some of the following areas might be covered in your introduction:
- Her exploration of extreme states of mind.
- Her exploration of death and dying.
- The importance of the soul.
- Her fondness for definition.
- Her observations of nature.
- The power and freshness of her language.
- Her epigrammatic style.
- Her creative use of the dash and capitalised nouns.

12. 'What Emily Dickinson's poetry means to me.' Write an essay in response to this title. You should include a discussion of her themes and the way she expresses them. Support the points you make by reference to the poetry on your course.

    Some of the following areas might be included:

    - Her treatment of hope and despair.
    - Her search for definition.
    - Her attitude to death and mortality.
    - The psychological drama of her poems.
    - The lack of a firm conclusion.
    - Her sense of nature.
    - The craft of her poetry.

13. Write a letter to a friend outlining your experience of studying the poetry of Emily Dickinson. You should refer to her themes and the way she expresses them. Support the points you make by reference to the poetry on your course.
    Material might be drawn from the following:

    - Her family and religious background.
    - The contrast between her sedate life and the drama of her poetry.
    - Her tone and style.
    - Her interest in extreme emotions and psychological states.
    - Her preoccupation with death.
    - Her painter's eye for the details of nature.
    - The lines and images that stay with you.

14. Write an essay in which you outline your reasons for liking or not liking the poetry of Emily Dickinson. You must refer to the poems on your course.

    Some possible reasons for liking the poetry:
    - The uniqueness of the poetic voice.
    - The striking perspective of many of the poems.
    - The vitality and energy of the writing.
    - The impact of the poetry upon the reader.
    - The wit and intelligence of Dickinson's writing.

    Some possible reasons for not liking the poetry:
    - The themes of death, isolation and despair.
    - The absence of happiness in many of the poems.
    - The sense of annihilation in many of the poems.
    - The obsession with her own mind.
    - The effect of the poems upon the reader.

Sample Essay

Write a letter to a friend outlining your experience of studying the poetry of Emily Dickinson. In your letter you should refer to her themes and the way she expresses them. Support the points you make by reference to the poetry on your course.

Dear Jane,

We have just finished reading the poetry of Emily Dickinson in class. What an amazing experience it has been. I feel I have been on an exhilarating but exhausting rollercoaster. What a fascinating poet and woman. I think Emily Dickinson proves the old saying true: never judge a book by its cover.

[Appropriate register used]

Viewing her life from the outside who could have guessed at the tumultuous seas of her mind? She came from a well-respected family in Amherst in New England. Her family were Calvinists. That makes me of think of a strict upbringing with a great deal of attention to saving your soul. But I don't think our idea of a religious tradition different from our own is ever really accurate, do you? It seems Emily enjoyed parties and visiting and dancing and several young men were interested in her. That doesn't seem too strict. In the school she attended, Mount Holyoke Female Seminary, she was a bit of a rebel, refusing to declare publicly her faith in God. That must have taken some courage. And I don't think she ever really settled the questions of belief in God and belief in the afterlife in her lifetime.

[Selective use of relevant biographical information]

She was a rebel in other ways, too. After she came home from boarding school, she opted out of some of the duties of someone in her position: receiving visitors and making endless social calls and doing mindless household chores. I like the sound of her – quietly determined and not bound by other peoples' rules. (She reminds me of you.) And then when she was around thirty, something must have happened to her, because she more or less withdrew into her own room, communicated with most of the outside world only through letters and began writing in a furious kind of way. I know I've often wanted to lock myself in my room but it doesn't last more than a few hours! And when I'm in a black mood I scribble in my diary, but she wrote 366 poems in 1862. What must have happened to her? We don't know and that adds to the fascination. Her sister and sister-in-law, Vinnie and Susan, destroyed all her correspondence after her death, as she had requested. I wish they hadn't! Luckily, they kept the thousand or more poems (a thousand poems!) they found in her writing desk.

[Personal response given]

And what poems they are – short sharp meditations on the world around her and the places she travelled to in her imagination. Those journeys were to the 'chillest land' and the 'strangest Sea' and she made them bravely and in solitude. I think I understand why hope was so important to her. If you undertake the kind of dangerous psychological journeys she took, you need to have something to fall back on, something that 'never stops – at all'. You want everything to turn out well for her. I almost cheered when I read 'I taste a liquor never brewed', how she drank in the happiness of summer days. Because those moments of happiness are rare enough in her poetry. And you hope that when she sent her beloved the little meadow flower, described in 'I could bring You Jewels – had I a mind to', her beloved sent her something equally charming back. Because more often than not the emotions in the poems are fearful and despairing. Even her little poem on the snake ends with the terrifying 'Zero at the Bone'.

[Good use of quotation in this paragraph]

The poems that made the greatest impact on me are the darker poems. 'After great pain, a formal feeling comes' is icy in its depiction of what I think was probably a broken heart and the numb feeling that comes with intense pain, so that you no longer want to cling to life: 'First – Chill – then Stupor – then the letting go – '. It is such a precise poem that you never doubt that Dickinson is writing about herself and her own experience even if she writes in an impersonal way. I think the impersonal style is a way of dealing with what would otherwise be too difficult to write about.

[More detailed discussion of a poem]

There is a similar feeling of chill in 'The Soul has Bandaged moments' (Isn't that the best title ever?!). I love the image of the 'freezing hair' and the dread caused by the unwanted advances of the Fright. Likewise the images of the 'shackles on the plumed feet' and the 'staples, in the Song'. It is like when Hope has been imprisoned and 'the little Bird that kept so many warm' is abashed in 'Hope' is the thing with feathers'. Is it a strange choice of word to say 'I love' such imagery? But that is the funny thing about a poem – even when it deals with psychological pain, you can admire the mind and the skill of the poet who created it. I feel a similar kind of admiration for the stately, stoical tone in which Emily describes the 'Heavenly Hurt' that comes with 'a certain Slant of light'. The light carrying the 'Seal Despair' cannot be countered or stopped and so must be endured. But she writes with such certainty and force that the poem carries Dickinson's own seal of authority. Her unusual punctuation adds to the sense that Dickinson will not be contradicted. She knows what she is talking about. It's as if she masters negative experiences by defining them so clearly.

[Uses several poems to make a point]

Of course, she doesn't always know what she is talking about. In her two great poems on death, she ends with the shuddering dash of 'I Felt a Funeral, in my Brain' and the darkness of 'I heard a Fly buzz – when I died'. That final dash is like a barrier that stops her and you from falling over a cliff. Somewhere beyond that dash is the place 'Where the meanings are', but despite her brave, maybe even her mad, effort, she cannot get there. When she pushes her imagination to 'Extremity', she still comes up short, at the end of knowing, facing the blank space beyond the dash, or a fly gets between her and the revelation she is waiting for. 'I heard a Fly buzz' is grimly comic, but I wonder how Emily felt when she finished 'I Felt a Funeral in my Brain'? I think she must have felt as 'wrecked' and 'solitary' as the persona of the poem. To put all that effort into imagining and understanding something and then to finish with that emptiness or 'Zero at the Bone'. I wonder did she take consolation from creating what I think is her finest poem? I hope she did.

[Opening sentence flows well from the previous paragraph and sets up this paragraph of comment and interpretation]

It's not the easiest poem to read or interpret. I think it is definitely an attempt to imagine a funeral from the perspective of the person in the coffin, before the moment when you are buried and lose the connection from the life you are departing. All your experiences contract and you can only hear the world ('And then I heard them lift a Box', 'Then Space – began to toll, As all the Heavens were a Bell, And Being, but an Ear') and then you lose even that connection and plunge into death. But it is also a description of Dickinson the poet undergoing the experience of imagining the funeral in her brain and persisting and succeeding, even if it is a terrifying and disturbing experience, until the point when the connection with life is severed and her imagination cannot travel any further:

> And then a Plank in Reason, broke,
> And I dropped down, and down –
> And hit a World, at every plunge,
> And Finished knowing – then –

I'm not sure I'd have the courage to make that kind of psychological and imaginative journey and record it as carefully as she has done. How it must have exhausted her and left her depleted.

[Personal response given to issues raised in the poem]

Please read these poems, Jane, and write back and let me know that you love them as much as I do! Having encountered them 'I feel for them a transport of cordiality'. I hope you will, too.

Your friend,

Sarah

[Keeps task in mind in concluding the essay]

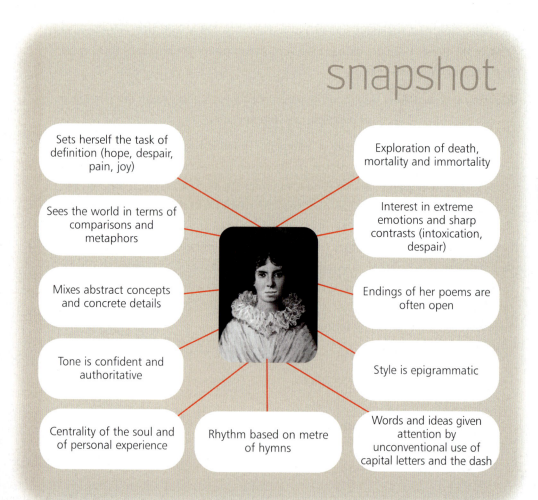

Seamus Heaney

b. 1939

THE FORGE
BOGLAND
THE TOLLUND MAN
MOSSBAWN: TWO POEMS IN DEDICATION: (1) SUNLIGHT
A CONSTABLE CALLS*
THE SKUNK
THE HARVEST BOW
THE UNDERGROUND*
THE PITCHFORK
LIGHTENINGS, VIII: 'THE ANNALS SAY'
A CALL*
POSTSCRIPT
TATE'S AVENUE

Biography

Seamus Heaney was born on 13 April 1939 on a farm called Mossbawn, situated between Lough Beg and Slieve Gallon in south Co. Derry. The Heaney family name has a long local history and can be traced back to a twelfth-century ancestor who founded a church in the northern part of the county. Heaney was the eldest of nine children (two girls and seven boys) born to Margaret and Patrick Heaney. Patrick Heaney farmed fifty acres and also worked as a cattle dealer.

By all accounts, the family home was a warm, affectionate place and the Heaneys were a close and loving family. The poems Heaney has written about his parents and his aunt reflect the quality of his family life. He was raised as a Catholic and steeped in the traditions and rituals of his religion.

Education

Heaney was educated at the local primary school in Anahorish, attended by both Catholic and Protestant children. In 1951 he won a scholarship to St Columb's College in Derry, a Catholic college and a Diocesan seminary about forty miles from his home. Heaney recalls it as an academic school, where the students were 'tuned like violins to play the tune of the exams'. The school has a distinguished roll of past pupils, including John Hume, Seamus Deane and Brian Friel. As he moved up the college, his talent was recognised and nurtured by a number of teachers. A summer in the Gaeltacht deepened his interest in and love of Irish.

Heaney won a scholarship to Queen's University Belfast, where he studied English literature and language, graduating with a first-class honours degree in 1961. The system of scholarships introduced by the Education Act 1947 allowed the children of small farmers and the urban working class to attend university for the first time. The influence of these students was particularly noticeable in the civil rights movement of the late 1960s.

Having trained as a teacher, Heaney took a job in a secondary school in Ballymurphy, Belfast.

Early success

Heaney began to write poems in a serious way in 1962. Shortly after his first poems had been published in newspapers and magazines, he came in contact with Philip Hobsbaum, who organised poetry workshops where participants read and discussed each other's work. The regular meetings of the Belfast Group, as it became known, over a period of seven years gave Heaney confidence and confirmed the importance of poetry in his life.

In 1966 the London publishers Faber & Faber published his first collection of poems, *Death of a Naturalist*. Heaney always remained deeply attached to his home place and to the values and traditions of his parents, which is evident in this award-winning collection. The acclaimed book contributed to his appointment as a lecturer in English at Queen's University in 1966. He also began to write for magazines and reviews in England, and to make broadcasts for the BBC.

In August 1965 Heaney had married Marie Devlin, who was also a teacher and a member of the Belfast Group. Their first child, Michael, was born in July 1966.

Situation in Northern Ireland

Heaney became a public figure as the situation in Northern Ireland grew tense and dangerous. The civil rights movement, campaigning for equality of treatment for Catholics, met with fierce resistance from extreme, Protestant loyalists and from the RUC (police). In October 1968, the year in which the Heaneys' second son, Christopher, was born, the first major, violent clash occurred in Derry. The following months were marked by periodic violence and sectarian clashes. When the British Army entered Derry in August 1969 they were welcomed as protectors by the Catholic community of the city. However, relations between the Catholic community and the army soon deteriorated and the Provisional IRA was formed in January 1970 in Dublin and quickly began its bombing campaign.

As a Catholic nationalist, Heaney was affected by the violence and the events in Northern Ireland. He had taken an active part in the civil rights movement, and he sought a way of reflecting his experiences in his writing. **With the publication of *North* in 1975, he addressed the divisions between the two communities and the pressure of history upon the present.**

In 1980 Heaney became a co-founder, with five others, of Field Day, a theatre company that soon expanded to become a forum for discussion. It contributed to the development of vigorous debate on cultural and political issues in Ireland, and Heaney's own work can be regarded as a contribution to that debate, from a mainly nationalist, Catholic perspective. 1980 and 1981 were turbulent years in Northern Ireland: the hunger strikes staged by republican prisoners in support of their demands for political status brought relations between the Irish and British governments to a low point. **The poems in Heaney's 1984 collection, *Station Island*, face up to the complexities of the situation and the feelings it called out in him.**

Moves west and south

Heaney taught at the University of California in 1970/71. **His time in the US coincided with student protests against government policies in Vietnam, and he saw how poetry could become 'a force, almost a mode of power, certainly a mode of resistance'.** This insight shaped the direction of his future writing.

When Heaney returned to Northern Ireland in 1971 the situation depressed him. He resigned from his job at Queen's University and moved south to Glanmore, a secluded spot in Co. Wicklow. Threats from loyalist extremists played some part in his decision. However, it was the general feeling of oppression within Northern Ireland that he sought to escape.

The period in Glanmore was one of domestic happiness. In 1973 his daughter, Catherine, was born. Many of the poems written at this time, including a sequence of sonnets, are love poems celebrating his marriage. Archaeological work on the Viking settlement in Dublin fuelled Heaney's interest in the culture of northern Europe and, with the encouragement of the poet Ted Hughes, he began work on 'The Tollund Man' and related bog poems.

In 1975 Heaney was appointed to the English department of Carysfort Teacher Training College in Dublin. Full-time employment gave him the financial security to buy a house and, in 1976, he and his family moved to Sandymount in Dublin. In 1981 he became a visiting professor at Harvard University. He has also taught and lectured at Oxford University.

Admired poet

Heaney is, without question, one of the most admired poets writing in English. The award of the Nobel Prize for Literature in 1995 is testament to his standing in world literature, while the celebrations in 2009 to mark his seventieth birthday show the affection in which he is held in Ireland.

Not surprisingly for a writer of Heaney's stature, there are conflicting claims made for his poetry, and there are some critics who dissent from the praise heaped upon his work. Some argue that Heaney has not been willing to act as the voice of the nationalist people of Northern Ireland, while others maintain that Heaney shows too much sympathy for his tribe. These dissenting views are, however, the exceptions rather than the rule. More typical of critical opinion is the assessment of Helen Vendler, who, writing in 1985 following the publication of *Station Island*, observed that 'it is arresting to find a poetry so conscious of cultural and social facts which nonetheless remains a poetry of awareness, observation, and sorrow'.

In a review of Heaney's prose collection *The Redress of Poetry* (1995), the reviewer referred to Heaney's character and his 'general benevolence'. And it is the generous, life-affirming vision of the poetry that is impressive and memorable. **Heaney might well have been writing about his own work when he said, 'We go to poetry to be forwarded in ourselves.'**

Changing poetry

Heaney's themes are large – the formation of the self; the individual's relationship with history; the relationship between past and present; the duty of the poet to his or her community; the nature of the poetic imagination – and he writes with an exquisite control of language.

Heaney's poetry has changed over the years. His early work is concerned with giving a faithful description of nature and reality. His middle work addresses the Northern Ireland situation in poems that are sometimes mythic in orientation and sometimes direct and documentary in style. And in his Nobel lecture, Heaney spoke of his more recent poetry as 'permitting myself the luxury of walking on air in spite of a temperamental disposition towards an art that was earnest and devoted to things as they are'.

Social and Cultural Context

The social and political dimensions of life in Northern Ireland are part and parcel of Heaney's inheritance and his poetry. The divided nature of the world into which he was born is reflected in the name of the family farm, Mossbawn. As Heaney says:

> Our farm was called Mossbawn. Moss, a Scots word probably carried to Ulster by the planters, and bawn, the name the English colonists gave to their fortified farmhouses . . . Yet in spite of the Ordnance Survey spelling, we pronounced it moss bann, and ban is the Gaelic word for white. So might not the thing mean the white moss, the moss of bog-cotton?

The question of response

History was and continues to be all around Heaney – whether in the family stories of sectarian assassinations in the 1920s, the murder of his cousin Colum McCartney in the 1970s or the death of his neighbour Francis Hughes on hunger strike – and his poetry addresses this reality. Indeed, a theme that runs through his work is the question of response: how should the poet respond to the circumstances in which he finds himself? These circumstances include events further afield such as the attack on the World Trade Centre and the bombing of the London Underground. A major achievement of Heaney is that, while he has sought to face up to his responsibilities as a writer, his work is not overwhelmed by the enormity of the events to which it responds.

Poetic influences

One of the most interesting features of Heaney's search for an adequate poetic response to the pressure of public events is the range of poets in whom he finds inspiration. **Heaney is open to the idea of learning from others and his poems and essays borrow from and refer to a wide range of writers.**

Heaney's main early influences were Thomas Hardy, William Wordsworth and Gerard Manley Hopkins. The example of *The Prelude*, Wordsworth's long, autobiographical poem charting his childhood and his relationship with nature, is reflected in the themes of Heaney's first collection, *Death of a Naturalist* (1966). As in Wordsworth, there is little separation between the poet and the persona of the poems. The influence of Hopkins is especially evident in the rhythms and forceful diction of the early poems.

In Queen's University, Robert Frost's autobiographical poems about life in a farming community pointed the way forward for Heaney's writing. The poetry of Patrick Kavanagh also influenced the direction and style of his work. **Heaney wrote, 'Kavanagh gave you permission to dwell without cultural anxiety among the usual landmarks of your life.'**

In the early 1960s Heaney also encountered the work of contemporary Irish poets, most notably John Montague, Richard Murphy and Thomas Kinsella. These poets gave Heaney further confidence in his own voice and in his own world as a resource for his poetry. Montague provided further examples of how the local might serve the universal in poetry and led Heaney to the tradition of *dinnseanchas* – poems and tales that relate to the original meaning of place names. As Heaney delved into the Gaelic tradition, he also looked to other sources such as Greek myths and Norse rituals and sagas. From an early stage in his career, he has shown a liking for a form that goes beyond the single poem, and his collections contain linked poems and poetic sequences.

At the University of California in the early 1970s Heaney read the poetry of Robert Lowell, William Carlos Williams and Gary Snyder, who opened his mind to the possibility of a looser form of poetry.

Heaney has inherited many of the features of Modernist poetry, especially in his use of classical poets and poetry as reference points for the present. **His poems do not stand as isolated artefacts but draw strength and power from other poems.** Thus, for example, Dante is a presence behind many of the poems in which Heaney addresses the dead. Heaney admires the mix of the political and the transcendent in Dante's work and tries to achieve a similar balance in his own. The balance between the practical and the poetic also draws Heaney to the ancient Irish annals.

Heaney finds inspiration and encouragement in the work of writers from Eastern Europe, who have sought to write in difficult and dangerous political circumstances. The Russian poet Osip Mandelstam is one such exemplary figure. He died in 1938, at the age of 47, as he was being transported to a prison camp. He was arrested for writing a poem against Stalin. Heaney acclaims him not for writing against the dictator, but for maintaining his inner freedom and his sense of delight and wonder in the world, which his poetry seeks to capture. In like manner he salutes the achievements of the Czech poet Miroslav Holub and the Polish writer Zbigniew Herbert.

From all the writers celebrated by Heaney, he draws the one lesson which he expressed thus in his essay 'The Government of the Tongue':

> Here is the great paradox of poetry and of the imaginative arts in general. Faced with the brutality of the historical onslaught, they are practically useless. Yet they verify our singularity, they strike and stake out the ore which lies at the base of every individual life. In one sense the efficacy of poetry is nil – no lyric has ever stopped a tank. In another sense, it is unlimited. It is like the writing in the sand in the face of which accusers and accused are left speechless and renewed.

Part of the excitement of reading Heaney is the way in which he leads you from the parish of Anahorish in Co. Derry outwards in space and time, making connections with kindred spirits, both living and dead, Dante or Holub, so that he verifies for us Kavanagh's belief that the local is universal. And it is impossible not to feel attracted to a poet who speaks of poetry as 'an agent of possible transformation, of evolution towards that more radiant and generous life which the imagination desires'.

Timeline

1939	Born on 13 April on Mossbawn farm, south Co. Derry
1944	Attends Anahorish Primary School
1951	Wins a scholarship to St Columb's College, Derry, where he boards for six years
1957	Begins studies in Queen's University Belfast
1963	Joins the 'Belfast Group' poetry workshop
1965	Marries Marie Devlin
1966	Publishes first collection, *Death of a Naturalist*; birth of first child, Michael
1968	Birth of second child, Christopher
1969	*Door into the Dark* published; visits United States, France and Spain
1972	Moves south to live in Wicklow; publishes *Wintering Out*
1973	Birth of third child, Catherine; travels in Jutland
1975	Publishes *North*
1979	Publishes *Field Work*; visiting lecturer in Harvard University
1984	Publishes *Station Island*; mother dies
1986	Father dies
1987	Publishes *The Haw Lantern*
1991	Publishes *Seeing Things*
1995	Awarded the Nobel Prize for Literature
1996	Publishes *The Spirit Level*
1998	Elected as Saoi by Aosdána, the highest award that can be bestowed on an artist in Ireland
2006	Publishes District and Circle; wins T. S. Eliot Prize and Irish Times Poetry Now Award
2010	Publishes twelfth collection, *Human Chain*; wins Forward Prize and Irish Times Poetry Now Award

The Forge

All I know is a door into the dark.
Outside, old axles and iron hoops rusting;
Inside, the hammered anvil's short-pitched ring,
The unpredictable fantail of sparks
Or hiss when a new shoe toughens in water. 5
The anvil must be somewhere in the centre,
Horned as a unicorn, at one end square,
Set there immovable: an altar
Where he expends himself in shape and music.
Sometimes, leather-aproned, hairs in his nose, 10
He leans out on the jamb, recalls a clatter
Of hoofs where traffic is flashing in rows;
Then grunts and goes in, with a slam and a flick
To beat real iron out, to work the bellows.

Glossary

11 | *jamb*: part of the door frame

Guidelines

'The Forge' comes from Heaney's second book, *Door into the Dark* (1969) – the title of the collection is taken from the first line of this poem. 'The Forge' recalls Heaney's boyhood fascination with the forge near his home. Here is how Heaney describes it: 'I was thinking of Barney Devlin's forge at Hillhead, on the roadside, where you had the noise of myth in the anvil and the noise of the 1940s in the passing car.' The poem uses the forge and the work of the blacksmith as symbols for artistic creation.

Literature often associates artistic creativity with the figure of the smith. The title of the poem calls to mind the declaration made by Stephen Dedalus, the hero of James Joyce's *A Portrait of the Artist as a Young Man*, that he is going 'to forge in the smithy of my soul the uncreated conscience of my race'. The poem also draws strength from the smiths of classical literature – Hephaestus, husband to Aphrodite, who crafted the armour of the gods, and Daedalus, who designed the Labyrinth at Knossos to house the Minotaur.

Commentary

'The Forge' is a celebration of the traditional craft of the blacksmith, and, appropriately, it is written in a traditional form: the sonnet. The first eight lines of the poem focus on the forge and its mysteries. The last six lines focus on the smith. **The craft of the blacksmith and the smith himself are presented as symbols of poetry and the poet.** The poem uses some precise evocations of the smith's craft in images that appeal to the senses of sight and hearing. However, the life of the smith is really secondary to its purpose in suggesting how the poet makes his poetry. It is Heaney's excitement in developing the analogy between the poet and the smith that drives the poem.

Poetry and the darkness of memory

At the time of writing this poem Heaney was speaking of poetry as something that lies in the darkness of memory and the subconscious (the forge), waiting to be discovered. When the discovery is made, the poet applies the traditional techniques of poetry to fashion the poem. To speak of technique is not to take the magical or sacred qualities away from the art of the blacksmith or the art of the poet. In the mind of the speaker, the 'I' of the poem, there is something mysterious and sacred in the transformations that take place in the forge. Indeed, the central symbol of the poem, the anvil, is described as a 'unicorn' (line 7) and 'an altar' (line 8), symbols of the mysterious and the sacred.

Writing about the title of the collection *Door into the Dark*, Heaney commented: 'Words themselves are doors, Janus is to a certain extent their deity, looking back to ramification of roots and associations and forward to a clarification of sense and meaning.' **The younger self, dramatised in 'The Forge', has not yet entered through the door of words into the darkness of the imagination.**

Heroic figure

'The Forge' laments the passing of traditional crafts. The smith is an heroic but doomed figure, out of place in a changing world, upon which, in disgust and defiance, he turns his back and continues his craft. However, the modern world is not interested in stopping at his door. Interestingly, 'The Forge' ends with the speaker still outside the door. The smith retires into the darkness as if he has escaped the poet, or if the poet's younger self has not yet entered the world of the forge where, in the dark interior, the smith works the magic of creation. **The ending opens out a range of possible interpretations.**

The contrast between the world outside of 'old axles and iron hoops rusting' (line 2) and that inside of the 'altar / Where he expends himself in shape and music' (lines 8–9) calls to mind Yeats's distinction between the sources of poetry – 'the foul rag-and-bone shop of the heart' – and their transformation in art.

Language of the poem

'The Forge' is remarkable for the effects Heaney achieves in the use of consonants, which give a muscularity to the language, in keeping with the energy and noise of the smith's work. Heaney has often made the association between consonants and masculinity, and vowels and femininity. In this poem, the strength of the consonants and the effort required in giving voice to their sounds imitate the energy and forcefulness of the smith's work.

Thinking about the poem

1. At the centre of the poem are the images of the anvil as a unicorn and as an altar. What is the significance of these images for the theme of the poem?
2. What view of the blacksmith emerges in the sestet of the sonnet?
3. Discuss the view that the portrait of the blacksmith is a caricature, owing more to literature than to life.
4. Trace the imagery of light and sound in the poem. What do they suggest about the art of the smith? Explain your answer.
5. The poem ends with the contrast between the traffic and the blacksmith's traditional craft. What is the thematic purpose of this contrast?
6. What, in your view, is the dominant tone of the poem? Explain your answer.
7. Heaney often refers to consonant sounds as masculine and vowel sounds as feminine. What kinds of sounds dominate this poem? Why, in your opinion, is this so?
8. The poem turns on a sharp contrast between outside and inside. What do you think are the symbolic implications of this contrast? Consider, in your answer, the rich possibilities of the phrase 'a door into the dark' (line 1).
9. Taking the forge and the blacksmith as analogies for the poet and his work, what does the poem say about the process of making a poem?
10. Compare this poem with 'Bogland' and 'Lightenings, viii' for variations on Heaney's exploration of the art of making poetry.

Bogland

for T. P. Flanagan

We have no prairies
To slice a big sun at evening –
Everywhere the eye concedes to
Encroaching horizon,

Is wooed into the cyclops' eye
Of a tarn. Our unfenced country
Is bog that keeps crusting
Between the sights of the sun.

They've taken the skeleton
Of the Great Irish Elk
Out of the peat, set it up
An astounding crate full of air.

Butter sunk under
More than a hundred years
Was recovered salty and white.
The ground itself is kind, black butter

Melting and opening underfoot,
Missing its last definition
By millions of years.
They'll never dig coal here,

Only the waterlogged trunks
Of great firs, soft as pulp.
Our pioneers keep striking
Inwards and downwards,

Every layer they strip
Seems camped on before.
The bogholes might be Atlantic seepage.
The wet centre is bottomless.

Glossary		
1	*prairies*:	the vast area of grassland in the central plains of North America, opened up by pioneers during the second half of the nineteenth century
5	*cyclops' eye*:	in Greek mythology a Cyclops is a member of a race of one-eyed giants
6	*tarn*:	a small mountain lake; the word comes from Old Norse and shows Heaney's many-sided interest in the Vikings
10	*Great Irish Elk*:	skeletons of huge deer were found preserved in the bogs
23	*pioneers*:	settlers in previously unknown or wild country; 'Bogland' suggests that the first settlers in Ireland explored by cutting down into the soil – digging is used by Heaney as a metaphor for the creative process and the process of remembering

Guidelines

'Bogland' is the final poem in *Door into the Dark* (1969). **It is widely regarded as one of Heaney's most important early poems, a poem that suggests new possibilities for the direction of the poet's writing.** This is what Heaney himself said about the origins of the poem:

> We used to hear about bog butter, butter kept fresh for a great number of years under the peat. Then when I was at school the skeleton of an elk had been taken out of a bog nearby and a few of our neighbours had got their photographs in the paper, peering out across its antlers. So I began to get an idea of the bog as the memory of the landscape, or as a landscape that remembered everything that happened in it and to it … Moreover, since memory was the faculty that supplied me with the first quickening of my own poetry, I had a tentative unrealised need to make a congruence between memory and bogland and, for want of a better word, our national consciousness … At that time, I had … been reading about the frontier and the west as an important myth in the American consciousness, so I set up – or rather, laid down – the bog as an answering Irish myth.

'Bogland' is one of the first poems in which Heaney speaks as a representative of his nationalist community.

Commentary

Contrast between prairie and bog
'Bogland' turns on a comparison between American prairies and Irish bogs. In America the eye has an unlimited vista, but in Ireland the eye is drawn to features of the landscape that close in and encroach on the view. As the poem presents it, the American pioneers moved across empty spaces of the prairies, but in Ireland the pioneers explore downwards, cutting through the layers of bog. The word 'pioneers' (line 23) suggests adventure and discovery: the adventure of poetry; the adventure of discovering your past and your national identity.

The contrast between prairie and bog allows the poet to reflect on bogs and what they contain. The bog is soft and accommodating. It is also generous. It preserves and returns the past to us in the form of ordinary, domestic gifts (butter) and traces of the marvellous (the elk). The emergence of the elk from the bog, this 'astounding crate full of air' (line 12), suggests lightness and buoyancy. Perhaps this is a symbol for the kind of elation that the poet feels when he excavates a poem from the bog of memory.

Bog as a symbol
'Bogland' is a poem in which Heaney opens himself to new possibilities, to deeper delving into the bog of autobiography and history. The bog contains the history of the island. Therefore, it acts as the memory of the race. To dig the bog, 'striking / Inwards and downwards' (lines 23–24), is to search into the bottomless centre of Irish history. Although not stated explicitly in this poem, it is clear that the action of digging the bog is seized by the poet as a symbol of his work as a poet. **The landscape of the poem is both the natural landscape of Ireland but also a cultural/visionary landscape.**

'Bogland' is a poem that is poised between the literal and the symbolic, and the reader must constantly shift between a literal and a metaphorical reading of the text.

The bog, as a symbol of Irish history, allows Heaney to speak, in future poems, about the Troubles in Northern Ireland. One of the insights gained in this poem, and developed in 'The Tollund Man', is that the soil of Ireland contains its past, including the spilled blood and the broken bones of its violent history, along with both domestic and marvellous relics. However, it is also important to note that in his later work Heaney dwells less on the idea of poems rooted in the yielding soil and gives more currency to the idea of poetry as flight.

Avoids closure
'Bogland' is one of the first of Heaney's poems to avoid a firm sense of closure. In describing the ground of the bog as bottomless, the poem is also describing itself, and the endless possibilities of the bog as a symbol. In this sense, as the critic Neil Corcoran points out, 'Bogland' offers a sophisticated commentary on itself. It suggests that poems are found, having lain in the subconscious of the poet, awaiting discovery.

Language and style of the poem

In 'Bogland' there is a new spareness in Heaney's poetic language. This is heightened by the use of short lines ('Every layer they strip'; line 25) and slant rhymes ('skeleton' and 'elk', lines 9 and 10). These ensure that the phrases of the poem open and melt into one another, in imitation of the yielding ground of the bog.

This unadorned style gives a sense of direct statement to the poem, an impression reinforced by the straightforward declaration that concludes 'Bogland': 'The wet centre is bottomless.' This line comes from the warning given by older people to keep children away from the bog. It is presented here with the force and excitement of illumination, as if the poet has gained an unexpected insight, which he offers to the reader with confidence and certainty. There is no bottom to the well of imagination. There is no end to the exploration of the past. Indeed, **the whole poem is delivered with a remarkable air of assurance and confidence**. Heaney speaks on behalf of the race ('We have no prairies', line 1; 'Our unfenced country', line 6; 'Our pioneers keep striking', line 23) with no hint of self-consciousness. In 'Bogland' he sets out to establish his own poetic myth, and does so with a confident excitement.

Thinking about the poem

1. Listen to a reading of the poem and note down all the words and phrases that strike you as memorable. What does this selection suggest are the themes and concerns of the poem?
2. What contrast does the poem establish between the American prairies and the bogs of Ireland? How, according to the poem, does the difference between the landscapes influence the way the world is viewed in the two places?
3. In the poem what qualities are ascribed to bogland?
4. How does the bog work as (a) a symbol of Irish history, and (b) a symbol of the imagination of the poet? In your view, is it a successful symbol? Explain your answer.
5. The last six lines of the poem are richly metaphorical. Explain some of their possible meanings.
6. What is the tone of the poem? In your answer, consider the poet's use of the communal pronouns 'Our' and 'We', and the declarative statements of the poem.
7. The poem speaks of the bog melting and opening underfoot. Select two examples where the short line and/or the sounds of the poem also melt and open.
8. The poem has a sense of excitement and possibility about it. Where, in your view, is this excitement most evident?
9. Compare the idea of poetry contained in 'Bogland' with the ideas in 'The Forge' and 'Lightenings, viii'.

The Tollund Man

I
Some day I will go to Aarhus
To see his peat-brown head,
The mild pods of his eye-lids,
His pointed skin cap.

In the flat country nearby
Where they dug him out,
His last gruel of winter seeds
Caked in his stomach,

Naked except for
The cap, noose and girdle,
I will stand a long time.
Bridegroom to the goddess,

She tightened her torc on him
And opened her fen,
Those dark juices working
Him to a saint's kept body,

Trove of the turfcutters'
Honeycombed workings.
Now his stained face
Reposes at Aarhus.

II
I could risk blasphemy,
Consecrate the cauldron bog
Our holy ground and pray
Him to make germinate

The scattered, ambushed
Flesh of labourers,
Stockinged corpses
Laid out in the farmyards,

Tell-tale skin and teeth
Flecking the sleepers 30
Of four young brothers, trailed
For miles along the lines.

III
Something of his sad freedom
As he rode the tumbril
Should come to me, driving, 35
Saying the names

Tollund, Grauballe, Nebelgard,
Watching the pointing hands
Of country people,
Not knowing their tongue. 40

Out there in Jutland
In the old man-killing parishes
I will feel lost,
Unhappy and at home.

	Glossary
1	*Aarhus*: a city in Jutland, Denmark
12	*the goddess*: Nerthus, a goddess of the earth and fertility; as Heaney describes her, she requires a bridegroom each year to make her germinate
13	*torc*: a necklace made of metal, usually bronze or gold
14	*fen*: bog or marshy land
27	*Stockinged corpses*: the image comes from Tom Barry's *Guerrilla Days in Ireland* (an account of a flying column in Cork during the War of Independence), which showed a farmer's family who had been shot in reprisals by the Black and Tans
31	*four young brothers*: Heaney has said that part of the folklore where he grew up concerned four brothers who were killed by Protestant paramilitaries during the sectarian troubles of the 1920s and whose bodies were 'trailed along the railway lines, over the sleepers as a kind of mutilation'
34	*tumbril*: a farm cart of the kind used during the French Revolution to bring condemned prisoners to the guillotine
37	*Tollund, Grabaulle, Nebelgard*: place names in Jutland; Heaney has written many poems on place names, following the Irish tradition of *dinnseanchas* – poems that bring to life the familiar names of places through the lore and legends associated with them

Guidelines

'The Tollund Man' comes from Heaney's third collection, *Wintering Out* (1972). Like many of the poems in the collection, **'The Tollund Man' was written in response to the violence and murders in Northern Ireland. P. V. Glob's** *The Bog People* **provided Heaney with an imaginative framework for thinking about the violence in his home place.** Heaney tells us:

> It was chiefly concerned with preserved bodies of men and women found in the bogs of Jutland, naked, strangled or with their throats cut, disposed under the peat since early Iron Age times. The author P.V. Glob argues convincingly that a number of these and, in particular, The Tollund Man, whose head is now preserved near Aarhus in the museum at Silkeburgchas, were ritual sacrifices to the Mother Goddess, the Goddess of the ground who needed new bridegrooms each winter to bed with her in her sacred place, in the bog, to ensure the renewal and fertility of the territory in the spring. Taken in relation to the tradition of Irish martyrdom for that cause whose icon is Cathleen Ni Houlihan, this is more than an archaic barbarous rite: it is an archetypal pattern. And the unforgettable photographs of those victims blended in my mind with photographs of atrocities, past and present, in the long rites of Irish political and religious struggles.

Heaney draws a parallel between the ritual killings in Iron Age Jutland and the killing of innocent victims in contemporary Ireland, which he sees as following a pattern of making sacrifices to the Mother Goddess, in this case Mother Ireland. In trying to make sense of events taking place around him, Heaney searches the past, and finds not only a long history of barbaric rites, but a recurrence of archetypal patterns.

Commentary

The entire poem has a religious feel to it and operates as a kind of prayer. The first part calls to mind the sacred figure of the Tollund Man. The second part invokes his power. The third part projects a pilgrimage to him.

Part 1

'The Tollund Man' opens with the poet making a declaration of intent to go to Aarhus in Jutland, to see the preserved body of the Tollund Man. The man had been hanged and his body placed in the bog, as a 'Bridegroom to the goddess' (line 12). The language of the opening stanza is simple and clear, and the vowel and soft consonant sounds create a feeling of whispered prayer.

Part II

The poet suggests that the miraculous preservation of the Tollund Man's body might make him into a kind of saint – a sacred ancestor – and the bog into a holy place. The poet considers invoking the Tollund Man to make the broken and scattered bodies of the victims of sectarian violence 'germinate', though the precise nature of this germination is not explained. The alliance in the poem is between the poet/speaker and the executed man. His preserved body becomes a sacred relic and its resting place a place of pilgrimage, to which Heaney promises to go.

In the movement from the past to the present and from Jutland to Ireland, there is a compacting of both time and space. The poem brings into relation the victims of the political/sectarian atrocities in Northern Ireland, and the Iron Age Tollund Man. However, whereas the Tollund Man was forewarned of his death, and perhaps was a willing victim, the four brothers had their bodies forcibly broken and shredded. Contemporary violence denies its victims the dignity that Heaney sees in the Tollund Man. **In contemplating an appeal to the Tollund Man, 'to make germinate / The scattered, ambushed / Flesh of labourers' (lines 24-26), Heaney searches to find some way of translating the death of these victims of savage, sectarian hatred into a positive, generative force.** While the reader can recognise the poet's wish to confer meaning and value on the deaths of local men, the precise nature of any possible germination is left unclear.

Part III

Heaney imagines himself driving through Jutland, en route to Aarhus, in a country where he does not speak the language. Not to know the language and to mispronounce names is to be outside the culture. He imagines experiencing some of the feelings of the Tollund Man as he rode in the cart, to his death. **In the country of Iron Age murder, the poet imagines he will feel as lost and unhappy as he feels in his own country.**

In the final part of the poem, the poet identifies with the Tollund Man, imagining himself retracing the final journey of the bridegroom to the goddess. The poet's imagined sense of disorientation, evident in the strange place names, and the implied threat in the pointing hands, captures something of the Tollund Man's experience. And then the poet understands something: that to travel on pilgrimage to Jutland would be to encounter his own desolate, disconsolate sense of home. And implicit in this desolation is the poet's desire for home – that is, Ulster – to be other than what it is.

Critical interpretation

'The Tollund Man' is a remarkably accomplished poem by any standards, but critics have raised questions about its achievement. Does the poem represent a refusal to confront the reality of violence in Northern Ireland? As with many of the questions of this kind raised in relation to Heaney's poetry, the poet asks these questions of himself. He admits that he found it easier writing about a victim of 2,000-year-old violence than about the barman at the end of his road who was killed carrying out a bomb attack:

> The barman at the end of our road tried to carry out a bomb and it blew up. Now of course there is something terrible about that, but somehow language, words didn't live in the way I think they have to live in a poem when they were hovering over that kind of horror and pity. They just become inert. And it was in these victims made strangely beautiful by the process of lying in bogs that somehow I felt could make offerings or images that were emblems.

So Heaney wants the Tollund Man to stand as an emblem, and in the poem the Tollund Man achieves a kind of beauty. Is this a dangerous myth to suggest that the victims of ritual killings achieve a kind of beauty, or is there something consoling in this idea? Is the poet/speaker ultimately identifying with the victim of violence?

Thinking about the poem

1. What, in your view, is the tone of the first stanza? How is this tone achieved?
2. The Tollund Man was a bridegroom to the goddess. What kind of bride was she? Look particularly at the images in stanzas 3 and 4 of the first part of the poem.
3. Where is this identification of the Tollund Man as a kind of sacred ancestor most evident in the poem?
4. The poet considers calling on the Tollund Man 'to make germinate' (line 24) the murdered victims of sectarian violence in Northern Ireland. What kind of germination, do you think, might the poet have in mind? Explain your answer.
5. In your view, what does the phrase 'sad freedom' (line 33) suggest about the bridegroom/victim?
6. What are the differences between the death of the Tollund Man and the deaths of the four brothers referred to in the second section of the poem? Explain your answer.
7. Some critics argue that the poem regards sectarian violence as the manifestation of dark, ancient forces. In your opinion, is this the case? Explain your answer.

8   What, in your opinion, does the Tollund Man represent? Is he, for example, a Christ-like figure, whose death and bizarre resurrection offer a kind of hope? Explain your answer.
9   The poet identifies closely with the Tollund Man's experience. Does the poet make the same identification with the victims of contemporary violence? Explain your answer.
10 The poem ends with a kind of revelation. What, in your opinion, has the poet gained from his imaginative pilgrimage to Jutland?

Mossbawn: Two Poems in Dedication: (1) Sunlight

For Mary Heaney

There was a sunlit absence.
The helmeted pump in the yard
heated its iron,
water honeyed

in the slung bucket   5
and the sun stood
like a griddle cooling
against the wall

of each long afternoon.
So, her hands scuffled   10
over the bakeboard,
the reddening stove

sent its plaque of heat
against her where she stood
in a floury apron   15
by the window.

Now she dusts the board
with a goose's wing,
now sits, broad-lapped,
with whitened nails   20

and measling shins:
here is a space
again, the scone rising
to the tick of two clocks.

And here is love   25
like a tinsmith's scoop
sunk past its gleam
in the meal-bin.

Glossary

title *Mossbawn*: the family home during Heaney's childhood

dedication *For Mary Heaney*: aunt of the poet who lived with the family in Mossbawn. Heaney said of her: 'She was a tower of emotional strength . . . I loved her dearly.' Elsewhere he said, 'She was the heart of the house in some way, and as a child I was "petted" on her, as they say. There were two women, as it were, in my life – happily there. Mary was always there as a kind of second mother.'

7 *griddle*: round, flat plate used for baking

Guidelines

'Sunlight' is the first of two poems under the collective title 'Mossbawn', which open the collection *North* (1975). 'Sunlight' delights in detail: like a rich Flemish painting, it paints a portrait of the farmyard and kitchen, with the poet's aunt as the central human figure. **The poem captures the stillness, tranquillity and warmth at the heart of the home.** Indeed, the central image – the baking of bread – symbolises nurturing and nourishment. The poem stands apart from many of the poems in *North*, which deal with the violence of the conflict in Northern Ireland.

Mossbawn was the family farm where Heaney grew up. He referred to it in a radio broadcast as 'the first place', the poet's version of Eden. The world of Mossbawn depicted in the poem is one of sunlight and feminine care, a world of grace and blessing. **Mossbawn stands as an antidote to the brutal reality of the wider society.**

Commentary

Lines 1–9

The empty yard is warmed by the sun, and transformed by its glow, so that the 'water honeyed / in the slung bucket' (lines 4–5). By comparing the sun to a griddle, Heaney prepares for the change of focus in the poem, moving from the sun baking the yard to the aunt's baking in the kitchen. The use of the initial letter 'h' in 'helmeted', 'heated' and 'honeyed' emphasises the heating process, as the reader exhales in saying the words.

At the heart of the sunlit, silent yard is the 'helmeted pump' (line 2). This pump was the central point of Heaney's boyhood world. In an evocation of his childhood in the early 1940s, in the midst of war, Heaney places the pump at the centre of a private world, untroubled by the historical events occurring around it:

> I would begin with the Greek word omphalos, meaning the navel, and hence the stone that marked the centre of the world, and repeat it, omphalos, omphalos, omphalos, until its blunt and falling music becomes the music of somebody pumping water at the pump outside our back door . . . There the pump stands, a slender, iron idol, snouted, helmeted, dressed down with a sweeping handle, painted a dark green and set on a concrete plinth, marking the centre of another world . . . That pump marked an original descent into earth, sand, gravel, water. It centred and staked the imagination.

The pump goes down into the earth and finds spring water, a symbol of purity and life. The 'helmeted pump' stands as a guardian of the domestic life and as a symbol of deep and hidden goodness.

Lines 10–24

The presiding figure in the poem is Heaney's Aunt Mary. Heaney paints a warm and tender portrait of his aunt at work. The stove itself seems to respond to her, sending out 'its plaque of heat' (line 13). The ordinary, domestic chore of baking is rendered with a painter's eye. The stillness of the penultimate stanza – 'the scone rising / to the tick of two clocks' (lines 23–24) – gives the scene a timeless quality, like that of a Dutch Renaissance interior. The timeless quality is emphasised by the sudden transition to the present tense in the first line of the fifth stanza, 'Now she dusts the board' (line 17).

Final thought

The mention of 'love' in line 25 is one of the few places in Heaney's poetry where the word 'love' is used. **Mary's benign love contrasts with the demanding, destructive traits of the Earth Goddess of 'The Tollund Man', and with the essentially male violence of sectarian hatred that affects the world beyond the domesticity of the farm. In 'Sunlight' the presiding spirit is nurturing, protective and gentle.**

The space in the penultimate stanza ('here is a space', line 22) is not only the space where the scones will rise, it is also the space where Heaney, the poet, can pause and come to understand the love shown by his aunt for his family, a love enacted every day in her domestic routine. It is the space that allows the final thought of the poem to grow and blossom, for the poem opens out emotionally in the final stanza.

Just as the water lies unseen beneath the soil, and the scoop is hidden in the meal, so his aunt's love is hidden but constant, as is the memory of her, sunk in the poet's consciousness but brought forth now in celebration. **And, in going on in the other poems in *North* to confront the darkness of the violence in Northern Ireland, Heaney draws strength from this invocation of his past, of Mossbawn, his childhood Eden.**

Form of the poem

The poem is written in short, four-line stanzas. The lines run into each other, which gives a momentum to the poem that flows until the pause in line 22, before the beautiful and elevating final stanza.

Thinking about the poem

1. The opening stanzas have the effect of a still-life painting. How is this effect achieved?
2. Where else, in the poem, is the suggestion of still life? Explain your answer.
3. The pump is described as 'helmeted' (line 2). In your view, what qualities does this adjective ascribe to the pump?
4. What, do you think, is the purpose of the image of the sun as a griddle? Is the image a successful one? Explain your answer.
5. Trace all the images of baking in the poem. In your view, does the poem succeed in linking the human activity to the natural processes of the weather? Explain your answer.

6   The final stanza commences with the declaration, 'And here is love' (line 25). Has the poem, in your opinion, built up to this declaration? Explain your answer.
7   In your view, what kind of love is suggested by the image of the tinsmith's scoop and the meal-bin (lines 26–28)?
8   Tone is clearly an important part of the poem's meaning. Trace the pattern of 'u' and 'o' sounds in the poem, noting how they contribute to the sense of slow time.
9   'Sunlight' is a celebration of the poet's home and of his aunt, Mary Heaney. Why, in your opinion, did Heaney choose this as the first poem in his collection North (1975), which deals, for the most part, with the theme of violence?
10 From your reading of the poem, what does the woman symbolise in the poem? Compare the female figure in this poem with the goddess in 'The Tollund Man' and with the male figure in 'A Constable Calls'.

A Constable Calls

His bicycle stood at the window-sill,
The rubber cowl of a mud-splasher
Skirting the front mudguard,
Its fat black handlegrips

Heating in sunlight, the 'spud'   5
Of the dynamo gleaming and cocked back,
The pedal treads hanging relieved
Of the boot of the law.

His cap was upside down
On the floor, next his chair.   10
The line of its pressure ran like a bevel
In his slightly sweating hair.

He had unstrapped
The heavy ledger, and my father
Was making tillage returns   15
In acres, roods, and perches.

Arithmetic and fear.
I sat staring at the polished holster
With its buttoned flap, the braid cord
Looped into the revolver butt.   20

'Any other root crops?
Mangolds? Marrowstems? Anything like that?'
'No.' But was there not a line
Of turnips where the seed ran out

In the potato field? I assumed   25
Small guilts and sat
Imagining the black hole in the barracks.
He stood up, shifted the baton-case

Further round on his belt,
Closed the domesday book,   30
Fitted his cap back with two hands,
And looked at me as he said goodbye.

A shadow bobbed in the window.
He was snapping the carrier spring
Over the ledger. His boot pushed off   35
And the bicycle ticked, ticked, ticked.

Glossary

title	*Constable*: a member of the Royal Ulster Constabulary (RUC), which was the police force of Northern Ireland from the beginning of the state in 1922 until the establishment of the Police Service of Northern Ireland (PSNI) in 2001; the RUC had a predominantly Protestant membership and was seen by many as pro-loyalist
11	*bevel*: a line or an edge left by the band of the constable's cap
30	*domesday book*: the record of a survey carried out by the commissioners of William I in 1086; here, the phrase refers to the official record of crop returns, registered by the constable. 'Domesday' also refers to the day of the Last Judgement, or any other day of reckoning

Guidelines

'A Constable Calls' is the second poem in a sequence of six called 'Singing School' that concludes the collection *North* (1975). Heaney uses an extract from Wordsworth's autobiographical poem, *The Prelude*, and one from Yeats's *Autobiographies*, as epigraphs for the sequence. Drawing on the example of Wordsworth ('Fostered alike by beauty and by fear') and Yeats ('When I began to dream of my future life, I thought I would like to die fighting the Fenians'), Heaney's sequence gives us moments of his autobiography that explain where he, as poet and citizen, has come from.

The poems in 'Singing School' are about fear and power. **In 'A Constable Calls' Heaney conveys the sense of implicit threat felt by the young boy during the official visit of the constable.** The poem shows the alienation of the Catholic, nationalist community from the agents of the state.

There is a difference between the mythic approach to the Troubles in 'The Tollund Man' and the documentary approach in 'A Constable Calls'. This change in approach indicates a feature of Heaney's writing that is worth bearing in mind – the constant revisiting of themes and concerns with sometimes radical changes in outlook and approach.

Commentary

Detailed description

The poem works by way of detailed description. The bicycle of the constable is first described, in the opening stanzas, in precise, cold language: 'rubber cowl of a mud-splasher . . . fat black handlegrips' (lines 2–4). The elements of the bicycle are associated, by clever word-play, with the power of the police to arrest and use force. The phrase 'handlegrips' suggests handcuffs, and the gleaming 'cocked back' dynamo (line 6) brings to mind a gun ready to fire. The phrase 'boot of the law' (line 8) gains an emotional force when read in the context of 1969 and the violence of the RUC towards the civil rights marchers. The harsh 'ck' sounds in the first two stanzas contribute to the cold, impersonal nature of the descriptions. Of course, one of the questions that arises in the context of the poem is: can description ever be regarded as neutral or is it always influenced by the assumptions and prejudices of the person who does the describing?

The description of the constable, as seen through the eyes of the boy, is made by reference to his uniform and his equipment, so that the man, like his bicycle, seems composed of separate pieces; this renders him inhuman. The boy notes that 'His cap was upside down / On the floor' (lines 9–10); he stares 'at the polished holster / With its buttoned flap' (lines 18–19); and he watches as the policeman 'shifted the baton-case / Further round on his belt' (lines 28–29).

Called to account

In the poem the father is obliged to give an account of his crop returns. This relatively minor matter is used by the poet to suggest the many ways in which the nationalist community was called to account by a police force that it regarded as oppressive. **The policeman is not an individual, but a shadowy figure whose armed presence in the domestic security of Mossbawn threatens the peace of the home. The poem dramatises the intrusion of public authority, embodied in the threatening male figure of the policeman, into the private world of feminine grace and warmth described in 'Sunlight'.** His presence is enough to cause doubt and guilt in the young child. The poem tells us that the boy's dread fascination with the gun turned to alarm as his father failed to mention a line of turnips, and the boy, feeling like an accessory to a crime, pictured a fearful place of punishment 'in the barracks' (line 27).

Ending of the poem

Even as the policeman cycles away, the sounds of his bicycle as it 'ticked, ticked, ticked' (line 36) carry menace – the menace of an explosive timing-device. The ending of 'A Constable Calls' highlights the contrast between this poem and 'Sunlight', where the only sound is the soothing ticking of the clocks as the aunt waits for the scones to rise. The domestic world is a place of love and security, but its peace is threatened by the presence of the policeman and all he represents of the world outside the home.

Form and tone of the poem

The poem is written in four-line stanzas and composed of short, concise phrases as in 'the boot of the law' (line 8). Heaney uses plosive 'p' and 'b' sounds and alliteration to create a sense of heaviness and threat, while the harsh 'ck' sounds of the final line add menace. There is no regular rhyming scheme in the stanzas and this creates an impression of control without harmony, which matches the theme of the poem.

Thinking about the poem

1. How, in your view, is the idea of menace and force conveyed in the first two stanzas of the poem?
2. The language of the opening stanzas is remarkable for its precision and harsh sounds. Select **two** words or phrases and comment on their effectiveness.
3. 'I sat staring at the polished holster' (line 18). In your view, what is the young boy's attitude to the constable? Explain your answer.

4   'I assumed / Small guilts' (lines 25–26). What, do you think, is the significance of this statement for your understanding of the poem?
5   The final three stanzas convey an atmosphere of fear. Which of the following, in your opinion, is/are the causes of this fear: the person of the constable; the imagination of the boy; the social and political situation in Northern Ireland? Explain your choice.
6   The constable is described in terms of his uniform and equipment. What does Heaney omit from his description? Why, in your view, does he do this?
7   Which of the following three statements about the poem is closest to your reading of the poem?
    The poem is about a small boy's fear.
    The poem is about the Troubles in Northern Ireland.
    The poem is about ordinary people's fear of the Law.
    Explain your choice.

Taking a closer look

1   Choose **two** phrases from the poem that you found especially appealing and say why you chose them.
2   'the domesday book' (line 30). What thoughts and feelings are prompted in you by this phrase?
3   'And the bicycle ticked, ticked, ticked' (line 36). What is the effect of the last three words of the poem, particularly in the context of Northern Ireland?

Imagining

1   Turn the events described in the poem into a short story.
2   You are asked to make a film of the poem. Describe the atmosphere you would create and the images, music and sounds you would use to create it.
3   You are the young boy in the poem. It is twenty years later and you are studying to become a journalist. You go to the home of the retired constable and interview him about this incident. Write the script of the interview.
4   Using the descriptions in the poem as a model, write a description of a machine, for example, a tractor or a mechanical digger, or a garden implement such as a spade or a fork.

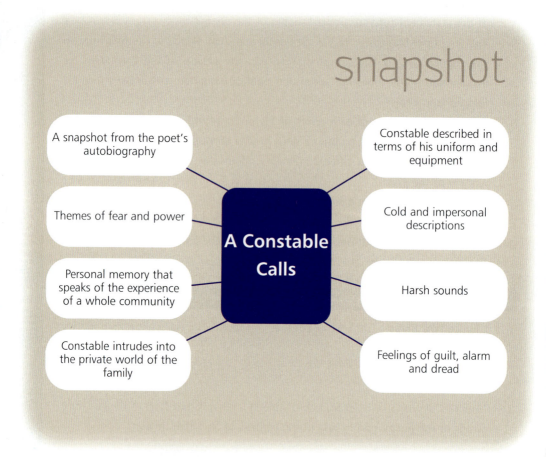

The Skunk

Up, black, striped and damasked like the chasuble
At a funeral mass, the skunk's tail
Paraded the skunk. Night after night
I expected her like a visitor.

The refrigerator whinnied into silence.   5
My desk light softened beyond the verandah.
Small oranges loomed in the orange tree.
I began to be tense as a voyeur.

After eleven years I was composing
Love-letters again, broaching the 'wife' 10
Like a stored cask, as if its slender vowel
Had mutated into the night earth and air

Of California. The beautiful, useless
Tang of eucalyptus spelt your absence.
The aftermath of a mouthful of wine 15
Was like inhaling you off a cold pillow.

And there she was, the intent and glamorous,
Ordinary, mysterious skunk,
Mythologized, demythologized,
Snuffing the boards five feet beyond me. 20

It all came back to me last night, stirred
By the sootfall of your things at bedtime,
Your head-down, tail-up hunt in a bottom drawer
For the black plunge-line nightdress.

Glossary

1	*damasked*:	damask is a reversible fabric with a design woven into it; like damask, the skunk's tail is reversible – it has markings on the underside
1	*chasuble*:	the outer vestment worn by a priest when saying Mass, usually with a decorative design in a different colour from that of the chasuble itself; at a funeral Mass, the chasuble is white with black markings
8	*voyeur*:	a person who takes sexual pleasure in watching another undress
11	*stored cask*:	the phrase brings to mind the story of Portia in Shakespeare's *The Merchant of Venice* – suitors could only win her through choosing successfully from three caskets, one of which contained her portrait; there is also the idea of broaching or opening a casket and releasing its essence so that it fills the surrounding air; and there is the ancient idea that the saying of a name invokes or summons the spirit

Guidelines

'The Skunk' comes from Heaney's fifth collection, *Field Work* (1979). This collection has a number of poems that deal in personal terms with the Troubles. They remember friends and family of Heaney who were murdered in Northern Ireland. In addition to the poems in which Heaney, drawing inspiration from Dante's *Divine Comedy*, encounters the dead, **Field Work contains a number of poems in which Heaney speaks in a natural, conversational voice about himself and his wife.**

'The Skunk' is a poem about the poet's love for his wife. It is a poem about the daily habit of love. It is a playful poem that combines irony and self-deprecating humour with genuine affection and love.

Commentary

The occasion of the poem is a bedtime scene, with the poet/speaker observing his wife hunt for her nightdress in a bottom drawer. As she searches she adopts a faintly comic posture, 'head-down, tail-up' (line 23). **This bedroom scene becomes a symbol for the nature of erotic intimacy in marriage, an intimacy that is warm, sometimes comic, and stirring.** His wife's posture, in searching for her nightdress, puts the poet in mind of the skunk that used to appear in the garden of his house in California, where he spent a year teaching, separated from his wife.

The poet recalls the air of expectancy that he experienced in waiting for the skunk's arrival. In his excited state, his senses are alert. **As the poem unfolds, the reader begins to understand that the poet's attitude to the skunk, the expectation and tension he felt waiting for her, mirrors his feelings for his wife.** When, in stanza 5, the poet describes the skunk as 'intent and glamorous, / Ordinary, mysterious' (lines 17–18), there is a shock of amusement in realising that this stanza refers to the poet's wife as she searches for her nightdress.

The separation of the poet and his wife works to bring her more sharply into his focus. Though distant from her, his wife fills his consciousness; away from home, he writes her a love letter. In her absence, the poet reclaims her, understanding how much he prizes and values her and discovering how much she is present to him in the very air he breathes. To say the word 'wife' is to release her presence into the air around him. She is like a 'stored cask' (line 11), the phrase suggests something valued, precious and mature.

The poem captures the mystery, which is almost sacred, at the heart of everyday relationships. This sense of mystery is conveyed in the image of priestly vestments in the first stanza, and in the magical effect of saying the word 'wife', described in stanzas 3 and 4, which causes her spirit to be present to the poet in the atmosphere and the objects around him. And there is an echo of the sacramental in lines 15 and 16: 'The aftermath of a mouthful of wine / Was like inhaling you off a cold pillow.' Finally, the black nightdress represents a vesting in preparation for the mysteries of married love.

Language of the poem

'The Skunk' has many delightful phrases and images, not least the coined word 'sootfall' (line 22), which captures the gentle noise of the clothes falling to the ground and picks up on the colour black that features throughout the poem. For the critic Neil Corcoran, 'sootfall' also contains the idea that the falling clothes are worn and soiled by everyday living. The poet is stirred by the fall of these clothes, a stirring that is all the more authentic for being caused by such a real undressing.

In the context of the poem as a whole, Heaney's use of the word 'voyeur' (line 8) is worth considering. A voyeur is usually a male who takes sexual pleasure in secretly watching a female undress, as in the Biblical story of Susanna and the Elders. Here, however, the ideas of undress and watching are placed in a domestic, affectionate context. The male still watches and the female undresses but the sense of intrusion or violation is removed. Reread the poem and decide if you agree with this reading.

The poem contains a number of unusual metaphors. In the first stanza, for example, the skunk's tail is compared to the priest's white and black robe at a funeral. However, the most startling of the images is the poet's identification of his wife with the skunk. By any standards this is a risky comparison, but in the context of the poem, and within the context of the confident, affectionate tone of the poet, it is a comparison that works.

Form of the poem

The poem is written in unrhymed four-line stanzas. Heaney uses lines of different length to create a conversational tone, though the language is carefully considered and phrased, as in line 14: 'Tang of eucalyptus spelt your absence'. The effect is to create a poem that is warm and affectionate in tone and rhythm, and that at the same time is highly wrought and carefully fashioned.

The long lines of the poems suggest ease – the ease of a poet relaxed and playful. This style of writing carries the influence of the great American writer Robert Lowell. The title of the 'The Skunk' and the reference to the poet as voyeur recall Lowell's 'Skunk Hour', though the two are very different in mood.

Thinking about the poem

1. In the first stanza the skunk's tail is compared to the priest's chasuble at a funeral. Identify other unusual images in the poem. What, in your view, is the effect of these images?

2. In the second stanza, what images convey a sense of expectancy? What, in your view, is the effect of the comparison 'tense as a voyeur' (line 8)?

3. The poet/speaker recollects a period of absence from his wife. How does the poem suggest that, despite this absence, he was aware and mindful of her?

4. In what way, do you think, might the word 'wife' be like a 'stored cask' (lines 10 and 11)? Explain your answer.

5. In the poem, the poet/speaker's wife is identified with the skunk.
   a) What, in your view, are the risks involved in this identification?
   b) Does the poem overcome them?
   c) The critic Christopher Ricks suggests that the comparison of his wife to a skunk reveals Heaney's trust in the love between them. Would you agree? Explain your answer.

6. a) Outline the possible meanings of the phrase 'the sootfall of your things' (line 22).
   b) Do you think that the phrase captures the ordinary and the mysterious in marriage? Explain your answer.

7. a) In your view, what does the final stanza reveal to be the source of the poet's recollection of the skunk's visit to his house in California?
   b) Select **two** words to describe the tone of the poem.

8. Read back over the poem. Identify the images that have a religious or magical association. Bearing these in mind, what, in your view, is the poem saying about the nature of marriage?

9. "The Skunk" is a poem that is full of irony and self-deprecating humour and genuine affection and love.' Give your view of this assessment of the poem.

The Harvest Bow

As you plaited the harvest bow
You implicated the mellowed silence in you
In wheat that does not rust
But brightens as it tightens twist by twist
Into a knowable corona, 5
A throwaway love-knot of straw.

Hands that aged round ashplants and cane sticks
And lapped the spurs on a lifetime of game cocks
Harked to their gift and worked with fine intent
Until your fingers moved somnambulant: 10
I tell and finger it like braille,
Gleaning the unsaid off the palpable,

And if I spy into its golden loops
I see us walk between the railway slopes
Into an evening of long grass and midges, 15
Blue smoke straight up, old beds and ploughs in hedges,
An auction notice on an outhouse wall—
You with a harvest bow in your lapel,

Me with the fishing rod, already homesick
For the big lift of these evenings, as your stick 20
Whacking the tips off weeds and bushes
Beats out of time, the beats, but flushes
Nothing: that original townland
Still tongue-tied in the straw tied by your hand.

The end of art is peace 25
Could be the motto of this frail device
That I have pinned up on our deal dresser—
Like a drawn snare
Slipped lately by the spirit of the corn
Yet burnished by its passage, and still warm. 30

Seamus Heaney

Glossary

1	*harvest bow*	a bow made from straw worn to the fair celebrating the end of the harvest
2	*implicated*	intertwined or woven
5	*corona*	the circle of light that surrounds the sun; here, although the father is silent, he is knowable in the bright circle of the bow that he plaits
6	*love-knot*	harvest bows were originally love tokens
17	*auction notice*	the notice announces the auction of Mossbawn, the family home; the family moved from this farm shortly after the death of Heaney's younger brother Christopher, an event commemorated in 'Mid-Term Break' – the sale of the house marked the end of the poet's childhood
25	*the end of art is peace*	a line from a poem by Coventry Patmore, a popular Victorian poet; Heaney said he read the line in one of Yeats's earlier books. While the sentiment is partly clichéd, there is an interesting ambiguity in the word 'end'
29	*spirit of the corn*	the spirit that makes the corn germinate each year; this is not only the spirit of nature itself, but also the patient spirit of humans, like the poet's father, who work the soil

Guidelines

The poem is addressed to the poet's father and comes from the collection *Field Work* (1979). It is one of many poems that Heaney has written about his father (including the much anthologised 'Digging'). In 'The Harvest Bow' there is a sense of the poet looking to the example of his father to draw inspiration and hope. Just as in 'Digging', his father provides the poet with an example that he wishes to follow.

Commentary

Portrait of his father

The portrait of Patrick Heaney presented in the poem is among the most affectionate to be found in Heaney's writing. The poet's father emerges as a man who is strong, robust and unsentimental. He is a man who has 'lapped the spurs on a lifetime of game cocks' (line 8) and strode with his stick 'Whacking the tips off weeds and bushes' (line 21); a 'tongue-tied' (line 24) man who expressed himself in action; a man now in 'mellowed silence' (line 2) whose hands, plaiting the straw, continue to be his means of self-expression.

As with many of the craftsmen celebrated in Heaney's poetry, the father in 'The Harvest Bow' becomes an exemplar, teaching the poet that the artist or the craftsman expresses himself through his work. The father's hands, harkening 'to their gift', work with a 'fine intent' (line 9). This attitude of joy and attention connects the father to the son, who sees in his father the qualities he wishes to bring to his poetry. There is an understanding between the father and the son, not reached through words, but expressed by the harvest bow, which Heaney fingers and reads 'like braille, / Gleaning the unsaid off the palpable' (lines 11–12). And then the poet translates what he has read in the harvest bow into words, which he, in his turn, fashions or plaits and weaves into a poem.

The end of art is peace

The motto that opens the final stanza, 'The end of art is peace' (line 25), expresses, among other things, the peace and harmony between father and son, arrived at through their respective arts. It can be read as stating either that the aim or purpose of art is the creation of peace or that peace, as in peace of mind, may lessen artistic inspiration. And, of course, the motto has wider and larger significance in the context of the political situation in Northern Ireland.

Symbol of love

The harvest bow is a symbol of the love between the father and the son. It is a 'love-knot' (line 6) that joins them. Holding it in his hands, and looking through 'its golden loops' (line 13), the poet sees the evenings he shared with his father: the boy walking towards his future, the father walking by the remnants of his past.

The bow celebrates the gathering in of the harvest, and the gathering in of the father–son relationship. The harvest bow is lifeless, 'the spirit of the corn' having slipped away from it (line 29), yet it retains its warmth and is enriched by the spirit that gave it life.

The harvest bow, 'this frail device' (line 26), is an emblem of agricultural labour and love of the land. The spirit of the corn is not only the spirit of bountiful nature, but it is also the patient spirit of agriculture, of the human being working the soil. As such, the harvest bow represents a strength of continuity and inheritance that is free of the pressures of tribal loyalties and communal strife. The harvest bow is a symbol of rural rituals tied to a love of the land, in a society where the harvest time is preceded by sectarian marches and divisions.

Form of the poem

The poem represents a poetic plaiting and weaving. It is a carefully structured and textured creation in six-line stanzas with interesting rhymes and half-rhymes. The son follows his father's example by combining sounds and images into a tightly woven creation. Heaney has remarked, 'I remember discovering a shape and then realising that it could be built on, and relishing the whole gradual, cumulative effect. But the texture of 'The Harvest Bow' is richer than many of the other poems in *Field Work*.'

Thinking about the poem

1. What, in your view, are the implications of the phrase 'mellowed silence' (line 2)? What does the phrase suggest to you about the relationship between father and son?
2. The plaiting of the straw emerges as a 'love-knot' (line 6). In your view, what is the tone of the poem as it announces this emergence? What words capture the tone?
3. From the evidence of stanza 2, what aspects of the father's personality are represented by the plaiting of the bow? From your reading, what view of the father emerges from the poem as a whole? Explain your answer.
4. 'Gleaning the unsaid off the palpable' (line 12). In your opinion, how much of what the poet gleans from the harvest bow is the result of his wish to glean it? Explain your answer.
5. What do the images of stanzas 3 and 4 say to you about the closeness and distances between father and son? Explain your answer.
6. Write a note on the phrase 'spirit of the corn' (line 29) and its relationship to the themes of the poem.
7. 'The end of art is peace' (line 25). What is the significance of this motto for (a) the father; (b) the relationship between father and son; (c) the poet; and (d) the North.
8. Explain your understanding of the image of the 'drawn snare' (line 28).
9. Like the harvest bow that it celebrates, the poem is a tightly made structure. Describe the stanza form and the variety of rhyme used in the poem.
10. 'The harvest bow, the "frail device" (line 26) woven by the father, becomes a rich and complex symbol within the poem.' Discuss this statement.

The Underground

There we were in the vaulted tunnel running,
You in your going-away coat speeding ahead
And me, me then like a fleet god gaining
Upon you before you turned to a reed

Or some new white flower japped with crimson   5
As the coat flapped wild and button after button
Sprang off and fell in a trail
Between the Underground and the Albert Hall.

Honeymooning, moonlighting, late for the Proms,
Our echoes die in that corridor and now   10
I come as Hansel came on the moonlit stones
Retracing the path back, lifting the buttons

To end up in a draughty lamplit station
After the trains have gone, the wet track
Bared and tensed as I am, all attention   15
For your step following and damned if I look back.

Glossary

title	*The Underground*: the London train system (the Tube), which operates in tunnels under the ground; Heaney has spoken of the dreamlike or nightmarish quality of travelling on the Tube – how 'the underground/underworld/otherworld parallels come into play', and of 'awareness of the mythical dimensions of all such journeys underground, into the earth, into the dark'
2	*going-away coat*: coat worn by the bride when leaving on her honeymoon
3–4	*fleet god . . . reed*: an allusion to the story of Pan and Syrinx. Pan was the Greek god of shepherds, fields and woods, hunting and music; he had the hindquarters, legs and horns of a goat and was associated with fertility and spring. The amorous Pan pursued the nymph Syrinx, a wood spirit with the form of a beautiful young woman, and she appealed to her sisters, the spirits of the river, to save her. As Pan was about to seize her, the river nymphs changed her into a reed. From this reed, Pan made musical pipes upon which he played sad and sweet melodies

Glossary

5	*japped*: Ulster-Scots word meaning spattered or splashed
8	*Albert Hall*: one of the most famous concert venues in the world, the Royal Albert Hall in South Kensington, London, was opened in 1871 and is named after the husband of Queen Victoria
9	*honeymooning*: a honeymoon is, traditionally, the holiday taken immediately after a wedding and is associated with harmony and happiness
9	*moonlighting*: doing something by the light of the moon, but the word has a host of interesting associations related to dangerous, secret or illegal activities; its use gives a humorous edge to the description of the honeymoon
9	*the Proms*: a season of summer concerts of classical music held at the Albert Hall. 'Prom' is an abbreviated form of 'promenade', a walk or stroll associated with display and dressing up. Today a promenade concert is one in which some of the audience stand. On the last night of the Proms, many of the audience attend in fancy dress
11	*Hansel*: character from the Grimm Brothers' fairy tale *Hansel and Gretel*. Hansel and his sister Gretel are the children of a poor woodcutter facing starvation. Having overheard their stepmother urge their father to abandon them in the woods, they gather pebbles from the garden and lay a trail as they are brought deep into the woods. In the moonlight, they find the pebbles and retrace the path home
16	*damned if I looked back*: echoes the story of Orpheus and Eurydice. Orpheus was a Greek musician and poet and it was said that he could charm birds, fish and animals and even move stones to tears. He visited the Underworld, where the souls of the dead reside, to plead for the return of his wife, Eurydice. His music moved Hades and Persephone, rulers of the kingdom of the dead, who allowed Eurydice to return with him on one condition: Orpheus was to walk ahead of his wife and not look back until they had reached the upper world. In his anxiety and love, no sooner had Orpheus reached the border of the two worlds than he looked behind him and Eurydice was lost to him forever

Guidelines

The poem comes from the 1984 collection *Station Island*, a book concerned with questions of guilt and the public responsibility of the poet. Many of the poems in the collection are severe and self-admonitory. 'The Underground' is something of an exception to the general rule. **It is a playful, celebratory love poem, which recalls a dash to a concert in the Albert Hall during the Heaneys' honeymoon in London and captures the energy and excitement of the newly-weds.** Here is Heaney's account of the poem:

> The last poem in *Field Work*, 'Ugolino', was an underground poem of a very different sort, [set in Hell] so we're into this next book at a run, heading up and away. I liked it because it seemed to have both truth to life and truth to love. It starts with a memory of running through a tunnel from the South Kensington tube station towards the Albert Hall, late for a BBC Promenade Concert. We were on our honeymoon and Marie was wearing her going-away coat. In the course of her sprint, the buttons started popping off. But in the end, the 'damned if I look back' line takes us well beyond the honeymoon. In this version of the story, Eurydice and much else gets saved by the sheer cussedness of the poet up ahead just keeping going.

Commentary

Pursuit and flight

The honeymoon described in the poem is defined by pursuit and flight, with the male persona doing the pursuing. At the end of the poem, the male is striding ahead, with the female following, though, by this stage, the poem has moved beyond the honeymoon and the relationship is one between two conflicting egos, with the ego of the male persona unwilling to concede or look back. The stubbornness described here is also evident in 'Tate's Avenue', a poem written two decades after 'The Underground', when no ground is conceded on the rug by either of the two lovers. **In both poems, love is portrayed as much as a matter of competing wills as an irresistible force of attraction.**

The idea of flight is captured in the phrase 'going-away coat' (line 2). Here, as elsewhere in his poetry, Heaney takes a common word or phrase and breathes new life into it. Apart from the bride going away on her honeymoon, she is also running ahead of her new husband. The accident of the buttons falling from the coat takes on an air of erotic abandonment with the use of words such as 'wild' (line 6) and 'sprang' (line 7).

Interestingly, for a poem that describes a honeymoon, 'The Underground' is about emerging from the Underground only to return to it, or somewhere very similar: 'a draughty lamplit station' (line 13). **The couple described in the poem seem constantly on the run, with neither the young husband nor the young wife at rest or together.** One pursues the other or one leads and the other follows.

In this poem of flight and return there is an erotic tension in the first two stanzas as the poetic persona, 'like a fleet-god' (line 3), pursues his beloved. This is replaced with a different kind of tension, possibly that between being a husband and a poet, in the last stanza, where the 'I' of the poem strides ahead of his wife and refuses to look back. Certainly the distance between 'There' in line 1 and the 'now' in line 10 seems immense and the placing of the word 'die' in line 10 seems to bring the honeymoon to an abrupt stop.

Classical allusions

The poem reminds us of one of Heaney's poetic methods. He takes a memory from ordinary life and overlays it with classical allusions, so that the young honeymooners and their race through London are linked to the classical lovers Orpheus and Eurydice and their journey from the Underworld, and also to the story of the god Pan and the nymph Syrinx. There is humour and ingenuity in Heaney's use of classical allusions. Orpheus, for example, was chief among poets and musicians and his journey to the Underworld in pursuit of his beloved wife is one of the most famous of all classical love stories. We can see the parallel between Heaney's poetic persona, full of love for his new wife, racing through the Underground en route to a concert of classical music and the mythical Orpheus.

The god Pan, renowned for his lusty passion and linked to fertility and spring, is often seen in the company of Eros, the god of love and romance. Pan, therefore, seems an appropriate reference for a man on his honeymoon. There is also a link between the music of Orpheus and of Pan: their compositions arose from their feelings of love and desire, in the same way that Heaney's poetry celebrates his marriage without sentimentalising it.

Encountering the world

'The Underground' describes the persona of the poet caught between the excitement and energy of a moment and a more guarded, closed way of encountering the world. The honeymoon is all rush and excitement. The final stanza 'well beyond the honeymoon' presents the persona of the poem as guarded and closed. The lesson of encountering the world off-guard is one that the poet learns again and again, as in 'The Pitchfork' ('the opening hand')

and 'Postscript'. In 'A Call' the impulse to open the heart is suppressed and the declaration of love never leaves the poet's lips.

A love poem

Although it is a love poem, Heaney does not use the word 'love' in the poem (he rarely does in his poetry) and the poem ends with the male persona waiting for his beloved who is following behind but 'damned if I look back' (line 16). The use of 'damned' in the final line echoes Patrick Kavanagh's use of 'blooming' in the final line of 'Iniskeen Road'. There is the formal meaning of 'damned' meaning lost, and the relevance of that meaning to the story of Orpheus and Eurydice, and there is the colloquial meaning of 'damned' suggesting that the poetic persona has no intention of looking back.

It is not a conventional end to a love poem but it may have the truth to life that Heaney refers to in his comments on the poem. **The love described in the poem is composed of many elements: desire, pursuit, excitement, escape, silence, complication and perseverance.**

Form of the poem

The poem is written in four-line stanzas with a variable rhyming pattern. The final rhyme of 'track' and 'back' provides a sense of ending and also catches something of the stubborn character of the poem's narrator.

Language of the poem

The energy of the poem and the excitement of the young couple is caught in the series of actions described with a present participle: 'running', 'speeding', 'gaining', 'honeymooning', 'moonlighting'.

The colours of the coat are crimson (deep red) on white, which is traditionally the colour of virginity. The image of the white flower splattered with red may suggest the bleeding that sometimes follows the breaking of the hymen when sexual intercourse takes place for the first time. In 'The Whitsun Weddings' Philip Larkin refers to the consummation of a marriage as 'a religious wounding'. Interestingly, the Heaneys briefly met Larkin in the London offices of the publishers Faber on 6 August 1965, the first day of their honeymoon.

Thinking about the poem

1. In a couple of sentences, tell the story of the poem.
2. How is the energy and excitement of the newly-weds captured in the first nine lines of the poem? Refer to language, imagery and sounds in your answer.
3. Look at the images of flight and pursuit in the poem. Who leads and who follows in the course of the poem?
4. Which of the following statements would best describe your view of the references and allusions in the poem?

    The ordinary story of running from the London Underground to catch the start of a concert is given weight by the classical allusions.

    The real lovers in the poem get buried under the weight of classical allusions.

    The poem never loses sight of the real world and the real couple on their honeymoon in London.

    Explain your choice.

5. Listen to a reading of the poem and note down all the phrases that stand out for you. Based on these phrases, consider the theme of the poem.
6. 'The love described in the poem is characterised by energy and an erotic charge though not by harmony and togetherness.' Give your response to this assessment of the poem.
7. In the poem there are allusions to the stories of Orpheus and Eurydice, Pan and Syrinx, and Hansel and Gretel. Which of these stories, in your opinion, is most suited to a honeymoon poem? Explain your answer.
8. How would you characterise the relationship described in the last six lines of the poem? Explain your answer.
9. Select one stanza from the poem. Comment on the music and rhythm of that stanza.
10. The London Underground has been a source of poetic inspiration for Heaney. Suggest some of the reasons why you think this is so.
11. From your reading of the poem, which of the following statements best describes the personality of the speaker?

    He is romantic.

    He is stubborn.

    He is determined.

    Explain your choice.

12. Based on your reading of the poem, which of these statements best describes the poem?

    It is a poem about the excitement of new love.

    It is a poem about the impossibility of re-creating the past.

    It is a poem about the difference between dreams and reality.

    Explain your choice.

Taking a closer look

1. Select your favourite image, line, phrase or sequence in the poem and say why you have chosen it.
2. In your view, what is the effect of the word 'die' in line 10?
3. The last two lines of the poem contain the pronoun 'I'. What is the significance of this in the context of the poem?

Imagining

1. Write a short poem of between three and six lines in the voice of the 'You' of the poem, spoken in the 'draughty lamplit station'.
2. Your class is compiling an anthology of love poems. Make a case for including or omitting 'The Underground' from the selection.

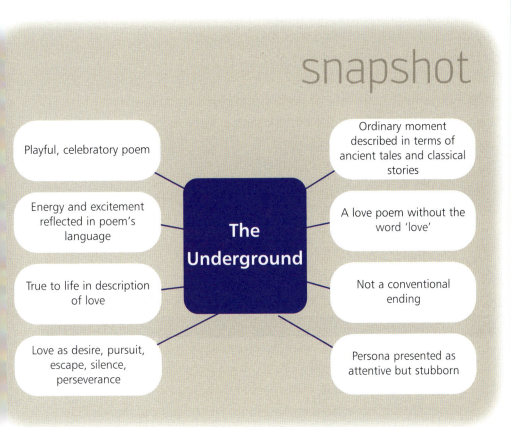

snapshot

- Playful, celebratory poem
- Energy and excitement reflected in poem's language
- True to life in description of love
- Love as desire, pursuit, escape, silence, perseverance

The Underground

- Ordinary moment described in terms of ancient tales and classical stories
- A love poem without the word 'love'
- Not a conventional ending
- Persona presented as attentive but stubborn

The Pitchfork

Of all implements, the pitchfork was the one
That came near to an imagined perfection:
When he tightened his raised hand and aimed high with it,
It felt like a javelin, accurate and light.

So whether he played the warrior or the athlete 5
Or worked in earnest in the chaff and sweat,
He loved its grain of tapering, dark-flecked ash
Grown satiny from its own natural polish.

Riveted steel, turned timber, burnish, grain,
Smoothness, straightness, roundness, length and sheen. 10
Sweat-cured, sharpened, balanced, tested, fitted.
The springiness, the clip and dart of it.

And then when he thought of probes that reached the farthest,
He would see the shaft of a pitchfork sailing past
Evenly, imperturbably through space, 15
Its prongs starlit and absolutely soundless –

But has learned at last to follow that simple lead
Past its own aim, out to an other side
Where perfection – or nearness to it – is imagined
Not in the aiming but the opening hand. 20

Glossary		
	1	*pitchfork*: a long-handled fork with two or three prongs used for tossing hay or other loose material such as dung; the word can also refer to a tuning fork and Heaney plays upon both meanings in the poem
	6	*chaff*: fine-cut hay or straw used as animal feed or bedding; the word can also refer to the dry outer casing of grain used in animal feed – traditionally, the chaff was separated from the grain by tossing the grain into the air

Guidelines

'The Pitchfork' comes from the 1991 collection, *Seeing Things.* It is a collection that has many poems that 'credit marvels'. It is also a collection that celebrates and mourns the poet's father, Patrick Heaney, who died in 1986. Although Heaney's father is not mentioned in 'The Pitchfork' and the poem can be read without reference to him, it is worth recalling that the first poem, 'Digging', in Heaney's first collection, *Death of a Naturalist*, was a celebration of the skill of his father and grandfather in handling farm implements.

Commentary

Connection to poet's father

The opening poem of *Seeing Things* is a translation of the *Aeneid,* Book VI, in which Aeneas asks permission to go to the underworld to meet his dead father. In Heaney's poem 'Crossings', the poet's father is associated with Hermes, the 'god of fair days, stone posts, roads and crossroads' and also a guardian of travellers and a guide to souls journeying to the other world. The poem concludes:

> . . . Flow on, flow on
>
> The journey of the soul with its soul guide
>
> And the mysteries of dealing men with sticks.

The imagery in 'Crossings' resonates with the imagery of the pitchfork sailing soundlessly through space in 'The Pitchfork'. **The pitchfork, like other objects in Heaney's poetry – spade, trowel, hammer, cane, speaks of masculine strength and solidity and is associated with the men in his family as well as with friends and neighbours.** Like the harvest bow, in the poem of the same name, the pitchfork is linked to his father and 'the opening hand' of the last line of the poem may well refer to the poet letting his father go, the flight of the pitchfork through space mirroring the father's soul travelling in an imagined afterlife, a placeless heaven, to borrow a phrase that Heaney has used elsewhere.

Implement of play and work

The pitchfork belongs to the poet's youth and childhood in rural Co. Derry:

> My heyday in the hay was when I was in my mid- to late teens, home from college, enjoying the camaraderie of the neighbours, the freedom of the holiday. And it would always be happening in sunshine, because you couldn't work at hay unless you had good weather.

I loved handling the fork and the rake, their lightness and rightness in the hand, the perfect suitedness to the jobs they had to do. It meant that the work of turning a swathe, for example, was its own reward; angling the shaft and the tines so that the hay turned over like a woven fabric – that was an intrinsically artistic challenge. Tasty work, as they say. Using the pitchfork was like an instrument. So much so that when you clipped and trimmed the head of a ruck, the strike of the fork on the hay made it a kind of tuning fork.

The pitchfork is an implement of both play and work, which combines natural 'dark-flecked ash' (line 7) with the man-made 'Riveted steel' (line 9). Holding it in his hands, the 'he' of the poem can pretend to be a warrior or an athlete or can use it to work 'in earnest' (line 6).

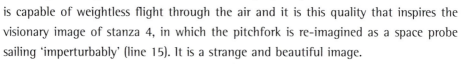

The poet is intent on capturing the physical quality of the implement, its real presence, in a series of brilliant descriptive phrases in stanza 3. In addition to the physical 'thereness' of the thing, the weight and feel of the material object, the pitchfork is capable of weightless flight through the air and it is this quality that inspires the visionary image of stanza 4, in which the pitchfork is re-imagined as a space probe sailing 'imperturbably' (line 15). It is a strange and beautiful image.

Symbol of poetry

Little surprise then that, according to the poem, of all the agricultural implements, the pitchfork 'came near to an imagined perfection' (line 2). The poem is not saying that the pitchfork was perfect but it came closest to what the young poet imagined perfection to be. **In its suitedness to the task, the pitchfork, the tuning fork, works as a symbol for the kind of poetry Heaney wants to write. It is rooted in the earth and in the ordinary things of a farm – hay and dung – yet it is capable of flight through the air, probing the empty spaces with its metal prongs.**

This poem also helps us to understand Heaney's attitude to real working objects and the ordinary lives of the people, including his father and grandfather, who used them. **In mixing the description of ordinary farm work with fanciful visions, the real sits side by side with the marvellous**, like the doctrine of the true presence in Catholicism, where the bread is simply the bread but is also something otherworldly and wonderful – the body and blood of the Saviour – so that the marvellous irradiates from a real object. **The pitchfork belongs to the real world of measurement, weight and balance, but it also belongs to the imagined world of visions, wonders and miracles. It serves as both farm implement and poetic tuning fork.** At the heart of the poem is the desire to translate, to transform.

Moral of final stanza

Interestingly, the poem concludes with a moral, an admission that the 'he' of the poem 'has learned at last' (line 17) to follow the lead of the pitchfork ship as it sails 'past its own aim, out to an other side' (line 18). The lesson is the lesson of acceptance and trust especially in relation to the work of poetry. **The 'opening hand', the phrase that concludes the poem, represents an openness to experience and a willingness to follow the imagination wherever it leads.** In 'The Pitchfork' that willingness leads to a calm floating through space.

Form and language of the poem

The poem is written in four-line stanzas. There is a pleasing sensuousness and lightness to the language that mirrors the lightness of the pitchfork. Indeed, line 12 of the poem ('The springiness, the clip and dart of it') might well serve as a description of the poem itself, with its alliteration, repetitions and balanced vowels.

Thinking about the poem

1. Make a selection of three or four of your favourite words, phrases or images from the poem and say why you chose them.
2. Having read the poem, why, in your opinion, did the pitchfork come near to an imagined perfection for the poet?
3. The third stanza is a brilliant listing of the physical qualities of the pitchfork. Comment on the stanza in detail, noting the patterns of sound that give the stanza its spring and dart.
4. 'In the fourth stanza the idea of the spring and lightness of the pitchfork is matched by the spring and lightness of the poet's imagination.' Comment on the imaginative process at work in this stanza.
5. Consider the meaning of the word 'probes' in line 13. In your view, how important is this word in considering the overall meaning of the poem? Explain your answer.
6. The end of the poem opens out into a wider meaning or moral. How do you interpret the reference to 'the opening hand' (line 20) and the lessons learned in relation to both life and poetry?
7. Having read the poem, why, do you think, does the poet use 'he' rather than 'I' or 'You' in referring to the persona of the poem?
8. 'In choosing to write about the pitchfork, Heaney is celebrating both his farming background and his father. Here as elsewhere in his poetry Heaney makes the ordinary into something extraordinary, visionary and poetic.' Give your response to this view of the poem.

9   'The pitchfork is admired as object, as implement and as symbol.' Give your response to this reading of the poem.
10 'Heaney has the gift of taking objects normally associated with earth and gravity and launching them into poetic flight, with startling effect.' Give your response to this assessment of the poem.
11 Do you like the fact that the meaning of the poem cannot be paraphrased in a simple way? Explain your answer.

Lightenings, viii: 'The Annals Say'

The annals say: when the monks of Clonmacnoise
Were all at prayers inside the oratory
A ship appeared above them in the air.

The anchor dragged along behind so deep
It hooked itself into the altar rails   5
And then, as the big hull rocked to a standstill,

A crewman shinned and grappled down the rope
And struggled to release it. But in vain.
'This man can't bear our life here and will drown,'

The abbot said, 'unless we help him.' So   10
They did, the freed ship sailed, and the man climbed back
Out of the marvellous as he had known it.

Glossary	
title	*Lightenings*: moments of vision, insight or illumination when the actual flows into the visionary
1	*The annals*: the Annals of Clonmacnoise is an early quasi-historical record written by monks in Irish; it survives now only in an English translation dating from the seventeenth century. Typically, annals detail notable events in a given year, such as the death of an important person, eclipses of the sun or similar natural phenomena, as well as miracles and other marvellous happenings

Glossary

1	Clonmacnoise: the monastery of Clonmacnoise, founded in 548 by St Ciaran, was one of the most important monasteries in early Christian Ireland and was renowned as a place of learning where many manuscripts were produced; it flourished until the sixteenth century
2	*oratory*: a small chapel in the monastery
3	*A ship*: in Anglo-Saxon poetry there are references to a ship that brings the souls of the dead from this world to heaven. Heaney's 1987 collection, *The Haw Lantern*, contains a translation from the Anglo-Saxon epic poem *Beowulf*, describing the placing of King Scyld in the ship of death and the launching of the ship on the sea – the journey appears as a magical adventure, whose ultimate destination is unclear and uncertain

Guidelines

The poem comes from the collection *Seeing Things* (1991). It is one of a sequence of forty-eight, twelve-line poems. Most of these poems derive from dreams, visions, old stories or quotations. The sequence is divided into four sections, each with twelve poems. The section from which this poem comes is called 'Lightenings'. **Lightenings are moments of vision, insight or illumination when the actual flows into the visionary.**

Station Island (1984), the collection that preceded *Seeing Things*, was written during a turbulent period in Northern Ireland and conscience and civic responsibilities are recurrent themes. **In comparison to *Station Island*, *Seeing Things* is characterised by a lightness of being and a freeing of the poet's spirit. While the poems in the collection deal with truth, they also celebrate mysteries.**

This poem is based on a story found in the *Annals of Clonmacnoise*. The annalists recorded events without comment or any effort at interpretation. In a matter-of-fact way, the wonders of the world were listed alongside mundane happenings. In some respects, the annalists provide Heaney with an example to follow – an example of how the commonplace and the visionary might exist side by side. Here is Heaney's account of the story:

> The story was unforgettable: it's there in Kenneth Hurlstone Jackson's *A Celtic Miscellany*, but the version I have is a bit different because I misremembered some of the details. In the original, the boat's anchor 'came right down to the floor of

the church', whereas I have it hooking on to the altar rails – somehow it enters miraculously through the roof and the crewman shins down a rope into the sanctuary. That wasn't a deliberate alteration, although I'm sure that the image in the first 'Lightenings' poem of an unroofed wallstead and an unroofed world must have prompted it.

The story has the 'there-you-are and where-are-you' of poetry. A boat in the air, its crewman on the ground, the abbot saying he will drown, the monks assisting him, the man climbing back, the boat sailing on. The narrative rises and sets, the magic casement opens for a moment only and the marvellous occurs in a sequence that sounds entirely like a matter of fact. The crewman is a successful Orpheus, one who goes down and comes back with the prize, which is probably what gives the whole episode its archetypal appeal.

Commentary

'Lightenings, viii' gives an account of an incident in which the monks of Clonmacnoise were disturbed at prayer in their oratory by a ship appearing above them in the air. **The poem brings together contrasting elements: the life of prayer and the life of action; the religious and the secular; a world that is earth-bound and one that floats free. The contrasts are captured in the images of weight, strain, anchorage, release, buoyancy and flight.** Amid these images of restraint and freedom, there is the desire of the imagination to loosen the binds of this world and float away.

Perspective
'Lightenings, viii'' suggests that **the marvellous is ultimately a matter of perspective.** For the sailor, the monks at prayer represent the marvellous, whereas for the monks, it is the ship sailing through the air that is marvellous. The ship itself is symbolic. It hints towards Anglo-Saxon poetry, which contains many references to a ship that brings the souls of the dead from this world to a world elsewhere.

Tolerance and acceptance
The earth-bound experience of the monks and the flight of the sailors are linked: the ship cannot continue its journey without the assistance and permission of the monks. **Read symbolically, the poem suggests that the high-flying imagination is dependent upon commonplace experience. Read in the light of the political situation in Northern Ireland, the abbot, another exemplary figure in Heaney's poetry, preaches a doctrine of tolerance and understanding that translates into an act of genuine friendship:** 'This man can't bear our life here and will drown,' / The abbot said, 'unless we help him' (lines 9–10). The poem, in offering the story of the ship, invites its readers to show the same tolerance and acceptance as that demonstrated by the abbot.

Interestingly, Heaney speaks of 'Lightenings, viii' in the context of the division and contradiction involved in being born in Northern Ireland and **the role of poetry as a vehicle of harmony – as a means of imagining a totally inclusive future**. He quotes with approval the historian Roy Foster's statement that 'the notion that people can reconcile more than one cultural identity may have much to recommend it'. Heaney goes on to say:

> Whatever the possibilities of achieving political harmony at an institutional level, I wanted to affirm that within our individual selves we can reconcile two orders of knowledge which we might call the practical and the poetic; to affirm also that each form of knowledge redresses the other and that the frontier between them is there for the crossing. All of which is implicit in this short poem ['Lightenings, viii'].

Form and tone of the poem

Heaney said this about the form of the poems in the sequence:

> The 12-line form felt arbitrary but it seemed to get me places swiftly. So I went with it, a sort of music of the arbitrary that's unpredictable, and can still up and catch a glimpse of the subject out of the blue. There's a phrase I use, 'make impulse one with wilfulness': the wilfulness is in the 12 lines, the impulse is in the freedom and shimmer and on-the-wingness.

As befits the telling of a traditional tale, the long lines and long vowel sounds create an unhurried, conversational feel to the poem. Here is the voice of the storyteller, claiming an authority that goes beyond his personal authority.

Thinking about the poem

1. Why, do you think, does Heaney begin the poem with 'The annals say'?
2. Identify the contrasting elements brought together in the poem. How in your view do these contrasting elements relate to the theme of the poem?
3. In your view, what does the final line of the poem suggest about the nature of the marvellous? Explain your answer.
4. What, do you think, is the effect created by the long lines employed in the poem?
5. In your opinion, what virtues does the abbot possess? What example does he offer to the poet and to the reader?
6. Writing of the poetry of Patrick Kavanagh, Heaney declared, 'When he writes about places now, they're the luminous spaces within his mind.' How in your view might this statement be applied to 'Lightenings, viii'?

7 Heaney said that the poem was 'a kind of image of poetry itself'. In your view, what image of poetry does it offer?
8 Although concerned with a visionary experience, examine how the verbs used by Heaney root the poem in the physical world.

A Call

'Hold on,' she said, 'I'll just run out and get him.
The weather here's so good, he took the chance
To do a bit of weeding.'
   So I saw him
Down on his hands and knees beside the leek rig,   5
Touching, inspecting, separating one
Stalk from the other, gently pulling up
Everything not tapered, frail and leafless
Pleased to feel each little weed-root break,
But rueful also . . .   10
   Then found myself listening to
The amplified grave ticking of hall clocks
Where the phone lay unattended in a calm
Of mirror glass and sunstruck pendulums . . .

And found myself then thinking: if it were nowadays   15
This is how Death would summon Everyman.

Next thing he spoke and I nearly said I loved him.

Glossary

16 *Everyman*: the central character in a late fifteenth-century English morality play of the same name. Morality plays were a form of religious theatre, usually performed around the feast of Corpus Christi, which encouraged their audience to lead better lives. The opening words of *Everyman* are: 'Here begins a story of how the high Father of Heaven sends Death to summon every man to give an account of their lives in this world.'

Guidelines

'A Call' comes from *The Spirit Level* (1996), the first collection published after Heaney received the Nobel Prize for Literature. It is a book written in the poet's middle age and is concerned with keeping going, with maintaining the spirit level. The title of the collection suggests, on the one hand, a poetry that is airy and free-floating, and on the other, a questioning of that impulse – a measuring of the spirit, a taking stock, a self-examination. The poems in *The Spirit Level* move back and forth between earth-bound realities and airiness. In 'A Call' the lift to the spirit comes from hearing the voice of the beloved after the dreaded thought of the loved one's absence through death.

Commentary

Dramatic opening (lines 1–3)

The poem opens with the dramatic 'Hold on' and we are immediately brought into the middle of things. The voice, 'she', asks the caller, the narrator of the poem, to wait while she runs out to get 'him', the poet's father. The line break after the word 'weeding' (line 3) signals a shift in the poem's perspective.

Visualising the father (lines 4–10)

The narrator imagines his father on his knees weeding. **The poem looks back to 'Digging', the first poem in Heaney's first collection, returning to the father, now no longer digging and handling a spade with vigour, but 'touching, inspecting, separating' (line 6) the plants. The loss of strength and the increasing frailty of the poet's father is caught in the contrast between the vigour of the early poem and the gentle activity of this one.** Indeed, the use of the word 'frail' (line 8) and the image of the root breaking (line 9) seem to describe the poet's father as much as the weeds he pulls. The adjectives 'pleased' (line 9) and 'rueful' (line 10) capture the mixture of pleasure in the work and sorrow at causing a living thing to cease to be. **The activity of weeding serves as a reminder to both the gardener and the narrator of the fragile hold we have on life, the constant threat posed by mortality to the living roots of family.**

Silence and absence (lines 11–14)

The next shift in the poem brings the narrator back to the present, listening to the hall clocks. Skilfully, the poet draws us in. The language of the poem at this point – the short words, with their long vowels and clear consonants – slows everything down so we hold our breath with the narrator and listen as he listens. **The placing of the word 'grave' (line 12) casts a shadow on everything else that follows.** The image of the amplified ticking of the clocks, which is, in effect, an amplified silence, and the image of the mirror glass reflecting nothing but the sunlight, emphasise the absence of the longed-for human presence. It is this emptiness and silence that lies at the heart of the poem.

Death's summons (lines 15–16)

What fills the silence is the thought of the phone call as death's summons. In a brilliant shift, Heaney throws the poem in a new direction. **Now the phone call from a son who is absent (remember the word 'here' in line 2 with the implication that the caller is elsewhere) is re-imagined as a contemporary version of Death summoning Everyman.** The reference to the medieval morality play evokes a world in which there were constant reminders of death and of the judgement of God that would follow it. These death reminders feature not only in literature but also in religious and secular art.

Heaney's gift, here and elsewhere, is to take a thoroughly modern object, in this case a phone, and an equally modern activity, making a phone call, and relate them to the medieval or the ancient world, reminding us that the modern world is not so distant, after all, from that of the Middle Ages. **Like our medieval ancestors we are faced with the mystery of death and the human emotions that surround it.** The phone call made by the poet in the late twentieth century brings to mind the call that will soon summon his beloved father to death. The choice of the word 'thinking' (line 15) is interesting: it is more guarded, more cautious, more distancing than words such as 'feeling' or 'fearing' that might have been chosen.

Final line

The final line of the poem ('Next thing he spoke and I nearly said I loved him.'), separated from the rest of the poem, conveys the relief of the narrator. **The line has a double effect of allowing us to see and hear the words that, we are told, were not spoken. It shows the middle-aged narrator shielding himself from feeling.** Here, as in other poems on the course, the poet notes his own tendency to be guarded, though openness is celebrated in both 'Postscript' and 'The Pitchfork'.

The line also succeeds in suggesting something of the character of the father, a silent man who was stoical in the face of life's vicissitudes. (In his poem 'The Stone Verdict' from the 1987 collection, *The Haw Lantern*, Heaney refers to his father's 'old disdain of sweet talk and excuses' and his 'lifetime's speechlessness'.) The last line reveals the taciturnity the son has inherited from the father. There is a gentle irony in the fact that a poem on the subject of a phone call is filled with silence.

Form of the poem

As in a sonnet, there is a clear progression through the poem marked by the connecting words 'So', 'Then', 'And', 'Next'. This organisation creates the dramatic tension and the relief felt in the final line. The language of the poem has an unfussy naturalness about it that masks the verbal patterns and the weight and balance in the phrasing.

Thinking about the poem

1. How does Heaney succeed in bringing us into the middle of the action in the opening lines of the poem?
2. What, in your view, is the significance of the world 'here' in line 2? How much does it tell us about the back story of the poem?
3. How does the poet picture his father between lines 5 and 10?
4. The word 'rueful' means sorrow or regret. It is a gentle emotion. Why, in your view, is the gardener described as 'rueful' (line 10) and what is the effect of this description?
5. As the poet waits for his father to come to the phone, he hears the ticking of 'hall clocks' (line 12). What, do you think, does the ticking of the hall clocks symbolise in the context of the poem?
6. What are the fears and the tension which govern the third stanza of the poem?
7. 'The final line is marked by feelings of relief and love.' Do you agree with this reading of the line? Explain your answer.
8. Consider the word 'thinking' in line 15. Suggest why, in your opinion, the poet chose to use it.
9. Here are five statements about the poem. Which **two** best describe your view of the poem.
    - It is a poem about a son's love for his father.
    - It is a poem about the sorrow felt at the idea of the death of a loved one.
    - It is a poem about the way the mind works.
    - It is a poem about frailty.
    - It is a poem about communication.

    Explain your choices.
10. Examine the shape of the poem on the page. Do you agree that the movement of thought and action is reflected in this shape? Explain your answer.

Taking a closer look

1. 'The amplified grave ticking of hall clocks' (line 12). Comment on the effect of the word 'grave' and its position and importance in the poem.
2. Look at the final line of the poem. What is your reaction to the statement, 'I nearly said I loved him.' In your view, is the poem stronger or weaker for having no direct declaration of love?
3. A student suggested that the poem could be titled 'The Silence at the End of the Phone'. Would this be a good title? Explain your answer.

Imagining

1. Based on what you know of the speaker from the poem, write the script of a short telephone conversation between the speaker and his father.
2. If you were to make a film, set in modern times, in which death comes to claim a soul, how would you represent death? Explain your answer.

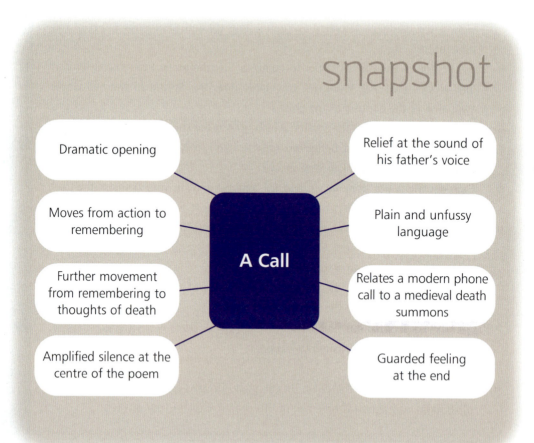

Postscript

And some time make the time to drive out west
Into County Clare, along the Flaggy Shore,
In September or October, when the wind
And the light are working off each other
So that the ocean on one side is wild 5
With foam and glitter, and inland among stones
The surface of a slate-grey lake is lit
By the earthed lightning of a flock of swans,
Their feathers roughed and ruffling, white on white,
Their fully-grown headstrong-looking heads 10
Tucked or cresting or busy underwater.
Useless to think you'll park and capture it
More thoroughly. You are neither here nor there,
A hurry through which known and strange things pass
As big soft buffetings come at the car sideways 15
And catch the heart off guard and blow it open.

Glossary	
title	*Postscript*: something added as an afterthought
2	*Flaggy Shore*: portion of the Atlantic shoreline between New Quay and Finavarra in the Burren region of Co. Clare
11	*Tucked or cresting*: some of the swans have tucked in their heads so that they rest on their bodies; some have their necks extended
15	*buffetings*: gusts of wind that push or knock against the car

Guidelines

'Postscript' is the final poem in the collection *The Spirit Level* (1996). **It is a record of a sightseeing drive in the west of Ireland. It is both a record of the journey and a record of the poetic harvest of that drive.** Reading 'Postscript' is like overhearing the end of a conversation in which someone offers advice to a friend (or a tourist) to take a car journey along the north Clare coast, especially in September or October, and describes the beauty of the journey and the feelings it inspires.

It recalls a real journey made by Heaney and his wife, Marie, and the playwright Brian Friel and his wife, Anne. This is how Heaney describes it:

> (The poem) came from remembering a windy Saturday afternoon when Marie and I drove with Brian and Anne Friel along the south coast of Galway Bay. We had stopped to look at Mount Vernon, Lady Gregory's summer house – still there, facing the waters and the wild; then we drove on into this glorious exultation of air and sea and swans. There are some poems that feel like guarantees of your work to yourself. They leave you with a sensation of having been visited, and this was one of them. It excited me, and yet publishing it in *The Irish Times* was, as much as anything else, a way of sending a holiday postcard – a PS of sorts – to the Friels.

Commentary

Dramatic journey

The journey is a dramatic one, with the wild sea on one side and a lake on which a flock of swans appear like 'earthed lightning' (line 8) on the other. Like a painter, the speaker appreciates the interplay between the light and the wind, and the way the wind ruffles the feather of the swans. The swans complement the landscape as they are powerful with 'fully-grown headstrong-looking heads' (line 10). **The world described in 'Postscript' is a world in flux, caught between wild things and settled things, between things earthed and things in flight.**

Like all journey poems, 'Postscript' can read in a metaphorical way, with the journey symbolising, to some degree, the journey of life and the journey of the poet, especially at those moments when we seem to be 'neither here nor there' (line 13) but exist on the edge of things – just as the car travels in the space between the lake and the sea and is blown off balance. **Therefore, the observation that it is 'Useless to think you'll park and capture it' (line 12) might well be read as the speaker's philosophy that life cannot be controlled or commanded because our hearts can always be blown open by the surprising and unexpected in our lives.** (This is similar to the 'opening hand' at the end of 'The Pitchfork'.) **The swans, 'the earthed lightning' (line 8), can be seen as symbolising poetry itself, the lightning strike that connects earth and sky.** The shore, too, has symbolic resonance. It stands as the boundary between land and ocean, earth and heaven.

World of change

The world of the poem is one of constant change in the interplay between wind and light. Even the months, September and October, are associated with changes, transformations and crossings. The critic Helen Vendler notes that the speaker of the poem remains anonymous so that the kind of elusive and fugitive moment that the poem describes is not one that belongs to the speaker alone but is made available to the reader as well.

Last line

In the last line the speaker seems to be referring to an experience of greater significance than the momentary heart-in-the-mouth experience of wind catching a moving car and blowing it slightly off course. It is a moment of ecstasy or exultation when the heart is surprised and open to experience. **The implication here is that the speaker's heart is often guarded and not open to the world.**

Going west

Interestingly, in introducing the poem at a reading, Heaney spoke of the significance of 'going west':

> The phrase, 'going west', from the First World War, has connotations of mortality, fatality, to 'go west'. And there's a very beautiful cadence in the last story of Joyce's *Dubliners*, 'The Dead', when Joyce says it was time for him to set out on his journey westward. So this is a memory of a vivid journey westward that we had.

Elsewhere, Heaney has spoken of imagining a phase in a writer's life that might involve 'solitary wandering at the edge of the mighty waters'. These remarks might lead you to read the poem in a new light.

Form of the poem

The poem has a sonnet-like structure in the division between description and reflection. The first eleven lines consist of the advice to 'make the time to drive out west' (line 1) and a description of what lies in store. The last five lines are more reflective. In these lines the speaker suggests there is little point in stopping the car in the hope of capturing the experience more fully. The sense of hurrying through the landscape, of being in motion and subject to the gusts of wind that catch the car sideways, is an essential part of the experience. The gusts of wind are not dangerous or threatening; on the contrary, they are 'big soft buffetings' that 'catch the heart off guard and blow it open' (lines 15–16).

Thinking about the poem

1. The poem is rich in description. Select **two** images which you think are particularly effective and explain your choice.
2. Much of the imagery in the poem suggests change and the crossings of boundaries. What is the thematic significance of this imagery?
3. The first eleven lines of description are written as one sentence. What effect is created by this?
4. Although conversational in tone, the poem has a feeling of strength about it. Examine the sounds of the poem and identify what you consider to be 'strong' sounds.
5. There is a sense of being between worlds in the poem. How is this conveyed in the imagery and descriptions of the poem?
6. 'A hurry through which known and strange things pass' (line 14). In the overall context of the poem, what, do you think, is the meaning of this line and what does it say about the nature of the self?
7. 'The speaker of the poem seems to enjoy the feeling of being off balance.' Do you agree with this statement? Explain your answer.
8. The poem reads like the advice of a wise man on how to lead your life. What is the wisdom that the speaker offers?
9. Why, in your opinion, is the poem entitled 'Postscript'? Does it suggest, for example, that the speaker is not claiming any great status for his advice and offers it modestly?
10. 'The poem is written in ordinary language which seems to take flight and lifts off, just as the car seems to lift off as the wind catches it sideways.' Do you agree with this statement? Support your answer by reference to the poem.
11. Just as the phrase 'going west' strikes a chord in Heaney's imagination, the reference to swans on a lake is rich in connotations. What ideas does the image generate in your imagination?
12. The poem recalls a car trip through the Burren. Comment on the symbolism of the car journey and the landscape through which the travellers pass.
13. Some critics have read the poem as a meditation on the fragility of life. Does the poem support this reading? Explain your answer.
14. 'catch the heart off guard' (line 16). What does this phrase tell us about the speaker of the poem?

Tate's Avenue

Not the brown and fawn car rug, that first one
Spread on sand by the sea but breathing land-breaths,
Its vestal folds unfolded, its comfort zone
Edged with a fringe of sepia-coloured wool tails.

Not the one scraggy with crusts and eggshells   5
And olive stones and cheese and salami rinds
Laid out by the torrents of the Guadalquivir
Where we got drunk before the corrida.

Instead, again, it's locked-park Sunday Belfast,
A walled back yard, the dust-bins high and silent   10
As a page is turned, a finger twirls warm hair
And nothing gives on the rug or the ground beneath it.

I lay at my length and felt the lumpy earth,
Keen-sensed more than ever through discomfort,
But never shifted off the plaid square once.   15
When we moved I had your measure and you had mine.

Glossary		
3	*vestal*: virginal or chaste; resembling the Vestal Virgins – a group of virginal priestesses who kept the sacred flame in the temple dedicated to Vesta, goddess of the hearth and the household, in Rome	
4	*sepia-coloured*: brown, like the colour in early photographs	
7	*Guadalquivir*: one of the great rivers of Spain, it flows through Andalusia and the cities of Seville and Cordoba are sited on its banks	
8	*corrida*: bullfight	

Guidelines

'Tate's Avenue' comes from the 2006 collection *District and Circle*. 'District' and 'Circle' are lines on the London Underground system. Two trains on the Circle line were bombed in the attack of 7 July 2005. The blasts killed fourteen people. This attack and that on the World Trade Centre in New York on 9 September 2001 influence some of the poetry in the book. Many of the poems are elegies or are set in the afterlife. Others circle back to the district of Heaney's childhood and cover the same ground explored in his first collection, *Death of a Naturalist*, published forty years earlier.

'Tate's Avenue' comes out of the poet's relationship with his wife, Marie, whom he met in Belfast in 1962 when both were completing their studies and starting out on their teaching careers. **The development of their relationship is traced through describing three rugs used by the young couple that mark different stages in their early life together.**

Commentary

Stanza 1
The first stanza refers to 'the brown and fawn car rug, that first one' (line 1), whose 'vestal folds' (line 3) were opened and 'Spread on sand by the sea' (line 2). The use of the adjective 'vestal' suggests the newness of the rug and the chasteness of the relationship. The rug does not breathe sea air but the tamer 'land-breaths' (line 2). The image of the comfort zone fringed with 'sepia-coloured wool tails' (line 4) suggests neatness and order rather than the wildness of young passion. **The impression is created of a relationship that is formal, careful and virginal.**

Stanza 2
The 'scraggy' rug of the second stanza is more used and more bohemian. There is a feeling of abandonment and intoxication, the intoxication of exotic food and drink, and the danger, passion and sexuality invoked by the Spanish setting: 'by the torrents of the Guadalquivir' (line 7) and 'the corrida' (line 8). **We have moved from the safety and chastity of the first stanza to something more wild, exciting and passionate.** In Spain, the corrida is a symbol of passion, courage and danger. In the rituals of the bullfight, death, bravery and cruelty are dressed as art and beauty. The corrida represents a different way of living and understanding life from that of the culture of Belfast.

Stanza 3

And it is to Belfast that the poem turns in the third stanza. This is 'locked-park Sunday Belfast' (line 9). The image connotes a puritanical culture and an atmosphere of suppression and inhibition, far removed from the wild romanticism of Spain. A prison-like sense of curtailment and drabness is suggested in the description of the 'walled back yard, the dust-bins high and silent' (line 10). It is against this backdrop that the young couple play out a love game or test. The rug is spread on the hard unyielding ground and, intent on reading, nothing is given away by the reader to the one observing. **The phrase 'nothing gives' (line 12) implies a battle of wills in which neither party is willing to concede or yield an inch.** In erotic terms, the phrase suggests that there will be no yielding of the 'soft' feminine to the 'hard' masculine.

From the poem it is clear that **love is influenced by where you come from and where you are.** In the poem 'Tollund', which is set in Jutland in a landscape that looks like the familiar landscape of Co. Derry, the persona describes himself and his beloved standing 'footloose, at home beyond the tribe'. In Belfast, with its locked gates, there is no escape from the tribe. In Belfast, lovemaking becomes a version of 'no surrender' and 'not an inch'.

Stanza 4

In the final stanza the pronouns 'I' and 'You' appear for the first time. Now the 'I' stretches out on the rug and feels 'the lumpy earth' (line 13). He is, we are told, 'Keen-sensed' (line 14). Though uncomfortable, he is not prepared to move, to give up his place on the rug beside her. Instead, he persists and stakes a claim to the territory. When eventually the pair move, we are told they each had the measure of the other. Nothing is said, but things are understood. **No one will be taken for granted in this relationship and both will bring determination and stubbornness to it.**

Interestingly, the final stanza of the poem is firmly rooted on 'the lumpy earth' (line 13). **This is not love as a flight of fantasy, but something altogether more grounded and careful, love as a measuring up, as an equal match.** If the rug itself symbolises love, then love is a patch of ground to be marked out and defended. The fact that nothing external happens and nothing is said seems to intensify the erotic frisson between the young lovers.

Form of the poem

'Tate's Avenue' is written using the same four-line stanza arrangement that is found in 'The Underground'. Like so many of Heaney's poems, it is richly patterned with half-rhymes, assonance, alliteration and consonance and delights in the shape and sound of words.

Thinking about the poem

1. What impression of the rug (and the relationship between the couple who shared it) do you form from stanza 1? What details influence your impression.
2. Comment on the use of the word 'vestal' in line 3.
3. Comment on the setting in stanza 1.
4. The rug described in the second stanza suggests an altogether different phase of the lovers' relationship. What details strike you as particularly revealing?
5. Comment on the effect of the Spanish words and setting in stanza 2.
6. Use **three** carefully considered adjectives to characterise the love described in stanza 2.
7. The third stanza moves the poem to Belfast. What impression of the city does it convey? What are the keys words and phrases that give this impression.
8. 'And nothing gives on the rug or the ground beneath it' (line 12). Would you agree that the relationship between the young lovers reflects an attitude of 'no surrender' and 'not an inch'? Explain your answer.
9. How does the last stanza convey the stubbornness of the persona of the poem?
10. The idea of love that emerges from the poem is one of measuring up and finding each equal to the other. Would you agree with this view?
11. 'It is clear from "Tate's Avenue" that love and the way lovers behave are related to where the lovers are.' Comment on this interpretation of the poem.
12. Examine one stanza and note how Heaney uses alliteration, consonance and assonance to create the music of the poem.

Exam-Style Questions

1. 'In Heaney's poetry we encounter contrasting female and male presences in a world that is, by turns, familiar and reassuring, and violent and unnerving.' Give your view of this assessment of Heaney's poetry.
2. 'Heaney's poetry is constantly engaged in finding images for the processes of the imagination and for poetry itself.' Discuss.
3. Do you agree that Heaney's poetry is rich in imagery and metaphor, expressed in a sensuous language? Support your point of view by reference to the poems you have studied.
4. Do you agree that Heaney's poetry seeks to find a balance between the demands of his social conscience, as a northern nationalist, and the freedom of his imagination?

5. 'I no longer wanted a door into the dark, I wanted a door into the light.' Discuss Heaney's poetry in terms of poems of darkness and poems of light.

6. Heaney's poetry is populated with exemplary figures from whom he learns. Give examples of three figures from the poems you have studied, outlining their importance to the poet.

7. Do you agree with the view that history and memory – personal, familial, racial – lie at the heart of Heaney's poetry? Support your opinion with references from the poems by Heaney that you have studied.

8. 'Many of Heaney's poems explore relationships: relationships of love; relationships of conflict; the relationship between the real and the imagined; and the relationship between the past and the present.' Discuss this view of Heaney's poetry in the light of the poems you have studied on your course.

9. The citation for his Nobel Prize refers to 'an authorship filled with lyrical beauty and ethical depth which brings out the miracle of the ordinary day and the living past'. Point to examples of Heaney's poetry where these qualities are to be found. Explain your choices.

10. 'What I find appealing in the poetry of Seamus Heaney.' Write an essay in which you outline the appeal that Heaney's poetry has for you.

    Some of the following points might be included:
    - His skill as a poet.
    - The themes – personal, familial and national.
    - The attachment to his home place.
    - The careful attention he pays to the actual and his delight in the visionary and marvellous.
    - The memorable lines and images that stay with you.

11. Write an introduction to the poetry of Heaney for readers new to his work.
    Your introduction should cover:
    - The themes and concerns of his poetry.
    - His use of language and your response to it.

    Some of the following might also be included:
    - The importance of exemplary figures in his poetry.
    - The marriage poems and the relationship they describe.
    - The metaphors for poetry.
    - The question of the response to the pressure of public events.
    - The relationship between the real and the imaginary.

12 Heaney is one of the most popular poets alive today. Why is this so?
    You could consider some of the following points in your answer:

    - Although often dealing with his home place his poetry has universal appeal.
    - His detailed descriptions of the real flow into flights of imagination.
    - His personality is revealed in the poems.
    - His celebration of love and family.
    - His courage in speaking as a representative of his people.
    - His delight in the sounds and shapes of words.
    - The hopefulness of his poetry.

Sample Essay

'Seamus Heaney's poetry moves between earth-bound realities and flights of poetic fantasy.' Discuss this view of Heaney's poetry, supporting your answer with references to the poems by Heaney on your course.

I think that Seamus Heaney's poetry does move between 'earth-bound realities' and 'flights of poetic fantasy'. However, it can be argued that it is only in his later writing that his poetry breaks free of earth-bound realities and takes flight.

[Introductory paragraph addresses the task straightaway]

Heaney's father farmed fifty acres in County Derry and also worked as a cattle dealer. He was a man of the earth, and the earth and the soil are central to Seamus Heaney's poetry. After primary school, Heaney won a scholarship to St Columb's College in Derry and there he came to love English literature and the literature of the Greeks and Romans. The mixture of a love of ordinary things and a love of literature is reflected in his poetry, where he often celebrates the life he knew as a child.

[A brief note on the poet's background helps make the case]

Take the example of his early poem 'The Forge'. What could be more real and down to earth than a detailed description of the local forge with its 'old axles and iron hoops rusting', where 'real iron' is beaten out? The young poet sees music in the solid objects and celebrates the music of ordinary life when he writes of 'the hammered anvil's short-pitched ring'. The poem is a celebration of a traditional craft and is written in a traditional form – the sonnet. The figure of the blacksmith in his leather apron, with 'hairs in his nose' is as earth-bound as they come. The language of the poem, with its alliteration and consonant sounds, suits the description of the blacksmith as a strong, masculine figure: 'Then grunts and goes in, with a slam and a flick'.

[Introduces first poem to be discussed; keeps the terms of the question in focus]

For the poet, the blacksmith's anvil becomes an altar, a magical object 'Horned as a unicorn'. Upon this altar the blacksmith beats out iron and 'expends himself in shape and music'. In other words, the blacksmith symbolises the poet, who takes the raw material of life and beats it into the shape and music of poetry. The door of the forge – 'a door into the dark' – symbolises the young poet entering through the door of words into the darkness of the imagination. At this early stage of his career, Heaney places his faith in describing real things in carefully shaped and musical poems. He is happy to stay earth-bound.

[In concluding the discussion of this poem, the answer goes back to the terms of the question]

Another early earth-bound poem is 'Bogland', which makes the association between the earth and the imagination. When Heaney was at school, the skeleton of an elk had been taken out of the bog near his home. This skeleton and the stories he had been told of butter buried for 'more than a hundred years', made him think of the bog as the memory of the landscape. To recover the past you dig 'inwards and downwards'. The last line of the poem, 'The wet centre is bottomless', implies that the young poet realises that just as there is no bottom to the bog, there is no bottom to the well of imagination, especially when the imagination explores the past of his childhood and his community. The final line of the poem suggests a poetry rooted in the soil, though beaten into shape by the imagination. What greater contrast could there be between poetry imagined as digging into the soil and poetry imagined as taking flight?

[Throughout the answer, short quotations are integrated into the argument]

'Mossbawn: Two Poems in Dedication: (1) Sunlight' is another poem dealing with the real. Like an artist painting a life portrait, Heaney portrays a domestic scene and places his much-loved aunt in the centre. The portrait is warm and affectionate, filled with images of light and heat, and while the beautiful last stanza is written with love, the image is of a love half-buried:

> And here is love
>
> like a tinsmith's scoop
>
> sunk past its gleam
>
> in the meal-bin.

The scoop is sunk and stuck in the meal-bin, just as, it can be argued, Heaney's imagination is stuck in the real.

'The Pitchfork' is a poem that recalls the poet's youth in Co. Derry, where he learned to handle a pitchfork. In many ways it is a poem that goes back to 'The Forge' in its celebration of a farm implement made of beaten metal and wood. To the young poet, the pitchfork was an implement of work and play. Holding it, he could imagine himself as a warrior or an athlete:

> When he tightened his raised hand and aimed high with it,
>
> It felt like a javelin, accurate and light.

The poem sets out to capture the physical quality of the pitchfork in a series of descriptive words and phrases:

> Sweat-cured, sharpened, balanced, tested, fitted.
>
> The springiness, the clip and dart of it.

However, the centre of the poem is inspired by the image of the pitchfork in flight through the air. On this occasion the imagination does not stay rooted in the earth but sails beyond it into space. The pitchfork becomes a space probe sailing:

> Evenly, imperturbably through space,
>
> Its prongs starlit and absolutely soundless –

It is a beautiful and striking image. Here we can see the poet's imagination take flight and leave the earth-bound realities behind. In the poem the visionary and the marvellous take over from the real and the earth-bound. At the end of the poem, Heaney seems to offer himself some advice on how his poetry might develop: he has to let the poem travel wherever it is bound. The 'opening hand' that concludes the poem suggests a willingness to follow the imagination where it leads. In this poem it leads far out into space on a soundless flight through starlight.

> *[Having established one line of argument, the answer moves on to set out a different line]*

Another poem celebrating the imagination in flight is 'Lightenings, viii: 'The Annals Say''. The poem comes from a collection entitled *Seeing Things*. The title hints at the theme of visions and marvels that lie at the heart of 'Lightenings, viii'. It is a poem written in a light-hearted way and the lightness allows the poem and the imagination to rise and take flight. The poem gives an account of an incident recorded in the *Annals of Clonmacnoise* in which the monks were disturbed at prayer by a ship sailing through the air above their heads. Heaney tells the story in a matter-of-fact way, describing how 'The anchor . . . hooked itself into the altar rails'. A crewman 'shinned and grappled down the rope' and the abbot ordered the monks to assist the sailor. The ship was released:

> and the man climbed back
>
> Out of the marvellous as he had known it.

The poem brings together a world that is earth-bound and one that floats free. The contrast between these two worlds is captured in the images of anchorage and of release.

[The fifth and final poem supports the new line of argument.]

The earth-bound monks and the flying sailors are linked: the ship cannot continue its journey without the assistance of the monks. Reading the poem as a metaphor for Heaney's poetry, we could say that the poem suggests that high-flying imagination is dependent upon earth-bound realities. However, these realities do not weigh the imagination down and the poem delights in the wonder quality of the story it tells.

In 'The Annals Say' the imagination takes flight, though it does not lose sight of the earth. The same may be said of all Heaney's poetry. There are dizzying moments of flight and lightness but the earth remains always in view.

[The concluding comments sum up the argument made throughout the essay]

New Discovery Poetry Anthology

snapshot

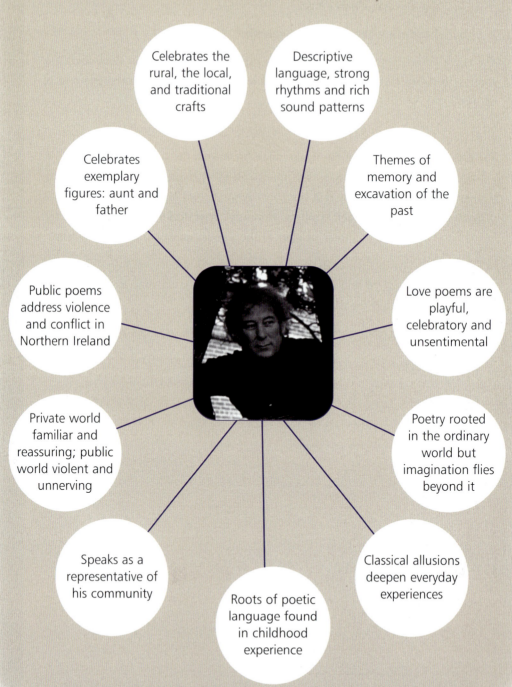

- Celebrates the rural, the local, and traditional crafts
- Descriptive language, strong rhythms and rich sound patterns
- Celebrates exemplary figures: aunt and father
- Themes of memory and excavation of the past
- Public poems address violence and conflict in Northern Ireland
- Love poems are playful, celebratory and unsentimental
- Private world familiar and reassuring; public world violent and unnerving
- Poetry rooted in the ordinary world but imagination flies beyond it
- Speaks as a representative of his community
- Classical allusions deepen everyday experiences
- Roots of poetic language found in childhood experience

Thomas Kinsella

b. 1928

THINKING OF MR D.*
DICK KING
CHRYSALIDES
MIRROR IN FEBRUARY*
HEN WOMAN
TEAR
HIS FATHER'S HANDS
from SETTINGS: MODEL SCHOOL, INCHICORE
from THE FAMILIAR: VII
from GLENMACNASS: VI LITTLEBODY
from BELIEF AND UNBELIEF: ECHO

Biography

Thomas Kinsella was born on 4 May 1928 in the Inchicore/Kilmainham area of Dublin. The eldest child of John and Agnes Kinsella, he was educated at the Inchicore Model School and the Christian Brothers' Secondary School on North Richmond Street. In 1946 he was awarded a scholarship to study at University College Dublin, but when he left to join the Irish civil service as a junior executive officer he began to study as a night student.

It was around this time that he started to write, contributing poems and reviews to student magazines and to the Irish language publication *Comhar*. In 1951 he moved to the Department of Finance as an administrative officer, but his primary interest was in literature and cultural matters.

In 1955 Kinsella married Eleanor Walsh. The couple have three children. His wife's ill-health at this period meant that Kinsella had to juggle his domestic responsibilities with an increasingly successful poetic career as well as his work in the Department of Finance.

Literary career

Poems, his first collection, appeared in 1956. However, it was *Another September* (1958) that brought him to wider attention as it won the Guinness Poetry Award. *Moralities* appeared in 1960, followed by *Downstream* in 1962. In 1965 an invitation to be writer-in-residence at Southern Illinois University at Carbondale allowed him to resign from the civil service to pursue a career in literature.

In 1970 he became a professor of English at Temple University, Philadelphia. The family lived in the United States until 1971 when they moved back to Dublin to live in the city centre at Percy Place. Kinsella's link with Temple University was strengthened in 1975 when he established a programme in Irish studies. This allowed him to divide his academic year between Philadelphia and Dublin. *Nightwalker and Other Poems* was published in 1968. *New Poems* appeared in 1973, as well as *Selected Poems 1956–68*.

In 1972 Kinsella established the Peppercanister Press. Named after the nickname of a local church, it operates from Kinsella's home and publishes his poems (with the collaboration since 1981 of John F. Deane's Dedalus Press).

Throughout his career Kinsella has worked to recover the lost tradition of Gaelic literature, through translations, including the great Irish epic the *Táin Bó Cúailgne* (1969) and *An Duanaire: Poetry of the Dispossessed 1600–1900* (1981).

In 1988 Kinsella and his wife moved from Dublin to Co. Wicklow where he still lives. In 1990 he retired from Temple University and the Irish studies programme; however, he still spends part of the year in Philadelphia. His *Collected Poems* appeared in 2001. Kinsella has won numerous awards and honours, including Guggenheim Fellowships, the Denis Devlin Memorial Award, the Irish Arts Council Triennial Book Awards and honorary doctorates from the University of Turin and the National University of Ireland.

Social and Cultural Context

The Ireland into which Kinsella was born and in which he was educated was economically depressed. He grew up during a time of high unemployment and emigration. His family background was urban working class. His father and his grandfather worked in Guinness's brewery and the extended family lived in the Inchicore/Kilmainham area of Dublin.

Secondary and third-level education was available only to those who could afford it. Scholarships enabled the young Kinsella to go to secondary school and to enter UCD, although he soon left to take up a position in the Irish civil service.

The influence of the Catholic Church was strong: he has said that its influence on his upbringing was 'so pervasive that it hardly counted as an influence at all; it was a reality like oxygen'.

Culturally speaking Ireland was in the doldrums during the early 1950s. The two most influential poets of the time were Patrick Kavanagh and Austin Clarke. Poets were dependent upon British companies to publish their work and on British critics to review it. Kinsella's initial association with Liam Miller and the Dolmen Press (founded in 1951) succeeded in breaking Irish writers' dependence upon British publishing houses.

Poetic influences

Kinsella has acknowledged that his early influences included the poets Ezra Pound, W. H. Auden and W. B. Yeats. Although he accepted the status of Yeats as a major Irish poet, and recognised the achievements of Kavanagh and of Clarke, he was not content to confine himself to only Irish concerns in his work. His earlier poems do not deal with Irish social or cultural issues to any great extent. However, he later referred to his earlier work as full of 'pointless elegance' in which he had failed to find his true voice as a poet.

As his career developed he began to confront many of the political issues of his day. Later still he made more use of personal material, exploring family relationships in recognisable settings in Ireland and especially in his native city, Dublin.

For Kinsella, poetry is a form of responsible reaction to the predicament one finds oneself in. When asked in an interview with the critic Donatella Abbate Badin, 'Why do you write?', he replied, 'To try to understand: to make sense. To preserve what I can and give it a longer hold on life.' These statements may enable us to understand the personal, social and cultural values behind a remarkable body of work.

Politics

Kinsella worked in the Department of Finance and was for a time secretary to T. K. Whitaker, who was instrumental in formulating the Irish government's Programme for Economic Development in 1958. Although inevitably involved in the programme, Kinsella saw the downside of emphasising material expansion to the detriment of any other.

He reacted negatively to the greed and what he saw as empty nationalism of Irish society as it developed in the 1960s. In 'Nightwalker' and in the 'Peppercanister One Fond Embrace' he satirised such attitudes and personalities in often savage verse. This disapproval was echoed in a practical way by his involvement in the protests concerning the destruction of the remains of Viking settlements in Dublin's Wood Quay in 1978. After a futile attempt to save the site for archaeological development, Kinsella and others occupied the site in a peaceful protest that came to no avail.

Kinsella was also involved in controversy following the publication of 'The Butcher's Dozen' in 1972. Although he had never espoused the strong nationalist views he encountered at school, he was outraged at the Widgery report on the killings of Bloody Sunday in Derry in January 1972. This was one of the most horrific events of the Northern Ireland conflict known as the Troubles. The Widgery report almost entirely exonerated the British paratroop regiment from culpability for the death of thirteen civilians on that day. Kinsella's nationalist outrage alienated many readers, especially in England. Some critics also reacted negatively, not only to his political views but also to what they saw as the biased nature of their expression.

Literature in Irish

Kinsella's achievement in promoting and fostering the study of Irish literature is well recognised. He has established Irish studies programmes in universities in the United States. In his editing of *The Oxford Book of Irish Verse* (1986) he brought many Irish poems (in translation) to a wider audience. In 1969 he published his translation of the

Irish epic the *Táin Bó Cúailgne*, an enormous task that had taken him fifteen years. He saw it as an 'act of responsibility . . . it's ours, Irish, and it deserved a new currency'. For him, it was a way of placing himself within an Irish poetic tradition.

In an interview in 1993 he spoke of the 'dual tradition' in Irish poetry, saying that he came to recognise that it is not necessary to abandon one aspect of Ireland's literature in order to deal with the other. He went on to say: 'We have a dead language with a powerful literature and a colonial language with a powerful literature. The combination is an extremely rich one.' In 1995 he published *The Dual Tradition*, in which he elaborated on these views.

Theories of Carl Jung

Kinsella has made fruitful use of his study of the theories of Carl Jung (1875–1961), one of the most influential of twentieth-century psychologists. For Jung, psychological well-being lay in a person's search for 'individuation', by which he meant personal growth and development. This involved confronting one's unconscious thoughts and feelings. Childhood experiences were crucial to adult development, in his view.

In the 1970s **Kinsella's exploration of his childhood memories and his social origins led to more personal and increasingly complex poems. This change of direction caused some readers to see his poems as challenging.** The poet Denis O'Driscoll has spoken of the 'lonely and courageous route' that Kinsella took as a poet when he abandoned lyric elegance and traditional form (rhyme, self-contained stanzas, for example) for a more self-focused and complex approach. These poems allow the reader to gain more of a sense of Kinsella's background and to enter more intimately into his experience.

A 'Dublin' poet

Kinsella has been called the 'quintessential Dublin poet'. Memories of his childhood in Dublin have been expressed in poems that meticulously detail his surroundings. Dublin is observed and celebrated in his work. Places are named and recognised – James's Street, Basin Lane, Inchicore.

The prestigious honour of Freedom of the City was awarded to him in 2007 (as well as to his former collaborator, artist Louis le Brocquy) in recognition of their 'enormous contribution to the city, in art and literature'. In his address to Dublin City Council as he accepted the award, Kinsella spoke of his native city: 'Dublin gave many important things their first shape and content for me. I learned to look at the world through the rich reality of the inner city – a living history . . . '.

Timeline

1928	Born on 4 May in Dublin
1934–46	Educated at Inchicore Model School and O'Connell CBS
1946	Joins Irish civil service as junior executive officer
1951	Begins association with Liam Miller, Dolmen Press
1955	Marries Eleanor Walsh
1956	Publishes first collection, *Poems*
1958	*Another September* wins Guinness Poetry Award
1965	Moves to Southern Illinois University as writer-in-residence
1969	Dolmen Press publishes *Táin Bó Cúailgne*
1971	Moves back to Dublin
1972	Establishes Peppercanister Press
1973	*Selected Poems 1956–68* appears
1975	Establishes Irish studies programme in Dublin
2001	Publishes *Collected Poems*
2007	Dublin City Council awards him Freedom of the City

Thinking of Mr D.

A man still light of foot, but ageing, took
An hour to drink his glass, his quiet tongue
Danced to such cheerful slander.

He sipped and swallowed with a scathing smile,
Tapping a polished toe.   5
His sober nod withheld assent.

When he died I saw him twice.
Once as he used retire
On one last murmured stabbing little tale
From the right company, tucking in his scarf.   10

And once down by the river, under wharf-
Lamps that plunged him in and out of light,
A priestlike figure turning, wolfish-slim,
Quickly aside from pain, in a bodily plight,
To note the oiled reflections chime and swim.   15

Glossary	
title	*Mr D.*: may be the poet Austin Clarke (see Guidelines)
3	*slander*: gossip or false reports
4	*scathing*: withering, scorching

Guidelines

This poem is from the collection *Another September* (1958). It is one of Kinsella's 'portrait' poems, in which he describes both ordinary and well-known people. **According to Donatella Abbate Badin, 'Thinking of Mr D.' is a portrait of the poet Austin Clarke, whom Kinsella admired but whom he considered to have been isolated as a poet in 1950s literary Dublin.**

Kinsella wrote about Clarke in similar terms in another poem, 'Brothers in the Craft':

> Again and again, in the Fifties, 'we' attended
> Austin Clarke. He murmured in mild malice
> and directed his knife-glance curiously among us.

Even though he portrays him as somewhat detached and isolated in literary circles, Kinsella is on record as admiring Clarke as a poet. In fact he edited Clarke's *Collected Poems* after the poet's death in 1974.

It has also been suggested that Kinsella had in mind the Italian poet Dante Alighieri as the subject of this portrait. A further interpretation has been that it is a portrait of Stephen Dedalus, the hero of James Joyce's novel *A Portrait of the Artist as a Young Man*, in his later years. However, the poem can be appreciated as a portrait of a complex individual in a literary context, without attempting to make too close a connection with an actual literary character.

Commentary

Stanzas 1 and 2

The poem describes 'Mr D.' as an ageing man who is nevertheless still lively – 'light of foot' (line 1) – and who enjoys being in company, but who remains somewhat detached from his surroundings and his companions. Polite and cheerful, he nonetheless falls short of engaging wholeheartedly in the conversations around him: 'his sober nod withheld assent' (line 6). Yet he is also capable of enjoying – perhaps even instigating – gossip, as suggested by the image of him as he drank, accompanied with a 'scathing smile' and 'tapping a polished toe' (lines 4 and 5).

Stanza 3

After the death of 'Mr D.' the speaker has two further lasting memories of him. One was the way in which he would take his leave of the company 'On one last murmured stabbing little tale' (line 9). Might he himself have told the story? The poem is ambiguous about this, but it adds to the portrait of him as a somewhat cynical man who may have taken pleasure in the downfall of others. There is a sarcastic tone in the phrase 'the right company' (line 10) that depicts neither 'Mr D.' nor his followers in a good light. His gesture as he leaves, 'tucking in his scarf' (line 10), after perhaps ruining someone's reputation, suggests someone who is indifferent. This is not an attractive aspect of the man.

Stanza 4

A second image of 'Mr D.', in the final stanza, is more sympathetic. In remembering 'Mr D.' as a solitary figure, walking down by the river, the speaker shows him to be lonely and sensitive. The adjectives Kinsella uses to describe him hint at the contradictions in his character. 'Priestlike' suggests someone prepared to sacrifice himself for his art, as well as someone who is set apart from others, but 'wolfish' suggests a predatory person, perhaps selfish or even cruel (line 13).

Kinsella also depicts 'Mr D.' as someone who never confronted sorrow or pain directly: he is seen as 'turning . . . quickly aside from pain.' (lines 13–14). What sort of 'pain' (physical or mental) is left unexplored. Yet 'Mr D.' still had the poet's urge to perceive and record his surroundings, the light reflected on the river and the sound of the water: 'the oiled reflections' that 'chime and swim' (line 15). **These contradictory aspects of his personality leave the reader with a sense of a complex, real person.**

'Mr D.' and poetry

Throughout the poem Kinsella has hinted at the poetic values of 'Mr D.'. There are subtle puns in the image of him as 'light of foot' (line 1) and 'tapping a polished toe' (line 5), which relate to poetic metre (feet) and rhythm, as well as his tendency to note the 'oiled reflections' that 'chime' (line 15). (One of the main characteristics of Austin Clarke's poems, arguably, was its musicality.) These are clearly poetic qualities that Kinsella admires. But there may also be an indication that Kinsella saw him as a poet who never truly confronted ugliness or pain in his work.

Another aspect of 'Mr D.'s' career that Kinsella does not fully admire was his role in the literary circle described in the poem. Kinsella recognises his status within the group. His detachment from it at times is also in his favour, although there is a suggestion that he plays a part in spreading literary gossip. He comes across as cynical and indifferent.

Most portrait poems indirectly reveal the values of the poet who writes them. In 'Mr D.' Kinsella conveys his own suspicion of the 'right company' (line 10), the literary group that 'Mr D.' belonged to. He sees it as negative and damaging.

It is in the final lines, however, that Kinsella's poetic values are seen most clearly. He sees that surface beauty and polish are not enough for poetry. It must not avoid difficult themes and unpleasant experiences.

Thinking about the poem

1. From the evidence of the poem, what sort of man was 'Mr D.'?
2. In your view, does the poet like 'Mr D.'?
3. Which detail of 'Mr D.'s' behaviour best conveys his personality to the reader, in your opinion?
4. From the following phrases choose the one which, in your opinion, best reveals the poet's attitude towards the literary group that 'Mr D.' belongs to:

    He thinks they are cruel and unfeeling.

    He thinks they are interesting.

    He dislikes them intensely.

    Explain your choice.
5. Would you agree that the poem presents 'Mr D.' as a complex, real person? Give reasons for your answer.
6. Choose **two** images from the poem that appeal to you and give reasons for your choice.
7. Does the poem suggest anything to you about Kinsella's views on the role of a poet in society? Would he like to be like 'Mr D.'? Explain your answer.

Taking a closer look

1. 'A man still light of foot' (line 1). 'Tapping a polished toe' (line 5). Comment on the effectiveness of these phrases in describing 'Mr D.'.
2. Kinsella uses the adjectives 'priestlike' and 'wolfish' about 'Mr D.' (line 13). Say what these words suggest to you.

Imagining

1. Imagine that you are 'Mr D.'. Write a short entry in your diary in which you give your honest opinion of the 'right company' you meet.
2. You are one of the members of the literary group described in the poem. Write out (in dialogue form) a conversation you have with another member, or with 'Mr D.'. Base your conversation on the poem.

snapshot

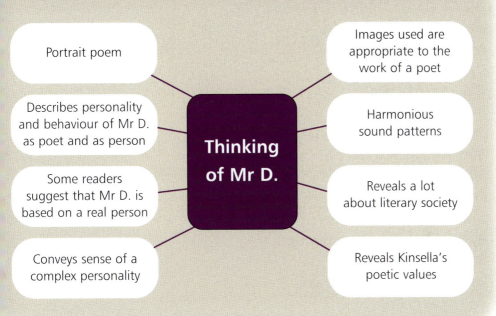

Thinking of Mr D.
- Portrait poem
- Describes personality and behaviour of Mr D. as poet and as person
- Some readers suggest that Mr D. is based on a real person
- Conveys sense of a complex personality
- Images used are appropriate to the work of a poet
- Harmonious sound patterns
- Reveals a lot about literary society
- Reveals Kinsella's poetic values

Dick King

In your ghost, Dick King, in your phantom vowels I read
That death roves our memories igniting
Love. Kind plague, low voice in a stubbled throat,
You haunt with the taint of age and of vanished good,
Fouling my thought with losses.   5

Clearly now I remember rain on the cobbles,
Ripples in the iron trough, and the horses' dipped
Faces under the Fountain in James's Street,
When I sheltered my nine years against your buttons
And your own dread years were to come: 10

And your voice, in a pause of softness, named the dead,
Hushed as though the city had died by fire,
Bemused, discovering . . . discovering
A gate to enter temperate ghosthood by;
And I squeezed your fingers till you found again   15
My hand hidden in yours.

I squeeze your fingers:

Dick King was an upright man.
Sixty years he trod
The dull stations underfoot.   20
Fifteen he lies with God.

By the salt seaboard he grew up
But left its rock and rain
To bring a dying language east
And dwell in Basin Lane.   25

By the Southern Railway he increased:
His second soul was born
In the clangour of the iron sheds,
The hush of the late horn.

An invalid he took to wife.   30
She prayed her life away;
Her whisper filled the whitewashed yard
Till her dying day.

And season in, season out,
He made his wintry bed.   35
He took the path to the turnstile
Morning and night till he was dead.

He clasped his hands in a Union ward
To hear St James's bell.
I searched his eyes though I was young,   40
The last to wish him well.

Glossary

2	*igniting*: setting alight
11	*named the dead*: may be the patriots who had died in the area (e.g. Robert Emmet in 1803)
13	*Bemused*: confused or lost in thought
22	*salt seaboard*: Dick King had been born in the west of Ireland
24	*dying language*: Dick King was an Irish speaker
25	*Basin Lane*: a street near the Guinness Brewery in Dublin
26	*Southern Railway*: the Great Southern Railway had works at Inchicore
38	*Union ward*: the workhouse, later a hospital
39	*St James's bell*: the bell of the foundry in James's Street (or of St James's Church)

Guidelines

'Dick King' is from the collection *Downstream* (1962). In *A Dublin Documentary* (2006) Kinsella tells us that Dick King was an elderly neighbour who lived in a nearby cottage with his wife:

> He seemed to be always there: a friend of the family, a protector of my unformed feelings . . . I wrote two poems for him, in memory of his importance during those early years. Neither of the poems achieved completeness, but their parts came together.

In this spirit of love and friendship Kinsella addresses Dick King's ghost and remembers incidents from his childhood.

Commentary

'Dick King' links two incomplete poems, written at different times, to form one poem.

Stanzas 1–4

From the beginning there is a sense of loss in the poem. Thinking of Dick King reminds Kinsella of how time has passed. He speaks directly to the man's ghost, calling it 'Kind plague' (line 3) as it seems to 'haunt' him with good memories (line 4), and yet leaves him with a terrible sense of loss (line 5).

Images of his childhood come into his mind. Their Dublin setting – rain on the cobblestones, the horses drinking from the fountain in James's Street – conjure up memories of his childish trust in the elderly man, which he expresses in the lovely image of himself as he 'sheltered my nine years against your buttons' (line 9). Dick King's own 'dread years' were yet 'to come' (line 10).

Dick King had been a link with previous generations as he 'named the dead' (line 11), keeping alive the memory of others who had died, perhaps neighbours and relatives, or even the patriot dead of the past.

Now the poet pays tribute to him. As once, as a nine-year-old boy, he had squeezed King's fingers in a gesture of affection, now he metaphorically does so again by tenderly recalling the details of the man's history.

Stanzas 5–10

The second part of the poem takes on a more jaunty rhythm – like that of a ballad – as it tells Dick King's story. An Irish speaker from the west of Ireland (he brought 'a dying language east', line 24), he had spent sixty years working for the Great Southern Railway at Inchicore. Kinsella portrays him as an uncomplaining, hard-working man, married to a pious wife who suffered from ill health. His admiration for the man is summed up in the compliment he pays him: 'Dick King was an upright man' (line 18).

Nonetheless, the poem also hints at the tragedy of Dick King's life, its unending routine and hardship. The phrase 'he made his wintry bed' (line 35) has connotations of the well-known expression 'he made his bed so he'll have to lie in it' – a rather harsh view of life, but one that is echoed in Kinsella's comment that he endured his routine 'season in, season out' (line 34).

Sadly, Dick King ended his days in what he knew as a workhouse, the Union on James's Street in Dublin now a hospital. These were the 'dread years' of line 10. But the tone of the final two lines softens the harsh picture to some extent, as Kinsella remembers how as a young boy he 'searched his eyes', wishing him, then as now, nothing but the best.

Elegy

The poem is an elegy (a poem lamenting a dead person). Kinsella mourns Dick King's loss as symbolic of 'vanished good' (line 4), his own childhood relationships. He praises him throughout, directly and indirectly. He finds some consolation in keeping Dick King's memory alive. **He has become part of the 'temperate ghosthood' (line 14) of the past, a symbol of continuity between past and present.**

Thinking about the poem

1. What is the dominant feeling in this poem: love, sorrow or fear? Perhaps you might suggest another emotion?
2. What sort of person was Dick King, as Kinsella suggests in the poem?
3. How would you describe the relationship Kinsella had with the dead man?
4. Would you agree that the poem succeeds in evoking a way of life that is gone? Explain your view.
5. Choose **three** images that appeal to you from the poem and explain your choice.
6. How does Kinsella use sound to convey meaning in the poem (e.g. onomatopoeia, rhyme, alliteration, repetition)? Give examples.
7. Explore the pattern of images of language throughout the poem (e.g. vowels, voice, named). How do they contribute to the meaning of the poem?
8. An elegy is a poem written to commemorate someone who has died. Is 'Dick King' effective as an elegy? Give reasons for your view.
9. Do you think that the two parts of the poem blend successfully? Support your view by reference to the poem.
10. 'Dick King' has been called 'a wonderful Dublin poem'. Do you agree with this view? Support your answer by reference to the poem.

Chrysalides

Our last free summer we mooned about at odd hours
Pedalling slowly through country towns, stopping to eat
Chocolate and fruit, tracing our vagaries on the map.

At night we watched in the barn, to the lurch of melodeon music,
The crunching boots of countrymen – huge and weightless   5
As their shadows – twirling and leaping over the yellow concrete.

Sleeping too little or too much, we awoke at noon
And were received with womanly mockery into the kitchen,
Like calves poking our faces in with enormous hunger.

Daily we strapped our saddlebags and went to experience 10
A tolerance we shall never know again, confusing
For the last time, for example, the licit and the familiar.

Our instincts blurred with change; a strange wakefulness
Sapped our energies and dulled our slow–beating hearts
To the extremes of feeling – insensitive alike 15

To the unique succession of our youthful midnights,
When by a window ablaze softly with the virgin moon
Dry scones and jugs of milk awaited us in the dark,

Or to lasting horror, a wedding flight of ants
Spawning to its death, a mute perspiration 20
Glistening like drops of copper, agonised, in our path

Glossary

title	*Chrysalides*:	plural form of chrysalis (pupa); this is the third, intermediate and transient, stage of development of an ant
1	*mooned about*:	wandered about aimlessly
3	*vagaries*:	ramblings
14	*sapped*:	drained
20	*spawning*:	generating or producing spawn

Guidelines

The poem is from the collection *Downstream* (1962). Like many of Kinsella's poems it begins with a vividly described, real experience: a cycling holiday he spent with his friends in his youth – probably the last summer they had before they began to study or work. Hence the significance of the title 'Chrysalides', which is an intermediate and transient stage of development. **The title indicates the theme and prepares us for the analogy from nature in the final lines.**

Kinsella does not say exactly who his companion or companions were, but it has been suggested that it may be a love poem, describing the innocence of young love. In this case it could be read as an awakening to the transient nature of human relationships, symbolised by the ants that die as they mate. On the other hand, the critic Brian John refers to the characters in the poem as

'the young boys' and suggests that it concerns adolescents on the verge of the transition into adulthood. Readers must make up their own mind as to which reading they prefer.

Commentary

Lines 1–12

The poem captures the carefree atmosphere of the time with details of what they ate and what they saw, how they pedalled from place to place with no real purpose, the different places they stayed in and the welcome they were given by the country people they met. The images and metaphors Kinsella uses convey the sense of freedom and wonder they felt. At night they slept in barns, watching the (adult) countrymen dancing to melodeon music, not yet ready to join in themselves.

In these descriptive stanzas Kinsella makes use of the senses to convey the vividness of the experience. There was the taste of 'chocolate and fruit' (line 3), the sound of music and 'crunching boots' (line 5) and the sight of men dancing with their 'shadows' on the 'yellow concrete' (line 6). He compares himself and his companions to 'calves poking our faces in with enormous hunger' (line 9) as they were given food in country kitchens. The effect of the simile is almost tactile if you imagine calves jostling one another at feeding time.

Lines 13–21

The tone of the poem becomes more reflective from the fourth stanza on. Looking back on that 'last free summer' (line 1), Kinsella realises how little experience of life he and his friends had. Caught up in their own world, they had no consciousness of the change that was taking place in their lives.

The daily routine of the holiday seemed to lull them into a false sense of timelessness in which their feelings were suspended, 'insensitive alike' (line 15) to the passage of time and to the horror of death and decay. He suggests that they were immune to the passing of their youth, the happiness and beauty of finding 'dry scones and jugs of milk' (line 18) on a window 'ablaze softly with the virgin moon' (line 17). Regret is the dominant feeling in these lines.

What brought them face to face with reality was their coming across a colony of ants, in which the male ants die even as they mate with the female. The 'wedding flight' is in fact 'spawning to its death' (lines 19 and 20). **This image of horror and death has stayed with Kinsella for the rest of his life.** But the poem suggests that the full implications of the scene, for their own lives, escaped them at that time. This was the realisation that the moment of death (for human beings as well as for ants) is inherent in the moment of birth.

Sound patterns in the poem

Although there is no end-rhyme, internal patterns of sound are established from the beginning. For example, assonance in the first stanza: the 'o' sounds in 'odd', 'stopping' and 'chocolate', and the 'a' sounds in 'tracing' and 'vagaries'. In the second stanza there is repetition of 'u' sounds in 'lurch' and 'crunching'; and in the third stanza 'e' sounds are repeated in 'sleeping' and 'received'. There are further examples throughout the poem.

Other sounds add unobtrusively to the musical quality, for example alliteration in 'melodeon music' (line 4) and consonance in 'experience' and 'tolerance' (lines 10 and 11).

Memories

This is one of Kinsella's poems recounting a memory that took hold in his imagination and fuelled later poems (see also 'Dick King', 'Hen Woman' and 'Tear').

As part of the collection *Downstream*, the poem has been seen by critics as representing Kinsella's intention to move from his earlier formal poems to more personal material that would also confront the disturbing and the horrific in his own experience.

Thinking about the poem

1. Would you agree that there is a sense of loss in the poem? What, precisely, has the poet lost?
2. Does the poem give a good picture of a youthful holiday? Support your answer by reference to the poem.
3. Explore the significance of the 'Like calves' simile (line 9) and 'virgin moon' (line 17) metaphor in the poem and say how they contribute to the poem's theme.
4. Select **three** images that appeal to you from the poem and explain your choice.

5. Comment on the title of the poem, 'Chrysalides'. Is it appropriate?
6. How do you interpret the final images in the poem?
7. How do you respond to these final images?
8. Is the poet critical of his youthful self or is he accepting of it? Give reasons for your answer.
9. Compare the poem with 'Hen Woman' or 'Dick King' as a poem of memory and say which poem you prefer and why.
10. You wish to include this poem in a talk entitled 'Introducing Thomas Kinsella'. Say why the poem is appropriate for the talk.

Mirror in February

The day dawns with scent of must and rain,
Of opened soil, dark trees, dry bedroom air.
Under the fading lamp, half-dressed – my brain
Idling on some compulsive fantasy –
I towel my shaven jaw and stop, and stare,   5
Riveted by a dark exhausted eye,
A dry downturning mouth.

It seems again that it is time to learn,
In this untiring, crumbling place of growth
To which, for the time being, I return.   10
Now plainly in the mirror of my soul
I read that I have looked my last on youth
And little more; for they are not made whole
That reach the age of Christ.

Below my window the awakening trees,   15
Hacked clean for better bearing, stand defaced
Suffering their brute necessities,
And how should the flesh not quail that span for span
Is mutilated more? In slow distaste
I fold my towel with what grace I can,   20
Not young and not renewable, but man.

Glossary

1	*must*:	mould, mustiness
6	*riveted*:	engrossed, attention fixed on
14	*age of Christ*:	Jesus Christ was aged thirty-three when he died
16	*hacked*:	pruned roughly
16	*better bearing*:	providing more fruit
16	*defaced*:	with spoiled looks
17	*brute necessities*:	required harsh treatment
18	*the flesh*:	human beings
18	*quail*:	flinch in fear
18	*span*:	period of time

Guidelines

'Mirror in February' is from the collection *Downstream* (1962). The speaker catches sight of his face in a mirror and reflects on the ageing process.

Commentary

Title

The title of the poem creates expectations and invites the reader to explore connotations of language and image. By drawing attention to the mirror, Kinsella prepares the reader for a confrontation of some sort. Mirrors have often been used as symbols of revelation or reflectors of the truth. They have been associated with luck and with one's shadow self – a mirror is where we may see ourselves more closely than anywhere else.

February is a transitional time of year. Winter is not yet over and yet there are signs of spring. We may be aware of both death (winter) and life (spring) at the same time. As we read through the poem we see how relevant this may be to Kinsella's moment of realisation.

Stanza 1

The setting of the poem is the speaker's bedroom, where he is shaving before a mirror. The intimate setting (in the next stanza we learn that it is his old bedroom in the house where he grew up) and the act of shaving prepare us for the personal nature of the poem.

From the beginning the speaker's surroundings play an important part. 'Dry bedroom air' (line 2) contrasts with the damp February day outside. He is aware of the sights and smells in the garden outside as the February day dawns. There is the sight of dawn although the trees are still 'dark' (line 2). There are smells of 'must and rain' and 'opened soil' (lines 1 and 2), an image that takes on connotations of death (i.e. a freshly dug grave) as the poem progresses.

Still half-asleep, his 'brain / Idling on some compulsive fantasy' (lines 3–4) – a vivid way of describing the dreamy start to the day – he suddenly catches sight of himself in the mirror. Like an artist's self-portrait, he sees himself in an objective and not very attractive way, looking tired and perhaps disappointed. He has 'a dry downturning mouth' (line 7). Assonance and alliteration help to establish the atmosphere of gloom, e.g. heavy consonantal 'd' sounds in 'day dawns', 'dark' and 'dry' as well as long vowel sounds in 'rain', 'air' and 'brain'.

Stanza 2
In a rather weary tone, the speaker accepts that he must 'learn' something 'again' in this place where he grew up – 'untiring' since it never stops teaching him lessons (lines 8 and 9). Looking into the mirror becomes a metaphor for inspecting the 'mirror of my soul' (line 11). He realises that he is no longer young, having reached the 'age of Christ' (line 14) – traditionally, Christ was thirty-three years old when he died. Even more painfully, he sees that death and decay await him. He will no longer be 'whole' (line 13).

Stanza 3
Once again he turns his attention to the trees outside in the garden. Now 'awakening' (line 15), as he has in the early morning, the trees have been cropped back for renewal in spring. This is part of their 'brute necessities' (line 17), it is what nature requires to be done. Contemplating this, he wonders how should human beings – in particular, himself – not feel afraid ('quail') as they also face ageing and death? Unlike the trees, however, he cannot be pruned in order to grow better. He deliberately uses strong language – 'hacked' (line 16), 'mutilated' (line 19) – to drive the point home. The thought upsets and frightens him.

He maintains a certain dignity in the face of ruin, however, by accepting his future as an inevitable part of his humanity. Although he experiences 'slow distaste' (line 19) for the lesson he has just learned, he proceeds to 'fold my towel with what grace I can' (line 20). The image suggests a possibility of order arising from the chaos of living. Coming after the honesty of the phrase 'not young and not renewable', the word 'man' bears a great deal of weight as an image of consolation and possibility (line 21).

Pathetic fallacy

The poem is one of many poems in which nature provides a means of expressing a sense of time passing and the inevitability of death. Kinsella makes use of what is known as the 'pathetic fallacy' (where natural phenomena are described as if they feel as humans do) in making an analogy between the trees and his situation. Although a relatively young man, he reveals an anxiety about death that is one of the main themes of his poetry.

Form of the poem

The poem is a lyric formally divided into three seven-line stanzas. End-rhyme is used throughout. **The longer stanza allows the poet to establish, develop and meditate on his theme.** In the first stanza the poet sets the scene, establishes his mood and prepares the reader for some revelation. In the second he develops the analogy with nature (the trees) and makes a discovery about his life. The final stanza reflects on this realisation and moves towards a certain closure in the last line.

Thinking about the poem

1. What is the speaker's mood in this poem?
2. How did you respond to the description of the weather and the trees?
3. How does the poem make us aware of death from the beginning?
4. What impression of the speaker do you gain from reading the poem?
5. What exactly has the speaker had to 'learn' from looking in the mirror?
6. The poem has images of suffering and grace. Give one example of **each** and explain why you chose it.
7. In this poem, it is clear that the speaker is:
    Afraid of old age and death.
    Hopeful because he is 'man', i.e. a human being.
    Choose the phrase which you think best describes the poet's feelings. Explain your choice.
8. Do you like this poem? Give a reason for your opinion.

Taking a closer look

1. Choose **two** of the following words that help to create the atmosphere in the third stanza: 'hacked' (line 16), 'suffering' (line 17), 'mutilated' (line 19). Comment on the impact made by these words in the poem.
2. Suggest a different title for the poem.

Imagining

1. You wish to make a short film of this poem. Describe what setting, music, lighting, etc. you would use to convey the atmosphere to viewers.
2. Your class is compiling an anthology called *Moments of Truth*. Make a case for including 'Mirror in February' in the anthology.

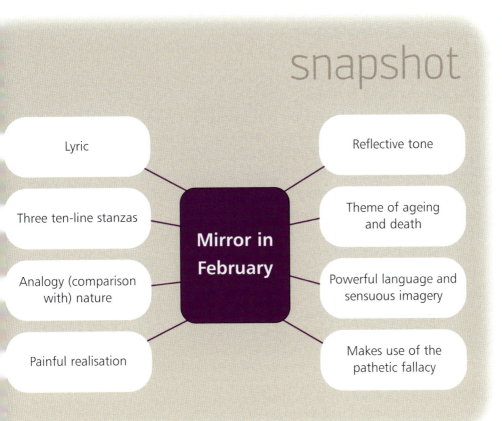

Hen Woman

The noon heat in the yard
smelled of stillness and coming thunder.
A hen scratched and picked at the shore.
It stopped, its body crouched and puffed out.
The brooding silence seemed to say 'Hush . . .'   5

The cottage door opened,
a black hole
in a whitewashed wall so bright
the eyes narrowed.
Inside, a clock murmured 'Gong . . .'

(I had felt all this before.)

She hurried out in her slippers
muttering, her face dark with anger,
and gathered the hen up jerking
languidly. Her hand fumbled.
Too late. Too late.

It fixed me with its pebble eyes
(seeing what mad blur).
A white egg showed in the sphincter;
mouth and beak opened together;
and time stood still.

Nothing moved: bird or woman,
fumbled or fumbling – locked there
(as I must have been) gaping.

      *

There was a tiny movement at my feet,
tiny and mechanical; I looked down.
A beetle like a bronze leaf
was inching across the cement,
clasping with small tarsi
a ball of dung bigger than its body.

The serrated brow pressed the ground humbly,
lifted in a short stare, bowed again;
the dung-ball advanced minutely,
losing a few fragments,
specks of staleness and freshness.

      *

A mutter of thunder far off
– time not quite stopped.
I saw the egg had moved a fraction:
a tender blank brain
under torsion, a clean a new world.   40

As I watched, the mystery completed.
The black zero of the orifice
closed to a point
and the white zero of the egg hung free,
flecked with greenish brown oils.   45

It fell and turned over slowly.
Dreamlike, fussed by her splayed fingers,
it floated outward, moon-white,
leaving no trace in the air,
and began its drop to the shore.   50

                         *

I feed upon it still, as you see;
there is no end to that which, not understood,
may yet be hoarded in the imagination,
in the yolk of one's being, so to speak,
there to undergo its (quite animal) growth,   55

dividing blindly, twitching, packed with will,
searching in its own tissue
for the structure in which it may wake.
Something that had – clenched in its cave –
not been now as was: an egg of being.   60

Through what seemed a whole year it fell
– as it still falls, for me, solid and light,
the red gold beating in its silvery womb,
alive as the yolk and white of my eye.
As it will continue to fall, probably, until I die,   65
through the vast indifferent spaces
with which I am empty.

                         *

It smashed against the grating
and slipped down quickly out of sight.
It was over in a comical flash. 70
The soft mucous shell clung a little longer,
then drained down.

She stood staring, in blank anger.
Then her eyes came to life, and she laughed
and let the bird flap away. 75

'It's all the one.
There's plenty more where that came from!'

Glossary

3	*shore*: a word used in Dublin for a sewer opening
15	*languidly*: listlessly
19	*sphincter*: ring-shaped muscle that opens and closes an orifice
29	*tarsi*: five-jointed foot in insects
31	*serrated*: notched like a saw
40	*torsion*: strain produced by twisting
42	*orifice*: opening
47	*splayed*: spread out
71	*mucous*: slimy
76	*It's all the one*: it makes no difference, it does not matter

Guidelines

'Hen Woman' is from *New Poems* (1973). It is a narrative poem that recalls an incident from Kinsella's childhood, when he saw an old woman pick up a hen just as it was laying an egg. Although the woman tried to catch it, the egg had fallen through the air, smashed through a grating and fallen down into the 'shore' (sewer's opening). The sight of the egg emerging from the hen astonished the child so much that he never forgot it. In *A Dublin Documentary* (2006) Kinsella described it as a 'scene ridiculous in its content, but of a serious early awareness of self and of process: of details insisting on their survival, regardless of any immediate significance'. In the same book he has described the setting of the poem:

> Also the yard outside, a silent square courtyard at the back, off Basin Lane, with a couple of whitewashed cottages in the corners, with half-doors. A separate world, with a few other people, and cats and hens and a feel of the country. A whole place that has long disappeared.

As well as the voice of the child who witnesses the event, we hear the voice of the adult who meditates on its significance.

Commentary

Lines 1–24

The first part of the poem sets the scene and describes what happens from the point of view of the young boy, of the old woman and indeed even that of the hen. Rich sensuous images – the heat of the day, the hint of thunder in the air, the movements of the hen, the sight of the old woman emerging from the darkness of her cottage – seem to suggest that something significant is about to happen.

The old woman, clearly annoyed that the hen is about to lay its egg outside in the street, tries to grab it before it does so. The hen, too, reacts in its own way to the event, while the young boy simply stands there, as he says, 'gaping' (line 24) in surprise at seeing the egg emerge, and close enough to the hen to register its 'pebble eyes' (line 17). It was as if time stood still. The moment is captured in all its drama.

Lines 25–35

The moment is so etched into his consciousness that the speaker's senses are heightened. He becomes acutely aware of what is happening around him, even the movement of a small beetle at his feet as it makes its way across the ground, carrying a ball of dung. (A dung beetle or scarab is a symbol of life in Egyptian mythology, and was considered sacred.)

Lines 36–50

In the third part of the poem his attention returns to the egg as it emerges from the hen. **The event is presented almost in cinematic slow motion.** The egg is realistically described. Like any new-laid egg it is 'flecked with greenish brown oils' (line 45), but it is also given metaphorical significance as a 'clean a new world' (line 40).

An egg is a source of life and a symbol of unity. For the watching child, it is a means of having the 'mystery' of the beginnings of life, of birth, 'completed' or finally understood (line 41), having seen the mechanics of how the egg was laid. As in a dream, he watches the woman's fumbling fingers miss the egg as it falls into the 'shore'.

Lines 51–67

The fourth part is the most abstract section of the poem. **The adult poet breaks away from the child's point of view to ponder on the significance that the event assumed for him.** Kinsella sees that this childhood incident had a greater impact on his imagination than one might have expected.

He makes use of the egg as a metaphor of how the imagination seizes upon an idea and then allows it to develop within the consciousness – just as an egg contains cells that multiply and divide once fertilised, in animals and humans alike. The experience has become part of his being, so that he can say he is able to 'feed upon it still' (line 51) in memory that makes him who he is, and in poems that express his inner consciousness. **He expects the experience to be more fruitful yet, even for the rest of his life.**

Lines 68–77

The final part of the poem reverts back to the past, to the tale of the old woman and the actual fallen egg as seen by the child. The atmosphere becomes lighter – the scene had its 'comical' side after all (line 70), which the old woman starts to appreciate.

After her initial annoyance at losing the egg she laughs and lets go of the hen, with the good-humoured comment, 'It's all the one. / There's plenty more where that came from!' (lines 76–77). Her words play wittily on eggs as symbols of unity (the yolk, the white, the shell, all in one container, so to speak). **This seems to give the story a sense of closure, but it also ironically points toward the endless possibilities of such childhood memories for the poet himself.**

Kinsella's change of direction

During the 1960s Kinsella embarked upon a study of the psychology of Carl Jung (1875–1961). **Jung placed great emphasis on the importance of childhood experience and memory** for the adult who seeks what he called 'individuation' or the realisation of one's own potential in life. According to Jung, in order to achieve personal growth in a psychological sense (individuation) it is necessary to bring to light our unconscious desires, as expressed in our dreams, for example.

Critics have pointed out that exploring these ideas changed the direction of Kinsella's poetry. His poems became more autobiographical and introspective. He became more interested in the origins of his creativity, whether it stemmed from certain specific childhood experiences (such as in 'Hen Woman' or 'Tear') or was part of a genetic and historical inheritance (such as in 'His Father's Hands'). Kinsella, of course, had always used memories as a basis for poems, as we have seen in 'Dick King' and 'Chrysalides'. However, in 'Hen Woman' we can see Jungian ideas applied more closely.

Jung and mythology
Jung placed great importance on the role of mythology in human civilisation. He saw that certain myths and legends occur time and time again in different cultures and eras. This led him to believe that myth is part of the human psyche and, as such, highly significant. For example, the story of the hero who undertakes a dangerous journey, the obstacles encountered on the quest and the opposing villain occurs time and again, so that these figures have come to be archetypes (or original models) of particular human behaviour.

There are many mythical echoes in 'Hen Woman'. The old woman is a neighbour, but as she emerges from the 'black hole' (perhaps connoting the pit of the underworld) of her cottage, muttering angrily, she becomes an archetype of the witch-like figure of the old hag (*cailleach* in Irish). The hag plays an important role in many myths, as a fearsome creature who may yet impart wisdom or teach a lesson.

It is significant that the poem ends with her words of wisdom and that the young boy has never forgotten them. Her light-hearted acceptance of the hen's future laying capacity highlights the potential for life that an egg symbolises. This might also be applied to the creative possibilities of experience for a poet, like Kinsella.

Thinking about the poem

1. Does the poet succeed in conveying the scene of the incident well? Refer to the poem in your answer.
2. 'Kinsella makes use of all his senses to re-create the experience in the poem.' Discuss this statement, supporting your answer by reference to the poem.
3. Which section of the poem do you prefer? Give reasons for your view.
4. Explore the imagery of light/darkness and colour throughout the poem and comment on its significance.
5. Would you agree that the poem skilfully combines realistic description with abstract meditation? Support your answer by reference to the poem, paying particular attention to the language the poet uses.
6. Why, do you think, does Kinsella say 'the egg still falls, for me' (line 62)?
7. Why, in your opinion, was the incident such a significant one for the young boy?
8. In line 70 the poet comments, 'It was over in a comical flash.' Did you find the incident to be comical in any way? Explain your response.
9. Does an awareness of the mythological aspects of the poem help or hinder your enjoyment of it? Give reasons for your view.
10. Compare this poem with 'Tear' in its treatment of Kinsella's memories of childhood. Which poem do you prefer and why?

Tear

I was sent in to see her.
A fringe of jet drops
chattered at my ear
as I went in through the hangings.

I swallowed in chambery dusk.
My heart shrank
at the smell of disused
organs and sour kidney.

The black aprons I used to
bury my face in
were folded at the foot of the bed
in the last watery light from the window

(Go in and say goodbye to her)
and I was carried off
to unfathomable depths.
I turned to look at her.

She stared at the ceiling
and puffed at her cheek, distracted,
propped high in the bed
resting for the next attack.

The covers were gathered close
up to her mouth,
that the lines of ill-temper still
marked. Her grey hair

was loosened out like a young woman's
all over the pillow,
mixed with the shadows
criss-crossing her forehead

and at her mouth and eyes,
like a web of strands tying down her head
and tangling down toward the shadow
eating away the floor at my feet.

I couldn't stir at first, nor wished to,
for fear she might turn and tempt me
(my own father's mother)
with open mouth

– with some fierce wheedling whisper –
to hide myself one last time
against her, and bury my
self in her dying mud.

Was I to kiss her? As soon
kiss the damp that crept
in the flowered walls
of this pit.

Yet I had to kiss.
I knelt by the bulk of the death bed
and sank my face in the chill
and smell of her black aprons.

Snuff and musk, the folds against my eyelids,
carried me into a derelict place
smelling of ash: unseen walls and roofs
rustled like breathing.

I found myself disturbing
dead ashes for any trace
of warmth, when far off
in the vaults a single drop

splashed. And I found
what I was looking for

– not heat nor fire,
not any comfort,

but her voice, soft, talking to someone
about my father: 'God help him, he cried
big tears over there by the machine
for the poor little thing.' Bright

drops on the wooden lid
for my infant sister.
My own wail of child-animal grief
was soon done, with any early guess

at sad dullness and tedious pain
and lives bitter with hard bondage.
How I tasted it now –
her heart beating in my mouth!

She drew an uncertain breath
and pushed at the clothes
and shuddered tiredly.
I broke free

and left the room
promising myself
when she was really dead
I would really kiss.

My grandfather half looked up
from the fireplace as I came out,
and shrugged and turned back
with a deaf stare to the heat.

I fidgeted beside him for a minute
and went out to the stop
It was still bright there
and I felt better able to breathe.

Old age can digest
anything: the commotion
at Heaven's gate – the struggle
in store for you all your life.

How long and hard it is
before you get to Heaven,
unless like little Agnes
you vanish with early tears.

Glossary	
5	*chambery*: of a room, a chamber
37	*wheedling*: coaxing
49	*Snuff*: powdered tobacco for sniffing, taken as stimulant or sedative
49	*musk*: strong-smelling perfume
50	*derelict*: in ruins
69	*tedious*: boring
70	*bondage*: captivity
95	*little Agnes*: the poet's infant sister

Guidelines

'Tear' is from *New Poems* (1973). As mentioned in the Guidelines for 'Hen Woman', **Kinsella's reading of the psychology of Carl Jung encouraged him to explore childhood experiences and memories in his poems** from the 1970s on. He has recalled the important role his grandparents played in his childhood:

> . . . it was in a world dominated by these people that I remember many things of importance happening to me for the first time. And it is in their world that I came to terms with these things as best I could, and later set my attempts at understanding.

In this poem the young Thomas is sent to visit his grandmother Kinsella, his father's mother, as she lay dying in her house in Bow Lane, on one side of James's Street, in Inchicore. It records the young child's first understanding of old age and death.

Commentary

Lines 1–44

This journey is depicted in both a realistic and a mythic way, as in 'Hen Woman'. First, the child has to pass through 'A fringe of jet drops' (line 2) into the darkness of the grandmother's room, just as a legendary hero had to journey down into the darkness of the underworld. The smells of decay and death in the room – of 'disused / organs and sour kidney' (lines 7–8) – make his heart shrink in fear and repulsion. In this atmosphere even familiar things – the grandmother's 'black aprons' (line 9) that he used to find such comfort in – become strange and frightening. There is a sense that the boy feels he is not in control of the situation, that he has been 'carried off / to unfathomable depths' (lines 14–15).

His grandmother, too, is described as both familiar and strange: her mouth is 'still / marked' by 'lines of ill-temper' (lines 23–24), but her hair is spread out on the pillow like that of a young woman. The young boy expresses a mixture of fear and guilt at not wishing to kiss the old woman whom he had once loved. Now she seems like a creature living in a 'pit' (line 44), a witch-like figure whose 'open mouth' (line 36) will lead him into danger. (We are reminded again of the hag figures of myth and legend, a source of danger for the unsuspecting heroes – see Guidelines for 'Hen Woman'.)

Lines 45–80

Forcing himself to show some kind of affection, he buries his head in his grandmother's black aprons, which smell of 'Snuff and musk' (line 49), but he cannot bring himself to kiss her face. Instead, he tries to find some expression of grief within himself, only to succeed in shedding a single 'tear' when he hears his grandmother talking from the bed (perhaps to herself). She is remembering the boy's father's grief when his infant daughter Agnes died. Her sympathetic words remind us that despite the association with darkness and danger that surrounds her, his grandmother had a soft heart.

The speaker recalls his own 'wail of child-animal grief' (line 67) when his little sister died, so different from the bleakness of his feelings now for his dying grandmother. He contrasts his early innocence with his new-found knowledge of the bitterness and hardship of life for someone like his grandmother. Managing to escape from the room ('I broke free', line 76), he soothes his guilt by promising that he would kiss her 'when she was really dead' (line 79).

Lines 81–96

Like all heroic journeys to the underworld, the 'hero' of the poem returns with some reward or insight that he has gained from what happens there. In many legends the hero's encounter with the hag or *cailleach* provides a glimpse of wisdom. So, as in 'Hen Woman', we see how Kinsella blends autobiographical material with mythic imagery, this time creating a moving poem about his grandmother's death and the insight it gave him.

Kinsella's insight is bleak. From his grandmother's words he now realises the yawning gap between the death of an innocent infant and the ugliness and struggle of death in old age, following a long and hard life. This realisation is reinforced by his grandfather's stoical silence by the fireplace as he comes out of the room. But, from a more hopeful perspective, he has also seen his grandmother's emotional side as well as that of his father at the death of 'little Agnes', who seemed to 'vanish' but is yet remembered.

Thinking about the poem

1. A critic has commented that the feeling in 'Tear' is 'a combination of intense revulsion and love'. Would you agree with this view? Give reasons for your answer.
2. Has Kinsella given an honest account of his experience? Support your answer by reference to the poem.
3. How does the poem convey the character of his grandmother? Does she surprise you at any stage?
4. How well does the poet convey the innocence and confusion of a child? Support your answer by reference to the poem.
5. Light, darkness, a journey, witch-like imagery associated with the old woman – what atmosphere do they all create in the poem? How did you respond to this atmosphere?
6. Look carefully at the description of the grandmother in lines 17 to 32. Discuss the view that in this description the grandmother resembles a figure from myth or legend.
7. What lesson did the boy learn from the experience, in your view? Support your answer with examples from the poem.
8. What is conveyed by the contrast between the dying old woman and the death of Kinsella's baby sister, Agnes?
9. From your reading of the poem, how would you describe the poet's vision of life in general?
10. 'Childhood experience is very significant in the poems of Thomas Kinsella.' Discuss this statement in relation to the poems 'Hen Woman' and 'Tear'.

His Father's Hands

I drank firmly
and set the glass down between us firmly.
You were saying.

My father
was saying.   5

His fingers prodded and prodded,
marring his point. Emphas–
emphasemphasis.

I have watched
his father's hands before him   10

cupped, and tightening the black Plug
between the knife and thumb,
carving off little curlicues
to rub them in the dark of his palms,

or cutting into new leather at his bench,   15
levering a groove open with his thumb,
insinuating wet sprigs for the hammer.

He kept the sprigs in mouthfuls
and brought them out in silvery
units between his lips.   20

I took a pinch out of their hole
and knocked them one by one into the wood,
bright points among hundreds gone black,
other children's – cousins and others, grown up.

Or his bow hand scarcely moving,   25
scraping in the dark corner near the fire,
his plump fingers shifting on the strings.

To his deaf, inclined head
he hugged the fiddle's body
whispering with the tune   30

with breaking heart
whene'er I hear
in privacy, across a blocked void,

the wind that shakes the barley.
The wind . . .   35
round her grave . . .

on my breast in blood she died . . .
But blood for blood without remorse
I've ta'en . . .

Beyond that.   40

                          *

Your family, Thomas, met with and helped
many of the Croppies in hiding from the Yeos
or on their way home after the defeat
in south Wexford. They sheltered the Laceys
who were later hanged on the Bridge in Ballinglen   45
between Tinahely and Anacorra.

From hearsay, as far as I can tell
the Men Folk were either Stone Cutters
or masons or probably both.

In the 18   50
and late 1700s even the farmers
had some other trade to make a living.

They lived in Farnese among a Colony
of North of Ireland or Scotch settlers left there

in some of the dispersals or migrations
which occurred in this Area of Wicklow and Wexford
and Carlow. And some years before that time
the Family came from somewhere around Tullow.

Beyond that.

*

Littered uplands. Dense grass. Rocks everywhere,
wet underneath, retaining memory of the long cold.

First, a prow of land
chosen, and wedged with tracks;
then boulders chosen
and sloped together, stabilized in menace.

I do not like this place.
I do not think the people who lived here
were ever happy. It feels evil.
Terrible things happened.
I feel afraid here when I am on my own.

*

Dispersals or migrations.
Through what evolutions or accidents
toward that peace and patience
by the fireside, that blocked gentleness . . .

That serene pause, with the slashing knife,
in kindly mockery,
as I busy myself with my little nails
at the rude block, his bench.

The blood advancing
– gorging vessel after vessel –

and altering in them
one by one.

Behold, that gentleness already
modulated twice, in others:
to earnestness and iteration;   85
to an offhandedness, repressing various impulses.

                              *

Extraordinary . . . The big block – I found it
years afterward in a corner of the yard
in sunlight after rain
and stood it up, wet and black: 90
it turned under my hands, an axis
of light flashing down its length,
and the wood's soft flesh broke open,
countless little nails
squirming and dropping out of it.   95

Glossary	
11	*Plug*: piece of tobacco
13	*curlicues*: fancy twists
16	*levering*: movement with a crowbar or other tool
17	*insinuating*: placing subtly or gradually
18	*sprigs*: headless or almost headless nails (used here in shoemaking)
34	*the wind that shakes the barley*: a traditional Irish tune
42	*Croppies*: Irish rebels of the 1798 rebellion (so-called because they cropped their hair short)
42	*Yeos*: Yeomen, the British cavalry volunteer force that quelled the Croppy rebellion
45–6	*Ballinglen between Tinahely and Anacorra*: three townlands in Co. Wicklow
48	*Men Folk*: male relatives
53	*Farnese*: a place in Co. Wicklow
55	*dispersals*: forced departure to new areas

55	*migrations*: movement from one region or country to another
58	*Tullow*: town in Co. Carlow
60	*uplands*: hilly country
62	*prow*: front part
72	*evolutions*: gradual developments
78	*rude*: crude, rough
80	*gorging*: feeding gluttonously; here, moving relentlessly through blood vessels as in genetic inheritance
84	*modulated*: softened or adjusted
85	*iteration*: repetition
86	*repressing*: keeping hidden or restrained
91	*axis*: straight line about which the parts of a figure are arranged

Guidelines

'His Father's Hands' was published in *Peppercanister One* (1974). **Kinsella's interest in his family history developed naturally from his decision, inspired by his study of Carl Jung's psychology, to look inwardly for material for his poems.** The information in the poem came to him from a letter from his uncle, Jack Brophy from Tinahely, Co. Wicklow. You can read the complete letter in *A Dublin Documentary* (2006).

Commentary

The poem is divided into five sections, each of which explores a different aspect of family history and relationships.

Lines 1–40

The poem begins with an image of the poet and his father talking and drinking together, possibly arguing, and using their hands in a similar way to make a point: the poet as he sets his glass down 'firmly', the father's finger prodding for emphasis. The imagery of hands creates associations in the poem, as the poet goes on to remember his grandfather's hands as he prepared tobacco for his pipe (significantly, he is remembered as 'tightening' the plug of tobacco) or skilfully mended shoes in his work as a cobbler. Kinsella then introduces the image of the cobbler's block of wood into which he and other cousins (another image of family links) used to knock little headless nails. He recalls, too, his grandfather's hands as they played a traditional tune on the fiddle and hears again how he would whisper the words of the old tune.

For Kinsella, the memory comes back to him 'with breaking heart' (line 31). But he wishes to go beyond his own memories into the earlier history of the family: 'Beyond that' (line 40).

Lines 41–59

In this section Kinsella does go 'beyond' the memory of his more immediate family. A speaker (his uncle, in a letter) recounts the family history to the poet. He tells how the Kinsella family helped many of the rebels of the 1798 rebellion, the Croppies, against the Yeos (Yeomen). Going back further in the eighteenth century, the Kinsellas were stone cutters or masons, or small farmers who lived among migrants from other parts of Ireland or Scotland.

Names of townlands in Wicklow (Ballinglen, Tinahely, Anacorra) convey the sense that these were real people rooted in real places. They were stone cutters and masons – significantly, these are trades that require manual skill. There is a hint of conflict or suffering as the family origins are traced to some of the forced movements of people ('dispersals', line 55) that occurred in the seventeenth century.

Lines 60–70

Here the poet imagines the family 'beyond that', in pre-historic times. **To him it is clear that the family would have had to struggle to establish themselves in their land.** Sacrifice and maybe violence would have been necessary to work the land and provide a living for the people. This realisation causes the poet to respond negatively to the place: 'I do not like this place' (line 66). Although he and his immediate ancestors never experienced that period of family history, in keeping with Jung's theories they share in a racial or unconscious memory of this time. This idea seems to disturb him.

Lines 71–86

Kinsella contemplates the genetic process by which traits are passed down through the generations. He wonders how history and evolution combined to bring about his grandfather's characteristics of patience and gentleness. This changed in the next generation in his son's (Kinsella's father's) seriousness and tendency to repeat himself, and finally produced the poet's 'offhandedness' (line 86), a trait he ruefully attributes to himself.

Lines 87–95

The poem comes full circle as it refers back to the block of wood mentioned in the first and fourth sections. His shoemaker grandfather had worked on it, and Kinsella and his cousins had knocked nails into it. Found many years later, it is now black and falling apart, but the image of the little nails that fall out of it as it breaks **suggests the potential for further life arising from the dead generations. It may also refer to the creative possibilities for the poet** as he continues to explore himself and his family relationships.

Personal experience

As he does in 'Hen Woman' and 'Tear', Kinsella skilfully blends personal material and universal concerns in 'His Father's Hands'. His childhood memories of his grandfather as well as his adult relationship with his father give a focus to the poet's exploration of aspects of his personality and the origins of his creativity. Running through the poem there is a moving awareness of the past, how family history influences later generations, and how family traits are inherited and mutated.

But Kinsella also contemplates questions that have more universal application. Underlying the poem is an awareness of Jung's theory of the collective unconscious (i.e. that people carry within themselves unconscious racial memory, perhaps of trauma or suffering in the past). Kinsella's interest in genetic inheritance mirrors many of the concerns of the twentieth and early twenty-first centuries.

Thinking about the poem

1. How does the poet make the link between himself, his father, his grandfather and his cousins in the poem's first section?
2. Would you agree that the image of 'hands' is particularly effective in conveying family history? Support your answer by reference to the poem.
3. Would you agree that the figure of the grandfather dominates the poem? What impression of him did you get? Support your answer by reference to the poem.
4. How would you describe the poet's father?
5. Explore the image of the cobbler's block as used throughout the poem.
6. How did you respond to the third section of the poem (lines 60–70)?
7. Explore the image of the block of wood and nails in the final part of the poem.
8. 'Kinsella's main concern in this poem is to understand himself.' Discuss this statement.
9. Does this poem succeed in conveying how important family history is? Use quotations from the poem to support your answer.
10. How did you respond to this poem?

from Settings: Model School, Inchicore

Miss Carney handed us out blank paper and marla,
old plasticine with colours
all rolled together into brown.

You started with a ball of it
and rolled it into a snake curling
around your hand, and kept rolling it
in one place until it wore down into two
with a stain on the paper.

We always tittered at each other
when we said the adding-up table in Irish
and came to her name.

*

In the second school we had Mr Browne.
He had white teeth in his brown man's face.

He stood in front of the blackboard
and chalked a white dot.

'We are going to start
decimals.'

I am going to know
everything.

*

One day he said:
'Out into the sun!'
We settled his chair under a tree
and sat ourselves down delighted
in two rows in the greeny gold shade.

A fat bee floated around
shining amongst us
and the flickering sun
warmed our folded coats
and he said: 'History . . . !'

*

When the Autumn came
and the big chestnut leaves
fell all over the playground
we piled them in heaps
between the wall and the tree trunks
and the boys ran races
jumping over the heaps
and tumbled into them shouting.

*

I sat by myself in the shed
and watched the draught
blowing the papers
around the wheels of the bicycles.

Will God judge
our most secret thoughts and actions?
God will judge
our most secret thoughts and actions
and every idle word that man shall speak
he shall render an account of it
on the Day of Judgement.

*

The taste
of ink off
the nib shrank your
mouth.

Glossary

title	*Model School*:	the primary school Kinsella attended in *Inchicore*, the Dublin neighbourhood in which he lived as a boy
1	*marla*:	a type of modelling material, similar to Plasticine
11	*her name*:	the teacher's name is Carney: lessons in the Model School were taught through the medium of Irish and, in the Irish-language addition tables, 4 (*ceathair*) + 9 (*naoi*) sounds rather like 'Carney'
12	*Mr Browne*:	Kinsella's teacher, George Browne
42	*Will God judge*:	a quotation from the Catechism, which children memorised at school

Guidelines

'Model School, Inchicore' is the first of three poems called 'Settings' that open Kinsella's Peppercanister sequence *Songs of the Psyche* (1985). As the title of the volume suggests, in these poems **Kinsella once again explores the childhood experiences and memories that have made him who he is** (i.e. that have influenced his psyche or mind). A 'setting' implies a background; it also has a musical connotation (as in words 'set' to music).

Kinsella began his education at the Model School, Inchicore, Dublin, near where he lived on Phoenix Street. The Model School had been established in 1811. In accordance with government policy following the foundation of the state in 1922, many of the lessons that Kinsella would have had in the 1930s were taught through the medium of Irish.

Commentary

Lines 1–11

In simple, childlike language and images Kinsella imaginatively re-creates the world of his primary school days. His first teacher, Miss Carney, gives out all the materials needed ('blank paper and marla', line 1) to set him on his way to knowledge. He learns how to make something out of something else (a snake from Plasticine) – a simple experience, but many commentators on the poem have pointed out that a snake is a symbol of knowledge, with mythic and psychological connotations. He is also introduced to the possibilities of language, as illustrated in the wordplay involving the sounds of Miss Carney's name. These are childish experiences, but they look forward to the creative world of the adult poet.

Lines 12–19
His next teacher, Mr Browne, had 'white teeth in a brown man's face' (line 13) – further evidence of the young Kinsella's awareness of wordplay. When Mr Browne begins to teach decimals, the young Kinsella, with a child's innocence, feels he is 'going to know / everything' (lines 18–19). The white dot in the centre of the blackboard seems to the young boy to contain all the seeds of knowledge.

Lines 20–29
Other memories have etched themselves into his consciousness: the happy day they learned about 'History', seated outdoors in the sun. We can almost feel the warmth of the sun and see the 'fat bee' that flew around them. (Might the 'greeny gold shade' of the day suggest the nationalist slant of the lessons?)

Lines 30–37
In autumn there were races and jumps in the playground. The language here re-creates the sheer physical fun and exhilaration the boys felt. Run-on lines without punctuation express the liveliness of their play, as do the verbs of movement: 'piled', 'ran', 'tumbled'.

Lines 38–48
In a moment indicative of Kinsella's later tendency to introspection, he remembers sitting alone in the bicycle shed pondering the lines from the Catechism about God's judgement, which the boys would have memorised in preparation for Confirmation. Here the young Kinsella seems to be waking up to morality and questions of religious importance. We notice the change of language from the simple expression of a child to the biblical-sounding words: 'he shall render an account of it / on the Day of Judgement' (lines 47–48).

Lines 49–52
The final short section contains only one image, but it is a very rich one. **The sensory image of the taste of the ink on the nib of the pen brings the poem back to the child's own experience.** It can also be read in a metaphorical way as the young boy's first encounter with the difficulty of learning, and by extension of writing. It certainly casts an ironic light over his earlier confident assertion 'I am going to know / everything' (lines 18–19).

What the poem reveals

The poem portrays Kinsella as an observant young boy, acutely aware of his surroundings, sensitive to language and keen to learn as much as he can about the world. Knowledge is first of all shown as sensory – the feel of the marla in his hands, the stain on the paper. Then it becomes more abstract, as he encounters mathematics, history and religious knowledge classes. The final image seems to be a metaphorical comment on his experience. But throughout the poem there is a sense of happiness. The boys 'tittered' (line 9), they sat down 'delighted' (line 23) in the sunshine, they 'ran races / jumping over the heaps / and tumbled into them shouting' (lines 35–37).

Thinking about the poem

1. Do you like Kinsella's description of his early schooldays? Which detail particularly appeals to you?
2. Would you agree that Kinsella has succeeded in getting inside the mind of a child in this poem? Refer to the poem in your answer.
3. How would you describe the tone of the poem?
4. How does the poem convey the growing maturity of the child during his primary school days?
5. Explore the sensory images throughout the poem. How do they contribute to the poem's atmosphere?
6. Compare the poem with 'Tear' as a depiction of childhood experience. Which poem do you prefer, and why?
7. Discuss the view that childhood experience has been a rich source of poetic material for Kinsella.
8. Using the poem as a model, write a short description (in poetry or prose) of your own early experiences at school.

from The Familiar: VII

I was downstairs at first light,
looking out through the frost on the window
at the hill opposite and the sheets of frost
scattered down among the rocks.

The cat back in the kitchen. 5
Folded on herself. Torn and watchful.

*

A chilled grapefruit
– thin-skinned, with that little gloss.
I took a mouthful, looking up along the edge of the wood

at the two hooded crows high in the cold 10
talking to each other,
flying up toward the tundra, beyond the waterfall.

*

I sliced the tomatoes in thin discs
in damp sequence into their dish;
scalded the kettle; made the tea, 15

and rang the little brazen bell,
and saved the toast.
Arranged the pieces

in slight disorder around the basket.
Fixed our places, one with the fruit 20
and one with the plate of sharp cheese.

*

And stood in my dressing gown
with arms extended
over the sweetness of the sacrifice.

Her shade showed in the door. 25
Her voice responded:
'You are very good. You always made it nice.'

Glossary

title	*Familiar*:	something known or understood; it also has connotations of a ghostly presence
12	*tundra*:	vast, level, treeless region with an arctic climate and vegetation; here, the terrain near the Sally Gap, Co. Wicklow
16	*brazen*:	brass
25	*shade*:	shadow

Guidelines

This is the final part of a seven-part sequence that explores the development of love between the speaker and his wife, Eleanor, from their earliest days in a flat in Baggot Street, to the time of writing (the poem appeared in 1999 in the collection entitled *The Familiar*). In the previous six sections of the poem the speaker portrays Eleanor as lover, poetic muse (source of inspiration) and guide. In this section he paints a more intimate picture of their life together in the domestic setting of their home in Co. Wicklow.

The title clearly conveys the fact that Eleanor is a familiar (intimate) person in his life and that the subject of the poem is the familiar life they lead together. But another meaning of the word 'familiar' is 'a spirit that attends on a person', and this interpretation is also relevant in Kinsella's depiction of their relationship.

Commentary

Lines 1–12
The early lines of the poem set the scene. The poet is up in the early morning and about to prepare breakfast. It is frosty outside. In the kitchen the cat quietly watches

him. As Kinsella works, he observes two crows outside as they fly up towards the treeless terrain of the Sally Gap ('tundra', line 12). They, too, like himself and his wife, are intimate, 'talking to each other' (line 11) as they fly.

Lines 13–21

Preparing breakfast for his wife becomes a sacrificial offering, like a religious ritual. As in many of his poems Kinsella uses sensuous images to convey atmosphere and feeling. He pays careful attention to the food, savouring the look, taste, feel and smell. For example, the 'sliced' (line 13) and 'damp' (line 14) of the tomatoes, the 'sharp cheese' (line 21). Like a priest taking Communion, he takes a mouthful and rings 'a little brazen bell' (line 16) to signal that the meal is ready. As in any ceremony, each action is given its own importance; the food is 'arranged' and 'fixed' (lines 18 to 20).

Lines 22–27

In the final section the priestlike image is even more explicit as he describes how he stretches out his arms 'over the sweetness of the sacrifice' (line 24). The exalted mood of the poem may seem somewhat deflated by the beloved's simple words: 'You always made it nice', but this response also expresses a great deal of love and appreciation. She appears as a 'shade' (line 25), with all the connotations of that word, as shadow, ghost, divine being, to whom reverence is due. **The image adds to a portrait of love as a spiritual experience as well as a physical and emotional one.**

Love poem

Love is a frequent theme in Kinsella's poetry. At the time of writing 'The Familiar' he and his wife were approaching old age; appropriately enough, the poem is set in winter, the end of the calendar year. Their relationship has arrived at the point where simple tasks undertaken for one another, in the ritual of routine (making breakfast, for instance), take on a spiritual dimension as symbols of love.

Religious sacrifice has always had an element of mystery about it. By using it as an analogy of love, Kinsella suggests that mystery also lies at the heart of love – the central theme of the poem 'Echo'.

Thinking about the poem

1. How did you respond to the poem as a love poem?
2. How do the details of the weather, landscape and cat contribute to the atmosphere of the poem?
3. Comment on the significance of the poem's title.
4. What is your interpretation of the image of the two crows that the speaker sees from his window?
5. What impression do you gain of the relationship between the speaker and his beloved?
6. How do the suggestions of priestly offering and sacrifice add to the depiction of the couple's relationship, in your opinion?
7. If you were the recipient of this love poem, would you be flattered? Give reasons for your answer.
8. Compare the poem as a love poem with 'Echo'.
9. You have decided to include this poem in an anthology of your favourite poems by Thomas Kinsella. Say why you would choose it, referring closely to the poem in your answer.

from Glenmacnass: VI Littlebody

Up on the high road, as far as the sheepfold
into the wind, and back. The sides of the black bog channels
dug down in the water. The white cottonheads
on the old cuttings nodding everywhere.
Around one more bend, toward the car shining in the distance.   5

From a stony slope half way, behind a rock prow
with the stones on top for an old mark,
the music of pipes, distant and clear.

*

I was climbing up, making no noise
and getting close, when the music stopped,   10
leaving a pagan shape in the air.

There was a hard inhale,
a base growl,
and it started again, in a guttural dance.

I looked around the edge   15
– and it was Littlebody. Hugging his bag
under his left arm, with his eyes closed.

I slipped. Our eyes met.
He started scuttling up the slope with his gear
and his hump, elbows out and neck back.   20

But I shouted:
            'Stop, Littlebody!
I found you fair and I want my due.'

He stopped and dropped his pipes,
and spread his arms out, waiting for the next move.   25
I heard myself reciting:

'Demon dwarf
with the German jaw,
surrender your purse
with the ghostly gold.'   30

He took out a fat purse,
put it down on a stone
and recited in reply, in a voice too big for his body:

'You found me fair,
and I grant your wishes.   35
But we'll meet again,
when I dance in your ashes.'

He settled himself down once more
and bent over the bag,
            looking off to one side.   40

'I thought I was safe up here.
You have to give the music a while to itself sometimes,
up out of the huckstering

– jumping around in your green top hat
and showing your skills   45
with your eye on your income.'

He ran his fingers up and down the stops,
then gave the bag a last squeeze.
His face went solemn,

his fingertips fondled all the right places,   50
and he started a slow air
                    out across the valley.

                *

I left him to himself.
And left the purse where it was.
I have all I need for the while I have left   55

without taking unnecessary risks.
And made my own way down to the main road
with my mind on our next meeting.

Glossary

title	*Glenmacnass*:	a waterfall in Co. Wicklow
title	*Littlebody*:	leprechaun (from the Irish *lú-chorpán*, 'little body')
1	*sheepfold*:	enclosure for penning sheep in
3	*cottonheads*:	plants
6	*prow*:	projecting front part
14	*guttural*:	a throaty sound; here, the deep sound of the uilleann pipes
28	*German jaw*:	probably a strong, pointed jaw
43	*huckstering*:	selling; here, prostituting your art

Guidelines

'Littlebody', the sixth part of the poem 'Glenmacnass', is from the collection *Littlebody* (2001). **It dramatises an encounter between the speaker and a traditional figure from Irish mythology, a leprechaun (*lú-chorpán* is Irish for littlebody).** In the previous sections of the poem the speaker has affirmed his choice of natural beauty over life in the city, and of domestic intimacy over public involvement. Kinsella made this choice when he left his home in Dublin's city centre to live near the Sally Gap in rural Co. Wicklow, also the setting for the poem 'The Familiar'.

Commentary

Lines 1–25

He describes how he climbs far up into the hills reaching an even more remote place, where he is surrounded by black bog and stony slopes. He hears the music of pipes (the traditional music of leprechauns) and comes across the leprechaun, playing his music. Like the landscape that surrounds him, the leprechaun's music is harsh. Its harshness is conveyed by the strong consonance (repetition of consonant sounds) and onomatopoeic effect of the 'g' sounds in 'growl' and 'guttural'.

Littlebody is described in the traditional way, with humped back, carrying his pipes and his bag. An elusive creature, he tries at first to escape from the speaker. But one of the traditions surrounding leprechauns is that they must hand over their purse or crock of gold if they are found, so the speaker duly stops him and demands his reward: 'I found you fair and I want my due' (line 23).

Lines 26–52

Up to this point the tone of the poem has been conversational, as is appropriate for a poem that tells a story. But the dialogue between the speaker and Littlebody is sing-song and ritualistic. The speaker addresses him as 'Demon dwarf / with the German jaw' (lines 27–28), a reference both to his supernatural aspect and the stern, pointed jaw of the traditional leprechaun figure. The 'ghostly gold' (line 30) is the 'magic' crock of gold that leprechauns were said to carry.

Littlebody also replies in a quatrain (four lines). While he is prepared to hand over his purse, ('You found me fair', line 34), he gives the speaker a grim warning: next time they meet it will be when the speaker dies. This is a reminder that leprechauns have an association with death as well as with good luck.

Rather surprisingly, Littlebody now veers away from his traditional role to speak more meaningfully. He tells the speaker that he felt safe in the hills (as indeed the speaker himself does) playing his music for himself rather than having to pander to onlookers or prostitute his art for money's sake. The image of him 'jumping around' in his 'green top hat' (line 44) might remind us of St Patrick's Day traditions. These revelations are followed by a 'slow air' of lament (line 51), perhaps for the times he was forced to do just that.

Lines 53–58

In the final section of the poem the speaker leaves Littlebody alone, realising that he has no need of the leprechaun's gold – in fact it might be a source of sorrow or ill luck for him. He realises that he has 'all I need for the while I have left' (line 55). Ominously, he concludes by saying that his mind is on their 'next meeting' (line 58), which as Littlebody has said, will take place when he dies.

Allegory

An allegory is a story with a second meaning hidden or partially hidden behind its literal one. Clearly Kinsella does not set out to convince us that he has met a leprechaun but decided not to take his purse of gold. There are, however, a number of possible allegorical interpretations we could make of this imagined encounter.

In the first part of the entire poem (not printed here) the speaker referred to how he 'turned away in refusal' from what he termed the 'hissing assemblies', seeking instead the calm and peace of the Wicklow countryside. His meeting with Littlebody dramatises the conflict inherent in this decision. In this context the 'fat purse' (line 31) may represent the material reward or the fame that he (as a poet) may have achieved if he had remained more publicly involved. **But the poem suggests that accepting fame or fortune inevitably leads to prostituting or squandering one's art.** Like Littlebody, then, he is better off seeking to pursue it in solitude, for the sake of the 'music'.

Kinsella the poet is so convinced by Littlebody's words that he leaves him alone. Allegorically speaking, his refusal of the 'ghostly gold' (line 30) represents his determination to avoid Littlebody's mistakes. This may be interpreted as Kinsella's refusal to engage with what has been called the 'business of poetry' (i.e. the public appearances and involvement required of a successful poet). For him, to do so might be one of the 'unnecessary risks' he mentions (line 56) of losing his sense of integrity as a poet.

The final lines remind us that death is a subject Kinsella returns to time and time again. The 'next meeting' (line 58), as in the old superstition, may be the speaker's last.

Thinking about the poem

1. How does the poem convey the remoteness of the place, in the first section?
2. How did you respond to the figure of Littlebody? Do you find him realistic in the context of the poem?
3. How would you describe the atmosphere created in the poem?
4. Bearing in mind the usual depictions of leprechauns, did you find anything surprising about Kinsella's portrayal of Littlebody?
5. What is your interpretation of the lines in the final section: 'I have all I need for the while I have left / without taking unnecessary risks' (lines 55–56)?
6. What is your interpretation of the lines 'You have to give the music a while to itself sometimes, / up out of the huckstering' (lines 42–43)?
7. From your reading of the poem, what have you learned of Kinsella's attitude to writing poetry?
8. Do you consider this poem to be hopeful or pessimistic? Give reasons for your view.
9. Discuss the view that the poem may be a satirical comment on Irish artistic or cultural circles.
10. Is allegory effective as a way of getting a point across? Support your answer by reference to the poem.

from Belief and Unbelief: Echo

He cleared the thorns
from the broken gate,
and held her hand
through the heart of the wood
to the holy well. 5

They revealed their names
and told their tales
as they said that they would
on that distant day
when their love began. 10

And hand in hand
they turned to leave.
when she stopped and whispered
a final secret
down to the water. 15

Guidelines

'Echo' was published in *Peppercanister 27* in 2007. **A love poem, it encapsulates the relationship between a man and woman in beautifully simple images.**

Commentary

A man and woman have returned, many years later, to the place where they first declared their love: a holy well deep in the heart of a wood. Symbolically, this is a place of pilgrimage. Perhaps they wish to express gratitude for the love they have shared. As they had both promised they would, they reveal themselves as intimately as possible: 'They revealed their names / and told their tales' (lines 6–7), in the same way as they had before. In this manner their love comes full circle, as the title 'Echo' might suggest.

But the underlying philosophy of love contained in the poem is not perhaps so straightforward. There are 'thorns' to be cleared (line 1). The 'heart of the wood' (line 4) is not easily found. Might these be metaphors for difficulty and effort? In the closing image we see how the woman has a 'final secret' (line 14) that she has kept. **Perhaps this implies the mystery of love**, the impossibility of ever knowing fully even a beloved partner.

Atmosphere of the poem

The atmosphere created in 'Echo' has the mythic quality of a fairy tale. The man and woman could almost be children wandering through a wood as in many old stories. Thorns feature as symbols in many tales. Holy wells have played a role in legends, Celtic and otherwise. While the title 'Echo' refers to the sound created by talking into the depths of a well, it may also refer to the mythical figure of Echo, who fell in love with the youth Narcissus in the Greek myth.

The tenderness of love is expressed in the couple's simple gestures and words. But there is also sadness in the insight expressed in the last image that is typical of Kinsella's honest appraisal of the love relationship. In an earlier poem (significantly, called 'Echoes') he had said: 'Love I consider a difficult, scrupulous art'.

Thinking about the poem

1. Would you agree that the poem is a celebration of love? Refer to the poem in your answer.
2. As well as celebrating love, would you agree that the poem is also realistic about it? Give a reason for your view.
3. Is the title an effective one? Give reasons for your view.
4. Suggest a new title for the poem and explain your choice.
5. Although the poem is short and simply expressed, do you agree that its vision of love is quite complex? Give reasons for your view.
6. Compare 'Echo' with 'The Familiar: VII' as love poems. Which poem do you prefer, and why?

Exam-Style Questions

1. In his poems, Kinsella has said that he 'attempted to make real, in whatever terms, the passing of time, the frightening exposure of all relationships and feeling to erosion'. With this statement in mind, discuss the poems of Thomas Kinsella.
2. 'Love, death and the artistic art are the main concerns of Kinsella in his poems.' Discuss this statement.
3. Kinsella's poems have been praised for their musicality and the power of his visual imagination. Explore these aspects of Kinsella's poems.
4. 'Kinsella is always alert and perceptive in his poems to details and their significance.' Discuss this statement.
5. 'Kinsella's poems have a strong sense of place but are also universal in their significance.' Would you agree with this view? Support your answer with reference to the poems.
6. 'Kinsella's poems see the bleakness of life but also its beauty.' Discuss this statement.
7. 'Kinsella gives us great insight in his poems into his childhood and his family relationships.' Choose the poems that you consider give the deepest insight into these family relationships and show how they are effective.
8. 'No one else writes like Kinsella.' Explore the aspects of Kinsella's poems that make his voice unique, in your view.
9. 'The Impact of Thomas Kinsella's Poetry.' Using this title, write a speech to be given to an audience of your fellow students.

Your speech could include some of the following points:
- Themes make a powerful impact on the reader (e.g. family relationships, childhood memories, love, death).
- Language used is highly effective (e.g. sensuous images, perceptive details, sound effects and patterns).
- Memorable atmosphere evoked in poems.
- Emotional honesty in dealing with difficult subjects.
- Creates vivid sense of time and place.
- Poems are both personal and universal.

10. 'Kinsella's poems add greatly to the understanding of the reader.' Do you agree with this assessment? Support your answer by relevant quotation and/or reference to the poems on your course.

Your answer might include some of the following ideas:
- Kinsella's exploration of childhood memories adds to the reader's understanding of this important time in life.
- The stylistic features he uses in evoking his childhood enable the reader to enter fully into his experience.
- He enhances our understanding of difficult issues such as death and suffering by confronting them with honesty.
- By dealing with personal and family relationships he broadens the reader's understanding of these issues.

Sample Essay

'In his poems Kinsella gives us great insight into his childhood experiences and his family relationships.'

Write a response to the poetry of Thomas Kinsella in the light of this statement.

I most certainly agree that reading Thomas Kinsella's poems gives us great insight into his childhood experiences and his family relationships. In 'Dick King', 'Hen Woman', 'Tear' and 'Model School, Inchicore' he evokes for us a world that has long since past, but which has been for him such a rich source of creative inspiration. His emotional honesty in dealing with his family relationships in 'Tear' and 'His Father's Hands', as well as in his experience of love and marriage in 'The Familiar', also made a great impact on me.

[First paragraph indicates the areas that will be covered in the essay and gives initial response]

For Kinsella, childhood experiences provided much material for future poems. In 'Dick King' he pays tribute to a neighbour who lived near the Kinsella family when the poet was a boy. Vivid images such as 'rain on the cobbles / Ripples in the iron trough, and the horses' dipped / Faces under the Fountain in James's Street' evoke a definite time and place: Dublin in the early decades of the twentieth century. He succeeds in giving us a real sense of the man's life and personality. Dick King's life may have been full of hardship – 'season in, season out / He made his wintry bed' – but he was also an 'upright' man who taught the young Kinsella a great deal about the history of their city. Now, as an adult poet, Kinsella acknowledges the kindness of his old friend and expresses his affection for him: he would like to 'wish him well'.

[First poem discussed in response to the question, suitable quotations included]

In 'Tear', however, Kinsella gives us a less positive insight into his childhood experiences. In the poem he recounts how he was 'sent in to see' his dying grandmother. As in 'Dick King', the sense of time and place is created by specific images: the 'fringe of jet drops' that were hanging at the entrance to the old woman's room, the 'smell of disused / organs' and 'the last watery light from the window'. His description of the old woman makes us almost see her, lying 'distracted' in her bed, the covers 'gathered close / up to her mouth'. Her hair was like that of a young woman, 'loosened out' on the pillow, but in the dim light it strangely 'mixed with the shadows / criss-crossing her forehead' so that it was 'like a web of strands'.

The impression we get is of a witch-like figure who is a source of potential danger to the young boy. It was as if his grandmother had ceased to be her familiar self ('my own father's mother') with whom he had a close relationship. She becomes instead someone who might 'turn and tempt me' 'with open mouth'. The image suggests that the boy feels he is being swallowed up in a situation beyond his control. We can identify with his mixed emotions here: he feels compelled to kiss her, but he also feels repelled and frightened at the sight of the dying old woman. With great emotional honesty Kinsella conveys the boy's dilemma. He solved it in his own way, when he 'sank' his face into the 'chill / and smell of her black aprons' at the foot of her bed, and found himself able to produce the single 'tear' of the poem's title.

[Second poem discussed in response to the question, suitable quotations included]

When we read 'Tear' we are conscious that Kinsella is describing a crucial moment in his childhood, and perhaps in everyone's childhood, when they become aware of death for the first time. The boy also learns another lesson from that experience. This could also be labelled a universal truth: that the death of an innocent infant, like that of his sister Agnes, is more affecting than that of an elderly person, whose life may be 'bitter with hard bondage'.

[Discussion of poem combines both aspects of the question and indicates response]

Kinsella's experience of being in primary school is the theme of 'Model School, Inchicore'. This poem is not as emotionally intense as 'Tear', but I was impressed and moved by the manner in which the poet brings us back to his childhood world. The language and imagery is simple and direct. In the earliest class the emphasis is on people and things: the marla they play with, Miss Carney the teacher and the silly pun on her name in Irish. Then we meet Mr Browne, who introduces them to 'decimals'. With a child's innocence Kinsella thinks he is 'going to know / everything'. For most people, childhood is a time when the senses are especially responsive, and Kinsella reflects this when he tells us of the 'flickering sun' that 'warmed our folded coats' and the 'big chestnut leaves' that they played with in autumn. He also succeeds in conveying the young boy's intellectual development as he sits in the shed contemplating what he had been taught in religious knowledge classes. He ends the poem with an image that may be interpreted in a number of ways: 'The taste / of ink off / the nib shrank your / mouth.' Might it suggest the disillusionment that lies in store for many people after their schooldays?

[Third poem discussed in response to the question, suitable quotations included]

Reading these poems it seems to me that Kinsella not only gives us an insight into his childhood experiences but that he goes beyond purely personal memories to give them a universal significance. One of the ways in which he does this is by using images and themes from mythology. In 'Tear', for instance, the boy's situation is described in terms of a journey into the dark, almost like the underworld, where the 'hero' will find something, or learn something. The description of his grandmother, too, has an otherworldly quality. Kinsella's study of the psychology of Carl Jung taught him that the stories in mythology reflect general human experience. Like the young boy in the poem, each of us must learn about death and suffering.

[Personal response given and background information provided]

In 'Hen Woman' there is a similar blend of autobiography and mythology. The young Kinsella sees an old woman grab a hen as it is laying an egg. The egg then smashes down into a 'shore' or sewer opening. This seemingly trivial incident takes on a mythological significance: the old woman emerges from the 'black hole' of her cottage, she is angry and threatening – again, a witch-like figure – and the watching boy not only learns a lesson about the origin of life itself but becomes aware that what he has seen will stay with him for the rest of his life. It will also provide material for poetry: 'I feed upon it still, as you see.' The poem suggests that memory and imagination are inextricably linked, and that childhood experience is crucial in developing artistic awareness.

[Fourth poem discussed in response to the question, suitable quotations included]

Just as I found myself identifying with Kinsella's childhood experiences, I also identified with his exploration of family relationships, especially in 'His Father's Hands', where the image of 'hands' allows him to examine the genetic link between himself, his father and his grandfather. He himself drinks 'firmly', his father's finger 'prodded and prodded', he saw his grandfather 'tightening' the tobacco plug in his pipe and making shoes.

[Links first aspect of discussion with second]

Throughout the poem, as he goes back further into his family's history, he describes how the generations before him worked with their hands – as stone cutters or masons – and earlier still how they seized their territory, 'wedged with tracks'. This leads him to wonder at the mystery of genetic inheritance:

> The blood advancing
> – gorging vessel after vessel –
> and altering in them
> one by one.

The image of the 'countless little nails' that fell from his grandfather's shoemaker's block that ends the poem may be a metaphor for how life continues, generation after generation. Although Kinsella's poem is rooted in his personal family history, I believe we can all respond to this idea, particularly since interest in genealogy and genetics has increased.

[Fifth poem discussed in response to the question, suitable quotations included]

One aspect of Kinsella's work that particularly appeals to me is his emotional honesty, as mentioned previously. This is expressed in his delicate love poems, such as 'The Familiar'. Addressed to his wife, the poem describes a seemingly mundane moment from their lives: preparing breakfast. As he goes through the motions of slicing tomatoes, making tea, fixing their places at the table, the routine becomes a ritual, a ceremony that celebrates their love without any fanfare or emotional drama. The language he uses – the 'little brazen bell', himself standing 'with arms extended' like a priest – creates a religious atmosphere, but the words of his wife that end the poem are plain and almost flat: 'You are very good. You always made it nice.' Placed alongside the religious imagery, these words evoke the simplicity of their life together. His wife is 'familiar' to him in the ordinary meaning of the word, but may also be a 'presence' or inspiration for him and his work. The poem seems to me to celebrate the mysteriousness that surrounds even those most familiar to us in a moving way.

To conclude, I found Thomas Kinsella's imaginative re-creation of childhood utterly convincing and his exploration of relationships emotionally satisfying.

[Final lines emphasise focus of answer and response]

snapshot

Thomas Kinsella

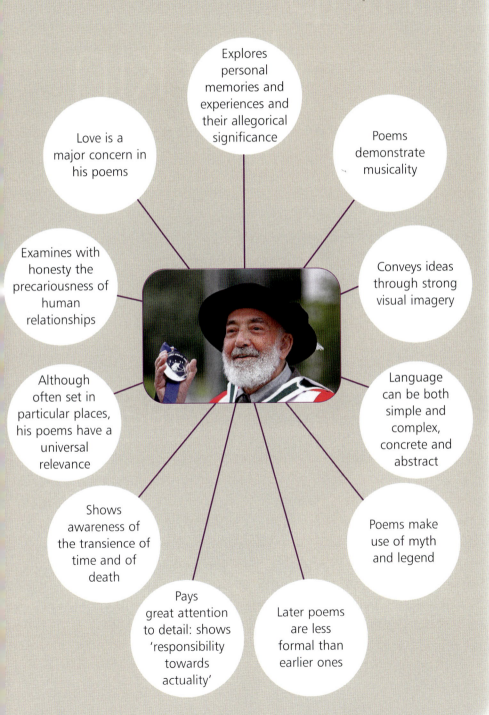

- Explores personal memories and experiences and their allegorical significance
- Poems demonstrate musicality
- Love is a major concern in his poems
- Conveys ideas through strong visual imagery
- Examines with honesty the precariousness of human relationships
- Language can be both simple and complex, concrete and abstract
- Although often set in particular places, his poems have a universal relevance
- Poems make use of myth and legend
- Shows awareness of the transience of time and of death
- Pays great attention to detail: shows 'responsibility towards actuality'
- Later poems are less formal than earlier ones

Philip Larkin

1922–1985

WEDDING-WIND
AT GRASS
CHURCH GOING
AN ARUNDEL TOMB
THE WHITSUN WEDDINGS
MCMXIV
AMBULANCES*
THE TREES
THE EXPLOSION*
CUT GRASS

Biography

Philip Larkin was born into a middle-class family in Coventry, England, on 9 August 1922. He was the second child of Sydney and Eva Larkin. The family name is common in Ireland and it was often assumed that the poet had Irish ancestry until Larkin's father established that their branch of the family was English and had lived in the same part of the Midlands for generations.

Family life

Sydney Larkin was an accountant and at the time of his son's birth he was treasurer of Coventry Corporation. He was well read, agnostic in outlook and outspoken in his convictions. Eva Larkin was intelligent but she was also nervous and timid and her husband ruled the household. There were constant tensions between Larkin's parents and this coloured his childhood, which he described as 'a forgotten boredom'. From an early age Larkin was ungainly and short-sighted. He was also shy and self-consciousness, so much so that, at age four, he developed a stammer.

By all accounts, the family home was a cold, lonely place. Because his sister, Kitty, was nine years older than him, Larkin felt like an only child. As he got older, his mother grew more anxious and his father more scornful, especially to Kitty, although he did communicate his love of literature and music to his son. **Reviewing his parents' relationship in the 1950s, Larkin wrote: 'Certainly the marriage left me with two convictions: that human beings should not live together, and that children should be taken from their parents at an early age.' He also said that although he liked his parents, 'they were rather awkward people and not very good at being happy. And these things rub off.'**

Larkin's father was an admirer of Adolf Hitler and of German efficiency and he brought the teenage Philip on holiday to Germany in the 1930s. Larkin said that these trips 'sowed the seed of my hatred of abroad'. His natural shyness was intensified by his inability to speak German and he was embarrassed by his father's enthusiasm for the National Socialists. **As Larkin grew to manhood, he rejected all interest in politics, though his outlook on life was decidedly conservative. From his father he inherited a 'total disbelief in Christianity'.**

Education

Larkin attended the local grammar school because his father despised the notion of elitist, private education. The school had a high academic standard and he did well without excelling or wanting to excel. He then studied at St John's College, Oxford, from 1940 to 1943. Although the war curbed the activities of the students, he enjoyed undergraduate life, adopting the pose of a dandy and listening to recordings of American jazz. It would be hard to overstate his love of jazz. In some respects Larkin was a flamboyant character at Oxford, but he still remained shy and self-conscious, especially with girls.

Larkin read widely. W.H. Auden was central to his view of literature, and his first poem, published as an undergraduate, reflects Auden's influence. He also admired D.H. Lawrence, W.B. Yeats (though he revised his opinion) and Dylan Thomas. Above all, **Larkin valued those writers who wrote without affectation and whose work remained close to ordinary, everyday life**. Thomas Hardy embodied all that Larkin looked for in a poet.

With his friend and fellow writer Kingsley Amis, Larkin developed a strong dislike of pomposity and a scathing, private disregard for 'respectability', which was to last a lifetime, although his public persona was polite and conformist.

Because of his poor eyesight, Larkin was not called up to the army. He was largely unaffected by the war and was disinterested in its progress. As he approached the end of his time in Oxford, he was sunk in depression. His writing was not progressing and he had no idea of a career and seemed indecisive and passive as the time came for him to choose. This pattern was to repeat itself at other critical junctures in his life.

Librarian and writer

He successfully applied in November 1943 for the post of librarian in a small town in Shropshire. Although his letters reveal his initial dislike and contempt for the job, he soon began to enjoy the life of a librarian and found time for his writing. In 1945 Larkin's first collection of poetry, *The North Ship*, was published, by a small publishing house called The Fortune Press, which also published his first novel, *Jill*, in 1946. The book describes, in fictional terms, Larkin's life as a student. Both the novel and the collection of poems met with a muted response.

In 1946 Larkin got a job in the library of University College, Leicester. **His second novel, *A Girl in Winter* (1947), received favourable reviews and Larkin believed that he had begun his writer's life in earnest. In fact, he was to write no more fiction and produced a small body of published work over his lifetime.** However, he maintained a voluminous correspondence with his many friends. In his letters he presented different aspects of his personality to each of his correspondents. **The letters, along with his diaries, reveal a complex personality and constitute an impressive and fascinating body of work.**

In 1950 Larkin moved to Belfast to work in the library at Queen's University. Belfast freed Larkin from the pressures of personal relationships and family obligations. He enjoyed university life and conversation and it was in Belfast that he prepared his first major poetry collection, *The Less Deceived* (1955). Larkin later recalled that Belfast provided him with the best conditions for writing: he was surrounded by interesting and stimulating company; he had comfortable accommodation provided by the university; and he formed a number of romantic attachments that did not threaten him or impede his writing.

In 1955 he applied for the post of librarian in the University of Hull. Larkin's quiet air of authority, his eloquence and the incisiveness of his mind impressed the interview board. They duly appointed him. During his time in Hull, the library underwent a transformation, growing from a staff of eleven to over one hundred. And while Larkin often spoke of his 'boring job', he took a professional pride in his stewardship of the library and was admired and respected within his profession. He oversaw the building of the new library in Hull and contributed many ideas to its design and decor.

Love life

Larkin's first love was Ruth Bowman, whom he met in 1943. To her, Larkin was witty, kind, outrageous and brilliant. To him, she was someone in whom he could confide and be himself. In 1948, when Larkin was twenty-five and struggling to come to terms with his father's death and his duty to his mother, he became engaged to Ruth, then aged twenty-one. The affair dragged on for two years before Bowman ended it.

Larkin never married, although he was involved in two more long-term relationships. One was with Monica Jones, a lecturer in English at the University of Leicester. The other was with Maeve Brennan, a colleague at the University of Hull. For years Larkin experienced conflict between his feelings for Brennan ('The woman I want to marry') and his loyalty to Jones ('The woman I should marry').

Recognition as a writer

As Larkin established himself as a librarian, he won increasing recognition as a writer. *The Less Deceived* was highly successful, selling over six thousand copies in the first years of publication and receiving favourable reviews. Selections of his poems appeared in all the major anthologies published in the late 1950s and early 1960s and he recorded a number of programmes for the BBC. He regularly reviewed poetry for *The Guardian* and became the jazz correspondent for *The Daily Telegraph*.

In a spirit of growing confidence, Larkin moved into a new flat in Hull in 1956 (and lived there until 1974). He preserved his solitude, rarely inviting guests and keeping his work separate from his life as a writer. The intention was to create a space for his writing but the space often remained empty and he wrote less poetry than he had hoped to write.

Larkin's literary reputation grew with the publication of the collections, *The Whitsun Weddings* (1964) and *High Windows* (1974), both of which were acclaimed as contemporary masterpieces, and awards and honours were heaped upon him, including a CBE in 1975. Following the publication of *The Whitsun Weddings*, he was invited to make a television programme for the BBC on his life and work, a project that gave him much delight and he made recordings of his poems.

Oxford University Press invited him to edit a new *Oxford Book of Modern Verse*, to replace the anthology edited by Yeats in 1936. On its publication in 1973 it proved to be every bit as controversial as the original. Larkin also served as a committee member for various poetry organisations, using his administrative know-how to good effect.

Recluse

By the age of fifty, he had the mien of an old man and was gripped by bouts of remorse and feelings of failure. He described his situation in the opening verse of 'Aubade':

> I work all day, and get half-drunk at night.
> Waking at four to soundless dark, I stare.
> In time the curtain edges will grow light.
> Till then I see what's really there:
> Unresting death, a whole day nearer now,
> Making all thought impossible but how
> And where and when I shall myself die.

As Larkin grew older, he became somewhat reclusive. **In the last ten years of his life, he wrote very little poetry. He believed that his inspiration had deserted him.** The onset of deafness restricted his social activities, and deepened his frequent bouts of melancholy. His love/hate relationship with his family lasted right up to his mother's death in 1977. In a letter he remarked: 'To escape from home is a life's work.' The economic cutbacks of the 1970s meant that the library in Hull was forced to curtail its services. To Larkin it seemed that everything was falling apart.

The end of his days was marked by a sense of failure. He believed that he had set out to perfect his work and was left with only a failed life. Not even the offer to succeed John Betjeman as poet laureate, which he declined, cheered him. In June 1985 he was diagnosed with cancer. After surgery and a short remission, he died in December, aged sixty-three. His final words were: 'I am going to the inevitable.' **On his death he was acclaimed as England's finest post-war poet, whose work transformed the contradictions, frustrations, fears and indignities of ordinary life into eloquent poetry.**

Social and Cultural Context

Poetic movements

Modernism

T.S. Eliot was the dominant figure in English poetry for the first third of the twentieth century. Eliot was a Modernist poet. Modernism arose out of the developments in psychoanalysis in the early part of the century and out of the crisis caused by the experience of World War 1. In all areas of life, old forms had failed and new ones needed to be invented. **Modernism rejected traditional practices in favour of new techniques and experiments.** In addition, as with most new movements in art, older traditions were revived. Thus, Greek mythology became a source for modern literature and works were written as if resuming a discussion that had begun two thousand years before. Borrowing from the model of the unconscious and its processes, Modernist poets used private symbols, allusions to other works of art and scraps and fragments of myth to make their poems. **The result was an exciting kind of poetry, often fragmentary and random in its organisation – a poetry that was neither popular nor easily accessible.**

Poetry of private experience

In the late 1920s Europe was in recession and fascism was on the rise. The experimentation of Modernism seemed indulgent to a generation of younger writers, many of whom were committed socialists. Their concern was to give expression to their political and social awareness and to speak to and for the poor and the working class within society. W.H. Auden became the leading figure in English poetry in the 1930s. For Auden, to be a writer was to be a citizen and to write was to put your insights at the service of your fellow citizens to give them strength to withstand their enemies. In some respects Auden's view of poetry was shared by Larkin, however, Larkin was not interested in the political awareness that shaped Auden's work. **For Larkin, poetry was concerned with private, individual experience**:

> I write about experiences, often quite simple, everyday experiences which somehow acquire some sort of special meaning for me, and I write poems about them to preserve them. You see, I want to express the experience in a poem so that it remains preserved, unchanging; and I then hope that other people will come upon this experience, pickled as it were in verse, and it will mean something to them, sound some chord in their own recollection, perhaps, or show them something familiar in a new light.

In Larkin's eyes, Modernism had destroyed the quality of delight that should accompany poetry: 'This is my essential criticism of modernism . . . it helps us neither to enjoy nor to endure.'

The Movement

The first coherent development in poetry after World War II was 'The Movement' – a loose grouping of poets who strove for clarity in their work and who used traditional forms in reaction against Modernism. They refused to abandon a rational structure and comprehensible language, even when the verse is highly charged with sensuous or emotional intent.

Everyday life as poetry

Larkin had little time for the experimentalism of Modernism or for poetry that was intellectually obscure. He rejected the example of Eliot in favour of the example of Hardy. Indeed, Larkin's work expresses nostalgia for the England evoked by Hardy, and Larkin admired the style of Hardy's writing, which is narrative, direct and personal.

Larkin thought that life, as it was lived by ordinary people, should and could provide the subject of poetry. He wanted his poems to address a non-academic audience in a language that was close to everyday speech and English in tone and manner.

Of course, this is not to say that Larkin's work does not reflect elements of the Modernist style or that it is simply an imitation of Hardy. Many of his own poems are complex and subtle, rich in symbolism and straining to go beyond the ordinary. In the words of the critic James Booth, Larkin pushes language 'to the limits of grammatical tolerance'. However, he admired poetry that was accessible and written with a keen sense of formality, using traditional verse patterns. He thought that life, as it was lived by ordinary people, should and could provide the subject of poetry.

A time of change

Larkin's life and career coincided with remarkable changes in English society. Yet these changes are almost totally absent from Larkin's poems. He lived through World War II and the economic depression of the 1950s. He was a librarian in Hull during the rapid expansion of the university system in England, and the changes in attitude and culture brought about by the affluence of the 1960s. Student unrest in the late 1960s and early 1970s won no sympathy from him. Nor was he sympathetic to the increasingly multiracial nature of British society. His cure for unemployment was to stop unemployment benefit. As he grew older, he expressed alarmingly reactionary views in his private correspondence. In his final collection, *High Windows* (1974), there is a coarseness in some of the poems that is striking. He admired the leadership of Margaret Thatcher, though, ironically, the financial policies pursued by her government led to cutbacks in university budgets, which in turn undid many of Larkin's professional achievements.

Whatever insights are won in his poetry arise from the observation of his own life and the ordinary lives around him. Perhaps it is only in the rueful tone of some poems in *High Windows*, where the persona of the poems envies the young their freedom, that we see the poetry reflecting public events.

Timeline

1922	Born on 9 August in Coventry into a middle-class family
1926	Develops a stammer
1930s	Visits Germany with his father, who admires Hitler
1940	Enters Oxford University to study English
1944	Begins work as a librarian in Shropshire
1945	Publishes first collection, *The North Ship*
1946	Publishes first novel, *Jill*
1947	Publishes second novel, *A Girl in Winter*
1948	Death of father; becomes engaged to Ruth Bowman
1950	Engagement ends; begins work in Queen's University, Belfast
1955	Publishes first major collection, *The Less Deceived*
1955	Becomes librarian at the University of Hull
1964	Publishes *The Whitsun Weddings* to wide acclaim
1974	*High Windows* greeted as a contemporary masterpiece
1975	Awarded a CBE
1977	Death of mother, aged 91
1985	Diagnosed with cancer in June; dies on 2 December

Wedding-Wind

The wind blew all my wedding-day,
And my wedding-night was the night of the high wind;
And a stable-door was banging, again and again,
That he must go and shut it, leaving me
Stupid in candlelight, hearing rain, 5
Seeing my face in the twisted candlestick,
Yet seeing nothing. When he came back
He said the horses were restless, and I was sad
That any man or beast that night should lack
The happiness I had. 10

    Now in the day
All's ravelled under the sun by the wind's blowing.
He has gone to look at the floods, and I
Carry a chipped pail to the chicken-run,
Set it down, and stare. All is the wind 15
Hunting through clouds and forests, thrashing
My apron and the hanging cloths on the line.
Can it be borne, this bodying-forth by wind
Of joy my actions turn on, like a thread
Carrying beads? Shall I be let to sleep 20
Now this perpetual morning shares my bed?
Can even death dry up
These new delighted lakes, conclude
Our kneeling as cattle by all-generous waters?

Glossary

5	*Stupid*:	here, drowsy or not fully awake, or stunned through lack of sleep
12	*ravelled*:	made clear; it also means to untangle and to entangle
14	*pail*:	a bucket
18	*borne*:	sustained, tolerated, endured; it also derives its force from its association with childbearing and birth
18	*bodying-forth*:	to give expression or form to something

Guidelines

'Wedding-Wind' was written in September 1946 and It appeared in *The Less Deceived* (1955). It was written during Larkin's engagement to Ruth Bowman. **'Wedding-Wind' is one of the few poems by Larkin that celebrates, in an unqualified way, passionate love. It is also one of the few poems in which the persona of the poem can be totally divorced from the poet himself.** In the poem the wind is a symbol of passion and change. The images of the wind and the wind-changed world suggest the powerful forces affecting the young bride.

Andrew Motion, Larkin's biographer, suggests that 'Wedding-Wind' was intended to ease the door open, through which Larkin could contemplate marriage. Yet, Larkin scribbled in his notebook during the period in which the poem was written: 'At 1.45 p.m. let me remember that the only married state I know, (i.e. that of my parents) is bloody hell. Never must it be forgotten.'

Commentary

Stanza 1

In the first stanza the bride tells us that her wedding night was the night of the 'high wind' (line 2). **In Larkin's work, the word 'high' is associated with experiences which are elevated and elevating and which have a spiritual resonance.** The joy of the bride on her wedding night makes her feel sympathetic to all creatures, 'man or beast' (line 9), who lack the happiness that she possesses.

Stanza 2

The second stanza speaks of the day after the wedding. Everything is bright and joyful. The wind continues to move through the world of 'clouds and forests, thrashing / My apron and the hanging cloths on the line' (lines 16–17). **Here, as elsewhere in the poem, the meaning advances by means of suggestion and indirect statement.** The verb 'thrashing', for example, suggests the forceful nature of the energy that affects the young bride and the violent strength of human passion.

The second stanza concludes with three questions. Surrendering herself to the images of the wind, she wonders if she can bear the joy of love, embodied in the wind, a joy that informs everything in her life. **However, paraphrasing lines 18 to 20 in this way fails to convey the richness of the language and imagery, which opens out in many directions.** For example, the verbs 'borne' and 'bodying-forth' suggest pregnancy and birth and link the wind to human passion, joy and generation. (See also the images of fruitfulness and generation in the concluding stanza of 'The Whitsun Weddings'.) The image of the beads suggests prayer and associates love with the sacred, as well as suggesting a necklace or a gift of love.

The second question (lines 20-21) suggests the radiance of the bride's new-found love and sexual passion, which are as bright as the 'perpetual morning'. In the third question, the bride, who knows that wind dries water, wonders, such is the intensity of her love, if the waters of 'these new delighted lakes' of love will ever be dried (lines 22-24). She questions whether death itself could force them to stop drinking from the generous waters of love.

In all of Larkin's poetry, this ending is unique in celebrating the possibility of love and joy outliving death. The concluding lines have the rhythm and syntax of liturgy, turning the poem into a hymn of praise to human love. The phrase 'all-generous waters' (line 24) is one of the poet's most memorable.

Language of the poem

The language throughout the poem is dignified and uplifting. Larkin skilfully uses long vowels, alliteration and repetition to give a sense of dignified eloquence to the simple vocabulary of the bride.

Note, how, in the last line of the poem, the bride speaks of 'Our kneeling', using the first person plural form of the pronoun for the first time in the poem.

Thinking about the poem

1. The bride describes her wedding night as 'the night of the high wind' (line 2). What, in your view, is the meaning of the adjective 'high', in the context of the poem?
2. Why does the bride say that she felt 'Stupid in candlelight' (line 5) when her husband went to shut the banging stable door?
3. Explain as clearly as you can what effect the joy of love has on the young woman.
4. What changes in the world and in the bride are described in the second stanza?
5. There are a number of interesting choices of word in stanza 2. Comment on the range of meaning in the following: 'thrashing', 'borne', 'bodying-forth'. Taken together, what do the words suggest?
6. The poem concludes with three questions. Consider the first of these, 'Can it be borne . . .' (lines 18-20). Paraphrase the meaning of these lines, and suggest some of the ways in which the language and imagery open out beyond one single meaning.
7. The waters of love are described as 'all-generous' (line 24). In your view, what possibility is contemplated by the bride in the final lines of the poem?

8   The language of the poem is simple. How, in your opinion, does Larkin manage to give it an eloquence and dignity?
9   Clearly the imagery of wind, storm and flood has a symbolic purpose in the poem. In your view, what complex of ideas and emotions does it express?
10 The poem has been described as a hymn to human love. Is this an apt description? Explain your answer.
11 Where else in Larkin's poetry is love presented in a positive light?

At Grass

The eye can hardly pick them out
From the cold shade they shelter in,
Till wind distresses tail and mane;
Then one crops grass, and moves about
– The other seeming to look on –   5
And stands anonymous again.

Yet fifteen years ago, perhaps
Two dozen distances sufficed
To fable them: faint afternoons
Of Cups and Stakes and Handicaps,   10
Whereby their names were artificed
To inlay faded, classic Junes –

Silks at the start: against the sky
Numbers and parasols: outside,
Squadrons of empty cars, and heat,   15
And littered grass: then the long cry
Hanging unhushed till it subside
To stop-press columns on the street.

Do memories plague their ears like flies?
They shake their heads. Dusk brims the shadows. 20
Summer by summer all stole away,
The starting-gates, the crowds and cries –
All but the unmolesting meadows.
Almanacked, their names live; they

Have slipped their names, and stand at ease,   25
Or gallop for what must be joy,
And not a fieldglass sees them home,
Or curious stop-watch prophesies:
Only the groom, and the groom's boy,
With bridles in the evening come.   30

Glossary

3	*distresses*: ruffles or upsets; here, it may suggest the nervousness of thoroughbred horses
4	*crops*: grazes or eats the grass
8	*Two dozen distances*: two dozen races or the distance of the race itself (a distance is a point 240 yards back from the winning post)
9	*fable*: to make famous in the lore of racing
10	*Cups . . . Handicaps*: types of horse race
11–12	*names . . . Junes*: Larkin takes a noun (artifice) and turns it into a verb; the formal, registered names of the horses were made fancy ('artificed') to decorate or ornament ('inlay') the important ('classic') races of the season, which were held in June and have now 'faded' from memory
13	*Silks*: the colourful garments worn by jockeys
23	*unmolesting*: not intrusive; the implied contrast is between the meadows and the crowds who swarm around the winning horse at the end of an important race
24	*Almanacked*: Larkin transforms a noun (almanac – an annual calendar giving information on particular topics) into a verb, which here means 'recorded in the racing records'
25	*slipped*: to be let loose from; Larkin plays with the idea of horses being freed from their bridles in this image of horses freed from their racing names and the obligation to race
28	*stop-watch prophesies*: the prospects of young race horses are determined by the times they register on the stop watch

Guidelines

Larkin wrote this poem in 1950 and it appeared in *The Less Deceived* (1955). The idea for 'At Grass' came to Larkin after he attended the cinema and saw a documentary on a retired racehorse.

Commentary

Stanza 1

The poem begins in a quiet, undramatic manner and captures the visual quality of the documentary which inspired the poem. The vocabulary, however, hints at themes beyond the level of description. The phrase 'the cold shade' (line 2) suggests death, and sets up an expectation that this meditation on the retired horses will involve an apprehension of death. The first line, 'The eye can hardly pick them out', suggests that the horses are becoming indistinct as, in the words of one critic, 'their fame recedes and their death approaches'.

Stanzas 2 and 3

In the second stanza we get an idea of Larkin's richly layered poetic method. Picking up on the idea of distance – the distance of the horses from the poet and the distance of the horses from their former lives – the poet thinks of the distances the horses ran to bring them into racing history. The final two lines of the stanza suggest the formal, registered names of the racehorses, as well as the inscription of each winning horse's name on racing trophies. The lines also contain the suggestion that horse racing itself is a kind of rich ornamentation or inlay to social life.

In stanza 3 Larkin uses a cinematic effect to evoke the fashion, wealth, hope, expectation and media interest that surrounds horse racing in England.

Stanzas 4 and 5

The opening of stanza 4 is whimsical: the horses shake their head in answer to the question, 'Do memories plague their ears like flies?' (lines 19 and 20). These lines bring into focus a major theme of the poem. However much human beings use horses for their sporting purposes, the horses themselves remain outside any understanding of that world. The racing names live on in the records of racing annuals, but 'they / Have slipped their names' (lines 24–25) and have returned to 'the unmolesting meadows' (line 23). **The fourth and fifth stanzas imply that the horses, now in the twilight of their lives, are free of the unwelcome attention of humans.**

The ending of the poem is beautifully achieved. The horses' names and their fame will live long after they have died. The thought of the final line of stanza 4 is left incomplete, 'Almanacked, their names live; they' . . . [will die]. However, before death comes, there is the freedom of the days at grass. Now the horses 'gallop for what must be joy' (line 26), away from the watchful eyes of racegoers. The final two lines take on an emotional resonance, through the use of mellow-sounding phrases and alliteration. The poetic effect is heightened by the inversion of the word order. The effect is to create a fine sense of closure, as the groom and the groom's boy come to take in the horses. **The ending suggests the final homecoming of horses whose lives have been safely and successfully concluded.**

Andrew Motion relates 'At Grass' to the personal crisis through which the poet was living. Larkin had yet to come to terms with the death of his father; his relationship with Ruth Bowman was coming to an end; and his relationship with his mother was beset by guilt and frustration. In these circumstances, the situation of the horses was to be envied.

Thinking about the poem

1. The opening stanza of the poem is quiet and undramatic. In your opinion, what words or phrases hint at themes beyond the level of description?
2. The first stanza suggests the distance of the horses from the observer. The concept of distance runs through the poem. What other types of distance are explored in 'At Grass'?
3. In stanza 3 the world of racing is suggested in a series of cinematic images. What kind of world emerges from these images?
4. The phrase 'unmolesting meadows' (line 23) is a startling one. What, do you think, does it contribute to the reader's understanding of the poem's themes?
5. The final stanza is rich and complex. Explain, as clearly as you can, how the images, language and rhythm suggest both freedom and the approach of death.
6. Which of the following, do you think, best describes Larkin's attitude to the horses?

    Larkin feels sorry for the retired horses.
    Larkin is happy that the horses are free from unwanted attention.
    Larkin envies the horses their freedom.

    Explain your answer
7. Some critics read 'At Grass' as expressing Larkin's nostalgia for an England that was disappearing. Others read it as expressing Larkin's personal sense of loss at the ending of his engagement to Ruth Bowman. Can you find evidence in the poem to support either of these readings?
8. What, in your opinion, are the main themes of 'At Grass'? What other poems by Larkin share these themes?

Church Going

Once I am sure there's nothing going on
I step inside, letting the door thud shut.
Another church: matting, seats, and stone,
And little books; sprawlings of flowers, cut
For Sunday, brownish now; some brass and stuff
Up at the holy end; the small neat organ;
And a tense, musty, unignorable silence,
Brewed God knows how long. Hatless, I take off
My cycle-clips in awkward reverence,

Move forward, run my hand around the font.
From where I stand, the roof looks almost new –
Cleaned, or restored? Someone would know: I don't.
Mounting the lectern, I peruse a few
Hectoring large-scale verses, and pronounce
'Here endeth' much more loudly than I'd meant.
The echoes snigger briefly. Back at the door
I sign the book, donate an Irish sixpence,
Reflect the place was not worth stopping for.

Yet stop I did: in fact I often do,
And always end much at a loss like this,
Wondering what to look for; wondering, too,
When churches fall completely out of use
What we shall turn them into, if we shall keep
A few cathedrals chronically on show,
Their parchment, plate and pyx in locked cases,
And let the rest rent-free to rain and sheep.
Shall we avoid them as unlucky places?

Or, after dark, will dubious women come
To make their children touch a particular stone;
Pick simples for a cancer; or on some
Advised night see walking a dead one?
Power of some sort or other will go on

In games, in riddles, seemingly at random;
But superstition, like belief, must die,
And what remains when disbelief has gone?
Grass, weedy pavement, brambles, buttress, sky,

A shape less recognisable each week,
A purpose more obscure. I wonder who
Will be the last, the very last, to seek
This place for what it was; one of the crew
That tap and jot and know what rood-lofts were?
Some ruin-bibber, randy for antique,
Or Christmas-addict, counting on a whiff
Of gown-and-bands and organ-pipes and myrrh?
Or will he be my representative,

Bored, uninformed, knowing the ghostly silt
Dispersed, yet tending to this cross of ground
Through the suburb scrub because it held unspilt
So long and equably what since is found
Only in separation – marriage, and birth,
And death, and thoughts of these – for which was built
This special shell? For, though I've no idea
What this accoutred frowsty barn is worth,
It pleases me to stand in silence here;

A serious house on serious earth it is,
In whose blent air all our compulsions meet,
Are recognised, and robed as destinies.
And that much never can be obsolete,
Since someone will forever be surprising
A hunger in himself to be more serious,
And gravitating with it to this ground,
Which, he once heard, was proper to grow wise in,
If only that so many dead lie round.

Glossary

4	*sprawlings*: arrangements of flowers that spread out in an irregular way
9	*cycle-clips*: metal clips that prevent the legs of trousers from flapping or catching in the chain of the bicycle
13	*the lectern*: a stand with a sloping surface for holding a book or Bible from which the readings from scripture are read during a church service
14	*Hectoring*: intimidating or bullying
15	*'Here endeth'*: the phrase that concludes each reading during services in the Anglican Church
17	*an Irish sixpence*: the 'Irish' coin is foreign currency and of little value
24	*chronically*: constantly
25	*parchment*: here, refers to all the sacred books kept in a church
25	*plate*: the gold and silver vessels used in church services
25	*pyx*: container or vessel in which the consecrated host is kept
28	*dubious*: uncertain, but also suspicious or untrustworthy
30	*simples*: herb used for medicinal purposes
31	*Advised night*: a night chosen deliberately
36	*buttress*: a stone support on the outside walls of the church
41	*rood-lofts*: galleries built above the altar in a church; a rood is a cross, especially one above the altar
42	*ruin-bibber*: Larkin coined this word for people who love to 'drink in' the atmosphere of ruins
44	*gown-and-bands*: a band is a large white collar, often with extensions, which hangs down over the gown; gown and bands are worn by the clergy and/or by members of the church choir
44	*myrrh*: the scent or fragrance in incense
46	*the ghostly silt*: this is a fine example of Larkin's ingenuity in his use of words: the phrase may be read as meaning, 'The deposit ('silt') of belief in spiritual ('ghostly') matters'
53	*accoutred*: decorated with all the appropriate trappings
53	*frowsty*: musty or stale-smelling
56	*compulsions*: impulses, deep-seated desires
61	*gravitating*: moving towards a centre of influence, as if drawn by a force; here, it combines the meaning of being attracted to the serious earth of the Church, the suggestion of weighty and solemn matters, and a reminder of the graves of the dead who lie round

Guidelines

This poem was written in 1954 and appeared in *The Less Deceived* (1955). **In 'Church Going' Larkin develops a style (and a poetic persona) that he was to use with great effect in several of his most important poems. The style is self-mocking, conversational and rich in detail.**

The poem arose out of a real experience, in which Larkin, on a cycling expedition, stopped to look inside a church.

Commentary

Title

The title, 'Church Going', is a pun. It describes both a visit to a church and the practice of attending religious services, but also suggests that religion is on the way out (i.e. that the Church itself is going).

Stanzas 1 and 2

The speaker of the poem, the Larkin persona, begins by presenting himself as an interloper, anxious to show no disrespect but uninformed. In stanza 2, as 'echoes snigger briefly' (line 16), the speaker appears as a faintly ridiculous figure, glad to be on his way. Like an ill-informed tourist, the speaker leaves the church noting that 'the place was not worth stopping for' (line 18) and admitting to feeling 'at a loss' (line 20). It is in the pursuit of an explanation for this feeling that the poem opens out in a rich, imaginative way.

Stanzas 3 and 4

In the course of the third stanza, the poem moves from the private 'I' to the communal 'we' and there is a corresponding shift from a descriptive to a reflective mode. The speaker considers a number of questions. What will happen 'When churches fall completely out of use' (line 22)? (The speaker presumes that religion will die and churches will fall into disuse. The questions project the successive stages in the process.) Will abandoned churches attract people who want to harness, in some superstitious way, the power that attended churches? Will churches be avoided 'as unlucky places' (line 27)? Will Christianity and belief be followed by superstition and disbelief? And when superstition dies, will the purpose of churches become obscure? What will follow after that? The vaguely mocking tone of stanzas 3 and 4 is unconcerned for the future of churches.

Stanza 5
The speaker considers who will be the very last person to seek the church where he stands for 'what it was' (line 40). The tone of the stanza, as the speaker considers the possible, future visitors, is sneering and dismissive.

Stanza 6
Just as suddenly as the satire surfaces, it disappears, and the speaker returns to the implied question of stanza 2: 'Why did I stop at this church?' The speaker now suggests that he is attracted to churches because they recognise and give meaning to the three most fundamental and vital experiences or necessities in our lives: love, procreation and death. The church is a space where these profound experiences may be contemplated in an appropriate way. And, as the stanza comes to an end, the voice of the speaker takes on a more confident tone, losing the awkwardness of the first stanza: 'It pleases me to stand in silence here' (line 54). This statement sets up the mood of the final stanza.

Final stanza
The speaker breaks completely with the scepticism of the earlier stanzas and speaks in a tone of elevated seriousness. The poem becomes solemn and resonant with the recognition of the deepest needs of human beings. Churches will attract individuals in the future for everyone has that 'hunger in himself to be more serious' (line 60) (perhaps including the poet). That seriousness will bring them to churches, because of the needs churches once served and because the dead lie buried round. The final stanza is written in a style that is weighty, dignified and quite removed from the earlier colloquialisms of the poem. Although churches may fall into ruin, and traditional churchgoing may become a thing of the past, the speaker sees that human beings will always hunger after seriousness and need to contemplate the mysteries of birth, love and death – the stages in human life that churches have recognised and made holy.

Andrew Motion says that the speaker in the poem 'speaks as someone without faith who is trying to recover the comfort that it used to give'. This comfort is not the usual one of love or other human beings. The speaker is alone and drawn to a place where 'so many dead lie round' (line 63).

Form and style of the poem

The poem is written in nine-line stanzas and follows a definite rhyming scheme – *ababcadcd*. Most of the lines contain ten syllables. The stanza form is big enough to incorporate the many changes of tone and language and the complex development of thought that occur in the poem. It is a measure of Larkin's skill that we read the poem without becoming aware of the tight structure that contains it.

Thinking about the poem

1. Comment on the appropriateness of the title of the poem.
2. Examine stanzas 1 and 2.
   a) How, in your view, does the speaker present himself in these stanzas?
   b) Is his attitude disrespectful?
   c) Is there, as some critics suggest, an ambivalence in his attitude?
3. List the questions that the speaker addresses in stanzas 3 to 5. These questions amount to a projected history of churches. Do you share the speaker's vision of the future of churches?
4. The poem takes on a savage tone in stanza 5. At whom is the speaker's contempt directed? In your view, does the poem supply a reasonable explanation of this anger?
5. The final two stanzas return to the question of why the speaker stopped at the church. What reason does the speaker give for gravitating to church grounds?
6. The final stanza achieves an impressive, elevated tone. What, in your opinion, contributes to this tone?
7. In your opinion, what truth or insight into human nature does the poem announce?
8. Is 'Church Going', in any sense, a religious poem? Explain your answer.
9. The voice of the poem clearly changes. Point out where the change is most notable. In your view, does this make the poem more or less interesting?
10. "Church Going" represents a highly selective, distilled, and disciplined use of language.' Comment on this view of the poem.
11. Read the opening stanza of the poem in minute detail. Examine each word. Note the precise nature of the descriptions; the observed details; the change in tone and attitude conveyed by a single word or detail. Note the use of colloquial phrases. Note the use of enjambment; the complex rhyme scheme; the syllable count. Now write a note on Larkin's poetic method in this stanza.
12. 'Church Going' and 'The Whitsun Weddings' are linked in terms of both style and the persona of the poem. From the evidence of 'Church Going' describe this persona.

An Arundel Tomb

Side by side, their faces blurred,
The earl and countess lie in stone,
Their proper habits vaguely shown
As jointed armour, stiffened pleat,
And that faint hint of the absurd –
The little dogs under their feet.

Such plainness of the pre-baroque
Hardly involves the eye, until
It meets his left-hand gauntlet, still
Clasped empty in the other; and
One sees, with a sharp tender shock,
His hand withdrawn, holding her hand.

They would not think to lie so long.
Such faithfulness in effigy
Was just a detail friends would see:
A sculpture's sweet commissioned grace
Thrown off in helping to prolong
The Latin names around the base.

They would not guess how early in
Their supine stationary voyage
The air would change to soundless damage,
Turn the old tenantry away;
How soon succeeding eyes begin
To look, not read. Rigidly they

Persisted, linked, through lengths and breadths
Of time. Snow fell, undated. Light
Each summer thronged the glass. A bright
Litter of birdcalls strewed the same
Bone-riddled ground. And up the paths
The endless altered people came,

Washing at their identity.
Now, helpless in the hollow of
An unarmorial age, a trough
Of smoke in slow suspended skeins
Above their scrap of history, 35
Only an attitude remains:

Time has transfigured them into
Untruth. The stone fidelity
They hardly meant has come to be
Their final blazon, and to prove 40
Our almost-instinct almost true:
What will survive of us is love.

Glossary

Line	Term
title	*Arundel*: a town in West Sussex in the south of England; the tomb, in nearby Chichester Cathedral, is a monument to the 10th Earl of Arundel, Richard FitzAlan (1313–76), and his wife, Eleanor of Lancaster (1318–72)
7	*pre-baroque*: a style of art that is plain and free from ornamentation; baroque is a style of art and architecture that flourished in the seventeenth century and is characterised by elaborate ornamentation
9	*gauntlet*: glove in a suit of armour
14	*effigy*: sculpted likeness or a portrait used in a monument
16	*grace*: elegance
20	*supine*: here, the pose of the sculptured couple who lie on their backs with their faces upwards
22	*tenantry*: tenants of an estate
33	*unarmorial age*: the post-medieval period, or an age that has no concern for social distinctions based upon the status of a family; 'armorial' relates to heraldry: coats of arms and genealogies
34	*skeins*: lengths of thread or yarn; also refers to locks of hair or, as here, wisps of smoke
40	*blazon*: coat of arms or symbol; also has the meaning of a public statement or proclamation

Guidelines

The poem was written in 1956, following a holiday visit to Chichester Cathedral in the company of Monica Jones. Larkin had spent time nursing his mother who had been seriously ill, and he had worries about his own state of health. **The poem is a meditation on transience, death and the survival of love.** 'An Arundel Tomb' appeared in the collection *The Whitsun Weddings* (1964).

Commentary

The poem is a meditation on the notion of the permanence of love, and the strong hope and desire of humans that love will remain – a hope which Larkin refers to as 'Our almost-instinct' (line 41). **The Arundel tomb, featuring sculptured effigies of the Earl of Arundel and his wife, is a reminder of the inevitability of death, and yet, in the clasped hands of the reclining figures, the tomb stands as a monument to enduring, faithful love.**

Conflict

In 'An Arundel Tomb' there is a clear conflict between the emotional force of the poem, which wants to proclaim 'What will survive of us is love' (line 42), and the intellectual honesty, which denies the truth of this sentiment and declares: 'Time has transfigured them into / Untruth' (lines 37–38). It is a familiar tension in Larkin's work.

Contemporary meaning of the tomb

The meditation on the tomb, and on the passing of time, is both aware of and alert to the ironic transformation which the tomb has undergone. The poem recognises that the contemporary meaning of the tomb is at odds with the original purpose that the monument was intended to serve. The tomb now expresses a meaning that neither the earl and countess nor the sculptor could have envisaged.

Now the couple serve as an emblem of faithful, tender love, an English version of Romeo and Juliet. The lesson that the speaker takes from this is that we, too, are subject to time. We have little control over the meaning of our lives after we have gone. And while the tomb stands as an emblem of love's survival, the individual identities of the earl and countess have been washed away. What remains of them is the sculptured pose.

Illusion of art

The poem points out an illusion of art: the illusion that art can preserve meaning and hold back time. The original intention of the tomb was to keep alive the names of the dead, to honour important people. Yet what remains is the gesture of affection and tenderness, the hands clasped in each other's. We have no way of knowing if the couple were the devoted lovers suggested by this gesture. A deeper irony is that, unknown to Larkin when he wrote the poem, the gesture upon which the poem depends is a late addition. It was added to the effigies some four hundred years after the burial of the earl and the countess during restoration work in the cathedral in the 1840s.

Meditation on falsehood

It is possible to read the poem as a meditation on falsehood. The gesture of affection is simply a lie and the poem reveals Larkin's doubts about the possibility of a long-lasting relationship. **Read in this way, the last two lines indicate Larkin's belief that no living couple could ever be truly happy and remain permanently in love.**

Larkin's attitude

Andrew Motion provides an interesting insight into Larkin's attitude to his own achievement in 'An Arundel Tomb'. He tells us that:

> At the end of the manuscript draft of 'An Arundel Tomb' Larkin wrote, 'Love isn't stronger than death just because statues hold hands for 600 years.' It is a remark which reinforced, privately, the sense of futility that hovers around the poem's conclusion in words like 'helpless', 'scrap', 'attitude', 'Untruth' and 'almost' (and it typifies his habit of writing cynical graffiti on his own most monumental lines.)

Form of the poem

The poem is written in six-line rhymed stanzas. The lines have eight syllables. The form of the poem lends itself to short complete statements: 'The little dogs under their feet' (line 6); 'Only an attitude remains' (line 36); 'What will survive of us is love' (line 42). The form is less suited to developing complex thought and this contributes to the difficulty in unravelling the thought in stanza 6.

Thinking about the poem

1. In your view, which of the following best describes the tone of the opening stanza: detached, disinterested, amused or superior? Explain your answer.
2. 'a sharp tender shock' (line 11).
   a) Why, in your opinion, is this a key moment in the poem?
   b) Do you agree that there is a successful blending of sound and sense in the phrase? Explain your answer.
3. The gesture of fidelity is now what gives meaning to the monument. What does the speaker suggest, in stanza 3, was the original purpose of the monument?
4. How throughout the poem, and in particular in stanzas 4 and 5, does the poet convey the idea that the monument serves less and less the commemoration of two individuals?
5. What, in your view, is the effect of the verb 'begin' in line 23?
6. Some readers have suggested that there are difficulties in reading stanza 4 in terms of grammar and syntax. Identify where such difficulties might arise.
7. There is a brilliant evocation of the passage of time, beginning in the last line of stanza 5, and continuing into the first line of stanza 7.
   a) Examine each of the images in this passage, and comment on its effectiveness.
   b) How, do you think, does the rhythm of these lines form part of their meaning?
8. 'The endless altered people' (line 30).
   a) In what way are the people altered?
   b) There is clearly a pun on the words alter/altar, explain it.
9. The lives and feelings of the earl and countess are gone. Now all that remains is 'a trough / Of smoke . . . Above their scrap of history' (lines 33–35). What, do you think, is the speaker's attitude to the loss of their identity?
10. The final stanza begins with the grave and dignified statement: 'Time has transfigured them into / Untruth'. In your view:
    a) What is the untruth?
    b) Is the untruth of the monument a beautiful untruth?
    c) Does the untruth fill a need in us?
    d) Is the poem suggesting that art is a form of self-delusion?
11. Read 'Wedding-Wind' and 'An Arundel Tomb' again. In your opinion, what view of love and marriage emerge from the two poems? What differences are there between them?

The Whitsun Weddings

That Whitsun, I was late getting away:
  Not till about
One-twenty on the sunlit Saturday
Did my three-quarters-empty train pull out,
All windows down, all cushions hot, all sense
Of being in a hurry gone. We ran
Behind the backs of houses, crossed a street
Of blinding windscreens, smelt the fish-dock; thence
The river's level drifting breadth began,
Where sky and Lincolnshire and water meet.

All afternoon, through the tall heat that slept
  For miles inland,
A slow and stopping curve southwards we kept.
Wide farms went by, short-shadowed cattle, and
Canals with floatings of industrial froth;
A hothouse flashed uniquely: hedges dipped
And rose: and now and then a smell of grass
Displaced the reek of buttoned carriage-cloth
Until the next town, new and nondescript,
Approached with acres of dismantled cars.

At first, I didn't notice what a noise
  The weddings made
Each station that we stopped at: sun destroys
The interest of what's happening in the shade,
And down the long cool platforms whoops and skirls
I took for porters larking with the mails,
And went on reading. Once we started, though,
We passed them, grinning and pomaded, girls
In parodies of fashion, heels and veils,
All posed irresolutely, watching us go,

As if out on the end of an event
  Waving goodbye
To something that survived it. Struck, I leant

More promptly out next time, more curiously,
And saw it all again in different terms:
The fathers with broad belts under their suits
And seamy foreheads; mothers loud and fat;
An uncle shouting smut; and then the perms,
The nylon gloves and jewellery-substitutes,
The lemons, mauves, and olive-ochres that

Marked off the girls unreally from the rest.
    Yes, from cafés
And banquet-halls up yards, and bunting-dressed
Coach-party annexes, the wedding-days
Were coming to an end. All down the line
Fresh couples climbed aboard: the rest stood round;
The last confetti and advice were thrown,
And, as we moved, each face seemed to define
Just what it saw departing: children frowned
At something dull; fathers had never known

Success so huge and wholly farcical;
    The women shared
The secret like a happy funeral;
While girls, gripping their handbags tighter, stared
At a religious wounding. Free at last,
And loaded with the sum of all they saw,
We hurried towards London, shuffling gouts of steam.
Now fields were building-plots, and poplars cast
Long shadows over major roads, and for
Some fifty minutes, that in time would seem

Just long enough to settle hats and say
    I nearly died,
A dozen marriages got under way.
They watched the landscape, sitting side by side
– An Odeon went past, a cooling tower,
And someone running up to bowl – and none
Thought of the others they would never meet
Or how their lives would all contain this hour.

I thought of London spread out in the sun,
Its postal districts packed like squares of wheat:

There we were aimed. And as we raced across
    Bright knots of rail
Past standing Pullmans, walls of blackened moss
Came close, and it was nearly done, this frail
Travelling coincidence; and what it held
Stood ready to be loosed with all the power
That being changed can give. We slowed again,
And as the tightened brakes took hold, there swelled
A sense of falling, like an arrow-shower
Sent out of sight, somewhere becoming rain.

Glossary	
title	*Whitsun*: Pentecost Sunday, the seventh Sunday after Easter, which celebrates the descent of the Holy Spirit upon the Apostles; traditionally, Whitsun was regarded as a lucky time to celebrate a wedding
19	*nondescript*: bland, characterless
25	*skirls*: high-pitched shrieks, shrill cries (like those made by the bagpipes)
26	*larking*: having fun, playing the fool
28	*pomaded*: perfumed
30	*irresolutely*: in a hesitant or uncertain manner
37	*seamy*: lined or wrinkled; it can also mean greasy or even disreputable
38–9	*the perms . . . jewellery-substitutes*: a perm was a popular hairstyle in the 1950s; nylon goods were an inexpensive alternative to many other fabrics. The list is an unflattering description of working-class taste in fashion
55	*a religious wounding*: the bleeding that sometimes follows the breaking of the hymen when sexual intercourse takes place for the first time; the 'wound' is a religious one in that it arises from the consummation of the marriage. The girls are staring into the future, and thinking about their own weddings. The marriage may also involve different kinds of wounding, which may be inferred from the poem as a whole
57	*gouts of steam*: drops or splashes of steam
65	*Odeon*: the name of a cinema
73	*Pullmans*: luxurious railway carriages, often with sleeping accommodation, named after their designer, George Pullman (1831–97)

Guidelines

'The Whitsun Weddings' was written over a two-year period and completed in October 1958. It appeared in the collection *The Whitsun Weddings* (1964). Larkin claimed that there was nothing of him in the poem. Andrew Motion suggests that 'there is everything of him in it – the yearning for love as well as the standing off.'

The poem was inspired by a journey Larkin took from Hull to London on Whit Saturday 1955. Larkin said that he caught:

> A very slow train that stopped at every station and I hadn't realized that, of course, this was the train that all the wedding couples would get on and go to London for their honeymoon; it was an eye-opener to me. Every part was different but the same somehow. They all looked different but they were all doing the same things and sort of feeling the same things. I suppose the train stopped at about four, five, six stations between Hull and London and there was a sense of gathering momentum. Every time you stopped fresh emotion climbed aboard. And finally between Peterborough and London, when you hurtle on, you felt the whole thing was being aimed like a bullet – at the heart of things, you know. All this fresh, open life. Incredible experience. I've never forgotten it.

Commentary

For most of the poem, the speaker is a detached observer. He notes the towns and countryside as the train speeds past, and also the wedding parties gathered on the station platforms at each stop. For the first five stanzas, the tone of the poem is amused to the point of disdain, but, **as the poem moves to consider the significance of the marriages whose beginnings the speaker has just witnessed, the tone becomes elevated and hopeful.**

Paradoxes

'The Whitsun Weddings' contains many paradoxes: the romantic ending that is preceded by a catalogue of ordinary, down-beat sights and sounds; the tone that is, in the words of Andrew Motion, 'both awe-struck and sharply conscious of absurdity'; a poem rich in concrete details that seems to reach for transcendence; a point-of-view that appears to dismiss the wedding parties as it celebrates what they represent. **In many respects, this is the quintessential Larkin poem, in which the poet satisfies the preconditions of his sceptical, almost brutal, intellect before surrendering himself to the imaginative possibilities of what the poem has recorded.**

Pivotal moment

The persona of the poem appears to sneer at the working-class culture he observes. However, **a pivotal moment in 'The Whitsun Weddings' occurs in the sixth stanza** when the speaker moves from being an observer to being a participant, sharing in the honeymoon journey of the couples. The 'frail' (line 74) coincidence of travelling on the same train is worked by the poet into something more substantial, something full of possibility, in the optimistic, regenerative images of the final stanza.

Final stanza

The final stanza is inspired by what Larkin called, in 'An Arundel Tomb', the 'almost-instinct' that love will survive. The physical sensation of being pitched forward by the braking train is transformed by Larkin into the image of the arrow-shower. It is a complex, compact and rewarding image. The ceremony of watching the couples embark on their wedding journey, of launching them, or aiming them, towards a future that includes human generation, is conveyed in the image of the arrow-shower 'somewhere becoming rain'. The couples on the train are the arrows aimed at London, mingling with the rain to germinate the future. The image contains a suggestion of strength, of something launched with great force, and also the idea of dispersal and gentle falling, at the flight's end. The couples will disperse to their separate destinies, in postal districts that are crowded but fruitful.

Dismissive

Characteristically, Larkin was dismissive of his own achievement in 'The Whitsun Weddings', remarking that the poem was 'just the transcription of a very happy afternoon. I didn't change a thing, it was just there to be written down.'

Form of the poem

The poem is one of the longest that Larkin ever wrote. Its length and the ten-line stanza form allow the speaker to capture both the journey and the movement and development of his responses to what he observes. Read aloud, the poem has a leisurely, colloquial feel, but Larkin achieves this effect without deviating from the rhyme or metre of the poem.

Thinking about the poem

1. From the tone and imagery of the first two stanzas what, in your opinion, is the observer's view of the urban landscape through which he passes?
2. Would you agree with the view that the observer is cruelly mocking in his description of the wedding parties (which begins in stanza 3 and continues into stanza 6)? Explain your answer.

3 In your opinion, what view of working-class English life emerges in the poem?
4 Larkin keenly observes the feelings that the marriages call out in the wedding guests. From the evidence of the poem, what feelings are evident in their actions? In your view, are the responses connected in any way to human sexuality?
5 What is the change of tone and perspective evident in stanza 6? Pinpoint the moment of change.
6 The final two stanzas move from description to meditation. What role does the observer take on himself in relation to the newly married couples on the train? Explain your answer.
7 From the evidence of 'The Whitsun Wedding', what is the poet's role in relation to ordinary lives?
8 The tone and language of the final stanzas are more elevated and excited than in the earlier stanzas. Where is the excitement and elevation most evident?
9 The final movement of the poem is dominated by the rich, complex and rewarding image of the arrow-shower. Discuss the image in terms of the various elements that it brings together:
   a) a sense of beauty;
   b) a sense of energy and dispersal;
   c) generation;
   d) a sense of lives being launched; and
   e) a sense of hope.
10 'The Whitsun Weddings' is noted for its method of detail-collecting and its observation of ordinary life. Comment on what you consider to be three of the most impressive and significant details of the poem.
11 Would you agree with the opinion that, despite the method of collecting details of social life, 'The Whitsun Weddings' is a poem that strives to go beyond the ordinary? Explain your thinking.
12 There are many changes of tone and changes in the stance of the poet/observer.
   a) Select what you consider to be three of the most important points of change in the poem.
   b) Describe how the transition from one viewpoint to another is achieved.
   c) Explain the significance of each of the changes.
13 Reviewing the poem, trace the emotional and the philosophical journey made by the speaker in the course of 'The Whitsun Weddings'.
14 Discuss the view that 'The Whitsun Weddings' is, ultimately, a celebration of marriage and a celebration of the hope and commitment to the future that it embodies.

MCMXIV

Those long uneven lines
Standing as patiently
As if they were stretched outside
The Oval or Villa Park,
The crowns of hats, the sun   5
On moustached archaic faces
Grinning as if it were all
An August Bank Holiday lark;

And the shut shops, the bleached
Established names on the sunblinds,   10
The farthings and sovereigns,
And dark-clothed children at play
Called after kings and queens,
The tin advertisements
For cocoa and twist, and the pubs   15
Wide open all day;

And the countryside not caring:
The place-names all hazed over
With flowering grasses, and fields
Shadowing Domesday lines   20
Under wheat's restless silence;
The differently-dressed servants
With tiny rooms in huge houses,
The dust behind limousines;

Never such innocence,   25
Never before or since,
As changed itself to past
Without a word – the men
Leaving the gardens tidy,
The thousands of marriages   30
Lasting a little while longer:
Never such innocence again.

Glossary	
title	*MCMXIV*: 1914, written in Roman numerals as it might appear on a monument; indeed, the poem might be described as a monument to life in England on the eve of World War 1
4	*Oval or Villa Park*: the Oval is the home of English cricket and Villa Park is the ground of the soccer team, Aston Villa; Larkin was a lover of all things English, including the English love of sport
6	*archaic*: from an earlier period, old-fashioned
11	*farthings and sovereigns*: British coins in use in 1914: a farthing was one-quarter of the old British penny and was the least valuable coin in circulation, whereas a sovereign was the most valuable coin, worth one pound
15	*twist*: a roll of tobacco
20	*Domesday lines*: lines of death comprising the millions of young men who registered to fight in the war and who were sent to their doom. 'Domesday' refers to the day of the Last Judgement; it reminds us of the Domesday Book, the record of a survey carried out by the commissioners of William 1 in 1086, in which the division and ownership of the land of England was registered and recorded – the register was considered as authoritative as the Last Judgement

Guidelines

This poem was completed in May 1960 and published in *The Whitsun Weddings* (1964).

Commentary

Stanza 1

In the first stanza of 'MCMXIV' the emphasis is on the men waiting in line to enlist in the army. There is awe and horror in Larkin's tone as he contemplates 'Those long uneven lines' (line 1). The 'archaic faces' (line 6) of the men belong to the past, to a different world. In the contemporary world, it is impossible to envisage lines of young men queuing so eagerly and patiently to enlist to fight in war, as if it were 'An August Bank Holiday lark' (line 8). However, the innocence of the men is not mocked. **'MCMXIV' is animated by the same gravitas evident in the treatment of the miners' death in 'The Explosion'.** The men are 'grinning' (line 7), a description with darker undertones that call to mind skeletal images of the dead, with the result that the image of the men is overshadowed by the poet's knowledge of what lay in store for them.

Stanzas 2 and 3

In stanzas 2 and 3 the poem evokes a wistful view of England on the eve of war. The town described in stanza 2 is on holidays, with its pubs 'Wide open all day' (line 16). The names on the shops are established names, suggesting a stable society. A similar impression of stability is achieved by the reference to 'farthings and sovereigns' (line 11), coins in use for centuries, but no longer current. In stanza 3 the reference to 'Domesday lines' (line 20) establishes continuity between the England of 1914 and the England of William the Conqueror. In a century of rapid change and discontinuity, it is easy to understand the appeal of such order. However, the idyll of stanza 2 is not maintained in stanza 3. The 'wheat's restless silence' (line 21), which shadows 'the Domesday lines', is a chilling reminder of the battlefields where the 'long uneven lines' of men from stanza 1 will die. As with the use of the word 'grinning' in stanza 1, the image is poised between past and future, between delight and horror. The poem shows us the countryside emptied of the men who stand in lines, men who signed up for a 'lark' (line 8), with no way of foreseeing that the war would drag on with unimaginable loss of life.

Final stanza

The final stanza makes an emotional appeal to the reader's sympathy in evoking the innocence of the men 'leaving the gardens tidy' (line 29) as they set out to war. The domestic detail works more powerfully than any rhetorical denunciation of war. The same emotional effect is achieved by the understatement of: 'The thousands of marriages / Lasting a little while longer' (lines 30–31). The final line of the poem, 'Never such innocence again', echoes the opening line of the final stanza.

Form of the poem

Interestingly, the poem is written as one sentence without a main verb. This creates an impression of timelessness, of a world divorced from historical change. It also suggests that the past is not over and, perhaps, it suggests that the line of men waiting to die represents a truth that is timeless. The poem is divided into four stanzas of eight lines. As with all Larkin's poetry, 'MCMXIV' is carefully phrased. There are fewer run-on lines than in other of his poems and the expression is straightforward. The long vowel sounds and the soft 's' sounds lend the poem an air of quiet regret.

Viewpoints

Some critics read the poem as an ironic view of innocence, the irony made gentle by Larkin's respect for those who died in the war. Here, as in 'An Arundel Tomb', Larkin is interested in the way in which the past is interpreted from the viewpoint of the present; in the way that the meaning of lives and events is changed over time. To borrow a phrase from 'An Arundel Tomb', **time has transfigured the England of 1914 into untruth**, into what the critic John Saunders calls 'a seductively false and unrepresentative image of reality'.

Thinking about the poem

1. The title of the poem is written in Roman numerals. Why, in your opinion, has Larkin chosen to do this? What effect does it have?
2. How are the 'long uneven lines' (line 1) of men portrayed in stanza 1? In what sense are their faces 'archaic' (line 6)? In your view, is there any irony in Larkin's depiction of the men?
3. Examine the images of stanza 2. How, do you think, is the continuity and joy of the social world conveyed?
4. Read through all the images used to evoke the past in the first two stanzas. Where is there evidence that the evocation of the past also contains intimations of a darker future? What words strike the darker note in the poem?
5. Look at the final lines of stanza 3. Would you agree that these lines paint a less idyllic picture of England on the eve of the war than the earlier images in the poem? Explain your answer.
6. The final stanza makes a direct appeal to the emotions of the reader. Do the repetition and the domestic imagery constitute a satisfying ending to the poem? Explain your answer.
7. In your view, is it intended that the reader accept the pre-war England evoked by the poem as real, or does the poem present us with a mythic England? (Compare the presentation of England in this poem with its presentation in 'The Whitsun Weddings'.)
8. 'Every comment about the past is also a comment about the present.' If this is true, what does the poem say about the present? Explain your answer.
9. 'MCMXIV' is written as one sentence without a main verb. What effect is achieved by this? How, do you think, does the absence of a main verb support the theme of the poem?
10. Innocence and the loss of innocence are clearly the major concerns of the poem. In your view, whose innocence is celebrated or lamented: the men who died, the nation or the poet? Explain your answer.
11. Describe the dominant mood of the poem.

Ambulances

Closed like confessionals, they thread
Loud noons of cities, giving back
None of the glances they absorb.
Light glossy grey, arms on a plaque,
They come to rest at any kerb: 5
All streets in time are visited.

Then children strewn on steps or road,
Or women coming from the shops
Past smells of different dinners, see
A wild white face that overtops 10
Red stretcher-blankets momently
As it is carried in and stowed,

And sense the solving emptiness
That lies just under all we do,
And for a second get it whole, 15
So permanent and blank and true.
The fastened doors recede. Poor soul,
They whisper at their own distress;

For borne away in deadened air
May go the sudden shut of loss 20
Round something nearly at an end,
And what cohered in it across
The years, the unique random blend
Of families and fashions, there

At last begin to loosen. Far 25
From the exchange of love to lie
Unreachable inside a room
The traffic parts to let go by
Brings closer what is left to come,
And dulls to distance all we are. 30

Glossary

1	*confessionals:*	the small enclosed stall in a church where the priest sits to hear confessions
4	*plaque:*	the medical crest on the side of the ambulance
13	*solving:*	unbinding, dissolving; an interesting choice of adjective, which may also suggest that the emptiness is the final answer to life's question
22	*cohered:*	came together, connected
25–30	*At last . . . all we are:*	the final sentence of the poem is difficult to read. In the ambulance, the logical connection of language begins to unravel. The critic James Booth suggests this reading of it: 'To lie far from the exchange of love, unreachable inside a room [which] the traffic parts to let go by, brings closer what is left to come, and dulls to distance all we are.'

Guidelines

The poem was written in 1961 and appeared in *The Whitsun Weddings* (1964). Larkin said of his poetry, **'Everything I write, I think, has the consciousness of approaching death in the background.'** This statement is certainly true of 'Ambulances'. **The poem is stark. It maintains that life is governed by the 'permanent and blank and true' (line 16) fact of death.** The ambulances of the title are a reminder of the way in which death visits everyone; a reminder that death underlies everything we do. And so the poem closes speaking of 'all we are'.

Commentary

The poem is carefully structured and formed. It works like a sonnet, with the first three stanzas presenting the subject of the poem in concrete terms, while the final two stanzas consider the deeper significance of what has been described.

Connotations

The poem is rich in words that carry multiple connotations. The word 'confessionals' in the first line, for example, suggests the closed secret world of the ambulance, as well as the soul preparing itself before God. The verb 'visited', which concludes the first stanza, suggests a ghostly visitation, turning the ambulance into a harbinger of death. The fact that the ambulance may come to rest at any kerb and that 'All streets in time are visited' (line 6) captures both the randomness of suffering and dying, and the inevitability of death.

Mercilessness of dying

The 'wild white face that overtops / Red stretcher-blankets' (lines 10–11) becomes the 'it' of line 12, a piece of cargo that is stowed and transported. **There is a brutality in this line that conveys the mercilessness of dying.** The children and women who witness the scene sense the 'solving emptiness' (line 13) that underlies all we do. The phrase 'solving emptiness' conveys the idea of solving life's riddle, but the solution is a dread emptiness. The word 'solving' draws in the meaning of related words: 'resolving', 'dissolving' and 'absolving'.

Final stanzas

The final two stanzas give expression to the meaning that the spectators sense. In the ambulance, the threads of life, the 'blend / Of families and fashions' (lines 23–24), begin to unravel, and the speeding ambulance brings its cargo towards its sure extinction, and away from all that it was. **The end of the poem, in its movement from 'it' (the person put into the ambulance) to the 'we' of the final line, collapses the distance not only between life and death, but also between those inside the locked room of the ambulance and those who see it pass by.** At the end of this journey poem, both Larkin and the readers have an uncomfortable sense of being co-travellers in the journey of the dying person in the ambulance.

The language of the poem is complex, as in the phrase 'the sudden shut of loss' (line 20). Here, Larkin has transformed a verb into a noun, so the reader must tease out its meaning. And the word 'shut' has many connotations in the context of the poem. It suggests the closing of the ambulance door, which may shut or stop the loss of life that has already gathered around the victim. Equally, the ambulance door shuts the spectators off from the drama of dying and carries it away, elsewhere. In doing so, the ambulance seals the loss of life within its locked room, confining it to something nearly at an end. And, perhaps, Larkin is hinting at the human capacity for detachment and self-preservation. We want death to be shut away. **Here, as in other moments of intensity in his poems, Larkin strains at the limits of language and grammar.**

Form of the poem

The poem is written in six-line stanzas, which rhyme *abcbca*. Most lines have eight syllables. The stanza form is very tight and this, added to the short line, means that Larkin has to twist language to express complex thoughts. For Larkin, the craft of poetry lies in making the language and the thought fit the structure of the stanza.

Thinking about the poem

1. Based on stanza 1, what impression do you form of the ambulances as they move through the cities?
2. The women and children who witness the victim being taken away in the ambulance sense a truth about life. What, in your opinion, is this truth and how do the women respond to it?
3. 'In stanzas 4 and 5, the poem suggests that death undoes the life that has been led and reduces it to nothing.' Is this a fair assessment of these stanzas? Explain your answer.
4. The critic James Booth, writing about the intricacy of thought in stanzas 4 and 5, suggests that Larkin takes the thought to the limits of grammar. Do you think that the poem gains from this strategy? Explain your answer.
5. In your view, what does the poem reveal about Larkin's attitude to life?
6. Is Larkin's use of the ambulance as a symbol successful? Explain your answer.
7. As in many of Larkin's poems, the language varies from colloquial to poetic. Select one example of **each** and say why it appeals to you.
8. What is the effect of Larkin's blending of these two forms of language, the colloquial and the poetic, in the poem?
9. The critic Andrew Gibson says of Larkin's poetry that it teeters on the edge and that Larkin is fascinated by impoverishment, loss, nullity. Is this assessment true of 'Ambulances'?
10. Read through the selection of Larkin's poetry in the anthology. What constants do you find in the poet's attitude to death?

Taking a closer look

1. Consider the possible meanings of (a) 'confessionals' and (b) 'visited' in stanza 1.
2. In line 12, the victim is described as 'it'. What in your view is the effect of this usage?
3. The phrase 'the solving emptiness' (line 13) is a striking one. How do you interpret it?

Imagining

1. Imagine that you are making a film of the poem. Describe the key images in your film and the music and lighting effects you would use to capture the atmosphere of the poem.
2. Listen to a reading of the poem and note any words or phrases that strike your ear. Using these words, write your own short poem.

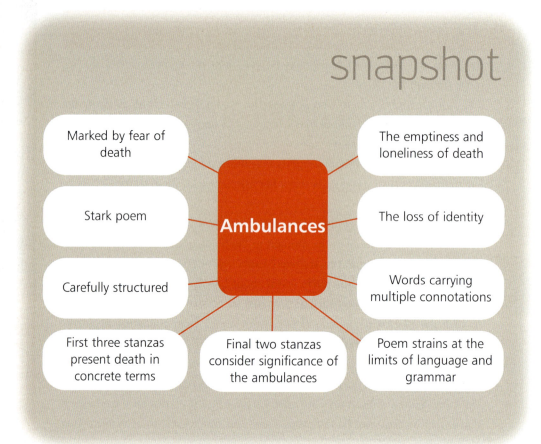

The Trees

The trees are coming into leaf
Like something almost being said;
The recent buds relax and spread,
Their greenness is a kind of grief.

Is it that they are born again   5
And we grow old? No, they die too.
Their yearly trick of looking new
Is written down in rings of grain.

Yet still the unresting castles thresh
In fullgrown thickness every May.   10
Last year is dead, they seem to say,
Begin afresh, afresh, afresh.

Guidelines

'The Trees' was written in 1967 and appeared in *High Windows* (1971). **The poem is a meditation on the theme of transience.** It was written during a period in which Larkin's personal relationships were vexed and complicated and his mother began to show the first signs of Alzheimer's disease.

Commentary

'The Trees', along with 'Cut Grass', deals with the classical theme of time and the decay it brings. The language of the poem is eloquent and harmonious. The careful phrasing and the use of long vowel sounds gives a sombre tone to the poem.

Stanza 1

Spring is given a qualified welcome. **The new leaves suggest a perpetual cycle of rejuvenation. No such renewal and rejuvenation occurs in the human life, so the sight of the new buds 'is a kind of grief' (line 4) to humans.**

Stanza 2

In the second stanza there is a realisation that the trees will die, too, and the appearance of renewing themselves is merely a 'trick' (line 7).

Stanza 3

Despite this realisation, the burgeoning trees offer an encouragement to humans of fresh starts and new beginnings. **Unusually for Larkin, having established the inevitably of death, the poem goes back to the attractive but false idea of renewal and concludes with the remarkably vibrant final line, 'Begin afresh, afresh, afresh'.** This line expresses an irresistible longing for life and may represent an act of self-persuasion.

In the final stanza Larkin allows himself to express a sense of awe. This allowance was short-lived. Larkin distrusted what he described in a letter as his 'astonished delight at the renewal of the natural world'. In his manuscript he wrote the words 'bloody awful tripe' after the date (2 June 1967) of the poem.

Thinking about the poem

1. The poem turns on a contrast between the trees and human beings. Why, do you think, is the appearance of the leaves on the trees described as 'a kind of grief' (line 4) by the poet?
2. The argument of the poem advances in an ordered way. Trace the thought through:
   a) the statements of the first stanza;
   b) the question and answer of stanza 2; and
   c) the qualification and tentative conclusion of stanza 3.
3. Comment on the phrase 'unresting castles' (line 9) to describe the trees.
4. Against the logic of the poem, the burgeoning trees, in the final stanza, are taken as an encouragement to begin afresh. The repetition of 'afresh' in line 12 gives an emphatic affirmation of the will to live. From your reading of Larkin's poetry, are there similar moments of affirmation in his work?
5. '"The Trees" can be read as an exercise in self-persuasion.' Give your view of this reading of the poem.
6. The poem is eloquent and harmonious throughout. Examine the phrasing, the vowels and the rhymes to explain how the harmony is created.
7. Larkin scrawled the judgement 'bloody awful tripe' at the end of the poem in his notebook. In your opinion, is this a fair assessment of 'The Trees'? Explain your answer.

The Explosion

On the day of the explosion
Shadows pointed towards the pithead:
In the sun the slagheap slept.

Down the lane came men in pitboots
Coughing oath-edged talk and pipe-smoke,   5
Shouldering off the freshened silence.

One chased after rabbits; lost them;
Came back with a nest of lark's eggs;
Showed them; lodged them in the grasses.

So they passed in beards and moleskins,
Fathers, brothers, nicknames, laughter,
Through the tall gates standing open.

At noon, there came a tremor; cows
Stopped chewing for a second; sun,
Scarfed as in a heat-haze, dimmed.

The dead go on before us, they
Are sitting in God's house in comfort,
We shall see them face to face –

Plain as lettering in the chapels
It was said, and for a second
Wives saw men of the explosion

Larger than in life they managed –
Gold as on a coin, or walking
Somehow from the sun towards them,

One showing the eggs unbroken.

Glossary		
2	*pithead:* the top of the mine shaft and the various buildings around it	
3	*slagheap:* the hill or mound made of the waste material from coalmining	
10	*moleskins:* a hard-wearing cotton used for work clothes; miners wore moleskin trousers to work	
16–18	*The dead . . . face:* the verse is taken from a prayer from the funeral service; these words formed part of the vision of the wives	

Guidelines

The poem was written over Christmas 1969 and appeared in *High Windows* (1971). It presents an account of a mine explosion in which many miners lost their lives. It was reported that, at the moment of the explosion, the wives of the miners had visions of their husbands. The source of the poem was a television documentary on the mining industry that Larkin watched with his mother. It may also have been influenced by his re-reading of the work of D.H. Lawrence.

Commentary

The poem is unusual in that there is no 'I' persona to supply the customary Larkin perspective on the events described. Instead, 'The Explosion' is a poem of observation and takes its tone from the event itself.

Stanzas 1 to 3

The first stanza paints a quiet scene, but there are hints of the disaster to come in the references to shadows and the sleeping slagheap. In stanza 2 the miners are portrayed as rough and ready as they make their way to the pithead. In stanza 3 a miner hurrying after the rabbit and returning with a nest of lark's eggs alerts us to the vitality of these men and to their closeness to nature.

Stanza 4

The fourth stanza suggests the close-knit community of the pit workers: family members, and friends and companions, laughing together as they pass 'Through the tall gates standing open' (line 12). The image of the gates suggests the entry into death's kingdom. The long vowel sounds of this stanza create an elegiac tone, as if the poet wishes to rouse our sympathy for these innocent men marching towards their death, without a care, or an intimation of what is to come.

Stanzas 5 and 6

In stanza 5 the explosion is registered on the surface by a mere tremor. This stanza suggests that much as we might wish it otherwise, sudden death does not stop the flow of life. However, the poem seeks to register the death of the men. Moreover, the poem provides comfort in stanza 6 in the quotation from the funeral service, which offers the hope of the eternal life to come. This comfort is unique in Larkin.

Final stanzas

The vision of the wives is used to give the poem a remarkably uplifting ending, which culminates in the final, floating line with its suggestion of Easter eggs and resurrection: 'One showing the eggs unbroken'.

In 'The Explosion' Larkin is back to the 'almost-instinct' of 'An Arundel Tomb', where what will survive of us is love. The poem does not declare that the men are transformed by death, but they are transformed in the visions of their wives. **The final, optimistic image contains a suggestion of continuity and generation. The poem, without stating anything directly, offers a testament to the power of love to withstand tragedy and death.**

Form of the poem

The poem is written in eight unrhymed, three-line stanzas. It concludes with a single line. This is an unusual form for Larkin. It is closest in tone to 'MCMXIV': both poems commemorate the premature death of innocent men and both reveal Larkin's respect and sympathy for the dead. These emotions are evident in the long vowel sounds, the alliteration and the verbal echoes throughout the poem. They are also evident in the beautiful phrasing of the poem.

Thinking about the poem

1. Unlike the most celebrated of Larkin's poems, 'The Explosion' does not have the customary Larkin narrator to comment and reflect on the action. In reading the poem, can you suggest why Larkin chose to dispense with his usual poetic persona?
2. From as early as the first stanza, the poem hints at the disaster to come. How is this done? Where else, in the first four stanzas, are there intimations of disaster?
3. In stanzas 2 to 4 Larkin deftly sketches the community of pit workers. What do we learn of the men and their relationship to each other?
4. One miner discovers a nest of lark's eggs and lodges them in the grasses (stanza 3). Why, in your view, does he do this? What is the point of this detail in relation to the impending disaster and the theme of the poem?
5. The sixth stanza consists of an extract from the funeral service. Do you think that this stanza fits in with the rest of the poem?
6. How does the poem deal with the reported visions of the wives about the explosion?
7. From your reading of the poem, which of the following best describes the poet's attitude to the victims of the explosion and their families?

    He is sympathetic.

    He wants to offer comfort.

    He wants to commemorate the men.

    Explain your choice.

8 The final four stanzas are difficult to read, both in terms of syntax and grammar. Attempt a paraphrase of these stanzas, supplying missing words where needed. What, in your view, is lost or gained in paraphrasing the lines?

9 The poem ends with an image of unbroken eggs. This image contains a suggestion of both continuity and generation. What does this line contribute to your understanding of the theme of the poem?

10 What similarities in theme and attitude can you find between this poem and 'Wedding Wind', 'The Whitsun Weddings', 'MCMXIV', 'Ambulances' and 'An Arundel Tomb', in relation to marriage and death?

Taking a closer look

1 'In the sun the slagheap slept' (line 3). Write a note on this line. Comment on (a) the way the line presents the slagheap and (b) the sounds of the line.

2 'a nest of lark's eggs' (line 8). In your view, what feelings are created by this image?

3 The poem ends with the word 'unbroken'. Is this a good word to conclude the poem? Explain your answer.

Imagining

1 Imagine that you are a child of one of the miners killed in the explosion. As an adult you read Larkin's poem. Write a diary entry capturing what the poem means to you.

2 Based on your reading of 'The Explosion', write a paragraph describing the kind of person whom you imagine wrote it.

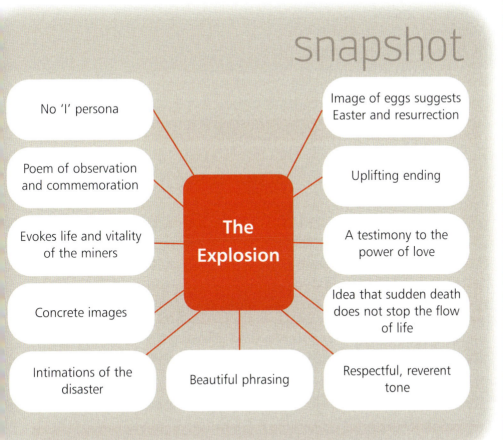

Cut Grass

Cut grass lies frail:
Brief is the breath
Mown stalks exhale.
Long, long the death

It dies in the white hours
Of young-leafed June
With chestnut flowers,
With hedges snowlike strewn,

White lilac bowed,
Lost lanes of Queen Anne's lace,
And that high-builded cloud
Moving at summer's pace.

10

Glossary

10	*Queen Anne's lace*: a wild flower with clusters of white flowers and a purplish centre; it is a species of wild carrot, though it is sometimes known as cow parsley

Guidelines

This short lyric on the theme of transience was composed in 1971 and appeared in *High Windows* (1971). The poem comes from the final third of Larkin's life, when he expressed dissatisfaction with life in England in virulent terms in his private correspondence.

Commentary

'Cut Grass' deals with a classical theme in a classical manner. The theme is announced without delay: 'Brief is the breath' (line 2) and 'Long, long the death' (line 4) sum up Larkin's attitude to life. The cut grass dies its death in mid-summer in a world that is in full bloom. But each of the flowers mentioned in the poem will last only a short time before they will also die. **The flowers teach us the brevity of life.** This lesson is a common one in classical literature, especially in the work of the Latin poet Ovid.

In Ovid the flowers also teach us the fragile nature of beauty and the relentless approach of death. However, there is no religious consolation in 'Cut Grass', nor does the poem advise us to live life passionately knowing that our time is short, as Ovid does in his poetry.

Distrust

Interestingly, **'Cut Grass' was written during a period when Larkin was expressing his most bitter right-wing views about the state of England**, complaining of socialism and the influx of black citizens into England. Not surprisingly, then, in his private correspondence, Larkin was dismissive or distrustful of the poem's lyrical impulse, describing it as 'pointless crap'.

Form and language of the poem

The poem is written in rhymed quatrains. There is little enjambment so each short line sounds complete in itself. The language of 'Cut Grass' is sweet and simple and the general sweetness is heightened by the use of long, vowel sounds, as if the poet wants to linger over the beauty that is fading. The combination of short lines, full rhymes and long vowels lends an air of tiredness or sadness to the poem.

Thinking about the poem

1. As with 'The Trees', this is a beautifully phrased and executed poem. Write a short note on the pattern of sound and phrasing in the poem. How, do you think, do the sound patterns contribute to the tone of the poem?
2. The grass dies in high summer, surrounded by a beauty that will also fade and die. Yet the poem offers no consolation. What does this suggest about Larkin's frame of mind at the time of writing? Explain your answer.
3. Compare this poem with 'The Trees'. Which of the poems do you prefer?
4. Larkin, writing about the poem, declared that the logical sense of the poem ceases at line 6, and the rest of the poem consists of no more than a succession of images. Is Larkin being fair to his own work in making this judgement?
5. Which of the following statements is closest to your own view of the poem?

    It is a poem about the inevitability of death and decay.

    It is a poem about the beauty of nature.

    It is a poem that laments the fading of beauty.

    Explain your answer.

Exam-Style Questions

1. What attitude to love emerges from the poetry of Philip Larkin? Support the points you make by reference to the poems that you have studied.
2. 'Loneliness and isolation are striking features of Larkin's poetry.' Do you agree with this statement? Support the points you make by reference to the poems on your course.
3. 'Although Larkin's poetry is not religious, the poems do convey a sense of the spiritual.' Give your view of this statement, supporting the points you make by reference to the poems on your course.
4. If you were asked to give a public reading of a small selection of the poetry of Philip Larkin, which poems would you choose to read? Give reasons for your choice, supporting them by reference to the poems on your course.

5   'We enjoy the poetry of Philip Larkin for its ideas and its language.' Using the above as your title, write an essay on Larkin's poetry. Support the points you make by reference to the poems on your course.

6   In many of Larkin's poems there are passages in which the thought is hard to paraphrase. Do you regard these difficulties as a failure of technique or an enrichment of meaning? Support your view by reference to the poems on your course.

7   Would you agree with Larkin when he described each of his poems as representing 'a composite and complex experience'? Support the points you make by reference to the poems on your course.

8   From your reading of his poetry, what kind of person do you imagine Larkin to have been? Support the points you make by reference to the poems on your course.

Your answer might consider some or all of the following:
- The ambiguity towards love.
- The self-mocking quality in some of the poems.
- The mixture of formal and colloquial language.
- The way the poems move from description to meditation.
- The sense of the spiritual in many of the poems.
- The sense of loneliness in some of the poems.

9   You have been asked to introduce the poetry of Philip Larkin to your fellow students. Write the speech you would make, referring to a representative selection of Larkin's poems.

Your answer might consider some or all of the following:
- The thematic range of his poetry: love; nostalgia for an older England; the consciousness of death.
- His skill as a poet.
- The traditional forms of many of the poems.
- The tone of the poems.
- The persona of the poet.
- The philosophy of life that emerges from the poetry.

10 'Philip Larkin: a Personal Response'. Using this title, give your view of the poetry of Philip Larkin.

Your answer might address some or all of the following:
- The themes of love and death.
- His portrait of England.
- The Larkin persona.
- The mixing of the colloquial and the formal.
- The effect of reading the poetry.

Sample Essay

'Philip Larkin's poetry is complex in both themes and style.'

Discuss this view of Larkin's poetry. Support the points you make by reference to the poems on your course.

I agree with the view that Larkin's poetry is complex and that this complexity refers both to the themes of the poems and to the style in which they are written. The complexity is reflected in the ambiguous treatment of love in the poetry. It is reflected in the contrasting tones that run through the poems. It is also reflected in the elaborate stanzas Larkin uses and the complex thoughts they contain.

[Answer is set up by the opening paragraph]

One of Larkin's early poems, 'Wedding-Wind', which was written in 1946 when Larkin was in his twenties, is the only poem on the course in which love is celebrated almost without reservation. It is probably no coincidence that it is one of the few poems in which the speaker is not identifiable with Larkin himself. The persona of the poem is a young bride speaking on the morning after her wedding. The night of the wedding is marked by a 'high wind' and the bride is sad 'that any man or beast' should not enjoy the happiness she experiences. In the second stanza of the poem, the young woman describes the day after the wedding. Everything in her world is filled with joy, even the laundry on the washing line, and she wonders if she can bear it:

> Can it be borne, this bodying-forth by wind
>
> Of joy my actions turn on, like a thread
>
> Carrying beads?

So in love is the young bride with love that she wonders if death itself can stop her and her love drinking from the waters of love:

> Can even death dry up
>
> These new delighted lakes, conclude
>
> Our kneeling as cattle by all-generous waters?

It is typical of Larkin that, in this hymn of praise to passionate love, the final lines of the poem are written as a question rather than as a statement. Larkin does not have the bride declare that death will not dry up the all-generous waters of love. No. Instead the bride wonders if this is the case. In subsequent poems, Larkin's ambiguity becomes more evident.

[First poem is discussed in relation to the ambiguous treatment of love in the poetry]

Ten years later Larkin wrote 'An Arundel Tomb' and again brought love and death into focus. In the later poem, the figures of an earl and his countess, carved on their tomb, are shown holding each other's hand. Larkin says that the moment of seeing this gesture is accompanied by 'a sharp tender shock'. Instead of the tomb serving as a reminder of death, the sculpted figures now serve as symbols of faithfulness and the endurance of love. Larkin views this transformation with an ironic eye. He says that 'Ttme has transfigured them into untruth'. And while the poem ends with one of Larkin's most memorable lines, 'What will survive of us is love', Larkin insists that this is not true. It is only when you read through to the end of the poem that you understand the force of the second line: 'The earl and countess lie in stone'. Indeed the poem is littered with negative or dismissive words such as 'lie', 'absurd', 'helpless', 'hollow', 'scrap' and 'untruth'. If ever a poem displayed a complex and ambiguous attitude to love, it is 'An Arundel Tomb'.

[Second poem introduced and discussed]

Another example of the complex nature of Larkin's poetry is evident in Larkin's longest poem, 'The Whitsun Weddings'. It is another poem dealing with marriage and the feelings that surround it. The voice of the poem is very much the voice of the poet, describing a real journey he took on the train from Hull to London. The journey took place on the Whit weekend in 1955. As the train pulled into the stations along the line, Larkin noticed wedding parties gathered on the platforms to wave off newly married couples. The couples were setting out to London on honeymoon. The early stanzas describe what Larkin the passenger sees out the window. He is not impressed by the towns 'new and nondescript' or the 'acres of dismantled cars'. Then he begins to notice the wedding guests on the platform. His tone is sneering and dismissive. He writes of young girls 'In parodies of fashion, heels and veils'. However, these wedding parties have caught his attention and he looks more carefully at the next station. Again the tone is mocking and cruel. He describes 'mothers loud and fat'. He describes 'an uncle shouting smut'. He mocks the fathers of the bride who 'had never known success so huge and wholly farcical'. And then at line 55 in the sixth stanza of the poem, something happens and the tone changes utterly. Maybe it is the use of the term 'religious wounding' that changes the tone, by giving a sacred and dignified air to the weddings. Now as 'a dozen marriages' get 'under way' Larkin makes himself part of the experience: 'We hurried towards London'. By the final stanza, as the train reaches London, Larkin has been transformed from a cynical observer to an excited witness who feels himself changed by 'this frail travelling coincidence'. The change is evident in the image of the 'arrow-shower', which concludes the poem. It is a beautiful image and suggests that the couples will disperse and their lives will blossom: 'an arrow-shower sent out of sight, somewhere becoming rain'. Who could have thought that the sneering observer of the early stanzas could conclude the poem with such an optimistic and elevating image? It is further evidence of the complexity at the heart of Larkin's writing.

[Second element of complexity discussed in relation to Larkin's longest poem]

A further area of complexity is Larkin's use of elaborate stanza forms, which sometimes has the effect of compressing thought and twisting language. An example is the last stanza in 'Ambulances'. The stanza contains short lines of eight syllables. The rhyming scheme is abccba. Given the strictness of the rhyming scheme and the shortness of the lines, it is hard to make everything fit. Larkin does not make things easy for himself. He does not describe something simple. Instead he expresses a complex thought about what it means to lie in an ambulance, shut off from all we know, as we move closer to death and to the loss of identity involved in dying. The final sentence of the poems reads:

> Far
>
> From the exchange of love to lie
>
> Unreachable inside a room
>
> The traffic parts to let go by
>
> Brings closer what is left to come
>
> And dulls to distance all we are.

Trying to unravel the thought is a challenge but it is easy to see how the poem gains from the contraction of thought and the pull of language. In the same poem, Larkin speaks of 'the solving emptiness'. It is a brilliant phrase. You can see how the word 'solving' takes meaning from other words and ideas in the poem. For example, in the first line the ambulances are compared to 'confessionals' and so 'solving' is immediately linked to 'absolving'. It is these little shocks of recognition that add pleasure to the experience of reading Larkin.

[Third element of complexity is discussed in relation to fourth poem]

Philip Larkin is a complex poet in an interesting way and, in my view, it is this complexity that makes the poems fascinating to read.

[Keeps the focus of the question in mind throughout the answer and returns to it in the conclusion]

New Discovery Poetry Anthology

snapshot

- Though not religious, the poetry conveys a sense of the spiritual
- There is an imaginative opening out in many of the poems
- Self-mocking observer present in many of the poems
- Consciousness of death in the background of all he wrote
- Believed ordinary life should be the subject of poetry, yet his poetry often goes beyond the ordinary
- Themes of love, loneliness and transience
- Poetry expresses affection for the English way of life
- Poems contain intricate thoughts in carefully crafted stanzas
- Social rather than political observations
- Movement from description to meditation in the poetry
- Distrustful of his talent and dismissive of his achievements and insights

Derek Mahon

b. 1941

GRANDFATHER*
DAY TRIP TO DONEGAL
ECCLESIASTES
AFTER THE TITANIC*
AS IT SHOULD BE
A DISUSED SHED IN CO. WEXFORD
THE CHINESE RESTAURANT IN PORTRUSH
RATHLIN
ANTARCTICA*
KINSALE

Biography

Derek Mahon was born on 23 November 1941 in Belfast and brought up in the suburb of Glengormley. His father was an engine-inspector in the Belfast shipyard of Harland and Wolff, where both his grandfathers had also been employed. His mother worked for a time in York Street Flax Spinning Company. He has noted that his parents thus 'embodied the two principal industries in Northern Ireland, shipbuilding and linen'.

Although Mahon's background was working-class Protestant, he played as a child with Catholic children, Glengormley being a mixed neighbourhood. He describes himself in one of his poems as having been a 'strange child with a taste for verse'. He went to secondary school at the Royal Belfast Academical Institution. The poet Michael Longley was a contemporary of his at school and remembers the younger Mahon as already being an accomplished poet at this time.

Like Longley, Mahon went on to study at Trinity College, Dublin. He studied modern languages there, specialising in French. He also began to work seriously at the craft of poetry. Mahon was part of a group of other gifted young poets studying at TCD at the time: Eavan Boland, Brendan Kennelly and Michael Longley. For the first time Mahon felt that there was a poetry-writing community that he could be part of, as well as a thriving literary scene in Dublin. He also studied for a year at the Sorbonne in Paris.

Career

Mahon worked as a teacher in the United States, in Canada and in Ireland, before becoming a journalist and writer in London. He was theatre critic for *The Listener* for a time, poetry editor for *The New Statesman* and features editor of *Vogue*. He was also involved in adapting Irish novels for television, among them Jennifer Johnston's *How Many Miles to Babylon?*, as well as radio adaptations and features. He was writer-in-residence in the University of Ulster (1978/79) and in TCD (1988). He has been a regular contributor of literary journalism and book reviews to *The Irish Times*.

For several years in the 1990s Mahon lived in New York and taught at New York University. Having by this time divorced his wife Doreen Douglas, whom he married in 1972, much of his work from New York was addressed to his two children, Rory and Katie, with whom he was no longer living. By 1996 he had returned to live in Dublin. He later moved to Kinsale, Co. Cork.

Poems 1962–78 brings together most of the poems from his first three collections, *Night Crossing* (1968), *Lives* (1972) and *The Snow Party* (1975). *Courtyards in Delft* was published in 1981, *The Hunt by Night* in 1982 and *Antarctica* in 1985. *Selected*

Poems (1991) was the winner of the Irish Times–Aer Lingus Irish Literature Prize for Poetry in 1992. In 1999 he published his *Collected Poems*, with updated versions of many of his poems. His recent collections include *Harbour Lights* (2005), *Life on Earth* (2008) and *An Autumn Wind* (2010).

Mahon edited *The Sphere Book of Modern Irish Poetry* (1972) and, with Peter Fallon, *The Penguin Book of Contemporary Irish Poetry* (1990). He has published several verse translations, including Molière's *School for Wives* and the poems of Philippe Jaccottet from French and a version of Euripides' *The Bacchae* from Greek.

A member of Aosdána and a fellow of the Royal Society of Literature, he has received numerous awards, among them the American Ireland Literary Award and the C. K. Scott-Moncrieff prize for translation.

Social and Cultural Context

Derek Mahon once said in an interview that he considers himself to be a European poet who happens to be Irish, and who just happens to have been born in Belfast. **Each of the three strands of his chosen cultural identity has its place in the development of his work.**

Irish influences

Mahon's work responds in a complex way to the society into which he was born. He is acutely aware of his roots, as the poem 'Grandfather' suggests, revealing a certain admiration for traits that have been associated with the Northern Irish character, such as a degree of rebelliousness and self-reliance. On the other hand, in a poem such as 'Ecclesiastes', he rejects the bigoted attitudes of the churchmen of his native Belfast – a rejection that is tinged with an admission of the attractions of that way of life.

Mahon has never sought to engage with the political problems or the conflict in Northern Ireland. He once said that he felt that as poets in Ulster 'we're supposed to write about the Troubles; a lot of people expect us to act as if it were part of our job – it's not, unless we choose to make it so'. And yet it is true to say that Mahon does not flinch from confronting the issue of violence, even if in a rather oblique way. For instance, in 'Rathlin' he contrasts the violent history of the island with its present peacefulness, but he is also aware of the contemporary conflict in Northern Ireland, the 'bombs that doze in the housing estates'. His attitude to the questions that have caused much grief in Ireland can be seen from his statement that 'whatever we mean by the "Irish situation", the shipyards of Belfast are no less a part of it than a country town in the Gaeltacht'.

The lesson of history is an important theme in his poems. In his long, complex poem 'A Disused Shed in Co. Wexford', he shows an awareness of the many conflicts of the past, from the French Revolution to the Jewish Holocaust, while his short poem 'Kinsale' can be read in the light of the historical battle of 1601 that signalled the end of Gaelic Ireland.

Mahon's education at Trinity College, Dublin widened his cultural experience. In the 1960s students at TCD were predominantly Protestant since Catholics were forbidden to attend by the Catholic Church. Mahon, however, met several southern Irish Catholic students at the university, among them the Kerry poet Brendan Kennelly and the Dublin poet Eavan Boland.

Having lived in Dublin while attending college and for some time afterwards, Mahon became familiar with life south of the border. An abiding love for the landscape of the west of Ireland is shown in his poems about Inis Oirr, Achill and Donegal. 'Day Trip to Donegal', for instance, is suffused with a love of the sea and a recognition of its power.

International influences

Mahon's assimilation of French literature at university led him to translate classical French texts and modern French poetry. As a student in Paris, he met the Irish writer Samuel Beckett, who had also been educated at Trinity. Like Beckett, Mahon's self-induced exile enabled him to write of his native country as an observer rather than as a participant in the Irish cultural scene.

Many of Mahon's poems reflect an interest in European art. He is conscious of the complex link between poetry and painting that is so important in his work. **His imagery is frequently concerned with the effects of light and shade, as an artist would be.**

Mahon has lived in the United States and some of his poems describe the US landscape and way of life. Although he has returned to Ireland, his poetic vision continues to be truly international. His themes are universal and his frame of reference and allusions contain many diverse cultural echoes.

Mahon has expressed the view that, for him, poetry is primarily an artistic activity rather than an expression of a particular cultural identity: 'for me, poetry is about shape and sound. It's about taking the formless and making it interesting; creating art out of formlessness.'

Timeline

1941	Born on 23 November in Belfast
1946–60	Attends Skegoneil Primary School and the Royal Belfast Academical Institution ('Inst')
1960	Begins studies at Trinity College, Dublin (TCD)
1964	Studies at the Sorbonne in Paris
1965	Completes BA degree at TCD
1968	Publishes first collection, *Night Crossing*
1968/9	Travels in North America and France
1970	Moves to London
1972	Marries Doreen Douglas; publishes second collection, *Lives*
1974–7	Works as a journalist and theatre critic in London
1975	Publishes third collection, *The Snow Party*
1977	Son Rory born
1977–79	Writer-in-residence at University of Ulster, Coleraine
1979	Daughter Katie born
1981	Publishes *Courtyards in Delft*
1982	Publishes *The Hunt by Night*
1985	Separates from wife Doreen
1985	Moves to Republic of Ireland
1990–96	Spends time in New York
1996	Returns to Ireland
1999	Publishes *Collected Poems*
2000s	Publishes *Harbour Lights* (2005), *Life on Earth* (2008) and *An Autumn Wind* (2010)

Grandfather

They brought him in on a stretcher from the world,
Wounded but humorous; and he soon recovered.
Boiler-rooms, row upon row of gantries rolled
Away to reveal the landscape of a childhood
Only he can recapture. Even on cold   5
Mornings he is up at six with a block of wood
Or a box of nails, discreetly up to no good
Or banging round the house like a four-year-old –

Never there when you call. But after dark
You hear his great boots thumping in the hall   10
And in he comes, as cute as they come. Each night
His shrewd eyes bolt the door and set the clock
Against the future, then his light goes out.
Nothing escapes him; he escapes us all.

Glossary

3 | *gantries*: overhead platforms for a travelling crane used in shipbuilding

Guidelines

'Grandfather' is from the collection *Night Crossing* (1968). Mahon's grandfather was a boiler-maker in Harland and Wolff, the shipbuilders in Belfast where the *Titanic* was built. **In this sonnet the poet paints an interesting portrait of the old man.**

Commentary

Lines 1–9

The poet tells us that his grandfather had been injured at work and then retired. Having recovered, he is no longer concerned with his working life (the 'boiler rooms' and 'gantries') but lives his own rich life, recapturing the freedom of his childhood (lines 3 to 5). He may now be isolated from the real world, and yet there are echoes of his adult work in the 'box of nails' and the 'banging' noises he makes around the house (lines 6 to 8). He behaves as if he were a young child. Like a 'four year old', too, he is 'never there when you call' (lines 8 and 9). Mahon paints a humorous portrait of a harmless old man.

Lines 9–14
The last six lines of the sonnet offer a slightly different perspective on his grandfather. His comings and goings seem to become rather more inexplicable, perhaps a little sinister. He does not say where he has been when he comes home 'after dark', but makes no effort to hide the noise of his 'great boots thumping in the hall' (lines 9 and 10). Again, he sees no need to apologise for or explain himself.

The colloquial phrase 'as cute as they come' (line 11) suggests that his behaviour is far from aimless. His actions are described now as having a purpose to them. He will 'bolt the door and set the clock' – ordinary everyday actions – but the poem goes on to say that he does them 'against the future' (lines 12 and 13). The word 'shrewd' (line 12) suggests that it is a clever form of self-preservation, an attempt to maintain his independence and dignity in the face of old age and inevitable death. Perhaps in his eccentric behaviour he has found a way of avoiding the problems of real life.

We are left with an impression of an old man who has stubbornly refused to adapt to the conventions of 'normal' elderly behaviour. It is impossible not to feel a certain admiration for the old man.

Tone of the poem

Mahon describes his grandfather with humanity and affection. He clearly identifies with the old man's rebelliousness, but his attitude is not patronising in any way. He seems to recognise his grandfather as an individual, as he accepts that his grandfather's childhood and working life remain a mystery to anyone except himself. He knows his grandfather is not about to explain his behaviour to his family: 'he escapes us all' (line 14). This may be exasperating for everyone else – he is 'never there when you call' (line 9) – but it is part of the old man's strategy for survival. He suggests, too, that his grandfather is perfectly well aware of the world around him: 'Nothing escapes him' (line 14).

Form of the poem

The poem is a sonnet – a poem of fourteen lines, usually divided into eight lines (octet or octave) and six lines (sestet). The octave generally presents a situation and the sestet comments further or develops it. Note that in this sonnet the octave extends into part of line 9. The basic rhyming pattern of a strict sonnet is *abba, abba, cde, cde*, but many poets deviate from this pattern or change it to suit their theme. For instance, 'Grandfather' does not conform exactly to this pattern. In the octave the pattern is *abababba*, in the sestet it is *cdeced*. These breaks with convention seem appropriate for a poem that describes an unusual and eccentric individual.

Sound patterns in the poem

Mahon makes use of sound to reinforce the picture he creates of his grandfather. Alliteration in 'row upon row', 'rolled' leads to 'reveal' and 'recapture' to create a seamless link between the grandfather's work and his childhood. The repetition of the 'u' sound (assonance) in 'wounded but humorous' echoes the sound of someone in pain, while the long 'o' sound in 'row after row' and 'rolled' might suggest wonder at the immensity of the shipyard.

Thinking about the poem

1. How is the grandfather portrayed in lines 1 and 2?
2. Why does the poet refer to his grandfather's working life in lines 3 and 4? Explain your answer.
3. Why also does he refer to his grandfather's childhood in lines 4 and 5?
4. What impression of the grandfather do we get in the last six lines (the sestet) of the sonnet? Is it different from the first eight lines (the octet)? Explain your answer.
5. What does the grandfather's ritual of bolting the door and setting the clock at night suggest about him? How would you explain the phrase 'against the future' (line 13)?
6. Which one of these words best describes the grandfather, as he is presented in the poem: secretive, eccentric, innocent, doddering, rebellious or clever. Explain your choice.
7. Do you think that Mahon loved his grandfather? Explain your answer.
8. Would the grandfather have been an easy person to live with? Give a reason for your answer.
9. Explore Mahon's use of sound patterns in the poem and say what effect it creates.

Taking a closer look

1. What do the phrases 'up to no good' (line 7) and 'as cute as they come' (line 11) contribute to the portrait of the old man?
2. Would you describe the tone of the phrase 'Never there when you call' (line 9) as: exasperated, annoyed, amused or accepting? Perhaps you would suggest another word? Explain your choice.
3. What is your interpretation of the last line, 'Nothing escapes him: he escapes us all'?

Imagining

1. Imagine that you are the grandfather in the poem. Write a letter to your grandson in which you describe some of your childhood adventures or your working life.
2. Using poetic means, Mahon has given us a vivid picture of his grandfather. From your reading of the poem, write a short descriptive portrait of the man as you imagine him to be.

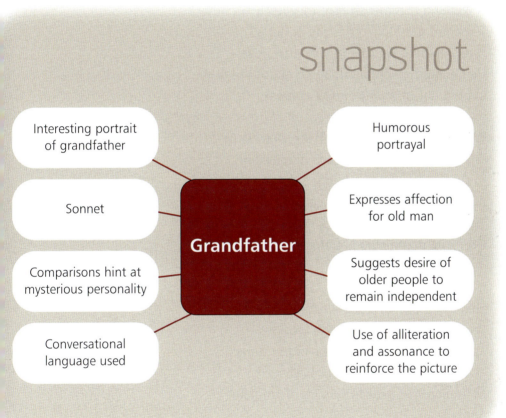

Day Trip to Donegal

We reached the sea in early afternoon,
Climbed stiffly out; there were things to be done,
Clothes to be picked up, friends to be seen.
As ever, the nearby hills were a deeper green
Than anywhere in the world, and the grave 5
Grey of the sea the grimmer in that enclave.

Down at the pier the boats gave up their catch,
A writhing glimmer of fish; they fetch
Ten times as much in the city as here,
And still the fish come in year after year – 10
Herring and mackerel, flopping about the deck
In attitudes of agony and heartbreak.

We left at eight, drove back the way we came,
The sea receding down each muddy lane.
Around midnight we changed-down into suburbs 15
Sunk in a sleep no gale-force wind disturbs.
The time of year had left its mark
On frosty pavements glistening in the dark.

Give me a ring, goodnight, and so to bed . . .
That night the slow sea washed against my head, 20
Performing its immeasurable erosions –
Spilling into the skull, marbling the stones
That spine the very harbour wall,
Muttering its threat to villages of landfall.

At dawn I was alone far out at sea 25
Without skill or reassurance – nobody
To show me how, no promise of rescue –
Cursing my constant failure to take due
Forethought for this; contriving vain
Overtures to the vindictive wind and rain. 30

Glossary	
6	*enclave*: a piece of a country that is entirely enclosed within foreign territory
8	*writhing*: twisting
21	*erosions*: eating away, wearing down
30	*overtures*: offers or proposals, especially in negotiations
30	*vindictive*: revengeful

Guidelines

'Day Trip to Donegal' is from the collection *Night Crossing* (1968). **In this poem we can see Mahon's love of the sea and his perception of it as a mysterious, creative force.**

Commentary

Stanza 1

The poem begins as a straightforward narrative with details of preparation for the trip. This is appropriate if we consider that the title is reminiscent of a school composition. At first the language used is conversational: 'things to be done, / Clothes to be picked up' (lines 2–3). The scene is set. The Donegal hills are still a 'deeper green' than anywhere in the world, 'as ever' – the phrase suggests how reassuringly familiar the place is to the poet and his companions (line 4). But words such as 'grave', 'grey' and 'grimmer' hint at a darker vision (lines 5 and 6). You may notice how the alliteration – the repetition of the hard 'g' sounds – in these words indicates this subtle change of mood.

Stanza 2

In the second stanza the poet focuses even more closely on his surroundings. Down at the pier, fish are being landed – a routine commercial event, as the poet recognises in his comment about the price they fetch. But his striking visual image of the fish as a 'writhing glimmer' (line 8) 'flopping about the deck / In attitudes of agony and heartbreak' (lines 11–12) seems to give human qualities and feelings to the fish. **These suggestions of pain and death add to the atmosphere of underlying unease set up in the first stanza.**

Stanza 3

The poet does not describe the actual day he spent at sea. Instead, he seems more interested in the return home, presumably to his native city of Belfast (although it is not named). Donegal seems to recede from his consciousness. The implication is that there is an essential difference in life as experienced in the suburbs and life as it is experienced close to nature in Donegal – the car 'changed-down' in gear as they approached the sleeping suburbs (line 15). Their peacefulness contrasts with the 'gale-force wind' (line 16) they had encountered at sea. **The change is not merely physical but also psychological, as the final two stanzas make clear.**

Stanza 4

All seems well as the companions take their leave of each other: 'Give me a ring, goodnight', and the phrase 'and so to bed . . . ' has echoes of a typical way to end an account of a day's adventures (line 19). **But the last two stanzas plunge us into the terrifying world of the subconscious.** In the speaker's dream the sea has appeared again, but different, as is the case in dreams. The imagery used to describe the experience is vividly sensuous. We can almost hear the sound of the sea and feel its power.

Mahon achieves this effect through the use of carefully chosen sounds and images. Alliteration as in 'slow sea' (line 20) and onomatopoeia as in 'immeasurable erosions' (line 21) and 'muttering' (line 24) reflect the sound and movement of the sea. The image of the water 'marbling the stones / That spine the very harbour wall' (lines 22–23) enables us to visualise its physical power. By deliberately blending the images of the sea with the experience of dreaming – 'spilling into the skull' (line 22) – Mahon conveys the surreal, and sometimes frightening, atmosphere of dreams.

Stanza 5

The dream experience becomes even more nightmarish as the speaker sees himself as lost, cut adrift from everyone and everything. **What is being described here goes beyond physical fear. It is as if being 'far out at sea' (line 25) is a metaphor for alienation, both psychological and spiritual.**

The atmosphere created in the final lines of the poem is utterly intense. The threat posed by the sea, wind and rain (elements of nature) may symbolise the wilderness of the subconscious or the imagination. It is a realm over which we can have no control, but it is central to the work of a poet. Or it may suggest the deepest human fears, of loss and ultimate death, which we must face alone. The fact that Mahon does not name specifically what his fears are adds to the sense of foreboding he conveys.

The imagery here recalls a long tradition in mythology and literature of representing the sea and wind as animate presences that are malevolent and powerful and will not easily be appeased, no more than the human sense of nameless dread can easily be overcome.

In this poem we see how Mahon's imagination works on the ordinary reality of a day trip to a place he knows well, and transforms it so that we are given an insight into the poet's deepest anxieties and fears. The 'trip' (the word has connotations of an out-of-body experience) to somewhere else has brought him back to a sense of himself in the most intense way possible, as a human being who must face his darkest fears alone, with 'no promise of rescue' (line 27).

Form of the poem

Mahon has organised this poem into five stanzas of six lines made up of rhyming couplets with the pattern *aabbcc* in each. **The very regular form of the poem contrasts with the chaotic feelings he expresses in the final stanza.**

Thinking about the poem

1. What expectations does the title of the poem set up? Are these expectations realised?
2. How would you describe the tone of the first two stanzas? How is it conveyed?
3. Why does the poet describe the fish in such detail? Support your answer by reference to the poem.
4. Was the poet's trip to Donegal as ordinary and uneventful as it seemed? How did it affect him in his later dreams?
5. In what terms does the poet describe the sea? Would you agree that the imagery here is sensuous and intense? Look carefully at words such as 'spilling', 'marbling', 'muttering' (lines 22 to 24).
6. Would you agree that the sense of danger and isolation intensifies in the last stanza? How is this reflected in the language used?
7. How would you account for the sense of fear and disorientation experienced by the speaker?
8. Look carefully at the sound patterns – the full end-rhymes, half-rhymes, alliteration, assonance, consonance – and say what they contribute to the overall impact made by the poem.
9. Discuss 'Day Trip to Donegal' as a nature poem.
10. What does the poem reveal to us about the personality of the speaker?

Ecclesiastes

God, you could grow to love it, God-fearing, God-
chosen purist little puritan that,
for all your wiles and smiles, you are (the
dank churches, the empty streets,
the shipyard silence, the tied-up swings) and   5
shelter your cold heart from the heat
of the world, from woman-inquisition, from the
bright eyes of children. Yes you could
wear black, drink water, nourish a fierce zeal
with locusts and wild honey, and not   10
feel called upon to understand and forgive
but only to speak with a bleak
afflatus, and love the January rains when they
darken the dark doors and sink hard
into the Antrim hills, the bog meadows, the heaped   15
graves of your fathers. Bury that red
bandana, stick and guitar; this is your
country, close one eye and be king.
Your people await you, their heavy washing
flaps for you in the housing estates –   20
a credulous people. God, you could do it, God
help you, stand on a corner stiff
with rhetoric, promising nothing under the sun.

Glossary

title	*Ecclesiastes*: one of the books of the Old Testament; an ecclesiast is a preacher or evangelist
2	*purist*: someone who insists on purity in language or art
2	*puritan*: a person of strict moral conduct
3	*wiles*: coaxing, pleasant ways
5	*tied-up swings*: it was formerly the custom in Northern Ireland to close playgrounds on Sundays
7	*woman-inquisition*: questioning by a woman

9	*zeal*: intense, sometimes fanatical, enthusiasm for a cause
10	*locusts and wild honey*: John the Baptist is said to have survived in the desert by eating locusts and wild honey (Matthew, chapter 3)
13	*afflatus*: divine inspiration
17	*bandana*: large handkerchief worn on the head or around the neck
18	*close one eye and be king*: alludes to the words of Erasmus, 'In the kingdom of the blind the one-eyed man is king'
21	*credulous*: gullible
23	*rhetoric*: art of using language to persuade others

Guidelines

'Ecclesiastes', first published in 1968, is contained in the collection *Lives* (1975). **The poem gives us an insight into the Protestant tradition in Ulster into which Mahon was born.** Northern Ireland, particularly in pre-Troubles time (before the late 1960s), had a great number of independent Protestant preachers who would travel around preaching the Bible. 'Ecclesiastes' vividly evokes their way of life and attitudes.

Commentary

Lines 1–8

The first thing we notice about the poem is its tone. You can hear the poet's passion as he addresses himself with a mixture of honesty and contempt. 'God-chosen' is heavily ironic (who knows God's real wishes?), while 'purist' and 'puritan' sound like insults (lines 1 and 2). He acknowledges that for all his outward amiability ('wiles and smiles', line 3) he could become a preacher, be attracted to a strict ('puritan', line 2) way of life, even as he focuses on its dreariness in images that evoke a gloomy Presbyterian Sunday in his native Belfast – the deserted streets and closed playgrounds. The advantages are that you might avoid the problems of the world or real human relationships with women or children. You may notice how the word 'from' is repeated three times in lines 6 and 7, as if the speaker is casting out these images from his mind.

Lines 8–16

The tone becomes even fiercer as the poet describes what his life as a preacher would be like. He would live simply – 'wear black, drink water' (line 9) – driven only by religious fervour and 'locusts and wild honey' (line 10). As described in the Bible, John the Baptist survived for forty days in the desert on a diet of locusts and wild honey.

This brand of religion would not require Mahon to preach forgiveness or understand the complexity of life. Religion, as practised by these preachers, offers no comfort. The word of God ('afflatus' suggests divine inspiration, line 13) is bleak, associated with rain and darkness, harshness and death. This is the tradition within which these preachers work. The poet accepts that it is his tradition, too, as the image of 'the heaped / graves of your fathers' (lines 15–16) suggests.

Lines 16–23
A few evocative images – the 'red / bandana, stick and guitar' (lines 16–17) – conjure up a completely contrasting way of life, that of the romantic 'hippies' of the 1960s and 1970s. Their philosophy revolved around peace and love rather than rigid rules or dogmatic beliefs. The speaker exhorts himself to leave this way of life and take his place among the preachers in his own country.

The phrase 'close one eye and be king' (line 18) recalls the saying of Erasmus: 'In the country of the blind the one-eyed man is king.' It implies religious ignorance allied to power – surely a damning indictment of a whole religious tradition, the evangelical Calvinism of Ulster Presbyterianism. But the fault lies not only with the preachers, but also with the gullible and bigoted people in the 'housing estates' (line 20) who blindly accept their teachings.

With heavy irony the poet suggests that he could easily stand on a street corner 'stiff / with rhetoric' (lines 22–23) but say nothing of value to anyone. This last line is utterly negative in tone. It recalls a line from the biblical Ecclesiates (chapter 1, verse 9): 'there is nothing new under the sun', and it suggests both self-righteousness and negativity. This preacher promises salvation but offers nothing for the here and now.

Personal experience

Mahon's themes are not often explicitly autobiographical, but 'Ecclesiastes' is one of the few poems in which he comes to terms in some way with his identity as a poet from Northern Ireland.

'Ecclesiastes' expresses a complex emotional relationship with Belfast and the religious tradition of Protestant Ulster. In actuality, Mahon's religious background was Church of Ireland, but in the poem he acknowledges his identification with a more puritanical religious inheritance. By constantly repeating the word 'God', and by the religious language he uses throughout, the poet forces the reader to examine the vision of God that is put forward in this society. In fact the word takes on different connotations as the poem progresses. In the first line it moves from expressing a sudden realisation – 'God, you could grow to love it' – to the irony in the compound adjectives 'God-fearing, God-chosen'. 'God, you could do it' in line 21 is forceful, but the final 'God help you' has overtones of contemptuous pity. However, because much of the irony and the pity are directed at himself, the poem stops short of condemning a whole society.

Form of the poem

You will notice that the poem is not divided into orderly stanzas. It is written in one long verse paragraph, unrhymed, with run-on lines reflecting impassioned speech. Mahon makes use of rhetorical devices such as repetition ('God', 'you could'), alliteration ('darken the dark doors') and biblical references ('locusts and wild honey') to reinforce his depiction of a preacher's oratory, so that the language and theme of the poem are inextricably linked. The exaggeration in the poem's final line reflects the utterly negative nature of the preacher's message.

Thinking about the poem

1. What exactly are the attractions of the preachers' way of life? Why might they appeal to the poet?
2. Mahon appears to be aware of the inadequacies of the preachers' way of life. How is this inadequacy suggested?
3. Would you agree that the poem satirises a certain kind of religious fanaticism? Look carefully at the religious references and the harsh adjectives used throughout.
4. How would you describe the tone of the poem? Is it consistent throughout?
5. What picture of the Protestant people of Ulster is created for the reader of 'Ecclesiastes'? How did you respond to it?
6. What are Mahon's feelings about his own people, as expressed in the poem?
7. Would you agree that the form of the poem – its language, organisation, rhythm and sound patterns – all contribute greatly to the forcefulness of its effect? Look in particular at the accumulation of images, the imperative mood of the verbs, the run-on lines that carry the poem forward to the implications of the last line.
8. If you were to choose the poem as one of your favourite poems by Mahon, what case would you make for your choice?
9. 'Mahon excels at giving a voice to unsympathetic or marginalised characters.' Based on the poems 'Ecclesiastes', 'As It Should Be' and 'After the Titanic', give your opinion of this view.

After the Titanic

    They said I got away in a boat
And humbled me at the inquiry. I tell you
    I sank as far that night as any
Hero. As I sat shivering on the dark water
    I turned to ice to hear my costly   5
Life go thundering down in a pandemonium of
    Prams, pianos, sideboards, winches,
Boilers bursting and shredded ragtime. Now I hide
    In a lonely house behind the sea
Where the tide leaves broken toys and hat-boxes   10
    Silently at my door. The showers of
April, flowers of May mean nothing to me, nor the
    Late light of June, when my gardener
Describes to strangers how the old man stays in bed
    On seaward mornings after nights of   15
Wind, takes his cocaine and will see no-one. Then it is
    I drown again with all those dim
Lost faces I never understood. My poor soul
    Screams out in the starlight, heart
Breaks loose and rolls down like a stone.   20
    Include me in your lamentations.

Glossary

Line	Term
2	*inquiry*: the formal investigation into why the *Titanic* sunk
6	*pandemonium*: chaos, confusion
7	*winches*: machinery used to lift heavy goods
8	*ragtime*: the popular jazz music played by the orchestra as the ship was sinking
15	*seaward mornings*: mornings when the wind blows towards the sea
21	*lamentations*: expressions of sorrow and grief

Guidelines

This poem comes from the collection *Lives* (1975). It was originally entitled 'Bruce Ismay's Soliloquy'.

In April 1912 the *SS Titanic* set sail from Southampton, bound for New York. It struck an iceberg off the coast of Newfoundland and sank with the loss of almost 1,500 lives. After the tragedy, an inquiry was held into the disaster. Among those questioned was Bruce Ismay, the president of the White Star Line (the ship's owners) and one of the few male passengers who had managed to escape in the lifeboats.

According to biographers, Ismay was not an articulate man and was unable to give an explanation for his action. (Some witnesses said he dressed as a woman in order to escape on the lifeboat, but this was not subsequently proved.) He was accused of cowardice and never recovered from the tragedy, becoming a recluse in Co. Galway. In this dramatic monologue, Mahon gives a voice to Ismay.

The *Titanic* was built at the Harland and Wolff shipyard in Belfast. Perhaps the fact that Mahon's grandfather was a boiler-maker for the ship – the poem contains references to boilers bursting – inspired the poet to reconstruct the events and enter imaginatively into the mind of the speaker.

Commentary

Lines 1–8
Bruce Ismay wants to give us his side of the story. From the beginning he distances himself from the verdict of the inquiry: 'They said' (line 1) suggests that he does not agree with the findings. He felt 'humbled . . . at the inquiry' (line 2) and wants to set the record straight, in his own mind. 'I tell you' (line 2) has an honest ring to it, but is there an element of self-delusion in comparing his plight the night that the *Titanic* went down to that of any other 'Hero' (line 4)? He tries to convince his listeners (and perhaps himself also) that he, too, was a victim of the tragedy.

In vivid images **he evokes the atmosphere of chaos as the ship was sinking.** From where he sat 'shivering' in his lifeboat he could hear a 'pandemonium' of sounds as 'prams, pianos' were destroyed, as well as the sounds of 'boilers bursting' and interrupted music: 'shredded ragtime' (lines 4 to 8).

Lines 8–21

Then **he describes his life in the aftermath of the disaster**. Feeling ashamed and guilty, he hides away from the world. Ironically, he has chosen to live by the sea, where the material washed up by the tide also seems to accuse him: 'broken toys and hat-boxes' are left 'silently' at his door (lines 9 to 10). One cannot help but have a sort of sympathy for him as he says that life or the wonders of nature no longer have any meaning for him. Significantly, hearing the sound of wind on the sea disturbs him emotionally, so that he has to numb his senses with cocaine and isolate himself (lines 14 to 16). All the time, too, people are curious about him. He is someone his gardener will gossip about with strangers (lines 13 and 14).

The metaphors and similes in the last few lines convey feelings of utter desolation. It is as if he is forced to relive his experience again and again, to 'drown again' (line 17) with all those who died. His 'poor soul / Screams out in the starlight', his 'heart / Breaks loose and rolls down like a stone' (lines 18–20). Although we can detect a note of self-pity here, the speaker seeks to justify why he should be included in any expressions of grief for those who suffered. However, his plea for understanding is diminished somewhat when he admits that he 'never understood' all the 'dim / Lost faces' (lines 17–18) – perhaps because most of those who drowned were the poorer passengers in steerage, not part of his own 'costly / Life' (lines 5–6).

Form of the poem

In a dramatic monologue the poet gives a voice to a certain character and tries to make us see things from his or her point of view. Ismay addresses the reader directly and constantly uses the first person, 'I'. His language is mostly conversational and simple, but the imagery at times is highly exaggerated, which adds to our sense of a man tortured by remorse (or wishing to seem as if he is).

A dramatic monologue will also give a glimpse of the views of other people. Ismay tells us that he is socially isolated and an object of curiosity to strangers. He also refers to the 'lost faces' of those who drowned. We must decide whether Ismay's remorse is convincing in the light of such an enormous tragedy for so many people.

Mahon uses alliteration to convey Ismay's experience. In the final lines, for example, the repetition of 's' sounds (sibilance) in 'soul', 'screams' and 'starlight' and the assonance in the long 'o' sounds of 'rolls' and 'stone' echo the sense of grief that pervades the poem.

Thinking about the poem

1. Why, do you think, does the speaker of this poem feel compelled to give his side of the story?
2. Does he paint a vivid picture of the disaster, in your view? Explain your answer.
3. Do you find it strange that he has chosen to live out his days beside the sea? Why might he have made this decision?
4. From the list of phrases that follows choose the one that is closest to your reading of the poem:
   > This man is trying to justify his own cowardly actions.
   > This speaker feels genuinely sorry for what he has done.
   > This speaker has suffered greatly; it would have been better for him to have drowned like the others.

   Explain your choice.
5. What does the speaker of the poem reveal about his personality? Do you find him a sympathetic character?
6. Has the speaker convinced you that he should be included in 'lamentations' (line 21) or grief for the victims? Give a reason for your answer.
7. 'Derek Mahon has a great ability to convey the thoughts of others.' Do you agree with this view in respect of 'After the Titanic'?
8. Give **two** examples **each** of alliteration and assonance and comment on the effect they create in the poem.
9. Do you like this poem? Give reasons for your opinion.

Taking a closer look

1. How would you explain the lines 'I turned to ice to hear my costly / Life go thundering down' (lines 5–6)?
2. Comment on the effectiveness of the simile 'like a stone' in line 20.
3. Choose **two** examples of interesting sounds from the poem and say why you chose them.

Imagining

1. Imagine that you are a survivor of the disaster. Write a letter to a friend telling of your memories of that night. Use details from the poem in your letter.
2. Imagine that you are a newspaper reporter covering Bruce Ismay's appearance at the inquiry into the *Titanic* disaster. Write a short report about what you heard and saw.

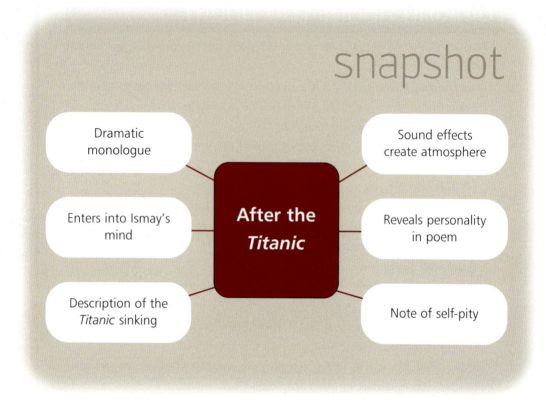

As It Should Be

We hunted the mad bastard
through bog, moorland, rock, to the star-lit west
And gunned him down in a blind yard
Between ten sleeping lorries
And an electricity generator.   5

Let us hear no idle talk
Of the moon in the Yellow River;
The air blows softer since his departure.

Since his tide-burial during school hours
Our children have known no bad dreams.   10
Their cries echo lightly along the coast.

This is as it should be.
They will thank us for it when they grow up
To a world with method in it.

Glossary
7 *Yellow River*: major Chinese river; possibly a reference to a play by Denis Johnston.

Guidelines

'As It Should Be' is from the collection *Lives* (1972). It is **another poem in which Mahon gives a voice to a persona who expresses a distinct and unpopular point of view.**

We enter into the mind of the speaker as he outlines his chilling justification of violence. Although the poem makes no direct reference to any particular conflict, the reference to the 'moon in the Yellow River' suggests a connection with the violence of the Irish Civil War, and, by extension, the conflict in Northern Ireland. Denis Johnston's play *The Moon in the Yellow River* (1931) deals with violence in Civil War times. It includes a particularly brutal episode in which the perpetrator of a plan to destroy a power plant was shot by one of his former comrades, a supporter of the Irish Free State. One of the characters in the play refers to the Chinese poet Lo Pi, who wished to embrace the moon in the Yellow River. This is interpreted as a metaphor for wishing to do the impossible, ideal thing.

Commentary

Stanza 1
From the beginning the speaker assumes an authority to kill that suggests official sanction for his actions. Possibly this is a hint that the speaker is identified with the Irish Free State character in Johnston's play. The enemy is insulted ('mad bastard') and dehumanised as he is 'hunted' like an animal (line 1). The manner of his death is described in chillingly factual terms. There is no sense of fair play: he is 'gunned down in a blind yard' (line 3), trapped between lorries and an electricity generator, from where he could not possibly have escaped.

Stanzas 2 and 3

No pity or remorse is expressed. It is as if the world is a better place without this human being. The speaker firmly rejects any possibility of idealism (the 'moon in the Yellow River', line 7) that may have been associated with his enemy's political views. In fact, he sees his violent death, ironically, as easing the fears of violence in the community: the children have had 'no bad dreams' (line 10) since this man's death.

Stanza 4

We hear the voice of fanaticism most clearly in the final stanza. The implications are quite chilling. The hunting down and murdering 'is as it should be' (line 12). There is no room for self-doubt or moral agonising. The world, according to the speaker, will now have 'method in it' (line 14) – a claim that casts an even more damning, ironic perspective on what he has described. What 'method' is there in the senseless killing of another human being?

Themes of the poem

Although the poem is short, it conveys a great deal about the psychology of the fanatic, whether he has the support of the state or not. An utter inability to consider any course of action other than the one that he sees as right, a total lack of moral questioning and an irrational justification of his actions are all suggested in the poem.

References to nature and the elements – bogs, moorland, stars, moon, air, tides, coast – reinforce the idea that the speaker sees his actions as part of the natural course of events, something that hardly needs to be explained.

His conviction that the children 'will thank us for it when they grow up' (line 13) assumes a right to act on behalf of others, even future generations, a belief that has been the basis of fascist regimes. It also betrays a total lack of awareness of how historical attitudes change over time.

As in 'After the Titanic', the poet allows the speaker to reveal the irony of his position, without direct authorial comment. The issues touched on may have their basis in historical events, but the picture of the speaker as it emerges is surely universally applicable to any conflict.

Thinking about the poem

1. How does the speaker of 'As It Should Be' justify the violent actions of himself and his companions?
2. Describe the tone of the poem. Look carefully at the use of the plural 'we' and the language and images the poet chooses when describing the events.
3. Which of the lines in the poem do you find the most disturbing? Give reasons for your choice.
4. Does the poem hint at another point of view? How does this affect your interpretation of the poem?
5. 'Ecclesiastes' and 'After the Titanic' are two other poems in which Mahon enters the mindset of other characters. Which of the three poems succeeds best in doing so, in your view?
6. Discuss the view that the poem is relevant to many contemporary events and conflicts.

A Disused Shed in Co. Wexford

'Let them not forget us, the weak souls among the asphodels.'
                                        Seferis, *Mythistorema*

(for J. G. Farrell)

Even now there are places where a thought might grow –
Peruvian mines, worked out and abandoned
To a slow clock of condensation,
An echo trapped for ever, and a flutter
Of wild-flowers in the lift-shaft,   5
Indian compound where the wind dances
And a door bangs with diminished confidence,
Lime crevices behind rippling rain-barrels,
Dog corners for bone burials;
And in a disused shed in Co. Wexford,   10

Deep in the grounds of a burnt-out hotel,
Among the bathtubs and the washbasins
A thousand mushrooms crowd to a keyhole.

This is the one star in their firmament
Or frames a star within a star.
What should they do there but desire?
So many days beyond the rhododendrons
With the world waltzing in its bowl of cloud,
They have learnt patience and silence
Listening to the rooks querulous in the high wood.

They have been waiting for us in a foetor
Of vegetable sweat since civil war days,
Since the gravel-crunching, interminable departure
Of the expropriated mycologist,
He never came back, and light since then
Is a keyhole rusting gently after rain.
Spiders have spun, flies dusted to mildew
And once a day, perhaps, they have heard something –
A trickle of masonry, a shout from the blue
Or a lorry changing gear at the end of the lane.

There have been deaths, the pale flesh flaking
Into the earth that nourished it;
And nightmares, born of these and the grim
Dominion of stale air and rank moisture.
Those nearest the door grow strong –
'Elbow room! Elbow room!'
The rest, dim in a twilight of crumbling
Utensils and broken pitchers, groaning
For their deliverance, have been so long
Expectant that there is left only the posture.

A half century, without visitors, in the dark –
Poor preparation for the cracking lock
And creak of hinges; magi, moonmen,
Powdery prisoners of the old regime,
Web-throated, stalked like triffids, racked by drought
And insomnia, only the ghost of a scream
At the flash-bulb firing-squad we wake them with
Shows there is life yet in their feverish forms.
Grown beyond nature now, soft food for worms,
They lift frail heads in gravity and good faith.

They are begging us, you see, in their wordless way,
To do something, to speak on their behalf
Or at least not to close the door again.
Lost people of Treblinka and Pompeii!
'Save us, save us,' they seem to say, 55
'Let the god not abandon us
Who have come so far in darkness and in pain.
We too had our lives to live.
You with your light meter and relaxed itinerary,
Let not our naïve labours have been in vain!' 60

Glossary	
Epigraph	*asphodels*: lily-like plants, associated with the dead in Greek mythology
Epigraph	*Mythistorema*: collection of short poems by the Greek poet George Seferis (1900–71) dealing with the myth of Odysseus in modern form; their themes are often political
Dedication	*J. G. Farrell*: novelist (1935–79)
6	*compound*: an enclosure around a house or factory
14	*firmament*: sky
20	*querulous*: complaining
21	*foetor*: a strong, offensive smell
24	*expropriated*: dispossessed
24	*mycologist*: someone who studies fungi
27	*mildew*: a disease on plants
43	*magi*: ancient priests or wise men; here, probably sorcerers
45	*triffids*: monstrous stinging plants invented by the writer John Wyndham in his science-fiction novel *The Day of the Triffids* (1951)
54	*Treblinka*: a Polish concentration camp in which Jews were incarcerated and killed during World War II
54	*Pompeii*: ancient city in Italy, buried when the volcano Vesuvius erupted in 79 ad
59	*light meter*: device for measuring light (in a camera)
59	*itinerary*: plan of a journey

New Discovery Poetry Anthology

Guidelines

This poem from *The Snow Party* (1985) has been called Mahon's masterpiece. Its impact depends upon our awareness of the symbolic significance the poet gives to the mushrooms in the old shed that he came across in Co. Wexford. **Lonely, abandoned, the mushrooms come to stand for the lost lives of those who have suffered through violence and neglect.** The Irish location of the poem links the suffering of the Irish people throughout history with the suffering of other peoples at other times.

Commentary

Epigraph and dedication

The epigraph 'Let them not forget us, the weak souls among the asphodels' is a plea for remembrance and is echoed throughout the poem.

The poem is dedicated to J. G. Farrell, author of the novel *Troubles* (1970). The subject matter of the novel may throw some light on the implications of the poem. A historical novel, set in Ireland in the 1920s, it evokes the fate of the Anglo-Irish Ascendancy class by describing the gradual ruin of a hotel, which is burnt down by republicans during the Civil War. This was a time when the Anglo-Irish community felt abandoned politically and emotionally by the British to whom they owed their allegiance.

Mahon has set his poem in a shed in the grounds of a burnt-out hotel, echoing Farrell's novel. Although the poem is not restricted to the theme of the novel, it is interesting that Mahon wrote it as the Protestant people of Ulster (his own people) began to express their sense of abandonment by the British government during the conflict in Northern Ireland in the 1970s.

Stanza 1

From the beginning there is a strong sense of place in the poem, which the language allows us imaginatively to enter. Like the opening shot of a film, the first stanza pans images of emptiness from across several continents – South America, India, Europe. These are places either once inhabited by people and now abandoned or places hidden from human consciousness. But these places rather eerily may become places where meaning is possible, and so the poem zooms in on the disused shed in Co. Wexford, before focusing more closely on the mushrooms that grow there. This first stanza sets the scene for the rest of the poem, ranging as it does throughout the world, preparing the reader for the historical insights that follow.

Stanza 2

The 'thousand mushrooms' (line 13) and their setting are described in a series of precise and rich images. At times we see the world from the mushrooms' point of view. Growing in the outhouse of a derelict hotel, they spend their days straining towards the source of light, which shines in through the keyhole. This source of light is the 'one star in their firmament' (line 14), an image that suggests their pathetic plight and sense of hopelessness.

The mushrooms take on a symbolic function as they are given human qualities and feelings. They are capable of 'desire' (line 16). Pent up in the shed for so long, they have accepted their isolation with 'patience and silence' (line 19). In contrast, the world moves on, 'waltzing in its bowl of cloud' (line 18).

Stanza 3

At times the mushrooms are presented simply as mushrooms: 'foetor / of vegetable sweat' (lines 21–22) suggests the foul smell of vegetable decay. **But their symbolic function is even more clear in this stanza as they are linked explicitly with 'civil war days'** (line 22).

The reference to the 'expropriated mycologist' (line 24) who never returned can be explained by an incident in Farrell's *The Troubles*. As in the novel, the decaying world seems to represent the Anglo-Irish who were displaced and ultimately abandoned. Mahon enables us to share in their experience. He names the things they can see and hear: the rusting keyhole, spiders and flies who also have 'dusted to mildew' (line 27), occasional sounds from the outside world: 'gravel-crunching' (line 23) steps, shouts or sounds of vehicles outside.

Stanza 4

The atmosphere becomes even more eerie in the fourth stanza. Powerful, sensuous imagery evokes suffering, death and decay. Visual, aural and tactile images are combined in the mushrooms' 'pale flesh flaking / Into the earth that nourished it' (lines 31–32). We can almost smell and feel the 'stale air and rank moisture' (line 34) in the shed.

Now the mushrooms are perceived as a multitude, symbolic of suffering people within a larger historical framework than those of the abandoned Anglo-Irish of the Irish Civil War. Like imprisoned people everywhere, they seek freedom. 'Elbow room! Elbow room!' (line 36) echoes the German '*lebensraum*' associated with the fate of the Jewish people under Nazi regimes during World War II. (Mahon makes the connection even more explicit in the final stanza, with the reference to the concentration camp at Treblinka.)

As the poem proceeds further, historical associations are established, so that the mushrooms take on their full symbolic weight as forgotten people, casualties of political cruelty or indifference. Like many oppressed people, all they can do is wait for their deliverance.

Stanza 5
In the fifth stanza the focus changes to the moment of discovery on the part of the poet/speaker and his unnamed companions. Hard consonant sounds in 'cracking lock / And creak of hinges' (lines 42–43) have an onomatopoeic effect as the door of the shed is opened. A series of imaginative metaphors follows.

The mushrooms are 'magi' and 'moonmen' (line 43) – mysterious and alien, like imagined inhabitants of the moon who have been without the light of the sun. The shape of the mushrooms also suggests the round moon.

'Powdery prisoners of the old regime' (line 44) has associations with the overthrow of the *ancien régime* during the French Revolution (1789–99). Both the 'p' sound of the alliteration and the word 'powdery' contribute to the richness of the metaphor, recalling both the powdered wigs worn by the French aristocrats and the fragility of the mushrooms.

In the image of the mushrooms as 'Web-throated, stalked like triffids' (line 45), there is a blend of the reality of mushrooms as fungi and the fantastic qualities Mahon sees in them.

As he does throughout the poem, Mahon personifies the mushrooms as he describes them: they suffer thirst and sleeplessness, they are ready to scream in fright when the shed door is opened. Weak and decaying, they 'lift frail heads in gravity and good faith' (line 50). Here the reader is reminded of many scenes of mass suffering that have been captured by the world's media in photographs and on television.

Stanza 6
In the final stanza the silence of the mushrooms is seen as a plea to the world to remember them and the multitudes of the oppressed that they symbolise, among them the Jewish prisoners at Treblinka and the buried inhabitants of Pompeii. The tone of the poem becomes almost biblical as the mushrooms pray that they will not be abandoned again, that their silence and suffering will not be in vain. They seem to acknowledge the power of the poet (notice the pun on the word 'meter', line 59) in speaking on behalf of the powerless.

Interpreting the poem

The poem has been interpreted as dealing specifically with the twentieth-century Anglo-Irish conflict that culminated in the Northern Ireland Troubles. It is set in Co. Wexford, makes explicit references to J. G. Farrell's novel about the Irish Civil War, and was published when the Northern Ireland conflict was at its height. From this point of view, the plight of the mushrooms may be an emblem of the stultifying political situation in Northern Ireland in the 1970s.

However, many commentators find this interpretation too restrictive. The poem ranges widely over many places and historical events. Indeed there is an almost epic time scale in the poem, with images of ancient burial customs, natural disasters (Pompeii), the French Revolution, the Jewish Holocaust, modern political oppression (the 'flash-bulb firing-squad', line 47) all telescoped into the dark intimacy of the disused shed. The perspective is constantly shifting, so that the mushrooms take on changing symbolic qualities as the poem progresses. Images of growth, death and rebirth remind us of the vegetable reality of the mushrooms, but are also symbolic of the ways in which history is constantly in flux, each moment arising organically from the last.

The image of speech and its opposite, silence, is significant in the poem. From the beginning the poem focuses on what can be heard: 'an echo' that becomes the 'silence' in the shed, the 'shout' heard by the mushrooms and how they are 'groaning', hear the 'ghost of a scream' and are 'begging us . . . to speak on their behalf'. The poem suggests that there is a responsibility to bear witness to the injustice of history. The mushrooms, begging the poet 'not to close the door again', are pleading for remembrance on behalf of oppressed people everywhere and of all times.

Form of the poem

The poem is organized into six stanzas of ten lines each. Apart from the introductory first stanza, the end of which is marked by a comma, each stanza is self-contained and end-stopped. In effect this means that each stanza works as a paragraph, allowing the poet to make his point or develop his description at some length. You will notice, too, the long line lengths (some have up to twelve syllables), which allow for development and expansion. **The form of the poem is particularly appropriate to its meditative tone and complex historical theme.**

Thinking about the poem

1. Would you agree that the imagery of the first stanza suggests desolation and abandonment? Do you find the effect melancholy or eerie? Explain your answer.
2. What human qualities are ascribed to the mushrooms in the second and third stanzas? How is their plight suggested?
3. How does the language of the poem reflect the passing of time in the second and third stanzas?
4. Is it significant that the mushrooms have been waiting since Civil War days, having been abandoned by the mycologist who never came back? What link does this reference create with the places and peoples mentioned in the first stanza?
5. How would you describe the tone and atmosphere of the fourth stanza? Look carefully at the language the poet uses. Do the mushrooms take on an even more poignant weight as metaphors of suffering and loss at this point in the poem?
6. What echoes of historical suffering are found in the fourth stanza?
7. The moment of entry by the humans, presented in terms of an invasion, provokes a reaction of passive terror in the mushrooms. How does the poet dramatise this?
8. Would you agree that the images in which the mushrooms are presented in the fifth stanza are imaginative, almost surreal? Discuss the contribution made by the sound-effects – alliteration, onomatopoeia – in building the images.
9. In the final stanza the full symbolism of the mushrooms is made apparent. What exactly do they represent? In considering this, take into account not only the explicit historical references of the poem but also the potential contemporary implications for the Protestant people of Northern Ireland.
10. Look carefully at how the six stanzas are formed. Why did the poet choose longer lines and ten-line stanzas for his theme?
11. You have chosen to speak about this poem in a talk entitled 'Introducing Derek Mahon'. Write out the talk you would give.
12. Write a short essay giving your response (positive or negative) to the view that this is 'one of Mahon's finest poems'.

The Chinese Restaurant in Portrush

Before the first visitor comes the spring
Softening the sharp air of the coast
In time for the first 'invasion'.
Today the place is as it might have been,
Gentle and almost hospitable. A girl   5
Strides past the Northern Counties Hotel,
Light-footed, swinging a book-bag,
And the doors that were shut all winter
Against the north wind and the sea mists
Lie open to the street, where one   10
By one the gulls go window-shopping
And an old wolfhound dozes in the sun.

While I sit with my paper and prawn chow mein
Under a framed photograph of Hong Kong
The proprietor of the Chinese restaurant   15
Stands at the door as if the world were young,
Watching the first yacht hoist a sail
– An ideogram on sea-cloud – and the light
Of heaven upon the mountains of Donegal;
And whistles a little tune, dreaming of home.   20

Derek Mahon

Glossary	
title	*Portrush*: seaside resort in Co. Antrim
13	*chow mein*: Chinese fried noodle dish
18	*ideogram*: in Chinese writing, a written character or symbol that stands not for a word or sound but for the thing itself

Guidelines

'The Chinese Restaurant in Portrush' is collected in the volume *Poems 1962–1978*.

Mahon rarely deals with the Northern Ireland conflict in his poems, but we cannot ignore the implications of the title. Portrush, a seaside town in north Co. Antrim, has been a predominantly Protestant, unionist area of Northern Ireland. This lyrical depiction of the resort as a peaceful, welcoming place must be set against the backdrop of violence and intransigence in Northern Ireland at the time the poem was written.

Commentary

Stanza 1

The poem celebrates Portrush but also sees its shortcomings. The image of spring with which the poem opens combines pleasant anticipation with an undercurrent of defensiveness: a 'visitor' (line 1) might be seen as part of an 'invasion' (line 3) of the town. The town is 'gentle' but 'almost hospitable' – not totally welcoming yet (line 5). There is a note of regret in line 4: 'the place is as it might have been'. Does the poet seek to recapture the memory of Portrush as it might have been in the past? Or might he be expressing a desire to recapture the town as it might have been had the violence in Northern Ireland not affected it?

Lively visual images – the girl, the gulls, the dog – bring the place to life for the reader. Words such as 'light-footed', 'swinging', 'open', 'window-shopping' and 'sun' set up a contrast to the town as it has been in 'winter', with the 'north wind', 'sea mists' and 'shut' doors. The town seems to be waking up at last.

Stanza 2

When we meet the figures of the poet and the owner of the Chinese restaurant in the second stanza, the scene is one of pleasure and relaxation. The lines that follow have the clarity of a painting. Sitting in the Chinese restaurant under a framed photograph of Hong Kong, the poet relaxes with his paper and his food. He seems then to enter imaginatively into the mind of the proprietor of the restaurant and describes what he sees from that particular perspective as he looks out to sea.

The first yacht on the sea becomes 'An ideogram on sea-cloud' (line 18), like a symbol in Chinese writing. In the background both the poet and the restaurant owner can see the 'mountains of Donegal' (line 19). The image suggests beauty and peace, and the owner of the restaurant responds happily, but there is some poignancy when we recall that he is far away from home.

Themes of the poem

Underlying the poem are themes of identity and belonging. Neither of the main characters in the poem – the poet or the proprietor of the restaurant – 'belong' in Portrush. The poet, a native of Belfast, is one of the town's 'visitors'. He eats his 'foreign' food in a Chinese restaurant, owned by a man who has travelled a long way from his original 'home'. The photograph of Hong Kong on the wall (presumably his former home) suggests that it still means a great deal to him, and yet he has chosen to buy a restaurant in Northern Ireland, and therefore he belongs now in Portrush. When he dreams of home, as the last line says, he 'whistles a little tune', but not in a sad or nostalgic way. So the idea of visiting, of movement from one place to another, is central to the poem. Even the background images – the yacht, the Donegal hills – contribute to this idea. **By placing the place names throughout the poem in such close proximity with each other, the poem makes us aware of how one place can be viewed from another.**

Another aspect of the theme of identity that the poem could be said to examine, in an indirect way, is the relationship between the counties of Northern Ireland and of the Republic of Ireland, divided as they are by the border and governed by two different jurisdictions. When we read the poem we are conscious of how close Portrush is to Co. Donegal, and yet the distance between them seems almost as far as that between China and Portrush.

Thinking about the poem

1. What atmosphere is created by the images in the first stanza? Take into account the description of the weather, the girl, the gulls, the dog.
2. What is the poet suggesting in line 4 when he says, 'Today the place is as it might have been'? What feelings may lie behind this?
3. What does the phrase 'as if the world were young' (line 16) suggest to you?
4. Discuss the significance of the notions of place, visitors and home in this poem.
5. Would you agree that the visual images in the second stanza have the clarity and vividness of a painting? What features combine to create this impression?
6. 'The poem celebrates the ordinary experiences of life amidst an awareness of their vulnerability to change.' Discuss this view of the poem.
7. Compare 'The Chinese Restaurant in Portrush' with 'Rathlin' and 'Kinsale' as poems that are concerned with place. Which do you prefer, and why?
8. 'Mahon is preoccupied with questions of belonging and identity.' Discuss this view in relation to the poem above and one of Mahon's other poems.

Rathlin

A long time since the last scream cut short –
Then an unnatural silence; and then
A natural silence, slowly broken
By the shearwater, by the sporadic
Conversation of crickets, the bleak
Reminder of a metaphysical wind.
Ages of this, till the report
Of an outboard motor at the pier
Shatters the dream-time, and we land
As if we were the first visitors here.

The whole island a sanctuary where amazed
Oneiric species whistle and chatter,
Evacuating rock-face and cliff-top.
Cerulean distance, an oceanic haze –
Nothing but sea-smoke to the ice-cap
And the odd somnolent freighter.
Bombs doze in the housing estates
But here they are through with history –
Custodians of a lone light which repeats
One simple statement to the turbulent sea.

A long time since the unspeakable violence –
Since Somhairle Buí, powerless on the mainland,
Heard the screams of the Rathlin women
Borne to him, seconds later, upon the wind.
Only the cry of the shearwater
And the roar of the outboard motor
Disturb the singular peace. Spray-blind,
We leave here the infancy of the race,
Unsure among the pitching surfaces
Whether the future lies before us or behind.

Glossary	
title	*Rathlin*: an island off the north coast of Co. Antrim
4	*shearwater*: an oceanic bird that skims the water
4	*sporadic*: occasional
12	*Oneiric*: relating to dreams
14	*Cerulean*: dark blue or sea-green
16	*somnolent*: sleepy
16	*freighter*: cargo-carrying boat
22	*Somhairle Buí*: Sorley Boy, chieftain of the MacDonnell clan of Antrim, whose castle was near Ballycastle, the nearest town on the Irish mainland to Rathlin

Guidelines

'Rathlin' is from the collection *Courtyards in Delft* (1981).

Rathlin Island, off the north coast of Co. Antrim, was the scene of a cruel massacre in 1575. The Earl of Essex, then Queen Elizabeth's marshal in Ireland, led his troops in a raid on the island. He and his soldiers succeeded in landing without being discovered, taking the inhabitants by surprise. They proceeded to destroy all the island's crops and cattle, before massacring in cold blood all the men, women and children on the island, including the wife and children of Somhairle Buí, chieftain of the MacDonnell clan. Their screams were said to have been heard by Somhairle Buí at his castle on the mainland at Ballycastle, Co. Antrim.

The poem is about a trip the poet takes to the island. His awareness of the island's violent history throws an ironic light on contemporary violence in Northern Ireland.

Commentary

Stanza 1

From the beginning the poet recalls the massacre that took place on Rathlin in a vivid image: the 'last scream cut short' was followed by 'an unnatural silence' (lines 1 and 2). For a long time the only sounds were the sounds of nature, the cries of the birds and the noise made by crickets. Only the 'metaphysical wind' is a reminder of the past (line 6). The phrase suggests the abstract power of the wind to evoke death and loss. (We might remember that in 'Day Trip to Donegal' Mahon described the wind as 'vindictive'.)

The arrival of the 'visitors' (line 10) and the sound (the 'report', line 7) of the boat's engine seems to disturb the silence of the place, its dreamlike atmosphere. When they land, it is as if they are the 'first visitors', like the first inhabitants of the Garden of Eden.

Stanza 2

Everything on the island is seen as if in a dream. Beautiful visual images convey how peaceful it is. The birds are part of some 'Oneiric' or dreamlike species (line 12), the sky is 'Cerulean', (intensely blue or sea-green, line 14). All that can be seen is the haze on the ocean and the occasional slow-moving freighter or cargo ship.

But the poem does not retain its dreamlike atmosphere for long. Line 17 – 'Bombs doze in the housing estates' – brings the reader back to reality with a jolt. Threats of violence underlie the lives of ordinary people, just as violence had once destroyed the people of Rathlin. The phrase 'through with history' (line 18) has complex implications that readers may like to tease out for themselves. Does it suggest that Rathlin represents some post-historical place in which history has no relevance, because it all happened so long ago? This would be a comforting thought if it did not follow the ominous reference to the 'bombs' that 'doze' on the mainland, where history is still being made, as it were.

As 'custodians of a lone light' (literally, the lighthouse on the island, line 19), the island and its inhabitants can be seen metaphorically to represent the light of imagination, 'dream-time' (line 9), which offers peace and simplicity. It 'repeats' a 'simple statement' of peace, in contrast to the 'turbulent' sea (lines 19 and 20).

Stanza 3

In the third stanza the mood of the poem changes as we are reminded again of the historical violence that took place on Rathlin, the 'screams' (line 23) of the women heard by Somhairle Buí. The 'cry of the shearwater' (line 25) and the 'roar of the outboard motor' (line 26) bring to an end the 'singular peace' (line 27) of the island as the poet and his companions leave what he calls the 'infancy of the race' (line 28). The phrase suggests a world of almost primordial innocence.

However, the final lines of the poem leave us with some questions. Does the poet suggest that the violence once known on Rathlin awaits them in the future, or that the peacefulness he experienced on the island is what the future holds? Or might the ambiguity here reflect his own uncertainty about the future? Just as the journey has made them 'Spray-blind' (line 27), is the future also confusing?

Themes of the poem

Mahon rarely deals directly in his poems with the violence of what came to be known as the Troubles, but there are many poems, such as 'Rathlin', in which he expresses his unease at the situation. By invoking the violent history of the island he reminds us of the ongoing hostility between the British and the Irish, the source of the contemporary problems in Northern Ireland. We become aware as we read the poem that this historical violence can and may erupt again at any time, and the disturbing implications of this fact.

Images and metaphors

You may notice that Mahon uses the image of speech and its opposite, silence, throughout the poem. 'Silence', 'conversation', even 'report' – although it literally means the backfire noise of the outboard engine it is also possible to see its other meanings as 'rumour' or 'formal account of a case' as relevant to this trip to the island where such atrocities took place. Birds 'whistle and chatter', light from the lighthouse 'repeats / One simple statement'.

As a metaphor for beauty and peace, the image of light occurs frequently in Mahon's poetry. For instance, in 'A Disused Shed in Co. Wexford' light was seen as the mushrooms' saviour. In 'The Chinese Restaurant in Portrush' it suggests hope. The sea and the wind, on the other hand, have represented turmoil in other poems besides 'Rathlin', for instance in 'Day Trip to Donegal'.

Form of the poem

The poem is written in three ten-line stanzas. As in 'A Disused Shed in Co. Wexford', the length of stanzas acts like a paragraph that allows the poet to develop his ideas in a reflective way, as befits a poem dealing with serious and complex issues. There is no regular rhyme pattern, but sounds are repeated throughout, in assonance (for example, the long 'o' sounds in 'custodians' and 'lone' in line 19), consonance (for example, 'Conversations of crickets' in line 5) and sibilance (for example, 'simple statement' in line 20) creating a musical effect.

Thinking about the poem

1. The poem speaks of 'the singular peace' (line 27) on the island of Rathlin. How does the language help to convey this sense of peace?
2. What other perspective on the island is suggested? Do the contrasting images of violence, past as well as present, for instance, contribute to the atmosphere presented throughout the poem?
3. Would you agree that the poem is remarkable for the vividness and sensuousness of its natural imagery? Explain your answer.
4. How would you explain the line: 'But here they are through with history' (line 18)? Is this idea echoed elsewhere in the poem?
5. The phrase 'dream-time' occurs in the first stanza. How is the notion of dreams elaborated upon in the poem?
6. What effect has the visit to the island had upon the speaker of the poem? Look carefully at the last two lines.
7. Why has the poet used the image of speech throughout the poem? Support your answer by reference to the poem.
8. Compare the poem with 'Day Trip to Donegal' as a description of nature and an evocation of mood. Which poem do you prefer, and why?
9. Would you agree that Mahon has a remarkable sense of place in his poems? Refer to the poem 'Kinsale' and 'The Chinese Restaurant in Portrush' as well as 'Rathlin' in your answer.
10. Critics have admired Mahon's 'acute eye and precise ear' as a poet. Discuss 'Rathlin' with this in mind.

Antarctica

(for Richard Ryan)

'I am just going outside and may be some time.'
The others nod, pretending not to know.
At the heart of the ridiculous, the sublime.

He leaves them reading and begins to climb,
Goading his ghost into the howling snow;
He is just going outside and may be some time.

The tent recedes beneath its crust of rime
And frostbite is replaced by vertigo:
At the heart of the ridiculous, the sublime.

Need we consider it some sort of crime, 10
This numb self-sacrifice of the weakest? No,
He is just going outside and may be some time –

In fact, for ever. Solitary enzyme,
Though the night yield no glimmer there will glow,
At the heart of the ridiculous, the sublime. 15

He takes leave of the earthly pantomime
Quietly, knowing it is time to go.
'I am just going outside and may be some time.'
At the heart of the ridiculous, the sublime.

	Glossary	
title	*Antarctica*: the Antarctic is the southern polar region	
dedication	*Richard Ryan*: an Irish diplomat and poet	
3	*sublime*: noble, awe-inspiring	
5	*goading*: urging on	
7	*rime*: frost	
8	*frostbite*: damage to body tissue exposed to freezing temperatures	
8	*vertigo*: dizziness, tendency to lose balance	
13	*enzyme*: a protein that causes a living organism to change but is not changed itself	
16	*earthly pantomime*: this world	

Guidelines

This poem comes from the collection *Antarctica* (1985).

In 1912 the explorer Captain Robert Scott led an expedition to the South Pole, but he and his men perished in the attempt. An entry in Scott's diary, found after his death, describes how one of the men, Captain L.E.G. Oates, sacrificed himself in order to save food for the others by crawling out into a blizzard, saying only, 'I am just going out and may be some time.' These words have become famous as an example of understatement and of a certain kind of heroism. Mahon dramatises the incident in this villanelle, which matches beautifully the dignity of Oates's last grim resolve.

Commentary

Stanza 1

Oates's words open the poem and form one of the two refrains used throughout.
Mahon depicts Oates's companions as nodding wordlessly, pretending that they do not know the true meaning of what he has said. They display the reserve and 'stiff upper lip' that the English were known for at that time.

In exploring the implications of Oates's words, and the reaction of his comrades, Mahon is writing from today's perspective where extreme heroic gestures have become rarer and even slightly suspect. The second refrain, 'At the heart of the ridiculous, the sublime', makes use of our familiarity with the expression 'from the sublime to the ridiculous'. We can see why Mahon might suggest that Oates's words are ridiculous in their failure to register even the smallest amount of emotion and in their glaring understatement. As we know, 'some time' means, in fact, for ever.

On the other hand, Mahon acknowledges the 'sublime' aspect of the event: the nobility and unselfishness with which Oates acted. From this point of view, the lack of emotion expressed by Oates's companions seems more like a brave acceptance of the inevitable.

Stanzas 2 and 3

As Oates climbs to his death, he is depicted in images of suffering and endurance that lend dignity to his famous words. He is seen to be 'Goading his ghost into the howling snow' (line 5), which captures the desperate nature of his situation. He suffers dizziness and frostbite. His experience is far from that suggested by his words 'just going outside', he is dying a lonely death in the cold snow.

Stanza 4

The poem questions present-day attitudes to such acts of 'self-sacrifice' (line 11). Why should they be seen as 'some sort of crime' (line 10)? Such a question would certainly never have been asked in the early twentieth century when the act took place. Generations of British children were brought up to admire Oates without qualification.

Stanzas 5 and 6

Mahon goes on to depict Oates, metaphorically, as a 'Solitary enzyme' or living thing that will glow in the night as a source of inspiration for others (lines 13 and 14). He knew the right thing to do and when to do it, leaving this world – described as an 'earthly pantomime' (line 16) – at a time of his own choosing. The refrain, ending finally with the word 'sublime', now appears as a tribute.

Form of the poem

A villanelle – said to have a singing line – is a form of poem in which there is a sequence of tercets (three lines), with rhyming scheme *aba, aba, aba*. Each tercet ends in a refrain, and there are only two refrains alternating throughout the poem. The set of tercets is rounded off with a quatrain in which the two refrains at last come together, one capping the other. A villanelle is a highly stylised, formal poem that has become associated with meditations on death or grief.

Mahon uses only two rhyme sounds throughout the nineteen lines of his poem: the rhyming 'time' and 'sublime' and the long 'o' sound of 'know', 'snow', 'vertigo' and other words. This could be said to enhance the feeling of emptiness and the sheer monotony of the Antarctic landscape in which the ill-fated expedition took place.

Thinking about the poem

1. Why might the words 'I am just going out and may be some time' be seen as 'ridiculous'?
2. Why are they also 'sublime'?
3. What picture of the members of the expedition do you get from reading this poem?
4. What sort of person was Oates, as suggested in the poem?
5. Choose which of the following phrases, in your opinion, best reveals the poet's attitude:

    He celebrates Oates's heroic act.

    He thinks Oates's act was foolish.

    Explain your answer.

6 Does the poem succeed in creating a sense of the awful climate that the explorers experienced? Choose the words and phrases that best create this sense.
7 What is your own response to the issues raised in the poem?
8 Would Oates's action be appreciated nowadays? Give a reason for your view.

Taking a closer look

1 Choose your favourite lines from the poem and give a reason for your choice.
2 Explain what you think Mahon suggests when he asks: 'Need we consider it some sort of crime, / This numb self-sacrifice of the weakest?' (lines 10–11).
3 What attitude to life is expressed in the phrase 'earthly pantomime' (line 16), in your view?

Imagining

1 Imagine that you are Captain Oates. In a diary entry for the night before you leave the tent, try to explain what you are about to do and why.
2 Imagine that you are one of Oates's companions. You do not want him to sacrifice himself for you and the others. Write what you would say to persuade him not to go.

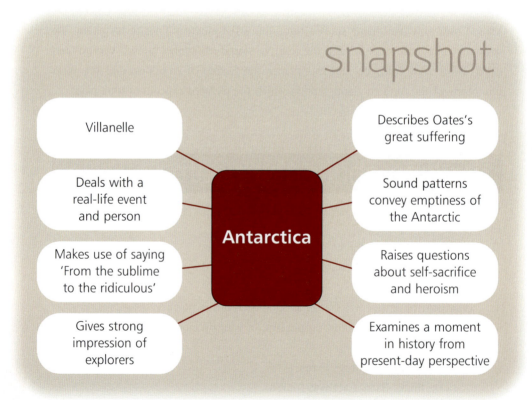

Kinsale

The kind of rain we knew is a thing of the past –
deep-delving, dark, deliberate you would say,
browsing on spire and bogland; but today
our sky-blue slates are steaming in the sun,
our yachts tinkling and dancing in the bay   5
like race-horses. We contemplate at last
shining windows, a future forbidden to no-one.

Glossary	
title	*Kinsale*: a fishing village, now a thriving resort in Co. Cork
3	*browsing on*: feeding on

Guidelines

This poem comes from the collection *Antarctica* (1985).

It is difficult to read this poem without remembering the battle that took place in Kinsale in 1601, in which the Irish, led by Red Hugh O'Donnell and Hugh O'Neill, were defeated by the army of Elizabeth I – a decisive victory that altered the course of Irish history. Historians have viewed the defeat as marking the end of the old Gaelic rule of Ireland. Kinsale is now a thriving, fashionable town, well known for sailing activities and tourism. **The contrast between past and present is depicted in the imagery Mahon uses to describe it.**

Commentary

Lines 1–3

There are rich connotations in the phrase the 'kind of rain we knew' (line 1). It was 'deep-delving, dark, deliberate' (line 2) and is perceived as having been 'browsing on spire and bogland' (line 3). The heavy 'd' sounds in the adjectives suggest death and gloom, the burden of remembered history of what happened in Kinsale and its effect on church ('spire') and countryside ('bogland'). As in the poem 'Rathlin', the implication is that Kinsale is 'through with history'. So the rain that we in Ireland once knew is symbolic of a time of suffering and lament in the Irish consciousness, the defeat of the old Gaelic and Catholic order.

Lines 4–6

The images of darkness and sorrow are followed by images of light and movement. The effect is celebratory and carefree. Light, as we have seen in a number of Mahon's poems, signifies hope. The vividly sensuous image of 'our sky-blue slates' 'steaming in the sun' (line 4) captures the new optimistic atmosphere visually and aurally, with sibilance and alliteration giving a musical effect to the words. This musical effect is reinforced by the images of the 'yachts tinkling and dancing' (line 5), while the simile 'like race-horses' (line 6) paints a very attractive picture of the movement of the yachts on the sea. End-rhyme, used throughout, contributes to the sense of harmony that the poem celebrates.

Lines 6–7

The final two lines make the contrast with the past even clearer by looking to the future, a future in which windows will be 'shining' – the image implies happiness and success and, significantly, it will be there for all to enjoy: 'forbidden to no one' (line 7). Is this the new Ireland, free from the shackles of the past, the burden of history? **The attractions of this idea in the Ireland of 1985 (when the poem was published) were obvious, offering a way forward from attitudes that have caused so much grief and strife.**

Might it be significant that the last idea is expressed in a rather sombre way, as the word 'forbidden' suggests? Does this undermine the confident optimism of the poem? It is possible to interpret the images in this poem from an ironic perspective. 'Spire' and 'bogland' contrast greatly with 'race-horses' and 'yachts' and may suggest the desire of the 'new' Irish people to leave aside the old ways of life (religion and the land). From this point of view, the final comment – 'a future forbidden to no-one' (line 7) – is ironic since access to yachts and race-horses requires money.

Thinking about the poem

1. Look carefully at the poet's use of contrast in this short lyric. Might the rain and the sun have a metaphorical significance? Can you say what associations they might carry?
2. Would you agree that the sound patterns of the poem create a musical effect? Explain your answer.
3. What is the dominant tone of the poem, in your view? Take into account the images of yachts and race-horses as well as those of spires and bogland.
4. Does the historical significance of Kinsale have any bearing on the theme of the poem, in your view?

5   Mahon has cited the work of the painter Raoul Dufy as an influence on his poetry, and on 'Kinsale' in particular. Dufy has painted watercolours and gouaches depicting harbour scenes, yachts and racecourses. You might like to find some illustrations of Dufy's work and comment on any connections you see between the two artists, painter and poet.

6   Do you like this poem? Give reasons for your opinion.

Exam-Style Questions

1   'Why read the poetry of Derek Mahon?' Write out the text of a talk you would give in response to this title. Support the points you make by reference to the poetry of Derek Mahon on your course.

In your talk, you might include the following reasons:

- His themes are interesting and varied (e.g. explorations of history, individual experiences, personal narrative).
- He is capable of writing from many different perspectives, even unpopular ones.
- His use of language is precise and vivid, his metaphors and images are carefully chosen, his use of sound is musical and evocative.
- He has a keen sense of place to which the reader can respond well.
- He raises important questions, directly or indirectly, about political issues and attitudes.

Remember that you must support your points by detailed discussion of individual poems.

2   'I like (or do not like) the poetry of Derek Mahon'. Respond to this statement, referring to the poetry by Derek Mahon on your course.

Reasons you could give for liking Mahon's poetry include:

- His themes are wide-ranging and relevant to modern life.
- He refuses to be pigeon-holed as a poet from Northern Ireland.
- He enters imaginatively into the minds of others in his poems.
- He uses language in a precise and fresh manner, and often with the eye of a painter.
- Imagery and sound are used to great effect in his work.
- He responds to the beauty of nature and the atmosphere of places.

Reasons you could give for not liking Mahon's poetry include:

- The poet reveals very little about himself in his work.
- He remains too detached from the historical issues and political questions of his time.
- There is a certain lack of emotion in his work.
- When he does engage with political issues, his approach is too indirect.

3. Discuss the importance of history in Mahon's poems.
4. 'In his poems Mahon is interested in giving a voice to those who are marginalised, no matter how unpalatable their views are.' To what extent is this true of the poems that are on your course?
5. Write a review of Mahon's poetry for a serious journal.
6. 'In his poems Mahon has a keen sense of place'. Discuss.
7. Mahon has been described as a poet of 'great richness, elegance, and technical brilliance'. Do you agree with this opinion of Mahon's poetry? Give reasons for your answer.
8. 'Although he rarely deals directly with the Troubles in Northern Ireland, Mahon is acutely aware of the effects of fanaticism and violence on society.' Do you agree with this point of view?
9. 'Mahon's poems appeal to both the intellect and the emotions.' Discuss this view.
10. 'A wide range of cultural reference makes Mahon's poetry appealing.' Would you agree with this statement?

Sample Essay

Derek Mahon explores people and places in his own distinctive style.

Write your response to this statement, supporting your answer with relevant quotation from or reference to the poems of Derek Mahon.

Derek Mahon's poetry appeals to me for many reasons. I particularly admire his ability to enter into the minds of other people and to communicate their experience. I also admire his gift of describing places so that they come to life for the reader.

[First statements refer directly to the terms of the question and indicate personal response]

The people who inhabit Mahon's poems range from those who are close to him, such as his grandfather in 'Grandfather', to those who are public figures, such as the hapless survivor of the *Titanic* in 'After the Titanic' or the zealous preacher in 'Ecclesiastes'.

[Introduces discussion of people, the first aspect of the question]

Mahon's distinctive style contributes to the effectiveness of these portrait poems. Even though he is describing a close relative in his sonnet 'Grandfather', Mahon shows very little personal emotion, allowing instead the images he uses to convey the personality of the old man. From the beginning of the poem he sets in motion the image of the old man as an outsider, someone who has refused to accommodate the needs and wishes of others. He is 'like a four-year-old' in the way he roams about the house early in the morning 'with a block of wood / Or a box of nails'. As Mahon says, he is 'up to no good' – but the word 'discreetly' hints at the essential privacy of the man, an idea reinforced in the sestet of the sonnet when we hear of his nightly escapades, how he returns home late 'as cute as they come'. This colloquial phrase and the image of him as he 'sets the clock / Against the future' suggest that there is a purpose to his activities. The word 'shrewd' implies that it is a clever form of self-preservation. The impression given is of someone who wishes to maintain his independence in the face of old age and impending death. Although the poem is short and at times wryly humorous, it succeeds in conveying a sense of a complex individual nearing the end of his life.

[First poem referred to, with suitable quotations; discussion includes content and style]

Mahon's poetic method is somewhat similar in 'After the Titanic', to the extent that the poet allows the images to speak for themselves without direct comment. In this poem the speaker is Bruce Ismay, president of the White Star Line, the owners of the *Titanic*. He had survived the disaster and was summoned to speak at the subsequent inquiry. Through the words he gives to Ismay, Mahon evokes the atmosphere of the disaster in vivid images. We can picture the speaker in his boat, 'shivering on the dark water'. A few well-chosen objects – 'prams, pianos, sideboards, winches' – crystallise the contents of the ship as it sinks, with onomatopoeic words and phrases – 'thundering', a 'pandemonium', 'boilers bursting' – conveying the chaos and terror of the event.

[Note how one paragraph links to the next]

Just as Mahon succeeded in capturing the essence of his grandfather's personality, he succeeds here in giving us an insight into the tormented mind of Ismay in the aftermath of the disaster. The metaphors and similes he uses convey a feeling of utter desolation. His 'poor soul / Screams out in the starlight', his heart 'breaks loose and rolls down like a stone'. It is impossible not to feel a certain compassion for the speaker as he now lives his life, isolated and vilified. And yet it is true to say that Mahon's poem has not justified Ismay's actions in any way.

[Second poem referred to, with suitable quotations]

A third poem in which Mahon explores the mind of another person is 'Ecclesiastes'. This poem appeals to me because it conveys not only the mindset of a particular individual, a zealous preacher, but also a whole way of life in a particular place: the Belfast of Mahon's youth. As such it could be said to show Mahon's ability to explore people and places at the one time. As he does in 'After the Titanic' with Bruce Ismay, the poet adopts the voice of another (this time a preacher) in 'Ecclesiastes', but the difference is that in 'Ecclesiastes' he identifies more closely with the speaker. He recognises that the preacher's way of life could have attractions for him. Something in his 'purist little puritan' personality accepts the dreariness of religion as it is practised in his native

Belfast: 'the dank churches, the empty streets, / the shipyard silence, the tied-up swings'. He could even 'grow to love it' if it offered a chance to avoid the problems of human relationships and feeling compelled 'to understand and forgive'. These damning words portray the essence of this strict religion preached in Northern Ireland, associated as it is with the 'January rains' and the 'dark doors' of the city. But the poem suggests that this form of religion is destructive. It preaches religious intolerance to a 'credulous' people. It promises them 'nothing under the sun'. 'Ecclesiastes' is one of the few poems in which Mahon comes to terms with his identity as a poet from Northern Ireland, acknowledging honestly the influence it had on his upbringing. The vivid images and impassioned tone of the poem leave us in no doubt about Mahon's complex emotional relationship with the city of his birth.

[Discussion of third poem includes reference to both people and places]

As we have seen, Mahon explores how people think and feel. Through his distinctive and imaginative use of language (what has been called his 'acute eye and precise ear') he also has the ability to make the reader experience a sense of place. We can see this in 'Rathlin', 'The Chinese Restaurant in Portrush' and 'Kinsale'.

[Introduces discussion of place, the second aspect of the question]

In 'Rathlin' he recounts a trip made to the island. It is a peaceful place where the 'natural silence' is 'slowly broken / by the shearwater' – sibilance echoes the sound of the sea – and we can hear the sound of the birds in the onomatopoeic phrase 'whistle and chatter'. Beautiful visual images re-create the atmosphere: the 'oceanic haze' that surrounds it, the 'sea-smoke' that seems to rise to the mountain tops, the 'lone light' of the lighthouse. But Mahon also recalls the violent past of the island, where a cruel massacre took place in the sixteenth century. Similarly, he places its peacefulness in the context of the present-day 'bombs' that 'doze in the housing estates' on the nearby mainland. By doing so he goes beyond surface description to awaken in the reader a sense of the complexity of places and how they have their part to play in the history of a people. The island, he says, is a place that is 'through with history', but it cannot offer reassurance for the future, as the last two lines suggest. It is not clear whether 'the future lies before us or behind'.

[Fourth poem referred to, with suitable quotations]

Mahon explores places not only by imaginative description but also by acknowledging the complex nature of their background and history. We see this at work in both 'The Chinese Restaurant in Portrush' and 'Kinsale'. Both of these locations have connotations within the context of Irish history and politics. Portrush is a seaside resort in Co. Antrim, which has been a predominantly Protestant, unionist area of Northern Ireland. The poem must be set against the backdrop of the Troubles, the Northern Ireland conflict of the late twentieth century. It opens with an image of the spring 'softening the sharp air of the coast / in time for the first 'invasion''. The image suggests the changing season, but the words 'sharp' and 'invasion' have connotations of defensiveness that give the place its own distinct Northern Ireland 'personality'.

The poem goes on to celebrate Portrush. Pleasant images of the carefree girl walking past the hotel, the 'window-shopping' gulls and the old wolfhound as it 'dozes' in the sun bring the place to life for the reader. When we meet the poet he is in a relaxed mood, in a Chinese restaurant, with his 'paper and prawn chow mein', while the proprietor of the restaurant is standing idly at the door, looking out, enjoying the view. The whole scene has the clarity of a painting. But beyond the picture is an awareness of complex connections between places. Mahon provides a number of actual place names – Portrush, the Northern Counties (the name of a hotel here, but nevertheless a geographical region), Hong Kong and Donegal. We cannot ignore the adjective 'Chinese' either. By putting these names in close proximity to each other, Mahon makes us aware of how one place can be viewed from another. It casts an ironic light on the last word of the poem, 'home', which is a subjective idea, varying from one person to another. Without direct comment, as is part of his distinctive style, Mahon leaves the reader to contemplate the complex relationship people have with place.

[Fifth poem referred to, with suitable quotations]

'Kinsale' is a short and in my view very attractive poem. This title has historical connotations as the site of the Battle of Kinsale in 1601, in which the Irish were defeated by the army of Elizabeth I. This decisive victory altered the course of Irish history. Mahon makes imaginative use of the contrast between the sorrows of the past in his image of the rain, 'deep-delving, dark, deliberate', and the present-day atmosphere of Kinsale with images of light and movement. Visually and aurally the imagery conveys happiness and freedom. Sibilance and alliteration combine in 'our sky-blue slates are steaming in the sun' to create a musical effect, as does the image of 'yachts tinkling and dancing in the bay'. They are 'like race-horses' – an unusual and attractive simile. End-rhyme, used throughout, adds to the sense of harmony. And unlike 'Rathlin', where the poet was unsure about the future, here he sees Kinsale as symbolic of a 'future forbidden to no-one'.

[Sixth poem referred to; note how quotations are incorporated into sentences throughout; as before, discussion includes both content and style]

In conclusion, in exploring people through his poetry Derek Mahon succeeds in conveying a sense of individual experience and personality, while recognising the complexity of the situations in which they find themselves. Similarly, in his exploration of particular places he goes beyond the surface description to convey a sense of their role in the history and emotions of a people. I greatly admire his achievement in doing so.

[Conclusion brings the two aspects of the question together and indicates a final response]

snapshot

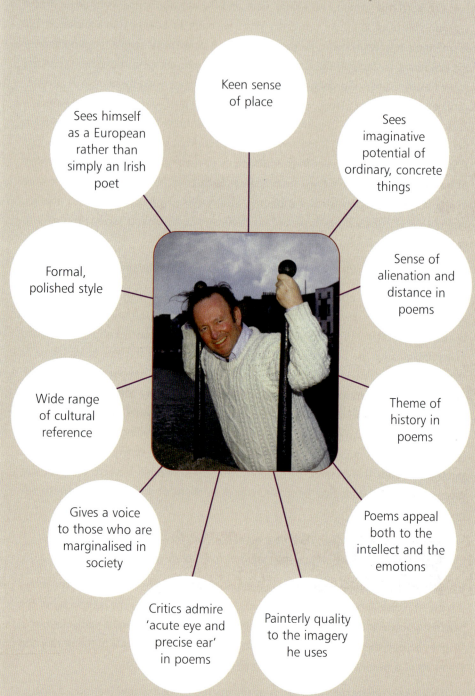

- Keen sense of place
- Sees imaginative potential of ordinary, concrete things
- Sees himself as a European rather than simply an Irish poet
- Sense of alienation and distance in poems
- Formal, polished style
- Theme of history in poems
- Wide range of cultural reference
- Poems appeal both to the intellect and the emotions
- Gives a voice to those who are marginalised in society
- Critics admire 'acute eye and precise ear' in poems
- Painterly quality to the imagery he uses

Sylvia Plath

1932–63

BLACK ROOK IN RAINY WEATHER
THE TIMES ARE TIDY
MORNING SONG
FINISTERRE
MIRROR
PHEASANT
ELM
POPPIES IN JULY*
THE ARRIVAL OF THE BEE BOX*
CHILD*

Biography

Sylvia Plath was born in a seaside suburb of Boston, Massachusetts, in 1932. Both her parents, Otto Plath and Aurelia Schober, were academics and had German ancestry. They believed in the virtues of hard work and were committed to education. Sylvia was a bright, intelligent child and won many school prizes and awards.

When she was eight years old, her father died. On learning of his death, Plath declared, 'I'll never speak to God again.' Anxious to spare Sylvia and her younger brother, Warren, any unnecessary upset, Aurelia did not bring them to the funeral. Her father's death haunted Plath for the remainder of her life.

Otto's death left the family in straitened circumstances. Aurelia took up a full-time teaching job to support her children and Sylvia's grandparents moved in with the family in a house in the prosperous suburb of Wellesley. Plath later wrote that the move to Wellesley marked the end of her idyllic childhood by the sea.

The young writer

All through High School, Plath published poems and stories in local and national newspapers and in her school magazine. In her final year at school *Seventeen*, a national teen magazine, published her short story 'And Summer Will Not Come Again'. It was an important landmark in the young writer's life.

In 1951 Plath won two scholarships, which allowed her to attend Smith College, an exclusive women's college in Massachusetts. Her talent and intelligence were nurtured by the teaching staff there and she continued to have her work published. During her second year at Smith she was awarded a fiction prize by *Mademoiselle*, a fashionable, upmarket magazine for young women.

Personal insecurity

Despite academic, personal and social success, Plath was deeply insecure. The beginning of her third year in college saw her beset by many doubts and uncertainties. A four-week guest editorship at *Mademoiselle* in New York did little to improve matters.

Failure to secure a place on a summer writing course run by Frank O'Connor at Harvard in 1953 caused a crisis, and she was sent for psychiatric treatment. A poorly supervised and administered series of electric shock treatments worsened her condition and she made an attempt to take her own life. She was missing for three days, unconscious in a narrow space under the family home. She recovered her health over a period of six months with the help of a sympathetic psychiatrist.

Smith College offered Plath a scholarship to allow her to finish her degree, and she returned to the college in spring 1954, graduating with distinction. By then she had acquired a growing reputation as a writer.

Cambridge and early career

More success came her way in the form of a prestigious Fulbright scholarship to study at Cambridge University in England. Plath entered Newnham College in October 1955. It was in Cambridge that Sylvia Plath met the poet Ted Hughes. After a whirlwind romance, the couple married on Bloomsday, 16 June 1956. Following a two-month honeymoon in France and Spain, Plath returned to Cambridge to complete her studies. She continued to write, while, at the same time, helping Hughes to organise and send out his work. 'Black Rook in Rainy Weather' was written in this period.

The couple moved to the United States in summer 1957, and Plath taught for a year at Smith College. She found the job taxing and considered herself to be a poor teacher. She was also frustrated that she had so little time to devote to her writing. At the end of the academic year in summer 1958 she resigned her teaching position.

Plath rented an apartment in Boston. It did not go well. She suffered from writer's block and depression. 'The Times Are Tidy' was one of the few poems she completed. She was worried by financial concerns and tried to supplement their income by taking part-time secretarial work.

By summer 1959 things had improved. Hughes continued to write and publish and Plath, too, completed some poems and short stories. The couple then decided to return to England. First, however, they spent two months at a writer's colony in New York state. Relieved of domestic duties, Plath wrote freely and finished a number of the poems that are included in *The Colossus*, the only collection of her work published during her lifetime.

Mother, wife and poet

Frieda Rebecca Hughes, the couple's first child, was born in April 1960 in London. By this time Heinemann had agreed to publish *The Colossus* and Hughes had won the prestigious Somerset Maugham Award. Plath, however, was disappointed by the lack of reaction to *The Colossus* and, while she loved her husband and new daughter, found that the roles of mother and wife took her away from her writing.

1961 was a topsy-turvy year for Plath. It began with the sadness of a miscarriage, followed by an operation to remove an appendix. She likened her recovery from this to a resurrection. A contract with the *New Yorker* magazine boosted her morale and she began work on her novel, *The Bell Jar*.

When Plath became pregnant the couple decided to look for a house in the country, eventually moving, in autumn, to Court Green in Devon, a rambling, crumbling old house with three acres of lawn, garden and orchard. Despite her pregnancy, the care of a young daughter and the practicalities of setting up home in an old house, Plath wrote with great energy in her first months in Devon, though the poems she completed, including 'Finisterre' and 'Mirror', are marked by a sense of threat, fear and menace.

In January 1962 Plath gave birth to her second child, Nicholas. Her experience of birth and her remembrance of her miscarriage in the previous year inform her radio play *Three Women*, which she wrote for the BBC in spring 1962. The poems written later in 1962, most notably 'Elm', are dark meditations on love and self-knowledge.

By summer 1962 Plath's marriage to Hughes had begun to unravel. Hughes became involved with Assia Wevill, the wife of a Canadian poet. He left Court Green. A holiday in Ireland in September failed to save Plath's marriage.

Failing health

Back in Court Green in October and November 1962, Plath, working early each morning, wrote forty of the poems that make up the collection *Ariel*, including 'Poppies in July' and 'The Arrival of the Bee Box'. *Ariel* was published after her death. By any standards, these are remarkable poems.

Writing to a friend, she said, 'I am living like a Spartan, writing through huge fevers and producing free stuff I had locked in me for years.' The strain of writing these intense, personal poems began to affect her health. Her letters to her mother, from this period, are touched with desperation.

In November Plath decided to move back to London. She found a flat in the house where W. B. Yeats had once lived. By December she had closed up Court Green and moved into her new home with her two young children.

In January 1963 some of the worst weather seen in London for decades, allied to the delay in obtaining a phone, and the colds and flu she and the children suffered, cast her down and left her feeling isolated. She was further disheartened by the fact that her new work was, on the whole, rejected by the editors to whom she sent it. The publication of her novel, *The Bell Jar*, under a pseudonym, did little to lift the gloom.

Plath's final poems (including 'Child'), written in late January and early February 1963, reveal that her will to live was almost spent. She sought medical help and was put on a course of anti-depressants. Arrangements were made for her to see a psychiatrist. However, in the early hours of Monday 11 February 1963, overcome by a despairing depression, she took her own life.

Ariel, a collection of her final poems, was published in 1965. Since that time, it has sold over half a million copies. Plath's life, death and poetry have been the subject of much controversy. Understandably, given the tragic circumstances of her death, much of the response to her poetry has sought to relate her work to her life – to find clues in her poetry to explain her suicide or to attribute blame.

The difference between the personality that Plath reveals in her letters home to her mother and the darker personality of her journals has also attracted the attention of critics. Rarely has a poet left such a disputed body of work.

Social and Cultural Context

Plath was born into a male-dominated world. Her father ruled the family. Her mother was the wife and homemaker. Plath attended a college for girls, where she wanted to achieve and be a perfect American girl. Magazines like *The Ladies Home Journal* defined this ideal. A woman should be a wife, a homemaker and a mother, but she was not expected to be a professional or to have her own career. She was to be respectable. There was, in this middle-class culture, a tolerance of male promiscuity but girls were expected to be modest and virginal. Not to marry was to risk being labelled 'unfeminine'.

Plath struggled to escape this ideal of perfection. Her letters to her mother are full of references to her attempts to make a home for herself and Hughes and to win her mother's approval. She was conscious of this tendency in herself, noting in her journal: 'Old need of giving mother accomplishments, getting reward of love.' Her biographer, Anne Stevenson, says of the letters Plath wrote to her mother:

> Letters Home can be seen as one long projection of the 'desired image' (the required image) of herself as Eve – wife, mother, home-maker, protector of the wholesome, the good and the holy, an identity that both her upbringing and her own instinctive physical being had fiercely aspired to.

Search for an identity

Much of Plath's poetry can be seen as a struggle to create a new identity for herself that transcended the cultural limitations imposed upon women. Given society's view of women, Plath found it difficult to find acceptance as a writer outside of women's books and magazines. In her lifetime, her work won serious admiration from only a small number of people. She was more famous for being the wife of the poet Ted Hughes than for being a talented, ambitious and dedicated poet, novelist and short story writer, in her own right.

Plath's desire to fit in at school and be an all-American girl was deepened by her consciousness of her German ancestry. Plath's use of Holocaust imagery and her reference to her father as a Nazi in her poem 'Daddy' indicate a feeling of displacement, a fear that she might, somehow, be tainted by her origins. She also employed Holocaust imagery to speak of the suffering of women.

More than is sometimes acknowledged by critics, Plath was attuned, in a personal way, to the major historical issues of her time. She lived during the period of the Cold War and the ever-present threat of nuclear warfare between the United States and the Soviet Union. She was conscious of the dangers of a nuclear conflict and concerned for the future safety of her children. Plath wrote of these fears in a letter to her mother in December 1961:

> The reason I haven't written for so long is probably quite silly, but I got so awfully depressed two weeks ago by reading two issues of *The Nation* all about the terrifying marriage of big business and the military in America . . . and the repulsive shelter craze for fallout, all very factual, documented and true, that I simply couldn't sleep for nights with all the warlike talk in the papers . . . I began to wonder if there was any point in trying to bring up children in such a mad, self-destructive world. The sad thing is that the power for destruction is real and universal.

The fears expressed here find their way into her poetry in the terrifying imagery of her last poems.

Displacement

For Plath, the opportunity to live and study in England was a partly liberating experience. From England she could view with clarity the consumerism and militarism of US culture. However, she did not always feel at home in England and disliked the shabby inefficiency that she saw in English life. Plath was caught between the two cultures, feeling ambivalent towards both. Her feelings of displacement are important in shaping the poetry she wrote.

Timeline

1932	Born on 27 October in Boston, Massachusetts
1940	Her father dies. Sylvia declares, 'I'll never speak to God again'
1950	*Seventeen* publishes her story 'And Summer Will Not Come Again'
1951	Wins scholarship to the exclusive Smith College for women
1953	Wins guest editorship at *Mademoiselle* magazine; attempts suicide after failing to gain a place on writing course in Harvard
1954	Graduates with distinction from Smith College
1955	Wins Fulbright Scholarship and goes to Cambridge; meets the poet Ted Hughes
1956	Marries Hughes on Bloomsday
1960	Gives birth to Frieda Rebecca Hughes, the couple's first child; publishes first collection, *The Colossus*
1961	Moves to Devon; writes with great energy in first months there; concerned by talk of nuclear warfare
1962	Gives birth to her son, Nicholas; Plath and Hughes separate; writes over 40 poems in October and November; moves to London
1963	Publishes her novel, *The Bell Jar*; takes her own life in February
1965	*Ariel*, a collection of her last poems, is published

Black Rook in Rainy Weather

On the stiff twig up there
Hunches a wet black rook
Arranging and rearranging its feathers in the rain.
I do not expect miracle
Or an accident

To set the sight on fire
In my eye, nor seek
Any more in the desultory weather some design,
But let spotted leaves fall as they fall,
Without ceremony, or portent.

Although, I admit, I desire,
Occasionally, some backtalk
From the mute sky, I can't honestly complain:
A certain minor light may still
Leap incandescent

Out of kitchen table or chair
As if a celestial burning took
Possession of the most obtuse objects now and then –
Thus hallowing an interval
Otherwise inconsequent

By bestowing largesse, honour,
One might say love. At any rate, I now walk
Wary (for it could happen
Even in this dull, ruinous landscape); sceptical,
Yet politic; ignorant

Of whatever angel may choose to flare
Suddenly at my elbow. I only know that a rook
Ordering its black feathers can so shine
As to seize my senses, haul
My eyelids up, and grant

A brief respite from fear
Of total neutrality. With luck,
Trekking stubborn through this season
Of fatigue, I shall
Patch together a content   35

Of sorts. Miracles occur,
If you care to call those spasmodic
Tricks of radiance miracles. The wait's begun again,
The long wait for the angel,
For that rare, random descent.   40

Glossary		
8	*desultory*: changing in a random way	
10	*portent*: omen, a sign or indication of a future event	
15	*incandescent*: red hot or white hot, shining, luminous	
17	*celestial*: heavenly	
18	*obtuse*: dull, insensitive	
19	*hallowing*: to make holy or sacred	
20	*inconsequent*: trivial, insignificant	
21	*largesse*: generosity	
23	*Wary*: alert, vigilant	
25	*politic*: discreet, prudent	
31	*respite*: rest, temporary relief	
33	*Trekking*: making a long, hard journey	
37	*spasmodic*: something that happens in sudden, brief spells	

Guidelines

'Black Rook in Rainy Weather' is contained in Plath's first collection, *The Colossus* (1960). It was originally published in the English journal *Granta*, while she studied at Cambridge.

The poem alerts us to many features of Plath's style:
- The confident handling of rhyme and stanza form.
- The exploration of emotions and states of mind.
- The use of weather, colours and natural objects as symbols.
- The dreamlike or surreal world of the poem.

This poem explores the nature of poetic inspiration, and the necessity of such inspiration to ward off the speaker's fear of total neutrality. There is no simple relationship between the 'I' of the poem (the persona or speaker) and the writer. In fact, many of her poems can be read as Plath trying out different identities.

Commentary

Describing the world

The poem begins with a clear description of the rook, sitting 'Arranging and rearranging feathers in the rain' (line 3). The sight is ordinary. The speaker of the poem tells us that she does not expect a 'miracle / Or an accident / To set the sight on fire' (lines 4–6). The words 'miracle' and 'fire' set up a contrast between the damp weather (the reality) and the fire of vision (the poet's imagination). The speaker is not expecting anything to happen. Her muse, her inner vision, seems to have deserted her. So she describes what she sees, content to let the world be as it is.

The word 'portent' (line 10) suggests the tradition of seeing the weather as a warning of things to come. The colour black is also associated with the ancient art of divination or prediction. In pre-Christian times a poet was considered to be a seer, a person possessed with the supernatural power of vision. This idea informs the poem's exploration of inspiration.

Inspiration

In stanza 3 the poet confesses that although she would like the sky to speak to her, she is not complaining. The reason for this is that the speaker believes that even the most ordinary object, such as a 'kitchen table or chair' (line 16), may appear transformed as if it was possessed by some heavenly fire. This visionary experience is described, in lines 19 to 22, in terms of heavenly generosity and love.

Although not stated directly, the poem suggests that poetic inspiration is like a gift from heaven. It is not within the control of the poet. It is not a matter of will

or determination. **Inspiration, when it happens, has the quality of accident, favour and giftedness about it.** Nor is it that the poet is inspired, but rather that the world is transformed in the poet's presence. The adjectives 'incandescent' (line 15) and 'burning' (line 17) suggest the force and power of the experience of inspiration.

The speaker tells us that she is waiting for the angel, the symbol of heavenly visitation and inspiration, 'to flare / Suddenly at my elbow' (lines 26–27). The description of the landscape as 'dull, ruinous' (line 24) suggests how much the poet wants the angel to appear, while the adjective 'sceptical' in the same line implies that she is trying not to hope too much.

Fear and hope

Yet, the rook gives her reason to hope, for in catching a sight of him, she feels a lifting of her spirit and 'A brief respite from fear / Of total neutrality' (lines 31–32). These two lines are key to understanding the emotional centre of the poem. **Without vision, without the inspiration to write, the poet fears 'total neutrality'.** The words suggest a state of non-being, a blank. (This kind of fear is expressed in a number of other poems, including 'Poppies in July'.)

In lines 32 and 36 the speaker's voice falters, overcome by fatigue but hoping, 'With luck', to 'Patch together a content / Of sorts'. **The final stanza is balanced between faith and scepticism, between 'miracles' and 'tricks' (line 38). However, the poet's belief, or desire to believe, or need to believe, is expressed in the beautiful ending.** The image of the angel's 'rare, random descent' (line 40) calls to mind Pentecost, when, according to the biblical account, tongues of fire appeared over the apostles and they were filled with the Holy Spirit.

It is clear from this poem that for the speaker/poet, the threat to her well-being is posed by a fear of 'neutrality' (line 32). She is afraid that without moments of vision and the reassurance of her creativity, life and identity will be intolerable.

Style and form of the poem

The poem is written in unrhymed five-line stanzas, a form that Plath also uses in 'The Times Are Tidy' and 'The Arrival of the Bee Box'. The form allows for flexibility in rhythm and pacing. Reading the poem aloud allows you to hear the intricate sound patterns that Plath creates and the way in which she marries sound to the emotional tone of the poem. Consider, for example, the long, vowel sounds and the alliteration in line 33, which capture the effort and drudgery in going on: 'Trekking stubborn through this season'.

Thinking about the poem

1. What attitude to the rook and the weather does the speaker of the poem express in the first two stanzas? What do these stanzas suggest to you about the speaker?
2. How do you understand the idea of celestial burning, as presented in the poem? In your experience can ordinary objects be seized in the way described in lines 14 to 22 of the poem?
3. Consider the character of the speaker of the poem, as suggested by the adjectives ('wary', 'sceptical', 'politic') in lines 23 to 25. Having read the poem, what additional adjectives would you use to describe the speaker?
4. What is the fear referred to at the outset of stanza 7? Consider the possible meanings of the word 'neutrality' (line 32). How might the rook allay this fear? What is the relationship between the rook and the celestial burning referred to in the fourth stanza?
5. What is it that the speaker hopes to achieve, 'With luck' (lines 32–35)? What is your reaction to this hope?
6. What belief is expressed in the final stanza? How is the belief qualified?
7. 'The wait's begun again' (line 38). Comment on the word 'again'.
8. 'Trekking stubborn through this season / Of fatigue' (lines 33–34). Write a note on these lines and the way in which sound and sense combine.
9. The beauty of the last two lines of the poem has been remarked on by critics. What, in your view, makes them beautiful?
10. Examine the stanza form employed by the poet and comment on it.
11. Comment on the images of heat and light in the poem, and their relevance to the theme of the poem.
12. Consider the title of the poem and its relevance to the theme of the poem.
13. What does the poem say to you about imagination and the vision of the poet?
14. 'The speaker of the poem is poised between hope and despair.' Comment on this view of the poem, supporting your answer by reference to the poem.
15. 'Behind the controlled language of the poem there is a glimpse of a fearful and nightmarish personal world.' Is this a fair assessment? Support your answer by reference to the poem.

The Times Are Tidy

Unlucky the hero born
In this province of the stuck record
Where the most watchful cooks go jobless
And the mayor's rôtisserie turns
Round of its own accord.   5

There's no career in the venture
Of riding against the lizard,
Himself withered these latter-days
To leaf-size from lack of action:
History's beaten the hazard.   10

The last crone got burnt up
More than eight decades back
With the love-hot herb, the talking cat,
But the children are better for it,
The cow milk's cream an inch thick.   15

Glossary		
	2	*province*: here, a historical period; the word also carries the derogatory suggestion of a place that is culturally backward
	2	*stuck record*: something that is going nowhere, as when a needle on a record player gets stuck on the vinyl surface of a record
	3	*watchful cooks*: from the Middle Ages onwards the poisoning of food was common in attempts on the lives of the powerful; thus, cooks had to be vigilant, wary and politic
	4	*rôtisserie*: traditionally, a pointed rod with a turning handle on which meat is skewered and roasted; today, an electric cooking apparatus, with a rotating spit
	7	*lizard*: used here as a synonym for dragon
	10	*hazard*: danger, risk; here, personal adventure
	11	*crone*: withered old woman, witch

Guidelines

'The Times Are Tidy' was published in the 1960 collection, *The Colossus*. The poem was written during the summer of 1958, after Plath had resigned from her job as a teacher at Smith College.

This is one of the few Plath poems in which the 'I' persona does not appear. **The poem is a straightforward social comment on the blandness of contemporary culture compared with the fairy-tale world of the past.** (As a way of keeping up her German, the language of her ancestors, Plath read *Grimm's Fairy Tales*.)

Commentary

Stanza 1

The tone of the poem is ironic. It begins with a statement: 'Unlucky the hero born / In the province of the stuck record'. The suggestion is that the present is an unheroic age, with little opportunity for adventure or valour.

Stanza 2

The second stanza introduces the figure of the knight riding to battle the dragon ('lizard', line 7). There is no career, we are told, in such heroism. The word 'career' (line 6) suggests the difference between the heroic age of the past (not specified in time or place) and the career-minded world of the late 1950s. The stanza concludes with the statement: 'History's beaten the hazard' (line 10). Adventure is dead. It is impossible to read Plath's assessment of the bland safety of public life without thinking of the hazards that she feared in her private world.

Stanza 3

There is an ironic edge to the regret that announces: 'The last crone got burnt up / More than eight decades back' (lines 11–12). Magic and mystery, it seems, have died with her. The 'but' that introduces the two last lines is unconvincing; the speaker does not really believe that 'the children are better for it' (line 14) or that the thick cream is compensation.

Interestingly, around the time Plath wrote 'The Times Are Tidy', she and Ted Hughes were experimenting with a Ouija board. Plath found these sessions both intriguing and entertaining. She also shared Hughes' interest in tarot cards and horoscopes. **The consumer culture, rapidly developing in urban America, was too sanitised and removed from the superstitious beliefs that attracted her.** Perhaps the poem hints at the difference between Hughes' home county of Yorkshire in northern England, where superstitions still survived, and the urban culture of the United States, where they had disappeared.

Form of the poem

The poem shows Plath's attention to the craft of poetry. In each stanza there are interesting patterns of sound. Look, for example, how the vowel sounds 'o' and 'u' are woven into stanza 1. The 'k' sound in the first word of the poem is repeated at intervals and concludes the poem. The stanzas and rhymes are carefully worked. You might like to consider if all the rhymes are successful. Consider the lizard / hazard rhyme of stanza 2. Are the words well chosen?

Thinking about the poem

1. How is the disappearance of the world of fairy-tale adventure suggested in the first stanza?
2. Comment on the phrase 'the stuck record' (line 2) and the attitude it conveys.
3. Give examples of the people of whom it might be said they rode 'against the lizard' (line 7).
4. What is the meaning of the statement 'History's beaten the hazard' (line 10).
5. How do you interpret the references to 'the love-hot herb' and 'the talking cat' (line 13)?
6. In your opinion, does the speaker believe that the gains referred to in the last two lines compensate for the losses mentioned in the rest of the poem? Support your answer by reference to the poem.
7. Describe the tone and mood of the poem and the attitude it expresses towards the contemporary world. Refer to the title of the poem, in your answer.
8. Is this a well-crafted poem? Explain your answer.
9. The poem is dismissed by some critics as a mere 'exercise'. What is your assessment of the poem?

Morning Song

Love set you going like a fat gold watch.
The midwife slapped your footsoles, and your bald cry
Took its place among the elements.

Our voices echo, magnifying your arrival. New statue.
In a drafty museum, your nakedness 5
Shadows our safety. We stand round blankly as walls.

I'm no more your mother
Than the cloud that distils a mirror to reflect its own slow
Effacement at the wind's hand.

All night your moth-breath 10
Flickers among the flat pink roses. I wake to listen:
A far sea moves in my ear.

One cry, and I stumble from bed, cow-heavy and floral
In my Victorian nightgown.
Your mouth opens clean as a cat's. The window square 15

Whitens and swallows its dull stars. And now you try
Your handful of notes;
The clear vowels rise like balloons.

Glossary	
3	*elements*: earth, air, water and fire
9	*Effacement*: obliteration, erasure
11	*flat pink roses*: presumably the patterned wallpaper
13	*cow-heavy*: the poet's amused reference to her breasts heavy with milk

Guidelines

Plath wrote 'Morning Song', a poem on the birth of her daughter, in spring 1961, ten months after Frieda's birth, and shortly after a miscarriage. It was first published in *The Observer* newspaper in May 1961 and was later included in her posthumous collection *Ariel*, published in 1965. In November 1962 Plath arranged the poems for her collection, placing 'Morning Song' first so that the manuscript would begin with the word 'love' and end with the word 'spring' from the poem, 'Wintering'. (The published collection does not follow her wishes.)

'Morning Song' is clearly a celebration of birth, but there is also a suggestion of loss and separation in the imagery of the poem. The poem begins with the word 'love' and ends with the music of the child's cry rising 'like balloons'. In between it charts the mother's journey from her initial disorientation to her joyful acceptance of her baby.

Commentary

Estrangement

'Morning Song' opens with a bold statement and a striking image: 'Love set you going like a fat gold watch.' There is little sense of the miraculous or the mysterious in the slap that sets the child crying. The child's cry is described as 'bald' (line 2). It seems to express a basic instinct and, therefore, takes 'its place among the elements' (line 3). **The voice of the narrator, the mother, seems puzzled by what is happening, even as she speaks to her child. The sense of estrangement is captured in the imagery of the second stanza, where things seem out of proportion.** For example, 'Our voices echo, magnifying your arrival' (line 4).

The baby is like an exhibit in a museum, around whom the adults stand, unable to make sense of what it is they are looking at. The museum imagery is striking. The description of the baby as a 'New statue' (line 4) may indicate that the baby resembles a perfect work of art. The baby's fragility, her 'nakedness' in the 'drafty museum' (line 5), causes the parents to feel anxious about their ability to protect and safeguard the child they have brought into the world. This doubt is suggested in the phrase 'Shadows our safety' (line 6); *a* line that will support many interpretations. The word 'blankly' (line 6) is particularly significant as it implies that the experience of birth has somehow robbed the parents of their identity.

The sense of estrangement leads to a declaration in stanza 3, which rehearses an often-expressed fear in Plath's work: the fear of effacement, of annihilation. She fears that the birth of her child will rob her of her identity, just as the rain creates a mirror (in the form of a puddle or pool of water) in which the cloud is reflected and can see its own dispersal by the wind. This is a complex image of the relationship between mother and daughter.

Mother's protective response

There is a change in tone in the fourth stanza. The sound of the child's breath, symbolising its fragile, though insistent, hold on life, evokes the mother's protective response. After the estrangement of the opening stanzas, where the mother's response was frozen into an attitude of a blank wall in a museum setting, a more recognisable, domestic world appears. In contrast to the immobility of the second stanza, the child's cry stirs the mother into activity. Having regained her composure and her sense of self, she can laugh at herself: 'cow-heavy and floral / In my Victorian nightgown' (lines 13–14).

The speaker is now involved with her child, filled with wonder as her 'mouth opens clean as a cat's' (line 15). The image resonates with amused delight. The quality of happiness continues in the imagery of the growing light. **The poem ends on a note of elation as the child's 'clear vowels rise like balloons'** (line 18).

Form of the poem

The poem is written is unrhymed three-line stanzas. The first line has ten syllables, which is the standard line length in English poetry. What is interesting in the poem is how Plath breaks the line to achieve certain effects. Look, for example, how the short line 10 creates a space that is filled by 'flickers' on line 11, so that that we almost hear the child's breath in the sound and rhythm of the stanza.

Thinking about the poem

1. Comment on the importance of the words 'love' and 'elements' in the first stanza of the poem.
2. In what way is the child a 'New statue' (line 4)?
3. Explain, as clearly as you can, the museum imagery in stanza 2. What does it suggest about the relationship between the adults and the new-born child?
4. Tease out the meaning of the statement, 'your nakedness / Shadows our safety' (lines 5–6).
5. What is the tone of the declaration, 'I'm no more your mother' (line 7)?

6   What kind of relationship between mother and child is described in the cloud, mirror and wind imagery of the third stanza? Is it a distinctive view or does it express a general truth?
7   What does the moth imagery in stanza 4 suggest about the child?
8   What picture of the new mother is created in stanzas 4 and 5?
9   What is your favourite image in the poem? Explain your choice.
10 'Although tender in tone, the poem is clear-sighted and unsentimental.' Discuss this view of the poem.
11 'Even though the poem celebrates motherhood, the mother appears as an isolated and estranged figure.' Do you agree with this assessment of the poem? Support your answer by reference to the poem.
12 How do you imagine Frieda Hughes reacting to this poem about her birth?

Finisterre

This was the land's end: the last fingers, knuckled and rheumatic,
Cramped on nothing. Black
Admonitory cliffs, and the sea exploding
With no bottom, or anything on the other side of it,
Whitened by the faces of the drowned.   5
Now it is only gloomy, a dump of rocks –
Leftover soldiers from old, messy wars.
The sea cannons into their ear, but they don't budge.
Other rocks hide their grudges under the water.

The cliffs are edged with trefoils, stars and bells   10
Such as fingers might embroider, close to death,
Almost too small for the mists to bother with.
The mists are part of the ancient paraphernalia –
Souls, rolled in the doom-noise of the sea.
They bruise the rocks out of existence, then resurrect them.   15
They go up without hope, like sighs.
I walk among them, and they stuff my mouth with cotton.
When they free me, I am beaded with tears.

Our Lady of the Shipwrecked is striding toward the horizon,
Her marble skirts blown back in two pink wings.   20
A marble sailor kneels at her foot distractedly, and at his foot
A peasant woman in black
Is praying to the monument of the sailor praying.
Our Lady of the Shipwrecked is three times life size,
Her lips sweet with divinity.   25
She does not hear what the sailor or the peasant is saying –
She is in love with the beautiful formlessness of the sea.

Gull-coloured laces flap in the sea drafts
Beside the postcard stalls.
The peasants anchor them with conches. One is told: 30
'These are the pretty trinkets the sea hides,
Little shells made up into necklaces and toy ladies.
They do not come from the Bay of the Dead down there,
But from another place, tropical and blue,
We have never been to.   35
These are our crêpes. Eat them before they blow cold.'

Glossary

title	*Finisterre*: English name for Finistère, the westernmost part of Brittany, France
1	*land's end*: the literal meaning of 'Finisterre'; from earliest times it was believed that the horizon marked the end of the created world
1	*fingers*: here, rocks jutting into the sea; the imagery suggests the desperate clinging of a drowning person
3	*Admonitory*: warning
7	*Leftover soldiers*: maimed veterans of the Algerian war
10	*trefoils, stars and bells*: wildflowers, identified by shape rather than name
13	*paraphernalia*: bits and pieces, miscellaneous items; here Plath is referring to the belief that the mists are the souls of the dead and associating this superstition with Finisterre
19	*Our Lady of the Shipwrecked*: statue commemorating lives lost at sea

Guidelines

'Finisterre' was among a group of poems that Plath wrote in autumn 1961, shortly after moving to Devon with her husband, Ted Hughes, and their daughter, Frieda. **Although this was one of the happiest periods of her personal life, the poems she wrote are dark.**

In June 1960 Plath and Hughes drove through Brittany, swimming along the rocky coastline of Finisterre. They also stopped at Berck-Plage, a seaside resort with a sanatorium for soldiers wounded in the Algerian war. Plath saw maimed soldiers limp among the holiday makers. The experience made a profound impression and called to mind her father's death, following the amputation of his leg. **The poems she wrote about Brittany – 'Finisterre' and 'Berck-Plage' – share a sense of death and menace, contrasting images of permanence and stability with those of formlessness and annihilation.** In this regard, it is worth bearing in mind that 'Finisterre' was written during a period when there was a serious risk of nuclear conflict between the Soviet Union and the United States. Plath wrote of her fears in a letter to her mother in December 1961.

The ocean played an important part in Plath's childhood and is a constant in the imagery of her poems. In a letter to her mother, written in 1958, she said, 'I am going back to the ocean as my poetic heritage.' She also wrote in her journal a note on the title of another of her poems, 'Full Fathom Five', which gives an insight into the importance of the sea for her:

> 'Full Fathom Five' . . . has the background of *The Tempest*, the association of the sea, which is a central metaphor for my childhood, my poems and the artist's subconscious, of the father image . . . and the pearls and coral highly wrought to art; pearls sea-changed from the ubiquitous grit of sorrow and routine.

As a twelve-year-old, Plath saw Shakespeare's *The Tempest*, a play that begins with a shipwreck, and she later associated Ariel's song, 'Full fathom five, thy father lies; / Of his bones are coral made', in that play with her own dead father.

Commentary

Different interpretations

At one level, 'Finisterre' is a description of a seaside resort. It depicts the rocky shoreline and the cliffs that surround the bay known as the Bay of the Dead. It describes the mists that rise from the sea, and the statue of Our Lady of the Shipwrecked, a memorial to the sailors who died at sea. The poem concludes with a description of the stalls and the trinkets sold by the local peasants. At another level,

'Finisterre' is a symbolic poem, in which the meeting of ocean and land is presented in terms of the recurrent drama of death and rebirth, of entrapment and freedom, and of form and formlessness. As with other Plath poems, the symbolic language sends the reader off in many directions. Thus, 'Finisterre' can support different interpretations.

Form and formlessness

The vocabulary of the opening stanza suggests a pattern of force – 'knuckled', 'cramped', 'exploding' and 'cannons' – and of annihilation – 'end', 'last', 'nothing', 'Black' and 'bottom'. It is as if the Bay of the Dead is a site of battle between the sea and the land.

In the second stanza Plath sees, in the relationship between the sea mist and the rocks, an archetype or symbol of death and resurrection. **In describing the rocks and the sea mist, the poem juxtaposes the fixed and the fluid. The fixed forms of the rocks seem threatened by the formlessness of the sea and the mist, but they survive.**

The imagery of fixed forms and formlessness appears in the third stanza where the statue of Our Lady of the Shipwrecked is said to be 'in love with the beautiful formlessness of the sea' (line 27).

Final stanza

There is a shift of tone in the fourth stanza. We are back in the world of the living, on firm land. The peasants sell 'pretty trinkets' (line 31) to the tourists. The locals do not want their souvenirs to be associated with the Bay of the Dead. They tell her that the trinkets come from 'another place, tropical and blue' (line 34).

This place is like the world of Plath's childhood or the world of her poetry. She takes elements from the sea of her unconscious and makes them into poems. The poem ends with the peasants offering her some sustenance. They urge her to eat before the food goes cold. Although eating is associated with nurture, the final word of the poem, 'cold', returns to the idea of death that haunts the poem.

Thinking about the poem

1. The first five lines give a vivid account of the beliefs/fears once held about the sea. Describe these. Is there a relationship between these fears/beliefs and the private fears of speaker of the poem?
2. How is Finisterre regarded now, according to lines 6 to 9? Comment on the rock imagery in these lines.
3. Examine the description of the flowers and the mist in stanza 2. How are both associated with death?
4. Comment on Plath's use of the verb 'bruise' in line 15. Is it effective?
5. 'I walk among them, and they stuff my mouth with cotton. / When they free me, I am beaded with tears' (lines 17–18). What do you make of these lines and the drama they describe? (Are the mists/souls presented as hostile? Do they prevent her from speaking? Is the speaker in the poem more in sympathy with the ancient or the modern view of the place . . . ?)
6. How is Our Lady of the Shipwrecked presented in the third stanza? Is it a surprising representation?
7. Comment on the phrase, 'the beautiful formlessness of the sea' (line 27).
8. In lines 31 to 35 the peasants speak of 'the pretty trinkets that the sea hides', which come from a place far away. How do you interpret these lines?
9. Does the poem end on a hopeful note? Give reasons for your answer.
10. In your view, is the speaker of the poem attracted to the sea? Plath regarded the sea as an image of the artist's subconscious. What does the description of the sea in the poem suggest about Plath's subconscious and its concerns?
11. The poem arose from a holiday visit to a seaside resort. What does her treatment of this visit in the poem suggest to you about the personality and imagination of the poet? Support the points you make by quotation from the poem.
12. Choose one stanza from the poem and write a response to the sounds and imagery of the stanza.

Mirror

I am silver and exact. I have no preconceptions.
Whatever I see I swallow immediately
Just as it is, unmisted by love or dislike.
I am not cruel, only truthful –
The eye of a little god, four-cornered. 5
Most of the time I meditate on the opposite wall.
It is pink, with speckles. I have looked at it so long
I think it is a part of my heart. But it flickers.
Faces and darkness separate us over and over.

Now I am a lake. A woman bends over me, 10
Searching my reaches for what she really is.
Then she turns to those liars, the candles or the moon.
I see her back, and reflect it faithfully.
She rewards me with tears and an agitation of hands.
I am important to her. She comes and goes. 15
Each morning it is her face that replaces the darkness.
In me she has drowned a young girl, and in me an old woman
Rises toward her day after day, like a terrible fish.

Glossary

1	*preconceptions*:	opinions or ideas formed in advance but not based on real knowledge or experience
14	*agitation of hands*:	hand wringing; a similar symbol of distress is used in 'Child' to convey the speaker's anguish

Guidelines

'Mirror' was one of a group of poems written in Autumn 1961, days before Plath's twenty-ninth birthday and shortly after she and Ted Hughes moved to Court Green in Devon. Plath was pregnant with her second child at the time. This was one of the last poems she wrote before the birth of her baby, Nicholas.

As in 'Elm', Plath employs the technique of personification to achieve a sinister effect. She was well read in folk and fairy tales and may have taken the idea of a talking mirror from this tradition. Mirrors occur in many of Plath's poems. Perhaps, they suggest the dangers of judging ourselves too harshly, or of seeking perfection. Or they may suggest the lonely drama of living and dying, as it was, in the end, for Plath herself.

Commentary

Opening statement

The poem begins with a precise statement: 'I am silver and exact.' 'Silver' connotes something valuable but it also suggests something inanimate and, therefore, heartless. The adjective 'exact' is ambiguous. It suggests accuracy and correctness. However, there is a more sinister meaning to the verbal form of the word. 'To exact' is to extort or demand payment. **So the opening statement can be read in quite different ways. The surface meaning: I am valuable and accurate. Or the implied meaning: I am heartless and demand payment. The opening statement succeeds in expressing both meanings simultaneously, moving back and forth between the ordinary and the symbolic.**

If we identify the mirror with the perceiving self, then the opening statement suggests a harsh and unforgiving way of viewing the self. It suggests a lack of self-love. Is the voice of the mirror to be interpreted as the voice of the woman whose image the mirror reflects? Is the voice of the poem an aspect of Plath's own voice? Or should we keep a distance between the poet and the speaker of the poem? There are no correct answers to these questions. Different readers read the poem in different ways. Moreover, Plath's poetry succeeds in communicating on a number of levels, in any individual poem, without losing its sense of focus.

Final image

In the final image of the poem (the 'old woman' rising 'like a terrible fish', lines 17 and 18), **Plath suggests many fears and insecurities: the fear of time and old age; the fear of annihilation; the fear of entrapment and alienation; and the fear of losing control.** The image may also perhaps suggest a daughter's fear of her mother, which is the reading that the critic David Holbrook gives to these lines.

World of the poem

The world of the poem is a bleak and unloving one. The perceiving and recording intelligence is cold and inhuman. It gives nothing creative, warm or assuring to the woman. The image of the lake in the second stanza is striking. Like the bottom in 'Elm', the sea in 'Finisterre' and the bee box in 'The Arrival of the Bee Box', the lake represents the dark and fearful inner life. The woman is alone and has no one else to turn to, except the moon and the candles.

Form of the poem

Plath uses the nine-line stanza, which she also used in 'Finisterre'. The line length is irregular but the lines are mostly long. On the page, the two stanzas of the poem appear to mirror each other. The cold tone of the poem is reflected in the carefully phrased statements and the harsh 'k' sounds of the first stanza.

Many of the lines form complete sentences. This contributes to the impression of exactitude that the mirror claims for itself. A sense that is also reflected in the many short words with final voiced consonants ('exact', 'just', 'god', 'pink', 'part' and so on), which create an impression of cold precision. For some readers, the controlled accuracy of the language of the poem emphasises the agitation and disturbed feelings that lie behind the carefully chosen words and phrases.

The run-on line (line 17) that continues with 'rises' in the last line of the poem works brilliantly to mirror the shock of the 'old woman' rising like a 'terrible fish'.

Thinking about the poem

1. What qualities does the mirror attribute to itself in the first four lines of the poem? What is your reaction to the claims the mirror makes for itself? What is your reaction to the tone of these lines?
2. In what sense might a mirror be said to 'swallow' what it sees (line 2)?
3. 'I am not cruel, only truthful' (line 4). Consider this statement. Is the voice of the poem cruel? Is it a masculine or a feminine voice? Are mirrors always truthful? What governs what a person may or may not see in a mirror?
4. Why does the mirror refer to the moon and candles as 'liars' (line 12)?
5. What is the woman's attitude to the mirror and the mirror's attitude to the woman? What is your attitude to the woman?

6 Comment on the images of the final lines of the poem and the impact they have on you. Where else is there a sense of dread or panic in the poem?
7 What does the poem say to you about fear and insecurity and the prospect of growing old?
8 'The exact and precise nature of the mirror is reflected in the language and structure of the poem.' In the light of this statement, comment on the language and form of the poem.
9 'The world reflected by the mirror is one in which the female persona suffers and is alone.' Do you agree with this reading of the poem? Support the points you make by quotation from the poem.
10 'The voice of the mirror is the harsh inner voice that every woman carries within herself.' Give your response to this statement, supporting the points you make by quotation from the poem.

Pheasant

You said you would kill it this morning.
Do not kill it. It startles me still,
The jut of that odd, dark head, pacing

Through the uncut grass on the elm's hill.
It is something to own a pheasant,
Or just to be visited at all.

I am not mystical: it isn't
As if I thought it had a spirit.
It is simply in its element.

That gives it a kingliness, a right.
The print of its big foot last winter,
The tail-track, on the snow in our court —

The wonder of it, in that pallor,
Through crosshatch of sparrow and starling.
Is it its rareness, then? It is rare.

But a dozen would be worth having,
A hundred, on that hill – green and red,
Crossing and recrossing: a fine thing!

It is such a good shape, so vivid.
It's a little cornucopia.   20
It unclasps, brown as a leaf, and loud,

Settles in the elm, and is easy.
It was sunning in the narcissi.
I trespass stupidly. Let be, let be.

Glossary

3	*jut of that odd, dark head*: jerky, forward movement of the head; the way the head of the pheasant leaned forward
12	*our court*: courtyard; Court Green is the name of the house in Devon where the poem is set; also suggests a royal court and picks up on the mention of the kingliness of the bird
13	*pallor*: paleness
14	*crosshatch*: shading by a series of intersecting lines; here, the prints left by the pheasant overlap those left by other birds to create a crosshatch pattern
20	*cornucopia*: treasure; literally means horn of plenty, a Roman symbol of abundance
23	*narcissi*: daffodil-like plants, with white or yellow flowers; there were thousands of bulbs planted around Court Green

Guidelines

Plath wrote 'Pheasant' in April 1962, in a period of enormous creativity in which she wrote a number of fine poems within days of each other. The poem had its origins in Plath's glimpse of a pheasant standing on a hill at the back of her house.

Some critics read the poem in terms of the relationship between the speaker and the person she addresses. The 'you' of the poem is often identified with Ted Hughes, Plath's husband, who came from a Yorkshire family that was well used to hunting and fishing.

Commentary

Dramatic opening

The poem opens in a dramatic fashion. The speaker reports the intention of 'you' to kill the pheasant, which she has seen on the hill behind their house. The opening line has the quality of an accusation: 'You said you would kill it this morning.' The repetition of the pronoun 'you' and the use of the verb 'kill' are striking. **'You' is associated with death, is a killer or a potential killer.**

The plea

The speaker pleads for the pheasant's life. The plea in line 2 is direct and simple, 'Do not kill it.' This is not an order as the speaker feels obliged to supply reasons for this request. She says that the pheasant has the capacity to startle her, as it paces through the grass on the hill. She is fascinated by the movement and shape of its head. And because the pheasant is on their land, she feels a pride of ownership. She feels it is an honour to be visited by this kingly bird. The adjective 'dark' (line 3) suggests that the pheasant is unknowable and therefore remains a mystery to her.

The speaker continues her plea for the bird in the third stanza, arguing that the pheasant 'is simply in its element' (line 9). To the speaker's mind, this naturalness gives the bird a kingly quality, a right to exist, without fear or favour. **The implicit argument is that it is the 'you' and the 'I' who are the outsiders, the interlopers.** In stanza 6 the speaker indulges in a flight of fancy, wondering what it would be like to have a hundred (dozen) pheasants 'green and red' (line 17) on the elm's hill. **The green and red hues of the pheasant are symbols of life and passion.**

Anguished voice

In stanza 7 the focus returns to the pheasant. This one alone is a source of delight. It is a 'cornucopia' (line 21), with its fine shape and vivid colouring. She watches as it unclaps its wings and makes itself comfortable in the tree. **There is almost envy in the statement that the pheasant 'Settles in the elm, and is easy' (line 22). This ease is not shared by the speaker.**

The tone of the poem takes on an edge as the speaker describes herself as trespassing stupidly on the pheasant, sunning itself in the narcissi. And then the emotion, which has been controlled throughout 'Pheasant', breaks out in the urgent plea that concludes the poem: 'Let be. Let be.' **The repeated phrase captures the**

anguish of the speaker, while the echoing rhyme of the final two lines captures the intensity of the plea. This is a trace of the anguished voice that we hear in 'Elm', 'Child', 'Mirror' and 'Poppies in July'.

Critical interpretation

For some critics, the plea is not for the pheasant but for the poet herself. Plath wrote 'Pheasant' in April 1962 during a tense period in her relationship with Ted Hughes. **Some critics read the poem as being about Plath's marriage.** She is the narrator and Hughes is the 'you' whom she addresses. **The pheasant represents the marriage itself, under threat from the male. It is he who is intent on destroying it.** Plath pleads for it. She pleads for its beauty and wonder, and for the life and passion that animate it. **The fact that it is the female who makes the plea suggests that the relationship of power is an unequal one, with the male possessing the authority to take or spare life, as he wills.** (In 'The Arrival of the Bee Box', the narrator says she will be a sweet god and spare the lives of the bees.) For the critic Linda Wagner-Martin, 'Pheasant' rests on the fear that the male will not listen to the female's plea for the life that deserves to exist. The male is a silent, powerful presence in the poem. The female is the pleading supplicant.

Form of the poem

'Pheasant' is a beautifully achieved poem. It has a conversational quality. Yet, apart from the final line, Plath uses a nine-syllable line, and there are subtle rhymes and half-rhymes throughout the poem. The rhyme scheme is a version of terza rima, a form in which the last word in the middle line of each stanza provides the rhyme for the next stanza. What is so impressive about 'Pheasant' is the way Plath follows a strict form while never losing the conversational feel of the poem.

Thinking about the poem

1. What is the dramatic situation suggested by the opening and closing of the poem?
2. What reasons does the 'I' give to support her plea, in stanzas 1 and 2?
3. From the evidence of stanzas 3 to 5, is the speaker sure of her reasons for wanting the pheasant spared? Quote from the poem in support of your answer.
4. In stanzas 7 and 8, what is the speaker's attitude to the pheasant and where is it most evident?

5. 'At the end of the poem, it is the speaker who feels like an outsider.' Do you agree with this reading of the poem? Give reasons for your answer.
6. 'The difference between "Pheasant" and "Black Rook in Rainy Weather" is that in the former there is no movement from the outside to the inside. It is the bird, rather than the poetic persona who is the centre of the poem.' *Or* 'In "Pheasant" the poetic persona pleads for herself in pleading for the bird.' Which of these two readings of the poem is closest to your own. Support the points you make by quotation from the poem.
7. In writing about 'Pheasant', Ted Hughes speaks of Plath achieving a 'cool, light, very beautiful moment of mastery'. Write a note on the kind of mastery achieved by Plath in 'Pheasant'. You might like to consider some or all of the following in your answer: the choice of verbs and their effect; the descriptions of the pheasant; the dramatic language; line length and syllable count; the stanza form. In considering these, be alert to the sounds of the poem and their effect.
8. If, as some critics suggest, the poem describes the relationship between the poet and her husband, what kind of relationship is portrayed? (In the above Commentary it is assumed that the speaker of the poem is a woman. Is this a fair assumption? Does the poem support it?)
9. If you were encouraging someone to read 'Pheasant' for the first time, how would you describe the poem and your reaction to it?

Elm

for Ruth Fainlight

I know the bottom, she says. I know it with my great tap root;
It is what you fear.
I do not fear it: I have been there.

Is it the sea you hear in me,
Its dissatisfactions?   5
Or the voice of nothing, that was your madness?

Love is a shadow.
How you lie and cry after it
Listen: these are its hooves: it has gone off, like a horse.

All night I shall gallop thus, impetuously,
Till your head is a stone, your pillow a little turf,
Echoing, echoing.

Or shall I bring you the sound of poisons?
This is rain now, this big hush.
And this is the fruit of it: tin-white, like arsenic.

I have suffered the atrocity of sunsets.
Scorched to the root
My red filaments burn and stand, a hand of wires.

Now I break up in pieces that fly about like clubs.
A wind of such violence
Will tolerate no bystanding: I must shriek.

The moon, also, is merciless: she would drag me
Cruelly, being barren.
Her radiance scathes me. Or perhaps I have caught her.

I let her go. I let her go
Diminished and flat, as after radical surgery.
How your bad dreams possess and endow me.

I am inhabited by a cry.
Nightly it flaps out
Looking, with its hooks, for something to love.

I am terrified by this dark thing
That sleeps in me;
All day I feel its soft, feathery turnings, its malignity.

Clouds pass and disperse.
Are those the faces of love, those pale irretrievables?
Is it for such I agitate my heart?

I am incapable of more knowledge.
What is this, this face
So murderous in its strangle of branches? –

Its snaky acids hiss. 40
It petrifies the will. These are the isolate, slow faults
That kill, that kill, that kill.

Glossary

dedication	*Ruth Fainlight*: writer and friend of Plath	
1	*the bottom*: the furthest point that can be reached; here, the deepest point in the subterranean world	
1	*tap root*: the main root that goes deep into the soil	
6	*voice of nothing*: silence, the absence of inspiration	
19	*clubs*: stout-ended sticks used as weapons	

Guidelines

'Elm' is a poem that went through numerous drafts before Plath completed it in April 1962. It follows on from the last line of 'Pheasant', in which the bird settles in the elm tree at the back of their house 'and is easy'. Plath took up the word 'easy' at the end of 'Pheasant' and began to explore the elm as something that is not easy.

Commentary

Title

The title refers to a wych elm that grew on a prehistoric mound at the back of Court Green, the house in Devon that Plath shared with Ted Hughes before the break-up of their marriage. In silhouette, the branches of the wych elm make strange, tangled shapes. Plath described the branches of the tree as an 'intricate nervous system'. She plays upon the visual appearance of the elm and its great age in giving it human characteristics. As Anne Stevenson, one of Plath's biographers, observes, the wych elm becomes 'witch' elm in the poem, a frightening, sinister presence.

Stanza 1

In the opening stanza the elm declares her knowledge. It is a dark and deep knowledge, one that has explored 'the bottom' (line 1), the thing that 'you' (the narrator) fears – implying the journey into the deepest part of the self or to the worst periods of one's life. The phrase also suggests the bed of a lake or river where the mud and sludge gather. The imagery here is reminiscent of that in 'Mirror'. The elm shows no sympathy and offers no comfort to the narrator. **The elm resembles an inner voice that is harsh and mocking.**

Stanza 2

In the second stanza the elm asks if the narrator hears the 'dissatisfactions' (line 5) of the sea, as the wind sounds in its branches. The sea is an important and complex symbol in Plath's poetry. It often represents formlessness and annihilation, as in 'Finisterre', or her childhood before the death of her father. After he died, Plath thought of him as drowned and described the creation of pearls as coming from the 'grit of sorrow and routine'. Thus, for Plath, the sea represents creativity and the subconscious of the artist.

The questions posed by the elm seem intended to taunt the narrator. The elm suggests that perhaps the sound is the 'voice of nothing' – the sound of silence, which it equates with the narrator's 'madness' (line 6). Silence – the absence of inspiration – was the cause of severe depression in Plath, who constantly feared that her poetic gift had deserted her.

Stanzas 3 and 4

Stanza 3 continues in a mocking vein. The elm compares its sounds to the pounding of horses' hooves. These hooves, it says, are the sound of love running away from the narrator. **The elm mocks the abandoned narrator's need and desire for it. Love's absence is a 'shadow' (line 7) that hangs over her life.** There is also an interesting ambiguity in the verb 'lie'. As with 'Pheasant', written during the same month, it is worth bearing in mind that Plath's marriage was in crisis at the time she wrote 'Elm'.

Stanza 5

The elm offers the narrator an alternative to the sound of the horse's hooves: 'the sound of poisons' (line 13). The movement from unattainable love to poison is similar to the movement in 'Poppies in July', where poison and annihilation are opposed to a life of intensity. Like the sound of madness, the sound of poisons is silent. Plath worried about the threat of nuclear warfare and the poisoning of the environment. Her fear is reflected in the imagery of this stanza, with its suggestions of acid rain and nuclear dust. The 'big hush' (line 14) may be the deathly silence induced by chemicals (arsenic is a component in many weed and insect killers) in the atmosphere and in the soil or it may be the hush following a nuclear explosion.

Stanzas 6 and 7

The nuclear imagery is continued into stanzas 6 and 7, where the sunset and the violent wind seem to characterise the flash and blast of a nuclear bomb. **The references to suffering – 'scorched', 'wires', 'violence', 'shriek' – speak as much to the suffering endured by Plath's body in the electric shock treatment she received for depression, as they do to the violence endured by the body of the elm.**

The difference established between the elm and the narrator in the first stanza becomes less apparent. In speaking of itself, the elm speaks for the narrator, and the narrator, increasingly, seems identifiable with Plath herself. This, in turn, leads to an intensifying of the emotional strain in the poem.

Stanzas 8 and 9

The elm/narrator continues to describe her suffering. Now it is the 'merciless' moon who is responsible. There are sixty-one references to the moon in Plath's poetry and none of them is benevolent. The moon is sterile and mocking. It is associated with women but it cannot create life (it is 'barren', line 23). 'Barren' is an adjective Plath uses often to indicate a strong dislike or horror of someone. A barren woman is, Plath suggests in another poem, like an empty museum. *'Diminished and flat, as after radical surgery'* is a startling and disturbing image that suggests a woman after a mastectomy.

Line 27 is a key line in interpreting the poem: **the elm suggests that the narrator's nightmares have taken them over and made them what they are: 'How your bad dreams possess and endow me.' From this point on, the elm and the narrator speak with one voice.** In 'The Moon and the Yew Tree', Plath says that the trees of the mind are black. The elm is black and expresses some of the dark, incomprehensible fears that occupy the narrator's mind.

Stanzas 10 and 11

The litany of the narrator's fears begins in stanza 10 and continues in stanza 11. **A bird-like predatory cry, 'this dark thing' (line 31), seems to represent the unconscious of the narrator.** It is fearful, threatening and malignant. It is as if she is a stranger to herself, terrified by forces that she cannot control and a destructive need for love. The imagery reminds us of the incomprehensible sounds in the box in 'The Arrival of the Bee Box'.

Stanzas 12 to 14

Stanza 12 returns to the need for love and the feeling that love, like the passing clouds, is unattainable. There is something pitiful in the question that concludes this stanza: 'Is it for such I agitate my heart?' (line 36).

But this question is not pursued, as the narrator admits she is incapable of more knowledge. However, even as she confesses to her inability to bear more knowledge, more knowledge must be borne. The elm's face forces itself into her consciousness bringing the knowledge of what that face represents. It is a Medusa-like face. Medusa symbolises duality, a double nature that is beautiful and horrifying, seductive and destructive. Is the narrator seeing her own nature in this face?

The 'snaky acids' of the branches 'hiss' (line 40) and the face freezes the will. Anyone who looked on Medusa (whose hair was a tangle of snakes) was turned to stone. The imagery also recalls the serpent in the Garden of Eden and suggests a correspondence between the elm and the Tree of Knowledge. The 'acids' of line 40 are the poisons that kill over time. The repetition of 'kill' in line 42 suggests both a violent frenzy and a hysterical fear of that violence.

The end of the poem, with its nightmarish imagery, a product of the narrator's imagination, suggests that it is the individual poisons ('the isolate, slow faults', line 41) that build up over time within the body (and the mind) that kill. **The repetition in the last line creates a feeling of inevitability, as if the narrator feels doomed, unable to escape the faults that kill.** It is interesting to note that the verb 'kill' also appears in the first line of 'Pheasant'.

Voice of the poem

In the poem, as in many others, Plath personifies a natural object (the elm) and gives it a voice. The voice is at once the 'voice' of a tree, as reported by the narrator, and the voice of the narrator herself.

The voice of the elm is knowledgeable, distressed and, at times, cruel and taunting. The elm addresses a 'you', the poetic persona of the poet, on the subject of fear, love, suffering and despair. Many critics read the second half of the poem as spoken by this 'you' and read the voice as anguished and fearful. The second part of the poem speaks of the need for love, its absence and a destructive inner force. However, to describe the poem in this way is, arguably, misleading. In each utterance of the tree, we can catch a trace of the woman's voice and, in effect, the voices blur and merge, as if the voice of the elm is the inner voice of the woman.

As with many of Plath's poems, the poetic persona seems very harsh in her view of herself. The end of the poem suggests the recognition of some inner faults that will lead to her death. The absence of love intensifies the activity of the dark owl-like thing, whose malignity she fears. As in 'Child', 'Mirror' and 'Poppies in July' the poetic persona is anguished and speaks in a voice that is, by the end of the poem, anguished and fearful.

Atmosphere of the poem

The technique of personification creates a surreal, even nightmarish effect. The world of 'Elm' is not unlike the world of a Brothers Grimm fairy tale, or the world of the subconscious: it is dark and frightening. The vocabulary of the poem captures this nightmarish world: 'terrified', 'dark' 'malignity', 'murderous', 'acid', 'kill'. It is also worth bearing in mind that, **in the heightened atmosphere of the Cold War, there was much discussion about the prospect of nuclear warfare,** so much so that Plath wrote to her mother a couple of months before she completed 'Elm' about the 'mad, self-destructive world' in which they lived. This atmosphere may also have contributed to the imagery of the poem, especially in stanza 5 where it suggests the aftermath of a nuclear bomb.

Form of the poem

Compared with the careful structure of 'Pheasant', 'Elm' is written in a looser manner, with lines of varying lengths. The lack of formal certainty mirrors the swarming content of the poem. Interestingly, the critic Hugh Kenner believes that Plath's abandonment of formal structures in her later poetry encouraged her to explore states of mind and emotions that were unsafe and which, ultimately, contributed to her suicide.

Thinking about the poem

1. What impression of the elm is created by its statements in the first stanza?
2. Examine the questions posed by the elm in stanza 2. What do they suggest about the elm and the person it addresses?
3. What image of love is created in stanzas 3 and 4? Is the elm comforting or cruel in these stanzas? Explain your answer.
4. Stanzas 5 to 9 describe the elements of rain, sun, wind and moon and their relationship to the elm. What aspect of each is emphasised? How does each affect the elm? What, in your view, is the most striking image in these stanzas?
5. What is the elm's attitude to the moon? Where is this attitude most apparent?
6. What do stanzas 5 to 9 suggest about the nature of the elm's existence? Select the words or phrases that strike you most forcefully.

7 What relationship is suggested between the elm and the 'you' of the poem in the statement: 'How your bad dreams possess and endow me' (line 27)? The line can be read as either the elm addressing the woman or the woman addressing the elm. What is the effect of each reading? How do you read it?

8 The last five stanzas are rich, complex and difficult. How does the narrator view herself? What images strike you as particularly disturbing or vivid? What is your reaction to the use of the word 'faults' (line 41)? What is the tone of the extraordinary last line of the poem?

9 'In "Elm" the boundary between outside and inside is blurred. It is as if the "you", the poetic persona, takes the elm into herself.' In the light of this statement, describe the poetic personae of 'Elm' and the nature of the world, physical and psychological, that they inhabit. Refer to the imagery and vocabulary of the poem in your answer.

10 There is no single reading of 'Elm' that will do justice to its rich complexity. Here are three of the many readings proposed for the poem. Give your opinion of each.

   (a) *The poem's narrator confesses that she is searching desperately for someone to love. Because of this hysteria, she realises that some deadly force within her has been triggered into action by the loss of love. The disintegration of love, the poem says, is a sure death warrant for the speaker.* (Paul Alexander)

   (b) *'Elm' describes the effects of nuclear and chemical damage upon a tree and a woman. 'I have suffered the atrocity of sunsets', the speaker explains, and further, 'My red filaments burn and stand, a hand of wires.' . . . 'Elm' is one of the many poems in which Plath explores the consequences of isolation, and argues against the impulse to hold oneself as separate from the rest of the world.* (Tracy Brain)

   (c) *In the poem, originally titled, 'The Elm Speaks', wych elm becomes witch elm, a frightening mother-double of the poet, who offers death as the only possible love substitute. Between the taproot of the tree and the murderous face of the moon, the poet, 'incapable of more knowledge' is forced into a terrible acknowledgement of 'faults' – suddenly a new word in Sylvia's poetic lexicon. The poem suggests them as somehow built into her nature, bent like a crooked tree by traumatic childhood events: 'These are the isolate slow faults / That kill, that kill, that kill.'* (Anne Stevenson)

11 'The poem vividly conveys suffering, self-doubt and despair.' Give your response to this assessment of 'Elm', supporting the points you make by quotation from the poem.

12 'Elm' is a poem with many striking visual images. Perhaps you might like to offer your own creative response to, or interpretation of, the poem, in visual form.

Poppies in July

Little poppies, little hell flames,
Do you do no harm?

You flicker. I cannot touch you.
I put my hands among the flames. Nothing burns.

And it exhausts me to watch you 5
Flickering like that, wrinkly and clear red, like the skin of a mouth.

A mouth just bloodied.
Little bloody skirts!

There are fumes that I cannot touch.
Where are your opiates, your nauseous capsules? 10

If I could bleed, or sleep! –
If my mouth could marry a hurt like that!

Or your liquors seep to me, in this glass capsule,
Dulling and stilling.

But colourless. Colourless. 15

Sylvia Plath

Glossary		
10	*opiates*:	opium comes from the unripe seed of the poppy
10	*nauseous capsules*:	tablets that cause sickness or discomfort
13	*liquors*:	a solution of a drug or chemical in water
13	*glass capsule*:	a bell jar, of the kind used in scientific experiments or to hold a specimen

Guidelines

Plath wrote 'Poppies in July' in July 1962, at Court Green in Devon, during the break-up of her marriage. The poetic persona addresses the flowers in a voice that is overwrought and anguished. Anne Stevenson, Plath's biographer, sets the poems that Plath wrote in the final months of her life in a biographical context. She says that these poems report on 'the weather of her inner universe' and the two poles that governed it: rage and stasis. 'At the depressed pole there was a turning in on herself, a longing for non-being as in "Poppies in July".'

Commentary

Title

Red poppies are a common sight in the English countryside in summer. The poppy is also a flower of remembrance for the war dead. In Keats' poem 'To Autumn', the poppy is associated with sleep and ease. As Plath develops the symbolism of the poppy, it takes on a dark and destructive resonance, indicative of a troubled state of mind.

Couplets 1–4

From the first line we realise that the speaker of the poem is troubled. The opening line greeting the poppies – 'Little poppies, little hell flames' – seems to be spoken by two different people. 'Little poppies' suggests a sentimental relationship to the flowers. However, this impression is immediately destroyed by the negative energy of 'little hell flowers' and the association that the speaker makes between the red poppies and the flames of hell. After only one line, we suspect that the poem is not really about the poppies. It is about someone in an excited and disturbed psychological state.

This disturbance is carried into the second line, where the speaker asks: 'Do, you do no harm?' **The word 'harm' is striking and from here on the speaker explores and contemplates the different kinds of harm that she associates with the flowers.** The poppies are associated with danger and death.

The second couplet (lines 3 and 4) continues the imagery of 'flames' begun in line 1. The movement of the red petals is like the flickering of flames. The speaker says she puts her hands among the flames (the petals of the flowers) but 'Nothing burns' (line 4). It is as if the speaker is cut off from feeling and sensation, an idea taken up later in the fifth couplet and linked to the imagery of being contained in the glass jar.

The speaker cannot touch the poppies but she can watch them, though she finds their movement exhausting (line 5). In a striking visual image, she compares the poppies to a mouth and immediately develops the comparison to bloodied mouths and bloodied skirts. The bloodied mouth may suggest violence. Plath often associated red with love, and love with violent emotion that incorporated danger, excitement and vitality. Famously, in her first meeting with Ted Hughes, she bit him on the cheek and he left with blood running down his face.

In poetry, blood is a complex symbol, suggesting hurt, violence, danger, excitement and vitality. The reference to  'little bloody skirts' (line 8) may suggest the stain of menstrual blood and the association of female sexuality with a wound. The tone of 'little bloody skirts' suggests disgust or irritation. It could also be an indirect and derogatory reference to Assia Wevill, the woman with whom Hughes was having an affair. Indeed, Ronald Hayman, one of Plath's biographers, suggests that 'Poppies in July' is directed at Assia Wevill.

Couplets 5–7

In the fifth couplet **the speaker changes tack and focuses on the by-products of poppies: the colourless fumes, their opiates**. She seems frustrated that she cannot inhale the fumes that bring drowsiness and ease, or find the opium tablets that make you feel sick or unwell.

In the sixth couplet we realise how distressed the speaker is. She expresses the wish that she could either bleed or sleep, suffer or escape. In other words, **the speaker seems trapped, unable to live life to the full or escape from it**. Either suffering or sleeping, it seems, would bring relief to her. The couplet concludes with the startling and passionate exclamation, 'If my mouth could marry a hurt like that' (line 12). It is a strange, wild and fascinating statement of longing and captures the desperation of the speaker to live life in a different way from the way she is living it now. **It** encompasses all the related imagery at work in the poem: life, death, violence, sexuality, addiction, sickness.

The seventh couplet (lines 13 and 14) expresses an alternative wish, namely that the fumes of the poppy will seep into the glass jar where she is trapped, dulling and stilling her senses. This is a death wish, which involves no blood or violence just a colourless fume that will drain the colour out of life. The image of the 'glass capsule' (the bell jar) is a recurrent one in Plath's work. References to bell jars and liquor suggest hospital and museum specimens kept in chemical solutions. Plath witnessed such specimens when she posed as a medical student and observed an anatomical dissection. The experience proved traumatic. In this case, the imagery suggests that the speaker sees herself as trapped in a glass jar, like an exhibit in a museum.

The poem concludes with a chilling wish for annihilation in place of her present inability to feel or experience life.

Interpreting the poem

The poem is complex and invites a variety of interpretations and you may not fully agree with the one offered here. It is clear that the speaker is distressed and acting out a psychological drama in her words. She is deeply unhappy and feels trapped. She wants something to change in her life or she wants her life to end. There are two impulses at work in the poem, one associated with the vibrant colour red and the other with the absence of colour. One symbolises a life of physical, even violent, intensity and the other the total annihilation of consciousness.

Style and form of the poem

The poem is dramatic. It progresses in short dramatic statements, governed by careful punctuation, which are organised into unrhymed, irregular couplets. The use of exclamation marks and question marks adds to the dramatic impact and the poem moves through a range of tones in its short fifteen lines, including fascination, frustration, disgust and repulsion, intense desire and longing. Plath is brilliant at weaving intricate patterns of sound that mirror the sense of the lines. You can almost hear the crackle of the flames in the opening six lines. This is achieved by the onomatopoeic effect of the 'c' and 'k' sounds used. A completely different effect is achieved in the final three lines of the poem where the soft 's' sounds and the long 'u' and 'ou' vowels create a sense of ease and quiet.

Thinking about the poem

1. Based on the first two lines of the poem, what is the state of mind of the speaker?
2. Why, in your view, does the speaker want to experience the sensation of burning by putting her 'hands among the flames' (line 4)?
3. In the fourth couplet, the speaker compares the poppies to 'a mouth just bloodied' and 'little bloody skirts'. What is the impact of these comparisons?
4. In the fifth couplet, the speaker says she cannot touch the fumes of the poppies. Why, in your view, can she not touch them?
5. The speaker asks about opiates and tablets in line 10. What do her questions tell us about what she is thinking?
6. 'If I could bleed or sleep!' (line 11). If the speaker is neither bleeding nor sleeping, what kind of existence is she experiencing? Explain your answer.

7. What does the reference to 'this glass capsule' (line 13) say to you about how the speaker views her life?
8. What is the wish expressed by the speaker at the end of the poem? How does the wish make you feel?
9. Which **two** of the following statements best describe your view of the poem?
   - It is a poem about feeling trapped.
   - It is a poem about wanting to escape.
   - It is a poem abut feeling numb.
   - It is about wanting to live life to the full.
   - It is a poem about annihilation.

   Explain your choice using reference to the text.
10. Which of the following statements is closest to your own feelings for the speaker of the poem?
    - I admire the speaker.
    - I feel sorry for the speaker.
    - I am fascinated by the speaker.

    Explain your choice.

Taking a closer look

1. Comment on the phrase 'little hell flames' (line 1) – considering each of the three words – and its impact upon you.
2. The phrase 'I cannot touch' is used twice in the poem (lines 3 and 9). How does it add to your understanding of the predicament of the speaker?
3. 'If my mouth could marry a hurt like that!' (line 12). In your opinion, what longing is expressed in this line?
4. 'The poem 'Poppies in July' has little to do with poppies and a great deal to do with the mind that perceives them.' Give your response to this statement, supporting the points you make by quotation from the poem.

Imagining

1. Imagine that you are asked to make a short film to accompany a reading of the poem. Explain how you would use music, sound effects, colour, images, etc. to capture the atmosphere of the poem.
2. Imagine that you are the poet. Write **two** diary entries that give your reaction to the poem a long time after you first wrote it.

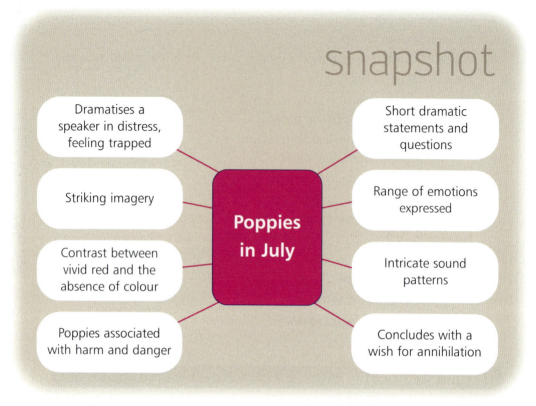

The Arrival of the Bee Box

I ordered this, this clean wood box
Square as a chair and almost too heavy to lift.
I would say it was the coffin of a midget
Or a square baby
Were there not such a din in it.   5

The box is locked, it is dangerous.
I have to live with it overnight
And I can't keep away from it.
There are no windows, so I can't see what is in there.
There is only a little grid, no exit.   10

I put my eye to the grid.
It is dark, dark,

With the swarmy feeling of African hands
Minute and shrunk for export,
Black on black, angrily clambering. 15

How can I let them out?
It is the noise that appals me most of all,
The unintelligible syllables.
It is like a Roman mob,
Small, taken one by one, but my god, together! 20

I lay my ear to furious Latin.
I am not a Caesar.
I have simply ordered a box of maniacs.
They can be sent back.
They can die, I need feed them nothing, I am the owner. 25

I wonder how hungry they are.
I wonder if they would forget me
If I just undid the locks and stood back and turned into a tree.
There is the laburnum, its blond colonnades,
And the petticoats of the cherry. 30

They might ignore me immediately
In my moon suit and funeral veil.
I am no source of honey
So why should they turn on me?
Tomorrow I will be sweet God, I will set them free. 35

The box is only temporary.

Glossary		
13	*swarmy*: moving in large numbers
22	*Caesar*: Roman emperor
29	*colonnades*: row of columns, in this case ringlets
32	*moon suit*: spacesuit, protective clothing worn by astronauts

Guidelines

In 1962 Plath and Hughes decided to take up beekeeping. (Plath's father had been an expert on bees.) In October, following their separation, Plath wrote a sequence of bee poems that explore the nature of the self and self-identity; personal fears; complex relations and attitudes towards freedom and control. Of the five poems in the sequence, 'The Arrival of the Bee Box' is the one that can stand on its own.

The poem may be taken at face value: it describes the arrival of the bee box and the speaker's response to it. **The box both frightens and fascinates the speaker of the poem. However, the bee box is often read as a symbol for the inner life of the speaker or a symbol for poetry itself, a formal shape which contains a swarm of ideas and feelings.**

Commentary

Stanza 1
The poem opens on a note of wonderment as the speaker seems surprised by the bee box and by the fact that she is responsible for its presence, 'I ordered this'. The verb 'ordered' introduces a major theme of the poem: the question of power and control.

Lines 3 and 4 introduce the first of the surreal images that run through the poem. The speaker says she would compare the box to 'the coffin of a midget / Or a square baby' except for the noise coming from it. The box, like the bell jar imagery that is evident in much of Plath's work, symbolises entrapment and confinement and, as the poem progresses, the noise coming from it is the sound of the bees agitating for release.

Stanza 2
The second stanza is the most straightforward in the poem. It opens with two direct statements: 'The box is locked. It is dangerous.' The speaker says she has to live with the box overnight and cannot keep away from it. Lines 9 and 10 describe the box in terms that bring to mind a windowless prison cell. **This stanza reveals the speaker's fascination with the contents of the box.** In Greek mythology, Pandora, out of curiosity, opened a container and released harm and sickness into the world. All the contents of the box escaped except hope. The box in this poem resembles Pandora's in the mixture of fear and hope that it excites in the speaker.

Stanza 3
Plath was influenced by the surrealist painter Giorgio de Chirico, and his use of symbols taken from the subconscious to create ominous, disturbing images. She was

also interested in African sculpture and folktales. Both interests – surrealism and Africa – come together in the imagery of the third stanza.

The speaker tells us that she can see only darkness when she puts her eyes to the grid. It is not an empty darkness but one which the speaker associates with 'African hands' (line 13), a reference to the Black slave-workers exported from Africa on slave ships to work as manual labourers on plantations. In a surreal, disturbing image, the speaker sees these 'hands' as 'minute and shrunk' (line 14).

Like the African slaves, the bees are workers and they must clamber over each other to move around in their cramped conditions. The use of the word 'angrily' (line 15) suggests the danger and aggression that the speaker senses within – the threat posed by the contained but angry bees. Some commentators have suggested that the series of images linking the bees to African slaves could only have been made by a White writer.

Stanza 4

The opening line of the fourth stanza, 'How can I let them out?', is ambiguous. Given the anger of the bees the question may mean 'How can I let them out *safely*?' On the other hand, it could mean 'How can I *possibly* let them out *now that I know what they are like*?' **It is as if the speaker doubts her capacity to cope with the bees, and their dangerous potential.** She tries to identify the source of her dismay and attributes it to the noise and its incomprehensibility: she fears what she does not understand. The potential for destruction that she senses in the bee box is captured in the comparison to the mob which, in Roman times, demanded public killings for their amusement (line 19).

Stanza 5

Listening to the 'furious Latin' (line 21), the speaker feels unable to control the mob, as Caesar did, by the power of his words. Their language is, after all, 'unintelligible' (line 18) to her. But then **the speaker grows more confident. She defines the situation and the solution to the problem with a new clarity** in lines 23–24: 'I have simply ordered a box of maniacs. / They can be sent back.' The situation is not out of control. In the final line of the stanza, another possibility occurs to her. The bees might be left in their box, without food. Then it will become a coffin. Ownership gives her the power of life and death. She is like a slave owner.

Stanza 6

The sixth stanza brings a change of tone. The possibility of allowing the bees to die is no longer entertained. Instead, she thinks of how they might be released without causing harm to herself. **The speaker is calmer, although still curious.** She wonders if the bees will forget her. It is an intriguing question. Does she mean 'forget' in the sense of not wanting to exact revenge upon her for bringing them there in the first place?

She thinks of the idea of escaping by becoming a tree. In Greek mythology, the God Apollo, mad with love and desire, pursued the nymph Daphne, who called on her father, Peneus, for help and was turned into a laurel tree.

The speaker seems to suggest that the laburnum and cherry trees may well be the result of a similar transformation. The drooping flower-covered branches of the laburnum are likened to blond ringlets and the blossom of the flowering cherry tree to the ruffled petticoats that were popular in the 1950s and 1960s (lines 29 to 30).

Stanza 7

The seventh stanza presents another possibility: the bees might ignore her in her beekeeper's suit, which she describes as a spacesuit topped with the type of veil traditionally worn by women mourners at a funeral, another comparison which shows that the speaker's mind swarms with ideas and associations.

Line 33 is a simple statement – 'I am no source of honey' – and it prompts the question, 'So why should they turn on me?' **This reveals the speaker's fear that the bees might hurt her.** The question is really an attempt by the speaker to persuade herself that the bees will not harm her. And taking comfort, she speaks with calm authority in line 35: 'Tomorrow I will be sweet God. I will set them free.' **She anticipates the pleasure of exercising her power in a generous way, though the action itself is postponed.**

Final line

There is a note of optimistic triumph in the final line of the poem, 'The box is only temporary.'

Interpreting the poem

The poem can be read as the story of an inexperienced beekeeper who orders a box of bees and is then afraid to release them. However, because Plath employs symbols and works by association, and because she was interested in the unconscious, her poems tend to be interpreted in a variety of ways. Here are examples of how some readers have interpreted this poem:

- The White female beekeeper wants to free the Black bees but she is appalled by them and frightened of what they might do to her.
- The poem depicts a psychological drama between the inner turmoil of the speaker, who is a version of Plath, and the outer, formal control that the speaker exerts on her feelings.
- It is about the kind of poetry that Plath wrote and the dangers involved in writing it. The bees represent her mind and all the repressed feelings, memories and ideas it contains. This is the dangerous subject-matter that both fascinates and appals her. The box represents the poem, the structure that contains and controls the dangerous swarming content of her mind.
- The beekeeper opening the box is like a person releasing repressed feelings or a poet exploring dark themes: all are likely to get hurt.

Style and form of the poem

The poem is written in five-line unrhymed stanzas. The language is direct and powerful. From the opening 'this', the speaker utters her words in short, sharp bursts. The dramatic impact is heightened by the repetition of key words such as 'dark', 'black' and 'I' ('I' appears five times in the fifth stanza alone).

The run-on lines and conversational words create the impression of someone telling a personal story. Look, for example, at the way the sound echoes in the first stanza in the words 'square', 'chair', 'were' and 'there'. The 'r' sound is repeated throughout the poem and occurs in the final word: 'temporary'. As always in Plath's poetry, there is an intricate pattern of sound woven through the text.

Because of the narrative structure and the use of the present tense, we get a sense of the flow of time and live the experience with the speaker.

Interestingly, the last line of the poem falls outside the five-line stanza structure. The speaker announces her intention to free the bees in a line that seems to escape the formal structure of the poem.

Thinking about the poem

1. How does the speaker describe the bee box in the first stanza? Do you find the imagery of the first stanza strange, disturbing or amusing? Explain your answer.
2. Based on the evidence of stanza 2, what is the speaker's attitude to the bee box?
3. Explain as clearly as you can the reference to 'African hands' (line 13) and the comparison the speaker makes between them and the bees.

4 What, according to the speaker in stanza 4, appals her most of all about the bees?

5 In stanza 5, the speaker grows more confident. Speaking as the 'owner' what actions are open to her?

6 In stanza 6, the speaker considers ways in which the bees might be released without causing harm to herself. What options does she consider?

7 What announcement does the speaker make in stanza 7? What is the tone of this announcement?

8 What, in your view, does the final line add to the poem? Does the poem end on a note of optimism?

9 Which one of the following statements best describes your view of the poem?

   It is a poem about bees.

   It is a poem about psychological fears.

   It is a poem about writing poetry.

   Explain your choice using reference to the text.

10 What impression of the poet do you form from reading the poem? What words or phrases help to create this impression of Plath?

Taking a closer look

1 'The box is locked, it is dangerous' (line 6). Comment on Plath's use of the word 'dangerous' and what you think it adds to the poem.

2 'With the swarmy feeling of African hands' (line 13). Describe the impact of this line on you.

3 'I will be sweet God' (line 35). Write a note on this statement and what it means in the context of the poem.

4 'In the poem, there is both a desire to trust the bees and a fear of trusting them, but in the end, the fear is overcome.' Do you agree with this reading of the poem? Explain your answer.

Imagining

1 You are the speaker of the poem. Write a diary entry describing your experience of having the bee box in your possession overnight. The entries should catch some of the conflicting feelings evident in the poem: fear, fascination, repulsion, intended kindness, etc.

2 Choose a song or a film that, in your opinion, has a similar atmosphere to that created in the 'The Arrival of the Bee Box'. Explain your choice.

3 Suggest an alternative title for the poem. Explain your suggestion.

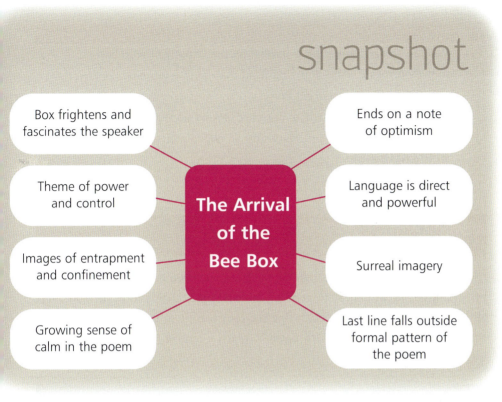

Child

Your clear eye is the one absolutely beautiful thing.
I want to fill it with colour and ducks.
The zoo of the new

Whose names you meditate –
April snowdrop, Indian pipe, 5
Little

Stalk without wrinkle,
Pool in which images
Should be grand and classical

Not this troublous 10
Wringing of hands, this dark
Ceiling without a star.

Glossary	
4	*meditate*: reflect upon; this is picking up the imagery of reflection
5	*snowdrop*: small, white-flowering plant that blooms in spring
5	*Indian pipe*: small, woodland flower
10	*troublous*: agitated, unsettled, disturbed; taking up the idea of classical and grand in the preceding line, Plath uses an old-fashioned, literary word

Guidelines

'Child' appeared in Plath's collection *Winter Trees*, published in 1971, eight years after her death. It was written at the end of January 1963, shortly after her son's first birthday and less than two weeks before she took her life at the age of thirty. It is a beautifully phrased and composed poem in which a mother expresses her frustrated wishes for her child.

Commentary

Stanza 1

'Child' opens dramatically with the mother addressing her child in what is the longest line in the poem. **She tells the child that its eye is the one thing in her life that is beautiful**: 'Your clear eye is the one absolutely beautiful thing.' The line tells us as much about the mother and the world she inhabits as it does about the child.

The mother then expresses her wishes for her child. She wants to create a world of excitement and colour to fill the child's eye: 'I want to fill it with colour and ducks. / The zoo of the new'. These lines work brilliantly. The random progression from 'colour' to 'ducks' captures the unpredictability and pleasure of the world she wants to show her child. The phrase 'the zoo of the new' expresses not only the potential of the world to delight, but also the humour and inventiveness of the mother who wants to bring this world to her child.

Stanza 2

The mother begins to describe the joyful world she wants to offer to her child: 'April snowdrop, Indian pipe' (line 5). The verb 'meditate' (to reflect upon, line 4) suggests that the child has not yet seen these beautiful flowers. The placing of the word 'Little' on its own in line 6 emphasises the smallness of the child. **For the mother, the child is her April snowdrop, the symbol of spring and new beginnings.**

Stanza 3

The child is also 'Little / Stalk without wrinkle' (lines 6–7) – delicate, young and unblemished like the flowers. Line 8 picks up on the imagery of reflection, which began with 'clear eye' in the opening line and continued in line 4 with 'meditate'. **Now the child's eye is a 'pool'. The mother thinks that 'grand and classical' images should fill it.** The image of a pool creates a different set of associations from the image of an eye: the world reflected in a pool is an unstable one that can quickly lose its shape and dissolve into formlessness.

Stanza 4

The final stanza gives us the image that fills the child's eye. It is a classic image of despair: the 'wringing of hands' (line 11). It symbolises the mother's anguish. Her anguish is intensified by her inability to give her child what she feels the child deserves. **The speaker is reduced to expressing her own anguish.** Her failure to fill the child's world with joy adds to her gloom: her world is now a 'dark / Ceiling without a star' (lines 11–12).

Interpreting the poem

It is difficult not to read this poem in the biographical context in which it was written – two weeks before Plath took her life. The poem presents a speaker who has lost confidence in her ability to create joy, a mother unable to escape her own anguish and despair, but anxious to spare her child the sight of it. She does not want the child's clear eye to witness the pain she endures, yet she lacks the strength and self-belief – not the humour, imagination or inventiveness – to make things otherwise.

Style and form of the poem

The poem is written in unrhymed, three-line stanzas. 'Child' is a testimony to Plath's skill and judgement as a poet. Every word is carefully chosen. The words 'Little' (line 6) and 'dark' (line 11), for example, are perfectly placed. The despair that underlies the poem is managed and controlled.

Thinking about the poem

1. 'The first line of the poem shows the mother's love for her child.' Do you agree? Explain your answer.
2. On the evidence of lines 2 and 3, what kind of world does the mother want to create for her child?
3. What is the effect of the flower names mentioned in the second stanza? Explain your answer.
4. What are the conditions in which the images in a pool might appear 'grand and classical' (line 9)? Do these conditions exist in the child's life?
5. What does stanza 4 tell us about the mother? What feeling does the mother have for her child? What feeling do you have for the mother?
6. 'This poem presents us with a picture of a woman who is deeply troubled.' Do you agree with this assessment of the poem? Explain your answer.
7. Which of the following statements is closest to your own view of the poem?

    It is a poem about love.

    It is a poem about despair.

    It is a poem about innocence.

    Explain your choice.

Taking a closer look

1. 'Your clear eye' (line 1). Comment on Plath's use of the adjective 'clear' at the beginning of the poem.
2. Comment on the use of the word 'zoo' (line 3) and the mood and ideas it generates.
3. Consider the phrase 'grand and classical' in line 9. Write a note on both words and the kind of images you associate with each.
4. Comment on the placing of the words 'Little' in line 6 and 'dark' in line 11.

Imagining

1. If you could write a letter to Sylvia Plath, after reading 'Child', what would you say to her?
2. What music would you select to accompany a reading of this poem? Explain your choice.

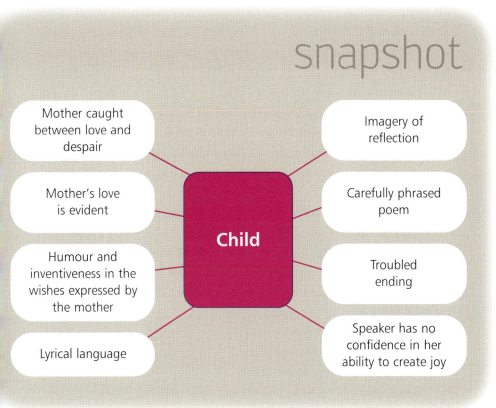

Exam-Style Questions

1. Give your personal response to the poetry of Sylvia Plath, describing the impact of the poems upon you. Support your answer by relevant quotation from the poems you have studied.

   Here are some possible areas that you might focus on in your answer:
   - Her themes, for example love and despair.
   - The anguished voice of some of her poems.
   - The startling imagery and symbolism employed in the poems.
   - Her skill as a poet.
   - The relationship between her life and her poetry.

2. What in your view are the emotions and the emotional experiences explored in Plath's poetry and how are these conveyed in the language and imagery of the poems? Support the points you make by quotation from the poems you have studied.

3. 'The poetic techniques employed by Plath succeed in making the world of her poetry a strange and terrifying one.' In the light of this statement, discuss the world of Plath's poetry. Support your answer by quotation from the poems you have studied.

4. 'Plath's poems make most sense when they are read as biographical.' Do you agree with this view of Plath's poetry? Explain your answer, supporting the points you make by quotation from the poetry by Plath on your course.

5. 'Death and annihilation are the themes that dominate Plath's poetry.' Is this an accurate assessment? Support your point of view by quotation from the poems you have studied.

6. 'Plath's poetry presents a vivid portrait of an individual whose life is tormented and anguished.' Do you agree with this reading of Plath's work? Support the points you make by quotation from the poems by Plath on your course.

7. Write an essay in which you outline your reasons for liking or not liking the poetry of Sylvia Plath. You must refer to the poems of Plath on your course.
Possible reasons for liking the poetry include:
- The uniqueness of the poetic voice.
- The striking imagery and symbolism.
- The vitality and energy of the writing.
- The exploration of emotions and extreme states of mind.
- The exploration of women's experiences.
- The impact of the poetry upon the reader.
- The variety of themes.
- Plath's skill as a poet.

Possible reasons for not liking the poetry include:
- The themes of isolation and estrangement.
- The cruelty of the world of many of the poems.
- The absence of happiness in many of the poems.
- The obscurity of the imagery.
- The troubled nature of the poetic persona.
- The complexity of the relationship explored in the poetry.
- The feeling of despair in many of the poems.
- The effect of the poems upon the reader.

8. 'The movement of Plath's poetry is from the outside world to the inner world, from landscape to mindscape.' Discuss this statement in relation to **two** of the poems by Plath on your course.

9. Select your favourite poems by Plath and explain what it is you admire about them. Support the points you make by quotation from the chosen poems.

10. 'In Plath's poetry, of course, this slightly old-fashioned point of view of the sanctity of domesticity is wedded to a tormented modern consciousness.' (Margaret Dickie)

'For all her harrowing and courageous record of suffering, Sylvia Plath died in the end because she could not sustain confidence in her true potentialities which could free her.' (David Holbrook)

Write an essay on Plath's poetry in support of **one** of the views above. Support the points you make by quotation from the poems you have studied.

Sample Essay

What in your view are the emotions and the emotional experiences explored in the poetry of Sylvia Plath and how are these conveyed in the language and imagery of the poems? Support the points you make by quotation from the poems you have studied.

Sylvia Plath's poetry is a poetry of emotional extremes and while there are moments of joy and optimism in her poems, the prevailing mood is dark and filled with fear, suffering and despair. The mood of her poetry is conveyed in dramatic monologues in which the speakers use memorable, haunting and sometimes terrifying imagery to convey their feelings.

[Opening paragraph sets up answer]

'Black Rook in Rainy Weather' was published during the time Plath spent in Cambridge as a student and probably captures the contrast between the sunny weather of Plath's Boston and the wet and dark atmosphere of autumn in England. The 'black' and 'rainy' adjectives of the title tell us all we need to know about the kind of experience that inspired the poem. However, the poem uses the dark colours of the bird and the gloomy atmosphere as symbols to represent the emotional mood of the speaker, the poetic persona of the poem. The landscape is described as 'dull, ruinous'. The autumn weather is now a 'season of fatigue' where the speaker is 'trekking stubborn'. The double consonant sounds and the long vowels capture the effort required by the speaker just to keep going. The speaker hopes for a break in the weather, for 'spasmodic tricks of radiance' that might give her 'A brief respite from fear / Of total neutrality'. Almost out of nowhere a poem that began by describing a bird in the rain gathers together all its imagery and poetic energy to announce its theme: the speaker's fear of a complete loss of identity. This theme runs through Plath's poetry and is expressed in striking imagery.

[Important theme introduced; first poem discussed]

Consider, for example, the museum imagery of 'Morning Song', where the newborn is described as a museum exhibit and the parents 'stand round blankly as walls'. The word 'blankly' is particularly striking. And it is immediately followed by the speaker of the poem announcing that she feels no more the mother of a child than a cloud is mother to a pool of water that shows the cloud 'its own slow / Effacement at the wind's hand.' As a reader, you want to shout 'Stop'. How can a poem that begins with the birth of a child move so quickly to the loss and disappearance of the mother? And while the poem ends on an optimistic note, it is the imagery of effacement and the word 'blankly' that stay in the mind.

[Reader response introduced; second poem discussed]

'Finisterre' is one of the few Plath poems that does not have a poetic persona or narrator and this results in the poem being less emotionally engaging than some of the others. However, what is clear is that the poem circles the theme of identity and fixed forms versus formlessness. The poem describes the statue of Our Lady of the Shipwrecked and says that 'She is in love with the beautiful formlessness of the sea'. It is a line that requires a bit of teasing out. What it seems to convey is an attraction to the loss of identity that was feared in the poems I have already discussed. The attraction is revealed in the long vowels and the soft sibilant sounds of the line, which reflect the seductive power of the formless sea. It is a dangerous form of seduction. This ambiguity towards annihilation becomes more pronounced in the poems that Plath wrote towards the end of her life.

[Third poem widens the discussion]

Of course, it is always dangerous to generalise about a poet's work, for as soon as we do, a poem appears that questions the validity of what we have claimed. Take, 'Pheasant', for example. The poem is brilliantly dramatic, with a woman pleading to a man to spare a pheasant he has threatened to kill. The basis of her plea is the definite shape and identity of the bird. Its solidity attracts her: 'it is such a good shape, so vivid.' And the poem itself is a good shape, written in carefully constructed three-line stanzas. The speaker sees the bird as belonging where it is. It is she who feels like a trespasser and pleads for the pheasant to be left alone: 'I trespass stupidly. Let be, let be.' Interestingly, the simplicity of the language indicates the heart-felt nature of the plea.

[Fourth poem introduced to show awareness of other aspects of the poet's work]

The repetition of 'Let be' at the end of the poem, suggests that the speaker is emotional and overwrought. The emotion is held in check by the tight structure of the poem. Certainly the speaker who addresses the poppies in 'Poppies in July' is anguished and emotional. The imagery is terrifying. The speaker sees the poppies as 'hell flames' and is disappointed that 'nothing burns' when she places her hands among them. The sinister, surreal imagery of the poem, conveys the distress of the speaker, who addresses the flowers as 'A mouth just bloodied' and 'Little bloody skirts'. Unable to feel pain or inflict harm upon herself, the speaker expresses a chilling wish for annihilation, where the fumes of the poppies would seep into her in her 'glass capsule' and dull and still her senses until life was drained of all its colour. The reference to a glass capsule suggests that the speaker feels trapped, and is so dissatisfied with life that death seems to be an attractive alternative to her current situation.

[Argument in new paragraph follows on from discussion in previous one; fifth poem discussed]

Of course at this stage the reader is asking, 'Why?' Why are the speakers in Plath's poems so fearful and afraid? Three poems offer two different answers. In 'Child', one of the last poems she completed before taking her own life, it is because the mother has lost confidence in herself and in her ability to create the kind of joyful world she would like for her child. She wants to fill her child's eye with 'The zoo of the new'. It is such a brilliant phrase – simple, zany, unforgettable. It shows a mother who is inventive and fun. But this is not enough for the speaker. She is anxious and in despair and does not want her child's 'clear eye' to witness her pain and distress. The speaker does not believe herself capable of being the mother she would like to be. It is such a sad poem.

[Sixth poem discussed; notice how short quotations are used throughout the answer]

In 'Elm', the speaker's terror is related to 'this dark thing / That sleeps in me.' This is the darkest imagery in all her poems, full of terror and self-hatred. The dark thing inside her is malignant and the poem concludes with an image of poisonous acids killing the self. The repetition of the verb 'kill' at the end of the poem suggests a frenzy of uncontrollable violence. This is a poem on the furthest edge of emotion and self-analysis.

[New paragraph continues the thread of argument running through the essay]

The idea of the uncontrollable violence and darkness that the speaker senses within herself is also evident in 'The Arrival of the Bee Box', where the bees represent a fascinating dark force that she senses within but which she does not understand. They speak in 'unintelligible syllables' and 'furious Latin'. The bees 'appal' her but she tells us that she 'can't keep away' from them. The box contains them but the speaker wants to see them free, even though she understands they could harm her, turn on her, just as the slow faults referred to in 'Elm' have the capacity to kill. However, 'The Arrival of the Bee Box' concludes with the speaker determined to release the bees. The last triumphant statement declares: 'The box is only temporary.' As a reader you fear for the safety of the speaker who would release such dark and dangerous things upon herself.

[Begins to draw entry to conclusion]

Reading the poetry of Sylvia Plath is to encounter a succession of speakers who live on the edge, who seem on the point of being overwhelmed by doubt and fear and a lack of belief. The wonder of the poetry is that out of such dark material Sylvia Plath makes such beautifully crafted poems. The tragedy for the poet was that, in her own life, she was not able to contain her personal fears within such tightly controlled structures.

[Strong conclusion]

snapshot

- Wrote all the poems within a period of seven years; died aged thirty
- Voice of the poems is sometimes anguished
- Writes about her life but no simple relationship between her life and her poetry
- Poems have a dreamlike or surreal quality
- Writes about the importance of love and motherhood
- Imagery influenced by the threat of nuclear warfare
- Writes about nature, the weather and children
- Images of entrapment and release
- Explores extreme emotions and extreme states of mind
- Poems carefully composed and beautifully phrased
- Poems are poised between celebration and despair

William Butler Yeats

1865–1939

THE LAKE ISLE OF INNISFREE
THE WILD SWANS AT COOLE*
AN IRISH AIRMAN FORESEES HIS DEATH*
SEPTEMBER 1913
EASTER 1916
THE SECOND COMING
SAILING TO BYZANTIUM
from MEDITATIONS IN TIME OF CIVIL WAR: VI:
THE STARE'S NEST BY MY WINDOW
IN MEMORY OF EVA GORE-BOOTH AND CON MARKIEWICZ
SWIFT'S EPITAPH
AN ACRE OF GRASS
POLITICS
from UNDER BEN BULBEN: V AND VI

Biography

William Butler Yeats was born on 13 June 1865 in Sandymount, Dublin. His father was the artist John Butler Yeats, his mother, Susan, was a member of a well-to-do Sligo merchant family. When Yeats was nine the family moved to London, where Yeats attended the Godolphin School, Hammersmith. In 1880 the family returned to Ireland and settled in Howth, where Yeats attended the High School in Dublin. He later studied at the College of Art in Dublin. Soon, however, his interest in art gave way to his enthusiasm for literature.

From his late teens he was writing poetry with the active encouragement of his father. Early in his career he began to explore mysticism and the occult, particularly Indian mysticism. This interest was to remain central to his outlook throughout his life. More significantly, however, he became active in helping to launch the movement known as the Irish Literary Renaissance, which saw a revival of interest in Ireland's literary heritage and was inspired by political and cultural nationalism.

In 1888 he met Maud Gonne, a committed Irish nationalist, whose influence on his personal life and work was to be considerable; she inspired his play *The Countess Kathleen* (1892) and a number of his great poems. He proposed marriage to her on several occasions. In 1896 he met Lady Augusta Gregory, the mistress of Coole Park estate in Co. Galway, where he composed many of his best poems, including the one that gives its name to his 1919 collection, *The Wild Swans at Coole*. In 1917 he bought an old Norman tower at Ballylee, close to Lady Gregory's house.

Yeats again proposed marriage to Maud Gonne following the execution of her husband, Major John MacBride, for his involvement in the 1916 Rising. Having been turned down by her, he proposed to her daughter, Iseult; again without success. In October 1917 another of his proposals of marriage was accepted by Georgie Hyde-Lees; he was fifty-two and she was twenty-five. The couple had two children: Anne, born in 1919, and Michael, born in 1921.

Following the establishment of the Irish Free State in 1922, Yeats took a lively interest in politics, becoming a member of the Irish Senate, and taking up such unpopular causes as divorce. In 1923 he was awarded the Nobel Prize for Literature. In the 1920s and 1930s he spent much of his time abroad, mainly for the sake of his health. He took a sympathetic interest in fascism during the 1930s, particularly in its Irish variety: the Blueshirt movement.

There is an important sense in which Yeats is the most remarkable of all poets who have written in English. There is no record in English literary history of another poet who produced his greatest work between the ages of fifty and seventy-four. Wordsworth represents the norm among poets in this regard: although he lived to be eighty, all his really significant work belongs to the first productive period of his life, between 1798 and 1810, that is before the age of forty. **In the case of Yeats, there is constant renewal, experimentation and utter dedication to the craft of poetry, leading to the ultimate command of words and images characteristic of his mature work.**

Yeats became seriously ill in France at the beginning of 1939 and died on 28 January of that year. He was buried in France, but in 1948 his body was taken to Drumcliffe Churchyard near Sligo.

Social and Cultural Context

Irish literary heritage

For convenience, Yeats's poetry is generally divided into three main phases. Only one of the poems in this anthology, 'The Lake Isle of Innisfree', belongs to the first phase, which extended from 1889 to 1909. Encouraged by the veteran Fenian John O'Leary, Yeats had broadened his knowledge of Irish history and folklore and during this phase his poetry is dominated by Celtic myths and motifs and much of it is escapist. During his visits to his uncle George Pollexfen in Sligo, he absorbed fairy lore and folk tales. He read, in translation, Irish legends such as the Cúchulainn saga and the stories of the Fianna, which inspired the poems in The Rose (1893), one of his early collections. The publication of The Wanderings of Oisin and Other Poems in 1889 established him as a literary figure. In the 1890s he was active in promoting the idea of a distinctively Irish literature for an Irish public.

Revolutionary Ireland

The transitional years, 1909 to 1914, represented in this anthology by 'September 1913', marked a change in Yeats's poetry, as well as in his life. **He gradually ceased to be a Romantic poet and his work became less decorative and musical, more harsh and realistic and, above all, more in tune with contemporary realities and public issues.** The Easter Rising of 1916 and the revolutionary turmoil that followed it had a profound effect on his mind and writings.

The 1916 Rising and the subsequent Irish Civil War inspired some of his finest poems. He invested these great and terrible public events and those who took part in them – such as Patrick Pearse, James Connolly, Maud Gonne, Countess Markiewicz, Kevin O'Higgins – with a mythic significance. In one of his Last Poems, called 'Beautiful Lofty Things', he shows how a commonplace, everyday happening can transform itself into an episode from a great personal mythology in which a woman he admires suddenly takes her place with great figures of ancient Greece:

> Maud Gonne at Howth Station waiting for a train
>
> Pallas Athene in that straight back and arrogant head
>
> All the Olympians, a thing never known again.

Political events in Ireland from 1916 onwards confronted Yeats with a series of acute personal dilemmas. On the one hand, his instinctive Irish nationalism responded with pride to the patriotic surge and heroic endeavour that inspired the 1916 Rising. On the other, he knew that triumphant nationalism was bound to destroy the Anglo-Irish civilisation that he regarded as the ideal embodiment of the aristocratic way of life. This explains the deep ambivalence that marks such poems as 'Easter 1916'.

Complex personal mythology

Yeats's great period dates from 1919 to the year of his death, 1939. This period witnessed the publication of his four outstanding books of poetry: The Wild Swans at Coole (1919), Michael Robartes and the Dancer (1921), The Tower (1928) and The Winding Stair (1933). The poems in these collections feature a comprehensive mythology of persons in which contemporaries who impressed Yeats appear larger than life. Yeats also draws from the great deposit of history and philosophy (the work of Plato and the art of the Byzantine empire) and universal symbolism (the tower, the moon and the swan, for example). The complex personal mythology behind these poems is elaborated at length in his prose work, A Vision (1925).

The Civil War led to Yeats's increasing disillusionment with Irish public life and caused him to question the patriotic, often fanatical, strivings of friends who had involved themselves in the nationalist cause. 'In Memory of Eva Gore-Booth and Con Markiewicz' is a splendid lament for the vanishing Anglo-Irish world and an exposure of the destructive effects of what Yeats regarded as misguided political activity on the minds and bodies of two once beautiful and elegant women.

The poetry written during the final twenty years of his life is notable for its vigorous rhythms within a generally plain, unornamented style with few adjectives and few, if any, of the luxuriant trappings of his earlier work. Even in his Last Poems (1939) Yeats retains his energy: the language and manner of 'An Acre of Grass' and 'Under Ben Bulben' are as emphatic as ever.

Timeline

1865	Born on 13 June in Sandymount, Dublin
1867	Moves to London
1880	Yeats family returns to Ireland
1884/5	Attends Metropolitan School of Art, Dublin
1886	Meets John O'Leary, mentioned in 'September 1913'
1889	Publishes *The Wanderings of Oisin and Other Poems*; meets Maud Gonne
1896	Meets Lady Gregory; meets John Millington Synge in Paris
1905	Abbey Theatre founded, with Yeats as a founder member
1917	Marries Georgie Hyde-Lees
1919	Birth of daughter, Anne; publishes *The Wild Swans at Coole*
1921	Birth of son, Michael; publishes *Michael Robartes and the Dancer*
1922	Made a senator
1923	Awarded the Nobel Prize for Literature
1928	Publishes *The Tower*
1933	Publishes *The Winding Stair*
1939	Dies at Cap Martin, France
1948	Body reinterred in Drumcliffe, Co. Sligo

The Lake Isle of Innisfree

I will arise and go now, and go to Innisfree,
And a small cabin build there, of clay and wattles made;
Nine bean-rows will I have there, a hive for the honey-bee,
And live alone in the bee-loud glade.

And I shall have some peace there, for peace comes dropping slow,   5
Dropping from the veils of the morning to where the cricket sings,
There midnight's all a glimmer, and noon a purple glow,
And evening full of the linnet's wings.

I will arise and go now, for always night and day
I hear lake water lapping with low sounds by the shore;   10
While I stand on the roadway, or on the pavements grey,
I hear it in the deep heart's core.

William Butler Yeats

Glossary	
title	*Innisfree:* an island in Lough Gill, Co. Sligo; the English version of the name of the island is derived from two Irish words: Inis (island) and fraoch (heather)
1	*I . . . now:* Yeats seems to have had the Gospel of Luke, chapter 15, verse 18 in mind: 'I will arise and go to my father', where the prodigal son in the parable wants to return home, just as the speaker in the poem does
2	*wattles:* flexible rods that can be interwoven and plastered with mud to form a building material
4	*glade:* open space in a wood
7	*Noon a purple glow:* heather grows profusely on the island and gives a purple glow to the light in the middle of the day
9	*always night and day:* an echo of the Gospel of Mark, chapter 5, verse 5: 'And always night and day, he was in the mountains'

Guidelines

Yeats wrote 'The Lake Isle of Innisfree' in London when he was twenty-five years of age. As he walked through Fleet Street, a fountain in a shop window reminded him of the sound of lake water and thus revived his dream of living alone on the island in Lough Gill, finding wisdom and peace in the tradition of the ancient hermits.

Commentary

The poem belongs to the Romantic phase of Yeats's early career, which was dominated by a quest for beauty in nature and in life. It celebrates a common and deep human impulse: the desire to find a way of escape from the sordid realities of city life into a pastoral Utopia where, free from care, the fortunate recluse can enjoy the simple, peaceful life amid the beauties of a natural landscape. **The attractions of the ideal island of Innisfree are heightened by the contrast with the drabness of London**, with its 'pavements grey' (line 11).

It is easy to see why this became one of Yeats's most popular poems and why it has remained so. It is pleasant, fluent, not particularly demanding and rich in texture. It is remarkable for its beauty of sound and its relaxed rhythms. **The movement, rhythm, repetition, alliteration and assonance combine to give the poem a soporific, dreamy quality, reminiscent of much Victorian escapist poetry in which ideal landscapes and states of living are evoked as alternatives to the unpleasantness of the real world.**

Thinking about the poem

1. Consider the poem as a pleasant piece of escapism. What does the speaker want to escape from?
2. The poem is remarkable for its beauty of sound and leisurely rhythms. How do such features help to convey the theme?
3. In what ways, do you think, might the kind of life imagined in the poem prove satisfactory? Would you enjoy the kind of life the speaker wants to create for himself?
4. This is perhaps the most popular of all Yeats's poems. Suggest possible reasons for this.
5. Over time, Yeats came to dislike the poem. Suggest reasons why.
6. In 'Sailing to Byzantium', Yeats imagines another ideal world. How do the two worlds compare? Which would you choose, and why?
7. Suggest an alternative title for the poem, and explain the reason or reasons for your choice.

8   Which of the following statements best describes your view of the speaker of the poem?
    The speaker is a wise man.
    The speaker is not a very practical man.
    The speaker shows good judgement.
    Explain your choice.
9   'In this poem, sound is more important than meaning.' Do you agree with this point of view? Give a reason for your opinion.

The Wild Swans at Coole

The trees are in their autumn beauty
The woodland paths are dry,
Under the October twilight the water
Mirrors a still sky;
Upon the brimming water among the stones   5
Are nine-and-fifty swans.

The nineteenth autumn has come upon me
Since I first made my count;
I saw, before I had well finished,
All suddenly mount   10
And scatter wheeling in great broken rings
Upon their clamorous wings.

I have looked upon those brilliant creatures,
And now my heart is sore.
All's changed since I, hearing at twilight,   15
The first time on this shore,
The bell-beat of their wings above my head,
Trod with a lighter tread.

Unwearied still, lover by lover,
They paddle in the cold   20
Companionable streams or climb the air;
Their hearts have not grown old;

Passion or conquest, wander where they will,
Attend upon them still.

But now they drift on the still water, 25
Mysterious, beautiful;
Among what rushes will they build,
By what lake's edge or pool
Delight men's eyes when I awake some day
To find they have flown away? 30

Glossary

12	*clamorous:* noisy
18	*Trod . . . tread:* walked with a lighter step

Guidelines

This is the title-poem of a collection first published in 1917, when Yeats was aged fifty-two and had become concerned about the exhausting effect of age on his imaginative powers. In the poem he reflects that he has been enjoying the beauty of the swans at Coole Park, the residence of his friend Lady Gregory, for nineteen years: his habit of counting them over that period reminds him of his own age. **Yeats is conscious of the gulf opening up between himself as the slave of time and timeless nature represented by the swans.** He ends the poem on a note of fear: one day the swans, which embody his creative relationship with nature, will have gone elsewhere, leaving him desolate.

Commentary

The poem is deeply symbolic. Like the subject of Keats's 'Ode to a Nightingale', Yeats's swans seem to defy time. They may age like the speaker, but they give the illusion of immortality. They are a Yeatsian symbol of eternity as they rise from the lake to wheel above him 'in great broken rings' (line 11).

The meaning of the poem depends to a large extent on the relationship the speaker establishes between the swans and himself. The speaker, conscious of his advancing age, looks at the fifty-nine swans. He has been counting these swans for nineteen years. Over all that time they, as if by a miracle, seem to have defied time ('Their hearts have not grown old', line 22). The speaker knows that individual swans are just as mortal as himself, but suggests they give the illusion of immortality: the pattern they establish survives.

Any interpretation of the poem must focus on the symbolism of the swans, without being over-precise about the meaning they generate. They anticipate the pattern of eternity as, before the speaker has finished counting them, they rise from the lake to wheel above him. They link the 'still water' (line 25) to the 'still sky' (line 4) that is mirrored in it. Unlike people, they are able to live in two elements: air and water. More importantly, they are able to live (in the symbolic sense created by the poem) on earth as well as in eternity. They are mortal – 'lover by lover' – and yet give the impression of immortality – 'Unwearied still' (line 19).

Throughout the poem, we are conscious of **the contrast between the speaker's sense of his own mortality and the perpetual youth and vitality enjoyed by the swans**. In stanza 2, for example, the swans resist the speaker's attempt to define them in terms of their number and to make them finite beings; instead, they assert their independence in a ritual flight symbolising their freedom from the constraints of time: 'All suddenly mount / And scatter wheeling in great broken rings' (lines 10–11).

The emphasis of the third stanza is on the changeless character of the swans and the all too evident decline in the speaker's vitality, which their animated movements underline for him. The speaker's response to the contrast between his sense of mortality and the ageless vitality of the swans is a self-regarding sorrow: his 'heart is sore' (line 14). By the end of the poem, however, he has come to terms with his own ageing and the eternity symbolised by the swans, who are outside time.

The final stanza raises complex questions, suggested in the speaker's description of the swans as 'mysterious' (line 26). The contemplation of these mysterious creatures leads him to wonder where they will be, to delight men's eyes, when some day he finds 'they have flown away' (line 30). The expression 'when I awake some day' in line 29 cannot be taken literally. The speaker is not simply saying that some day he will awake to find that the swans have gone. The question then arises: what kind of awakening is he describing? Is he talking about awakening into death to find that the pattern of immortality represented by the swans has vanished, as he himself has become immortal?

Or, given that the swans symbolise youthfulness, is he saying that their eventual flight from his life will signal his decline into old age and approaching death?

The poem's references to autumn and the passage of time ('The nineteenth autumn has come upon me', line 7) may suggest that the swans represent his passionate youth, or at least mirror that part of his past. The final stanza may, in the light of this, imply that when the speaker is old, perhaps dead (having awakened in eternity), the swans will delight other men in other places who enjoy the youth and passion that he has lost. Lines 23 and 24 suggest that the 'passion or conquest' associated with youth and vitality are an intimate part of their significance, that wherever they wander, these 'Attend upon them still'. Those human beings whose youth makes them capable of passion or conquest will always ('still') find in the swans a symbolic representation of their feelings and impulses.

Different interpretations

The poem ends on the optimistic notion that the swans will always be symbols of beauty, love, youth and vitality. The poet finally comes to terms with the swans' freedom and with his own ageing. This reading is not universally accepted. Some interpreters see the poem as ending on a note of pessimism, and expressing the fear that the day will come when the swans, symbolising the speaker's creative relationship with nature, will desert him, leaving him bereft of inspiration and creativity.

Thinking about the poem

1. The autumn setting is important. Why?
2. What does the counting of the swans signify?
3. What meaning do the swans have for the speaker?
4. The poem is partly based on a contrast between the speaker and the swans. What is this contrast? Mention some other contrasts in the poem.
5. Why is the speaker troubled as he contemplates the swans?
6. Does the speaker have reason to envy the swans?
7. Describe the impression the poem has made on you.
8. Choose your favourite image from the poem, and explain why you have chosen it.
9. There are changes in the poet's feeling and attitude in the course of the poem. Describe these changes.
10. Yeats explained that lonely birds such as the heron, hawk, eagle and swan are the natural symbols of subjectivity. In 'The Wild Swans at Coole', do the swans symbolise other things?

Taking a closer look

1. Is the poem more about the speaker than about the swans? Explain your answer.
2. In what sense is this poem about time and eternity?
3. Is the ending of the poem hopeful or sad? Explain your answer.
4. What impression of the speaker do you get from reading this poem?
5. This is a great descriptive poem. Choose **two** descriptions that appeal to you, and give reasons for your choice.

Imagining

1. Write a response to a landscape you are familiar with, emphasising its features and what they mean to you.
2. You have been asked to make a short film to accompany a reading of this poem. Say how you would use music, sound effects, colour, images, etc. to convey the atmosphere of the lake.

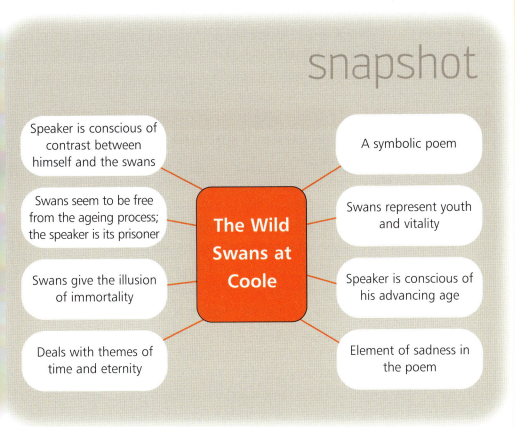

snapshot

The Wild Swans at Coole

- Speaker is conscious of contrast between himself and the swans
- Swans seem to be free from the ageing process; the speaker is its prisoner
- Swans give the illusion of immortality
- Deals with themes of time and eternity
- A symbolic poem
- Swans represent youth and vitality
- Speaker is conscious of his advancing age
- Element of sadness in the poem

An Irish Airman Foresees His Death

I know that I shall meet my fate
Somewhere among the clouds above;
Those that I fight I do not hate,
Those that I guard I do not love;
My country is Kiltartan Cross,   5
My countrymen Kiltartan's poor,
No likely end could bring them loss
Or leave them happier than before.
Nor law, nor duty bade me fight,
Nor public men, nor cheering crowds,   10
A lonely impulse of delight
Drove to this tumult in the clouds;
I balanced all, brought all to mind,
The years to come seemed waste of breath,
A waste of breath the years behind   15
In balance with this life, this death.

Glossary	
title	*Irish Airman:* the subject of this poem is Major Robert Gregory (1881–1918), the only child of Lady Gregory
1–2	*I know . . . above:* Yeats makes Gregory 'know' what the future holds for him. To understand this we have to bear in mind that Gregory was reputed to possess psychic second sight, which gave him a premonition of death; Yeats believed that people could possess this faculty, and admired it
4	*Those . . . I guard:* the Allied peoples in World War 1
5–6	*My country . . . poor:* the Gregorys lived on the Coole Park estate, Kiltartan, Co. Galway; Kiltartan Cross is a few miles from Coole
7	*end:* result of the war
9	*Nor . . . fight:* I enlisted neither because I was legally compelled to do so, nor out of a sense of patriotic duty
10	*public men:* politicians whose warlike oratory encouraged young men to fight
11	*lonely impulse:* his impulse to join in the fight is lonely because it comes from within himself; he will choose a hero's death in a war that is otherwise without meaning for him.

Guidelines

This poem is part of Yeats's 1919 volume, *The Wild Swans at Coole*. Its subject is Major Robert Gregory, the only son of Lady Gregory. Like his mother, Robert had been extremely close to Yeats. He learned Irish at Coole, his mother's home, and was a stage designer for Yeats at the Abbey Theatre in Dublin. An accomplished artist, he became a member of the Royal Flying Corps during World War 1. In January 1918 he was shot down as he returned to base in northern Italy.

Commentary

The sixteen lines of this poem are not a conventional lament for a dear friend, but a presentation, or definition, of Gregory as the perfect man of Yeats's imagination.

Lines 1–8

From Yeats's point of view, the quality that best defined the perfect man was balance, and this quality is central to his presentation of Gregory. From his lofty position in the clouds, Gregory is able to view the war with detachment and poise. He is not motivated to fight by partisan political emotions: he neither hates the Germans nor loves the Allies (lines 3–4). He balances the future prospects of his poor countrymen living on or near his family estate at Kiltartan, Co. Galway, against the outcome of the war, concluding that, regardless of the war's outcome, they will neither lose nor gain (lines 7–8).

Lines 9–16

Gregory's detachment is further shown in his indifference to the cheering crowds encouraging men such as himself to go to war and to the warlike speeches of politicians (line 10). Instead, he is able to resolve the tensions of his life by finding fulfilment in the 'tumult in the clouds' (line 12), which will inevitably lead to his extinction. There is a sense in which Yeats presents the war purely as an opportunity for Gregory to gratify his impulse and to resolve his personal problems. Yeats sees Gregory as a man fated to find his ultimate delight in the experience of death in life. Given his hero's impulse to balance 'all' at the expense of life itself, it is appropriate that Yeats should ask in another poem, 'In Memory of Major Robert Gregory': 'What made us dream that he could comb grey hair?'

The structural impulse behind the poem is indicated in line 13: 'I balanced all, brought all to mind'. **Yeats makes his speaker take a balanced, unemotional view of his involvement in the war.** This involvement is explained in lines 9 to 12, which are all the more remarkable when we consider the historical background against which they were written. Young men went to war because they were conscripted (by 'law') or because they saw it as their 'duty' to fight for their country. Alternatively, many of them were caught up in a patriotic surge, created by the passionate speeches of politicians ('public men'), who had launched the war and were willing to sacrifice the youth of all nations to keep it going. This patriotic nationalism was further inflamed by the multitudes who cheered the doomed young men on to their deaths.

The speaker of Yeats's poem is unmoved by the emotions generated by the public rhetoric of war and the mass hysteria of patriotic crowds. These themes were rehearsed in innumerable war poems – many poets were prepared to debase their art in the service of propaganda by supplying recruiting verses to correspond to the government's recruiting posters. Most of the pro-war poetry is simple-minded in the extreme. The following from 'To You Who Have Lost' in John Oxenham's All's Well: Some Helpful Verse for these Dark Days of War is typical:

> He died as a few men get the chance to die –
> Fighting to save a world's morality.
> He died the noblest death a man may die,
> Fighting for God, and Right, and Liberty –
> And such a death is Immortality.

The speaker's participation in the war has nothing to do with such impulses, or with a belief in whatever goal the war was supposed to achieve, or with the notion that one side was right and the other wrong. He is above and beyond such absurd oppositions.

The war has, however, a purpose for the speaker. It gives him a splendid opportunity to resolve his own tensions, to live with the utmost intensity and to experience the paradox of death in life, which will give him his greatest fulfilment. His decision to fight, and die, in the skies is made coldly, rationally and without passion. Yeats makes Gregory see life and death as equivalent to each other: he will find his life's meaning in the manner of his death (line 16). His experience of death will not, however, be without passion: it will involve both 'delight' (line 11) and 'tumult' (line 12). **Gregory thus becomes the kind of man Yeats most admired: one who can combine passion and detachment, joy and loneliness.**

Second thoughts

Yeats wrote a sequel to 'An Irish Airman Foresees His Death' in 1921, but the sequel, 'Reprisals', was suppressed until 1948, nine years after Yeats's death, for fear of offending the Gregory family. 'Reprisals' was written during the Irish War of Independence, when British soldiers were shooting tenants on the Gregory estate. Yeats imagined Robert Gregory's ghost visiting Kiltartan, bitterly contemplating what the soldiers of the country he had fought for are now doing to his own people. Yeats addresses Gregory's ghost:

> Yet rise from your Italian tomb,
>
> Flit to Kiltartan Cross and stay
>
> Till certain second thoughts have come
>
> Upon the cause you served, that we
>
> Imagined such a fine affair:
>
> Half-drunk or whole-mad soldiery
>
> Are murdering your tenants there.
>
> Men that revere your father yet
>
> Are shot at on the open plain.
>
> Then close your ears with dust and lie
>
> Among the other cheated dead.

Thinking about the poem

1. Describe the speaker's attitude to the war. Does he think it is worthwhile?
2. Consider the idea of balance as central to the poem.
3. Yeats greatly admired Major Robert Gregory, the subject of the poem. Does the poem suggest why?
4. Does the speaker emerge as a self-centred, even selfish man? Give reasons for your answer.
5. Does the poem give the impression of a man who feels superior to those around him? Give reasons for your answer.
6. How would you describe the tone of the poem?
7. How would you describe the language of the poem?
8. Might the poem be described as an anti-war poem? Give reasons for your answer.
9. Write a short piece outlining your response to the poem and its speaker.
10. Given his attitude to the parties fighting the war, was the speaker justified in becoming involved? Give reasons for your answer.

Taking a closer look

1. Is the speaker's military mission an escape from solitude? Explain your answer.
2. Select **two** details from the poem that capture the personality of the speaker.
3. What is the speaker's attitude to death?
4. What, in your opinion, is the significance of 'An Irish Airman' in the title of the poem?

Imagining

1. Imagine that you are a newspaper reporter. Using details from the poem, write a brief account of the airman's approach to life and death, as if you had interviewed him.
2. Imagine that you are one of those who took part in the war. Explain your motives for doing so.

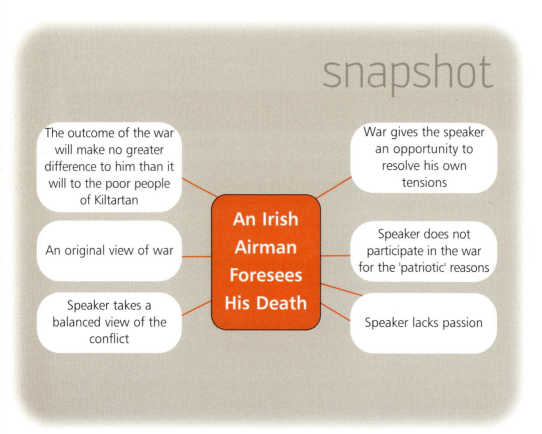

September 1913

What need you, being come to sense,
But fumble in a greasy till
And add the halfpence to the pence
And prayer to shivering prayer, until
You have dried the marrow from the bone?   5
For men were born to pray and save:
Romantic Ireland's dead and gone,
It's with O'Leary in the grave.

Yet they were of a different kind,
The names that stilled your childish play,   10
They have gone about the world like wind,
But little time had they to pray
For whom the hangman's rope was spun,
And what, God help us, could they save?
Romantic Ireland's dead and gone,   15
It's with O'Leary in the grave.

Was it for this the wild geese spread
The grey wing upon every tide;
For this that all that blood was shed,
For this Edward Fitzgerald died,   20
And Robert Emmet and Wolfe Tone,
All that delirium of the brave?
Romantic Ireland's dead and gone,
It's with O'Leary in the grave.

Yet could we turn the years again,   25
And call those exiles as they were
In all their loneliness and pain,
You'd cry, 'Some woman's yellow hair
Has maddened every mother's son':
They weighed so lightly what they gave.   30
But let them be, they're dead and gone,
They're with O'Leary in the grave.

Glossary

1	*you:*	the Irish merchant and business classes of the early twentieth century
5	*dried . . . bone:*	lost all human feeling, allowed emotion to wither
8	*O'Leary:*	John O'Leary (1830–1907), a Fenian veteran whose devotion to Irish independence forced him into exile in France, where Yeats came to know him
9	*they:*	self-sacrificing Irish patriots
17	*wild geese:*	Irish soldiers who served in foreign armies in the seventeenth and eighteenth centuries; these included such patriotic leaders as Patrick Sarsfield
20	*Edward Fitzgerald:*	(1763–98) Lord Edward Fitzgerald took part in the 1798 Rebellion; he died of wounds sustained while he was being arrested for treason
21	*Robert Emmet:*	(1778–1803) Irish revolutionary who spent his personal fortune on weapons to be used against the British government in Ireland; he was hanged in September 1803 following the failure of the rising he led
21	*Wolfe Tone:*	(1763–98) Theobald Wolfe Tone organised a French military expedition to Ireland in support of a planned revolution; he was captured, tried and condemned to death as a traitor, but committed suicide in prison while waiting to be hanged. Line 13 ('For whom the hangman's rope was spun') is especially appropriate to Tone, as well as to Emmet

Guidelines

An angry speaker is addressing people he dislikes. These are middle-class Irish merchants, whose lives, he suggests, are focused on two occupations: praying and saving. They have no love for their country and have made Ireland a selfish, materialistic society. As always with Yeats, there is a contrast. This is provided by the unselfish, patriotic heroes of the past, who were prepared to die for the freedom of their country. The speaker recognises that these past idealists would be regarded by leaders of modern opinion as foolish, even mad, and best forgotten.

Commentary

Stanza 1

The central impulse behind the poem is the disparagement of the present by setting it in opposition to a romanticised past. The 'you' of line 1 is the group to whom the poem is mockingly and ironically addressed: the nationalist merchant class, characterised here by the qualities of religious devotion and attachment to money. The speaker is asking the people he despises, 'What more do you need than to spend your time praying and saving, and so dehumanising yourselves? What else, after all, were men born for?' The rhetoric is all the more effective for its vivid, concrete imagery. The image of the merchant fumbling 'in a greasy till' (line 2) conveys just the right note of contempt for the whole class he represents, making its activities appear sordid, mean and squalid.

Refrain

Against this presentation of crass materialism allied to debased religious practice, **the speaker offers a nobler vision of Ireland represented by the Fenian John O'Leary, who had a vital influence on Irish cultural nationalism.** When Yeats first met him, O'Leary was a venerable Fenian. He had served five years in prison and fifteen years in exile in Paris. He introduced Yeats to the work of such Irish nationalist poets as Thomas Davis and James Clarence Mangan. In Yeats's personal mythology, O'Leary represented all that was finest and most idealistic in the Irish poetic tradition. In the scheme of the poem, the tradition represented by the dead O'Leary belongs to a vanished age.

Stanzas 2 and 3

The 'they' at the beginning of Stanza 2 are the patriots of the heroic past, whose mere names are enough to bring the play of children to a halt, and who are universally honoured. Line 12 ('But little time had they to pray') and line 14 ('And what, God help us, could they save?') contrast sharply with the preoccupations of the speaker's contemporaries described in stanza 1. The 'this' of line 17 is contemporary Ireland with all its imperfections. The 'wild geese' were the Irish soldiers who served in the armies of Europe after the Treaty of Limerick in 1691. The speaker wonders whether their sacrifice, or the sacrificial deaths of Fitzgerald, Emmet and Tone, were worthwhile if the only result is a nation of prayerful materialists.

His choice of models of Irish patriotism, apart from O'Leary, is significant. The three he mentions in lines 20 and 21 – Fitzgerald, Emmet and Tone – were all members of the Anglo-Irish Protestant Ascendancy, a class to which Yeats was proud to belong.

The phrase 'delirium of the brave' (line 22) is not intended to suggest that the Irish heroes of the past were delirious, but that their sacrifice was emotional and instinctive rather than calculating and rational. Had they been rational they would, presumably, have prayed and saved like merchants: instead, they gave their lives for a dream.

Stanza 4

The ironic tone persists in the final stanza. Yeats is imagining a return to life of the heroic dead to confront the unheroic living, who would probably dismiss the sacrifices of the past as mere madness, inspired by romantic love for a woman (or for Ireland in the traditional guise of a woman). The calculating merchants who now hold sway would find the activities of patriotic Irishmen ridiculous because they gave everything they had without counting the cost. The final two lines set a seal on the mocking irony to which Yeats has exposed his contemporaries throughout the poem. The speaker imagines his merchants thinking that past heroes are best forgotten since they are safely dead and buried with O'Leary.

Dispiriting vision

'September 1913' offers a dispiriting vision of an Ireland lacking in spiritual values, 'a little greasy huxtering nation groping for halfpence in a greasy till', as Yeats expressed it elsewhere. The poem is a rousing celebration of past patriotic glory, but it also reflects Yeats's strong anti-democratic feelings, his elitist view of Irish history and his lack of faith in the possibility of a wise and civilised democratic government. Less than three years later, in 'Easter 1916', he was to discover and record a more optimistic vision of Ireland.

Thinking about the poem

1. There is a clear contrast in the poem between past and present. Show how Yeats manages this contrast. Mention other contrasts in the poem.
2. Irony plays a significant part in the poem with one thing being said but another meant. Give examples of this feature. Is it effective?
3. How does Yeats convey the modern absence of human feelings and idealism?
4. Does Yeats present an ideal for his readers' approval? If so, how can it be described?
5. What does 'Romantic Ireland' mean in the context of this poem?
6. Does the poem have a significance for the Ireland of the present day? Are the issues it raises of interest to you?
7. Do you think that the patriots mentioned in the poem were fools? Did the poet think so?
8. Yeats lists a number of patriots in the poem. What did they have in common?
9. There is a suggestion in the poem that extreme patriotism might be seen as a form of madness. Do you think that the poet agrees with this view? Explain your answer with reference to the poem.
10. Comment on the reference to 'Some woman's yellow hair' (line 28). Who do you think the woman might be?

Easter 1916

I have met them at close of day
Coming with vivid faces
From counter or desk among grey
Eighteenth-century houses.
I have passed with a nod of the head
Or polite meaningless words,
Or have lingered awhile and said
Polite meaningless words,
And thought before I had done
Of a mocking tale or a gibe
To please a companion
Around the fire at the club,
Being certain that they and I
But lived where motley is worn:
All changed, changed utterly:
A terrible beauty is born.

That woman's days were spent
In ignorant good-will,
Her nights in argument
Until her voice grew shrill.
What voice more sweet than hers
When, young and beautiful,
She rode to harriers?
This man had kept a school
And rode our winged horse:
This other his helper and friend
Was coming into his force;
He might have won fame in the end,
So sensitive his nature seemed,
So daring and sweet his thought.
This other man I had dreamed
A drunken, vainglorious lout.
He had done most bitter wrong

To some who are near my heart.
Yet I number him in the song;
He, too, has resigned his part.
In the casual comedy;
He, too, has been changed in his turn,
Transformed utterly:
A terrible beauty is born.

Hearts with one purpose alone
Through summer and winter seem
Enchanted to stone
To trouble the living stream.
The horse that comes from the road,
The rider, the birds that range
From cloud to tumbling cloud,
Minute by minute they change;
A shadow of cloud on the stream
Changes minute by minute;
A horse-hoof slides on the brim,
And a horse plashes within it;
The long-legged moor-hens dive,
And hens to moor-hens call;
Minute by minute they live:
The stone's in the midst of all.

Too long a sacrifice
Can make a stone of the heart.
O when may it suffice?
That is Heaven's part, our part
To murmur name upon name,
As a mother names her child
When sleep at last has come
On limbs that had run wild,
What is it but nightfall?
No, no, not night but death;
Was it needless death after all?
For England may keep faith

For all that is done and said.
We know their dream; enough 70
To know they dreamed and are dead;
And what if excess of love
Bewildered them till they died?
I write it out in a verse –
MacDonagh and MacBride 75
And Connolly and Pearse,
Now and in time to be,
Whenever green is worn,
Are changed, changed utterly:
A terrible beauty is born. 80

Glossary		
	1	*them:* the people who secretly planned the 1916 Rising
	4	*Eighteenth-century houses:* many of the houses in central Dublin date to the Georgian era (1714–1830) when the city experienced rapid growth
	14	*motley:* the dress of the fool in a play
	17	*That woman:* Constance Markiewicz (1868–1927), one of the daughters of the Gore-Booth family of Lissadell House, Co. Sligo, and a Volunteer officer during the 1916 Rising (see also 'In Memory of Eva Gore-Booth and Con Markiewicz')
	24	*This man:* Patrick Pearse (1879–1916), schoolmaster, lawyer and poet, President of the Republic declared in 1916, who was executed as a leader of the Rising
	24	*a school:* St Enda's in Rathfarnham, Dublin, where the pupils were taught to value their Gaelic heritage
	25	*winged horse:* Pegasus, traditionally associated with poetic inspiration
	26	*This other:* Thomas MacDonagh (1878–1916), poet, teacher, dramatist and critic, who was executed as a leader of the Rising
	31	*This other man:* Major John MacBride (1868–1916), estranged husband of Yeats's muse Maud Gonne; he was executed for taking part in the Rising
	76	*Connolly:* James Connolly (1870–1916), whose Citizen Army, the military force of the labour movement, took part in the 1916 Rising; although severely wounded, he was executed as a leader of the Rising

Guidelines

The subject of this poem is the Easter Rising of 1916, the central event in twentieth-century Irish history, whose consequences are still felt. On 24 April 1916 a small group of Irish republicans occupied buildings in the centre of Dublin and their leaders proclaimed an Irish Republic. The Rising collapsed within a week and its leaders were executed by firing squad. Their idealism, bravery and chivalry impressed even their enemies. They were soon seen as martyrs and as heroic champions of the cause of Irish freedom.

Yeats was with Maud Gonne in France when he heard the news, and was at first shocked, believing that what the patriots had died for might be conceded peacefully by the British. Against this, he acknowledged that Maud Gonne might have been justified in arguing that with the Rising, in which her estranged husband died, 'tragic dignity has returned to Ireland', an idea expressed in the poem's most memorable line, 'A terrible beauty is born'. The Rising, which he saw as a tragic drama, moved Yeats as no other public event ever did. The first manuscript of the poem is dated 25 September 1916.

'Easter 1916' may be read as a retraction of the more cynical view of Irish public life expressed in 'September 1913'. Maud Gonne recalled that when Yeats read the newly composed 'Easter 1916' to her in France, he urged her to abandon her patriotic intensity, imploring her 'to forget the stone and its inner fire for the flashing, changing joy of life'. See lines 41 to 56 of the poem for the context of Yeats's plea.

Commentary

Like 'September 1913', this poem is based on contrast and antithesis (a balancing of opposing ideas). **The central antithesis is between the speaker's attitude to the people who were secretly planning the 1916 Rising and his attitude to the same people after they had displayed an unexpected heroism and become nationalist martyrs.**

Stanza 1

Yeats evokes the spirit of pre-revolutionary Ireland, when he could detect no serious commitment to patriotism, which seemed a matter of show rather than substance. Before 1916, he could not take either the patriots or their cause seriously, as the first fourteen lines make clear. They seemed to be merely posing as revolutionaries. He characterises their seemingly ineffectual activities as no more significant than those of well-meaning patriots who might dress in bright colourful costumes for a pageant, the 'motley' of line 14 being the multi-coloured dress of a clown or the fool in a play, a way of suggesting that the planners of revolution were merely playing at it, without any real intention of carrying it out. He had even thought of making fun of them with his sophisticated friends at the gentleman's club to which he belonged.

Refrain

'Easter 1916' is a profoundly ambiguous poem as suggested by the refrain in three of the four stanzas: 'A terrible beauty is born'. The poem is not a single-minded celebration of what the leaders of the Rising have done. The key phrase 'terrible beauty' suggests that the beauty of what has been achieved has been purchased at the expense of life. The patriots have transcended the changing world, but only by making themselves immune from normal human impulses; their concentration on 'one purpose alone' (line 41) has turned their hearts to stone.

Stanza 2

The second stanza is a catalogue of the revolutionary men and women the speaker had so seriously undervalued in the years before the Rising. His presentation of the first of these, his friend Countess Markiewicz, is based on an antithesis: Yeats contrasts her younger days as a beautiful aristocratic woman of leisure with her later ones as a fanatical nationalist. The revolutionary countess had allowed her voice to become shrill in political argument, thus becoming a different, and less attractive, person from her earlier self who enjoyed aristocratic sports and had a sweet voice. There is loss and gain: her earlier good will was 'ignorant', but her later patriotism involves a coarsening of voice and appearance. The speaker next introduces two men: Patrick Pearse and Thomas MacDonagh, both of them teachers and poets. MacDonagh, as the speaker remarks with some regret, had the qualities of mind and imagination that might have brought him fame as a writer had he lived. The speaker's fourth figure is quite different. He is Major John MacBride, the husband of Maud Gonne, the woman Yeats loved in vain. He is characterised as a drunken, boastful lout who had wronged people whom Yeats holds dear.

In lines 36 to 41, these four figures are considered as characters in a drama, with the speaker returning to the earlier suggestion that before 1916 they had been acting out trivial parts in the play of life. Now, as he recognises, they have 'resigned' the parts assigned to them in 'the casual comedy' and transformed themselves into noble, beautiful actors in a new drama. This new drama is tragic rather than comic – it is the drama of violent, redemptive revolution leading to the deaths of all but the Countess. No longer half-hearted or faintly ridiculous casual patriots, they became noble, tragic participants, terrible and violent but beautiful in their self-sacrifice. The Rising is characterised by the speaker as 'terrible' as well as beautiful, since it involves great loss and waste as well as the regeneration of Ireland's soul.

In the first two stanzas, the idea of change has been dominant. The change in question is also one affecting the speaker: his perception of the participants in the Rising has changed. Yeats must even revise his opinion of his rival MacBride, whose sacrifice of his life in the cause of the Republic is evidence of his commitment and genuine patriotism.

Stanzas 3 and 4

The notion of change (or the appearance of change) gives way in stanza 3 to its opposite: the unchanging reality of patriotic devotion. The patriots of the poem have dedicated themselves exclusively and obsessively to the cause of Irish freedom. The price of this is that they become stone-hearted, devoid of everyday human emotion. The relation of the 1916 martyrs to the world around them is conveyed in the images of the stream and the stone.

The stone in the midst of the flowing stream is a powerfully effective image: the patriots remain unchanging, inflexible, immovable in a world of contrast and change. Pearse and his followers have turned their backs on life (the stone is a dead thing) in their fanatical concentration on a single cause. These lines are based on a powerful contrast between the constantly changing face of nature in a world of flux (whose image is the 'living stream', line 44) and the obsessive resistance to change that characterises the patriots, whose hearts, 'with one purpose alone' (line 41), are the only fixed objects.

The onward movement of daily life, in which all things alter from minute to minute, is the living stream, around and in which the rider and his horse, the birds, the cloud, the moor-hens and moor-cocks are part of a constant process of change. The stone stands firm in the midst of all this movement, to trouble and challenge it, as the patriotic rebels confront the changes and compromises of their world with their inflexible principles. This inflexibility exacts a terrible price: 'Minute by minute they live: / The stone's in the midst of all' (lines 55–56). The stone is a dead thing in the midst of the living things around it. This idea is clarified in the following lines. The heroic dreams of the patriots have deprived them of life. The metaphor becomes a reality: they are as dead as stones as a result of their inflexible heroism: 'Too long a sacrifice / Can make a stone of the heart' (lines 57–58).

The third stanza is a celebration of the joy of life to which the patriots have deliberately blinded themselves and makes us wonder whether they sacrificed too much. The speaker raises a more disturbing question in lines 67 to 69: 'Was it needless death after all? / For England may keep faith / For all that is done and said'. The 1916 patriots, in other words, may have wasted their lives in the cause of Irish independence, something the speaker suggests might have been granted by England in any case, even had there been no 1916

Rising. Yeats is here referring to the belief at the time that the British authorities would soon give Ireland a measure of freedom, as promised in the Home Rule Bill.

Yeats's speaker retains an impersonal attitude and refuses to pass judgement on the prudence or otherwise of what the rebels have done, preferring to leave this to the deeper wisdom of providence ('That is Heaven's part', line 60). The speaker is content to assume the role of chorus: 'To murmur name upon name, / As a mother names her child' (lines 61–62).

Thinking about the poem

1. Two worlds clash in 'Easter 1916'. Describe these two worlds. In what ways do they clash?
2. Discuss Yeats's evolving attitudes to the people who participated in the 1916 Rising.
3. Yeats expresses reservations about the people who sacrificed their lives in the Rising. What are these reservations? How does he express them?
4. Comment on the symbols used in the poem (the stone and the stream, for example). Consider the function of these symbols. How do they contribute to the meaning of the poem?
5. Having read the poem carefully, do you get the impression that Yeats, on the whole, approves of the Rising? Is 'Easter 1916' a patriotic poem? Explain your answer.
6. The poem has many striking images. Choose **two** of these and explain how they contribute to the effect of the poem.
7. What kind of person is the speaker of the poem? Support your answer with reference to **three** phrases or lines from the poem.
8. Consider the relationship between 'Easter 1916' and some of Yeats's other 'political' poems, such as 'September 1913', 'The Stare's Nest by My Window', 'In Memory of Eva Gore-Booth and Con Markiewicz'. Outline some resemblances and differences of outlook and treatment of political issues in these.
9. 'Easter 1916' and 'An Irish Airman Foresees His Death' both deal with war. Are the attitudes expressed in both similar or are there differences?
10. "Easter 1916" offers a balanced view of the Rising and of those who participated in it.' Would you agree with this verdict on the poem? Explain your answer.
11. Why does Yeats repeat the notion that the Rising has given birth to 'a terrible beauty'? What does this beauty consist of? How can it be described as 'terrible'?
12. In the last stanza the poet raises a number of questions. What are these questions and what do they suggest about his attitude to his theme?

The Second Coming

Turning and turning in the widening gyre
The falcon cannot hear the falconer;
Things fall apart; the centre cannot hold;
Mere anarchy is loosed upon the world,
The blood-dimmed tide is loosed, and everywhere   5
The ceremony of innocence is drowned;
The best lack all conviction while the worst
Are full of passionate intensity,

Surely some revelation is at hand:
Surely the Second Coming is at hand,   10
The Second Coming! Hardly are the words out
When a vast image out of Spiritus Mundi
Troubles my sight: somewhere in sands of the desert
A shape with lion body and the head of a man,
A gaze blank and pitiless as the sun,   15
Is moving its slow thighs, while all about it
Reel shadows of the indignant desert birds.
The darkness drops again; but now I know
That twenty centuries of stony sleep
Were vexed to nightmare by a rocking cradle   20
And what rough beast, its hour come round at last,
Slouches towards Bethlehem to be born?

Glossary

title	*The Second Coming:* here Yeats combines two elements of Christian scripture: the Second Coming of Christ to judge humankind on the Day of Judgement, and the coming of the Antichrist, foretold in the Apocalypse	
1	*gyre:* in Yeats's mythology, gyres are conical spirals of history through which events and people move; he saw history in terms of cycles, each lasting for two thousand years, and this poem visualises the destruction of the two-thousand-year Christian cycle	
5	*blood-dimmed tide:* bloody wars	
10	*Second Coming:* not the coming of Christ but of His opposite, the Antichrist	
12	*Spiritus Mundi (Spirit of the World):* a storehouse or reservoir of images built up in the course of human history; such images can have a universal meaning	
14–16	*shape . . . thighs:* the Sphinx-like beast represents the horrors to come	

Guidelines

This prophetic poem was written in January 1919, in the immediate aftermath of worldwide war and during a period of revolution. It was a time that saw the collapse of a political order that had survived for centuries. **The poem is based on Yeats's cyclical view of history and his conviction that the Christian era was ending.** This era is associated in the poem with innocence, order, maternal love and goodness. The era about to succeed it will be pitiless and destructive, with the 'rough beast' (line 21) and predatory birds representing its characteristic violence – what Yeats called 'the growing murderousness of the world'.

Commentary

An understanding of what is happening in the poem requires some biblical knowledge as well as an acquaintance with Yeats's vision of history.

Biblical references

The poem blends Christ's prediction of his own Second Coming with St John's vision of the coming of the Antichrist, the beast of the Apocalypse. This is the 'rough beast' of line 21 of the poem. Yeats makes the rough beast more disturbing and sinister by assigning its place of birth to Bethlehem, the place of Christ's birth, associated over the course of two thousand years with peace, mercy, gentleness and forgiveness.

Yeats's vision of history

The explanation of the Antichrist's birth at Bethlehem lies in Yeats's cyclical theory of history. In his philosophical, mystical work, A Vision, he foretold the birth of a new, violent, bestial anti-civilisation and the simultaneous destruction of the two-thousand-year Christian cycle. The 'Second Coming' of the poem is thus not that of Christ but that of his opposite: the slouching, revolting figure of the beast whose birth will herald a new age of anarchy to be 'loosed upon the world' (line 4).

What happens in the poem accords perfectly with Yeats's treatment of history in A Vision, where he thinks of each period of history as overthrown by some massive upheaval. He symbolised this process in what he called the gyres. A gyre is a cone-shaped spiral movement, which begins at a fixed point in history (such as the birth of Christ) and expands to its fullest circle. In the middle of this circle is the point at which the next historical phase begins, the new age that will be the antithesis of all that has preceded it. Yeats believed that the twentieth century would mark the violent end of the Christian phase of history.

Stanza 1

It is in the light of Yeats's mythology that the opening lines of the poem should be read. The falcon is an image of mankind moving along the widening gyre of history. It circles in such widening sweeps that it can no longer hear its master's call. Yeats wants us to imagine the widening base of the cone that marks the end of an age: the falcon is like humanity rapidly losing contact with Christ the falconer.

The following six lines convey a grim picture of the beginning of a new age, marked by worldwide anarchy and violence ('The blood-dimmed tide is loosed', line 5). Yeats probably had in mind events such as the Great War, the Russian Revolution and the Irish Troubles. In 1923 Kevin O'Higgins would declare that 'anarchy was loosed in this country' by opponents of the Free State Government.

The poem gives a frightening account of the fate in store for the post-Christian world. As the gyre widens and there is a collapse of order, 'Things fall apart; the centre cannot hold' (line 3). The end of the Christian age is granted the revelation of the character of the next age. The tide of violence and personal and social revolution has already begun to move, and as it does, it begins to drown the 'ceremony of innocence' (line 6), which, in Yeats's symbolic system, stands for order, obedience and harmony (i.e. established institutions such as monarchies and empires). Social anarchy and massive destruction are made worse by the collapse of moral values among the leaders of nations: good people (the 'best', line 7) have grown cynical and sceptical and lack the strength and commitment to resist the fanatics ('the worst', line 7) who have seized power. Evil will triumph in the public sphere because those leaders who might be expected to defend humane values lack the determination to resist those who preach violence and intolerance.

The more terrible events associated with the Antichrist are yet to come, but in lines 3 to 8 Yeats makes it clear that the world is already experiencing a foretaste of the grim future heralded by the birth of the rough beast. **The year of the composition of 'The Second Coming' was an appropriate one in which to contemplate the effects of the anarchy that war and revolution had loosed upon the world: war, revolution and the collapse of great empires and dynasties were very recent events in 1919, while the Irish War of Independence was threatening to uproot the Anglo-Irish Ascendancy and the civilisation it represented, many elements of which appealed to Yeats.**

Stanza 2

Yeats took the view that these terrible events must mean that the birth of a violent, beastly, anti-civilisation is about to be revealed. The 'vast image out of Spiritus Mundi' (line 12) is a favourite Yeatsian idea. The Spiritus Mundi is a storehouse of ideas deriving from the great universal memory common to all humankind, and is also the source of prophecy, since history repeats the same predestined cycles.

In contemplating the terrifying beast and its meaning for the future of humankind, Yeats becomes aware how dramatically Christ's birth ('a rocking cradle', line 20) reversed the previous historical cycle ('That twenty centuries of stony sleep', line 19) before He was born. The new Bethlehem will reverse the significance of the Bethlehem of Christ's birth: the slouching, pitiless 'rough beast' (line 21) about to be born there will be a prophet of evil and universal anarchy. Its sinister possibilities are hinted at in the suggestion that even the predatory desert birds, for all their savagery, are 'indignant' (line 17) at its coming.

Thinking about the poem

1. The poem dramatises a clash between two contrasting ways of life. Describe these and discuss the poet's attitude to them.
2. In 'The Second Coming', Yeats presents his ideas in terms of images. Describe the kinds of images that dominate the poem and discuss their effect on the reader's imagination.
3. This is a political poem. What kind of political vision does it convey?
4. How does Yeats convey the idea that good is about to be overcome by evil?
5. In 'The Second Coming', Yeats suggests a reason why the forces of evil will overcome the forces of good. What is this reason?
6. Why does Yeats refer to Bethlehem in the final line of the poem?
7. How does Yeats work out the implications of the title of his poem?
8. Bearing in mind that the poem was written early in the twentieth century, can it now be seen as prophetic? Why do you think it is so often quoted? Mention some features of present-day civilisation to which the poem seems to look forward.
9. How would you describe the mood or tone of the poem?
10. Is the speaker more or less detached from his subject matter than the speakers in Yeats's other 'political' poems? Does he offer a murderous, despairing vision, unrelieved by any kind of hope?
11. What does the poem suggest to you about Yeats's view of Christianity?
12. 'The Second Coming' has been described as 'a poem about history', and also as 'a poem about image-making' and as 'an occult experiment in imagination'. Which of these three descriptions best represents your own impression of the poem? Give reasons for your choice.

Sailing to Byzantium

That is no country for old men. The young
In one another's arms, birds in the trees
Those dying generations – at their song,
The salmon-falls, the mackerel-crowded seas,
Fish, flesh, or fowl, commend all summer long
Whatever is begotten, born and dies
Caught in that sensual music all neglect
Monuments of unageing intellect.

An aged man is but a paltry thing,
A tattered coat upon a stick, unless
Soul clap its hands and sing, and louder sing
For every tatter in its mortal dress,
Nor is there singing school but studying
Monuments of its own magnificence;
And therefore I have sailed the seas and come
To the holy city of Byzantium.

O sages standing in God's holy fire
As in the gold mosaic of a wall,
Come from the holy fire, perne in a gyre,
And be the singing-masters of my soul.
Consume my heart away; sick with desire
And fastened to a dying animal
It knows not what it is; and gather me
Into the artifice of eternity.

Once out of nature I shall never take
My bodily form from any natural thing,
But such a form as Grecian goldsmiths make
Of hammered gold and gold enamelling
To keep a drowsy Emperor awake;
Or set upon a golden bough to sing
To lords and ladies of Byzantium
Of what is past, or passing, or to come.

Glossary		
title	*Byzantium:*	the ancient city was one of the glories of civilisation, a famous centre of religion, art and architecture; Yeats wrote that if he could be given a month in an ancient place, he would choose to spend it in Byzantium
1	*That:*	Ireland
17	*sages:*	wise men; referring to ancient Byzantine martyrs
19	*perne in a gyre:*	move in a circular spinning motion; 'perne' is another name for the spool on which thread is wound and to 'gyre' is to gyrate or whirl; see also the notes on 'The Second Coming'

Guidelines

'Sailing to Byzantium' confronts the problems posed by advancing age. Yeats found the idea of bodily decay and decrepitude intolerable and in this poem he outlines a means of escape: to travel in the imagination to an ideal place in which he will be exempt from decay or death, a civilisation in which he can spend his eternity as a work of art. See 'The Lake Isle of Innisfree' for another version of a happy future.

Commentary

Title
The title of the poem expresses the notion of a voyage to perfection: in many of Yeats's works sailing is a symbol of such a voyage. In this case, the voyage is to a country of the mind, firmly situated in an ideal past: the ancient city of Byzantium. This inner voyage is prompted by the speaker's consciousness of increasing age and decrepitude. **The ageing man, falling victim to the ravages of time, is in a quest for a timeless existence in a timeless paradise of art.**

Stanza 1
The country of this stanza is Ireland, with its 'salmon-falls' and 'mackerel-crowded seas' (line 4). Yeats probably had Co. Sligo or Co. Galway in mind. However, the geographical location is not really important. What does merit attention here is the imagery of full and abundant natural life: the 'sensual music' (line 7) of the birds sounding mockingly in the ears of an old man whose waning physical powers make him feel out of place in a world in which vitality and energy are the supreme values. The real birds singing in real trees, with which the speaker contrasts the artificial golden

birds and boughs of Byzantium in the final stanza, are, for all their joyful music, symbols of the transience of natural life: they are the 'dying generations' (line 3). So, too, are the other creatures, 'Fish, flesh, or fowl' (line 5): all are doomed to death and decay.

Against these, the speaker sets up the uncompromising contrast of 'Monuments of unageing intellect' (line 8), symbols of the life of the spirit, of contemplation, of art. In their preoccupation with the life of the senses, the inhabitants, whether human or animal, of the natural world that the speaker rejects, and is about to abandon, ignore ('all neglect', line 7) the inner life (of the mind and spirit that can create the enduring works of art associated with Byzantium).

Stanza 2

In the second stanza the speaker develops the theme of the uselessness of the old in relation to the life of the senses. Confronted by the teeming life of youth, an old man is no better than a poor scarecrow (lines 9–10). The images of the ageing body, the soul's 'mortal dress' (line 12) in tatters, become more cruel as the poem progresses: the speaker is one of the 'old men' in the first stanza, a decrepit scarecrow in the second and 'a dying animal' in the third.

But if the condition of the body is a source of despair, the soul can rise above the sad condition of its 'mortal dress' (lines 10–12). It must listen, not to the 'sensual music' of the first stanza, but to the immortal singing of the holy sages of Byzantium. There is no more perfect exercise ('singing school', line 13) for the soul than to assert itself and break free from the limitations of bodily life and lose itself in the study of the timeless art of previous generations ('Monuments of its own magnificence', line 14). With this purpose in view, the speaker will undertake his inner voyage to Byzantium, the beautiful world where human limitations are transcended.

Stanza 3

Here the speaker addresses Byzantine sages who are also martyrs ('Come from the holy fire', line 19). These sages are exemplars of spiritual wisdom and perfection. The scene described in the first three lines of this stanza is of the kind Yeats admired on the Byzantine mosaics in Ravenna. To 'perne in a gyre' (line 19) means to move in a circular, spinning motion. These Byzantine sages will heal the speaker's sufferings and agonies ('Consume my heart away', line 21), and having instructed him in their kind of perfection (having been his 'singing-masters', line 20), will absorb ('gather', line 23) his soul, now artificially joined to a wasting body ('dying animal', line 22) into an eternity of beauty. The sages are being asked to re-enter this world of change and decay long enough to take him away to their world, which, like them, is immune from decay.

Stanza 4

Having shaken off his human nature and become an inhabitant of the heavenly city of Byzantium, the speaker will take on a shape that will ensure him an eternity of freedom from change and decay. The golden bird on the golden bough of the final stanza is an ageless, incorruptible thing, the antithesis of the 'dying animal' (the body he must occupy) of the third stanza.

Contradictory emotions

The 'official' theme of the poem is that the speaker feels obliged to make a choice between two worlds. The world he rejects is the cruel world of birth, generation and death, splendidly evoked in the richly concrete first stanza, where life is celebrated. The world he embraces as he turns away from life is a timeless world of art. He longs to spend eternity, after he has cast away his mortal body, in a Byzantine palace of art, taking the form of an imperishable artefact, a golden bird perched on a golden bough, which will sing as a way of passing the time for the nobility of this ideal place.

The feeling of the poem, however, reflected in its imagery and rhythms, suggests that the speaker, despite his longing to escape from reality, finds that the alternative fails to compensate for the vigorous excitement of actual life. Another look at the first stanza, notable for its rhythmic vitality and 'sensual music', confirms this impression. **The real theme of the poem is that art is not a substitute for life. The speaker's metamorphosis into a golden bird at the end seems an elaborate triviality when compared with the scenes from the real world presented in stanza 1.**

Thinking about the poem

1. Many of the poem's images suggest that the soul is superior to the body. List these. Do these images tend to make us see Yeats's point of view?
2. Is there anything in the poem to suggest that the ageing speaker regrets his bodily decay? Explain your answer.
3. Choose **two** images from the poem that strike you as particularly impressive. Say why you admire these images.
4. Choose an alternative title for the poem, and explain the reason for your choice.
5. Is this a religious poem? Could a Christian poet write as Yeats does here?
6. Is this a sad or a happy poem? Explain your answer with reference to the text.
7. 'This poem is a powerful exercise in imagination'. Agree or disagree with this statement. Refer to features of the poem in your answer.
8. Consider the poem as a splendid exercise in escapism.
9. The poem is an attempt to overcome the horrors associated with old age. What does this attempt involve? Compare the response to old age offered in this poem to that offered in 'An Acre of Grass'. Which of the responses makes more sense to you?

10 Discuss the poem as a meditation on time and eternity.
11 The poem is built on contrasts between different states of being. Examine it in this light.
12 Why do the 'dying generations' of Stanza 1 neglect 'Monuments of unageing intellect'. Why does the speaker take a different view of them?
13 One of the themes of the poem is the relationship of art and life. Develop this idea.
14 'This poem is Yeats's vision of an anti-world'. Is this a good description? Explain your answer.

from Meditations in Time of Civil War: VI: The Stare's Nest by My Window

The bees build in the crevices
Of loosening masonry, and there
The mother birds bring grubs and flies.
My wall is loosening; honey-bees,
Come build in the empty house of the stare.   5

We are closed in, and the key is turned
On our uncertainty; somewhere
A man is killed, or a house burned,
Yet no clear fact to be discerned:
Come build in the empty house of the stare   10

A barricade of stone or wood;
Some fourteen days of civil war;
Last night they trundled down the road
That dead young soldier in his blood:
Come build in the empty house of the stare.   15

We had fed the heart on fantasies,
The heart's grown brutal from the fare;
More substance in our enmities
Than in our love; O honey-bees,
Come build in the empty house of the stare   20

Glossary

5	*stare:* starling
6–7	*the key . . . uncertainty:* there is a similar image in T.S. Elliot's The Waste Land (1922): 'I have heard the key / turn in the door once and turn once only' (lines 412–13).

Guidelines

The setting of the poem is the Tower, Thor Ballylee, near Gort in south Co. Galway, which Yeats used as a retreat. In a time of Civil War, the tower, as the poem makes clear, could offer no sanctuary from the harsh realities outside. Word of killings and burnings reaches him in his tower, as well as accounts of terrible incidents such as that involving the dead young soldier (lines 13–14). The reality of this young man's fate was much more terrible than the poem suggests. He had been dragged down a road near the tower, his body so mangled that his mother could recover only his torn, disembodied head. **The poem is a vision of a disintegrating society (note the symbolism of the 'loosening masonry' of line 2).**

Commentary

In 'The Stare's Nest by My Window' there is a sense that the poet-speaker is overawed by the crude power of the men who fight the Civil War, compared with whom he is a powerless dreamer. In the first stanza he expresses his consciousness of the disintegration of his personal values in the midst of the war. This consciousness is conveyed in terms of symbolism, as he calls on the honey-bees, emblems of sweetness, to build in the 'loosening masonry' (line 2) of his tower, swept by violence and bitterness. **The loosening of the wall of the tower is an image of the collapse of order in the world outside, reminding us of the descent into anarchy visualised in 'The Second Coming'.**

As the speaker sees the bees building in the masonry, he senses that he must rebuild his imagination and that he must do this on a foundation of love rather than on a dangerous fantasy, the cause of the destructive bitterness that underlies the Civil War (lines 16–19). The consequences of this diet of fantasy are made real in the poem by means of images of war: 'A man is killed, or a house burned' (line 8) and 'Last night they trundled down the road / That dead young soldier in his blood' (lines 13–14).

The tower in which the speaker lives might have been a sanctuary, a place of detachment from the imperfect, troublesome world outside. During the Civil War, however, it offers the speaker no protection from reality. This is because stories of killings and burnings continue to intrude on his peace of mind. All these outside horrors force their way into the speaker's consciousness even though: 'We are closed in, and the key is turned / On our uncertainty' (lines 6–7).

Thinking about the poem

1. What kind of atmosphere does the poem convey?
2. Why does Yeats introduce the image of the honey-bees? What do they represent?
3. This poem deals with the collapse of a civilisation and of its values. How does the speaker convey this collapse? Refer to relevant details from the poem in support of your answer.
4. Comment on the relevance to the speaker of what is described in the poem.
5. Judging from what he says in this poem, what kind of Ireland would the speaker like? How would it differ from the Ireland he describes?
6. In stanza 2, the speaker makes the point that living in his tower does not protect him from sharing in the horrors of the world outside. How does he convey this idea?
7. Yeats connects the 'fantasies' (line 16) on which Irish hearts have been fed with the events described in the poem? Consider the nature of the connection.
8. The poem raises questions about the nature of nationalism, particularly in its extreme forms. What are these questions? Are they still topical in Ireland or elsewhere?
9. What has this poem in common with 'The Second Coming'? Does it offer a more balanced account of evil?
10. What, in your opinion, do the images of nature in the poem represent?

In Memory of Eva Gore-Booth and Con Markiewicz

The light of evening, Lissadell,
Great windows, open to the south,
Two girls in silk kimonos, both
Beautiful, one a gazelle.
But a raving autumn shears 5
Blossom from the summer's wreath;
The older is condemned to death,
Pardoned, drags out lonely years
Conspiring among the ignorant.
I know not what the younger dreams – 10
Some vague Utopia – and she seems,
When withered old and skeleton-gaunt,
An image of such politics.
Many a time I think to seek
One or the other out and speak 15
Of that old Georgian mansion, mix
Pictures of the mind, recall
That table and the talk of youth,
Two girls in silk kimonos, both
Beautiful, one a gazelle. 20
Dear shadows, now you know it all,
All the folly of a fight
With a common wrong or right,
The innocent and the beautiful
Have no enemy but time: 25
Arise and bid me strike a match
And strike another till time catch;
Should the conflagration climb,
Run till all the sages know.
We the great gazebo built, 30
They convicted us of guilt;
Bid me strike a match and blow.

Glossary

1	*Lissadell:*	the early nineteenth-century mansion near Sligo that was the home of the Gore-Booth sisters, Constance and Eva; Yeats visited the house as a young man in the winter of 1894/95
3	*kimonos:*	Japanese ankle-length, wide-sleeved garments that wrap around the body and are secured with a sash
7	*The older:*	Constance Markiewicz (1868–1927) (see also 'Easter 1916')
11	*Utopia:*	an ideal place or state; Yeats shows his scorn for political Utopias by invoking Eva's old, withered body as an image of them
16	*Georgian mansion:*	Lissadell
21	*shadows:*	ghosts; here means the dead women, Constance and Eva, who are now in a position to know what they could not know on earth
27	*catch:*	here means 'catch fire'
28	*conflagration:*	massive fire
29	*sages:*	wise people
30	*gazebo:*	a building commanding a view, probably a summer-house

Guidelines

The poem was written after the two Gore-Booth sisters, Eva and Constance, had died, the first in 1926, the second in July 1927. The poem was completed in October 1927.

The 'gazelle' (line 4), an image of graceful femininity, was Eva, the younger sister who, in Yeats's opinion, showed 'some promise as a writer of verse'. She was, like Yeats, interested in mysticism. She later rejected her privileged lifestyle and devoted herself to the service of the poor. Eva moved to England in 1897 to be with her partner, Esther Roper, and together they were involved in the trade union movement and the campaign for the emancipation of women.

Constance became a painter, married a Polish Count called Casimir Markiewicz, and settled in Dublin. A disciple of James Connolly, the Dublin Labour leader, she had joined his Citizen Army. She was second-in-command of a group that fought in St Stephen's Green during the 1916 Rising (see 'Easter 1916'). She was condemned to death, but later pardoned, for her part in the Rising. On her release, she became involved once more in revolutionary politics. She was elected to the British parliament, but did not take her seat. She became Minister for Labour in the first Dáil Éireann cabinet. She supported the republican cause in the Civil War of 1922/23.

Commentary

'folly of a fight'

This poem is built on a striking contrast between two ways of life. The first belongs to the elegant, beautiful civilisation in which the sisters grew up, which Yeats found immensely attractive. The second began when they took up another kind of living as servants of the cause of Irish freedom and of social reform, or as Yeats contemptuously puts it, spent their time 'Conspiring among the ignorant' (line 9) and dreaming of 'Some vague Utopia' (line 11). Their youth and beauty were spoiled in their struggle. Revolutionary politics made them appear crude and ugly. Yeats's terrible 'image of such politics' (line 13) is that of Eva, 'withered old and skeleton-gaunt' (line 12). **The poem marks the disappearance of a civilisation whose images are two beautiful sisters elegantly dressed, and a pleasant gazebo. This civilisation, Yeats suggests, has given way to democratic ignorance and ugliness.**

The poem is less a memorial to the Gore-Booth sisters than a nostalgic recollection of what they had been when the young Yeats had visited them at Lissadell in their youth, before they involved themselves in political and social agitation. The poem contemplates the radical change undergone by the two sisters with bitterness: two once beautiful, elegant aristocratic women grew prematurely old and miserable by devoting themselves to what the speaker sees as pointless, futile political activity. Yeats had no faith in the efforts of liberal aristocrats such as the Gore-Booths to build a world for the benefit of the lower orders of society. And he abhorred their 'folly' (line 22) in wasting their youth and beauty in violent acts.

'no enemy but time'

The speaker, however, has another target. Lines 5 to 6 offer a beautiful image of the destruction of human beauty by its enemy, time. The violence of time is the 'raving autumn' (line 5) that shears off youth from the 'innocent and the beautiful' (line 24). Time converts the sisters into 'Dear shadows' (line 21) of the selves they once were, ghosts clinging to withered bodies. The final seven lines of the poem are addressed to these 'Dear shadows' or ghosts, both those of the sisters and of the speaker's younger self. The task of these ghosts is not made totally clear and has been interpreted in a variety of ways.

Lines 26 to 32 are so difficult to interpret because the poem offers no obvious context for the command to set the 'great gazebo' alight. However, the key to the passage may be found in Yeats's view of time, life and death. For example, he believed that time was merely a construction of the human mind, and not an independent reality. He called pure time and pure space 'abstractions or figments of the mind'. In 'The Tower' (part III: lines 28–29) he wrote that 'Death and life were not / Till man made up the whole'. Another reference to time is helpful: 'Time drops in decay, / Like a candle burnt out' ('The Moods', lines 1–2). If time is only a construction of the human mind, or the human imagination, it can also be deconstructed, or burnt away, as the first two lines of this passage suggest: 'Arise and bid me strike a match / And strike another till time catch [fire]'.

By burning up the time that is the enemy of youthful innocence and beauty, the poet can restore these qualities, bringing back to life the 'Two girls in silk kimonos, both / Beautiful, one a gazelle' (lines 3–4 and 19–20). In other words, Yeats uses the power of his poetic imagination to re-create the former beauty of Constance and Eva. Thus, his achievement in this poem is to undo the ravages of time: to restore the blossom of summer (youthful beauty) that a 'raving autumn' (the passage of time) has sheared away (lines 5–6).

'the great gazebo'

A gazebo is generally a building commanding a view and here probably refers to a summer-house. If we take lines 30 to 32 literally, they refer to an arsonist setting fire to such a building. However, it seems more appropriate to interpret the gazebo as a reference to the dreams and ambitions of youth associated with the Gore-Booth sisters and their involvement in the 'folly of a fight' (line 22). Yeats is here returning to his theme of the damaging effect of political fanaticism on the sisters, and the hopelessness of the causes they followed. The 'We' in line 30 seems to unite Yeats with the two sisters in a common cause: that of building up a 'great gazebo' of youthful hopes. The 'They' of line 31 would thus seem to be their critics, the would-be 'sages' or wise people of line 29, who found them guilty of entertaining such hopes.

In his monumental biography of Yeats, R.F. Foster has offered an alternative interpretation. This interpretation is partly prompted by the fact that in an early draft of the poem Yeats had written: 'I the great gazebo built / They brought home to me the guilt'. To Foster's mind, the 'great gazebo' is an image of the achievement of the Anglo-Irish Ascendancy of which Yeats was always proud, and to which he and the Gore-Booth sisters belonged. He goes on to suggest that the people who convicted 'us' of guilt are not the sages but the Gore-Booth sisters themselves, who denounced the Anglo-Irish world from whence they came, and to which Yeats still felt loyal and for which he expressed public admiration, as he does for the Anglo-Irish patriots in 'September 1913': Tone, Fitzgerald and Emmet.

Thinking about the poem

1. This is a poem of contrasts. Develop this idea.
2. Comment on the tone of the poem. Does the tone change as the poem progresses?
3. Does Yeats approve of politics as a career for beautiful women? Give reasons for your answer.
4. Is this an optimistic or a pessimistic poem? Give reasons for your answer.
5. This poem has some impressive images. Select **three** of these and comment on their effectiveness in the context of the poem.
6. This poem has elements in common with 'The Stare's Nest by My Window'. Comment on this idea with reference to both poems.
7. On the evidence supplied by the poem, how would you describe Yeats's attitude to the two sisters? Can you sympathise with this? Why did the sisters give up their pampered way of life?
8. The passing of time and its effects are at the heart of the poem. Show how Yeats deals with this idea.
9. The poem betrays Yeats's social and political attitudes. How would you describe these on the evidence it provides? Consider also the insight offered by 'Politics'.
10. Like 'September 1913' and 'Easter 1916', this a political poem. How does it fit into the context created by each of the others?
11. The speaker's main objective in the poem is to bring back the delights of the past. How does he do this?
12. If Eva Gore-Booth and Con Markiewicz could be conjured back to life and were shown Yeats's poem, what, do you think, might they say?

Swift's Epitaph

Swift has sailed into his rest;
Savage indignation there
Cannot lacerate his breast.
Imitate him if you dare,
World-besotted traveller; he   5
Served human liberty.

Glossary	
title	*Swift:* Jonathan Swift (1667–1745), writer and Dean of St Patrick's Cathedral, Dublin
title	*Epitaph:* commemorative inscription on a tombstone or plaque; Swift wrote his own epitaph and in this poem Yeats offers a poetic translation of Swift's Latin text

Guidelines

The first line of the poem is by Yeats. The remainder is Yeats's translation of Swift's Latin epitaph, now in St Patrick's Cathedral, Dublin, where Swift was Dean. Yeats was particularly attracted to the notion that Swift had fought for the cause of human liberty, but he interpreted this in a sense that suited his own aristocratic view of society. Yeats had little respect for popular opinion, or the liberty of expression linked to democracy, which he tended to associate with organised mobs of ignorant people.

Swift had a strong hold on Yeats's imagination. Yeats liked to 'wander and meditate' in St Patrick's Cathedral, or sit beside Swift's monument on which his epitaph was carved, sensing that Swift was 'always just round the next corner'.

Commentary

Swift was a moralist, who advocated a society in which vice should be punished and virtue rewarded. Vices such as cruelty, hypocrisy, selfishness and aggression aroused his intense anger or, as Yeats puts it, 'Savage indignation' (line 2). This reaction found ironical expression in some of the greatest satires written in the English language, among them Gulliver's Travels.

The meaning of Yeats's poem can be seriously misunderstood, particularly the significance of the ending: 'he / Served human liberty' (lines 5–6). The sense in which this was true for either Swift or Yeats is limited. It is true that both Swift and Yeats were devoted to some forms of liberty, particularly the liberty of the artist. Both defended the liberty of Ireland, or at any rate of the Anglo-Irish Ascendancy, against English domination. Neither Yeats nor Swift, however, had much faith in the liberty of the masses. Yeats admired Swift for isolating himself from the mass of common men to give voice to the human spirit. **As Yeats saw it, Swift served human liberty by freeing the artist from the mob and not by being a champion of the**

rights of all the people. In 1930 Yeats recorded in his diary that he interpreted Swift's epitaph as meaning that 'the liberty he served was that of intellect, not liberty for the masses but for those who could make liberty visible'.

Yeats's political outlook in the 1930s helps to account for his admiration for Swift's elitist position. In April 1934, with Hitler in power in Germany and Mussolini in Italy, Yeats was advocating 'force, marching men' to 'break the reign of the mob' in Ireland. Here he was thinking of a role for the Blueshirts, the Irish movement modelled on continental fascism, for which he wrote anti-democratic songs ('What is equality? Muck in the yard'). Yeats lost interest in Irish fascism only when it became evident that it was a lost cause. The Irish politician he admired most, indeed without qualification, was Kevin O'Higgins, the ruthless 'strong man' of the 1920s, and he associated this admiration with the rise of fascism in Europe.

As an Anglo-Irishman, Yeats felt that he belonged to a superior caste. In a famous speech in the Senate in 1925, he denied the right of the elected majority to make laws affecting the rights of people such as himself. Speaking of the members of the Protestant Ascendancy, he told his fellow-senators, 'We are one of the great stocks of Europe. We are the people of Burke; we are the people of Grattan; we are the people of Swift, the people of Emmet, the people of Parnell. We have created the most of the modern literature of this country. We have created the best of its political intelligence.' These sentiments are reflected in many of Yeats's poems (see especially 'September 1913' and 'In Memory of Eva Gore-Booth and Con Markiewicz').

Thinking about the poem

1. Compare this epitaph with the one Yeats chose for himself in 'Under Ben Bulben'.
2. On the evidence of the epitaph, what kind of man was Swift?
3. Why is the 'World-besotted traveller' being addressed in the epitaph?

An Acre of Grass

Picture and book remain,
An acre of green grass
For air and exercise,
Now strength of body goes;
Midnight, an old house
Where nothing stirs but a mouse.

My temptation is quiet,
Here at life's end
Neither loose imagination,
Nor the mill of the mind
Consuming its rag and bone,
Can make the truth known.

Grant me an old man's frenzy,
Myself must I remake
Till I am Timon and Lear
Or that William Blake
Who beat upon the wall
Till Truth obeyed his call:

A mind Michael Angelo knew
That can pierce the clouds,
Or inspired by frenzy
Shake the dead in their shrouds;
Forgotten else by mankind,
An old man's eagle mind.

Glossary

9	*loose*:	relaxed
11	*rag and bone*:	the flesh, or body, the emotions
15	*Timon and Lear*:	Shakespearean tragic heroes; Timon of Athens rages against humanity in frenzied language and King Lear attacks vice, hypocrisy and injustice during his spell of madness
16	*William Blake*:	(1757–1827) mystic, poet, printmaker and prophetic figure
19	*Michael Angelo*:	Michelangelo Buonarroti (1475–1564), one of the supreme artists and figures of the Renaissance
24	*eagle mind*:	sharp, penetrating mind

Guidelines

The main themes of 'An Acre of Grass' have something in common with those of 'Sailing to Byzantium'. The speaker is preoccupied with old age. He wants to associate himself with those figures from art and life who retained powerful creative energy as they aged, who refused to remain quiet and passive. He insists on his right to break free of the limits of old age, to experience the whole of life and living and to have visions and dreams so compelling that they will shake the dead in their shrouds.

Commentary

Stanza 1

In the opening stanza the speaker expresses anger at the restraints imposed on old men by society. He imagines himself like a harmless, superannuated horse, and is reluctant to be put out to pasture on 'An acre of green grass / For air and exercise' (lines 2–3) as if he were in need of rest and quiet.

Stanza 2

He is tempted to adopt the attitude of philosophical detachment ('My temptation is quiet', line 7) that might be considered appropriate to an old man's retirement. In this kind of quiet condition, however, he cannot produce any work of lasting merit. **Living a quiet life may give the speaker truth, but it cannot help him to work that truth into poems.** Neither his relaxed imagination nor its casual focus on the body (the 'rag and bone' it consumes, line 11) 'Can make the truth known' (line 12).

Stanzas 3 and 4

If he wants to assert himself as a great poet and write 'true' poetry, he must achieve mystical insight, which will come only if he can model himself on those inspiring figures from art (such as Timon and Lear) and life (such as William Blake and Michelangelo) who retained creative energy (were 'inspired by frenzy', line 21) well into old age. What the speaker needs is indicated in his account of Blake 'Who beat upon the wall / Till Truth obeyed his call' (lines 17–18). He must cease to be the quiet man he has become in old age and remake himself in the form of a mad old prophet. Possessed and inspired by this frenzy, his quiet, relatively uninspired self will give way to an impassioned, prophetic self with 'An old man's eagle mind' (line 24) that can excite the world or 'Shake the dead in their shrouds' (line 22). **He insists on his right, in spite of old age, to experience the fullness of life, and will not be forced to live the quiet, limited life normally associated with someone 'at life's end' (line 8).**

Thinking about the poem

1. What kind of condition is suggested in the first stanza?
2. How would you describe the tone of lines 2 to 3: 'An acre of green grass / For air and exercise'?
3. Why is the speaker dissatisfied with his quiet life?
4. In the third and fourth stanzas, the poem becomes a kind of prayer. What kind of prayer?
5. How would the speaker like to pass his old age? Explain the significance of the title.
6. Reread the first four lines of the second stanza of 'Sailing to Byzantium' (lines 9–12) and explore the common elements of that poem and 'An Acre of Grass'. Does the latter poem offer any new insights?
7. Yeats mentions four names in the poem. What do these names mean to him? What purpose do they serve in the poem?
8. In stanza 3, the speaker writes: 'Myself must I remake' (line 14). For what purpose must he 'remake' himself?
9. Choose **two** images from the poem that strike you as particularly effective. Explain your choice.
10. Do you think that the speaker deserves our admiration? Give reasons for your answer.

Politics

'In our time the destiny of man presents its meaning in political terms.'
Thomas Mann

How can I, that girl standing there,
My attention fix
On Roman or on Russian
Or on Spanish politics?
Yet here's a travelled man that knows   5
What he talks about,
And there's a politician
That has read and thought,
And maybe what they say is true
Of war and war's alarms,   10
But O that I were young again
And held her in my arms!

Glossary

epigraph | *Thomas Mann:* (1875–1955) German writer

Guidelines

Yeats wrote this poem as an answer to an article about his work that had appeared in an American journal, the *Yale Review*. The article suggested that Yeats should devote his attention to political subjects. The poem is also an answer to the claim made by Thomas Mann in the epigraph. The poem shows how insignificant the great issues of Italian, Russian or Spanish politics can seem when human realities (in this case represented by the sight of a beautiful girl) intrude on the poet's consciousness.

Commentary

Yeats originally called this poem 'The Theme', and wrote it as an answer to the Yale Review article about his work written by the poet and playwright Archibald MacLeish, who praised the language of Yeats's poetry for being 'public'. This pleased Yeats, whose constant desire was to communicate with a popular audience and 'to move the common people'. However, he disagreed with MacLeish's claim that his public language might have more profitably been used on political themes.

Yeats had long considered politics as fundamentally dishonest and superficial, defining the activities of professional politicians as 'the manipulation of popular enthusiasm by false news'. This attitude explains the ironic contemplation in the poem of his experience of their public pronouncements: 'And maybe what they say is true' (line 9).

In contrast to this display of half-truth and pretended expertise, Yeats presents another kind of truth, one which makes Roman, Russian and Spanish politics appear of little importance. **The essential truths are those involving live human relationships, not the abstractions mediated by politicians. The girl in the poem is of considerably more significance in the scheme of reality than all the politicians in the world**, which is why the sight of her can make the speaker forget about politics and focus exclusively on her: 'O that I were young again / And held her in my arms!' (lines 11–12).

Thinking about the poem

1. This poem can be considered in relation to Yeats's other 'political' poems. What has it in common with them?
2. Does Yeats make a convincing point in the poem? Give reasons for your answer.
3. What does the young girl in the poem represent?
4. Is the speaker in this poem impressed by world affairs and by what people say about these?
5. Describe the impression the poem has made on you.
6. Suggest an alternative title for this poem and give reasons for your suggestion.

from Under Ben Bulben: V and VI

V
Irish poets, learn your trade,
Sing whatever is well made,
Scorn the sort now growing up
All out of shape from toe to top,
Their unremembering hearts and heads   5
Base-born products of base beds,
Sing the peasantry, and then

Hard-riding country gentlemen,
The holiness of monks, and after
Porter-drinkers' randy laughter;
Sing the lords and ladies gay
That were beaten into the clay
Through seven heroic centuries;
Cast your mind on other days
That we in coming days may be
Still the indomitable Irishry.

VI
Under bare Ben Bulben's head
In Drumcliff churchyard Yeats is laid,
An ancestor was rector there
Long years ago, a church stands near,
By the road an ancient cross.
No marble, no conventional phrase;
On limestone quarried near the spot
By his command these words are cut:
    Cast a cold eye
On life, on death.
Horseman, pass by!

	Glossary	
2	*Sing*: write about
6	*Base-born . . . beds*: low-born descendants of low-born parents; this idea may reflect Yeats's interest in contemporary theories of improving the racial stock, morally, mentally and physically, by means of selective breeding, and the elimination of people deemed unfit or inferior – such ideas were popular in Hitler's Germany
13	*seven heroic centuries*: the seven centuries that followed the Norman invasion of Ireland in 1169
16	*indomitable*: unconquerable
17	*Ben Bulben*: the mountain that dominates the landscape around Drumcliffe churchyard, Co. Sligo, where Yeats was later buried

Guidelines

This poem is generally read as Yeats's farewell to the world, his poetic last will and testament. Section V expresses his hopes for the future course of Irish poetry, and provides advice for Irish poets on the themes they should choose and on the proper way to give them expression. Section VI gives his reasons for being buried at Drumcliffe and provides the words for his tombstone.

Yeats died at Cap Martin, on the French Riviera, on 28 January 1939 and was buried there. In September 1948 his body was reinterred in Drumcliffe churchyard, and his chosen epitaph was engraved on his tombstone.

Commentary

Throughout his career, Yeats wrote many elegies, that is, poems celebrating the significance and achievements of dead friends. This poem is his own elegy, a statement of his beliefs as he approaches death and of the inscription he wanted on his gravestone as an epitaph.

Section V

Yeats offers a pessimistic comment on contemporary poetry: the great poetic tradition represented by such visionary poets as William Blake had, in the course of time, become corrupted. He believed that modern poetry was the product of a historical cycle nearing its end and was thus confused, formless and unworthy of imitation. (For Yeats's more detailed exploration of the end of the two-thousand-year Christian cycle, see 'The Second Coming'.) Modern poets had forgotten or neglected the great tradition of poetry so that their language had become awkward and their themes degraded. For these reasons, **the poem encourages Irish poets to ignore their modern contemporaries and become technically competent**.

Yeats advises the Irish poets who will succeed him to feel contempt for the shapeless, badly constructed work of the latest generation of writers. The 'sort now growing up' (line 3) are the middle-class makers of post-independence Ireland, for whom Yeats had little respect. Instead, he encourages new Irish poets to learn their craft by turning to the past and dealing with themes associated with peasants and aristocrats, which will impart vigour and authenticity to their poems.

Section VI

In contrast to the rhetorical, dogmatic, even shrill tone of section V, section VI is a tranquil lyric in which Yeats gives reasons for being buried at Drumcliffe. His grandfather John Yeats had been Rector at Drumcliffe church. Yeats refers to himself in the third person as a dead man ('In Drumcliff churchyard Yeats is laid') and provides a short and simple but enigmatic epitaph.

It is not clear what the epitaph means, and we cannot be sure to whom it is addressed. The horseman may be one of the visionary beings of local folklore, described for Yeats by Sligo people. It has also been suggested that the horseman is Yeats's ghost, or any passing rider. The injunction given to the passer-by, to 'Cast a cold eye / On life, on death' (lines 25–26) is characteristic of Yeats's thinking and of his fondness for balancing opposites. Notice that the sentiments expressed here echo those of the speaker in 'An Irish Airman Foresees His Death' (lines 13–16). The reader of the epitaph is encouraged to see life and death as coldly, if paradoxically, balanced.

We can also view the epitaph as belonging to an ancient tradition. Since classical times, passing travellers have been encouraged by those who carved inscriptions on monuments to the dead to pause or stop, if only to consider their own mortality, and to recognise that as the dead man is, they will some day be. The brevity of Yeats's epitaph is such that the horseman would be able to read it as he passed. Many commentators have suggested that Yeats should have retained his earlier version of the final line, which was 'Draw rein, Draw breath', thus asking the horseman to pause and contemplate the words.

There is an interesting parallel between Yeats's epitaph in this poem and his version of Jonathan Swift's epitaph, where the traveller is encouraged to imitate Swift if he dare. Yeats's epitaph may offer a similar inducement to the horseman to imitate its author's dispassionate attitude to life and death.

Thinking about the poem

1. What attitude to contemporary writers does Yeats express here?
2. What kind of Irish poetry would he like to see in the future?
3. Does Yeats see himself as an Irish patriot?
4. How would you describe the tone of section V of the extract?
5. Why has Yeats chosen the three-line epitaph at the end of section VI? What does it tell us about him?
6. Describe the impression the poem has made on you.

Exam-Style Questions

1. Yeats's poetry presents a consistent tension between projected ideal states and actuality. Is this an accurate generalisation?

2. Consider various versions of the past as central themes of Yeats's poetry. Why do you think he usually makes the past seem better than the present?
3. Discuss the ways in which Yeats uses his poetry as a means of escape from unpleasant realities such as old age and decay.
4. Examine the versions of Ireland that emerge from Yeats's poems. Do these versions form a consistent pattern?
5. Consider Yeats as a poet of conflict.
6. Explore the significance of art in the poetry of Yeats.
7. Comment on the ways in which many of Yeats's poems convey a sense of loss.
8. Discuss Yeats's quest for a sense of permanence in the midst of change.
9. Do his poems as a whole suggest that Yeats was a pessimist?
10. It has been remarked that Yeats conveys his meanings by means of images and symbols to a greater extent than through statement and argument. Would you agree? Give reasons for your answer.
11. What do Yeats's poems, taken as a whole, tell us about the man who wrote them?
12. Outline the qualities of Yeats's poetry you admire or dislike. You might discuss Yeats's ideas, his images, his descriptive power, his power of suggestion, his relevance for our time, his emotional and intellectual power, his patriotism, his honesty, his skilful depiction of human beings.
13. Write an essay in which you give your reasons for liking and/or not liking the poetry of W.B. Yeats. You must support your points by reference to, or quotation from, the poems that are on your course.

The following are reasons you might give for liking Yeats's poetry:

- The subject matter of the poems is of interest to Irish readers.
- The poems deal with an interesting variety of subjects.
- Many of the poems enable us to understand history and politics, especially Irish politics.
- The poems are full of powerful images and impressive descriptions.
- The poems are remarkable for their profound and original ideas, etc.

Here are some reasons you might give for not liking Yeats's poetry:

- Some of the allusions in the poems are extremely obscure.
- The poems seldom convey a sense of happiness.
- There is an undue emphasis on the poet in Yeats's poems.
- Younger readers may be alienated by the emphasis on old age in the poems.
- Too much background reading is required for an understanding of Yeats's philosophical themes.

Sample Essay

'Much of the poetry of W.B. Yeats is based on contrast'.

Discuss this comment with reference to, and quotation from, some of the poems by Yeats on your course.

The first kind of contrast I would like to discuss is that between past and present in two of Yeats's 'patriotic' poems: 'September 1913' and 'Easter 1916'. The main structural feature of 'September 1913' is the opposition created by Yeats between an unattractive present and an admirable past. The present is unattractive because it is inhabited by a set of people with little or no concern for the welfare of their country. Instead, they are content to occupy themselves with accumulating money: they 'fumble in a greasy till' and they 'add the halfpence to the pence'. They spend the rest of their time praying: they add 'prayer to shivering prayer', as if people were born for no other reason than to 'pray and save'.

[First sentence of answer immediately addresses the point of the question]

Then comes the contrast with these selfish, unpatriotic people. The contrast is provided by a number of patriotic Irishmen of the past, who fought for the freedom of their country. They had little time to pray because they were in constant danger of death: the 'hangman's rope' had been spun specially for them. They were too busy fighting to think of saving: 'And what, God help us, could they save'. Yeats sees that the 'Romantic Ireland' of these patriots, Edward Fitzgerald, Robert Emmet, Wolfe Tone and John O'Leary, belongs strictly to the past, while the materialists dominate the present. These unpatriotic cynics are given the last word, as they dismiss the dead patriots as foolish individuals who 'weighed so lightly what they gave' and failed to consider their own interests. The patriots can now safely be forgotten: 'But let them be, they're dead and gone'.

[Contrast has been outlined between past and present in the case of one poem]

The contrast between past and present in 'Easter 1916' is different. It relates to the difference between the poet's opinion of the leaders of the 1916 Rising before and after its outbreak. For the purposes of the poem, the Rising marks a dividing line between past and present. In the past (the period preceding the Rising), Yeats had found it difficult to take the leaders of the Rising seriously, to the extent that he considered mocking their efforts when he spoke to friends at his gentlemen's club, thinking that Patrick Pearse, Thomas MacDonagh, James Connolly and John MacBride were not serious revolutionaries, but merely play-acting. When the Rising did take place, and when those who planned and took part in it showed themselves to be agents in the regeneration of Ireland's soul, Yeats was obliged to acknowledge that what they had done would change the course of Irish history. Pearse and the rest of the revolutionaries, now and in future time, are, and will be seen as having been, 'changed, changed utterly'. They took part in a terrible, violent event, which their nobility and self-sacrifice made beautiful. The contrast between the earlier opinion of the poet that they were simply playing games, and his subsequent view of them as heroes in a great national event, could not be more stark.

[Another contrast has been discussed, using a different poem]

A second kind of contrast in Yeats's poetry is between ideal, imagined states of being and realities. Here, a good example is to be found in 'Sailing to Byzantium'. One side of the contrast is presented in the first two stanzas of the poem. These reveal the reality of old age lived out in an Ireland 'that is no country for old men'. The body of an old, or ageing, man is no better than a scarecrow, 'a tattered coat upon a stick'. At this stage of life, the old can find consolation for their physical decay only if their souls rise to the contemplation of an ideal world presented through the medium of great works of art. An escape from the physical reality of bodily decay can be achieved by making an imaginative voyage to some ideal country of the mind like Byzantium. On this voyage, the soul will no longer be fastened to the 'dying animal', which is the body, but will be gathered 'into the artifice of eternity'. In eternity ('out of nature') the poet would like to take on a new 'bodily form', not that of the ageing man he now is, but that of a beautiful, incorruptible golden bird made by Grecian goldsmiths, perched on a 'golden bough', singing forever to the immortal 'lords and ladies of Byzantium'. The contrast between real and ideal is reinforced by the opposing images of the body as a scarecrow and the soul escaping from that body to join itself to a splendid everlasting work of art.

[A new example of contrast has been outlined, with reference to a third poem]

'The Second Coming' deals with the stark contrast between two cycles, or periods, of human history, each two thousand years long. The first of these cycles, the Christian one, Yeats sees as soon coming to an end, as humanity, symbolised by the falcon, is rapidly losing touch with Christ, the falconer ('the falcon cannot hear the falconer'). Yeats implies that Christianity stood for order, peace and harmony. The imminent destruction of its two-thousand-year cycle, in contrast, will be marked by a new cycle of disorder. It will be a period during which 'mere anarchy is loosed upon the world'. Christ's rule will be followed by that of his opposite, the Anti-Christ, who will preside over a time of bloody war and revolution against established governments and institutions and the general collapse of order throughout the world. The reign of the Anti-Christ will signal the collapse of civilised values:

> The blood-dimmed tide is loosed, and everywhere
>
> The ceremony of innocence is drowned.

Just as the pagan cycle ended with Christ's birth ('twenty centuries of stony sleep' vexed by a 'rocking cradle'), the cycle of the Anti-Christ is heralded in a fearful image:

> And what rough beast, its hour come round at last,
>
> Slouches towards Bethlehem to be born?

[A fourth poem is used to provide another example of contrast]

In other poems, the principle of contrast is maintained. In 'The Lake Isle of Innisfree', we have a contrast between the commonplace, uninspiring realities of city life, indicated in images of the roadway and 'the pavements grey', and the contrasting beauties of a natural landscape to be enjoyed on a lake island by a solitary lover of nature, whose senses are continually stimulated by lovely sights and sounds, the 'purple glow' of noon and the 'lake water lapping with low sounds by the shore'. In 'The Wild Swans at Coole', Yeats is conscious of the troubling constrasts between the swans and himself. He is conscious of ageing and the passage of time. In contrast the swans give the illusion of immortality. They are, for Yeats, a symbol of eternity as they rise 'in great broken rings'. In 'In Memory of Eva Gore-Booth and Con Markiewicz', there is a painful, moving contrast between two phases in the lives of these women. In their early lives they were 'two girls in silk kimonos, both beautiful, one a gazelle'. Their beauty soon fades, as time, in the form of 'a raving autumn', shears away the blossoms of youth. The fate of the beautiful younger sister is to become 'withered old and skeleton-gaunt'.

[Summary of other examples of contrast from other poems on the course]

As this essay has illustrated, much of the poetry of W.B. Yeats is indeed based on contrast. We find this both within individual poems and between one poem and another.

[Brief concluding paragraph referring back to the question]

snapshot

W.B. Yeats

- Many poems are based on the opposition between reality and imagination
- Uses symbols (e.g. tower, swan) to express profound ideas
- Contrasts ideal past and sordid present
- Balances opposing ideas and leaves many questions open
- Some poems suggest an ambivalent attitude to Irish patriots
- Violence and conflict are central to his vision
- Many poems are inspired by Ireland, its history and landscape
- Creates his own mythology
- Several poems suggest a need to escape from reality
- Makes effective use of imagery to convey themes
- Many poems are taken up with arguments

Patricia Beer

1919–99

THE VOICE

Biography

Patricia Beer was born in Devon, England in 1919. Her family were Plymouth Brethren, a religious sect founded in 1827 that has a strict moral code and emphasises the dangers of sin. She grew up in Devon and settled there for the last decades of her life. She taught English literature in Italy and in Goldsmith's College, London.

Her first book of poetry, *The Loss of Magyar*, was published in 1959. During the 1960s and early 1970s she published three additional poetry collections. In 1968 she resigned from her teaching job to become a full-time writer. Her autobiography, *Mrs Beer's House* (1968), evokes her childhood in Devon. She also published a critical study of women writers. Her 1978 novel, *Moon's Ottery*, described life in a Devon village at the time of the Spanish Armada. When her collection *Friend of Heraclitus* won an award on its publication in 1993, she said that the recognition gave her 'an agreeable sense of persistence'.

> Given that Beer's career as a poet extended over forty years, much of her poetry has the traditional element of rhyme, but she also wrote syllabic verse and free verse. She was writing up to the time of her death. Her last book of poetry, *Autumn*, was published in 1997.

The Voice

When God took my aunt's baby boy, a merciful neighbour
Gave her a parrot. She could not have afforded one
But now bought a new cage as brilliant as the bird,
And turned her back on the idea of other babies.

He looked unlikely. In her house his scarlet feathers   5
Stuck out like a jungle, though his blue ones blended
With the local pottery which carried messages
Like 'Du ee help yerself to crame, me handsome.'

He said nothing when he arrived, not a quotation
From pet-shop gossip or a sailor's oath, no sound   10
From someone's home: the telephone or car-door slamming,
And none from his: tom-tom, war-cry or wild beast roaring.

He came from silence but was ready to become noise.
My aunt taught him nursery rhymes morning after morning.
He learnt Miss Muffett, Jack and Jill, Little Jack Horner,   15
Including her jokes; she used to say turds and whey.

A genuine Devon accent is not easy. Actors
Cannot do it. He could though. In his court clothes
He sounded like a farmer, as her son might have.
He sounded like our family. He fitted in.   20

Years went by. We came and went. A day or two
Before he died, he got confused, and muddled up

His rhymes. Jack Horner ate his pail of water.
The spider said what a good boy he was. I wept.

He had never seemed puzzled by the bizarre events 25
He spoke of. But the last day he turned his head towards us
With the bewilderment of death upon him. Said
'Broke his crown' and 'Christmas pie'. And tumbled after.

My aunt died the next winter, widowed, childless, pitied
And patronised. I cannot summon up her voice at all. 30
She would not have expected it to be remembered
After so long. But I can still hear his.

Glossary

8	*Du . . . handsome:*	Do help yourself to cream, my handsome; tourism in Devon plays upon its past associations with pirates and smugglers
16	*turds and whey:*	recalls the opening lines of the nursery rhyme 'Little Miss Muffett': 'Little Miss Muffett sat on a tuffet / Eating her curds and whey'; curds are the thickened or cheese part of milk, and whey is the remaining liquid; a turd is a lump of excrement or dung
30	*patronised:*	treated kindly by those who considered themselves her superiors

Guidelines

'The Voice' was published in *Friend of Heraclitus* (1993). It tells the story of the poet's aunt, who lost a baby boy, and the parrot given to her by a neighbour. The story is told in a direct, non-sentimental way, with flashes of humour and irony. The setting of the poem is Devon, a part of England associated with pirates and pirate ships.

Commentary

Stanza 1

The opening stanza tells the reader how the parrot came to the narrator's aunt. Some readers might find it amusing; others might find it cruel or shocking. **The question of tone is central to interpreting the poem** and readers differ in their understanding of the tone of the poem. Readers may also differ in their assessment of the style of the poem. Is the language too flat and ordinary, or does it capture the flow of everyday speech?

Stanza 2

The opening statement of stanza 2, **'He looked unlikely' (line 5), shows Beer's talent for pithy, clever summations of a situation**. The stanza suggests that the parrot both stands out and blends in in the aunt's house.

Two worlds

The idea of belonging to two worlds is developed in stanza 3. The parrot, we are told, did not speak when he came to the aunt's house. He said nothing of the things he might have heard in his adopted home, nor did he imitate the sounds of home. The opening of the fourth stanza is a well-balanced line, neatly contrasting silence and noise: 'He came from silence but was ready to become noise' (line 13).

Stanza 5

Stanza 5 is one of the most interesting stanzas in the poem. It is developed from another contrast, this time between the 'court clothes' (line 18) of the parrot and his Devon farmer's accent. The narrator says the parrot 'sounded like our family' (line 20). More tellingly the narrator says that the parrot 'sounded like a farmer, as her son might have' (line 19). **This is the emotional centre of the poem.** Behind the story of the aunt's parrot, is the story of her lost baby.

Stanzas 6 and 7

The story gathers pace in the sixth stanza and we are brought to the day before the parrot died. **The tone softens, as the narrator describes the parrot's confusion. The final 'I wept' (line 24) of the stanza appears to be without irony.** The account of the parrot's death continues into stanza 7. **Arguably lines 25 to 27 are the best lines in the poem, with their array of sounds and sound correspondences and the admirable phrase 'the bewilderment of death'.**

Stanza 8

The final stanza is unsettling and deserves careful reading. Does the aunt live on in the remembered voice of the parrot? Or is the narrator's remembrance of the parrot a final insult to the 'pitied / And patronised' aunt (lines 29–30)? Is 'The Voice' an exercise in warm affection, or an exercise in cruel indifference? Or is it something in between? For all the simplicity of the story it tells, 'The Voice' is a complex poem.

Themes of the poem

You might also like to consider the themes that emerge from the poem and from the story it tells. Some readers identify commemoration as the main theme. Others select loneliness and grief. It is also possible to identify the theme of companionship. You might take account of the title of the poem when considering the theme and reflect on the poet's statement, 'I cannot summon up her voice at all' (line 30).

Exam-style questions

Thinking about the poem

1. The first stanza tells us the story of how the parrot came to the poet's aunt. Comment on the story and the tone in which it is told.
2. What, do you think, caused the aunt to turn away from 'the idea of other babies' (line 4)?
3. 'He looked unlikely' (line 5). What, in your view, is the tone implied in this statement? Where else in the poem is this tone apparent?
4. In your view, what is the importance of the parrot's Devon accent referred to in stanza 5?
5. From reading stanza 5, what part does the parrot play in the aunt's life?
6. The final stanza begins, 'My aunt died the next winter' (line 29). Do you think the poet wants us to connect the aunt's death with the death of the parrot? Explain your answer.
7. In the final stanza, the poet says her aunt died 'pitied / And patronised' (lines 29–30). In your view, does the poet display these attitudes towards her aunt?
8. Which one of the following words best describes the tone of the poem: humorous, cruel, ironic, insulting or affectionate? Explain your choice.
9. 'In remembering the parrot, the poet remembers her aunt.' Do you agree with this reading of the poem? Explain your point of view.
10. Do you think that 'The Voice' sounds enough like a poem? Explain your answer.
11. Suggest an alternative title for the poem and explain your suggestion.
12. Which of the following statements is closest to your own reading of the poem?

    It is a poem about loneliness.

    It is a poem about companionship.

    It is a poem about death.

    It is a poem about remembering.

    Explain your choice.

Taking a closer look

1. Comment on the poet's use of the adjective 'merciful' in line 1 and describe the impact of the word on you.
2. At the end of stanza 6, the poet says 'I wept' (line 24). Give your response to this statement.
3. Comment on the effectiveness of the phrase 'the bewilderment of death' (line 27).
4. What phrases or lines do you like most in the poem? Explain your choice.

Imagining

1. Writing in the voice of the aunt, prepare a short response to the poem beginning with the line, 'I know how others see me.'
2. Write a letter to a friend describing the poem and your response to it.

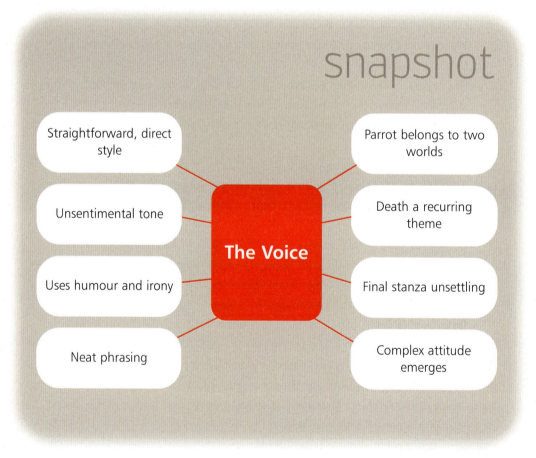

Carol Ann Duffy

b. 1955

VALENTINE

Biography

Carol Ann Duffy was born in Glasgow in December 1955. She grew up in Staffordshire in England, where she was educated at Stafford Girls' High School. She studied philosophy at university in Liverpool before moving to London to work as a freelance writer. She has written plays as well as poems, edited books of poetry and been writer-in-residence at the Southern Arts, Thamesdown.

Duffy's books of poetry include *Standing Female Nude* (1985), *Selling Manhattan* (1987), *The Other Country* (1990) and *Mean Time* (1993). In 2000 she published *The World's Wife*, a collection of dramatic monologues in the voices of the wives of famous men (Mrs Midas and Mrs Aesop, for example). She has written picture books for children and edited two anthologies for teenagers: *I Wouldn't Thank You for a Valentine* and *Stopping for Death*. *Rapture* was published in 2006, and *New and Collected Poems for Children* appeared in 2009.

In 1999 Duffy became a Fellow of the Royal Society of Literature. She was awarded an OBE in 1995 and a CBE in 2001. She became Britain's Poet Laureate in May 2009, the first woman to hold the position in its 300-year history.

She lives in Manchester, where she is Creative Director of the Writing School at Manchester Metropolitan University.

Valentine

Not a red rose or a satin heart.

I give you an onion.
It is a moon wrapped in brown paper.
It promises light
like the careful undressing of love.   5

Here.
It will blind you with tears
like a lover.
It will make your reflection
a wobbling photo of grief.   10

I am trying to be truthful.

Not a cute card or a kissogram.

I give you an onion.
Its fierce kiss will stay on your lips, possessive and faithful
As we are,   15
for as long as we are.

Take it.
Its platinum loops shrink to a wedding-ring,
if you like.
Lethal.   20
Its scent will cling to your fingers,
Cling to your knife.

Glossary	
18	*platinum:* white, valuable metal used in jewellery
20	*Lethal:* deadly, dangerous

Guidelines

'Valentine' is from the collection *Mean Time* (1993). Like a traditional valentine, the poem contains a proposal of marriage. But unlike a traditional valentine, the proposal is expressed in unromantic terms. Also unlike a conventional valentine's poem, Duffy's version does not try to rhyme.

Commentary

The title prepares us for a romantic love poem, but Duffy rejects traditional symbols of love.

Lines 1–10

Instead of the usual gifts that a lover gives to a beloved – 'a red rose or a satin heart' (line 1) – this poem offers an onion (line 2).

The speaker makes a case for the onion as an appropriate gift. **She uses the image of the onion as a metaphor for love**, keeping the extended metaphor going throughout the poem. She mixes romantic images – the onion is a 'moon' in shape – with ordinary things – an onion comes 'wrapped in brown paper' (i.e. onion skin) (line 3). Yet underneath its dull appearance an onion 'promises light' (line 4) (perhaps meaning hope or happiness) just as love does. It can be peeled to reveal beauty, just as lovers also undress each other. The different layers of the onion are also like the layers of someone's personality as it is discovered in a relationship.

As an onion may do, too, love may cause tears that will blind your eyes in grief. Your reflection will become 'a wobbling photo of grief' (line 10). Here the poet cleverly plays on the 'wobbling' or blurring of vision that occurs as we peel an onion and our eyes water.

Lines 11–19

The speaker thinks that an onion is a more 'truthful' (line 11) symbol of love than any other more conventional Valentine's Day gift, such as a 'cute card or a kissogram' (line 12). 'I give you an onion' (line 13) echoes the ceremony of marriage ('I give you this ring'). The smell and taste of the onion, its 'fierce kiss' (line 14), will last on the lips of the beloved, just as the speaker's love will last. An onion, too, has rings, and this brings the speaker to compare its 'platinum loops' to a 'wedding-ring' (line 18), adding hesitantly, 'if you like' (line 19). This is the proposal for a long-term relationship, even if it is expressed in a rather casual and off-hand manner.

She does undermine her own proposal rather by using the word 'shrink' (line 18). Might she be suggesting that marriage can be experienced as something negative, something less than love itself?

Lines 20-22
Throughout the poem the speaker has stressed her desire to be honest about love. We can read the final three lines in a number of ways. 'Lethal' (line 20) might suggest the fierceness of love, but it has underlying suggestions of destruction. And is there a threatening tone in the image of the onion's 'scent' that 'will cling to your fingers / Cling to your knife'? (lines 21-22). 'Knife' is a strange word to finish a poem about love. It has suggestions of hurt and betrayal.

What the poem says about love
The poem is honest about love. It sees love as sexual, passionate and hopeful. But it also sees that love can cause pain and grief and that it may not last, after all – it will only be 'possessive and faithful' (line 14) for as long as the lovers remain true to each other. This is a more realistic view of love than is usually found in a valentine's poem.

The speaking voice
The mixture of ordinary and romantic images gives 'Valentine' an ironic, bittersweet tone, so that we are never quite sure what the feelings of the speaker are. Duffy creates a sense of an intimate conversation taking place between the 'I' and 'you' of the poem. The abrupt tone of the first line, 'Not a red rose or a satin heart', gives the impression of a conversation that has been going on for some time. It is as if the gift is being given at this present moment ('Here', line 6) and the reader is witnessing the event.

At times the speaker seems confident and in control ('Take it', line 17), whereas at other times she seems unsure ('if you like', line 19). It is possible to read the final lines as expressing doubts about the future of the relationship (the image of the knife may make sense in terms of an onion, but it suggests pain and betrayal in terms of a relationship).

Despite the casual and even slightly comical tone of the poem, it is clear that the speaker is not avoiding the darker side of love. How we respond to the poem may depend on our personal experience, but we cannot fail to see how original and honest it is.

Exam-style questions

Thinking about the poem

1. Why, according to the poem's speaker, is the onion suitable as a gift for the beloved on Valentine's Day?
2. Which of the metaphors and similes that the poet uses do you find the most unusual and effective?
3. Do you think that the relationship between the lovers in this poem is a happy one?
4. What attitude to love and relationships in general is suggested in this poem?
5. With which of these statements would you most agree:
   The speaker is very honest about love.
   The speaker is very bitter about love.
   The speaker's attitude to love is refreshing and enjoyable.
   Give reasons for your view.
6. Do you think that this is a good love poem?

Taking a closer look

1. Write down one line or phrase from the poem that tells you the most about the kind of relationship the lovers have. Say why you think it is an important line.
2. 'Its fierce kiss will stay on your lips, possessive and faithful / As we are, / for as long as we are' (lines 14–16). What do these lines suggest to you about the speaker's view of love?
3. 'Its scent will cling to your fingers, / Cling to your knife' (lines 21–22). How do these lines affect your reading of the poem? Give a reason for your view.

Imagining

1. Imagine that you are the person who has received the onion (and the poem) as a valentine. Write out the response you would make.
2. Write out (in dialogue form) the conversation that may have taken place after the onion has been given as a gift.

snapshot

Valentine

- Extended metaphor of onion as metaphor for love
- Complex vision of love
- Tone changes throughout
- Creates sound of speaking voice
- Mixture of ordinary and romantic images
- Written in unrhymed, conversational language
- Rejects traditional valentines
- Clever and original love poem

Tess Gallagher

b. 1943

THE HUG

Biography

Tess Gallagher was born in 1943 in Port Angeles, a small port town in the Pacific state of Washington on the north-west coast of the United States. She is a poet and a short-story writer and was married to Ray Carver one of America's greatest short-story writers.

Gallagher's childhood was marred by her father's alcoholism. For the young woman, words and writing were a means of escape from poverty and gave her the power to 'direct and make meaning' in her life. She attended university where she studied creative writing with the celebrated poet Theodore Roethke.

Her 1992 collection, *Moon Crossing Bridge*, was written after Carver's death from cancer in 1988 and is considered among her finest work. Since his death, Gallagher has edited and written introductions to collections of Carver's work. She also worked with Robert Altman on the 1993 film *Short Cuts*, which was based on nine of Carver's short stories.

Gallagher has won numerous awards for her poetry and has taught creative writing at a number of colleges in the United States.

Gallagher has Irish connections. She has been coming to Ireland since 1968 and is a frequent visitor to Lough Arrow in Co. Sligo. She collaborated with a local story-teller, Josie Gray, to compile an anthology of stories, *Barnacle Soup and Other Stories from the West of Ireland*.

The Hug

A woman is reading a poem on the street
and another woman stops to listen. We stop too,
with our arms around each other. The poem
is being read and listened to out here
in the open. Behind us   5
no one is entering or leaving the houses.

Suddenly a hug comes over me and I'm
giving it to you, like a variable star shooting light
off to make itself comfortable, then
subsiding. I finish but keep on holding   10
you. A man walks up to us and we know he hasn't
come out of nowhere, but if he could, he
would have. He looks homeless because of how
he needs. 'Can I have one of those?' he asks you,
and I feel you nod. I'm surprised,   15
surprised you don't tell him how
it is – that I'm yours, only
yours, etc., exclusive as a nose to
its face. Love – that's what we're talking about, love
that nabs you with 'for me   20
only' and holds on.

So I walk over to him and put my
arms around him and try to
hug him like I mean it. He's got an overcoat on
so thick I can't feel   25
him past it. I'm starting the hug
and thinking, 'How big a hug is this supposed to be?
How long shall I hold this hug?' Already
we could be eternal, his arms falling over my
shoulders, my hands not   30
meeting behind his back, he is so big!

I put my head into his chest and snuggle
in. I lean into him. I lean my blood and my wishes
into him. He stands for it. This is his
and he's starting to give it back so well I know he's   35
getting it. This hug. So truly, so tenderly
we stop having arms and I don't know if
my lover has walked away or what, or
if the woman is still reading the poem, or the houses –
what about them? – the houses.   40

Clearly, a little permission is a dangerous thing.
But when you hug someone you want it
to be a masterpiece of connection, the way the button
on his coat will leave the imprint of
a planet on my cheek   45
when I walk away. When I try to find some place
to go back to.

Glossary

8	a *variable star*: a pulsating star, its brightness varies considerably

Guidelines

The poem tells a story. The female narrator of the poem recalls an incident when she and her lover stopped on the street to listen to a woman reading a poem. On an impulse the woman hugged her lover and continued to hold him. Out of nowhere a homeless man approached and asked the lover if he, too, could have a hug. To the woman's surprise, the lover nodded his assent. So the woman walked over to the man and put her arms around him. She gave him a hug and he hugged her back and the woman lost herself in the hug and the connection between them. **Out of this story the poet creates a meditation on love, possession, connection, presence, tenderness and commitment.**

Commentary

Stanza 1

The first stanza sets up the situation. A woman is reading on the street; another woman stops to listen and the narrator and her lover stop, too. There seems no apparent connection between the four people. They are strangers to each other who meet by accident. In this open public place, the narrator and her lover stand with their arms around each other. It is as if the normal activity of the world is suspended, as they listen to the woman reading.

Stanza 2

The narrator describes being possessed by the desire to give her lover a hug. She gives the hug and then continues to hold on to her lover. **The image of the hug and holding suggests an exclusive love shared between the two of them.** The narrator then describes a man, possibly a homeless man, approaching them. **Audaciously, speaking man to man, he asks the lover if he, too, can have a hug. To the surprise of the narrator, her lover gives his permission** and does not insist that their love is exclusive and that the woman (the narrator) is his alone. It is hard to decide if the narrator's surprise is born of anger or disappointment or if it is simply surprise.

Stanza 3

The narrator describes going over to the man, the stranger, and preparing to give the hug. She is uncertain, wondering how hard she should hug the man and for how long. The man is so big that when she puts her hands around his back, they do not meet.

Stanza 4

In the fourth stanza **the narrator describes how she settles into the hug, putting her head on the man's chest and leaning into him. The gesture is one of trust and tenderness.** The gesture is not only physical. The narrator declares that she leans her blood and her wishes into him. This is an arresting statement. 'Blood' suggests something warm and heartfelt. 'Wishes' suggest that the woman wishes the stranger well. The man, we are told, 'stands for it' (line 34). In other words, he is not overcome by her gesture but accepts it. And then he returns the hug to her so that they meet now not as donor and recipient but as equals.

The phrase 'This hug' (line 36) concentrates all the power of the poem on the moment of contact between the two strangers. Lines 36 to 40 describe the trance-like state the narrator enters in surrendering herself to this hug and the feelings of tenderness and truth. In this state, she has almost no consciousness of her lover, or the woman reading the poem, or the houses on the street.

Stanza 5

The final stanza contains both narrative and reflective elements and moves between the particular hug given to the stranger and all hugs. The statement, 'Clearly, a little permission is a dangerous thing' (line 41) has a sly humour about it. The word 'permission' is interesting. In one sense the permission for the hug has been given by the lover to the stranger. However, it is also the narrator and the stranger who give permission to themselves and to each other. Lines 42 and 43 read as the narrator justifying the kind of hug she gave the man and explaining the motivation behind all hugs: 'But when you hug someone you want it / to be a masterpiece of connection'. If connection is the aim of all hugs, even those given to strangers, what implication does this have on the idea of love as something exclusive and proprietorial?

The image of the button leaving the imprint of a planet on her cheek is beautiful and rich and will repay thinking about. The imprint is like a sign or a seal of the connection that has been made between the man and the woman. **Because the hug is a masterpiece, the connection is intense, absorbing and brief.**

The future tense 'will' (line 44) and the phrase 'when I walk away' (line 46) suggest that the narrator is still lost in the hug and has not yet found the place to which she will return. At this point in the poem the lover of the earlier stanzas seems absent. **This element of disorientation and loss creates a sense of mystery.** Will the woman return to her lover, the 'you' of the first two stanzas, or has the hug broken the bond between them? In surrendering herself to the hug, has everything else been left behind?

A love poem

The poem begins as a conventional love poem, based on the exclusive love of a man and a woman, but then the nature of the love described in the poem changes, and the woman reaches out to a stranger in a spirit of loving tenderness. Ironically, it is the lover, the one who gave 'permission' for the hug, who now seems excluded. Overall, the poem conveys a sense of accident, grace and giftedness about the situation. This is a small but good thing that takes place between strangers and it makes the world a more human and tender place.

Style of the poem

The poem has no rhymes and uses irregular stanzas. The voice of the narrator is natural and close to everyday speech. It is a gentle, thoughtful voice. The careful phrasing, the choice of words, the run-on lines and the absence of harsh sounds give the poem a smooth, flowing rhythm. The poem tells its story in a cinematic way with a strong emphasis on the visual. It has a number of arresting images, images of love and moments of pause. Gallagher says that rhythm and the image are important elements in her poetry, as well as mystery.

Exam-style questions

Thinking about the poem

1. From the first stanza what is your impression of the relationship between the narrator and her lover?
2. Explain the image of the star in stanza 2. Is it effective?
3. What is the reason for the woman's surprise in stanza 2? What surprises you about the events related in stanza 2?
4. As outlined in stanza 3, what kind of thoughts are going through the narrator's head as she prepares to hug the man?
5. What effect does the hug have on the narrator, based on the evidence of stanzas 4 and 5?
6. Many people admire the button imagery of the final stanza. Why, do you think, is this so?
7. The poem is written in the present tense. What is the effect of this? Explain your answer.

8   'The poem explores a moment of loving tenderness that is all the more powerful because the man and woman are strangers to each other.' Give your view of this reading of the poem. Support the points you make with quotations from the poem.

9   From the list, select **three** words which, in your view, capture the mood of the poem: gentle, thoughtful, tender, mysterious, confused, sad. Explain your choice.

10 The woman hugs the man because:

   She has no choice.
   She wants to spite her lover.
   She pities the man.
   She is generous.

Which of these explanations is closest to your reading of the poem? Explain your choice.

Taking a closer look

1   'He looks homeless because of how / he needs' (lines 13–14). Write a note on this statement teasing out its full implications.

2   A 'masterpiece of connection' (line 43). Write a short piece giving your definition of this phrase.

3   'When I try to find some place / to go back to' (lines 46–47) Do you think the narrator goes back to the place from where she started? Explain your answer.

4   How are the personal pronouns (I, you and we) used in this poem? Do they change over the course of the poem?

5   'The moral of the poem is that no human being ever belongs to another.' Discuss.

6   Choose your favourite image from the poem and say why you chose it.

Imagining

1   If the poem were a film, then stanza 4 would be where the camera zooms in on the couple who are embracing. Using the details in the stanza, describe how you would portray this scene on film.

2   Turn the events described in the poem into a short story written from the perspective of the man who asked for the hug.

3   Write **two** diary entries in the voice of the narrator's lover describing the day of the hug and the impact of the incident on you.

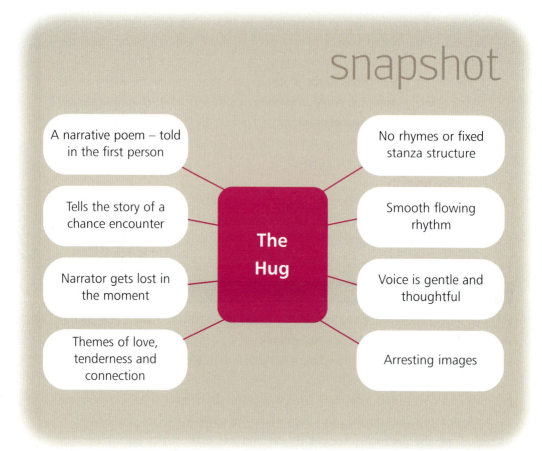

Kerry Hardie

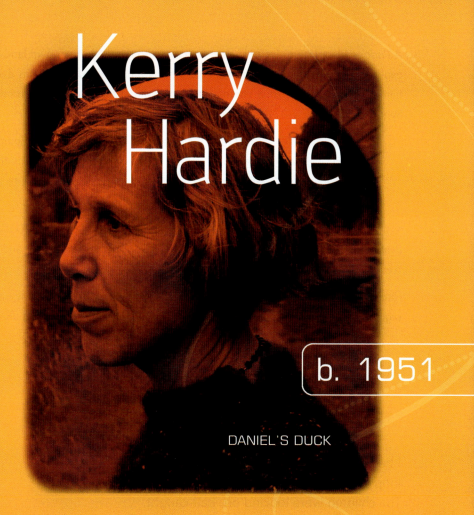

b. 1951

DANIEL'S DUCK

Biography

Kerry Hardie was born in 1951 in Singapore and grew up in Co. Down. She studied English at York University in England and then came back to Ireland to work as a researcher and radio interviewer for the BBC in Belfast and Derry:

> This period coincided with the most violent years of the Troubles, and through my job I had access to situations and people I might not otherwise have known. I became fascinated with people who found themselves in a hard place and with how they reacted to this place. Some people adapted astonishingly fast to their new realities, but others spent their energies resisting and could only change to meet them when they had in some way been broken by them.

Hardie has published several collections of poetry. Her first novel, *A Winter Marriage*, was published in 2002, and her second novel, *The Bird Woman*, was published in 2006.

A Furious Place (1996) includes poems that record people in their own landscapes and explores the way in which landscape permeates their lives. Other poems dwell on the hardships and lessons of a chronic illness. Hardie suffers from ME (Chronic Fatigue Syndrome):

> Being chronically sick makes you an observer rather than a participant. Before I was sick, I lived very hard and my life was very outgoing; now my life is quiet and disciplined and reflective. . . . It took me a long time to come to terms with the change, but now I find my life immensely rich and rewarding.

Many of the poems in *The Sky Didn't Fall* (2003), from which 'Daniel's Duck' is taken, deal with grief and loss and the contrast between the outside world and our inner feelings.

Hardie has won major literary awards and she is a member of Aosdána, the national arts organisation. She lives in Kilkenny with her husband, Sean Hardie, who is also a writer.

Daniel's Duck

(for Frances)

I held out the shot mallard, she took it from me,
looped its neck-string over a drawer of the dresser.
The children were looking on, half-caught.
Then the kitchen life – warm, lit, glowing –
moved forward, taking in the dead bird,   5
and its coldness, its wildness, were leaching away.

The children were sitting to their dinners.
Us too – drinking tea, hardly noticing
the child's quiet slide from his chair,
his small absorbed body before the duck's body,   10
the duck changing – feral, live –
arrowing up out of black sloblands
with the gleam of a river
falling away below.

Then the duck – dead again – hanging from the drawer-knob   15
the green head, brown neck running into the breast,

the intricate silvery-greyness of the back;
the wings, their white bars and blue flashes,
the feet, their snakey, orange scaliness, small claws, piteous webbing,
the yellow beak, blooded, 20
the whole like a weighted sack –
all that downward-dragginess of death.

He hovered, took a step forward, a step back,
something appeared in his face, some knowledge
of a place where he stood, the world stilled, 25
the lit streaks of sunrise running off red
into the high bowl of the morning.

She watched him, moving to touch, his hand out:
What is it, Daniel, do you like the duck?
He turned as though caught in the act, 30
saw the gentleness in her face and his body loosened.
I thought there was water on it –
he was finding the words, one by one,
holding them out, to see would they do us –
But there isn't. 35
He added this on, going small with relief
that his wind-drag of sound was enough.

Glossary

1	*mallard*:	a wild duck (the male or drake has the markings described in the poem)
6	*leaching away*:	seeping or draining away; disappearing
11	*feral*:	wild; not tame or domesticated but fending for itself
12	*arrowing up*:	flying upwards with wings outstretched the duck resembles an arrow shape
12	*sloblands*:	mudflats or land reclaimed from the sea
19	*scaliness*:	the quality of being covered in scales or scab-like, thin plates that provide protection on the legs of birds and the skin of fish and reptiles
19	*piteous*:	deserving or giving rise to pity; heartrending; pathetic
37	*wind-drag*:	when birds fly they use their wings to push the air out of the way and the sound made by their wings is the result of the drag or resistance of the wind

Guidelines

The poem tells a story, a little drama from daily life. In a kitchen, where the children sit down to their dinner and the adults drink tea, **a young boy encounters death in the form of a shot mallard and tries to make sense of his experience.** The poem focuses on the moment when the boy begins to understand something, though he has not the words to express his new knowledge. Standing absorbed before the bird, he enters a private world and feels something like guilt when he becomes aware of the attention of the adults. To his relief, the adults are satisfied by the words he finds to explain his fascination for the duck.

Within the narrative, the poem encompasses many ideas and contrasting themes: the contrast between the living wild duck and the dead bird hanging in the kitchen; the contrast between the duck 'arrowing up out of black sloblands' and the force of death dragging the body down; the dawning of knowledge in the child; the private, interior world of the child; the contrast between things we can describe and those experiences for which we struggle to find words.

Commentary

Stanzas 1 and 2

The narrator tells us that the handing over of the duck to the woman of the house and the hanging of the bird on the dresser was something that 'half-caught' (line 3) the attention of the children before the life of the kitchen, the warm domestic life of the household, moved on and the duck began to lose its 'wildness' (line 6).

We learn that one child, the Daniel of the title, has slid from the chair and is standing in front of the duck. Reading between the lines, the poem suggests that Daniel is seeing the duck as though it was alive in its wild or feral state.

Stanzas 3 and 4

There is a detailed description of the duck as it is now, hanging dead on the drawer-knob. The description emphasises its intricate colouring, including the blood on its 'yellow beak' (line 20), and the way in which the duck is weighed down and dragged down by death.

The young boy tries to make sense of what he sees. The verb 'hovers' suggest that his thought is moving back and forth and he is absorbed in the moment, so much so that the world is 'stilled' (line 25). **The idea that he understands something for the first time is suggested in the imagery of the dawn and the sun rising.**

Stanza 5

As he reaches out his hand to touch the dead duck, the boy is interrupted by a woman's voice. He seems almost guilty: 'as though caught in the act' (line 30), but he relaxes when he sees 'the gentleness in her face' (line 31). **He tries to find the words to explain himself and is relieved when no more questions are asked.**

Form and style of the poem

The story is narrated by an adult, possibly the person who shot the duck. Clearly the narrator's account is sympathetic to Daniel and, arguably, parts of the poem are written as if seen through the child's eyes. **'Daniel's Duck' brings us into the middle of a small drama, but intriguingly it leaves a number of questions unanswered.** Who speaks the words: the poet or a persona like a narrator in a novel? Is it a man or a woman? What is the speaker's relationship to the 'she' of the poem and to Daniel? Is the 'she' Daniel's mother?

Although the poem is written in irregular stanzas with no rhyme scheme, Hardie pays great attention to sound and rhythm and there are many examples of alliteration as well as consonance and assonance. Look, for example, at how the 'l' sound is repeated throughout the first stanza, or how 'b' and 'd' sounds echo through the second stanza and into the first lines of stanza 3. You will also notice the words which end with '-ness'. Note, too, the succession of noun phrases that are used to great effect in stanza 3 to describe the duck.

Exam-style questions

Thinking about the poem

1. According to the speaker of the poem in the first stanza, what happened to the duck once it was hung from the drawer-knob of the dresser?
2. There is a reference in stanza 2 to 'the duck changing' (line 11). Where and how does the duck change?
3. The third stanza is a detailed description of the appearance of the shot duck. Comment on each detail and its significance.
4. The fourth stanza focuses on the young boy. In your own words explain what happens to the boy and the 'something' that 'appeared in his face' (line 24).
5. In the final stanza, what was Daniel's initial reaction when the woman called out to him?
6. Think about the meaning of the last word of the poem 'enough'. In what sense was Daniel's answer 'enough'?
7. There are many contrasts in the poem. Identify as many of them as you can and comment on each.
8. Having read the poem, what age is Daniel, in your opinion?
9. Here are three views of what the poem is about. Which one of them is closest to your view?

    A child's first encounter with death.
    The difference between the things we can describe and those which are beyond words.
    The difference between the private world of children and the world of adults.
    Explain your choice.

10 'Good poetry creates vivid pictures in our minds.' In your opinion, is this true of 'Daniel's Duck'? Support your view by reference to the poem.

Taking a closer look

1 Give your view of the effectiveness of the phrase 'that downward-dragginess of death' (line 22).
2 'the lit streaks of sunrise running off red / into the high bowl of the morning' (lines 26–27). In your view, why has the poet included these lines at this point in the poem?
3 Comment on the phrase 'his wind-drag of sound' in the last line of the poem.
4 There are many interesting uses of words in the poem. Select **two** which you like and say why you like them.

Imagining

1 Imagine that you are Daniel. You are now a young man. Write a diary entry in which you record your experiences and feelings on the day described in the poem.
2 If you were to make a film that interprets the poem, what images would you include and what kind of music would you select as a musical score?

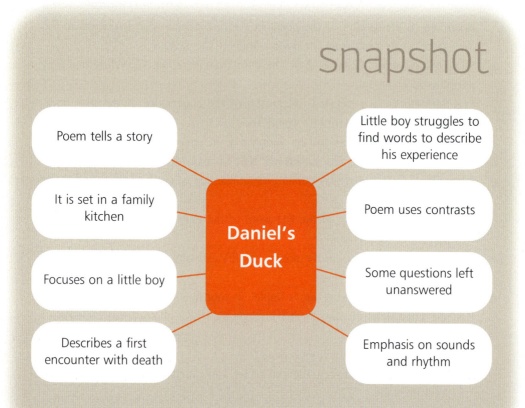

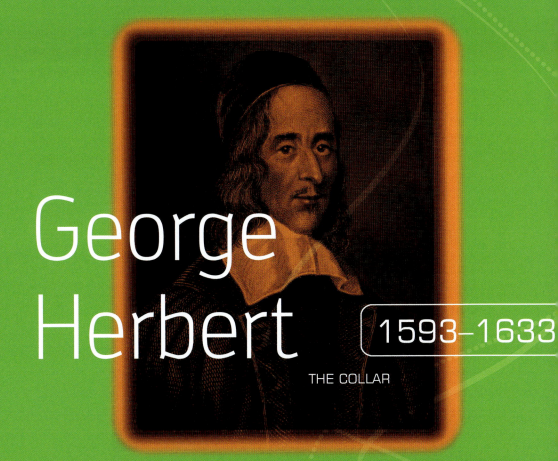

George Herbert
1593–1633

THE COLLAR

Biography

George Herbert was born in Wales into a distinguished military family. His father died when he was three years old and he grew up under the watchful eye of his mother, who was a friend of the poet and preacher John Donne. Herbert won distinction at Trinity College, Cambridge, where he became a Fellow and lecturer. In or before 1626 he was ordained deacon in the Church of England. He married in 1629. In 1630 he was ordained priest and appointed rector of Bemerton, near Salisbury, in southern England.

Herbert was first and foremost a religious poet, and he devoted his life and his work to the service of God. He was troubled by failing health and by thoughts of unfitness and futility. The seventeenth-century commentator Richard Baxter remarked, 'Herbert speaks to God like one that really believeth a God, and whose business in the world is most with God'.

Herbert has always been admired for the purity of his diction. He maintains a homely, colloquial quietness of tone, and peace brings quiet endings. He did not cultivate scientific or learned classical imagery; rather, nature and everyday life, the Bible and the liturgy of his church were his chief sources. He said more than once that the highest truth must be plainly dressed.

Herbert's poems circulated only in manuscript form during his lifetime. On his deathbed he sent a volume of his manuscript poems to his friend Nicholas Ferrar, who had founded a religious community in nearby Little Gidding. He asked Ferrar to decide whether to publish or destroy his work. Ferrar published the poems in 1633.

The Collar

I struck the board, and cry'd, No more.
I will abroad.
What? shall I ever sigh and pine?
My lines and life are free; free as the road,
Loose as the winde, as large as store. 5
Shall I be still in suit?
Have I no harvest but a thorn
To let me blood, and not restore
What I have lost with cordiall fruit?
Sure there was wine 10
Before my sighs did drie it: there was corn
Before my tears did drown it.

Is the yeare onely lost to me?
Have I no bayes to crown it?
No, flowers, no garlands gay? all blasted? 15
All wasted?
Not so, my heart: but there is fruit,
And thou hast hands.
Recover all thy sigh-blown age
On double pleasures: leave thy cold dispute 20
Of what is fit, and not; forsake thy cage,
Thy rope of sands,
Which pettie thoughts have made, and made to thee
Good cable, to enforce and draw,

And be thy law, 25
While thou didst wink and wouldst not see
Away; take heed:
I will abroad.
Call in thy death's head there: tie up thy fears.
He that forbears 30
To suit and serve his need,
Deserves his load.

But as I rav'd and grew more fierce and wilde
At every word,
Me thought I heard one calling, *Childe*: 35
And I reply'd, *My Lord*.

Glossary

1	*board:* the altar or the table of the father's house
2	*abroad:* away from home
3	*pine:* long for something not achieved
4	*My lines . . . road:* I am free to do as I wish and go where I wish
5	*store:* plenty
6	*Shall . . . suit?:* Am I always going to be in service to the will of God? Am I always going to be God's slave?
8	*let me blood*: spill my blood
8–9	*restore . . . fruit*: compensate me for my losses with achievements to restore my spirits
10–11	*wine . . . corn*: these stand for lawful pleasures
14–15	*bayes . . . garlands*: symbols of achievement
17	*there is fruit*: life has its pleasures
18	*And . . . hands*: you can have the pleasures of life if only you will reach out for them
19–20	*Recover . . . pleasures*: compensate yourself for your period of misery by enjoying a double share of pleasure
20	*cold dispute*: debate that brings no comfort
21	*fit*: proper
22	*rope of sands*: bonds that are liable to come apart easily, so ending the heart's imprisonment

Glossary

23–25	*Which pettie ... law*:	you have imposed your own petty or childish limits on yourself and observed these limits as the law of your life
26	*While ... see*:	you ignored the means of escape from your self-imposed limits
29	*deaths head*:	a skull, which served as a reminder to religious people of the certainty of death, intended to ensure strict behaviour
30–32	*He that ... load*:	the man who fails to put his own needs first deserves the burdens others place on his shoulders
35–36	*I heard ... My Lord*:	these two lines express the traditional Christian idea that human beings are God's children

Guidelines

The speaker of this poem is a Christian priest. **The poem is mainly concerned with a conflict between the speaker's will and the will of God.** The title expresses discipline, control and service to God. For the priest-speaker this service is performed through following his religious vocation. He makes it clear that this vocation means that he must suffer a certain loss of freedom. He is strongly tempted to regain his freedom by giving up his priesthood and leaving for some unnamed region. The more he thinks of the opportunities for pleasure he is missing and of the narrowness of his way of life, the more angry and frustrated he becomes. He talks wildly and excitedly, like a child who has been deprived of something he badly wants. At the height of his angry outburst, the voice of God sounds in his ears, calling him back to Him and to His service. The speaker immediately submits to God's demand. The rebellion is over.

Commentary

Lines 1–16

In this section the speaker expresses the complaints of his heart against his unhappy life of service to God. He is determined to find happiness and freedom in some unnamed place ('abroad', line 2). He feels that the courses of action open to him are without limit: his 'lines and life are free' (line 4). The road and the wind suggest freedom. The world outside is full of possible benefits, having plenty ('store', line 5) to offer him. He wonders why he must always be a slave ('in suit', line 6) to God's will. He has given up the pleasures of the world, represented in the poem by corn and wine. All he has got in return is a harvest of pain and sorrow ('thorn ... blood ... sighs ... tears', lines 7–12). The 'bayes', 'flowers' and 'garlands' of lines 14 and 15 are symbols of success and achievement. He has none of these rewards because he has wasted his talents on a vocation that has given him only misery and disappointment.

Lines 17–26

Here the speaker's will answers the complaints made by the heart in the first section of the poem. The will suggests strongly that there is no need for the speaker's heart to despair. Life has its pleasures (its 'fruit', line 17), but the speaker must reach out for them. He will be able to do so ('thou hast hands', line 18). He can even make up for all the miseries he has suffered so far ('thy sigh-blown age', line 19). He can do this by enjoying increased ('double', line 20) pleasures. He must give up his useless debate ('cold dispute', line 20) about what may be right or wrong for him ('what is fit, and not', line 21). His conscience is a prison from which he must break free, as a bird or animal might escape from its cage. His doubts and fears have bound him like a rope, which is not as strong as he thinks: it is merely a 'rope of sands' (line 22). He has refused to accept the means of escape, which has always been there.

Lines 27–32

These lines belong to the speaker's heart, which repeats the earlier complaints it made in lines 1 to 16. It is now determined to break free. Up to now the speaker's life has been controlled by thoughts of death. The 'death's head' (line 29), or skull, was a constant reminder of death. When he casts this skull aside, he will be able to enjoy himself without fear. He has been tied up by his fears; now he will be able to tie up these fears. He decides that he will serve his own needs rather than serve God. A slave deserves whatever burdens his master places on his shoulders. Here, the master is God.

Lines 33–36

The speaker's language has been growing more and more excitable and wild. In the final four lines, the voice of God restores peace and calm to his soul, and the speaker addresses God as a child would address a father. He puts aside his complaints and is ready to follow his vocation as a priest.

Deeper meanings

'The Collar' offers new layers of meaning on each new reading. God is presented as a father, and the speaker as his child who wants to leave home. Here, Herbert is glancing at Christ's parable of the prodigal son. 'Board' in the first line can mean 'altar' as well as 'table'. Since the man striking the board is a priest, his action in striking the board is a sacrilege. The priestly collar of the title is a symbol of service and even enslavement. There may also be a pun on 'choler' (anger), which would fit the speaker's state of mind. Notice that Herbert uses unpleasant sounds and images that seem odd and out of place ('sigh-blown', 'cold dispute', 'cage', 'rope of sands'). The same applies to the very first rhyme we hear ('board' / 'abroad'). It is as if the speaker is too impatient and angry to find a proper rhyme.

Imagery

At first glance it might be difficult to tell from the imagery that this is a deeply Christian poem. This is because the Christian imagery on which the poem is based can be read as the imagery of nature, food and drink. The wine and corn of lines 10 and 11 are the bread and wine of the Eucharist. The thorn and blood of lines 7 and 8 are intended to recall Christ's crowning with thorns. The child and lord of the two final lines are the Christian and God, in this case the Christian priest and his heavenly Father.

Imagery has a vital part to play in expressing the speaker's thoughts and feelings. Until the final two lines, the speaker's mind is disordered, even chaotic. The imagery reflects this. The board of the first line is the altar, normally a focus of peace and quietness. 'The Collar' opens with an image of a rebel priest violently striking the altar with his hand in a gesture of defiance. As the poem proceeds, the speaker's anger increases, and the imagery becomes more violent. The early lines feature pleasant images of 'cordiall' fruit, wine, flowers and garlands. These give way to the menacing images of the 'cage', the 'rope of sands', the 'cable' and the 'death's head'.

Rhymes and rhythms

The rhymes and rhythms of 'The Collar', like its imagery, mirror the chaos and confusion of the speaker's mind. The arrangement of the lines and rhymes provides a perfect image of revolt. Notice the irregular appearance of the poem as you look at it on the page. Notice that as you read it aloud, it lacks an even, rhythmic pattern. This is deliberate on Herbert's part. The chaotic rhythms match the chaos in the speaker's mind and spirit. In the first thirty-two lines there are different patterns of rhyme (six) and line lengths (seven). The rhyming scheme lacks any kind of pattern. Of the nine groups of four lines, only the final one has a regular rhyming scheme ('wilde' / 'Childe'; 'word' / 'Lord'). This return to a normal rhyming pattern comes only when the speaker returns to an orderly state of mind from his earlier confusion.

Exam-style questions

Thinking about the poem

1. For almost the entire poem, the speaker is in a state of revolt. What is he revolting against? Explain your answer with reference to the poem.
2. Why does the speaker submit at the end of the poem?
3. The speaker is a Christian priest. Comment on some details in the poem that suggest this.
4. 'The poem as a whole is a depiction of violence and disorder.' Comment on this idea with reference to the poem.
5. The poem is based on a dialogue between the speaker's heart and his will. Comment on it from this point of view.
6. In what way does the speaker blame himself for his problems? Refer to relevant details of the poem in your answer.
7. Some of the images in the poem convey the idea that the speaker is in captivity. Explain how these images work.
8. Do you think that the speaker's inner conflict is resolved too easily? Refer to the poem in support of your answer.
9. How would you describe the relationship between God and the speaker?
10. 'In Herbert's opinion, harmony and order represented God and goodness.' Comment on 'The Collar' in the light of this opinion.
11. In which part of the poem is harmony restored? Explain how this is done.
12. 'Throughout the body of the poem, God's love has been working within the speaker despite his rebellious agitation.' Consider the evidence provided in 'The Collar' for this point of view.

Taking a closer look

1. It has been said that the structure of the poem and its shape on the page offer a representation of what the speaker is trying to communicate. Examine this idea with reference to the text.
2. Discuss the religious imagery of 'The Collar', with reference to the text.
3. Choose a phrase or a line from the poem that impressed you. Explain your choice.

Imagining

1. You are forced to confront a situation in which duty points you in one direction and personal inclination points you in the opposite one. Describe such a situation and explain how you might deal with it.
2. Imagine that you are Herbert. Write a letter to a friend giving reasons for writing this poem.

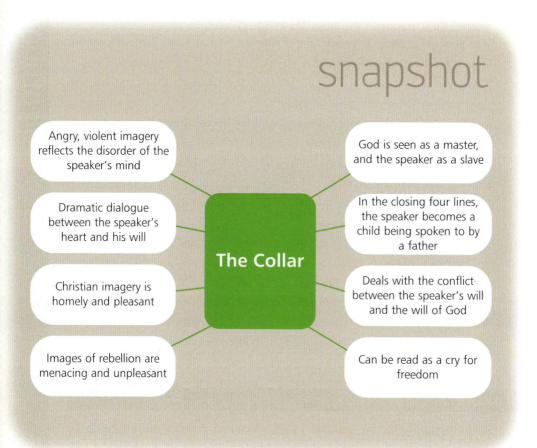

Brendan Kennelly

b. 1936

NIGHT DRIVE

Biography

Brendan Kennelly was born in 1936 in Ballylongford, Co. Kerry. He was educated at St Ita's College, Tarbert, Co. Kerry, and Trinity College, Dublin. He also studied at Leeds University in England.

He has lectured at the University of Antwerp, at Barnard College, New York, and at Swarthmore College, Pennsylvania. He was Professor of Modern Literature at Trinity College, Dublin, for over thirty years, and retired from that post in 2005. He now teaches part-time in the United States and lives in Dublin.

Kennelly has published over thirty books of poetry, among them *My Dark Fathers* (1964), *Cromwell* (1983), *Breathing Spaces: Early Poems* (1992), *Poetry Me Arse* (1995), *Familiar Strangers: New and Selected Poems 1960–2004* (2004) and *Now* (2006).

He has also translated poems from Irish, and these are collected in the volume *Love of Ireland* (1989). He edited *The Penguin Book of Irish Verse* (1981) and published two novels. He is a well-known dramatist whose plays include versions of the Greek plays *Antigone* and *Medea*, and a stage version of his poem *Cromwell*. He is a renowned and popular broadcaster on radio and television where he has done a great deal to bring poetry to a wider audience.

Night Drive

I
The rain hammered as we drove
Along the road to Limerick
'Jesus what a night!' Alan breathed
And – 'I wonder how he is, the last account
Was poor.' 5
I couldn't speak.

The windscreen fumed and blurred, the rain's spit
Lashing the glass. Once or twice
The wind's fist seemed to lift the car
And pitch it hard against the ditch. 10
Alan straightened out in time,
Silent. Glimpses of the Shannon –
A boiling madhouse roaring for its life
Or any life too near its gaping maw,
White shreds flaring in the waste 15
Of insane murderous black;
Trees bending in grotesque humility,
Branches scattered on the road, smashed
Beneath the wheels.
Then, ghastly under the headlights, 20
Frogs bellied everywhere, driven
From the swampy fields and meadows,
Bewildered refugees, gorged with terror.
We killed them because we had to,
Their fatness crunched and flattened in the dark. 25
'How is he now?" Alan whispered
To himself. Behind us,
Carnage of broken frogs.

II
His head
Sweated on the pillow of the white hospital bed.
He spoke a little, said
Outrageously, 'I think I'll make it.'
Another time, he'd rail against the weather,
(Such a night would make him eloquent)
But now, quiet, he gathered his fierce will
To live.

III
Coming home
Alan saw the frogs.
'Look at them, they're everywhere,
Dozens of the bastards dead.'

Minutes later –
'I think he might pull through now.'
Alan, thoughtful at the wheel, was picking out
The homeroad in the flailing rain
Nighthedges closed on either side.
In the suffocating darkness
I heard the heavy breathing
Of my father's pain.

Glossary		
14	*gaping maw*: a stomach that devours its prey	
17	*grotesque*: bizarre	
23	*gorged*: made fat	
28	*carnage*: slaughter	
33	*rail*: to scold or curse	
34	*eloquent*: expressive	
44	*flailing*: striking out in all directions	

Guidelines

'Night Drive' is from *Breathing Spaces* (1992). **In this poem, Kennelly describes his feelings as he travels with his brother, Alan, to visit their dying father.**

Commentary

Part I

The dreadful weather is described in a series of powerful images, as if it has a life of its own: the rain can 'spit' (line 7), the wind has a 'fist' (line 9). Strong verbs reinforce the violence of the weather: the rain that 'hammered' (line 1), the wind that seemed to 'pitch' (line 10) the car against the ditch.

It is as if nature is in tune with the turmoil of the two brothers' feelings, although it is Alan who is given the direct speech. The poet himself says simply in line 6: 'I couldn't speak.'

The River Shannon, which they pass on their journey to Co. Kerry, is compared to a 'boiling madhouse' (line 13) with a 'gaping maw' (line 14) or stomach that would devour all in its path. The metaphors prepare us for the images of destruction that follow: the stark white and black of the water is 'murderous' (line 16), the branches of the trees are 'smashed' (line 18) beneath the wheels of the car. The trees themselves are 'bending in grotesque humility' (line 17), helpless before the strength of the storm.

Another 'ghastly' (line 20) sight is that of the frogs, driven out of the flooded fields like 'refugees' (line 23) searching for safety but being killed underneath the wheels of the car. 'Crunched and flattened' (line 25) expresses the sound and sight of what the poet describes as 'carnage of broken frogs' (line 28).

Again, it is Alan who voices his concern about their father. **The sights and sounds of death and destruction in the world outside the car are subconsciously related to the father's struggle for life.**

Part II

There is a moving description of their dying father as he lies in his hospital bed. He is struggling against the inevitable end. His fierce will to live is reflected in what he says, 'I think I'll make it' (line 32) but the poet seems to know that he speaks 'outrageously' – there is little hope that he will survive. We get a glimpse of him as having been a strong man who would once have cursed such weather, but now he needs all his energy to stay alive.

Part III

As the poet and his brother make their way home after the hospital visit, their attitudes to their father's illness seem to differ. Alan appears quite hopeful about his recovery, in contrast to the lifeless frogs that are strewn on the roadway. But the poet does not appear to share his optimism. As he describes his brother driving carefully home, words such as 'flailing', 'closed' and 'suffocating' (lines 44 to 46) remind us that the poem is about the struggle with death that is part of nature, for the frogs as well as human beings.

The poem ends with an image that does not flinch from the hopelessness of this struggle: the 'heavy breathing' of their 'father's pain' (lines 47 and 48). **His desire to survive will end with the 'suffocating darkness'** (line 46) **of the grave.**

Exam-style questions

Thinking about the poem

1. In what way does the weather reflect the human situation that is described in the poem?
2. Do you think that the image of the frogs is significant in the poem? Explain your answer.
3. Why, do you think, does the poet describe the journey in more detail than the actual visit to his father? Give a reason for your answer.
4. What impression of the poet's father do you get when you read the poem?
5. Do you think that the father had a good relationship with his sons? Explain your answer.
6. How do the images of death and destruction contribute to the mood of the poem?
7. Choose the word which in your opinion most closely describes the atmosphere created in 'Night Drive': tense, depressing, sad, hopeful or confused. Explain your choice.
8. 'The poem deals with the theme of death in a powerful and moving way.' Write a paragraph in which you agree or disagree with this statement.

Taking a closer look

1. Comment on the effect of the following phrases in the poem:
   - 'the Shannon – / A boiling madhouse roaring for its life' (lines 12–13)
   - 'Trees bending in grotesque humility' (line 17)
   - 'Carnage of broken frogs' (line 28).
2. Suggest a new title for the poem, giving a reason for your choice.

Imagining

1. You have been asked to make a short film of the first part of the poem. Describe the sort of atmosphere you would like to create, and say what music, sound effects and images you would use.
2. A collection of poems called *Last Memories* is being put together. Explain why you would or would not recommend the inclusion of 'Night Drive' in the collection.

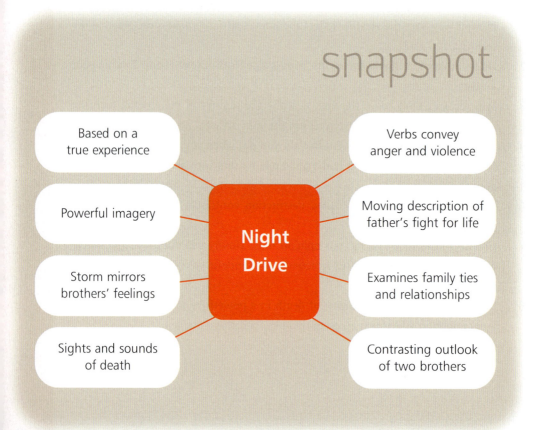

Liz Lochhead

b. 1947

KIDSPOEM/BAIRNSANG

Biography

Liz Lochhead was born in Motherwell, Scotland in 1947 into a Presbyterian family. At the local secondary school, her essays were praised by her teachers and she won the lead parts in school plays. Against her headmaster's advice, she studied art in Glasgow, and later taught art at schools in Glasgow and Bristol. She describes herself as having been a 'terrible' teacher. Her first collection of poems, *Memo for Spring*, was published in the early 1970s and won a Scottish Arts Council Award. In 1978 she left teaching to become a full-time writer. At a time when most Scottish poets were men, Lochhead was a fresh, original and witty voice on the literary scene.

Lochhead has described her writing as 'female-coloured as well as Scottish-coloured'. Her poetry celebrates Scots, the version of English spoken by many ordinary Scottish people, and gives expression to it as a valid language in its own right. Her poetry also celebrates women as a marginalised community within Scottish society.

Apart from her poetry, Lochhead is well known as a playwright. Her plays include *Blood and Ice* (1982), *Mary Queen of Scots Got Her Head Chopped Off* (1989) and *Dracula* (1989). The titles give an indication of her humour and her interest in Gothic horror. As well as writing new plays, she has translated and adapted existing plays into Scots and English.

Lochhead is married and lives in Glasgow. In 2005 she was appointed Glasgow's Poet Laureate. The announcement of her appointment described her as someone who 'is generous in her sympathies, sharp in her observation, and moves her audiences to tears and laughter'. In 2011 she became Scots Makar, or Scotland's national poet.

Kidspoem/Bairnsang

it wis January
and a gey driech day
the first day Ah went to the school
so my Mum happed me up in ma
good navy-blue napp coat wi the rid tartan hood   5
birled a scarf aroon ma neck
pu'ed oan ma pixie an' my pawkies
it wis that bitter
said noo ye'll no starve
gie'd me a wee kiss and a kid-oan skelp oan the bum   10
and sent me aff across the playground
tae the place A'd learn to say
it was January
and a really dismal day
the first day I went to school   15
so my mother wrapped me up in my
best navy-blue top coat with the red tartan hood,
twirled a scarf around my neck,
pulled on my bobble-hat and mittens
it was so bitterly cold   20
said now you won't freeze to death
gave me a little kiss and a pretend slap on the bottom

and sent me off across the playground
to the place I'd learn to forget to say
it wis January 25
and a gey driech day
the first day Ah went to the school
so my Mum happed me up in ma
good navy-blue napp coat wi the rid tartan hood,
birled a scarf aroon ma neck, 30
pu'ed oan ma pixie an' ma pawkies
it wis that bitter.

Oh saying it was one thing
But when it came to writing it
In black and white 35
The way it had to be said
Was as if you were posh, grown-up, male, English and dead.

Guidelines

'Kidspoem/Bairnsang' is from Lochhead's 2003 collection, *The Colour of Black and White: Poems 1984–2003*.

Lochhead's work shows an interest in everyday speech and accent. Her poetry is characterised by its conversational quality, which deliberately seeks to capture the idioms and rhythm of Scots. **For Lochhead, language and accent are part of the politics of class, gender and nationality.**

Commentary

The poem is written in the first person. The narrator describes her mum getting her ready for her first day at school. The day is cold and dismal and her mum wraps her up warmly before sending her off across the playground to school. **This description occurs twice in the poem, once in Scots and the second time in Standard English.** In this way, the poem explores how schooling substitutes Standard English for the child's own language. Not only does the child learn to speak in a new way, but she learns to forget the old way.

In relation to writing, **the child learns that the 'correct' way to write is to use a style that belongs to a different class, a different nationality and a different gender from her own, and which lacks the vitality of the language of home.** In school she learns to write 'as if you were posh, grown-up, male, English and dead' (line 37). **The effect of school, then, is to make Scots seem an inferior language or a childish language, in comparison with Standard English.** However, the effect of the poem is to show the vitality and energy of Scots and to question the wisdom of an educational system that suppresses it.

Language of the poem

Much of the poem's energy comes from the sounds of the language, with the emphasis on consonants, like the 'ch' in 'dreich'; the voiced 'd' and 't' in words such as 'rid' and 'coat'; the alliteration and plosive sounds in the phrase 'pixie and pawkies'; and the rolling, rumbling sound of the 'rl' in 'birled'. Part of the pleasure of the language is the expressive effect of pronouncing these sounds.

Exam-style questions

Thinking about the poem

1. What words are effective in capturing the weather on the narrator's first day at school?
2. What picture of the little girl do you get from the poem? Explain your answer.
3. In your view, which of the following words describes the relationship between the child and her mother: loving, mocking or cruel? Explain your answer.
4. In your view, what kind of place is school, as described in the poem? Explain your answer.
5. 'What the poem says is that for someone who was not raised as a speaker of Standard English, school is where you learn to become someone else.' Give your response to this statement.
6. In your view, what would be the advantages and disadvantages of speakers of Scots writing their language as they speak it?
7. Lochhead considers each poem as a voice, as something to be heard out loud. Read the poem out loud and describe the difference between the Scots and the Standard English parts of the poem.
8. Identify what you consider to be the elements that make 'Kidspoem/Bairnsang' a poem.

9　Which of the following statements is closest to your view of the poem:
　　　It is a poem about the difference between home and school.
　　　It is a poem about the power of language.
　　　It is a poem about identity.
　　Explain your choice.

Taking a closer look

1　Select **two** of your favourite words or phrases from the poem and say why you chose them.
2　Using the Standard English part of the poem, write a glossary for the following Scots words: 'gey'; 'dreich'; 'birled'; 'pixie'; 'pawkies'; and 'kid-oan'.

Imagining

1　Imagine that you are making a film to accompany a reading of the poem. Describe the visuals you would use and the music you would select for the soundtrack.
2　Using 'Kidspoem/Bairnsang' as a model, write your own twelve-line poem about your first day at school.

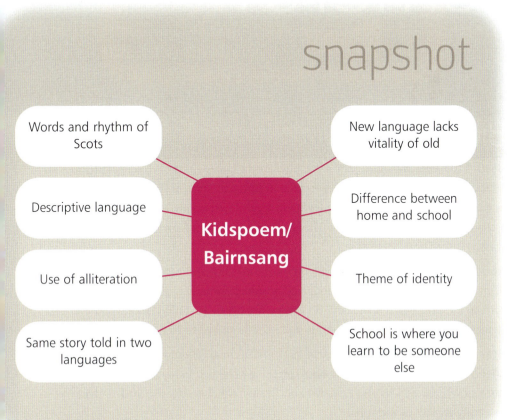

Howard Nemerov

1920-91

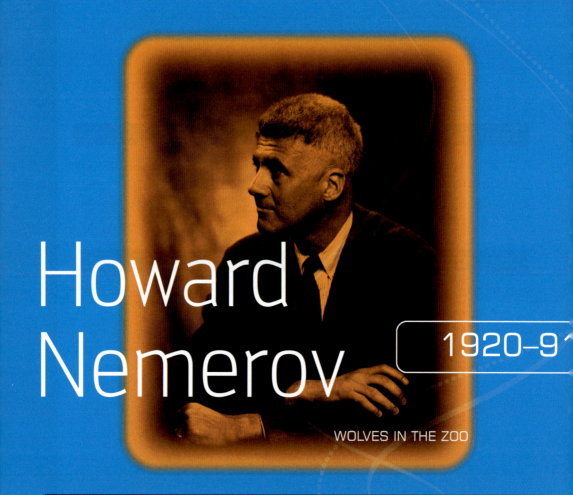

WOLVES IN THE ZOO

Biography

Howard Nemerov was born into a wealthy Jewish family on 29 February 1920 in New York city. His parents owned a fashionable department store on Fifth Avenue and were interested in art and theatre. He grew up in a privileged home, with two maids, a cook, a chauffeur and a German nanny. The family was untouched by the 1929 stock market crash and the Great Depression.

Nemerov was accepted into Harvard University in 1937 and earned a Bachelor of Arts degree in English. After college, he joined an American unit of the Canadian Air Force, earning the rank of first lieutenant. He flew combat missions during World War II. In 1944 Nemerov married and after the war he and his wife moved to New York.

He published his first book of poetry in 1947 and his final collection was published shortly after his death in 1991. During his long career, he published thirteen books of poetry and three novels, as well as short stories and literary criticism. He also had a career as a university teacher of literature.

Nemerov won many awards and prizes for his writing, including the Pulitzer Prize and the National Book Award. He was the Poet Laureate for the Library of Congress in America from 1988 to 1990, a position given in recognition of outstanding achievement in poetry. Despite these honours, Nemerov, an intensely private man, remained insecure about his achievement as a writer. Of his poetry he remarked: 'I do insist on making what I hope is sense so there's always a coherent narrative or argument that the reader can follow instantly the first time through and then if there's something more to occupy the reader, I've been lucky.'

As a poet, Nemerov is known for his intelligence and his irreverence. His friend and fellow poet James Dickey said: 'Nemerov is a poet of great wit and deep resources. He's the most unboring poet I know. He can say funny and serious things at the same time, and is the best of both wit and seriousness we have now.'

Nemerov died of throat cancer in 1991.

Wolves in the Zoo

They look like big dogs badly drawn, drawn wrong.
A legend on their cage tells us there is
No evidence that any of their kind
Has ever attacked man, woman, or child.

Now it turns out there were no babies dropped   5
In sacrifice, delaying tactics, from
Siberian sleds; now it turns out, so late,
That Little Red Ridinghood and her Gran

Were the aggressors with the slavering fangs
And tell-tale tails; now it turns out at last   10
That grey wolf and timber wolf are near extinct,
Done out of being by the tales we tell

Told us by Nanny in the nursery;
Young sparks we were, to set such forest fires
As blazed from story into history   15
And put such bounty on their wolvish heads

As brought the few survivors to our terms,
Surrendered in happy Babylon among
The peacock dusting off the path of dust,
The tiger pacing in the striped shade. 20

Glossary		
	2	*legend:* here, a notice giving information and explanation; it also means a traditional story or a popular belief, and the poem contrasts the 'scientific' information given about wolves with the beliefs expressed in stories and fairy tales
	7	*Siberian sleds:* Siberia is a vast area of northern Russia, where many of the native people were traditionally nomadic, living off hunting and fishing; because the winters are harsh and cold, and because a large portion of the territory is within the Artic, sleds are a common form of transport; there are many tales of nomadic people sacrificing the frailest member of their group so that the others might survive. The Siberian wolf is famed for its resourcefulness in surviving in a harsh wilderness. In Mongolian mythology (Mongolia borders Siberia), Genghis Khan is said to have descended from a wolf
	9	*slavering fangs:* saliva running from long, sharp teeth; suggests that the teeth are moist in greedy anticipation of the feast to come
	11	*grey wolf:* the most common species of wolf, with a distribution across North America, Europe and Asia
	11	*timber wolf:* a sub-species of the grey wolf, found in North America
	16	*bounty:* money paid as a reward; in the Middle Ages there was widespread fear of wolves in Europe, which settlers brought with them to America, and many governments (or wealthy farmers) paid a bounty to hunters for every wolf that they killed
	17	*our terms:* the imagery suggests a war, in which the defeated survivors, the wolves, accept the terms of surrender

Glossary

18 *Babylon:* an ancient city in what is now known as Iraq. The city was the centre of a kingdom bounded by two great rivers, the Tigris and the Euphrates. The Hanging Gardens of Babylon were one of the wonders of the ancient world. It was reputed to be a place of fruits and flowers, rivers and waterfalls, exotic plants and animals. In many ways, it was a forerunner of the modern zoo. The kingdom of Babylon played an important part in Jewish history: for seventy years (586–516 bc) the Jews lived in captivity in Babylonia; they accepted the exile as a punishment from God ('For because of the anger of the Lord this happened in Jerusalem and Judah, that He finally cast them out from His presence', Kings 2, chapter 24, verse 20) and lived quietly without complaint

Guidelines

'The wolf at the door.' 'To cry wolf.' 'Don't wolf down your food.' 'A wolf in sheep's clothing.' Conventional attitudes to the wolf are expressed in many everyday sayings and in popular stories and legends. In fairy tales such as *Little Red Riding Hood* and *The Three Little Pigs*, the wolf is greedy and cruel. And the wolves howling in the forests around the castle of Count Dracula symbolise everything that humans fear about the dark. In the Middle Ages some humans were thought to be able to transform themselves into wolves. These werewolves were considered to be the servants of the devil. Nemerov's poem contrasts the rich imaginative view of the wolf in legend and folklore with the tame, scientific version offered by the 'legend' on the wolves' cage in the zoo.

Commentary

Loss of identity
The wolves in the zoo hardly look like wolves, they look like 'dogs badly drawn' (line 1). They resemble the remnants of a great army that has surrendered to its conquerors. They accept their new conditions, their new surroundings in 'happy Babylon' (line 18). **Here the wild animals almost lose their identity.** The wolves no longer look like wolves; the peacock's tail dusts the path; the tiger seems to have lost its stripes.

Old and new

The wolves are not really the centre of attention in the poem. Nemerov is more interested in playfully teasing out the difference between the old view and the new view of something, between folklore and science. He takes delight in suggesting that Granny and Little Red Riding Hood were the real aggressors, with their 'slavering fangs' (line 9). He is amused by the idea that the tales told 'by Nanny in the nursery' (line 13) have been the ruination of wolves. There seems to be more scepticism than guilt in the statement, 'Young sparks we were, to set such forest fires / As blazed from story into history' (lines 14–15). With a lightness of touch, the poem questions the nature of truth and the difference between science and legend. The tone is sceptical and playful.

Form of the poem

The poem is organised into five stanzas of four lines. It is written in blank verse, that is, in unrhymed lines of ten syllables. This was the style Shakespeare used in writing his plays. While the poem is unrhymed, it does contain half-rhymes and many examples of sound and wordplay, as in the first line where alliteration and consonance create a big booming sound: 'They look like big dogs badly drawn, drawn wrong.' See also the wordplay in phrases such as 'tell-tale tails' (line 10) or in 'story into history' (line 15).

Exam-style questions

Thinking about the poem

1. Does the poet believe what the legend on the cage says about wolves? Explain your answer. Support the points you make by quotation from the poem.
2. The phrase 'Now it turns out' is used three times in the poem. In what tone(s) of voice should this be phrase be recited? Give reasons for your answer.
3. Does the poem make you feel sad for the wolves in the zoo? Explain your point of view.
4. Here are three views of the poem:
    - It is a poem about wolves.
    - It is a poem about zoos.
    - It is a poem about old and new ways of seeing things.

    Which is closest to your view of the poem? Explain your choice.
5. What impression of the poet do you form from the poem? Refer to the poem in your answer.
6. 'He can say funny and serious things at the same time.' Is 'Wolves in the Zoo' an example of Howard Nemerov saying funny and serious things at the same time? Explain your answer.

7   Is this poem different from other poems you have read on animals in zoos? Explain your thinking.
8   Do you like the poem? Give a reason for your answer.

Taking a closer look

1   'tell-tale tails' (line 10). Comment on the effectiveness of this phrase in the poem.
2   Comment on the effectiveness of the word 'aggressors' (line 9) to describe 'Little Red Ridinghood and her Gran'.
3   Select **two** phrases from the poem that you really like. Explain your choice.

Imagining

1   Imagine that you are one of the wolves in the zoo. Write a response to the poem describing your feelings about living in the zoo.
2   Write a short prose piece under the title 'In Praise of Zoos'.

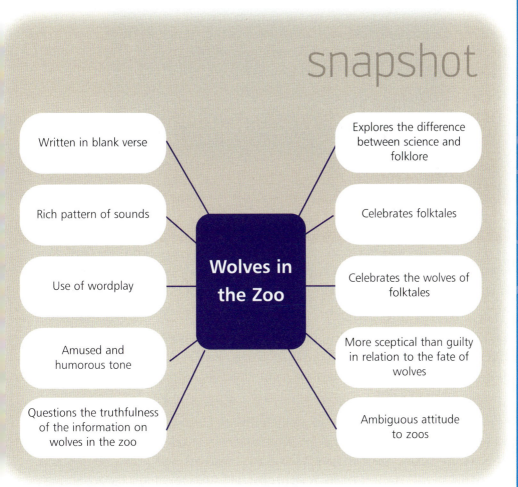

snapshot

Wolves in the Zoo

- Written in blank verse
- Rich pattern of sounds
- Use of wordplay
- Amused and humorous tone
- Questions the truthfulness of the information on wolves in the zoo
- Explores the difference between science and folklore
- Celebrates folktales
- Celebrates the wolves of folktales
- More sceptical than guilty in relation to the fate of wolves
- Ambiguous attitude to zoos

Julie O'Callaghan

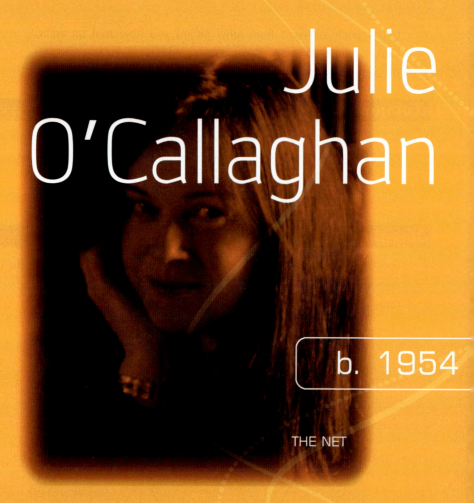

b. 1954

THE NET

Biography

Julie O'Callaghan was born in Chicago in 1954 into an Irish-American family. The family lived five minutes from the beach at Lake Michigan and the children spent the summer swimming and playing in the sand. She attended a Catholic primary school and, later, Sullivan High School. English was her favourite subject and she enjoyed writing stories, articles and poetry.

O'Callaghan has lived in Ireland since 1974. She works in the library in Trinity College, Dublin and is married to the poet Denis O'Driscoll. On being a poet in Ireland, she says: 'Poetry in Ireland comes from an ancient tradition and is part of the culture. You don't have to apologise for it. I can't think of a better place to be writing.'

She has published several collections of poetry for children and young adults as well as her work for an adult audience, including *The Book of Whispers* (2006) for children, and *Tell Me This Is Normal* (2008). She has earned numerous distinctions and awards for her work, including the Michael Hartnett Poetry Word in 2001 and a number of Arts Council bursaries. She is a member of Aosdána, the national arts organisation.

The Net

I am the Lost Classmate
being hunted down the superhighways
and byways of infinite cyber-space.
How long can I evade the class committee
searching for my lost self?   5

I watch the list
of Found Classmates
grow by the month
Corralled into a hotel ballroom
festooned with 70s paraphernalia,   10

bombarded with atmospheric
hit tunes, the Captured Classmates
from Sullivan High School
will celebrate thirty years
of freedom from each other.   15

I peek at the message board:
my locker partner,
out in California, looks forward
to being reunited with
her old school chums.   20

Wearing a disguise, I calculate
the number of months left
for me to do what I do best,
what I've always done:
slip through the net.   25

Glossary

3	*infinite:*	vast, limitless
3	*cyber-space:*	here, the Internet; generally, the environment or space in which communication takes place over computer networks
9	*Corralled:*	herded in and confined as if in a corral or animal enclosure; it can also mean captured
10	*paraphernalia:*	trappings, accessories
13	*Sullivan High School:*	the second-level school in Chicago that O'Callaghan attended

Guidelines

'The Net' was inspired by a real event, when O'Callaghan saw that Sullivan High School was organising a thirtieth anniversary reunion for her class. In her words, 'It gave me the creeps having people hunting for me in the cyber-world.'

The poem deals with two interesting themes. **The first is the sinister nature of the Internet in terms of tracking and locating individuals and making it difficult to remain invisible; the second is the pressure on people to celebrate school reunions and subscribe to the myth that their school days were the best days of their life**, especially if, like the poet, you are shy and retiring by nature.

Commentary

The poem works by playing on the meaning of the word 'net'. **In the poem, the 'Net' is not viewed as an exciting worldwide form of communication, but as a sinister worldwide form of entrapment and tyranny.** The net catches people. However, the speaker of the poem does not want to be caught and hopes, as she says in the last line of the poem, 'to slip through the net'. **The poem is also a humorous account of the oppressive nature of school reunions where individuals are forced to celebrate their time in school.** The poem employs a mock serious tone to make its point. In the first line, the speaker declares herself 'the Lost Classmate'. She is a fugitive on the run.

Sinister air

In the poem the class committee takes on a sinister role, chasing down and capturing former classmates, like the intelligence service of a totalitarian state. For the speaker of the poem, the growing list of 'Found Classmates' (line 7) is not a cause for rejoicing. Like an escaped prisoner reading that her fellow escapees have been recaptured, the Lost Classmate feels the net tightening. However, she is determined to stay in hiding and slip through the net. As portrayed in the poem, the Internet creates a nightmarish society in which the individual never feels safe and secure. There is the constant fear of being discovered and subjected to unwelcome attention.

Form of the poem

The poem is written in five five-line stanzas. The stanzas are unrhymed and irregular. This gives a conversational feel to the poem. However, part of the pleasure of reading it is to recognise the many sounds that repeat and echo through the poem. Look, for example, how the 'c' and 'l' sounds feature throughout.

Exam-style questions

Thinking about the poem

1. How does the speaker of the poem feel about the search for lost classmates? Where are her feelings most evident?
2. Trace the imagery of escape and capture, flight and pursuit in the poem. Do you think that the imagery is effective? Explain your answer.
3. According to the poem, what will be the fate of 'Found Classmates' (line 7)?
4. Which of the following best describes the feelings of the speaker as she watches the list of found classmates?
   - She is alarmed.
   - She is determined.
   - She is flattered.

   Explain your choice.
5. The poem suggests that the Internet is part of the technology of surveillance and tracking. Do you agree with this point of view? Explain your answer.
6. Having read the poem, what, do you imagine, were the speaker's feelings on leaving Sullivan High School?
7. The poem is written in five-line stanzas. Why, do you think, has O'Callaghan broken the lines in the way that she has? You might find it helpful to read the poem aloud a number of times before answering the question.

Taking a closer look

1. Comment on the phrase 'the Lost Classmate' (line 1) and suggest what it means to you.
2. Comment on the use of the verbs 'corralled' (line 9) and 'bombarded' (line 11) in the poem.

Imagining

1. Write a letter to Julie O'Callaghan in which you either (a) encourage her to attend the class reunion or (b) offer support for the point of view she expresses in the poem.
2. Compose a short poem inspired by the phrase 'infinite cyber-space' (line 3).
3. You have been asked to make a short film version of the poem. Describe the atmosphere you wish to create. Outline the images, the shots and camera angles and the soundtrack you would use to create this atmosphere.

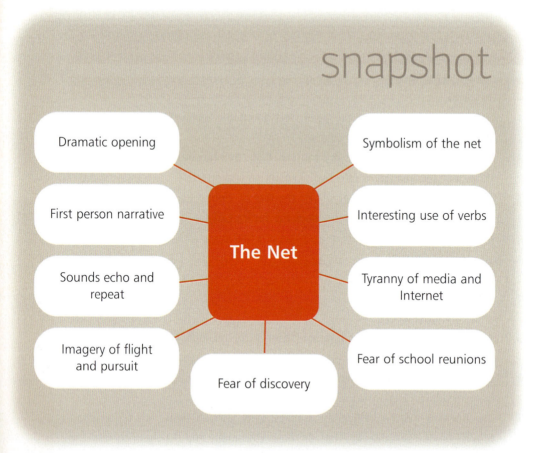

Marge Piercy

b. 1936

WILL WE WORK TOGETHER?

Biography

Marge Piercy was born in 1936 in Detroit, Michigan. The Piercy family lived in a working-class neighbourhood in Detroit. Her childhood was affected by the Great Depression, during which her father struggled to find employment. He eventually found a job installing and repairing machinery. Although Piercy's father was not Jewish, her mother and maternal grandmother raised her in their Jewish faith.

Piercy was educated at public school in Detroit and later won a scholarship to the University of Michigan; she was the first person in her family to go to college. During her career Piercy has been involved in the feminist movement and other political issues such as the protests against US involvement in the war in Vietnam. She has lived in France, Chicago and New York. She now lives in Cape Cod, Massachusetts, with her third husband, writer Ira Wood.

She has written plays and novels as well as poetry. She has also edited anthologies. Along with her husband, she founded a small literary publishing company. Among her many publications are *The Moon Is Always Female* (1977), *Circles on the Water: Selected Poems of Marge Piercy* (1982) and *Colors Passing through Us* (2003).

Will we work together?

You wake in the early grey
morning in bed alone and curse
me, that I am only
sometimes there. But when
I am with you, I light   5
up the corners, I am bright
as a fireplace roaring
with love, every bone in my back
and my fingers is singing
like a tea kettle on the boil.   10
My heart wags me, a big dog
With a bigger tail. I am
a new coin printed with
your face. My body wears
sore before I can express   15
on yours the smallest part
of what moves me. Words
shred and splinter.
I want to make with you
some bold new thing   20
to stand in the marketplace,
the statue of a goddess
laughing, armed and wearing
flowers and feathers, like sheep
of whose hair is made   25
blankets and coats. I want
to force from this fierce sturdy
rampant love some useful thing.

Glossary

20	*bold*:	daring, brave
27	*sturdy*:	strong
28	*rampant*:	out of control

Guidelines

'Will we work together?' is from the collection *The Moon Is Always Female*, published in 1977. In the poem the speaker expresses her strong feelings for her beloved and her desire to love him as best she can.

Commentary

Lines 1–18

The speaker says that her beloved 'curses' her when he finds she is not there in bed with him in the morning (lines 1 to 4), but the rest of the poem leaves him in no doubt as to the strength of her feelings for him. The tone of the poem is highly emotional.

Similes and metaphors of light and heat, as well as of loud sound, convey how passionately she loves him. She is 'bright / as a fireplace roaring / with love' (line 6–8), her bones are 'singing / like a tea kettle on the boil' (line 9–10). Physical images – 'bone', 'back', 'fingers', 'heart', 'body' – combine with the senses of sight and touch to express her passion for this man.

Piercy uses some interesting and original metaphors in seeking to express her strong feelings in lines 11 to 18. Her heart is compared to a 'big dog / with a bigger tail' (lines 11–12), generous with his affection. She is 'a new coin printed with / your face' (lines 13–14), an image that surely suggests the close relationship between them – and perhaps the newness of their relationship too. She goes on to say that she can scarcely find the words to express 'the smallest part / of what moves me' (lines 16–17), as words seem to 'shred and splinter' (line 18) in the attempt to convey how she feels for him. Again, we get an indication of the explosive nature of these feelings.

Lines 19–28

Moving beyond her immediate feelings, **the speaker describes the kind of relationship she wishes to create with her beloved**. Two unusual images suggest the creative possibilities of their love. The first is that of a 'statue of a goddess / laughing, armed and wearing / flowers and feathers' (lines 22–24). This, she says, will 'stand in the marketplace' (line 21).

As we know from history, statues are objects of respect, erected to commemorate or symbolise some great person or event. A statue represents public recognition and endurance. Goddesses were powerful, respected figures. Piercy wants to 'make' such a statue: a relationship that will be publicly acknowledged and that will last. It will also be beautiful, 'wearing flowers and feathers' (lines 23-24), and happy, 'laughing' (line 23).

The second image that she creates is more unexpected. She hopes that their love will produce 'some useful thing' (line 28), as useful as woollen 'blankets and coats' (line 26). This cosy domestic image contrasts greatly with the public nature of the statue image. The suggestion is that both aspects of their love – the public and the intimate – are essential to her. The three adjectives she uses in the final two lines – 'fierce sturdy / rampant' each emphasise how fiery and passionate this love is, but there is also a sense in these lines that it is greater than them both. From its energy can spring something good and lasting.

Title

At this stage we can see why the poem is called 'Will we work together?' **She is asking her lover to 'work' with her to produce this beautiful, lasting, creative relationship.**

Exam-style questions

Thinking about the poem

1. What sort of relationship does the poet have with her beloved?
2. How does the language she uses (similes, metaphors, images) convey her feelings?
3. Do you think that the relationship is a new one, or has it existed for some time? Give a reason for your opinion.
4. How would you describe the relationship that the poet hopes to have with her beloved in the future?
5. With which of the following statements would you agree most?
    - The speaker is too much in love for her own good.
    - The relationship seems to be too one-sided.
    - The relationship has great potential for both the man and woman.

   Explain your choice.
6. Do you like the way in which the speaker expresses her feelings in the poem? Give a reason for your answer.
7. From your reading of the poem, describe the personality of the speaker.
8. Do you think the title of the poem is appropriate? Give a reason for your view.
9. 'I think "Will we work together?" is a wonderful love poem.' Write a paragraph in which you agree or disagree with this view.

Taking a closer look

1. Choose **two** images from the poem that you find most effective in expressing love. Explain your choice.
2. What do lines 22 to 24 – 'the statue of a goddess / laughing, armed and wearing / flowers and feathers' – suggest to you about the kind of relationship the speaker would like to have with her beloved?

Imagining

1. Imagine that someone (male or female) has written the above poem for you. In your diary, say how you felt when you received the poem.
2. Your class is compiling a selection of love poems and songs. You wish to include the above poem. Say why you think it is suitable for the collection.

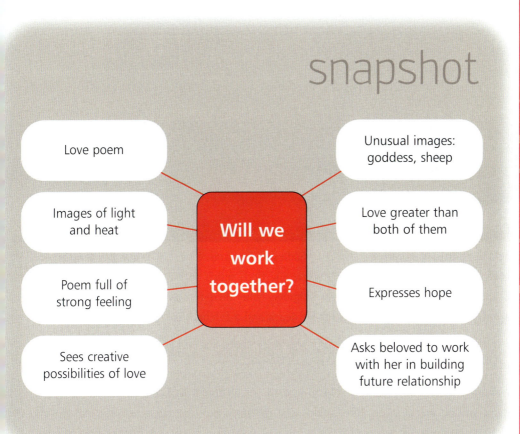

Penelope Shuttle

b. 1947

ZOO MORNING

Biography

Penelope Shuttle was born in 1947 in Middlesex, England. Since 1970 she has lived in the seaside town of Falmouth, Cornwall, where she finds much of the inspiration for her work. She was married to the poet Peter Redgrove, who died in 2003. Her poetry collection *Redgrove's Wife* (2006) is a lament for his death and a celebration of his life.

She has published thirty collections of poems since 1968. She has been awarded a number of important poetry prizes and been shortlisted for others.

For Shuttle, writing and reading help to give shape and order to her life. She has said that without writing and reading, 'life would be a drifting chaos for me, a series of losses and forgettings. My sense of being would have no meaning, no inner or outer geography.' She has also endorsed the comment of US poet Wallace Stevens that 'the whole world is material for poetry, that all our ideas come from the natural world'.

Zoo Morning

Elephants prepare to look solemn and move slowly
though all night they drank and danced, partied
and gambled, didn't act their age.

Night-scholar monkeys take off their glasses,
pack away their tomes and theses,
sighing as they get ready for yet another long day
of gibbering and gesticulating, shocking
and scandalizing the punters.

Bears stop shouting their political slogans
and adopt their cute-but-not-really teddies' stance
in the concrete bear-pit.

Big cats hide their flower-presses, embroidery-frames
and watercolours;
grumbling, they try a few practice roars.
Their job is to rend the air, to devour carcasses,
to sleep-lounge at their vicious carnivorous ease.

What a life.
But none of them would give up show-business.
The snakes who are always changing,
skin after skin,
open their aged eyes and hinged jaws in welcome.

Between paddock and enclosure
we drag our unfurred young.
Our speech is over-complex, deceitful.
Our day out is not all it should be.
The kids howl, baffled.

All the animals are very good at being animals.
As usual, we are not up to being us.
Our human smells prison us.

> In the insect house 30
> the red-kneed spider dances on her eight light fantastics;
> on her shelf of silence she waltzes and twirls,
> joy in her hairy joints, her ruby-red eyes.

Glossary

4	*Night-scholar monkeys:*	monkeys, more learned and scholarly than other animals, spend their nights in study and research
5	*tomes:*	large volumes
5	*theses:*	scholarly exercises on research topics, presented for a higher degree at university
8	*Scandalizing the punters:*	causing offence to those who paid to look at them
10	*adopt . . . stance:*	the bears pose as lovable, appealing teddy bears, thus giving a false impression of their true nature
15	*rend the air:*	make ear-splitting noises
16	*sleep-lounge . . . .. ease:*	the sense here is that the big cats (lions, tigers, etc.) eat their supplies of meat with vicious enthusiasm and then take their ease by sleeping and lounging; 'carnivorous' means 'flesh-eating.
18	*show-business:*	their roles as entertainers of the public
20	*skin after skin:*	snakes shed their skin, replacing each layer with a new one
22	*paddock:*	a small field
22	*enclosure:*	a fenced-off space
23	*unfurred young:*	human children who, unlike most of the animals on display, are not covered in fur
26	*baffled:*	bewildered, extremely puzzled
29	*Our . . . us:*	we human beings are prisoners of our own bodies and lack self-awareness, unlike the zoo animals
31	*dances . . . fantastics:*	dances on her eight light, nimble toes; there is a reference here to John Milton's poem 'L'Allegro': 'Come and trip it as you go / On the light fantastic toe'; here, 'fantastics' refers to imaginative or extravagant movements, the kind Shuttle's red-kneed spider makes
32	*shelf of silence:*	unlike most other creatures in the zoo, the spider makes no sound as she waltzes and twirls

Guidelines

'Zoo Morning' is from the collection *Taxing the Rain* (1992). The poem makes a serious point, but does so light-heartedly and humorously. Shuttle's humour has a distinctive quality. Here it is based mainly on a surreal vision of the animal world, in which elephants dance and hold parties throughout the night, monkeys involve themselves in academic study, while lions and tigers practise embroidery and paint pictures. By day, they all abandon these pursuits and devote themselves to their business of entertaining visitors to the zoo.

Commentary

The key to 'Zoo Morning' may be found in lines 22 to 29. These lines contrast animals with human beings. The contrast is unfavourable to human beings. Human offspring, 'our unfurred young' (line 23), have to be dragged along, howling and baffled by their experience. The speech of human beings is 'over-complex, deceitful' (line 24), designed to conceal rather than reveal the truth about themselves. They are incapable of properly enjoying a day at the zoo, as the behaviour of the children shows. While human beings are incapable of portraying their true selves, all the animals in the zoo are 'very good at being animals' (line 27). Elephants, for example, 'look solemn and move slowly' (line 1) as their natures require them to do, while big cats emit their characteristic roars, and the monkeys do what is expected of them by 'gibbering and gesticulating' (line 7). The human spectators, being perverse, are 'not up to being' themselves (line 28).

The zoo animals have a greater capacity for enjoying themselves than do the people who are watching them. They even enjoy their everyday lives in 'show-business' (line 18). This is indicated in the statement that none of them would give their work up, even if they had the choice, and in the humorous reference to the snakes opening up 'their aged eyes and hinged jaws in welcome' (line 21). They derive their real enjoyment from their nightly leisure hours. During these hours, their fantasy lives are spent pursuing a variety of pastimes: the elephants enjoy juvenile entertainments, the monkeys favour intellectual pursuits, and the lions and tigers have artistic tendencies. As the red-kneed spider dances, there is 'joy in her hairy joints' and 'ruby-red eyes' (line 33). Contrast this with the baffled howling of the child-spectators, who are supposed to be enjoying themselves but have to be dragged along.

Exam-Style questions

Thinking about the poem

1. There is a significant contrast between the behaviour of the elephants during the night and their behaviour in the presence of a human audience. Describe this contrast.
2. Comment on a similar set of contrasts between the night-time and day-time behaviour of the monkeys, bears and big cats.
3. What do the contrasts referred to in questions 1 and 2 tell us about the animals?
4. Are the night-time pursuits of the various animals mentioned in the first four stanzas appropriate to each of the animals? Explain your answer.
5. Why does the poet suggest that 'All the animals are very good at being animals' (line 27)?
6. Why does the poet think that we human beings 'are not up to being us' (line 28)?
7. Does the poem suggest that zoo animals have talents that human beings lack? Explain your answer.
8. Write a piece entitled 'We have a lot to learn from animals about how life should be lived'.
9. Which of these words best describes the animals: attractive, ridiculous, talented or happy? Explain your choice.
10. You have been asked to explain to the members of your class why you like or dislike this poem. What would you say?
11. 'The poet is being unfair to human beings.' Write a short piece in which you agree or disagree with this statement.

Taking a closer look

1. The animals in the poem are a rich source of comedy. Choose **two** examples of this, and explain where the comedy lies.
2. Why would none of the zoo animals give up 'show-business' (line 18)? Is 'show-business' a suitable term for what the animals do? Explain your answers.
3. Write out **three** descriptions from the poem that you find particularly impressive. Comment on your choices.

Imagining

1. Imagine that you are one of the animals. Write a short account of your experiences during a single twenty-four-hour period.
2. Imagine that you are a news reporter and have been given access to the zoo at night. Write a brief report on what you have seen and heard, basing this on the first four stanzas of the poem.

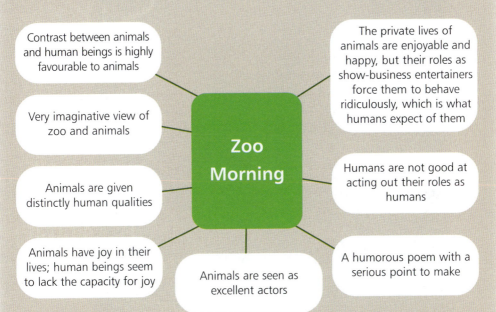

Peter Sirr

b. 1960

MADLY SINGING IN THE CITY

Biography

Peter Sirr was born in Waterford in 1960. He lives in Dublin, where he is a freelance writer and translator. He is project manager of the Liffey Project, a multilingual literature site. He is also a part-time lecturer at Trinity College, Dublin. He is a former director of the Irish Writers' Centre and a former editor of *Poetry Ireland Review*. He lived in Holland and Italy for a number of years before returning to settle in Dublin. He is married to the poet Enda Wyley.

His collections of poetry are *Marginal Zones* (1984), *Talk, Talk* (1987), *Ways of Falling* (1995), *The Ledger of Fruitful Exchange* (1995), *Bring Everything* (2000), *Nonetheless* (2004), *Selected Poems 1982–2004* (2004), *The Thing Is* (2009).

Sirr is a member of Aosdána. In 1982 he won the Patrick Kavanagh Award for his poetry; he won the O'Shaughnessy Award of the Irish-American Cultural Institute in 1998; and in 2011 he won the Michael Hartnett Poetry Award for *The Thing Is*.

Madly Singing in the City

after Po-Chü-i

And often, when I have finished a new poem,
I climb to the dark roof garden
and lean on a rail over an ocean of streets.
What news I have for the sleeping citizens
and these restless ones, still shouting their tune   5
in the small hours. Fumes rise from the chip-shop
and I am back at the counter, waiting my turn.
Cod, haddock, plaice, whiting.
The long queue moves closer;
men in white coats paint fish with batter,   10
chips leap in the drying tray.
There's a table reserved for salt and vinegar
where the hot package is unswaddled,
salted, drenched, wrapped again
and borne out into the darkness.   15
In darkness I lean out, the new words ready,
the spires attentive, St Werburgh's, St Patrick's, Nicholas
of Myra. Nearby, the Myra Glass Company
from where we carried the glass table-top.
In a second I will sing, it will be as if   20
a god has leaned with me, having strolled over
from either of the two cathedrals, or from the green
and godly domes of Iveagh Buildings.
Ever since I was banished from the mountains
I have lived here in the roar of the streets.   25
Each year more of it enters me, I am grown
populous and tangled. The thousand ties of life
I thought I had escaped have multiplied
I stand in the dark roof garden, my lungs swelling
with the new poem, my eyes filled with buildings   30
and people. I let them fill, then,
without saying a word, I go back down.

Peter Sirr

Glossary

	Dedication	*Po-Chü-i*: a Chinese poet
13	*unswaddled*: unwrapped, opened	
17	*St Werburgh's*: a church on Werburgh Street, backing on to Dublin Castle; the chip-shop mentioned in line 6 is also on Werburgh Street	
17	*St Patrick's*: St Patrick's Cathedral on Patrick Street	
17–18	*Nicholas of Myra*: a church on Francis Street	
22	*two cathedrals*: Christ Church Cathedral is close to St Patrick's Cathedral and the other places mentioned in the poem	
23	*Iveagh Buildings*: blocks of flats on Patrick Street	
27	*populous*: abundantly populated, full of people	

Guidelines

The poem 'Madly Singing in the City' is from *Bring Everything*, a collection in which several of the poems are inspired by Sirr's reading of poetry from many countries and historical periods. 'Madly Singing in the City' is a narrative poem (it tells a story). The story is an unusual one. It is about a poem composed but not shared with an audience. It is short on incident. **A poet, having composed a poem, stands on a roof garden looking down on the streets of Dublin, ready to read his poem. Attracted by the fumes of a chip-shop in a street below him, he visits the shop. He returns to his roof garden and thinks about the disadvantages of living in a city. He abandons the idea of reading the poem aloud. We are left to guess why.**

Commentary

Dedication

The dedication, 'after Po-Chü-i', indicates that Sirr's poem is written in imitation of, or was inspired by, a Chinese poet named Po-Chü-i who lived from 772 to 846 AD. Po-Chü-i believed that poetry should be understood by the common people. His poems were notable for their simple diction, natural style and social content. These influences can be seen in Sirr's poem. For example, 'I climb to the dark roof garden' (line 2), 'The long queue moves closer' (line 9), 'In darkness I lean out' (line 16).

Po-Chü-i used his poems to attack government corruption, heavy taxation and abuse of the common people by powerful officials. He favoured the simple life. 'In Madly Singing in the City', the speaker associates a new poem he has completed with news he has for the citizens. Since Sirr's model for this poem is Po-Chü-i, we may guess that the new poem contains a political message for the citizens of Dublin, perhaps some social comment or criticism of life in the city, a place that the speaker claims has made him 'populous and tangled' (line 27).

The speaker tells us that he was 'banished from the mountains' (line 24). Po-Chü-i was banished from the capital city of his country for taking a stand against dishonest people in power. One of his beliefs was that poems and songs should be written 'to influence public affairs'. Is this the poet's purpose in Sirr's poem?

Source for Sirr's Poem

One poem by Po-Chü-i, 'Madly Singing in the Mountains', is the obvious model for Sirr's poem. In his poem, the Chinese poet explains his present circumstances : 'Ever since the day I was banished to Hsün-yang / half my time I have lived among the hills'. In his case, the banishment is from the capital city to the provinces. In Sirr's poem, this process is reversed : 'Ever since I was banished from the mountains / I have lived here in the roar of the streets' (lines 24–25). This change accounts for the difference between the titles of the two poems.

Po-Chü-i cannot resist writing verses. He tells us that each time he looks at a fine landscape or meets a loved friend, 'I raise any voice as though a God had crossed my path'. Sirr's version of this is: 'In a second I will sing, it will be as if / a god has leaned with me, having strolled over / from either of the two cathedrals' (lines 20–22). In his time of banishment, Po-Chü-i still writes poems: 'And often when I have finished a new poem / Alone I climb the road to the Eastern Rock'. This is rendered by Sirr as: 'And often, when I have finished a new poem, / I climb to the dark roof garden' (lines 1–2). Po-Chü-i recites his poem to an audience of wild creatures: 'My mad singing startles the valleys and hills: / The apes and birds all come to peep'. He mentions his motive for doing this: 'Fearing to become a laughing-stock to the world, / I choose a place that is unfrequented by men'. Sirr's poetic message ('What news I have for the sleeping citizens', line 4) remains unspoken: 'I stand in the dark roof garden, my lungs swelling / with the new poem, my eyes filled with buildings / and people I let them fill, then, / without saying a word, I go back down' (lines 29–32).

Sense of mystery

The poem retains a sense of mystery throughout. We do not know what the speaker's newly finished poem is about. We do not know why the speaker does not recite his poem. Particularly since he seems ready and even eager to do so at a number of points: 'In darkness I lean out, the new words ready, / the spires attentive' (lines 16–17); 'In a second I will sing' (line 20); 'I stand in the dark roof garden, my lungs swelling / with the new poem' (lines 29–30).

The final lines may give a clue to his failure to speak his poem. His lungs may be full of his new poem, but his eyes are 'filled with buildings / and people' (lines 30–31). We already know that city life does not appeal to him. Are we to understand that he is so overcome by dislike for what the city stands for that his enthusiasm for communicating his 'news' to its people quickly fades?

Form and style of the poem

Notice that the lines do not rhyme, and that they are of uneven length. There is no fixed rhythm. If the poem is read aloud, it can be made to sound like a passage of prose. It might even have been composed as prose, and simply broken up to resemble a poem. It would be interesting to re-write it as a series of prose sentences, and to read it aloud in that form.

The tone of the poem is matter-of-fact. The diction is that of everyday speech. The poem has little in the way of poetic ornament such as imagery or sound patterns.

Exam-style questions

Thinking about the poem

1. Why, do you think, did the poet choose 'Madly Singing in the City' as the title for this poem?
2. The speaker mentions two groups of citizens: the sleeping ones and the restless ones, and the news he has for each kind. What kind of news, do you think, might he have?
3. Halfway through the poem the speaker says: 'In darkness I lean out, the new words ready, / the spires attentive' (lines 16–17). What are 'the new words'? Have they been mentioned already in the poem? What does the expression 'the spires attentive' suggest?
4. What does the speaker mean when he says, 'In a second I will sing' (line 20)? What will he sing?

5   From line 24 on, the speaker is conscious of two contrasting phases in his life. What are these? Which one would he prefer? Explain your answer.
6   What does the speaker mean when he says he has grown 'populous and tangled' (line 27)? What has caused him to be like this, do you think?
7   Why, do you think, does the speaker 'go back down' 'without saying a word' (line 32)?
8   Do you think that this poem has a single theme? Explain your answer.
9   Based on your reading of the poem, give your overall impression of the kind of person the speaker is.
10 Did you find this poem difficult? Explain your answer.

Taking a closer look

1   Who are 'these restless ones' (line 5)? What tune are they shouting in the small hours?
2   Who are the 'men in white coats' (line 10)?
3   More than one-quarter of the poem is devoted to events in a chip-shop. What has this to do with the rest of the poem?
4   The speaker tells us that when he sings, 'it will be as if / a god has leaned with me' (lines 20–21). Why does the speaker introduce a god here?
5   The god the speaker mentions is imagined as strolling over to join him from 'either of the two cathedrals' (line 22). What do you think this image signifies?
6   What are the 'thousand ties of life' (line 27) the speaker thought he had escaped but which have now multiplied?
7   Does the poem suggest that the speaker is happy with his present life? Base your answer on details from the poem.
8   Choose **two** images from the poem that you find appealing. Explain your choice.

Imagining

1   The speaker does not tell us why he 'was banished from the mountains' (line 24). Write a paragraph setting out one or more reasons why he might have been banished.
2   Choose an alternative title for the poem, and explain your choice.

snapshot

Madly Singing in the City

- A narrative poem with some personal reflections
- Poem written in a matter-of-fact way
- Informal style, similar to prose
- Little use of poetic imagery, simile, metaphor or alliteration
- Deals with urban life
- Language is generally simple and contemporary
- Creates a sense of mystery, particularly regarding the speaker's 'news' for the citizens
- Expresses disillusionment

Dylan Thomas

1914–53

DO NOT GO GENTLE INTO THAT GOOD NIGHT

Biography

Born in 1914, Dylan Thomas was the son of a senior English teacher at Swansea Grammar School in Wales, where Thomas completed his formal education before he was seventeen. He was not interested in academic studies. He became a newspaper reporter for a year, and did some acting. His main occupation from the age of sixteen was the writing of poems.

By 1923 his poems were being published in reputable journals. His first collection, *Eighteen Poems*, was published when he was twenty, and his second, *Twenty-Five Poems*, followed a couple of years later. The response of reviewers to these poems was enthusiastic. His admirers found his work obscure, and acknowledged that much of it did not make much sense, but they were taken by the force and energy of his language.

Thomas became a 'character' and a cult figure, embodying the predominant idea of what a poet should be: wild, disorderly, eccentric. One hostile critic remarked that 'he relied on beer and genius'. His behaviour generated valuable publicity for his poetry, which was extremely popular and still attracts attention. Thomas was also in demand as a broadcaster and his readings of his poems on radio attracted large and appreciative audiences.

His addiction to alcohol helped to bring about his early death, which occurred in the United States in 1953, when he was thirty-nine, during a lecture tour.

Do Not Go Gentle into that Good Night

Do not go gentle into that good night,
Old age should burn and rave at close of day;
Rage, rage against the dying of the light.

Though wise men at their end know dark is right,
Because their words had forked no lightning they   5
Do not go gentle into that good night.

Good men, the last wave by, crying how bright
Their frail deeds might have danced in a green bay,
Rage, rage against the dying of the light.

Wild men who caught and sang the sun in flight,   10
And learn, too late, they grieved it on its way,
Do not go gentle into that good night.

Grave men, near death, who see with blinding sight
Blind eyes could blaze like meteors and be gay,
Rage, rage against the dying of the light.   15

And you, my father, there on the sad height,
Curse, bless, me now with your fierce tears, I pray.
Do not go gentle into that good night.
Rage, rage against the dying of the light.

Glossary

1	*gentle*:	meekly, without a fight
1	*that good night*:	death
3	*light*:	soul, hope, will to live
4	*at their end*:	immediately before their death
4	*dark*:	death
4	*right*:	natural, inevitable
5	*forked no lightning*:	failed to shake or astound the world (with spectacular ideas or creativity)
7	*last wave*:	final farewell
10	*sun in flight*:	passage of time
13	*Grave men*:	serious men (who are also soon to be in their graves)

Guidelines

The subject, as we learn from the final stanza, is the speaker's father, who is close to death. **The poem is a passionate appeal to the dying man to resist death with all his might.** Although the theme of the poem is straightforward, the language is not, with Thomas preferring to locate meaning in images rather than in statements.

Commentary

Stanza 1

The poem opens with a strong command to the listener: do not submit to death; older people must work hard to retain their passions and strength in order to resist fading away or losing the will to live.

Stanza 2

The second stanza tells of 'Wise men' who recognise that death must come, but still fight to live 'Because their words had forked no lightning' (line 5). When a stroke of lightning divides into different branches it is described, metaphorically, as forked lightning. Forked lightning is a powerful and dramatic spectacle. The suggestion in the poem is therefore that the men's words have failed to make a strong impact.

Stanza 3
The third stanza tells of 'Good men' who resist death because they recognise that they should have achieved more with their lives, that 'Their frail deeds might have danced' (line 8).

Stanza 4
The fourth stanza tells of 'Wild men' who resist death because they recognise that they allowed time to pass without making the most of it.

Stanza 5
The fifth stanza tells of 'Grave men' who resist death because they recognise they have been too serious and that, even if they have now lost their sight, they can still light up the world with joy.

Stanza 6
The final stanza is a direct address to the poet's father. Thomas wants his father to curse him with 'fierce tears' (line 17). If he did, the curse would be a blessing because it would demonstrate that he still has the strength to fight.

Secondary theme

The meaning of the poem becomes clearer when we learn that the poet's father was blind when he died (line 14), that he was a serious man (line 13) and that he had an ambition to be a poet, although his efforts in that direction were not notably successful (line 5).

His father's qualities and characteristics reveal the poem's secondary theme, which might be described as 'talent frustrated'. Underlying the poem is the sad contrast between the life lived by the father and the life he might have lived, had fate given him the means or the drive to exploit his talents. This gives the poem a sense of regret and loss.

Form of the poem

This poem is a villanelle. The standard form of the villanelle was fixed in the sixteenth century. A few modern poets, including W. H. Auden and Derek Mahon, have experimented with it, but this is the best-known example.

The rules for the villanelle are strict. The first and third lines of the first tercet (group of three lines) recur alternately in the following stanzas as a refrain, and come together at the end to form a rhyming couplet (in a quatrain).

Exam-style questions

Thinking about the poem

1. In this poem, Thomas deals with death and with individual lives. How does he connect the two themes?
2. Why does Thomas refer to death as 'that good night'?
3. Why should old age 'burn and rave at close of day' (line 2)? What does 'close of day' mean here?
4. What impression of the poet do you get from this poem?
5. Is this an entirely sad poem? Give reasons for your answer.
6. Does the poem suggest that the father's fate is a tragic one?
7. Choose **two** images that you find appealing from the poem. Explain your choice.
8. Which of the following statements would best describe your view of the poem?

    It is a poem about failure.

    It is a poem about human endurance.

    It is a poem about pity.

    Refer to the text of the poem in support of your choice.
9. What is this poem about?

Taking a closer look

1. One critic remarked that in the poetry of Dylan Thomas, words are 'hurled around in a way which does not make much sense'. Does this remark apply to 'Do Not Go Gentle into that Good Night'?
2. Thomas conveys his meanings through images rather than logical statements. Does this mean that the reader is not sure of precisely what he is trying to say? Can you give examples?
3. It is often said that the success of poems such as this comes mainly from brilliant sound effects and exciting rhythms rather than from the expression of ideas. Would you agree in the case of this poem?
4. Many readers find Thomas's poems extremely difficult. Why do you think this might be so? Describe your own experience of reading this one.
5. In this poem, Thomas balances positive words and images against negative ones, as part of a pattern of plusses and minuses. Consider this idea, giving examples.

6   Thomas thinks of joy and grief, birth and death, as necessary to each other, and this is why he weaves them together in this poem. Consider how he does this.
7   Does this poem suggest that Thomas had an optimistic view of life and death? Does he give the impression that he considers life worth living?

Imagining

1   Try to compose a prose paraphrase of the poem.
2   Compose a short speech that the poet might have made at his father's graveside.

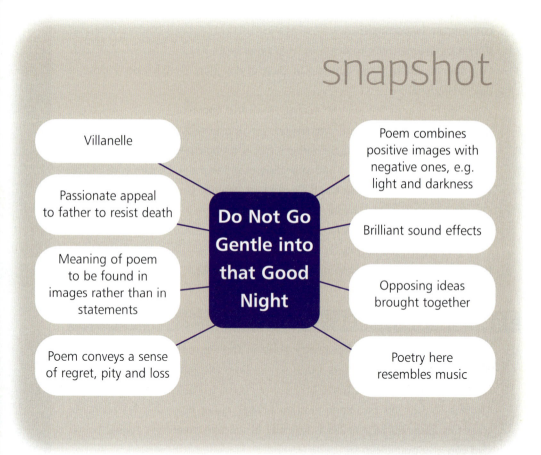

David Wheatley

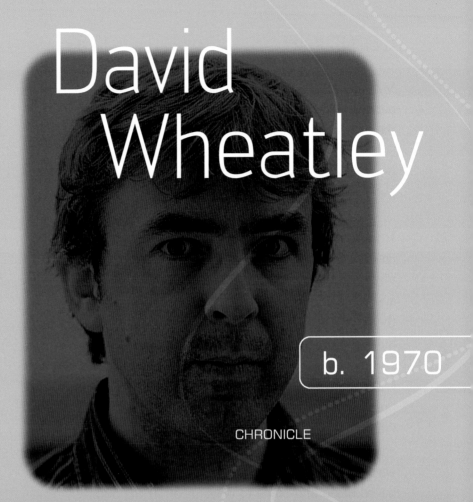

b. 1970

CHRONICLE

Biography

David Wheatley was born in Dublin in 1970 and grew up in the seaside town of Bray, Co. Wicklow. He was educated at Trinity College, Dublin, where he wrote a PhD on the poetry of Samuel Beckett. He edited the student magazine *Icarus* and was co-founder, with fellow poet Justin Quinn, of the literary magazine *Metre*.

Wheatley's first collection, *Thirst* (1997), was awarded the Rooney Prize for Irish Literature and was also shortlisted for the Forward Prize. His second collection, *Misery Hill*, was published in 2000. *Mocker* appeared in 2006, and in 2010 he published *A Nest on the Waves*. He has been writer-in-residence in Co. Wicklow, during which time he edited *Stream and Gliding Sun: A Wicklow Anthology*, and *I am the Crocus*, a volume of children's verse. He has also translated a number of poems from medieval and early-modern Irish for *The Penguin Book of Irish Verse*.

A distinguished reviewer and critic, Wheatley is a lecturer at the University of Hull, England.

Chronicle

My grandfather is chugging along the back roads
between Kilcoole and Newtown in his van,
the first wood-panelled Morris Minor in Wicklow.
Evening is draped lazily over the mountains;
one hapless midnight, mistaking the garage door 5
for open, he drove right through it, waking my father.

The old man never did get to farm like his father,
Preferring to trundle his taxi along the back roads.
Visiting, I stand in his workshop door
and try to engage him in small talk, always in vain, 10
then climb the uncarpeted stairs to look at the mountains
hulking over soggy, up-and-down Wicklow.

Cattle, accents and muck: I don't have a clue,
I need everything explained to me by my father.
Clannish great-uncles somewhere nearer the mountains 15
are vaguer still, farming their few poor roods,
encountered at Christmas with wives who serve me oven-
baked bread and come to wave us off at the door.

My grandfather pacing the garden, benignly dour,
a whiskey or a Woodbine stuck in his claw, 20
a compost of newsprint in the back of his van.
You're mad to go live in Bray, he told my father,
somewhere he'd visit on rare and timorous raids,
too close to 'town' to be properly *Cill Mhantáin*.

All this coming back to me in the mountains 25
early one morning, crossing the windy corridor
to the Glen of Imaal, where schoolchildren read
acrostics to me of 'wet and wonderful Wicklow',
and driving on down to Hacketstown with my father
we find grandfather's grandfather under an even 30

gravestone gone to his Church of Ireland heaven,
and his grandfather too, my father maintains,
all turned, long since turned to graveyard fodder
just over the county line from their own dear Wicklow,
the dirt tracks, twisting lanes and third-class roads   35
they would have hauled themselves round while they endured,

before my father and I ever followed the roads
or my mountainy cousins first picked up a loy
or my grandfather's van ever hit that garage door.

Glossary		
title	*Chronicle*: a history of events
2	*Kilcoole and Newtown*: villages in Co. Wicklow
3	*Morris Minor*: a popular vehicle in the 1950s and 1960s
5	*hapless*: unfortunate
12	*hulking*: towering
15	*Clannish*: closely united through family ties
16	*roods*: an old measurement of land, about 400 square metres
19	*benignly*: kindly
19	*dour*: sullen, grim
20	*Woodbine*: a brand of cigarette
21	*compost*: decaying mixture
21	*newsprint*: the type of paper on which newspapers are printed
22	*Bray*: a seaside town in Co. Wicklow
23	*timorous*: timid
24	*Cill Mhantáin*: the Irish name for Wicklow
27	*Glen of Imaal*: a scenic valley in west Co. Wicklow
28	*acrostics*: poems or puzzles in which the first letters of each line spell a word or sentence
29	*Hacketstown*: town in east Co. Carlow
33	*fodder*: food, usually for livestock
34	*line*: border
38	*loy*: long, narrow spade

Guidelines

'Chronicle' is from the collection *Misery Hill* (2000). The poet's experience of working as writer-in-residence in Co. Wicklow summons up history and memories of his family, long established in the mountains of Wicklow. **Like most family histories or 'chronicles' the poem is made up of personal memories, anecdotes and hearsay.**

Commentary

Stanza 1

The poet remembers his grandfather as he drove along the Wicklow roads in his van, the 'first wood-panelled Morris Minor' in the county. 'Chugging' is an expressive word that suggests the actual sound of the van, and by using this and writing in the present tense ('is') the poet makes us feel as if it is still happening rather than being a memory of a time gone by (line 1). A sense of remembered family pride in the car and a story of how his grandfather had driven it one night through the garage door bring his family history to life for us even more. **The figures of grandfather, father and son (the poet) are closely linked.**

Stanza 2

The poet's grandfather is seen in relation to his own father, a farmer, which brings the family chronicle back further in time. We are reminded of time passing as the poet remembers himself as a child 'visiting' (line 9) – he is not really a part of the life that is lived here – and trying in vain to communicate with his grandfather. **For the poet as a child, it was the mountains and landscape of Wicklow, always in the background, that held his interest.**

Stanza 3

Once more the poet describes himself as somewhat of an outsider in Wicklow, not understanding about cattle or how people talked unless his father explained it to him. Other relatives too (great-uncles and their wives) are remembered as the 'clannish' people (line 15) he met only at Christmas and who were vaguely kind and welcoming to him. It may be significant that he remembers them as they waved him 'off at the door' (line 18), the word echoing his sense of being an outsider as he stood at the 'door' of his grandfather's workshop in line 9.

Stanza 4

The focus is once again on the grandfather, remembered as he walked in the garden with his whiskey or his cigarette in hand, while newspapers rotted in the back of his van. He is 'benignly dour', a contradictory phrase that nevertheless conveys a kindly personality behind his silence. We get another glimpse of him as a somewhat reclusive man, set in his ways. To him, even a small town like Bray seemed an intimidating place, not 'properly *Cill Mhantáin*' (the original Irish name for Co. Wicklow) and therefore to be avoided (line 24). It is the poet's father who must have told him of the grandfather's opinion that he would be 'mad' to go and live there (line 22). (Wheatley was brought up in Bray.)

Stanza 5
In this stanza the poet is remembering 'all this' (line 25) as he crosses the mountains in his car, in the course of his work as writer-in-residence in Wicklow. Part of his duties would have been to visit schools and listen to the children's poems about 'wet and wonderful Wicklow' (line 28), poems which echo the love his father and grandfather have for their native county.

Stanza 6
The poet goes further back again into his family history as he describes finding the graves of his forebears (his grandfather's grandfather and 'his grandfather too', line 32). Once they may have 'turned' to their Church of Ireland faith (perhaps from Catholicism), now they have 'turned' to graveyard soil (what he calls 'fodder' in line 33) in the neighbouring county (Carlow), just beyond where they lived and travelled during their lifetimes.

Stanza 7
There are only three lines in this final stanza, but in them **the poet evokes the sense of time long past**. He imagines his long-dead relatives, who existed before any of things he remembers had happened. The word 'ever' in line 37 seems to suggest a long span of time. By ending the poem with the word 'door', might the poet suggest the barrier between the living and the dead that can only be opened to a certain extent, and that we can never fully understand those who lived in the past?

Theme of the poem

Genealogy has become a very popular pastime. The poet's interest in his family history clearly inspired him to write the poem. In doing so he succeeds in conveying a sense of the connections and also the distances between the generations. These distances may not have been solely caused by time, they are also due to temperament and circumstances. But throughout the poem he makes us aware of the landscape of Co. Wicklow as a backdrop to the lives of everyone he mentions, including himself, which gives a great sense of the continuity of generations of the Wheatley family.

Form of the poem

Wheatley has chosen to write 'Chronicle' in the form of a sestina. A sestina is a rather old form of poem in which there are six stanzas of six lines each, followed by a three-line seventh stanza. This means there are thirty-nine lines in the poem.

The main feature of a sestina is that the poet uses six particular words throughout the poem as end words of each line, but in a different order each time. Finally, in the 'triplet', he uses all six words, in no particular order and not necessarily as end words. The six main words in this poem are: roads, van, Wicklow, mountains, door, father. (These are all established as the end words of each line in the first stanza.)

However, Wheatley has cleverly played around with the form by sometimes changing the words in a subtle way, making use of how sounds of words echo each other. For instance, whereas 'roads' is one of the key words, it becomes 'roods' (line 16), 'raids' (line 23), 'read' (line 27). 'Van' becomes 'vain' (line 10), 'oven' (line 17), 'even' (line 30), 'heaven' (line 31). 'Mountains' becomes 'Cill Mhantáin' (a witty pun that depends on how you look at the word) in line 24, 'maintains' in line 32, and 'mountainy' in line 38. 'Wicklow' is also echoed in a clever manner: 'clue' (line 13), 'claw' (line 20), 'loy' (line 38). The sound of the word 'door' is echoed in 'dour' (line 19), 'corridor' (line 26) and 'endured' (line 36). The word 'father' remains the same, however, with the one exception of 'fodder' in line 33.

It is possible to enjoy the poem without looking too closely at how the effects are achieved, but in the case of a sestina the form is usually so rigid that it is interesting to see how Wheatley varies it. In the poem he refers to the schoolchildren writing their 'acrostics' or word-puzzles – he has done a similar thing in writing this sestina.

Repetition is an important part of a sestina, so it is an appropriate form in which to write of family connections and continuity.

Exam-style questions

Thinking about the poem

1. What impression of the poet's grandfather do you get from reading the poem?
2. From your reading of the poem, how would you describe Co. Wicklow?
3. What sort of people are the poet's relations? Explain your answer.
4. How do the place-names contribute to the atmosphere of the poem?
5. Images of roads and journeys occur throughout the poem. Do you think that they are effective? Give a reason for your opinion.

6. What, in your opinion, does the poem say about families and where they live?
7. Would you agree that the word 'father' is a significant one in the poem? Can you say why this might be?
8. 'The poem gives a great sense of how the past and the present are linked.' Would you agree with this view? Give reasons for your opinion.

Taking a closer look

1. Choose **two** details that appealed most to you from the poem and say why you chose them.
2. 'Clannish great-uncles somewhere nearer the mountains / are vaguer still, farming their few poor roods' (lines 15–16). What do these lines suggest to you about the poet's relatives and their lives in Co. Wicklow?

Imagining

1. You have discovered a long-lost relative who emigrated to Australia fifty years ago. Write a letter asking him or her about the life they have led abroad, and giving them some (fictional) news about the family as it is at present.
2. Write out the conversation that might have taken place between the grandfather and his son (the poet's father) when he said that he'd be 'mad to go live in Bray (line 22)'.

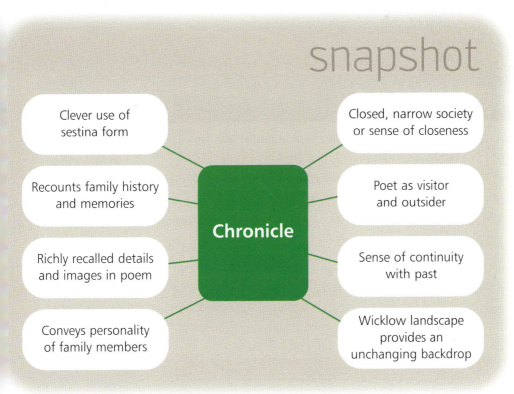

William Carlos Williams

1883–1963

THIS IS JUST TO SAY

Biography

William Carlos Williams was born in the town of Rutherford, New Jersey, 20 miles from New York city. His father, who had English and Danish ancestry, earned his living as a travelling salesman in the Caribbean and in Latin America; he met his future wife in Puerto Rico. William and his younger brother grew up speaking both English and Spanish. His mother passed on her love of art to her children, and his father read poetry aloud.

Williams began to write poetry when he was in secondary school, and decided at an early age that he wanted to be a writer and a doctor. He studied medicine at the University of Pennsylvania in Philadelphia from 1902 to 1906. While there he met the poet Ezra Pound and was influenced by the ideas of Imagism, a movement in poetry that emphasises concentrated images presented in clear and simple language. Imagist poems often take their shape from the objects they describe.

After graduation Williams returned to Rutherford and began general practice. He married in 1912 and lived out his long life as a doctor in his hometown.

Throughout the 1920s and 1930s Williams published poetry. His work was admired by a small number of people, but it was not until the publication of his long poem, *Paterson*, published in five books between 1946 and 1958, that his reputation began to grow in the United States. His work was less known in Europe, and the first British edition of his poetry appeared after his death.

Williams wanted to write in a fresh and original way. He believed that ordinary, everyday life should be the subject of poetry. He was open to new ideas and acted as a mentor to many young poets. He suffered a heart attack and a series of strokes in the late 1940s and early 1950s. Despite these setbacks he continued to publish poetry, and he wrote plays, novels and short stories, as well as essays, reviews and an autobiography. He died in 1963.

This is just to say

I have eaten
the plums
that were in
the icebox

and which
you were probably
saving
for breakfast

Forgive me
they were delicious
so sweet
and so cold

Glossary

4   *icebox:* refrigerator

Guidelines

The poem is written in the form of a note left on a refrigerator. Writing about the way the imagination works, Williams said, 'Imagination creates an image, point by point, piece by piece, segment by segment into a whole. But each part as it plays into its neighbour, each segment into its neighbouring segment and every part into every other . . . exists naturally in rhythm.' 'This is just to say' shows the imagination at work in the manner Williams described.

Commentary

There is no agreement or way of agreeing on the theme of the poem. Some readers take it at face value – a playful 'apology' for a minor event, equivalent to someone apologising to you for taking your last Rolo. Others give it a 'deeper' meaning. They suggest that the poem shows the male figure apologising to the female for his weakness in succumbing to temptation. A further version of this interpretation suggests that the male succumbs to sexual temptation, represented by the soft fruit.

The variety of interpretations is related to the tone that emerges in an individual reading of the poem. Some readers regard the final word 'cold' as an indication of the nature of the relationship between the 'I' and the 'you' of the poem, a relationship so cold that forgiveness must be sought for eating a few plums. An opposite view suggests that it is the 'I' who is cold, who enjoys stealing the plums and feels no remorse for doing so. In this view, the poem is more an expression of triumph than a real apology. A different interpretation suggests that the poem, and its description of eating the plums, is payment for what has been taken. The poem is a fair exchange for the fruit.

Real life
The very existence of the poem leads some readers to speculate on the nature of the relationship between Williams and his wife. In real life, the poem would have been successful if his wife had been amused and had forgiven him the transgression. You might like to consider this angle in the light of the answering poem written by Williams's wife, Floss, which ends with the lines:

> Plenty of bread in the bread-box
> and butter and eggs–
> I didn't know just what to
> make for you. Several people
> called up about office hours–

> See you later. Love. Floss.

> Please switch off the telephone.

Form of the poem

The poem is composed of twenty-eight words arranged into three stanzas of four lines, with no line having more than three words. There is no rhyme or regular beat. **The arrangement of words on the page guides our reading and encourages us to pay full attention to the sound and shape of every single word. In this way, as each word and line falls into the next, the rhythm of the poem unfolds in a slow, delicious way that imitates the eating of the plums.**

Sound effects

For such a short poem, Williams achieves interesting sound effects through clever repetition. Note, for example, how the explosive 'p' and 'b' sounds echo in the first two stanzas. Note also, how various forms of 's' sounds snake their way through the poem. When you combine these sounds with the long vowel sounds and the more precise 't' and 'd' sounds in the final stanza, you begin to see the artfulness behind the short poem. The sounds capture the physical and sensual pleasure of eating a soft fruit.

Exam-style questions

Thinking about the poem

1. In your view, what is the relationship between the 'I' and the 'you' in the poem? Explain your point of view.
2. Here are two opposing views of the motives behind the writing of the poem:
   - The poem is intended to charm and disarm the 'you'.
   - Having taken her plums, the 'I' makes matter worse by describing how delicious they were.

   Which of the two readings do you prefer? Explain your thinking.
3. How would you feel if you were the 'you' and found this poem on the door of your fridge?
   - I would feel offended.
   - I would feel amused.
   - I would feel delighted.
   - I would feel angry.
   - I would feel cheated.

   Explain your choice.

4. Which of the following best describes the theme of the poem?
    - It is a poem about love.
    - It is a poem about guilt.
    - It is a poem about selfishness.

    Explain your choice.
5. Do you like the poem? Give reasons for your answer.
6. 'Williams is the poet of the everyday. He captures the small but important moments in life.' On the evidence of 'This is just to say', would you agree with this assessment of Williams? Explain your answer.
7. Do you think that a poem of small details can speak about bigger themes? Explain your thinking.

Taking a closer look

1. Comment on the effectiveness of the phrase 'the icebox', which forms the last line of stanza 1.
2. What, in your view, is the impact of placing the word 'cold' at the end of the poem?
3. The poem has twenty-eight words. Which, if any, of the words would you replace? Explain your thinking.

Imagining

1. Imagine that you are the 'You' of the poem. Write a poem in response to this one and suggest where you would leave it for the 'I' to find.
2. Write a poem to a friend or relative confessing that you have borrowed and lost something that belongs to him or her. Ask forgiveness of your relative. Imitate Williams's method of using no more than thirty words. Give consideration to the placement of each word on the page and the sound of each word.

snapshot

William Carlos Williams

- Contains only 28 words
- Carefully phrased and arranged
- Sensuous language
- No rhyme or regular beat
- Written as a note of apology
- **This is just to say**
- Tone open to different interpretations
- No agreement on theme
- Nature of the relationship is a source of interest
- Ends on a word that is precise and clear

Enda Wyley
b. 1966

POEMS FOR BREAKFAST

Biography

Enda Wyley was born in Dublin in 1966; she grew up in Glenageary and went to school in Dalkey. Her family home was a place filled with books, where reading for pleasure was a natural part of the daily routine. When she was nine she won first prize in a national poetry competition and from then on, she began to take writing more seriously – her notebooks quickly filling with poems and stories. She trained as a primary school teacher and took English and History as her degree subjects. The study of English at Carysfort Teacher Training College proved to be vital to the young poet. She says that during this time she read to learn and to observe how others wrote. Afterwards she undertook a Master of Arts degree in creative writing at the University of Lancaster.

It was in Lancaster that Wyley prepared her first collection, *Eating Baby Jesus* (1994). She has since published three further collections: *Socrates in the Garden* (1998), *Poems for Breakfast* (2004) and *To Wake to This* (2009). She has won a number of national and international awards and bursaries. She has also written books for children, including *Boo and Bear*, *The Secret Notebook* and *I Won't Go*.

Wyley is married to the poet Peter Sirr. *To Wake to This* celebrates the birth of their daughter and the first months of motherhood. She is currently the website poet for the Coombe Maternity Hospital in Dublin and writer-in-residence at Coláiste Mhuire, Marino Institute of Education.

In Wyley's view, the poet is the poem's first critic. Writing involves a willingness to edit out every spare word and phrase.

Poems for Breakfast

Another morning shaking us.
The young potted willow
is creased with thirst,
the cat is its purring roots.
Under our chipped window   5
the frail orange flowers grow.
Now the garden gate clicks.
Now footsteps on the path.
Letters fall like weather reports.
Our dog barks, his collar clinks,   10
he scrambles, and we follow,
stumble over Catullus, *MacUser*,
Ancient Greek for Beginners,
cold half-finished mugs of tea,
last week's clothes at the bed's edge.   15
Then the old stairs begin to creak.

And there are the poems for breakfast –
favourites left out on the long glass table.
We take turns to place them there
bent open with the pepper pot,   20
marmalade jar, a sugar bowl –
the weight of kitchen things.

Secret gifts to wake up with,
rhythms to last the whole day long,
surprises that net the cat, the dog,
these days that we wake together in –
our door forever opening.

Glossary

12	*Catullus*: (84–54 bc) Latin poet, born in Verona, who is famous for his love poems
12	*MacUser*: a fortnightly magazine for people who use Apple computers

Guidelines

'Poems for Breakfast' comes from Wyley's 2004 collection of the same name. **It is a love poem that celebrates both romantic love and poetry. The relationship described in the poem is marked by grace and hopefulness.** The idea for the poem came following a visit made by the poet to see Francis Bacon's studio in the Hugh Lane Gallery, Dublin. Bacon's working space is renowned for its chaos, and he wrote, 'I feel at home here in this chaos because chaos suggests images to me. And in any case I just love living in chaos.' This quote stayed with Wyley, who later wrote:

> Then, one morning I woke in my bedroom, saw the chaos of my own life scattered around me – the half-finished mugs of tea, the clothes flung in piles, the array of books – and I felt that from the mess of my own ordinary life a poem might come. When I stumbled downstairs, I found on our kitchen table a poem my husband had left open there – like a startling morning gift, making order out of our lives. Suddenly joy filled my page in the rhythms of a new poem.

Commentary

Setting the scene

The poem begins with a new morning. The lovers are shaken into wakefulness as if the house and everything within it wants and needs them to be awake, from the willow plant 'creased with thirst' (line 3), to the purring cat and the barking dog. The 'chipped window' (line 5) suggests the modesty of their home – this is not a modern, perfect place but an old, worn one.

The window marks the boundary between outside and inside, between the private world of the lovers and the public world beyond them. The clicking gate and the footsteps of the postman bridge these two worlds. The letters arriving from the outside are 'like weather reports' (line 9). The barking dog and the messages from the outside world bring the couple, the 'We' of the poem, stumbling into the world of day. As they stir, the old house creaks into wakefulness. Interestingly, the opening lines have a number of adjectives that suggest frailty: 'creased' (line 3), 'chipped' (line 5) and 'frail' (line 6). However, there is nothing frail or uncertain about the relationship described in the first stanza and elaborated in the second.

A vignette of their lives
As the lovers stumble into the day, they fall over books, 'half-finished mugs of tea' (line 14) and 'last week's clothes at the bed's edge' (line 15). The selection of books – the Roman poet Catullus and *Ancient Greek for Beginners* – indicates a life of literature and scholarship, while the reference to *MacUser* suggests the habit and practice of writing. **The lovers inhabit a world that looks back to the ancient world but is also thoroughly modern.** The unfinished mugs of tea and the worn clothes suggest a sense of happy disorder and the mingling of work and home. The reference to the bed reminds us that this is a portrait of a couple, joined by love. **Deftly in these four lines (lines 12–15), Wyley creates a vignette of their busy life together, lived in happy chaos.**

Stanza 2
The second stanza of the poem opens with the statement: 'And there are the poems for breakfast'. The poems feed the soul of the lovers. They are set out on the table in the way that cutlery might be set out before a meal. They are kept in place by 'the pepper pot', the 'marmalade jar' or 'a sugar bowl', ordinary 'kitchen things' (lines 20 to 22), so that **poetry is not something apart from everyday life, but something which adds to it and which is found in what Wyley has referred to elsewhere as 'the objects and simple happenings' of the lovers' world.** The poems are 'Secret gifts' (line 23) shared with each other, 'favourites' (line 18) that delight them and remind them of their life together. **The poems grant a sense of grace and giftedness to each new day.** The couple's whole world, including their cat and dog, their unwashed clothes and mugs of tea, is caught in the 'net' (line 25) of poetry, in the surprise and pleasure of it, so that it is a joyful experience to 'wake together in' (line 26) these days. **The poems for breakfast both contribute to and record the sense of possibility that greets each day, captured in the final image of the poem, 'our door forever opening'.**

World of possibility
The final line of the poem encapsulates the mood of optimism that pervades the poem. With this lovely image, the poem opens out beyond the intimate space of the lovers' small world, reaches beyond the window, the gate and the door into a constantly renewed world of possibility.

Surprise

Although written in irregular verse, the poem is full of carefully balanced phrases, which create pictures of the details of the lovers' life, from the 'chipped window' to **the 'cold half-finished mugs of tea'. The poem celebrates the joy of poetry, while remaining firmly rooted in the ordinary objects of the everyday world.**

Just like the old house in which the lovers live, sounds echo and creak through the poem, as in 'creak', 'Greek', 'clinks' and 'clicks'. **Like the poems which surprise the lovers at breakfast, the sounds in the poem surprise and delight.**

Exam-style questions

Thinking about the poem

1. What shakes the lovers in the poem into wakefulness?
2. The lovers wake to a series of small obligations. What are they?
3. What impression of the lovers' life do you form from lines 11 to 15?
4. How does the poet show that the poems they share are part of their everyday world?
5. What effect do the poems have on the couple?
6. 'The days that the couple "wake together in" are full of possibility and joy.' Do you agree with this statement? Explain your answer.
7. What impression of the poet do you get from reading the poem?
8. Would you like to have poems for breakfast? Explain your answer?

Taking a closer look

1. Comment on the word 'shaking' in line 1 and its impact upon you.
2. 'our door forever opening' (line 27). Write a brief note on the last line of the poem.
3. Select **two** phrases from the poem that you particularly like and say why you chose them.

Imagining

1. If you decided to leave a favourite poem for your best friend to find, what poem would you choose? Explain your choice.
2. Suggest **two** pieces of music that you think would make a suitable accompaniment to this poem? Explain your choices.
3. Write a letter to Enda Wyley expressing your thoughts and feelings on the poem.

snapshot

Enda Wyley

Poems for Breakfast

- Carefully worded phrases
- Small details of everyday life
- Celebrates love
- Celebrates poetry
- Poems are lovers' gifts
- Intimate portrait of couple's life
- Mix of ancient and modern
- Mingling of work and home
- Poetry part of the everyday world
- Pervasive mood of optimism
- Ends on a note of possibility

Reading Unseen Poetry

Reading the Unseen Poem

Reading a poem is an activity in which your mind, your beliefs and your feelings are called into play. As you read, you work to create the poem's meaning from the words and images offered to you by the poet. This process takes a little time, so be patient. However, the fact that poems are generally short – much shorter than most stories, for example – allows you to read and re-read a poem many times over.

As you read a poem, jot down your responses. These notes may take the form of words or phrases from the poem that you feel are important, although you may not be able to say at first why this is so. Write questions, teasing out the literal meaning of a word or a phrase. Write notes or commentaries as you go, expressing your understanding. Record your feelings. Record your resistance to, or your approval of, any aspect of the poem – its statements, the choice of words, the imagery, the tone, the values it expresses.

Begin with the title. What expectations does it set up in you? What does it remind you of? Consider the different expectations set up by Elizabeth Bishop's 'The Fish' and Derek Mahon's 'After the Titanic'.

Next, read the poem and jot down any ideas or associations brought to mind by any element of the poem, such as a word, a phrase, an image, the rhythm or the tone.

Be alert to combinations of words and patterns of repetition. Look for those words or images that carry emotional or symbolic force. Try to understand their effect.

Note other poems that are called to mind as you read the unseen poem. In this way, you create a territory in which the poem can be read and understood.

Poems frequently work by way of hints, suggestions or associations. The unstated may be as important as the stated. Learn to live with ambiguity. Learn to enjoy the uncertainty of poetry. Don't be impatient if a poem does not 'make sense' to you. Most readers interpret and work on poems with more success than they know or admit! Learning to recognise your own competence, and trusting in it, is an important part of reading poems in a fruitful way. Remember that reading is an active process and that your readings are provisional and open to reconsideration.

Do not feel that you have to supply all the answers asked of you by a poem. In a class situation, confer with your fellow students. Words and images will resonate in different ways for different readers. Readers bring their own style, ideas and experiences to every encounter with a poem. Sharing ideas and adopting a collaborative approach to the reading of a new poem will open out the poem's possibilities beyond what you, or any individual, will achieve alone.

In an examination situation, of course, you will not be able to talk with your fellow students or return to the poem many times over a couple of days. **Trust yourself.** The poem may be new to you, but you are not new to the reading of poems. Draw on your experience of creating meaning.

Poetry works to reveal the world in new ways. D. H. Lawrence said, 'The essential quality of poetry is that it makes a new effort of attention and "discovers" a new world within the known world.' In an examination answer, you are looking to show how a poem, and your reading of it, presents a new view of the world. Read the poem over, noting and jotting as you do so, and then focus on different aspects of the poem. **The questions set on the poem will help direct your attention.**

Possible Ways into a Poem

There are many ways to approach a poem, here are some suggestions.

The words of the poem

Remember that every word chosen by a poet suggests that another word was rejected. In poetry some words are so charged with meaning that everyday meaning gives way to poetic meaning. Often there are one or two words in a poem that carry a weight of meaning – these words can be read in a variety of ways that open up the poem for you. Think, for example, of how the words 'rocks' and 'sea' come to signify fixed forms and formlessness in Sylvia Plath's poem 'Finisterre'.

Here are some questions you might ask yourself:
- Are the words in the poem simple or complex, concrete or abstract?
- Are there any obvious patterns of word usage, for example words that refer to colours, or verbs that suggest energy and force?

- Is there a pattern in the descriptive words used by the poet?
- Are there key words – words that carry a symbolic or emotional force, or a clear set of associations? Does the poet play with these associations by calling them into question or subverting them?
- Do patterns of words establish any contrasts or oppositions, for example night and day, winter and summer, joy and sorrow, love and death?

The music and movement of the poem

In relation to the sounds and rhythms of the poem, **note such characteristics as punctuation, the length of the lines, or the presence or absence of rhyme**. A short line can create a feeling of compressed energy; a long line can create an impression of unhurried thought.

Look carefully at the punctuation in a poem and the way in which it affects your reading. Think of Emily Dickinson's 'I felt a Funeral in my Brain' and the way in which the punctuation works with the line endings and the repetition to influence the flow and energy of the poem.

Consider how sound patterns add to the poem's texture and meaning. For example, do the sound patterns create a sense of hushed stillness, or an effect of forceful energy?

Ask yourself the following questions:
- What is the pattern of line length in the poem?
- What is the pattern of rhyme?
- Is there a pattern to vowel sounds and length? What influence might this have on the rhythm of the poem or the feelings conveyed by the poem?
- Are there patterns of consonant sounds, including alliteration? What is their effect?
- Are there changes in the poem's rhythm? Where and why do these occur?
- What part does punctuation play in controlling or influencing the movement of the poem?

The voice of the poem

Each poem has its own voice. When you read a poet's work, you can often recognise a distinctive, poetic voice. This may be in the poetry's rhythms or in the viewpoint the poems express. Sometimes it is most evident in the tone of voice. Sometimes you are taken by the warmth of a poetic voice, or its coldness and detachment, or its tone of amused surprise.

Try to catch the distinctive characteristic of the voice of the poem, as you read. Decide if it is a man's voice or a woman's voice and what this might mean.

Try to place the voice in a context; for example, is it the voice of a child or an adult? This may help you to understand the assumptions in the poem's statements, or the emotional force of those statements.

The imagery of the poem

Images are the descriptive words and phrases used by poets to speak to our senses. They are mostly visual in quality (word pictures) but they can also appeal to our sense of touch, smell, taste or hearing.

Images and patterns of imagery are key elements in the way that poems convey meanings. They create moods, capture emotions and suggest or provoke feelings in the readers.

Ask yourself these questions:

- Are there patterns of images in the poem?
- What kind of world is suggested by the images of the poem – familiar or strange; fertile or barren; secure or threatening; private or public; calm or stormy; generous or mean? (Images often suggest contrasts or opposites.)
- What emotions are associated with the images of the poem?
- What emotions might have inspired the choice of images?
- What emotions do the images provoke in me?
- If there are images that are particularly powerful, why do they carry the force they do?
- Do any of the images have the force of a symbol? What is the usual meaning of the symbol? What is its meaning in the poem?

The structure of the poem

There are endless possibilities for structuring a poem, for example:

- The obvious structures of a poem are the lines and stanzas. Short lines give a sense of tautness to a poem. Long lines can create a conversational feel and allow for shifts and changes in rhythm.
- Rhyme and the pattern of rhyme influence the structure of a poem.
- The poem is also structured by the movement of thought. This may or may not coincide with line and stanza divisions. Words such as 'while', 'then', 'and', 'or' and 'but' may help you to trace the line of thought or argument as it develops through the poem.
- In narrative poems, a simple form of structure is provided by the story itself and the sequence of events it describes.
- Another simple structure is one in which the poet describes a scene and then records his or her response to it.

- A poem may be built on a comparison or a contrast.
- A poem may be structured around a question and an answer, or a dilemma and a decision.
- The structure may also come from a series of parallel statements, or a series of linked reflections.

The structure of a poem can be quite subtle, perhaps depending on such things as word association or changes in emotions. **Be alert to a change of focus or a shift of thought or emotion in the poem.**

Quite often there is a creative tension between the stanza structure (the visual form of the poem) and the emotional or imaginative structure of the poem. Think, for example, of the three-line stanza form of Sylvia Plath's 'Elm', which gives an impression of neat tidiness, and the alarming changes of tone that occur within this structure. For this reason, **look out for turning points in poems – these may be marked by a pause, a change in imagery or a variation in rhythm.**

If the poem is in a conventional form such as a sonnet or a villanelle, consider why the poet chose that structure for the subject matter of the poem. Also note any departures from the traditional structure and consider why the poet has deviated from the convention. For example, Derek Mahon's sonnet 'Grandfather' does not conform to the strict rhyming patterns and structure of the sonnet form, however, these breaks with convention seem appropriate for a poem that describes an unusual and eccentric individual.

Five Poems for You to Try

In each case, answer **either** Question 1 **or** Question 2

Thistles by Ted Hughes

Thistles

Against the rubber tongues of cows and the hoeing hands of men
Thistles spike the summer air
Or crackle open under a blue-black pressure.

Every one a revengeful burst
Of resurrection, a grasped fistful   5
Of splintered weapons and Icelandic frost thrust up

From the underground stain of a decayed Viking.
They are like pale hair and the gutturals of dialect.
Every one manages a plume of blood.

Then they grow grey, like men.   10
Mown down, it is a feud. Their sons appear,
Stiff with weapons, fighting back over the same ground.

1   (a)   What in your view is the poet's attitude to thistles and where is it most
          evident? Refer to the text in support of your answer.
    (b)   Choose one image in the poem that appealed to you. Explain your choice.

OR

2   Give your personal response to the poem, highlighting the impact it made upon
    you. Support your answer with close reference to the text of the poem.

Eating Poetry by Mark Strand

Eating Poetry

Ink runs from the corners of my mouth.
There is no happiness like mine.
I have been eating poetry.

The librarian does not believe what she sees.
Her eyes are sad   5
and she walks with her hands in her dress.

The poems are gone.
The light is dim.
The dogs are on the basement stairs and coming up.

Their eyeballs roll,   10
their blond legs burn like brush.
The poor librarian begins to stamp her feet and weep.

She does not understand.
When I get on my knees and lick her hand,
she screams.   15

I am a new man.
I snarl at her and bark.
I romp with joy in the bookish dark.

1. (a) What in your view is the mood of the poem and how is it conveyed by the poet?
   (b) Choose an image or idea from the poem that appealed to you and explain your choice.

OR

2. Write a response to the poem, explaining the impact it made on you. Support your answer with reference to the poem.

Lay Back the Darkness by Edward Hirsch

Lay Back the Darkness

My father in the night shuffling from room to room
on an obscure mission through the hallway.

Help me, spirits, to penetrate his dream
and ease his restless passage.

Lay back the darkness for a salesman   5
who could charm everything but the shadows,

an immigrant who stands on the threshold
of a vast night

without his walker or his cane
and cannot remember what he meant to say,   10

though his right arm is raised, as if in prophecy,
while his left shakes uselessly in warning.

My father in the night shuffling from room to room
is no longer a father or a husband or a son,

but a boy standing on the edge of a forest   15
listening to the distant cry of wolves,

to wild dogs,
to primitive wingbeats shuddering in the treetops.

1 (a) What impression of the father–son relationship do you get from reading the poem?
  (b) Briefly describe the mood or feeling you get from reading the poem.

OR

2 Write a personal response to the poem. Support your answer with close reference to the poem.

Dreams by Langston Hughes

Dreams

Hold fast to dreams
For if dreams die
Life is a broken-winged bird
That cannot fly.

Hold fast to dreams 5
For when dreams go
Life is a barren field
Frozen with snow.

1   (a)   Give your response to the imagery in lines 3–4 and 7–8.
     (b)   In your view, does the poem create a mood of optimism or pessimism?

OR

2   Describe the impact that the poem makes on you. Refer to the poem in your answer.

A Blessing by James Wright

A Blessing

Just off the highway to Rochester, Minnesota,
Twilight bounds softly forth on the grass.
And the eyes of those two Indian ponies
Darken with kindness.
They have come gladly out of the willows 5
To welcome my friend and me.
We step over the barbed wire into the pasture
Where they have been grazing all day, alone.
They ripple tensely, they can hardly contain their happiness
That we have come. 10
They bow shyly as wet swans. They love each other.
There is no loneliness like theirs.
At home once more,
They begin munching the young tufts of spring in the darkness.
I would like to hold the slenderer one in my arms, 15
For she has walked over to me
And nuzzled my left hand.
She is black and white,
Her mane falls wild on her forehead,
And the light breeze moves me to caress her long ear 20
That is delicate as the skin over a girl's wrist.
Suddenly I realize
That if I stepped out of my body I would break
Into blossom.

1 (a) Do you think that the poem describes an interesting experience? Explain your answer.
  (b) Comment on the image that most appeals to you in the poem.

OR

2 Give your personal response to the poem.

Exam Advice from the Department of Education and Skills

The Department of Education and Skills published this advice to students on answering on the unseen poem in the Leaving Certificate Examination.

> As the Unseen Poem on the paper will more than likely be unfamiliar to you, you should read it a number of times (at least twice) before attempting your answer. You should pay careful attention to the introductory note printed above the text of the poem.

It has also issued an explanation of the following phrases, which may be used in the exam questions on poetry:

'Do you agree with this statement?'

You are free to agree in full or in part with the statement offered. But you must deal with the statement in question – you cannot simply dismiss the statement and write about a different topic of your choice.

'Write a response to this statement.'

As above, your answer can show the degree to which you agree/disagree with a statement or point of view. You can also deal with the impact the text made on you as a reader.

'What does the poem say to you about . . . ?'

What is being asked for here is your understanding/reading of the poem. It is important that you show how your understanding comes from the text of the poem, its language and imagery.

Last Word

The really essential part in reading a poem is that you try to meet the poet halfway. Bring your intelligence and your emotions to the encounter with a poem and match the openness of the poet with an equal openness of your mind and heart. **And when you write about a poem, give your honest assessment.**

In responding to the unseen poem in the exam, never lose sight of the question you have been asked. Make sure that you support every point you make with clear references to the poem. Your answers do not have to be very long, but they must be clearly structured in a coherent way. For this reason, **write in paragraphs. Write as clearly and accurately as you can.**

Guidelines for Answering Questions on Poetry

Phrasing of Examination Questions

Questions may be phrased in different ways in the Leaving Certificate English examination. In the earlier years of the examination questions were usually phrased in a general way. Some examples include:

- Poet V: a personal response.
- What impact did the poetry of Poet W have on you as a reader?
- Write an introduction to the poetry of Poet X.

However, in recent years students have been presented with more specific statements about a poet, to which they are then invited to respond. Some examples include:

- 'The poetry of Sylvia Plath is intense, deeply personal, and quite disturbing.' Do you agree with this assessment of her poetry? Write a response, supporting your points with the aid of suitable reference to the poems you have studied. (2007)
- 'Elizabeth Bishop poses interesting questions delivered by means of a unique style.' Do you agree with this assessment of her poetry? Your answer should focus on both themes and stylistic features. Support your points with the aid of suitable reference to the poems you have studied. (2009)
- 'Derek Mahon explores people and places in his own distinctive style.' Write your response to this statement supporting your points with the aid of suitable reference to the poems you have studied. (2008)

Answering the full question

You will notice that these questions refer to more than one aspect of the poet's work. For example, one asks you to consider Bishop's 'interesting questions' (i.e. the issues that concern her, her themes) as well as her 'unique style'.

Pay special attention to the guidelines for answering that follow the opening statement. For example, 'Your answer should focus on both themes and stylistic features.' Examiners will expect discussion of both aspects of the question, although it is not necessary to give both equal attention.

Do not neglect the final aspect of the questions asked. 'Support your points with suitable reference to the poems you have studied.' This may take the form of direct quotation or paraphrasing of the appropriate lines.

Whatever way the question is phrased, you will need to show that you have engaged fully with the work of the poet under discussion.

Marking criteria

As in all of the questions in the examination, you will be marked using the following criteria:

- *Clarity of purpose* (30% of marks available). This is explained by the Department of Education and Skills as 'engagement with the set task' – in other words, are you answering the question you have been asked? Is your answer relevant and focused?
- *Coherence of delivery* (30% of marks available). Here you are assessed on your 'ability to sustain the response over the entire answer'. Is there coherence and continuity in the points you are making? Are the references you choose to illustrate your points appropriate?
- *Efficiency of language use* (30% of marks available). This concerns your 'management and control of language to achieve clear communication'. Aspects of your writing such as vocabulary, use of phrasing and fluency will be taken into account – in other words, your writing style.
- *Accuracy of mechanics* (10% of marks available). Your levels of accuracy in spelling and grammar are what count here. Always leave some time available to read over your work – you are bound to spot some errors.

Preparing for the Examination

In order to prepare well for specific questions such as those above, it is necessary to examine different aspects of the work of each poet on your course.

The poet's choice of themes

Be familiar with the issues and preoccupations of each poet on your course. **In writing about themes in the examination, you will need to know how the poet develops the themes, what questions are raised in the poems and how they may or may not be resolved.** Bear in mind that the themes may be complex and open to more than one interpretation.

Write about how you responded to the poet's themes. In forming your response, questions you should ask yourself include:

- Do the poet's themes appeal to me because they enrich my understanding of universal human concerns such as love or death?
- Do the themes offer me an insight into the life of the poet?
- Do I respond to the themes because they are unusual or unfamiliar?
- Do the themes appeal to me because they reflect my personal concerns and interests?
- Do I respond to themes that appeal to my intellect as well as to my emotions, for example politics, religion or history?

The poet's style or use of language

Any discussion of a poet's work will involve his or her style or use of language. In preparing for the examination you should study carefully the individual **images** or **patterns of imagery** used by each of the poets on your course.

When you write about imagery, try to analyse how the particular poet you are dealing with creates the effects he or she does (i.e. what the poet's unique or **distinctive style** is). Ask yourself the following questions:

- Do the images appeal to my senses – my visual, tactile and aural senses, and my sense of taste and of smell? How do I respond? Do I find the images effective in conveying theme or emotion?
- Are the images clear and vivid, or puzzling in an unusual or exciting way?
- Are the images created by the use of **simile** and **metaphor**? Can I say why these particular comparisons were chosen by the poet? Do I find them surprising, precise, fresh, painterly . . . ?

- Has the poet made use of **symbol** or **personification**? How have these devices added to the poem's richness?
- Does the poet blend poetic and conversational language? Has language been used to **denote** (to signify) and/or to **connote** (to suggest)?
- Does the poet use simple expression to convey his or her ideas or complex language to express complex ideas?

An exploration of language may include style, manner, phraseology and vocabulary, as well as imagery and the techniques mentioned above.

The sounds of poetry

Many people find that it is the sound of poetry that they respond to most. It is an ancient human characteristic to respond to word patterns like **rhyme** or musical effects such as rhythm. This may be one of the aspects of a poet's work that makes it unique or distinctive.

Sound effects such as **alliteration, assonance, consonance** and **onomatopoeia** may be used for many reasons – some thematic, some for emotive effect, some merely because of the sheer pleasure of creating pleasant musical word patterns.

Look carefully at how each of the poets you have studied makes use of sound. Your response will be much richer if it is based on close reading and attention to sound patterns and effects.

The poet's life, personality or outlook

Since poems are often written out of a poet's inner urgency, they can reveal a great deal about the personality of the poet. An examination question may ask you to discuss this aspect of a poet's work. (See, for example, the question on Sylvia Plath mentioned earlier.)

Poems can be as revealing as an autobiography. Read the work of each of the poets carefully with this in mind. Ask yourself the following questions:

- Can I build up a profile of the poet from what he or she has written, from his or her personal voice?
- Is this voice honest, convincing, suggesting an original or perceptive view of the world?
- Do I find the personal issues revealed to be moving, intense, disturbing? What reasons can I give for my opinion?

It may also be that you like the work of a particular poet for a contrasting reason: that he or she goes beyond personal revelation to create other voices, other lives. Many poets adopt a different persona to explore a particular experience. Might this enrich our understanding of the world? Your response may also take this aspect into account.

Poetry and the emotions

At their best, poems celebrate what it is to be human, with all that being human suggests, including confronting our deepest fears and anxieties. **Very often it is the emotional intensity of a poem that enables us to engage with it most fully.**

Questions to consider include:

- What is the tone of the poem? Tone conveys the emotions that lie behind the poem. All of the elements in a poem may be used to convey tone and emotion. Each stylistic feature – such as the poet's choice of imagery, language and sound patterns – contributes to the tone of the poem. Look at the work of the different poets with this in mind.
- What corresponding emotions does the work of each poet on the course create in you as a reader? Do you feel consoled, uplifted, disturbed, perhaps even alienated?
- Does the poet succeed in conveying his or her feelings effectively, in your view?

These are issues you should consider in preparing to form your response to a specific question in the examination.

Conclusion

It is worth remembering that you will be rewarded for your attempts to come to terms with the work of the poets you have studied in a personal and responsive way. This may entail a heartfelt negative response, too. But even a negative response must display close reading and should pay attention to specific aspects of the poems mentioned in the question. Do not feel that you have to conform to the opinions of others – even the opinions expressed in this book!

Read the question carefully. Some questions may direct your attention to specific aspects of a poet's work – make sure you deal with these aspects in your answer.

Some questions may simply invite you to include some aspects of a poet's work in your response. It would be unwise to ignore any hints as to how to proceed!

You will be required to support your answer by reference to or quotation from the poems chosen. The Department of Education and Skills has published the following advice to students on answering the question on poetry:

> It is a matter of judgement as to which of the poems will best suit the question under discussion and candidates should not feel a necessity to refer to all of the poems they have studied.

Remember that long quotations are hardly ever necessary.

Good luck!

Glossary of Terms

Allegory: a story with a second symbolic meaning hidden or partially hidden behind its literal meaning. Poems such as Elizabeth Bishop's 'Filling Station' or Thomas Kinsella's 'Littlebody' may be considered allegorical.

Alliteration: repetition of consonants, especially at the beginning of words. The term itself means 'repeating and playing upon the same letter'. Alliteration is a common feature of poetry in every period of literary history. It is used mainly to reinforce a point. A good example is found in Emily Dickinson's 'I felt a Funeral in my Brain' where the speaker expresses her growing despair, "And I, and Silence, some strange Race / Wrecked, solitary here – "

Allusion: a reference to a person, place or event or to another work of art or literature. The purpose of allusion is to get the reader to share an experience that has significant meaning for the writer. The title of Elizabeth Bishop's poem 'The Prodigal' is an allusion to Christ's parable of the prodigal son told in the gospel of St Luke. The poem alludes to some of the themes of that parable.

Ambiguity: ambiguous words, phrases or sentences that are capable of being understood in two or more possible senses. In many poems, ambiguity is part of the poet's method and is essential to the meaning of the poem. The title of Philip Larkin's celebrated poem 'Church Going' involves a suggestive ambiguity. It means both 'going to church' and 'the church going' (i.e. disappearing, going out of use, or becoming decayed).

Assonance: repetition of identical or similar vowel sounds, especially in stressed syllables, in a sequence of words. Assonance can contribute significantly to the meaning of a poem. An example is 'with tiny white sea-lice' from Elizabeth Bishop's 'The Fish'.

Ballad: concentrates on the story and the characters. They are usually composed in quatrains with the second and fourth lines rhyming. Their meaning can be easily grasped. The second part of Thomas Kinsella's 'Dick King' exhibits ballad-like features.

Colloquialism: using the language of everyday speech and writing. The colloquial style is plain and relaxed. In much poetry of the twentieth and twenty-first centuries, there is an acceptance of colloquialism, even slang, as a medium of poetic expression.

Consonance: repetition of consonant sounds that are not confined to the initial sounds of words, as in alliteration, though they may support and echo an alliterative pattern. In Shakespeare's Sonnet 18 ('Shall I Compare Thee to a Summer's Day?'), the sound of the consonant 'l' features throughout the poem in words such as 'lovely', 'darling', 'lease', 'gold', 'complexion', 'declines' and 'eternal'.

Convention: any aspect of a literary work that author and readers accept as normal and to be expected in that kind of writing. For example, it is a convention that a sonnet has fourteen lines that rhyme in a certain pattern.

Diction: the vocabulary used by a writer – his or her selection of words. Until the beginning of the nineteenth century, poets wrote in accordance with the principle that the diction of poetry had to differ, often significantly, from that of current speech. There was, in other words, a certain sort of 'poetic' diction, which, by avoiding commonplace words and expressions, was supposed to lend dignity to the poem and its subject. This is entirely contrary to modern practice.

Genre: a particular literary species or form. Traditionally, the important genres were epic, tragedy, comedy, elegy, satire, lyric and pastoral. Until modern times, critics tended to distinguish carefully between the various genres and writers were expected to follow the rules prescribed for each.

Imagery: this is a term with a very wide application. When we speak of the imagery of a poem, we refer to all its images taken collectively. The poet Cecil Day Lewis puts the matter well when he describes an image as 'a picture made out of words'. If we consider imagery in its narrow and popular sense, it signifies descriptions of visible objects and scenes, as, for example, in Derek Mahon's 'After the Titanic': 'Where the tide leaves broken toys and hat-boxes / Silently at my door'. In its wider sense, imagery signifies figurative language, especially metaphor and simile.

Lyric: any relatively short poem in which a single speaker, not necessarily representing the poet, expresses feelings and thoughts in a personal and subjective fashion. Most poems are either lyrics or feature large lyrical elements.

Metaphor and simile: the two commonest figures of speech in poetry. A simile contains two parts – a subject that is the focus of attention, and another element that is introduced for the sake of emphasising some quality in the subject. In a simile, the poet uses a word such as 'like' or 'as' to show that a comparison is being made. Sylvia Plath's 'The Arrival of the Bee Box' features a striking metaphor in which the bee box is described as 'the coffin of a midget'. Metaphor differs from simile only in omitting the comparative word ('like' or 'as'). If in a simile someone's teeth are like pearls, in a metaphor they are pearls. While in the case of a simile the comparison is openly proclaimed as such, in the case of a metaphor the comparison is implied. A metaphor is capable of a greater range of suggestiveness than a simile and its implications are wider and richer. One advantage of metaphor is its tendency to establish numerous relationships between the two things being compared. In Sylvia Plath's 'Poppies in July', the poet compares the red flowers to 'little hell flames'.

Metre: the rhythm or pattern of sounds in a line of verse. The metrical scheme is determined by the number and length of feet in a line. A foot is a unit of poetic metre that has one unstressed syllable followed by one stressed syllable. The number of feet in a line determines the description of its length, for example a line of five feet (or five stresses) is described as a pentameter.

Onomatopoeia: the use of words that resemble, or enact, the very sounds they describe. In Thomas Kinsella's 'Mirror in February' the phrase 'hacked clean' captures the sound of the axe cutting in the wood of the tree.

Paradox: an apparently self-contradictory statement, which, on further consideration, is found to contain an essential truth. Paradox is so intrinsic to human nature that poetry rich in paradox is valued as a reflection of the central truths of human experience. Derek Mahon's 'Antarctica' explores the paradox that the ridiculous can contain the sublime.

Personification: involves the attribution of human qualities to an animal, concept or object. Derek Mahon's 'A Disused Shed in Co. Wexford' makes use of this technique.

Sestina: a poem with six stanzas of six lines each, followed by a three-line seventh stanza (known as an envoy). The poet uses six particular words throughout the poem as the end words of each line, but in a different order in each stanza. David Wheatley's 'Chronicle' is a sestina.

Sibilance: the hissing sound associated with certain letters such as 's', 'sh'. The sound is used to good effect by the poet Mary Oliver when she tells us how the sun 'slides again / out of the blackness' in her poem 'The Sun'.

Simile: see 'metaphor and simile'.

Sonnet: a single-stanza lyric, consisting of fourteen lines. These fourteen lines are long enough to make possible the fairly complex development of a single theme, and short enough to test the poet's gift for concentrated expression. The poet's freedom is further restricted by a demanding rhyme scheme and a conventional metrical form (five strong stresses in each line). The greatest sonnets reconcile freedom of expression, variety of rhythm, mood and tone and richness of imagery with adherence to a rigid set of conventions. The Petrarchan sonnet, favoured by Milton and Wordsworth, falls into two divisions – the octave (eight lines rhyming *abba, abba*) and the sestet (six lines generally rhyming *cde, cde*). The octave generally presents a problem, situation or incident; the sestet resolves the problem or comments on the situation or incident. In contrast, the Shakespearean sonnet consists of three quatrains (groups of four lines rhyming *abab, cdcd, efef*) and a rhyming couplet (*gg*).

Style: the manner of expression characteristic of a writer – that is, his or her particular way of saying things. Consideration of style involves an examination of the writer's diction, use of figures of speech, order of words, tone and feeling, rhythm and movement. Traditionally, styles were classified as: high (formal or learned), middle and low (plain). Convention required that the level of style be appropriate to the speaker, the subject matter, the occasion that inspired the poem and the literary genre.

Symbol: anything that stands for something else. In this sense, all words are symbols. Literary symbolism, however, comes about when the objects signified by the words stand in turn for things other than themselves. Objects commonly associated with fixed ideas or qualities have come to symbolise these: for example, the cross is the primary Christian symbol, and the dove is a symbol of peace. Colour symbols have no fixed meaning, but derive their significance from a context: green may signify innocence or Irish patriotism or envy. In W.B. Yeats' 'Sailing to Byzantium', the golden bird symbolises the timelessness of art.

Tone: the expression of the speaker's attitude to the listener or the subject. When one is trying to describe the tone of a poem, it is best to think of every poem as a spoken, rather than a written, exercise. A poem has at least one speaker who is addressing somebody or something. In some poems, the speaker can be thought of as meditating aloud, talking to himself or herself. We, the readers overhear the words. Every speaker must inevitably have an attitude to the person or object being addressed or talked about, and must also see himself or herself in some relationship with that person or object. This attitude or relationship will determine the tone of the utterance.

Villanelle: a highly stylised formal poem. It has five stanzas of three lines (tercets) and a final stanza of four lines (quatrain). In the tercets the rhyme scheme is *aba*. Each of these three-line stanzas ends in a refrain and there are two refrains that alternate throughout the poem. In the quatrain the two refrains come together. It is often used for poems that deal with death and grief, such as Derek Mahon's 'Antarctica'.

Poets Examined at Higher Level in Previous Years

2011
Eavan Boland
Emily Dickinson
Robert Frost
W.B. Yeats

2010
T.S. Eliot
Patrick Kavanagh
Adrienne Rich
W.B. Yeats

2009
Derek Walcott
John Keats
John Montague
Elizabeth Bishop

2008
Philip Larkin
John Donne
Derek Mahon
Adrienne Rich

2007
Robert Frost
T.S. Eliot
John Montague
Sylvia Plath

2006
John Donne
Thomas Hardy
Elizabeth Bishop
Michael Longley

2005
Eavan Boland
Emily Dickinson
T.S. Eliot
W.B. Yeats

2004
G.M. Hopkins
Patrick Kavanagh
Derek Mahon
Sylvia Plath

2003
John Donne
Robert Frost
Sylvia Plath
Seamus Heaney

2002
Elizabeth Bishop
Eavan Boland
Michael Longley
William Shakespeare

2001
Elizabeth Bishop
John Keats
Philip Larkin
Michael Longley

At a glance

Elizabeth Bishop Revision Chart

	Theme	Tone	Imagery	Language	Form	Mood	Effect
The Fish	Struggle and freedom	Admiring, respectful, marvelling	Numerous unusual comparisons throughout	Conversational, descriptive, detailed	Narrative	Elation, transcendence	Teaches a lesson, allegorical
The Bight	Creative act, power of subconscious, achievement	Rueful, realistic yet hopeful	Vivid and unusual comparisons and details	Descriptive, detailed, vivid use of sound	Personal lyric	Humour, acceptance, optimism	Personally revealing, celebratory
At the Fishhouses	Nature of knowledge and imagination	Exploring, tentative, wondering	Sea as symbol of knowledge, imaginative descriptions	Heightened, metaphorical	Personal lyric, meditation	Exploration, transcendence	Mysterious, uplifting
The Prodigal	Personal degradation and despair	Despairing, hopeful	Light, darkness, parts of body, squalor	Descriptive, sensuous, detailed	Double sonnet of 28 lines, allusive	Acceptance and horror	Disturbing, emotional
Questions of Travel	Why people travel, cultural experience	Questioning, tentative, wryly humorous	Vivid descriptions of place, unusual comparisons	Blend of poetic and conversational	Personal lyric, long stanzas allow complex ideas	Speculation	Thought-provoking, personally revealing
The Armadillo	Man's cruelty to creatures of natural world	Admiring, horrified, indignant	Sensuous, vivid descriptions of nature	Uses number of poetic devices to great effect	Nature lyric with possible allegorical undertones	Horror, anger, empathy	Makes powerful case against cruelty to animals
Sestina	Childhood sorrow, grief	Sad, uncomprehending	Emphasis on objects	Atmospheric, simple	Sestina (see commentary)	Sorrow and loss	Moving, emotional
First Death in Nova Scotia	First experience of death, childhood memory	Confused, wondering	Childlike, emphasis on colours, objects	Simple yet atmospheric, imaginative	Narrative based on personal experience	Mixture of innocence and awareness	Disturbing, moving
Filling Station	Love amidst squalor	Light-hearted yet serious	Sensuous, detailed	Conversational, descriptive	Lyric with possible allegorical undertones	Tolerance, hope, speculation	Reveals personality of poet
In the Waiting Room	Cultural diversity and awareness of identity	Serious, speculative	Describes diversity of world, waiting room as symbol	Descriptive, discursive, revelatory	Personal narrative	Philosophical	Thought-provoking, complex

At a glance

Emily Dickinson Revision Chart

	Theme	Tone	Imagery	Language	Form	Mood	Effect
'Hope' is the thing with feathers	Hope	Buoyant, solemn	Flight	Precise, metaphorical	Lyric, hymn-like	Optimism	Striking, vivid and Immediate
There's a certain Slant of light	Despair	Oppressive, authoritative	Blurring of senses	Solemn, weighty	Lyric statement	Affliction	Sobering
I Felt a Funeral, in my Brain	Death, breakdown, the limits of the imagination	Intense, disoriented	Sounds, falling	Sparse, repetitive	Intense lyric	Incomprehension	Startling
A Bird came down the Walk	Nature, harmony	Amused, whimsical, gentle	Movement, flight	Playful, gentle, metaphorical	Descriptive lyric	Grace	Calming
I Heard a Fly buzz — when I died	Death, faith	Ironic	Light and dark	Solemn, legal	Dramatic monologue	Ambiguity	Revelatory of the poet
The Soul has Bandaged moments	Elation/despair	Chilling, delirious,	Freedom, entrapment	Gothic	Lyric meditation	Oppression	Chilling
I could bring You Jewels — had I a mind to	Love	Confident, playful	New world, treasures	Colourful, allusive	Love lyric	Assurance	Heartening
A narrow fellow in the Grass	Nature	Conversational, terrified fascination	Secrecy, unpredictability	Formal, poised	Lyric description	Wariness	Quietly chilling
I taste a liquor never brewed	Joys of summer	Joyful, rapturous	Intoxication, extravagant imagery	Playful, ornate	Lyric	Dizzy happiness	Cheering
After great pain a formal feeling comes	Suffering	Dignified, solemn	Immobility, freezing	Formal, fragmented	Lyric meditation	Anguish	Sobering

Seamus Heaney Revision Chart

	Theme	Tone	Imagery	Language	Form	Mood	Effect
The Forge	Craft, imagination	Wonder, lament	Light and dark, sacred	Strong, rich in sound	Sonnet	Celebration	Transforming
Bogland	Landscape, memory, poetry	Assured, confident	Bogs and prairies	Spare, musical	Lyric meditation	Excitement	Opening up possibilities
The Tollund Man	Violence, ancestry, imagination	Sadness, longing	Burial, sacrifice, germination, pilgrimage	Simple, clear, prayer-like	Lyric meditation	Sombre contemplation	Raising questions
Mossbawn: Two Poems in Dedication (1) Sunlight	Love, family, nurture	Affectionate, loving	Baking, warmth	Flowing, descriptive	Lyric description	Tenderness	Warming
A Constable Calls	Fear, power, alienation	Fearful, guilty	Precise, inhuman	Clear, impersonal, harsh	Narrative	Oppression	Threatening
The Skunk	Married love, erotic intimacy	Humorous, ironic, affectionate	Unusual metaphors, sensuous, sacramental	Descriptive, full-sounding, symbolic	Lyric meditation	Love	Amusing, startling
The Harvest Bow	Father-son relationship hope	Nostalgic, loving, harmonious	Craft and making	Richly descriptive	Lyric addressed to poet's father	Admiration	Inspiring
The Underground	Marriage, love	Playful, celebratory, erotic, honest	Classical allusions, flight and pursuit	Allusive, energetic	Love lyric	Celebration, perseverance	Energising
The Pitchfork	The real and the marvellous	Uplifting, admiring	Visionary, weight, weightlessness	Light, sensuous, symbolic	Lyric meditation	Trust	Transforming
Lightenings, viii: 'The Annals Say'	The real and the marvellous	Tolerant, understanding, definite	Fligth, anchorage	Clear, matter-of-fact	Narrative	Lightness	Freeing of the spirit
A Call	Love, death	Fearful, apprehensive, relieved	Silence, waiting	Clear, dramatic	Dramatic narrative	Relief	Involving
Postscript	Openness, the unexpected	Thoughtful, excited	Land and sea, light and air	Conversational, descriptive, symbolic	Sonnet-like	Openness	Being in two worlds
Tate's Avenue	Love, influence of place	Intoxicated, cautious	Rugs, picnics, home and abroad	Descriptive, sensuous	Love lyric	Fond remembrance	Revealing of the lovers

At a glance

Thomas Kinsella Revision Chart

	Theme	Tone	Imagery	Language	Form	Mood	Effect
Thinking of Mr D.	Portrait of an individual and a group	Detached, sombre, judgmental	Light/darkness, poetic references	Precise and careful	Sonnet "portrait poem"	Seriousness, regret, honesty	Conveys sense of complex personality
Dick King	Childhood memory, love and friendship	Happy memories mixed with awareness of loss	Images of particular place and time	Vividly descriptive, celebratory	Elegy	Nostalgia, regret and celebration	Moving tribute
Chrysalides	Ageing, death	Rueful, pessimistic, accepting	Analogy with nature throughout	Metaphorical, sensuous	Personal lyric	Reflection	Pessimistic yet powerful
Mirror in February	End of youth and innocence	Carefree yet underlying awareness of death	Youth, freedom, natural world	Heightened, rich in sound, sensuous	Personal lyric, memory poem	Nostalgia, reflection	Powerful description of long-lasting memory
Hen Woman	Awareness of self, memory as part of artistic process	Observant, involved, reflective	Significance of egg, mythic images	Cinematic, detailed, blends concrete and abstract	Narrative poem based on childhood experience	Heightened awareness, meditation	Raises awareness of how imagination works
Tear	Youthful experience of death, awareness of hardship	Fearful, repulsed, guilty, sorrowful	Blends familiar and autobiographical with mythic	Vivid, emotional, evocative description of experience	Lyric based on childhood memory	Bleakness, pessimism	Insightful, moving
His Father's Hands	Family history, genetic inheritance and relationships	Reflective, self-aware, honest	Bodily images, place, time, people (history)	Blend of autobiographical and general, concrete and abstract	Dramatic evocation of family history	Speculation and awareness	Thought-provoking
from Settings: Model School, Inchicore	Childhood memories of school	Hopeful, reflective	Images familiar to child at school	Simple, evocative,	Lyric of personal experience	Childlike wonder, growing awareness of life	Imaginative re-creation of childhood
from The Familiar: VII	Exploration of love relationship, artistic muse	Loving, devoted, grateful	Imagery of sacred as analogy of relationship	Heightened, metaphorical	Lyric of love and devotion	Elevation, transcendence	Moving depiction of relationship
from Glenmacnass: VI Littlebody	Artistic integrity	Hard-hitting, honest, bitter	Realistic and mythic	Mixture of conversational and ritualistic	Allegorical narrative	Cynicism, realism, disdain	Dramatic
from Belief and Unbelief: Echo	Love	Tender, honest	Fairy-tale like	Direct, simple lyric	Celebration	Mysterious	Mythic

At a glance

Philip Larkin Revision Chart

	Theme	Tone	Imagery	Language	Form	Mood	Effect
Wedding-Wind	Marriage, passionate Love	Joyful, sympathetic, intense	Storm, wind, generation	Rich, prayer-like, symbolic	Lyric meditation	Radiance	Energising
At Grass	Freedom, happiness, death	Whimsical, regretful, envious	Racing, cinematic	Descriptive	Lyric mediation	Thoughtfulness	Calming
Church Going	The spiritual instinct	Mocking, thoughtful, questioning, serious	Cinematic, churches	Controlled, elevated	Long narrative, reflective	Philosophical	Uplifting
An Arundel Tomb	Survival of love, change, death	Quiet, surprised, thoughtful	Sculpted figures, monuments, fidelity	Descriptive, gentle, dignified	Lyric meditation	Poised between doubt and belief	Revealing of the poet
The Whitsun Weddings	Marriage, beginnings	Bored, mocking, excited, celebratory	Journey, dispersal, generation	Colloquial, dignified, poetic	Narrative, reflective	Awe	Involving
MCMXIV	Innocence, war, the past	Nostalgic, mournful	English way of life	Plain, dignified	Lyric lament	Gravity, sadness	Commemorating
Ambulances	Fear of death	Brutal, stark	Detailed, metaphorical	Descriptive, dense, complex	Dramatic lyric	Despair	Depressing
The Trees	Time and decay	Grieving, encouraging, longing	Contrast – decay and growth	Eloquent, harmonious	Short lyric	Determination	Affirming
The Explosion	Sudden death, power of love	Respectful, sympathetic	Resurrection, transformation	Beautifully phrased	Lyric narrative	Commemoration	Uplifting
Cut Grass	Brevity of life	Lyrical, regretful	Nature, countryside	Sweet, simple	Short lyric	Regret, sadness	Saddening

At a glance

Derek Mahon Revision Chart

	Theme	Tone	Imagery	Language	Form	Mood	Effect
Grandfather	Portrait of grandfather	Affectionate, humorous	Interesting comparisons used	Conversational	Sonnet	Seriousness combined with lightheartedness	Conveys sense of complex personality
Day Trip to Donegal	Alienation and fear, subconscious anxieties	Uneasy, fearful	Sea and wind as mysterious, powerful, malevolent	Combination of literal and metaphorical	Lyric	Disturbance, nightmare	Unsettling, almost surreal
Ecclesiastes	Power and attraction of preacher's way of life	Fierce, contemptuous, ironic	Contrasting religious /secular	Allusive, Biblical, rhetorical	Lyric	Bitterness, self-righteousness	Evocative of way of life in particular society
After the Titanic	Bruce Ismay's account of Titanic disaster	Self-justifying, self-pitying	Disaster, sea, chaos	Direct, descriptive	Dramatic monologue	Desolation	Powerful evocation of disaster and aftermath
As It Should Be	Justification of violent act	Cold, unrelenting, authoritative	Violence, nature	Simple yet powerful	Dramatic monologue	Moral certainty	Conveys psychology of fanatic
A Disused Shed in Co. Wexford	Plight and struggle of oppressed peoples throughout history	Sombre, pleading, empathetic	Highly metaphorical, wide-ranging historical references	Sensuous, balanced, allusive	Meditative lyric	Sombre meditation	Thought-provoking
The Chinese Restaurant in Portrush	Identity, home, belonging	Cheerful, hopeful	Light, nature	Conversational, sensuous	Lyric	Pleasure and relaxation, celebration	Uplifting
Rathlin	Relation of past violence to contemporary events	Dream-like, becoming uneasy	Nature, violence, speech /silence	Sensuous, metaphorical	Lyric	Peacefulness changing to unease, reflection	Unsettling
Antarctica	Self-sacrifice, heroism	Qualified admiration	Suffering/ endurance	Allusive, sensuous	Villanelle (see commentary)	Sombre questioning	Thought-provoking
Kinsale	Contrast of past and present	Glad, hopeful	Light/darkness, sea	Sensuous, evocative sound-patterns	Lyric	Elevation and happiness	Celebratory

At a glance

Sylvia Plath Revision Chart

	Theme	Tone	Imagery	Language	Form	Mood	Effect
Black Rook in Rainy Weather	Inspiration	Fearful, hopeful, cautious	Light and radiance; transformation	Heightened, metaphorical, controlled	Lyric meditation	Ambiguity	Exhilarating
The Times Are Tidy	Blandness of contemporary culture	Dismissive	Fairytale	Clear, patterned	Lyric, confident statements	Irony	Low-keyed
Morning Song	Motherhood, birth	Joyful amazed, protective	Museum, separation, baby's cry	Clear, direct, musical	Lyric, expressive	Elation	Surprising, elevating
Finisterre	Life and death	Anxious, calm	Surreal images of the ocean	Detailed, symbolic	Lyric-description and meditation	Heightened emotion	Fascinating
Mirror	Judgement, fear, ageing	Detached, cold	Personification rising fish	Precise, accurate	Dramatic monologue	Darkness	Disturbing
Pheasant	Preciousness of life, fear of destruction	Accusing, pleading, admiring	Visual, descriptive	Intense	Dramatic monologue in terza rima	Anguish	Revealing of the poet
Elm	Fear, love, self hatred	Mocking, fearful, threatening	Subconscious, dreams, nightmares	Powerful, symbolic, rich	Dramatic monologue	Terror	Overpowering
Poppies in July	Fear and longing	Dramatic, disturbed, emotional	Sickness, violence, annihilation	Intense, passionate, onomatopoeic	Concentrated lyric	Darkness	Unsettling
The Arrival of the Bee Box	Personal fears	Frightened, fascinated	Entrapment and freedom	Direct, powerful	Present tense narrative	Triumphant optimism	Unsettling
Child	Love and despair	Frustration, longing	Whimsical, images of reflection	Inventive, composed	Short lyric	Anguish	Heart-breaking

At a glance

W. B. Yeats Revision Chart

	Theme	Tone	Imagery	Language	Form	Mood	Effect
The Lake Isle of Innisfree	Desire for peace amid beauty of nature	Celebratory	Beautiful sights and sounds	Fluent, descriptive	Pastoral lyric	Contentment	Relaxing
The Wild Swans at Coole	Time, death, immortality	Initially regretful, finally resigned	Symbolic	Musical, harmonious	Lyrical meditation	Reflective, wistful	Exhilarating
An Irish Airman Foresees His Death	One man's attitude to war, life and death	Detached, stoical	Drawn from common life	Unadorned, controlled	Reflective lyric	Detached, almost casual	Exhilarating
September 1913	Betrayal of a noble ideal	Ironical, mocking	Images of thrift and sacrifice	Energetic	Ballad	Resentful, bitter	Disturbing
Easter 1916	Transportation of casual patriots into heroes	Questioning, enquiring	Play-acting and sacrifice	Partly symbolic, partly descriptive	Meditation	Reflective	Thought-provoking
The Second Coming	End of order, coming of anarchy	Deeply pessimistic	Repulsive	Heightened, dramatic	A prophetic poem	Fearful	Terrifying
Sailing to Byzantium	Journey to ideal world, curse on old age	Passionate	Decaying nature and immortal art	Forceful, energetic	A lyric	From despair to celebration	Fascinating
from Meditations in Time of Civil War: VI: The Stare's Nest by My Window	Damaging influence of civil conflict	Disillusioned, fearful	Balance of repulsive and gentle images	Colloquial, drawn from nature and common life	Lyric, description and meditation	Depressed and bitter	Deeply depressing
In Memory of Eva Gore-Booth and Con Markiewicz	Past contrasted with present of two women	Critical	Decaying human nature and fashional social life	Descriptive	Analogy	Bitter, regretful	Disturbing closing lines
Swift's Epitaph	Swift as champion of liberty	Celebratory	Enemy of oppression	Dignified	An epitaph	Solemn	Challenging
An Acre of Grass	Limits imposed by old age	Emotional	Images of great artists of the past	Plain words, strong rhythms	A meditation	Frustration rage	Exhilarating
Politics	Regret over lost youth	Frustration, longing	Abstract images of politics	Colloquial	Lyric	Regret	Inducing nostalgia
from Under Ben Bulben: V and VI	Guidance for future Irish poets; desire for a plain monument	Celebratory, affirmative	Drawn from everyday life	Lively, energetic in Part V; obscure in Part VI	A valediction or farewell poem	Generally optimistic	Stimulating

Notes

Notes

Notes

Notes